D1548112

"By the Blood of Our Alumni"

Norwich University Citizen Soldiers
in the Army of the Potomac

Robert G. Poirier

Manufactured in the United States of America

©1999 by
Maps ©1999 by Theodore P. Savas

Includes bibliographical references, index, and appendices.

Savas Publishing Company
202 First Street, SE, Suite 103A
Mason City, Iowa 50401   1-800-732-3669

Printing Number
10 9 8 7 6 5 4 3 2 1

ISBN 1-882810-21-X
First hardcover edition

This book is printed on 50-lb., acid-free stock.
The paper in this book meets or exceeds the guidelines for permanence and durability of the Committee on Production Guidelines for Book Longevity of the Council on Library Resources.

To the Citizen-Soldiers of Norwich University
Who have served the republic in all her wars.

1832-1999

Especially those alumni who made the ultimate
sacrifice in the war to preserve this union.

CAPTAIN ALDEN PARTRIDGE, U. S. A.
Founder of Norwich University.

TABLE OF CONTENTS

List of Illustrations

PHOTOGRAPHIC GALLERIES ARE FOUND ON PAGES
143-152 AND PAGES 243-252

FOREWORD

The illustrious heritage of Norwich University, The Military College of Vermont, is captured in Robert G. Poirier's important historical examination of the courageous, proud, and often final service of her alumni in the Civil War. Gaining an appreciation for the record of our former cadets in that conflict will serve as a source of inspiration for all Americans, particularly those who believe in the importance of America's citizen-soldier tradition.

For nearly two hundred years Norwich University has faithfully served this great nation. Founded in 1819 by Capt. Alden Partridge in Norwich, Vermont, it is the Republic's oldest private military college and is recognized as the birthplace of the Reserve Officer Training Corps concept. Continually challenged by their founder's educational tenets to lead wherever they might be, her cadet corps and alumni, who since 1974 include Norwich women, have excelled in all peacetime fields of endeavor and have served with distinction in all our nation's wars since the Blackhawk War of 1832.

No challenge in that long and noble history, however, was greater than the one faced less than fifty years after the first cadets matriculated. After many years of tension, the very fabric of our nation was torn asunder by regional strife and America's sons were cast into the fires of a great civil war. Norwich trained citizen-soldiers donned uniforms and marched off to serve; most wore blue, some wore gray. She stood alongside the United States Military Academy at West Point as the only other military college faithful to the Union. Following the death in battle or from disease of hundreds of thousands of the flower of America's youth in the bloodiest war in our history, the nation stood united once again. In 1865, Norwich University was rightly viewed as "second only to West Point," and the fame of her sons and their battlefield deeds had spread far and wide throughout the land. With the passage of time, the neglect of historians, and Norwich's own modesty regarding her historical legacy, her rightful place in the storied history of that conflict is largely forgotten. Robert G. Poirier's *By the Blood of Our Alumni: Norwich University's Citizen-Soldiers in the Army of the Potomac*, marks a significant step towards correcting this oversight.

There is strength to be found in this wonderful book about the Civil War service of Norwich alumni and those men they influenced and led. As these citizens wrestled with the realities of their day, so have Norwich men and women courageously and resolutely faced challenges in the years which followed. As important and well done as is the history of those who served in the Army of the Potomac, it is no more important than the early history of Norwich itself, recounted herein, and the principles which have guided those attending the university since its founding. That is, "to give youth an education that shall be American in character—to enable them to act as well as think—to execute as well as to conceive—to tolerate all opinions when reason is left free to combat them—to make moral, patriotic, efficient, and useful citizens, and to qualify them for all those high responsibilities resting upon a citizen of a free republic—all of these goals were the design of the founders of this college."

By the Blood of Our Alumni enhances my pride in my alma mater's role in the War to Preserve the Union. The lessons in courage, leadership, and sacrifice found in this book are important to all Americans. For generations, justifiable honor has been rendered to West Point, the Virginia Military Institute and The Citadel for their respective wartime roles. I hope that this book will lead students of the greatest of American conflicts, as well as future generations of Americans and Norwich cadets, to give Norwich University her legitimate share of recognition.

Gordon R. Sullivan (Class of 1959)
General and Chief of Staff
United States Army (Retired)

PREFACE

*I*t was not a goal I had set for myself. While I have always been fascinated by the Civil War and consider myself a historian and student of military history, my previous writing experiences centered on World War II and the Soviet Army. Why then, did I decide to write a book about the Civil War?

That conflict is justifiably regarded as the defining moment in our national history and collective experience. The issues involved were fundamental: would we exist half-slave and half-free? Would the Republic evolve into a united, slave-free entity? For that matter, would we continue to exist as a nation at all? As a former army officer, I remain intrigued with the details of the war, its units, commanders, battles, troop movements, and the experiences of men in combat. Reading extensively on the subject over many years, I invariably see references to this or that officer being a West Pointer. Less often, a Virginia Military Institute (VMI) or Citadel man is referred to. Rarely mentioned is an alumnus of the Union's "other" military academy: Norwich University. While it is true that the national academy supplied more officers to the service of the United States, Norwich ranked second only to West Point—despite its small student body. As the years passed, this oversight—a maddening lack of recognition of Norwich's achievements—bothered me.

The turning point came when I read Howard Coffin's book, *Full Duty: Vermonters in the Civil War* (Woodstock, 1993). While Norwich and her sons were mentioned and credited more than in other Civil War books, many of her most outstanding Vermont-born citizen-soldiers, including three Congressional Medal of Honor winners, drew scant mention. In addition, a number of officers who received their initial, and sometimes extensive, training at Norwich prior to entering the United States Military Academy, were presented solely as West Pointers. "Well," interrupted my wife Terry in the middle of one of my frequent outbursts on the subject, "why don't you stop complaining and do something about it!" The date was September 15, 1994, and I remember it clearly to this day. We headed for Gettysburg the very next morning, discussing the concept for the book and the form it should take. The result of Terry's challenge to me is the work you are now holding, a presentation of an important and largely forgotten aspect of the War of the Rebellion.

The research and writing of *By the Blood of Our Alumni: Norwich University's Citizen-Soldiers in the Army of the Potomac* has been a test of perseverance, frustration, joy, and a self-reeducation in the basic concepts and beliefs which have made our country, my university, and their mutual tradition of a citizen-soldiery great. In the early stages of research, my plan was to include all Norwich alumni in all theaters of the war. As the project and the quest for materials progressed and my understanding of the intricacies and scope of the subject broadened, I realized I had neither the time nor the resources to do justice to all of Norwich's Civil War veterans. I therefore decided to narrow the scope of the book and focus only on those Norwich men who served in the Army of the Potomac. As a result, *By the Blood of Our Alumni* serves as the initial baseline for others to build upon.

By studying Norwich alumni in the North's primary (and best-known) field army, I sought to validate my basic thesis that the contributions rendered by Norwich men in the Civil War are undervalued and under reported, little understood, and in some cases rival those of the Virginia Military Institute and The Citadel to the Confederacy. I also provided a brief overview of some of the more noteworthy alumni in other armies and theaters, and summarize their service in several appendices. In reducing the original scope of the project, I trust I have not done them an injustice.

The names of alumni associated with various battles, as well as the numbers wounded, breveted, and cited for gallantry, are conservative. Similarly, the number of alumni identified as having served on both sides in all theaters is undoubtedly higher than presented here. (My decision to concentrate my research effort on Norwich men in the Army of the Potomac necessarily limited my research on those alumni who served outside the Army of the Potomac.) Tragically, the destruction of many early Norwich records has at times confused and complicated the correct identification of alumni participants in the war. Any errors, omissions, and misidentifications that follow are, of course, my own. However, during the course of my research, previously unknown alumni have been identified using cadet matriculation records, thus opening new and potentially rewarding avenues of future study. These findings have been encapsulated in one of the appendices. In cases where evidence confirming a suspected alumnus' matriculation at Norwich was insufficient or conflicting, such as for James A. Hall and Alfred H. Terry, accounts of their wartime service have been deliberately minimized.

It is my hope that *By the Blood of Our Alumni* provides insightful reading to students of the Civil War, and at the same time educates future generations of Norwich cadets as to their alma mater's role in that conflict while emphasizing the best traditions of our citizen-soldiery past. It is important to note, however, that this study is neither a history of the Army of the Potomac nor a single volume account of the Civil War in the Eastern Theater. Others have already produced outstanding works on these topics. Instead, my study is intended to describe and convey the role Norwich alumni played within the Army of the Potomac. This goal is achieved by presenting a general framework of the history of the war in the East and the campaigns and battles that comprised it. Given the length and scope of this topic, the strategies and tactics of the opposing armies are given less ink than the roles played by the alumni.

Hopefully readers will come to realize that the path these men chose to follow in that great conflict, as well as the lessons in courage and sacrifice which their service conveys, are still relevant today. Their experiences have been a privilege for me to rediscover. There is a genuine humanity to them, and I trust you will learn to understand and appreciate, as I have, their service to the Republic.

Norwich Forever!

ACKNOWLEDGEMENTS

here are dozens of persons who made this book possible, and I apologize in advance if I overlooked someone. With sincere thanks and appreciation to all the following for their guidance, assistance, and advice: Dr. Richard Schneider, President, Norwich University; Dr. Gary T. Lord, Norwich University Historian and Charles Dana Professor of History; Commandant of Cadets Colonel Craig Lind (Class of '71) and his staff; Paul Heller, Director of Libraries and the staff of the Kreitzberg Library, Norwich University; Julie Bressor, Norwich University Librarian of Special Collections; Lieutenant Colonel David Olson (Class of '86), Director of Alumni Affairs; Cadet Francine Ippolito (Class of '96) for her research on my behalf; my Norwich roommate Kerry Shea (Class of '66) and Mary Ann Shea for their role in obtaining materials on Massachusetts men; my friends and colleagues Albert Z. Conner, Frederick G. Myer, and William D. Pratt for their comments and criticisms; Robert K. Krick, Chief Historian, Don Pfanz and Elsa Schemmer, staff historians, at the Fredericksburg-Spotsylvania National Military Park for allowing access to materials held there; Jerry T. Wooten, park historian at Pamphlin Park Civil War Site; Wayne Motts, staff historian for artist Dale Gallon, Bob Needham (Class of '56), David Watson (Class of '71), Mark Gudalis (Class of '78), Eric Ward (Class of '86), Ed Sullivan (Class of '91), Dr. Elliot Hoffman, Dave Long, Robert Lohman, and Nick Picerno, for so generously sharing materials, photos of alumni, and for either assisting in my research effort or sharing their own research with me.

Special thanks are also due to Steven J. Nitch, the great-great-great-grandson of Brig. Gen. Edmund Rice (Class of '60), for generously allowing the use of material from his private collection; and to Roger D. Hunt for so generously sharing his tremendous knowledge of Union colonels with me. Linda Margaret Farr Welch generously allowed me to use material on Norwich alumni from her forthcoming book *Families of Cavendish* (Vermont). I would also like to thank the staff of the State Historical Society of Wisconsin; Steven Hill, the former Curator of the Battle Flag Collection at the Massachusetts State House, and the staff of the United States Army's Military History Institute at Carlisle Barracks, particularly Louise Arnold-Friend, for their assistance. Robert Maher and the staff of the Civil War Education Association provided much needed support, information leads, and assistance in touring the battlefields where Norwich alumni fought. Gary Gallagher, the epitome of Civil War scholars and authors, provided me with valuable guidance and kindly consented to read and critique the draft manuscript. He assisted me in controlling my "Norwich Pride," and in (correctly) allowing the deeds of Norwich alumni to speak for themselves. Ted Savas, my publisher, was willing to take a chance on a first time Civil War author. He taught me much about the process of researching and writing about that great conflict. Hopefully, his tireless efforts will bear fruit in my next book.

Very special thanks are also due to former Army Chief of Staff, General Gordon R. Sullivan (Class of '59) for writing the foreword to this story of our alma mater. Additionally, I wish to extend my heartfelt and very special thanks to the ladies and gentlemen of the 1996-97 Norwich University Corps of Cadets. In particular, Cadets Mark Annese, Jason Hartling, Matt Westcott, Sean Coulter and the fine lads who allowed me to join the Harmon Hall "shade table." Also, to Cadets Tricia Goff, Allison Babineau, Emily Van Arman, Brigette Paddock, and Alexandra Etsell who, with many other young ladies, amply justify the confidence Alden Partridge had in the abilities of American women. Heartfelt thanks for making my research time on campus so enjoyable and for allowing me, a member of the "Old Corps," to feel a part of the current Corps of Cadets. Norwich's future is in good hands as long as cadets of their caliber staff the corps. Their predecessors would be very proud of them. I know I am.

Last and by no means least my wife, colleague, and friend Teresa Carol Selnack Poirier. Terry was the catalyst for this project and worked with me at Norwich and in numerous dusty research facilities. She gamely trooped over many rugged battlefields and manages to live her life with the ghosts of Norwich alumni. Terry has become a Civil War and Clara Barton expert in her own right. I look forward to following the ghostly blue columns of the Army of the Republic with her for many years to come.

Robert Poirier
Woodbridge, Virginia

I. Origins

"A citizen-soldiery is the cornerstone."
K.R.B. Flint '08

he Confederates flooded over the wall. The roar of battle was deafening and smoke obscured many details of the epic struggle. For an instant on that July afternoon it appeared as though the gallant Southerners of Lewis Armistead's Brigade were going to break the center of the Federal line and carry the day, and perhaps the war, for the Confederacy. Hand-to-hand combat broke out and raged for what seemed an endless period as the breakthrough expanded along the ridgeline into a small copse of trees.

At that moment a young officer sprinted into the fray leading a small band of soldiers from Massachusetts and New York. The reinforcements smashed into the Southern spearhead, stopping it cold. Men from both sides were bayoneted, clubbed, and shot. Many were struck down by fire from their own infantry and artillery. Literally standing breast-to-breast with the foe, the young major, sword in hand and a flag bearer by his side, thrust his blade forward and signaled for his men to follow. He fell severely wounded within the enemy's lines just a few seconds later, as his men pressed deeper into the crowded mass of gray and brown Confederates. The color bearer of the 19th Massachusetts Infantry struck down his opposite number in the 14th Virginia Infantry and seized the Rebel battle flag. The stiffening Federal resistance shattered the grand attempt by Robert E. Lee to crush the center of the Army of the Potomac, and the assault known forever after as "Pickett's Charge," was over. While virtually every Federal fighting on Cemetery Ridge on July 3, 1863, played a role in the Republic's victory at Gettysburg, Norwich University had cause for special celebration. For his actions that afternoon, 20-year-old Maj. Edmund Rice, of the 19th Massachusetts and a Norwich alumnus (Class of '60), became one of the youngest officers ever to win the Congressional Medal of Honor.[1]

*   *   *

The seeds of Rice's deed of valor were sown on another field in Norwich, Vermont, almost half a century earlier on August 6, 1819. The rich harvest of young citizen-soldiers that developed from this educational innovation on the banks of the Connecticut River, later proved its worth on the bloody fields of the War to Preserve the Union. From its inception in 1819, Norwich University—the nation's oldest private military college—has educated and trained its cadets to be leaders in peace and citizen-soldiers in war. The unique educational ideas developed by Capt. Alden Partridge (1785-1854), the founder of Norwich, are recognized by the Department of the Army as the basis for the concept behind the nation's Reserve Officer Training Corps (ROTC). Beginning with the Blackhawk War of 1832, Norwich alumni (which since 1974 include Norwich women), have served in all of our nation's conflicts and currently have the opportunity to seek a commission in any branch of our armed forces. The greatest single trial confronted by Norwich graduates has been the Civil War. Their contributions to the Republic in that conflict, while extensive, have received scant modern recognition and are appreciated and understood by few. They deserve better.[2]

University founder Alden Partridge was a native Vermonter who attended Dartmouth College and graduated from the United States Military Academy at West Point in October 1806. Partridge remained at West Point teaching mathematics and engineering, served as Acting Superintendent from 1808-1815, and as Superintendent from 1815-1817. One of the nation's best known army officers at the time, he was an important factor in the early development of the nation's Military Academy. It was Captain Partridge who replaced the blue uniforms at West Point with the now famous "cadet grey," the color most commonly associated with American militia forces. He selected grey as the

Academy's uniform color in honor of the citizen-soldiers and regulars who defeated the British in the Battle of Chippewa in 1814. His work at West Point and his plans for reforming the Academy and establishing a national system of citizen-soldier colleges, however, conflicted with the views of some elements in the Army as well as Congress. Following Partridge's departure from the Academy, his service and achievements at West Point were denigrated by writers seeking to enhance the importance and impact of Sylvanus Thayer, the erstwhile "Father of the Military Academy," who served as superintendent from 1817-1833. Partridge's inability to implement his ideas on military education at West Point led to his resignation from the United States Army in 1818 and a decision to found his own military college in his native state. While the Partridge-Thayer philosophical conflict raged for an extended period in the 19th century, a detailed discussion of that conflict is beyond the scope of this work. A more balanced and favorable view of Partridge's years at West Point and the positive impact of his ideas on American education, however, has emerged in recent years.[3]

The education and leadership development of America's youth has been the business of Alden Partridge's school since its establishment in 1819 at Norwich, Vermont. The institution was founded as The American Literary, Scientific, and Military Academy (A.L.S.& M.A.). The name was deliberately selected to define the characteristics of the school and to contrast it with contemporary American colleges and universities. It was the first private institution of higher learning organized in a military mode in the United States. In the four decades following the matriculation of the first cadet, Cyril Pennock of Hartford, Vermont, on September 4, 1820, Norwich implemented the educational ideas its founder termed "The American System of Education." Essentially, Partridge's concepts challenged the contemporary American college and university system. He argued for a pragmatic balance of physical and intellectual training, an emphasis on the liberal arts, and the use of practical field work—all within a military structure. Simply put, his goal was and remains the preparation of young people for the fulfillment of their obligations as citizens in a democratic society. A key building block of Partridge's ideas was a preference for the establishment and maintenance of a large body of trained citizen-soldiers rather than reliance on a professional army and regular officers, such as those trained at West Point. Such a force, he argued, was dangerous to the maintenance of a democracy and the antithesis of the principles of the Founding Fathers. Mindful of the strategic importance of the nation's ocean frontiers, Partridge's cadets were also prepared for service in the navy. "Let practical and scientific military instruction be a part of our system of education," wrote Partridge on the regular-militia issue, "and we shall become a nation of citizen-soldiers . . . . Scarcely ever has a nation lost her liberties when her armies were composed of her own citizens, who fought for preservation of their liberties and property."[4]

If he had still been alive during the early part of the 20th century, Partridge surely would have agreed with the summation of his ideas on the American militia soldier's importance to the Republic as laid out in K. R. B. Flint's (Class of 1908), "A Norwich Man's Creed": "I believe that the fundamental problem of society is to maintain a free government wherein liberty may be secured through obedience to law, and that a citizen-soldiery is the cornerstone upon which such a government must rest." Even today, new Cadet Recruits (called "Rooks" in the Norwich vernacular) memorize these words.[5]

Recognizing that his ideas were both new and difficult to implement, Partridge systematically trained his students to rise to the varied challenges he placed before them. He adopted as his school's motto the words "I Will Try." The phrase was a promise made by New Hampshire's Col. James Miller to his commander at the Battle of Chippewa during the War of 1812, when Miller was asked to assault a particularly dangerous battery. The pledge was redeemed in victory. This motto, which symbolizes perseverance in the face of adversity, came to epitomize the actions of Partridge's educational descendants in the years and battles to come. Indeed, these same three words are today prominently displayed on the Norwich University seal, the cadet class ring, and the regimental colors of the Norwich University Corps of Cadets.[6]

The early years of the Academy on the banks of the Connecticut River at Norwich were consumed with building construction, student recruitment, and the implementation of new academic programs. By August 1821, one hundred cadets from eleven states and Canada were on campus. A significant percentage of students from the institution's early years hailed from southern states, with nearly 150 cadets attending from South Carolina alone. In the first decades of it existence the Academy would lay claim to such "firsts" as fielding the nation's first collegiate band, offering the nation's first engineering instruction, and providing extensive field work and training for its students. No specified period for completing the course of study was required, and each student advanced at his own pace and according to his own abilities. Typically it took cadets from one to six years to graduate and receive a diploma. A number of cadets—more than three dozen—either graduated from Norwich or attended the Academy before transferring to the United States Military Academy at West Point. By 1825, when the Academy had relocated to Middletown, Connecticut, 480 cadets had matriculated. Ten years later in 1835, by which time the school had returned to Norwich, Vermont and been renamed and chartered as Norwich University, surviving school records indicate a total of 1,202 cadets had attended The American Literary, Scientific, and Military Academy. Alden Partridge's Academy and educational system were well received in his day, drawing wide acceptance and praise from contemporary politicians, newspaper editors, and educators.[7]

Partridge's detailed thoughts for educational reform are documented in an extensive "Lecture on Education," which was first published in the *Middlesex Gazette*, in Middletown, Connecticut, in 1826. Among his proposals for reforming American higher education as it existed in the 1820s, was a description of what the heart of the new "model" educational institution should look like: "1st. The organization and discipline should be strictly military," and "2dly. Military science and instruction should constitute a part of the course of education. . .every American citizen. . .is emphatically a citizen soldier, and. . .should be equally prepared by education to discharge. . .his duties in times of war and peace."[8]

The Academy's curriculum embraced numerous branches of literature, science, practical instruction and, of course, military science. These classes included: Latin, Greek, Hebrew, French and English; composition, rhetoric, logic, education, and elocution; history, geography, maps, globes, ethics, metaphysics, natural and political law, the law of nations, the Constitution of the United States and the states, chemistry, electricity, optics, all aspects of mathematics, surveying, engineering, navigation, weather, mechanics, agriculture, physical fitness, and music. In military science, instruction was provided in all aspects of field engineering and fortifications, artillery tactics and gunnery, infantry tactics, the attack and defense of fortified places, modern and ancient tactics, fencing and swordsmanship, military drawing, topography, and the school of the soldier.[9]

One of Partridge's major innovations was an attempt to foster individual initiative, "risk taking" in today's vernacular. This was achieved by placing substantial command responsibilities upon cadet officers and by including practical field exercises and work as an integral part of the educational process. Academy field work included engineering surveys, the study and construction of field fortifications, navigation, and extended practice marches and pedestrian tours. Over the years, these marches would take cadets as far afield as Boston, Niagara Falls, Fort Ticonderoga, the White Mountains, and, with some travel by boat, to the nation's capital at Washington, where they were reviewed by President John Quincy Adams and the Secretary of War.[10]

While all the reasons for the relocation of the Academy from its original home in Norwich, Vermont, on April 1, 1825, to a location on the Connecticut River in Middletown, Connecticut are not known, there is no doubt that Captain Partridge deemed the latter location beneficial to his efforts to train naval officers. In addition, Commodore Thomas Macdonough of Middletown, a naval hero of the War of 1812, probably personally influenced Partridge's decision to relocate. The Academy flourished in its new home, and for a time the Academy's Corps of Cadets was actually larger than that of West Point (297 versus 250). Political disputes in the Connecticut legislature, however, prevented the Academy from being chartered by the state. The unfortunate end result was that Partridge abandoned the Connecticut site and buildings in 1829 and moved his institution back to Norwich. Unlike Connecticut, Vermont chartered the school and it was renamed "Norwich University" on November 6, 1834. It remained at its original site in Norwich until a devastating fire destroyed the principal building on March 14, 1866. After much debate the university was relocated to "The Hill," in Northfield, Vermont. To this day Norwich University—officially labeled "The Military College of

Vermont" in 1898 continues its educational mission and the preparation of citizen-soldier leaders.[11]

The dislocation and turmoil in the 1825-1834 period negatively affected academic development of the Academy and the growth of the Corps of Cadets, which dwindled to as few as 30 members. In addition, during these difficult years following its return to the banks of the Connecticut River in Vermont, anti-military feeling ran high in New England and the tide of contemporary social influence ran against the military school. Anti-military feelings had been rampant in the northeast for several decades following the War of 1812. Referencing that trend, a cadet of the period remembered that "At this time, the martial spirit in New England at least was dormant. . . .On training days and muster days in certain localities, military manouevres degenerated into the burlesque." To many, Norwich "was regarded. . .not only as out of tune with the age, but as a promoter of that wild war spirit which, under military chieftains, had deluged the earth with blood." Alden Partridge's partially successful effort to create a string of military schools across the South on the Norwich University model caused further disruption. These academies, which opened in the 1830s and 1840s, drained off potential Norwich cadets and allowed Partridge but little time to focus on the affairs of the primary campus.[12]

The prewar military organization and daily administration of the corps of cadets was different from that of other military schools. One student offered a detailed glimpse into this instructional world when he wrote:

> No cadet officers or non-commissioned officers were known, except an adjutant, whose duties were little different from those of a first sergeant, and who fell into ranks with a rifle, like any private, at all drills. He called the rolls, marched the battalion to meals and church, read the reports of himself and the officer of the day at morning parade for prayers, and performed certain clerical duties required by the president. Two adjutants were usually appointed annually, one holding office from the beginning of the year to the middle, and the other from the middle of the year to Commencement.

> . . . .A stranger looking on at drills would have seen companies and battalions properly officered and everything conducted according to tactics. This was provided for at the close of each drill, when the commandant announced for the following day the commissioned officers from the Senior

and the non-commissioned officers from the Junior classes. By this method, every graduate had an opportunity to perform the duties of all grades from private to battalion commander. . . .it was the system under which generations of cadets were instructed.[13]

The uniform required for all cadets in 1841 was described as "A coat of dark blue cloth with three rows of white bullet buttons in front, the two outside rows terminating a little past the top of the shoulder. . . . standing collar, to rise as high as the tip of the ear with a button on each side . . . The skirts to have two buttons behind, at the bottom of the waist and two at their lower extremity; then four set on the center, extending up and down" and "at the half distance between the buttons at the bottom of the waist and the buttons of the skirt, to be two buttons placed close together near the edge of each fold." The uniform trousers were "Pantaloons, dark blue for winter, white for summer. Vests, dark for winter, white for summer. Caps and trimmings can be obtained at the University." This uniform is essentially the same as that worn as "full dress" by Norwich cadets on parade today.[14]

The student population grew very slowly in the decades following the receipt of the University Charter in 1834, and between 1850-1861, the size of the Corps of Cadets never exceeded 100 members. Partially as a result of Partridge's absences, Col. Truman B. Ransom (Class of '25), one of Partridge's former students and a close associate, succeeded to the university presidency in 1844. Partridge's basic educational philosophy, however, was continued by his successor.[15]

While Norwich was the first and principal school founded by Alden Partridge, it was not unique. Aided by a strong supporting cadre of former students, Partridge established a network of schools based on his "American System of Education." A total of nineteen academies were founded and flourished for some time. Thirteen of these were located in the North and West, and six were constructed in the South. These schools were under the tutelage of thirteen of Partridge's former students, all of whom, interestingly enough, were Northerners. Partridge's philisophy may have had a profound impact upon the development of military schools in Virginia. He spent much of 1834-1836 lecturing and drilling students at the University of Virginia. In 1834 he discussed his educational concepts before the Virginia General Assembly.

In that speech, he pointed out that Virginia had the opportunity to establish the nation's first state-funded military school or "institute." Just a few years later that state established the renowned Virginia Military Institute at Lexington in 1839.[16]

The most successful of the Partridge-inspired academies was the Virginia Literary, Scientific and Military Academy and its successor institute, the Virginia Collegiate Institute. Founded in 1839 at Portsmouth, Virginia, the same year the Virginia Military Institute opened in Lexington, the Portsmouth school remained in operation until the opening of the Civil War. It was one of nine military colleges in the South, two of which were in the Old Dominion. These schools graduated thousands of students, many of whom went on to serve in the Civil War. Ironically, that conflict brought about the termination of all of Partridge's academies except Norwich University. In addition to these military schools, Partridge pioneered the implementation of ROTC-like military training on civilian campuses, including the University of Virginia at Charlottesville, an institution which sent large numbers of her alumni to fight for the Southern Confederacy. One of the students to whom Partridge taught the science of war was Edmund Ruffin, an agricultural reformist and Southern nationalist who purportedly pulled the first artillery lanyard at Fort Sumter.[17]

Captain Partridge's system of education was also successful north of the Mason-Dixon Line. The most effective of these institutions—other than Norwich—was the Collegiate and Commercial Institute, founded at New Haven, Connecticut, in September, 1836. The institute was established and maintained under the leadership of William H. Russell (Class of '28), one of Partridge's disciples. Between three and four thousand students attended the New Haven school, a large number of whom went on to serve in the Union Army. Russell, who later became a major general commanding Connecticut state troops, played a key role in the raising, drilling, and equipping of that state's regiments, many of which carved out fine combat records. Hundreds of these men were Collegiate Institute alumni.[18]

As earlier alluded, the War to Preserve the Union was not the first conflict in which Norwich's citizen-soldiers participated. Its graduates served on active duty in both the army and navy from the 1820s. Incomplete university records indicate that at least nine Norwich alumni served in the Blackhawk War of 1832, while some 26 saw service during the Seminole and Creek Wars. At least 82 graduates fought in the Mexican War, many in the famed 9th United States ("Old 9th New England") Infantry.[19]

When war with Mexico was declared in 1846, Norwich University President Truman B. Ransom resigned and, in the spirit of the "American System of Education," went off to serve as a lieutenant colonel in the 9th New England Infantry (later redesignated the 9th United States Infantry). The regiment, which was initially commanded by Norwich Trustee (and later President of the United States) Col. Franklin Pierce, boasted numerous Norwich men in its ranks, many serving as officers. Ransom became colonel of the 9th U.S. upon Colonel Pierce's promotion, and led the regiment in the successful assault on the fortress of Chapultepec. Leading his men with much gallantry and panache, Ransom fell at the head of the assaulting column. Major Thomas H. Seymour (Class of '28) assumed command after Ransom was shot down and is credited with being the first man to enter the fortress. One of Ransom's sons, Brig. Gen. Thomas E. G. Ransom (Class of '51), would achieve fame and a corps command in the Civil War. Like his father before him, he too would perish from the effects of wounds received in battle.[20]

A nineteenth century cadet's daily life on campus tended to be spartan and a bit grim, particularly by modern standards. Like students of all ages, Norwich's managed to find time for occasional mischief. The focus of considerable attention was the relationship of Norwich to its older and more famous neighbor across the Connecticut River in Hanover: Dartmouth College. Surviving tales of conflict and glorious deeds surround the rivalry. One cadet wrote of an 1859 encounter popularly known as the the "Battle of the Torn Coats." One of the cadets, "venturing over to Hanover alone, was seized by the bellicose 'Darties' who ripped his dress coat up the back. The next day the corps was marched to Hanover and after a severe fight a large number of Dartmouth men received the same treatment." A full account of the "battle" is given in Rev. Homer White's novel, *The Norwich Cadets*.[21]

Even this longstanding rivalry mellowed somewhat as talk of secession and war brought about Northern unity. When fighting actually erupted in the spring of 1861, a truce between the schools was declared. Even Dartmouth men conceded that a military institution such as Norwich had its uses after all. At a joint meeting held in Hanover, one Dartmouth student graciously proclaimed: "We must acknowledge that you are not only our equals in classical and scientific attainments, but our superiors in this, that you can buckle on a sword and lead men in this conflict, while we must shoulder the musket."[22]

As tension between free and slave states grew in the 1850s, a beneficial effect of the impending conflict was the development of a more positive attitude towards military schools in general, and Norwich in particular. The daily routine of the pre-war Corps of Cadets, which hovered at 100 members between 1850-1861, appears to have continued generally unaffected by the increasing political strife and tensions between the North and South. One cadet wrote that ". . . life ran on pleasantly at Norwich, with no premonition of the tremendous events soon to occur. The routine was not much unlike that of other colleges, except the cadets kept regular hours, according to military system." The cadets of those years were not attending Norwich in order to prepare for an imminent civil war. Why, then, were young men attending the university?

In 1858, Cadet Charles A. Curtis (Class of '61) honestly opined that other factors were at work. "When our Dartmouth friends. . .questioned cadets upon the subject, some confessed to a love of a handsome uniform, a pleasure in handling fire arms, sword, and sabre; others to a desire for regular hours for study, meals, sleep, and exercise." It was also advantageous that "others. . .sought the ease of manner, grace of carriage, and erect figures which military drill was here to give." These reasons are not altogether unlike those provided by young men and women today. In hindsight, however, Curtis indicated that "No one claimed that he was learning the art of war, to be prepared to defend his country in time of need, and yet at every drill we touched elbows with future generals, colonels, majors, captains and lieutenants, gallant lads who left their blood, limbs, or bodies on every hard-fought field from Bull Run to Appomattox." As war clouds gathered and the sound of distant fifes and drums were heard on the wind, the student journal *University Reveille* editorialized with just a tad of irony that ". . .the foundation of Military Colleges. . .(and) institutions, are now regarded with a higher degree of favor than was formerly accorded them."[23]

While the level of civil strife increased, Norwich remained relatively immune from the turmoil and continued the education and training of its cadets. As late as April 1861, the *University Reveille* held that Norwich existed ". . .in the temperate zone of tranquility, and though the news is read with a lively interest. . .amicable relations exist between those from different sections of the country." A lone South Carolina Palmetto Flag had been displayed from a barracks window that spring, undoubtedly by a cadet from that state ". . .but was furled without a murmur at the order of the Adjutant."[24]

When the drum beat "Lights Out" on campus the evening of April 11, 1861, none of the retiring cadets could have imagined what the coming dawn would bring. Certainly none realized the extent to which their lives, their alma mater, their families, their respective states, and their very country were about to be permanently changed by a single mortar shell fired by a Confederate gun crew.

II. BULL RUN & BALL'S BLUFF

1861: *"Aye, deem us proud."*
Frederick W. Lander '41

Early on the morning of April 12, 1861, Secessionist gunners opened fire on Fort Sumter in Charleston harbor, South Carolina. The fort's guns were manned by Federal artillerymen, one of whom was Capt. Truman B. Seymour (Class of '44). After thirty four hours of intensive bombardment, the small garrison from the 1st United States Artillery was allowed to withdraw with honor, and the Union, shocked and outraged by the event, had its first heroes. Norwich's Seymour was one of them. The captain was breveted major for "gallant and meritorious service" during the engagement, the first—though certainly not the last—Norwich alumnus to be so honored.[1]

The attitude of Norwich alumni at the time (and probably many peace-loving Union men), is well summarized in an extract of a letter written April 14, 1861, by George B. French (Class of '55) to his parents. "I am willing to go and help enforce the laws and sustain the government if it becomes necessary," he wrote. "How a man who has taken the 'oath of Allegiance' and is willing to do his whole duty as a citizen can say less than this I do not see." Perhaps sensing the implications of such a duty, French added, "May an overruling Providence hear the petitions which this day have been offered, and avert that most horrible of all calamities, Civil War."[2]

The regular United States Army in April 1861 consisted of only a few hundred officers and about 16,000 men. This small standing army, wholly incapable of putting down a large scale insurrection, was scattered across the vast expanse of the country. Although a few state militia units in the North were sufficiently organized and trained to be immediately useful, it was clear that the burden of supplying military manpower would be borne by those citizens who stood by the national government. President Abraham Lincoln's initial call for 75,000 volunteers to suppress the rebellion prompted hundreds of thousands to rally to the Stars and Stripes. These men had to be organized into units, uniformed, equipped, trained, and led into combat—a difficult mission for which the "American System of Education" had specifically prepared Norwich alumni.

Wherever the outbreak of hostilities found them, Norwich University men were among the first to answer the call. In addition, Norwich was unique among the colleges and universities within those states remaining loyal to the Union, since it was the only non-Federal military college. According to the Census of 1860, besides West Point and Annapolis, ten military colleges were in operation in the country. Unfortunately for President Lincoln and the Union, eight of these were in Southern states and one was in a border state. Alabama, Kentucky, Louisiana, Mississippi and Tennesse each held one institution, and both South Carolina and Virginia hosted a pair of such schools. Norwich, which had struggled at times to maintain its very existence, suddenly found itself as the singular non-Federal asset for training Union officers.[3]

The effect of armed rebellion on the Norwich University campus and in the Corps of Cadets was immediately apparent. The *University Reveille* appealed to the cadets' patriotism: ". . . our country calls, and her brave sons are ready to do their duty . . . . Let others come and prepare themselves either for peace or war." Pointing out those things that made Norwich unique from other Union colleges, the paper added, "All may come and take a thorough collegiate course, which, together with military discipline, will fit their minds as well as bodies for the good of their country, in whatever sphere it may be."[4]

Those governing the institution believed their cadets and graduates were ready for the contest confronting them. The Norwich submission to the July 1861 national publication *University Quarterly* reported that "no College in the land has felt more severely the shock which civil war has produced, than Norwich University." The initial impact of the war had gutted the institution's cadet population. "Our condition at present is truly novel. All our seniors have gone from us, and but four Juniors remain. . . .we hope and believe that their deeds in the coming contest will speak well for us and for our military discipline and training, and make the name of N.U. to be known widely as the institution of its kind, second only to the U.S. Military Academy at West Point."[5]

The words of the cadets were prophetic. Actually, by the time these words were published, the entire Norwich Class of 1861 and all but four of the Class of 1862 were on active duty and no commencement was held in 1861. By the end of that summer, more than 200 Norwich alumni were to be found in Union combat units, gone from campus, home, and job "to uphold the cause of Right."[6]

On April 18, six days after Fort Sumter was fired upon, the cadet corps escorted Sgt. Maj. Samuel J. Shattuck (Class of '60), lately their tutor of mathematics and military science, to the train station at White River Junction. Shattuck was departing to join the ranks of the mobilized and soon to be famous 6th Massachusetts Volunteer Infantry (Militia) Regiment. Concurrently, Norwich University's Brig. Gen. Alonzo Jackman (Class of '36), who had commanded all of the Vermont militia troops at the state musters of 1860 and 1861, had been among the first Vermonters to offer his sword to his state. Governor Erastus Fairbanks, however, refused to allow him to go on active service and urged him to remain at Norwich. "There is a duty, a very patriotic duty for you to perform," he wrote, ". . . to remain at the Military College and qualify young men for duty as officers, and thus you will do your State the best service."[7]

Jackman reluctantly complied, and throughout the war traveled the state of Vermont with hand-picked contingents of cadet officers to organize and drill troops of newly-mustered regiments. For instance, the companies for the 1st Vermont Volunteer Infantry, with at least nine Norwich alumni in its ranks, were personally selected and drilled by Jackman and his cadets prior to their deployment. Many of the officers and enlisted men of this three-month regiment went on to distinguished wartime careers in other units, particularly within the crack Vermont Brigade.[8]

In the following months, it became routine to dispatch detachments of cadets from the Norwich campus to train Vermont troops. For example, during 1863, in what had become by then a common wartime practice, fifteen cadets were assigned to Vermont training camps as state drillmasters with the rank of first lieutenant. It was later acknowledged that the proficient service performed by Vermont units in the war was largely due to the instruction rendered by Jackman and his cadets. By war's end, at least 108 Norwich alumni would serve with Vermont troops, and every Vermont regiment had at least one alumnus in its ranks at some time during its existence. Twelve of eighteen Vermont regiments had at least one Norwich man serving in field grade rank. In addition, as hostilities loomed, special detachments of Norwich cadets were formed and dispatched to drill and train companies of Bowdoin, Colby, and Dartmouth students. As a result of their Norwich-provided instruction, many college men were aided in qualifying for commissions in regiments of the various states.[9]

Major General William T. Sherman later stated that the efficiency and outstanding combat reputation of the New England regiments was largely due to the Norwich men in their ranks. The men of whom Sherman wrote numbered at least 304 alumni, broken down by state service as follows:

> Vermont - 108
> Massachusetts - 95
> New Hamsphire - 37
> Rhode Island - 33
> Connecticut - 16
> Maine - 15
>
> Total - 304[10]

The role played by drillmasters in the Civil War was critical to the success of the Federal armies and has been largely ignored by historians of the conflict. One need only read battle reports or skim through the text, diagrams, and steps for troop maneuvering and firing the regulation rifle in *Gilham's Manual for Volunteers and Militia* and William J. Hardee's *Rifle and Light Infantry Tactics* to appreciate their importance to the cause. No fewer than 122 Norwich alumni served as drillmasters in every state in the Union, and one, Capt. George Tucker (Class of '47), served for a time as drillmaster general of the Army of the Potomac in 1863. Untold thousands of citizen-soldiers were drilled by Norwich men. As alluded to above, the presence and influence of these alumni drillmasters was especially widespread and effective in the New England states and regiments.[11]

As the men of the North and South rushed off to war, how did the participation of Norwich men compare to that of other established colleges and universities? While it is true that Norwich was a military college and as such its alumni might well be expected to serve, in relation to other colleges of the era it had one of the nation's smallest prewar student and alumni populations. A few comparative figures indicate an exceptionally high level of wartime service by Norwich alumni:

SCHOOL	ALUMNI	SERVING	% SERVING	OFFICERS	% of OFFICERS
Bowdoin	1,770	443	25.02*	353	79.69
Dartmouth	2,800	669	23.89	450	67.26
Norwich	1,351	658	48.63	569	86.47*[12]

Taking the Union as a whole, 17.6% of the male population of the United States, for ages 15-50, took part in the war. A sampling of a similar age group for alumni of the following universities shows:

SCHOOL	CLASSES	% SERVING
Harvard	1841-61	24
Yale	1841-61	23
Norwich	1841-61	72[13]

The Civil War participation statistics for Norwich alumni listed above represent minimum participation and do not include 241 military-age alumni for whom no service data is available or those who

---

*The author has been able to determine the rank of only 642 of these men. These totals do not include "more than 100" special military students who became officers after these courses but does include both Union and Confederate service. If the special students were included the percentage of Norwich alumni participation would increase to 52.23 and the percentage serving as officers to 88.09.

died before the war. To this total must be added those alumni (total number unknown) who cannot be identified as matriculating due to the loss of their attendance records, and the unknown war record of many of our numerous Southern alumni. Undoubtedly, some of these alumni whose service records are not known not only served in the war, but also served in the Army of the Potomac. While these statistics may be minimized by saying that it was logical for the alumni of a military school to participate in the war, the figures are nevertheless impressive. Furthermore, the fact that most of these alumni left civilian pursuits and employments for military service must be recognized.[14]

Volunteers flocked to enroll and the loyal states competed with each other to raise, equip, and train units. The enthusiasm to serve proved contagious, and patriotic fervor ran at a fever pitch. When a Massachusetts unit passed through New York on its way to Washington in April 1861, where the military threat to the Union's seat of power was viewed as both grave and imminent, one of the soldiers, when asked how many Bay Staters were coming, shouted "How many? We're all a-coming!" In the North, perhaps war fever ran hottest in Massachusetts, a stronghold of abolitionism. Lieutenant Charles Bowers (Class of '52), Company G, 5th Massachusetts Infantry, wrote to his son Charlie from Boston on April 21, 1861, that "We are now in Faneuil Hall. The Brigade Band is playing patriotic and inspiring music, we are all in excellent spirits and are momentarily expecting the order to march." Conjuring up the shades of the state's revolutionary forefathers, Bowers spoke of "The glorious associations of the past that are called up by this place, the momentous issues of the present, both conspire to fill us all with intense desires to do our whole duty, and be worthy of the confidence that is placed in us. . . ." To his family Bowers wrote that he hoped ". . . before many months I may return and then the fact of a free country and a glorious destiny, and a joyful greeting with you all will more than compensate for all our Sacrifices." Sensing that he and his comrades might not be sufficient to put down the rebellion, Bowers wrote ". . . I hear a meeting is to be held tonight to form a new Company. I am glad to hear it. I want dear old Concord to be foremost in the conflict. Tell all to stand ready to come if necessary. No sacrifice is too great to make when freedom is in peril."[15]

Lieutenant Bowers, who later served in the 32nd Massachusetts, kept his family abreast of developments during his tour of duty. He wrote his wife from Washington on May 4, 1861 that "Another week of camp life has ended. . . .I don't know how it is that I can endure such wear and tear and suffer no more from it. It must be the Cause in which I am enlisted . . ." Charles was excited by what he saw in the national capital. "All anxiety is dismissed concerning every thing . . . The tone of the sentiment in Washington is all I can desire." Abolitionist in temperament and confident of the war's outcome, he stated, "Let the north pour down her 500,000 men all armed for the fight, and their simple presence will strike terror and dismay into the ranks of the rebels. I feel that 'the day of their deliverance is drawing nigh,' and the words of the faithful hated Abolitionists that were `Sown in weakness are being raised in power.' This must be a day of jubilee to Garrison and his faithful coadjutors . . . . Cannon balls and bayonets are the strong arguments that will strike off the fetters from every bondsman."[16]

From his father in Vermont, Oscar A. Learnard (Class of '55), a strong abolitionist and Union man residing in Kansas, received a letter informing him of what was transpiring in the east: ". . . .Ere this you have learned that our Nation is engaged in Civil (or uncivil) war—there (is) much excitement in the vicinity. . .Fort Sumter is taken &. . . that a large force are on the march to take Washington." Do not worry, explained his father, as "Thousands of men are marching to defend the Capital" and "God speed them & long may the Stars & Stripes our emblem of Liberty, wave over the Capital of those now distracted states." In line with the anti-slavery feeling prevalent in the state, the elder Learnard added that "Persons not acquainted with our History would enquire, what is the cause of all this commotion—There is but one answer, that is—slavery." With the conviction of a preacher he confessed that "Some think I am rather obstinate when I said that I had rather see this nation drenched in Blood, then secumb (sic) to Slavery—We have raised a lofty liberty pole & have a splendid flag—under whose banner we hope to rally men to aid in the cause of Freedom." Worrying as only parents can about their children, no matter what the age, he closed by writing "PS . . . Mother says don't go (to) War . . . I think you have done your part."[17]

In the Spring of 1861, Rebel troops were ensconced across the Potomac River from the District of Columbia, and from the White House their flags could be seen daily flying in Alexandria. Spurred by the April 15 appeal from President Abraham Lincoln for 75,000 militia to serve for three months, the most combat ready state militia units rapidly deployed to the capital. Among the first to arrive was the 6th Massachusetts Volunteer Infantry (Militia). This regiment, which referred to itself as the "Minutemen of 1861," had to fight its way through mobs in the streets of Baltimore on April 19 (ironically, the anniversary of the Revolutionary War battles of Lexington and Concord). Seven Norwich men were in its ranks during that encounter. One of them, Cpl. Abbot A. Shattuck (Class of '64), was with Company C, one of the four rifle companies attacked by the mobs on their way through the city. Theirs was the first of many regiments to come to the capital, and they were the vanguard of the 235 alumni who would later serve in 133 regiments and several additional independent artillery batteries of the Army of the Potomac.[18]

Many believed that much of the preparation was unnecessary. Indeed, prevailing Union and Confederate civilian and military opinion predicted a short, glorious, and victorious war. As a result, most state-activated and federally-mustered units deploying to Washington at the time were called into service for only three months (90 days). The regiments arriving in response to the President's call contained at least 30 alumni spread across infantry units including the 2nd Maine, 1st, 5th, and 6th Massachusetts, 1st and 2nd New Hampshire, 2nd and 11th New York, 2nd and 4th Pennsylvania, 1st and 2nd Vermont, and the 1st and 2nd Wisconsin. These regiments, many of which reenlisted for three years when their initial tour of duty expired, would be among the troops constituting the all-volunteer core during the Army of the Potomac's formative days. Additional calls for volunteers—which included plans for a major expansion of the Regular Army and navy and the first enrollment of three-year men—were issued by President Lincoln on May 24, 1861.[19]

In early June, Brevet Lt. Gen. Winfield Scott, the United States Army's General-in-Chief, tasked Brig. Gen. Irvin McDowell to submit "an estimate of the number and composition of a column to be pushed towards Manassas Junction." This order initiated a chain of events which led to the first major battle and large scale casualties of the war at Bull Run on July 21, 1861. However, the first real land encounter in the Eastern Theater, in hindsight a militarily insignificant clash, occurred on June 10 at Big Bethel, Virginia. This skirmish was triggered when troops from Fortress Monroe under Brig. Gen. Benjamin J. Butler marched inland to destroy or force away a Southern artillery battery under construction near Yorktown at Big Bethel. The attack was made by five New York regiments and five companies of the 1st Vermont, in which four Norwich alumni served. Butler's thrust was a failure, and Federal troops suffered 76 casualties in the event, with Confederate losses totalling only eight men. Southern success at Big Bethel raised Southern morale and gave birth to the first Northern concerns about the conduct of the war. Displaying growing impatience, congressional and public opinion, coupled with an anxious Northern press, called for the army to move "Forward to Richmond!"[20]

In and around Washington, the business of organizing and training a large army was well underway. Thousands of raw troops, too many of them of the three-month variety, were slowly becoming accustomed to army life. Demands for action and the limited time within which to utilize the 90-day regiments pressured the Union high command to commit the army to an offensive movement despite significant doubts as to the army's actual combat readiness.

As these events were unfolding, a new three-year regiment, the 12th Massachusetts, passed through New York City on its way to the front. Several Norwich men marched with the regiment, including Capt. Edward C. Saltmarsh (Class of '61), Capt. Jedediah H. Baxter (Class of '56), and Pvt. William H. Hooper (Class of '67), Company K. As the Bay Staters paraded down Broadway, they sang a song they had learned during their initial activation and training in Massachusetts:

> John Brown's body lies a-moldering in the grave,
> John Brown's body lies a-moldering in the grave,
> John Brown's body lies a-moldering in the grave,
> But his truth goes marching on.

The tune was electrifying and an immediate sensation. In the months to come, after new lyrics were provided by Julia Ward Howe, it would pass into the nation's consciousness as our national war song, "The Battle Hymn of the Republic."[21]

When General McDowell's army finally marched on July 16, it consisted of some 45 regiments grouped into 20 brigades and five divisions. Included in this force were eight understrength companies of United States Regular Army infantry and a small battalion of United States Marines. None of the units had any training above the brigade level, and no road marches had been conducted prior to the movement. Indeed, few officers had ever commanded anything larger than a regiment. In McDowell's ranks were at least 28 Norwich alumni serving in the 1st Minnesota, 2nd Connecticut, 2nd New York, 2nd Wisconsin, 2nd Vermont, 3rd New Jersey Volunteers, 4th Michigan, 5th Massachusetts, 11th New York, 16th New York, the U.S. Army Regulars and Marines, and on a brigade staff. The march from Washington toward Manassas was exhausting, largely because most of the men wore wool uniforms in the oppressive July heat and humidity. The staffs had no experience handling large units and few of the soldiers had marched more than a few miles with their full combat equipment. Their lack of field training was aptly demonstrated by the trail of discarded supplies and straggling troops left to the sides and rear of the army. Nevertheless, by the evening of July 20, McDowell's expedition faced the Confederates across Bull Run Creek.[22]

The Battle of Bull Run (or Manassas, as the Confederates called it) proved equally confusing for both combatants. The hastily trained troops were unaccustomed to active field service, and the hard marching and fighting completely disorganized the respective armies. The uniforms worn by both sides compounded problems, as some Federal units were clothed in gray and thus mistaken for Southerners, while some Secessionists were dressed in blue and mistaken for Federals. The flags carried by both armies were also similar in design, adding to the chaos of the field.

After a long and tiring march around the Confederate left flank on the morning of July 21, Brig. Gen. Samuel Heintzelman's three-brigade Federal division joined the heavy fighting along the Sudley Road designed to turn the Southerners from their position along Bull Run Creek. By the time Heintzelman arrived the fighting had grown confused and the units intermingled. He dispatched regiments from

Col. William B. Franklin's brigade to support the faltering Federal line. The 5th Massachusetts (3rd Lt. Charles Bowers, Class of '52 and Cpl. George B. Buttrick, Class of '56, both of Company G) and 11th Massachusetts were employed to strengthen the line along the Warrenton Turnpike, while the 1st Minnesota (1st Lt. James Hollister, Company E, Class of '55) joined in the battle in support of Ambrose Burnside's weakened command. The regiments were hit hard, largely by Southern artillery, which broke up their advance. Heintzelman then ordered up the 11th New York, known as "Ellsworth's Zouaves" (1st Lt. Edward K. Aldrich, Class of '66), and a battalion of United States Marines (2nd Lt. Robert E. Hitchcock, Class of '59) from Andrew Porter's brigade to their assistance and to support a threatened Union artillery battery. These units and others forced the Confederates from positions on Matthews Hill. For a time, despite the piecemeal nature of the fighting, it seemed the Federals had won. The 5th Massachusetts and 1st Minnesota fought well at Henry Hill, even though their disjointed attacks and counterattacks were driven back by the fire of several Southern regiments and guns. The wounded included the 1st Minnesota's Lieutenant Hollister.

After two hours of indecisive fighting on the hill, General McDowell committed Brig. Gen. William T. Sherman's 3,000-man brigade to the desperate action. Unfortunately for the Federals, Sherman launched his regiments into the battle east across the Sudley Road and against Henry Hill one at a time rather than as a body. The members of one of his regiments, the 2nd Wisconsin (1st Lt. Charles K. Dean, Company C, Class of '45, and Sgt. Julius C. "Shanghai" Chandler, Company G, Class of '45), deployed for action in gray uniforms. Destined to win future fame as part of the legendary "Iron Brigade," the Wisconsoners fought well and suffered heavy losses from both enemy and friendly fire. Among the casualties was Sergeant Chandler, who fell with a serious wound in the head at the height of the action. The regiment's command situation had recently undergone a change in the top position. Norwich alumnus Col. Squire Park Coon (Class of '42), formerly the commanding officer of the 2nd Wisconsin, had engaged in a disruptive internal dispute with his officers just a few weeks earlier. The intercine feud—fueled by unsubstantiated rumors of alcohol abuse—was at least temporarily resolved when Coon was ordered up to serve on Sherman's brigade staff, in which capacity he served during the battle. Coon performed well enough under fire at Bull Run to earn a personal commendation from both Sherman and his division commander, Brig. Gen. Daniel Tyler.

Another Norwich graduate who fought in support of Sherman's brigade that afternoon was 1st Lt. Dunbar R. Ransom (Class of '51). Ransom served with Battery E, 3rd United States Artillery, and earned his first citation for gallantry while covering the brigade's attack and the army's subsequent disastrous retreat from the battlefield. According to the lieutenant's commanding officer, ". . .the coolness and gallantry of First Lieut. Dunbar R. Ransom on all occasions, and particularly when under fire of three pieces. . .when the battery was about to be charged by a large body of cavalry, and also when crossing a broken bridge in a rough gully, and fired upon in the rear by the enemy's infantry, were conspicuous."[23]

Brigadier General Oliver O. Howard's brigade, the last of Heintzleman's division to engage at Bull Run, arrived on the field as the battle for Henry Hill was ending, about 3:00 p.m. Many of Howard's men had fallen from the ranks because of the intense heat and 10-mile forced march. Howard formed his regiments north of the Warrenton Turnpike and ascended Chinn Ridge with the intent of turning the left flank of the Confederate line on Henry Hill. Unfortunately for Howard, Southern reinforcements were arriving in relatively large numbers. The first line of Howard's brigade consisted of the 2nd Vermont (1st Lt. Walter A. Phillipes, Company F, Class of '62 and Sgt. Van Buren Sleeper, Company E, Class of '61) and the 4th Maine, followed by a second line consisting of the 3rd and 5th Maine. By the time Howard's advance reached the crest of Chinn Ridge advancing Confederates opened fire on it. A stand-up affair ensued for some time during which the Federals discharged about half of their ammunition before being relieved by the remaining pair of Maine regiments. The fight continued for a while until the 5th Maine's commanding officer miscontrued an order to relign a portion of his regiment as a call for a general withdrawal. The troops began pouring rearward, and Howard's "realignment" developed into a general retreat. This retrograde movement, in turn, exposed the flank of a line of Regular troops, which were also forced to fall back.

The thin varnish of discipline present in the untested units disintegrated. What began as an organized and orderly retreat became a full-fledged panic and rout which did not end until the remnants of the army staggered back into Washington. Even in retreat some units, like Sykes' Regulars, stood and fought well and covered the withdrawal. The 16th New York, under the direct command of Lt. Col. Samuel Marsh (Class of '39), was the last Union unit to leave the field. When it retreated, it did so in good order and without undue panic, one of a very few units that can claim such a distinction. Fortunately for McDowell, the Confederates were as disorganized by their victory as the Northerners were in their defeat, and did not follow up their hard-won success.[24]

The Norwich alumni, all things considered, fought as well as anyone at Bull Run, where they suffered their first combat casualties and fatalities of the war. Second Lieutenant Robert E. Hitchcock (Class of '59), United States Marine Corps, became the first Vermont officer and the first marine to give his life for the Union. During the battle the marine battalion had broken three times but rallied after each retreat. In his shirt-sleeves with a lighted cigar in his mouth, Lieutenant Hitchcock dressed his men to take part in another attack, calling out "Come on with your fighting geese!" As he advanced his men yet again, a cannon shot whizzed through the air and struck him in the head, severing it above the eyes. Hitchcock's casual dress and the fact that the Federals did not retain possession of the field made it impossible to later identify his remains.[25]

The nation was stunned by the disaster at Bull Run. For the vast majority of Northerners, the defeat acted as a gigantic reveille. Dreams of a short and glorious war disappeared and were replaced by the realization that a long and bloody conflict was in the offing. Within days a dynamic new commander, fresh from a series of minor victories in west Virginia which were much inflated by the press and his personal dispatches, was summoned to Washington to command the growing Union war machine. Thirty-five-year old Maj. Gen. George B. McClellan, soon nicknamed the "Young Napoleon" by an admiring media and public, would be the Union's key military personality for the next fifteen months.[26]

While McClellan has been faulted by historians for many failings, instilling discipline, restoring morale, and preparing troops for battle are not among them. By his ability, youthful looks, dash, and a knack for establishing a close rapport with the men, "Little Mac" quickly became the darling of the troops who had survived Bull Run and of the new units pouring into the capital in ever increasing numbers. Comprehensive training programs were implemented for both officers and soldiers, camp life became strictly regulated, selection boards to eliminate unfit officers were instituted, and regular army-style discipline was introduced and enforced.

Concurrent with these events on July 25, 1861 was the birth of the Army of the Potomac, which was brought about by the consolidation of the Departments of Washington and Northeastern Virginia. Serving with distinction on the staff of that army from its inception was Lt. Col. Albert V. Colburn (Class of '53), described in contemporary accounts as a "bold soldier of the Green Mountain State." Colburn was a favorite and highly valued aide-de-camp of McClellan's, handled all the headquarters correspondence, and remained with the general during his entire tenure with the Army of the Potomac.[27]

As part of McClellan's fall training program, a major dress review of 70,000 troops was held at Bailey's Crossroads, Virginia, on November 20, 1861. The lone brigade of "Western" troops to parade that day (which would later be recognized as the "Iron Brigade"), contained three Norwich alumni: Lt. Col. William W. Robinson of the 7th Wisconsin (Class of '41), Capt. David Noyes (Class of '45), Company A, 6th Wisconsin, and 1st Lt. Charles K. Dean (Class of '45), Company C, 2nd Wisconsin. As the men marched back from the ceremony to their training camp at Arlington Heights, a soldier in the 6th Wisconsin began the great marching song, "John Brown's Body." Soon the entire brigade was singing as it tramped back to camp. Julia Ward Howe was among those attending that day's review who heard the troops singing enthusiastically. She was so moved by the event that she could not get the tune out of her mind. That night, while a guest in the brigade's camp on Arlington Heights, Howe penned the following words:

> Mine eyes have seen the glory of
> the coming of the Lord;
> He is trampling out the vintage where
> the grapes of wrath are stored;
> He hath loosed the fateful lightning of His
> terrible swift sword,
> His truth is marching on.

After finishing the initial stanza, Howe looked out from the hill, over the misty valley aglow with the flicker of many campfires and continued:

> I have seen Him in the watch-fires of
> a hundred circling-camps;
> They have builded Him an altar in
> the evening dews and damps;
> I can read His righteous sentence by
> the dim and flaring lamps.
> His day is marching on.

These words, of course, would become part of the "Battle Hymn of the Republic," one of the most popular military songs in history.[28]

Life in the camps of the Army of the Potomac in late summer and early fall was relatively pleasant. Among the numerous army regiments picketing the banks of the Potomac River was the 20th Massachusetts ("The Harvard Regiment"), commanded by Col. William R. Lee (Class of '25). After graduating from Norwich Lee attended West Point, where Southern Cadet Jefferson Davis was numbered among his classmates. Lee's handpicked officers for the 20th Massachusetts included an obscure young captain (and future Supreme Court justice) Oliver Wendell Holmes, Jr., in addition to many other Harvard men. Colonel Lee was one of the oldest field officers in the service, and probably the second oldest in the army after Brig. Gen. Edwin V. "Bull" Sumner. The 20th Massachusetts was considered an elite regiment (at least by its own members). For example, when Brig. Gen. Charles P. Stone, Lee's division commander, asked if the unit had everything it needed, Lee replied: "My regiment, sir, came from

Massachusetts!" Lee was hard on his men but well-liked. Lieutenant Henry Livermore Abbot cried the eternal complaints of army second lieutenants in a letter home on September 25, 1861, when he wrote that "Very few of the (honors), I notice do the ignoble second lieuts. get. The col. roughs us poor second lieuts. awfully." As an example, noted Abbott, ". . . he makes a general remark to all officers assembled about their conduct, & then adds, 'of course all you capts. are all right. It is these young lieuts. (pointing to us) that I mean particularly. They are very heedless & need a great deal of looking after." Despite his complaints, Abbot added a caveat to his griping by claiming that ". . . the colonel is a regular old brick & I think we could all bear being snubbed every day for the sake of being commanded by such a bully old fighter . . . ."[29]

Like most of the army's regiments, the 20th Massachusetts trained hard and yearned for action. On October 20, General Stone was informed by McClellan that the Confederates might be evacuating Leesburg, and that "perhaps a small demonstration on your part would have the effect to move them."[30]

Four days later, Lieutenant Abbott wrote home that just before the battle of Ball's Bluff Colonel Lee was ". . .in the merriest of moods, he joked & quoted Shakespeare & appeared transported at the idea of at last getting into action." Despite this levity, "At the same time, he didn't omit mention of a single circum(stance) that would help make us safe. I never heard of a more clearsighted, cooler, or more satisfactory statement of a plan than was his. He discussed every possible emergency & suggested the action appropriate for it. Nothing escaped him. . . ." When Lee finished his pep talk with his men, "He wound up every thing by the assertion that it must be distinctly understood beforehand that in case of defeat, no retreat was possible. We must either conquer or die."[31]

At dawn on October 21, two companies of the 20th accompanied by Colonel Lee crossed the Potomac and climbed a dominating bluff to join a portion of the 15th Massachusetts which had crossed the night before. Union intelligence, however, proved faulty, for the Confederates had not evacuated the area at all. A day long battle developed under the overall command of former United States Senator Col. Edward D. Baker, a personal friend of President Lincoln's. The two regiments, joined by the 42nd New York and 71st Pennsylvania, made a hard fight of it. Late in the day, however, Baker was killed and the Federal line began to unravel. Superior numbers of Rebel troops pushed the Northerners off the steep bluff and down to the river bank below. A fighting withdrawal across a river is a difficult endeavor under the best of circumstances, let alone with green troops. While most escaped, large numbers of men panicked and drowned trying to swim back to Union lines or were overrun and captured before reaching the river. One of the captured Northerners was Colonel Lee. Mindful, perhaps, of his pre-battle speech, Lee had refused to leave the field and save himself before all his wounded could be evacuated. The withdrawal was supported from the northern bank by troops under the command of Brig. Gen. Frederick W. Lander (Class of '41), whose brigade included the 19th Massachusetts (Capt. Edmund Rice, Company F, Class of '60, and 1st Lt. Henry A. Hale, Company H, Class of '61), and the 1st Minnesota (1st Lt. James Hollister, Company E, Class of '55). Both Edmund Rice and Henry Hale (and their respective companies) were directly involved in ferrying troops over the Potomac River into the battle, covering the retreat, ferrying wounded back to the northern bank, and in nighttime picket duty.

General Lander would be severely wounded in the leg during skirmishing operations on October 22 and die from pneumonia and the effects of his wounds. In the immediate aftermath of the battle, however, Lander was extremely impressed by the bravery of his brigade's Massachusetts members. It was reported to him that the Confederates had observed that fewer Massachusetts officers would have been killed if they had not been too proud to surrender. Lander, deeply moved by their sacrifice, wrote an eight stanza poem, very popular at the time, which began:

> Aye, deem us proud, for we are more
> Than proud of all our mighty dead. . .
> Old State—some souls are rudely sped—
> This record for thy Twentieth Corps—
> Imprisoned, wounded, dying, dead,
> It only asks, "Has Sparta more?"

On Christmas Day 1861, the 20th Massachusetts was presented a silk state memorial flag, a gift from the sisters of an officer of the regiment killed at Ball's Bluff. It bore on one side the name "Ball's Bluff," the state pine tree, and the motto "Stand in the Evil Day." The regiment went on to become one of the most prominent regiments in the Army of the Potomac.[32]

Colonel Lee had a particularly rough time following his capture. Despite his age, he refused to accept a Rebel offer of parole which would have required him to sit out the rest of the war. Confined in Richmond within the walls of Libby Prison, Lee was one of seven officers selected by lot to be hung if Southern privateers were executed as pirates. One soldier of the 20th Massachusetts who was about to be released, on asking Colonel Lee if he had any last message for his regiment, received the emotional reply: "Tell the men—tell the men—tell the men—that their colonel died like a brave man." Fortunately for Lee and his fellow prisoners, however, they were paroled after the Federal government announced it would not execute captured Rebel privateers. Colonel Lee rejoined his regiment on May 2, 1862, in time for General McClellan's expedition up the Virginia peninsula.[33]

The remainder of the year and the early months of 1862 were used by McClellan to perfect the organization and training of the Army of the Potomac. The training was critical, for scores of new units were flocking to the army. The men and their regiments had to be prepared for field and combat duty and organized into brigades and divisions, a difficult task that kept the army's drillmasters busy. As discipline gradually tightened during the fall of 1861, 2nd Lt. Walter Phillipes (Class of '62) of the 2nd Vermont Infantry fell afoul of military justice following a minor scrap at Lewinsville, Virginia. He and a 100-man picket force had just returned to camp and an expected well-earned rest when a regimental muster was held. Being volunteers, and acting on the theory that American volunteers need not respond to unreasonable orders, the men remained in their tents. The regimental commander was furious when he heard of the incident. Phillipes was court-martialed and dismissed from the service. Unwilling to sit out the rest of the war, however, he enlisted (after changing the spelling of his name) in Company H, 13th Vermont. The enterprising former officer, who later earned a commission and fought at Gettysburg, would go on to serve as a 1st lieutenant in the 3rd Vermont Light Artillery, where he earned a citation for gallantry.[34]

In the 7th Wisconsin, Col. William W. Robinson (Class of '41) experienced disciplinary problems of a different kind. His daughter fell in love with a lieutenant in his regiment. After forbidding them to see each other, the colonel was thwarted in his efforts when love triumphed and the couple eloped and got married in Washington. Despite his initial unhappiness with his future son-in-law, Robinson apparently learned to live with the situation, as no further problems are recorded.[35]

Dozens of Norwich alumni were scattered throughout the ranks of the new regiments joining the Army of the Potomac that fall. Before the end of the war, at least 235 alumni would serve in the ranks of that army in 133 different regiments. As might be expected, large numbers of Norwich University alumni were found in Vermont units. At least 108 alumni served the Union in that state's regiments and batteries. The combat reputation, casualties, and accomplishments of the Vermonters were well-known both inside and outside the ranks of the army.[36]

On November 2, George McClellan officially replaced the aged Maj. Gen. Winfield Scott as General-in-Chief of the Armies of the Republic. Over the course of the fall and winter, while great work was being done to prepare the army for field duty, virtually no offensive activity took place in the Eastern Theater. Rightly or wrongly, an offensive was what the President, Congress, and the nation demanded. The lack of combat operations by the army during that time, moreover, led to a deterioration of good will and trust towards the commander of the Army of the Potomac, which did not bode well for McClellan's relationship with President Lincoln, his cabinet, or Congress.[37]

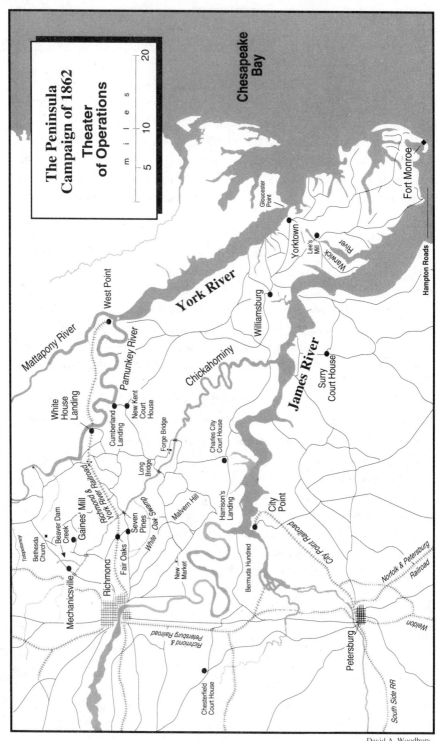

The Peninsula Campaign of 1862
Theater of Operations

miles

5   10   20

Chesapeake Bay

Fort Monroe

Hampton Roads

Gloucester Point

Yorktown

Lee's Mill

Warwick River

Williamsburg

York River

West Point

Mattapony River

Pamunkey River

Chickahominy

James River

Surry Court House

White House Landing

Cumberland Landing

New Kent Court House

Forge Bridge

Charles City Court House

Long Bridge

Richmond & York River Railroad

Beaver Dam Creek

Gaines' Mill

Seven Pines

White Oak Swamp

Malvern Hill

Harrison's Landing

City Point

City Point Railroad

Bethesda Church

Totopotomoy

Mechanicsville

Fair Oaks

Richmond

New Market

Bermuda Hundred

Norfolk & Petersburg Railroad

Richmond & Petersburg Railroad

Chesterfield Court House

Petersburg

Weldon

South Side RR

David A. Woodbury

III. The Peninsula Campaign through Fredericksburg

"They are bright and untarnished"
Colonel William R. Lee '25

After the carnage of Bull Run and Ball's Bluff, the relatively quiet winter months were welcome ones for the Army of the Potomac. As the early months of 1862 slipped past, much of the Republican administration's confidence in General McClellan waned. Since the previous fall, every attempt to prod McClellan into action had failed. In the early days following Bull Run and Big Bethel, "Little Mac's" arguments in favor of delay made sense. The new units and officers needed training, and the logistics and administrative problems of an army the size of the Army of the Potomac were staggering. As the end of winter approached, however, Lincoln's patience, as well as that of many in Congress and the press, wore thin. The Union could only suppress the rebellion by offensive action, and thus far McClellan had done little other than drill and organize his army.

By late winter it appeared as though McClellan was ready to commit his army to battle. After a plan to move the Army of the Potomac to Urbanna, Virginia, became obsolete when Joe Johnston's Confederates evacuated Manassas on March 8-9, 1862, McClellan devised a strategically innovative and daring combined operation against the Southern capital of Richmond. Massive in scope, its objective was nothing less than the capture or destruction of the Confederacy's Eastern power base. McClellan's concept called for a strategic regrouping of the Army of the Potomac by water to the tip of the Virginia peninsula, a narrow strip of land flanked by the York and James rivers. Once opposite Yorktown, McClellan intended to march the Army of the Potomac up the peninsula and seize Richmond before Johnston could be redeployed from northern Virginia to defend it. Success depended largely on celerity of movement. The Peninsula Campaign officially got underway on March 17, 1862, when the leading elements of the Army of the Potomac set sail for Fortress Monroe in what was the largest military movement of any kind ever seen in North America. In fact, McClellan's juggernaut involved more than three times the total number of troops mobilized for the entire Mexican War.[1]

The army that disembarked at Fortress Monroe—a move which initially surprised the Confederates—contained at least 79 Norwich men ranging in grade from private to brigadier general (and division commander). Many of these men served in units which would soon play prominent roles in the developing campaign. One of the alumni worthy of mention is 2nd Lt. Edward B. Williston (Class of '56), Battery D, 2nd United States Artillery. His initiation to combat would come while serving as a gun section commander under 1st Lt. Emory Upton, who would rise to high rank and fame during the war as an innovative tactician.[2]

Once the advance of the army from Fortress Monroe began on April 4, however, three factors destined to plague McClellan throughout the Peninsula Campaign decisively entered into play: miserable weather, bad luck, and faulty intelligence. The Federal advance bogged down as heavy rainstorms turned roads into deep mud, and incorrect intelligence (which held that a network of good roads was available upon which to march the army toward Richmond) further slowed and confused the operation. By the time McClellan approached Yorktown, Confederate Maj. Gen. John B. "Prince John" Magruder further complicated Federal plans by splitting his weak force into segments and parading them repeatedly across the front of the Union lines, a clever tactic that caused McClellan to overestimate the strength of the Rebel forces opposing him. Magruder's artful presentation behind powerful earthworks, combined with the bad weather and Lincoln's decision to withhold Irvin McDowell's First Corps from the campaign for the defense of Washington, reinforced McClellan's natural tendency to exaggerate his enemy's strengths while downplaying his own. Thus, instead of a rapid and overwhelming advance against Yorktown and an immediate thrust against Richmond, the Army of the Potomac settled for a quasi-siege against Magruder's numerically inferior force.[3]

The heaviest fighting of the Siege of Yorktown took place on April 16 close to the Warwick River at Dam Number 1 near Lee's Mill. There, William F. Smith's Federal division moved out with orders to stop the Confederates from strengthening their works. Elements of the Vermont Brigade, which included an exceptionally literate private of the 2nd Vermont named Wilbur Fisk, received their baptism of fire in the action. According to Fisk, "The battle-field was in an opening surrounded by woods composed mostly of pine. The rebel fort was on the west side of the clearing, situated back in a kind of bay formed by the trees, and in front of it was a creek with a wide dam, which drank the blood of many of our men in one brief hour." The Vermonters, including several Norwich men, "quickly formed in line of battle, sheltered by a piece of pine woods bordering on the creek which separated us from the enemy," wrote one participant. "The Fourth [Vermont] also participated actively in the fight. Part of them. . .had advanced to the creek on the right, and when the Third and Sixth retreated, the enemy's attention was directed to the Fourth." The regiment, according to Fisk, was in "the most critical position with nothing to cover their retreat. . . .Nearly twenty of their number were killed or wounded." The probing reconnaissance conducted by Smith, whom McClellan had directed to avoid a general engagement, resulted in little other than the waste of artillery ammunition and the killing and maiming of 165 Federals. Southern losses were negligible. The fiasco, wrote one Federal, "took place at Dam No. 1. . .and was a Dam failure."[4]

Although the action proved militarily insignificant, the Vermonters had distinguished themselves in the affair. Many of the Sons of Ethan Allen and the Green Mountain Boys now rest side by side in the Yorktown National Cemetery. Their bravery was noted by friend and foe alike. During a temporary truce to recover the dead and wounded, Union and Confederate officers discussed the fight. The commander of the 2nd Louisiana asked what regiment it was that assaulted his fortifications. When told it was a detachment of the 3rd Vermont he is said to have replied: "It was lucky for us that you did not send over many such detachments." According to the *New York World*, "the fighting and the bravery of the Vermont boys covered the arms of their State with glory." Two Norwich alumni are worthy of special mention, albeit for widely varying reasons. First Lieutenant George B. French (Class of '55), 4th Vermont, was cited for gallantry in carrying dispatches and evacuating wounded comrades from the field. Another lieutenant, Edward A. Chandler (Class of '61), was not so fortunate. A member of Company F, 3rd Vermont, Chandler was severely wounded when a minie ball destroyed three bones in his hand and penetrated his thigh.[5]

Not all of the casualties suffered during the affair at Lee's Mill were the result of Confederate shot and shell. It was determined soon after the fighting that Capt. William H. H. Hall (Class of '46), Company G, 6th Vermont Infantry, was "Ill from exposure." According to Hall's own writings, "while lying helpless in the field, after the enemy had charged, Hiram Hosland, six foot four inch in his stocking feet, picked [me] up and carried [me] back four miles. [I] was then placed in a wagon and taken to Washington, discharged." The details of Hall's medical discharge related the effects of his contribution to the Republic. "While in the service of the United States and in line of his duty at Warwick creek or Lee's Mills in the State of Virginia. . .on or about the 18th day of April, 1862, contracted a physical disability, produced by exposure to wet and cold which resulted in fever, nasal catarrh, a long difficulty, and rheumatism." Unfortunately, "at the same time, [Hall] had mumps and [the] resultant loss of a left testicle on account of which he was obliged to resign."[6]

As the armies continued glaring at each other across the Yorktown earthworks, the men of the 20th Massachusetts rejoiced over the return of the recently-paroled Colonel Lee, who had been captured at Ball's Bluff the preceding October. He rejoined his old regiment on the second day of May. Lieutenant Henry L. Abbott wrote his mother on May 18 that "Col. Lee is enormously popular with the regiment. He certainly has a charm of conciliating every body about him. All old cliques surrender to him unconditionally." Abbott and his comrades appreciated Lee's contributions to the 20th Massachusetts, which included hard work. "It is good to see the head officer work just as hard as his subordinates, always up before anybody, & 3 o'clock in the morning is no joke for a man who, though not very old, has suffered so many hardships." Abbott recognized that Lee's advanced age (Class of '25) caused him no little difficulty: "Some days too, he has been in his saddle all day long, so stiff at night that he can hardly get off."[7]

By the time the April-long siege stretched into early May, Joe Johnston determined that he had squeezed as much benefit as possible by holding the line at Yorktown. McClellan had spent weeks placing heavy guns in position in order to pry the Rebels from their lines with a massive artillery and mortar bombardment. How much longer would it be before he opened fire? Johnston knew that when that day arrived his army could not stand long under such a barrage. In the hopes of finding a location from which to more favorably oppose McClellan, Johnston quietly slipped his divisions out of the line on the night of May 3 and marched them up the peninsula toward the Confederate capital. Although some criticized this withdrawal, he did not leave too soon. McClellan later reported that he was ready to open fire with his heavy artillery by May 6.

Colonel Jesse A. Gove (Class of '49), commander of the 22nd Massachusetts, was one of the first Federals to reach historic Yorktown. Gove's regiment, together with 150 soldiers from the 13th New York, advanced without opposition, the enemy's works being "entirely evacuated." According to Gove, he "planted the first national flag upon the ramparts, the men giving three hearty cheers as it unfolded to the breeze." His actions during the campaign and particularly during a brisk skirmishing action had earned the admiration and praise of his superiors. Gove's brigade commander commented in a report dated April 11 that the 22nd Massachusetts "was under severe fire, and but for the cool, discreet, and fearless conduct of its commander would have suffered still more from their exposure."[8]

Gove appeared to be marked for higher command. His time on the peninsula would include an association with Professor Thaddeus Lowe's observation balloon, the army's first efforts at aerial reconnaissance. Colonel Gove is also credited by the United States Army as the first officer in the Civil War to have his men dig field entrenchments during active operations and the first to encounter (during the occupation of Yorktown) "land torpedoes," or what are commonly known as land mines. "It is my painful duty to report the wounding of 6 of Company G, Captain Whorf, from the explosion of a torpedo embedded in the surface of the ground," wrote Gove after he came into contact with the deadly explosives. Many believed that the use of subterranean "infernal machines," as the soldiers referred to them, conflicted with the general rules of civilized warfare, and thus it is not surprising that their use outraged Gove. "These inhuman missiles of war were placed in the field in front, in several houses, and in the roads and thoroughfares in the town," he complained. "One of the telegraph corps stepped on one of them, which exploded with deadly effect. It was a 10-inch shell concealed in the sand, and in the middle of the road."[9]

By the afternoon of May 4, much of the retreating Confederate army was camped near Williamsburg, a small town about eleven miles northwest of Yorktown. Months earlier Major General Magruder had erected a series of crude field works a couple miles east of the town which included a powerful earthwork near the center of the line named in his honor. James Longstreet's Division, which composed the rear guard of Johnston's army, filed into this line on the evening of May 4, while the balance of Johnston's force continued moving up the peninsula with the bulk of his slow-moving trains. The Federal vanguard of two divisions under Joseph Hooker and William F. Smith caught up with the withdrawing Southerners and struck Longstreet's line on May 5.

At the Battle of Williamsburg, Brig. Gen. Winfield S. Hancock led his Sixth Corps brigade in a long flanking march around the Confederate left flank. Once in position, Hancock drove his regiments forward and captured two unoccupied redoubts which he defended against vicious Southern assaults, earning in the process his first laurels of the war, his nickname ("Hancock the Superb"), and a superior reputation as a combat commander. Several Norwich alumni contributed to Hancock's gallant exploits, including Lt. Col. Harvey W. Emery (Class of '52), 5th Wisconsin, Capts. Charles A. Curtis (Class of '61) and Frank C. Peirce (Class of '62), both of the 6th Maine, and the 7th Maine's 1st Lt. Albert P. Titcomb (Class of '57).

Darkness eventually ended the action, which was followed by a renewal of the Rebel withdrawal toward Richmond. After the capture of Williamsburg on May 5, McClellan submitted a petition to Secretary of War Edwin Stanton requesting permission for his soldiers to place the names of battles on their regimental colors. This practice became a general and popular one in the army and was followed for the rest of the war.[10]

As the Peninsula Campaign dragged on, the soldiers gradually became accustomed to living in the field under difficult conditions in the face of the enemy. Reputations for dash and valor, or for that matter cowardice and inefficiency, were also being established by the army's officers. In addition, units began to establish their individual identities, personalities, and reputations on the field of battle. At Lee's Mill before Yorktown on April 16, for example, Federal soldiers assaulted an entrenched line for the first time. The Vermont Brigade's attack demonstrated that it was composed of quality material, and the engagement was but the first serious action in a long string of performances which would eventually transform the unit into one of the best combat brigades in the Army of the Potomac. The Vermont Brigade, in which at least 44 Norwich men eventually served, would finish the war as one of the few "pure" state brigades. It suffered more combat-related deaths than any other similar unit in the Union Army. Two Norwich men led regiments in the Vermont Brigade during the Peninsula Campaign: Lt. Col. Charles B. Stoughton (Class of '61) commanded the 4th Vermont, and Col. Henry A. Smalley (Class of '51), led the 5th Vermont.[11]

While Norwich men participated in combat operations on the peninsula, other alumni from the institution dedicated themselves to activities more mundane but no less important. One of these men was Lt. Col. William H. Pettes (Class of '27), the second in command of the 50th New York Engineers. He and his comrades labored long and hard to repair roads and build bridges to aid the army's advance to Richmond. Pettes had been hand picked to provide initial military training to the 50th Engineers when the regiment organized at Elmira, New York, in the summer of 1861. His Norwich training in drilling and engineering served him well, for he was later cited for his important field contributions and eventually took command of his regiment. The often overlooked commissaries and quartermasters also played an important role on the peninsula. Captain Brownell Granger (Class of '57), who transferred to the commissary department after line service in the 11th Massachusetts, was cited and singled out for his contributions. According to the chief of the Army of the Potomac's

Commissary Department, Granger's overall performance on the peninsula was exemplary. He "was always ready and willing, and ever discharged his duties with promptness, intelligence, and entire success."[12]

With the exception of the sharp May 5 engagement at Williamsburg, where Lt. Col. Harvey W. Emery (Class of '52) of the 5th Wisconsin distinguished himself, and Capt. Alonzo B. Hutchinson (Class of '62) of Company B, 6th Vermont was wounded, no serious combat took place until the end of the month. McClellan's army continued its inexorable advance up the peninsula on narrow roads, as Johnston's Confederates withdrew into a defensive network just outside the Southern capital. The Federal army continued moving at a snail's pace, burdened by the heavy rains that saturated the terrain and transformed the roads into ribbons of axle-deep mud. By May 21, Federal troops in a driving rainstorm began crossing to the south side of the Chickahominy River, a slow moving waterway that ran north from the James River for several miles before meandering in a northwest direction toward Richmond. The river bisected the peninsula and was its dominant geographic feature below the city. The Chickahominy was the last major natural obstacle before the Army of the Potomac reached Richmond.

McClellan retained three of his five corps north of the Chickahominy in order to protect the Richmond and York River Railroad, an important supply line utilized to feed and outfit his men. This force also served to establish a link with a Federal corps supposedly moving in McClellan's direction from Fredericksburg under General McDowell. It was a rather bold alignment, for McClellan had divided his army in the face of the enemy, leaving but two corps—the Third under Samuel Heintzelman and the Fourth under Erasmus Keyes— below or south of the Chickahominy. Much as he had at Yorktown, McClellan's strategy to capture Richmond centered on his big siege guns, which he planned utilize in the reduction of the Confederate defenses.

Seemingly unable to halt McClellan's army, General Johnston informed President Jefferson Davis that he would have to rely on unforeseeable circumstances or a unique opportunity in order to strike a decisive blow against the enemy. That opportunity arrived sooner than even Johnston expected. The steady rain spilled the Chickahominy River over its banks and effectively separated McClellan's army into two unequal segments. On the evening of May 30, McClellan's army—separated by a widening river and only six miles from Richmond—was dealt a severe blow without the firing of a shot. That Friday night a violent rain and thunderstorm inundated the region, transforming the normally sluggish Chickahominy into a rushing torrent of muddy water. The downpour left Heintzelman and Keyes stranded below the river, essentially isolated from their supports. To his credit Johnston seized the opportunity and devised a complicated plan of attack for the following day. The plan committed two-thirds of his army to the offensive, three separate commands ordered to attack from three separate directions on different roads. While it looked workable on a map table, it was a recipe for disaster for the green soldiers and officers called upon to execute it.

The two Federal corps Johnston planned to fall upon had established a string of fortified positions near the vital road hub of Seven Pines. Others were thrown up at Fair Oaks, about one mile north of Seven Pines on the Richmond and York River Railroad. Although the battle began much later than Johnston intended, when it finally got underway, the fighting was prolonged and savage. Brigadier General Henry W. Wessells (Class of '28), who commanded a brigade in Silas Casey's division in the action at Seven Pines, was personally cited by his commanding officer for his gallantry on the field. In addition to having his horse shot out from under him and taking a wound in the shoulder, Wessells "encouraged by [his] example [his] men to do their duty on the field," complimented Casey in his report. Wessells was also breveted lieutenant colonel in the regular army for his role in the fighting. Another Norwich graduate, Col. William W. H. Davis (Class of '42), was severely wounded on May 31 at the Battle of Fair Oaks while in command of the 104th Pennsylvania Infantry. Davis' regiment had stood in the path of the approaching Confederates, and was the first Union unit to receive the attack. The 104th had ten officers and 166 enlisted men killed and wounded, and 61 captured (nearly 50% of those engaged).[13]

Colonel William R. Lee's 20th Massachusetts Infantry, which arrived as a reserve contingent and formed on the left of the first line of battle, continued to enhance its reputation as a gallant and reliable combat regiment. Its brigade commander Brig. Gen. N. J. T Dana reported, "I may be pardoned a feeling of pride when I can report that the Massachusetts men, the veteran's of Ball's Bluff. . .came into action with a bearing of which their State may well be proud, and before the movement was fully executed received a withering volley from the enemy's right at short range with steadiness."[14]

The Battle of Seven Pines-Fair Oaks witnessed the end of Johnston's tenure with the Army of Northern Virginia when he was badly wounded on the evening of May 31. President Davis appointed his military advisor, Gen. Robert E. Lee, to head the army on the afternoon of June 1, 1862. Lee immediately ordered a general withdrawal to the original position held by the army before the battle opened. Although Federal losses were heavy (around 5,000), they had prevented the destruction of the pair of isolated corps and had beaten back the Confederates, whose casualties exceeded 6,100.

The bloody fighting of May 31-June 1 did not alter significantly the relative positions of the armies. Lee, who had realized for some time that vigorous offensive action was required to drive the Army of the Potomac away from Richmond, planned his strategy accordingly and launched a massive strike on June 25. The resultant several engagements, known collectively as the Seven Days' Battles, were designed to turn McClellan's right flank and crush his army in detail. The fighting lasted until the first of July and was the bloodiest and largest series of battles up to that time ever fought on American soil. The fighting rolled across swampy and wooded terrain, with the heaviest combat often confined to a single corps or division. Norwich men saw more than their fair share of the action at places like Oak Grove, Mechanicsville (Beaver Dam Creek), Gaines' Mill, Garnett's Farm, Savage Station, Glendale, and Malvern Hill. The soldiers were finally cured of any ideas that they may still have retained about the glory of battle.

Among those making the ultimate sacrifice for the preservation of the Union was Col. Jesse A. Gove, commander of the 22nd Massachusetts and the first Union officer to step into abandoned Yorktown several weeks earlier. The 1849 Norwich graduate fell on June 27 at Gaines' Mill, the bloodiest of the peninsula battles. He was shot through the heart with a minie ball as he rallied his regiment. Unfortunately, Gove's corpse was never recovered. According to the historian of the Fifth Corps, "Colonel Gove fell in front of his men, a gallant leader in the van of those whose unknown graves await the sounding of the final reveille." His death was a shock to his regiment, whose chronicler described him as "a thorough tactician, with the bearing of a courageous soldier, he impressed the men with the idea that he was a leader it was an honor to follow." As a commander, "No order of his was ever questioned, much less disobeyed, because every man in his command believed that the colonel could not make a mistake and always meant what he said. . . ." The regimental historian later wrote what many felt: If Gove had not fallen at Gaines' Mill, "there can be no doubt, he would have been found high in rank among the generals of the army."[15]

As mentioned earlier, the campaigning on the peninsula developed or brought to the fore unique characteristics in many organizations. For example, the 16th New York was easily recognized by friend or foe because its colonel's wife had generously provided each officer and man with a distinctive white straw hat to protect them from the Virginia sun. The headgear also made them particularly conspicuous targets. Most of the 16th's casualties at Gaines' Mill were struck in the head or upper part of the body. Lieutenant Colonel Samuel Marsh (Class of '39), led the 16th New York in the battle, where his New Yorkers, together with the 2nd United States Infantry, saved the guns of consolidated Battery L/M, 3rd United States Artillery. Shortly thereafter Marsh fell severely wounded when a minie ball entered his neck and penetrated his spinal cord, paralyzing him. He died on the James River aboard the hospital steamer *S. R. Spaulding* on Independence Day, 1862.[16]

Another regiment with a Norwich graduate at its head, the 83rd Pennsylvania under the command of Lt. Col. Hugh S. Campbell (Class of '59), also suffered heavily in the battle, losing 196 casualties within but a short time. Trapped by James Longstreet's Division, rather than surrender, Campbell and his men opted to fight their way back to Union lines. The Norwich men of Gaines' Mill served the Republic well, a privilege paid for dearly in blood.[17]

The Battle of Savage's Station two days later on June 29 was also a bloody affair, one which set a melancholy record for a Vermont regiment. The 5th Vermont, officially commanded by Col. Henry A. Smalley (Class of '51) but led into action by Lt. Col. W. G. Veazey on account of Smalley's illness, suffered the highest casualties of any Vermont regiment in a single battle during the war. Veazey's unit lost 72 officers and men killed and mortally wounded, and another 116 wounded or missing, or almost 44% of its total effective strength. Company E alone suffered horribly in the fighting, losing 44 of its 59 members, 25 of whom were killed outright. Another Norwich alumni, the 3rd Vermont's Cpl. John G. Fowler (Class of '58), Company C, was so badly wounded at Savage's Station that he would be discharged for disability.[18]

In Brig. Gen. George McCall's soon to be famous division of Pennsylvania Reserves, two of its three brigades at the fighting at Glendale on June 30 were led by Norwich alumni. Colonel Seneca G. Simmons (Class of '29), commander of the 5th Pennsylvania Reserves, who took command after Brig. Gen. John Reynolds was captured, fell while leading a counterattack at the height of the battle. He became a casualty in the seesaw fight for possession of Capt. James H. Cooper's guns of Battery B, 1st Pennsylvania Light Artillery. Simmons, who had distinguished himself at Gaines' Mill and Mechanicsville, was mortally wounded and fell into enemy hands. He died in captivity in Richmond soon thereafter. The second Norwich alumni leading a brigade of the Pennsylvania Reserves in the Seven Days' fighting was Brig. Gen. Truman B. Seymour (Class of '44). Seymour's troops suffered heavy casualties at Glendale, and the general's horse was killed under him and he was thrown to the ground. A Union staff officer eventually found Seymour (who had almost been killed by a bullet that had pierced his hat), walking along a road in a dazed and confused state while searching for his corps commander. The incident prompted some to question his whereabouts during the battle, but eyewitness accounts and his multiple wartime citations and brevets for gallantry appear to rule out any misconduct at Glendale.[19]

Other Norwich graduates also performed well during the horrendous fighting at Glendale. Captain Frank P. Amsden (Class of '59), commanding Batteries "B" and "G," 1st Pennsylvania Light Artillery, was cited for gallantry. He was singled out by General Seymour (who took command of the division when General McCall was captured), for maintaining his position under heavy attack. "Amsden," wrote his superior, " stood fast, doing excellent service until his ammunition was exhausted, then withdrew." Colonel William R. Lee (Class of '25), whom his brigade commander called "The gallant old veteran," was "entirely disabled by an artillery horse falling on him." The dedicated officer refused to be evacuated and remained in command of his unit during the remainder of the campaign. Captain Edmund Rice (Class of '60), Company F, 19th Massachusetts, received his first of many citations for bravery in the fight.[20]

Numerous other alumni gained various forms of recognition during the Seven Days' Battles. Brigadier General George W. Taylor (Class of '26), the commander of the New Jersey Brigade, was singled out for personal courage at both Gaines' Mill and Glendale. At the former action, Taylor encountered the French Prince de Joinville, an aide to General McClellan. The prince, who spoke English very well, was so excited during the fight that he rattled on in French to Taylor, who did not speak the language. An aide finally translated the orders, which directed Talyor to send the 4th New Jersey as reinforcements to another part of the field. Taylor's actions at Glendale and throughout the campaign were reported in glowing terms by his division commander, Maj. Gen. Philip Kearny. When Kearny found a gap in his line at Glendale, he "placed in it the First New Jersey Brigade. . . .I then knew it to be in true hands." Kearny was "proud to give thanks and to include in the glory of my own division, the First New Jersey Brigade, General Taylor, who held McCall's deserted ground. . ." Ironically, General Taylor's son, Lt. Archibald S. Taylor (Class of '58) served in the New Jersey Brigade's 3rd New Jersey Infantry, his father's old regiment.[21]

It seems the soldiers from New Jersey earned a reputation for more than courage. General Kearny once told President Lincoln that if he really wanted to capture Richmond, he should put a hen house and a peach orchard on the far side of the city's fortifications, and the New Jersey Brigade on the other; the brigade, assured Kearney, would pass through all the fortifications to get to the chickens and peaches![22]

The last major action of the Seven Days Battles was fought at Malvern Hill on July 1, where Lee attempted to smash McClellan with a grand frontal assault. The Army of the Potomac had fallen back to the relative safety of the James River, leaving Fitz John Porter's Fifth Corps to occupy the plateau, upon which were emplaced some 250 artillery pieces. Despite advance warnings about its natural strength and virtual impregnability, Lee launched a series of piecemeal assaults against the position that were torn apart by the Federal artillery, which completely dominated Southern guns. Numerous Norwich men took a hand in the victory at Malvern Hill. Lieutenant Colonel Hugh S. Campbell (Class of '59) fell wounded while leading a charge by the 83rd Pennsylvania. Between the Battles of Gaines' Mill and Malvern Hill, Campbell's regiment lost 363 of its 554 officers and men, a casualty rate of 65.5%. Captain Edmund Weston (Class of '48) of Company F, 1st United States Sharpshooters, and Capt. John W. Dewey (Class of '55), Company C, Second United States Sharpshooters, performed particularly important and difficult duty on the ground north and west of Malvern Hill. Weston's company completely devastated a battery of the elite "Richmond Howitzers" by picking off its men and horses with small arms fire. "We went in a battery and came out a wreck," remembered one a Confederate artilleryman after the war. "We staid ten minutes by the watch and came out with one gun, ten men and two horses, and without firing a shot."[23]

Similar courage and resolve was demonstrated by the members of the 4th Michigan, which was led by Col. Jonathan W. Childs (Class of '58). Childs' Wolverines, planted squarely in the front ranks, stood firm and assisted in driving back Brig. Gen. William "Billy" Mahone's attacking Confederate brigade.[24]

The members of the 22nd Massachusetts had not forgotten the lessons in field fortifications taught them by the late Colonel Gove, the Norwich graduate who had fallen at Gaines' Mill. The Bay Staters cleverly used the furrows on a plowed patch of sloping ground at Malvern Hill as defensive cover. The front rank of the regiment deployed in a prone position in the first furrow, with the second line in a furrow behind them. The regiment's officers positioned themselves above in a third furrow, from which they exercised control of the regiment. The tactic worked well and went a long way toward allowing them to fire off 60 rounds per man and hold their position under the pressure of a powerful infantry attack. The Massachusetts men also rated comment from nearby artillerymen, who remembered that they loudly sang "John Brown's Body" and "We'll hang Jeff Davis on a sour apple tree" even as the battle raged around them.

The furrows weren't deep enough, however, to prevent death or serious injury to their occupants. Captain Samuel J. Thompson (Class of '48), commanding Company F, fell severely wounded and was later captured. The 22nd's regimental history relates his particularly poignant story: "Corp. Thompson, of Company F, Captain S. J. Thompson's only son. . .fell dead on the field of honor. His father sought him everywhere during that night and the next day, and eagerly grasped at any rumor which held out hope. As the days wore on. . . Captain Thompson. . .subsequently taken prisoner. . .came to Libby. . .He wrote me a note asking about Frank, and I replied, telling him the painful truth as tenderly as possible. Refusing to accept the harsh truth, the heartbroken father insisted I was mistaken, and died in the belief that the missing one would yet be returned to his home. Frank sleeps in an unknown grave, and his father among the kindred, while on Fame's eternal camping ground their spirits walk in glory."[25]

The Regulars of Brig. Gen. George Sykes' division also performed to their usual high standards. Fighting with Charles S. Lovell's brigade were Capt Solon H. Lathrop (Class of '52), Capt George W. Smith (Class of '64), Company A, 2nd Battalion, and Sgt. Eldridge H. Babbitt (Class of '64), and Sgt. James W. Buel (Class of '64), all of the 17th United States Infantry.[26]

A solitary Norwich alumnus played a bit part in the anti-climactic conclusion of the fighting at Malvern Hill. Although the battle had been a clear-cut Federal victory (Lee lost nearly 5,500 men killed wounded, missing and captured, while McClellan suffered some 3,200 casualties and still held the field), the cautious Federal commander still believed he faced an overwhelming enemy and that further retreat was in order. Fitz-John Porter, the commander of the Fifth Corps, believed otherwise. Porter dispatched one of McClellan's own staff officers, Lt. Col. Albert V. Colburn (Class of '53), to McClellan with a message that the position at Malvern Hill could be held and that no further retrograde was necessary. McClellan, however, was not in the frame of mind to heed such advice, and shortly thereafter issued an order for retreat. By the 4th of July, the Army of the Potomac was safely within the

Harrison's Landing perimeter, protected by field fortifications and Union gunboats. McClellan's massive Peninsula Campaign offensive was over.[27]

Routinely overlooked in the army's operations on the Peninsula is the role of Federal cavalry. Alumnus Capt. Elisha S. Kelley (Class of '54) distinguished himself in command of a squadron of the 8th Illinois Cavalry during the weeklong fighting withdrawal from the gates of Richmond to the area surrounding Harrison's Landing—a difficult undertaking which, to their credit, McClellan and his subordinates carried out in fine fashion. At one point Captain Kelley and his men held off approaching Confederates at Bottom's Bridge on June 29 until a Union field hospital was successfully evacuated.[28]

Twelve-year-old Private and drummer Willie Johnston (Class of '70), Company D, 3rd Vermont Infantry, was with the Vermont Brigade when it finally reached Harrison's Landing. The drummer, remarkably, had retained his instrument during the entire Seven Days' Battles and the gruesome retreat to McClellan's new base camp. While many stronger and older men had thrown away their weapons and equipment, Willie clung to his drum, the only musician in his division to do so. As a result, he enjoyed the honor of drumming for division parade at Harrison's Landing. His example of "gallantry in the Seven Days fight and the Peninsula campaign," worked its way up the chain of command to Secretary of War Edwin Stanton, who presented the lad with the Congressional Medal of Honor on September 16, 1863. Willie Johnston was the youngest soldier to ever win the coveted decoration, and the first Norwich alumnus (and first Vermonter) so honored. Johnston, who was only the seventh medal winner in the award's history, entered Norwich in 1866, where he served as a drummer in the cadet band.[29]

The Army of the Potomac spent July and much of August refitting at Harrison's Landing,. Unfortunately, the swamps, heat, dust, and mosquitoes, together with the tens of thousands of soldiers, made it a miserable place to encamp. Sergeant Charles E. Bowers, serving under his father, Capt. Charles Bowers (Class of '52) in Company G, 32nd Massachusetts, described the disagreeable conditions in a letter home on August 8, 1862. "[Some claimed it] was no warmer in Virginia then in Mass.," he wrote, "but don't you believe it, it is awful hot out here & if we had anything to do we should suffer." In addition to the heat ". . .the worst of it is the horrible stench which rises from the swamp. It is perfectly sickening & I have no doubt is the cause of most of the sickness in camp. I have been quite sick for 2 or three days & have had a stern time of it."[30]

An extensive series of reviews were conducted along the James River, including one for President Lincoln on July 8, just one week after Malvern Hill. Lincoln held numerous strategy meetings with McClellan, the results of which further weakened the president's confidence in his field commander. The lack of any likelihood that McClellan would renew the offensive from his current position at Harrison's Landing prompted Lincoln to withdraw the Army of the Potomac to northern Virginia, where Maj. Gen. John Pope and his Army of Virginia was coalescing in preparation for an offensive. Perhaps Pope, who had scored some victories in the Western Theater, might have better luck against Robert E. Lee.[31]

The army's redeployment came none to soon for men like Charles Bowers. Despite the failure to capture Richmond and the poor conditions in camp along the James River, morale remained high and the men still believed in ultimate victory. Rumors of a transfer of troops swept through the ranks, and the idea of an offensive operation appealed to many. Few yet realized, however, that they were being shifted away from Richmond rather toward it. On August 12 Bowers' son wrote that "We are just about leaving our Camp here & I am very glad of it . . . . No one knows sure where we are going but all rejoice at leaving this Camp as we couldn't get a worse one." Bowers summarized the frenzied activity: "Sunday we received the orders to march & take nothing but our blankets & 3 days rations. . . .I suppose we shall march today & I hope it will be on to Richmond. If it is we shall take the city & rout the Rebels if it is a possible thing. But you know the Rebels fight well & unless we are on the lookout we may get whipt ourselves." Despite hopes of victory, he was forced to continue waging his own Seven Days' Battles. "The flies are so thick down here you can hardly see & they bite with a vengeance. When I eat dinner the flies get into our food & we can't scare them off but have to pick them out with our fingers before they will leave." The weather also continued to drain the strength from the men. "It is terrible hot down here," penned Bowers, "and between the hours of 9 A.M. & 4 P.M. persons can't be out much as they are liable to sun-stroke."[32]

Bowers— "Charlie," as he was known to his parents—soon discovered the ancient army tradition of "hurry up and wait." In a letter home to Concord, Massachusetts on August 14, he explained that they still "haven't left camp yet and are living on our own hook entirely. . . .I hope we shall start soon for I dislike this place worse than you can imagine." Summarizing the result of the army's stay on the James River, he noted that "Harrison's Landing has become a perfect desert as barren a one as there ever was."[33]

It was while the army was entrenched at Harrison's Landing that Maj. Thomas O. Seaver's (Class of '59) wife fell seriously ill back in Vermont. Seaver tried to resign in order to be with her, but his resignation was rejected. General McClellan and other commanders claimed that he was "too valuable" an officer to lose and that his departure would be "prejudicial to the service." As we shall see, it was fortunate for the Union, the Vermont Brigade, and the 3rd Vermont Infantry that Seaver remained with them at the front.[34]

By mid-August 1862, Northern enthusiasm for the war, which had soared to great heights following major victories in the West and the initial success of McClellan's offensive, had dropped off sharply. President Lincoln was similarly dejected. He could not announce his embryonic plan to declare freedom for at least some slaves—he called it an emancipation proclamation—until one of his generals scored a strong Union victory.

As McClellan reluctantly withdrew troops from the Peninsula to the environs of Washington, albeit at a snail's pace, General Lee rapidly redeployed his army to face the new threat posed by General Pope's Army of Virginia. By using interior lines of communcations, Lee ordered Stonewall Jackson's "wing" of his army to march north to keep an eye on Pope, while the balance of the Confederates under James Longstreet watched over McClellan. As the Army of the Potomac slowly began to arrive at Alexandria, word spread through the ranks that there was trouble up the railroad tracks in the direction of Manassas. Pope's army had marched up the line of the Alexandria Railroad towards the Rappahanock River. Advance elements of the army under Nathaniel Banks had waged a sharp meeting engagement at Cedar Mountain on August 9 against Jackson. Lee, realizing that McClellan no longer posed a serious threat against the Southern capital, moved the remaining bulk of army north to link up with Jackson. The result of these movements culminated in the Manassas Campaign, or the Second Battle of Bull Run (Second Manassas) on August 27-31, 1862. As pieces of the Army of the Potomac arrived in Alexandria they were ordered west to support of Pope and, after he was defeated, to cover his withdrawal from Manassas towards Washington.

Forty-six Norwich alumni served in the series of actions known as the Second Bull Run Campaign. Among them was Brig. Gen. George Taylor (Class of '26), who had distinguished himself in the Peninsula Campaign. Taylor was dispatched via rail from Alexandria with his New Jersey Brigade to chase away a small unit of Rebel "raiders" from the vicinity of Manassas. The small raiding party turned out to be much of Stonewall Jackson's corps. Taylor unloaded his 1,200 men, detached one regiment to guard the bridge, and moved along the tracks in the direction of Manassas Junction with the rest of his brigade, oblivious to what was waiting for him.

Within minutes, Taylor's well-trimmed battleline was inundated with Confederate artillery fire, including deadly canister from a battery positioned beyond his left flank. He had marched his men into a deadly trap, and Jackson was closing the door behind him. After suffering under this fire for about one-quarter hour, Taylor noticed Confederate cavalry riding around his flanks. Realizing he could no longer hold his position, the general ordered a retreat and his battered regiments fell back in good order toward Bull Run Bridge. Unable to quickly climb a steep hard-packed hill near the span, the New Jersey soldiers began to panic as Confederate cavalry thundered into them. Taylor was fatally wounded in the leg in the ensuing melee.[35]

Somehow a stretcher was found and Taylor was carried from the battlefield. The old soldier called to his men to stand firm and make a fight for the bridge, ordering one of his colonels to "rally the men and for God's sake to prevent another Bull Run." Taylor lost both his leg and his life, dying in a hospital in Alexandria a few days later. His actions and personal popularity at the time inspired a contemporary poem by Joseph O'Connor entitled "The General's Death." The poem, intended as a tribute to Taylor's courage and the affection shown him by his men, incorrectly—though certainly more dramatically—has the general dying instantly on the field, felled by a bullet in the brain rather than from complications ensuing from the loss of a leg. Historian Henry C. Ropes, in his postwar book, *The Army Under Pope*, claims that Stonewall Jackson says of "[Taylor's] advance, that it was made with great spirit and determination and under a leader worthy of a better cause."[36]

The initial fighting at Manassas Junction, and Jackson's subsequent sacking and destruction of the place, prompted General Pope to order his subordinates to find and destroy the Confederates. Jackson, however, eluded his pursuers and by the time Pope reached the junction on August 28, the enemy was no where to be found. When reports came in that Jackson was at Centreville, Pope ordered his men to march there. The movement triggered one of the sharpest actions of the campaign at Brawner's Farm (Groveton).

Unbeknownst to Brig. Gen. Rufus King, his march down the Warrenton Turnpike late on the afternoon of August 28 carried his division across the front of Jackson's corps, which was hidden north of the road. The aggressive Jackson could not resist the temptation to smash into the moving column. His attack ran squarely into Brig. Gen. John Gibbon's all-western brigade, which was leading the division. The affair was a bloody stand up fight that lasted until past sundown, as both sides stood toe-to-toe and poured small arms and artillery rounds into one another. Gibbon's 2,100 men of the 2nd, 6th, 7th Wisconsin and 19th Indiana fought Jackson's 6,400 men (four Southern brigades, including the famed "Stonewall Brigade," under the personal command of Stonewall Jackson) to a standstill, suffering 37% casualties in the process.

Two Norwich alumni served with the brigade that day. The right flank of the brigade was held by the 6th Wisconsin, whose Company A was ably led throughout the engagement by Capt. David K. Noyes (Class of '45). To the left of the 6th battled Col. William W. Robinson (Class of '41) and his 7th Wisconsin, which held the right center of the brigade front. During the height of the action, as the brigade advanced and threw back Jackson's attack, Robinson was shot from his horse with a severe wound in the leg. His wound was so serious he was unable to rejoin his regiment for several months. While in the hospital Robinson wrote the governor of Wisconsin about the Battle of Brawner's Farm:

Our Brigade formed a line of battle under a galling fire from the enemies batteries, he penned, and advanced upon them for the purpose of
taking them, where we were met by twelve regiments of their infantry,
then followed the hottest fire that any troops ever stood up under, lasting about one one and a half hours, when their fire was silenced. In the
heat of the engagement it became necessary for the Seventh to change
front forward on its tenth company, in order to get an enfilading fire
upon the heavy masses of the enemy, who were pressing forward to
charge the Second Regiment. The evolution was executed with as much
precision as they ever executed the movement in drill. This brought us
within 30 yards of the enemy. Our line never gave an inch during the
fight. The enemy made three different attempts to charge upon the 2nd
and the 7th. In each attempt they fell under our fire like grass before
the scythe. Our loss was heavy, as a necessary consequence of such a fire
at close quarters. . . .With regards to individual officers and men,
whose conduct was especially meritorious, I shall have to report at
some future time. But I will say here that the noble conduct of all, both
officers and men, was all that could be wished, and beyond my most
sanguine expectations.[37]

After the battle Stonewall Jackson queried Union prisoners about
the troops in the "Black Hats." It is rumored that "Old Jack" refused to
believe he had been fighting only one reinforced brigade. Brawner's
Farm (Groveton) was the first major battle for three of Gibbon's four
western regiments, and they had performed well beyond expectations.
Within a few weeks Gibbon's brigade would blaze its way into Civil
War legend, earning the name by which they have been known ever
since: the Iron Brigade.[38]

Again alerted to the strategic situation by the sound of combat,
General Pope ordered a concentration against Jackson at Groveton.
Pope, however, was not aware that Longstreet's Corps had also reached
the field that night after a march through Thoroughfare Gap. By the
29th he was essentially facing Lee's entire army. As Pope's divisions arrived on the field, he hurled them piecemeal against Jackson's front.
Brigadier General Robert H. Milroy (Class of '43), an aggressive
Indiana native, learned the strength of the Confederate position the
hard way. He foolishly divided his brigade of West Virginia and Ohio
troops into two parts and lost control of his units. Two of his regiments
dispatched to the right to support another brigade ended up assaulting
Jackson's position along the unfinished railroad cut alone and head-on,
as did his remaining two regiments. Within a few minutes Milroy's

brigade was a bloody wreck and falling back into the Groveton Woods. Caution, wrote one of the general's staff officers, "was [not] a virtue. . .known to Milroy."[39]

Sergeant George T. Carter (Class of '54), Company B, 2nd New Hampshire, suffered the first of his four wartime wounds in the attack against Jackson's position. The New Hampshire troops, part of Cuvier Grover's brigade, Joe Hooker's division, held the center of the first line of the brigade's attack. Advancing blindly through thick woods, the New Englanders did not see the unfinished railroad embankment before it was too late. Confederates from Edward Thomas' Georgia brigade rose from behind it and delivered a withering fire into the regiment. Shaking it off, Carter's regiment, together with the two Massachusetts regiments flanking it, charged Thomas' Confederates and sliced through into the line. The fight on the embankment, reported Grover, was "a short, sharp and obstinate hand to hand conflict." Within minutes the Southerners were fleeing in all directions. Continuing on, Grover pushed his three lead regiments into Thomas' second line, where another hand-to-hand fight was waged. After a brief melee, the Georgians again fled to the rear. A single brigade had overrun a portion of the railroad embankment, bayoneted and captured dozens of the enemy, and caused a momentary crisis amongst the defenders. The momentum of their attack could not be sustained, however, and when no reinforcements came up to engage the swelling enemy numbers confronting them, the Federals fell back under heavy enemy fire, leaving about one-third of their number on the field. Like so many other Union units that day, their blood and courage was wasted.[40]

Major General Fitz John Porter, ordered to attack Jackson's right flank, moved forward late in the day and ran into elements of Longstreet's deployed divisions. Pope, however, refused to believe that the Army of Northern Virginia was united. The action sputtered on until darkness brought an end to the bloody day. With his entire army now on the field, General Lee withdrew his lines to a more compact position and offered battle again the following morning. Pope interpreted the retrograde movement as a retreat and ordered a pursuit, selecting Porter's corps to lead the advance. After a morning of skirmishing, light fighting, and repositioning, Porter's Federals moved forward about 3:00 p.m. in concentrated lines. Instead of light rear guard opposition, they discovered massed Confederate artillery and Jackson's veteran infantry waiting for them. August 30 was a repeat of the preceding day—with even worse consequences for the Federals.

Part of Porter's assaulting column that afternoon contained Lt. Col. Hugh S. Campbell (Class of '59) and his 83rd Pennsylvania. Campbell's regiment, part of Henry Weeks' brigade, Maj. Gen. George Morell's division, drove forward against the right-front of Jackson's Confederate line. The Pennsylvanians, with several other regiments, managed to reach the cut and drive away some Virginians, where they settled into a furious and deadly exchange of small arms fire (described by a modern historian of the action as "the most intense combat of the battle"). Lieutenant Colonel Campbell did not make it to the embankment, but instead fell wounded for a second time while leading his regiment in the assault. The Pennsylvanians passed over the fallen Norwich alumnus and continued their attack. It was during the fighting on this portion of the line that defending Louisiana troops resorted to hurling stones at the attacking Northerners when their ammunition ran out. Another alumnus, Capt. James A. Hall (Class of '62), was positioned in the rear with his 2nd Maine Battery, offering what little support he could provide to the futile infantry assaults in this sector.[41]

As the Federal assaults climaxed and receded, James Longstreet launched a sweeping corps-level attack that crushed the exposed left of Pope's Army of Virginia. Brigade after brigade dissolved in disorder under the weight of the Confederate onslaught. Only a last-ditch defense on Henry Hill saved the army from complete disaster, and a number of Norwich alumni and their units were present on the hill and along the Sudley Road. What was left of General Robert Milroy's independent brigade stood with Truman Seymour's brigade of Pennsylvania Reserves and Brig. Gen. John Buford's Federal brigade of cavalry along the Sudley Road and helped repel Longstreet's final attacks. Both units were supported by Capt. Dunbar Ransom's Battery C, 5th United States Artillery. The 4th and 17th United States Infantry, with six alumni in their ranks, deployed with the brigade of Regulars on the extreme left flank and fought gallantly against overwhelming odds. Major Josiah Hall (Class of '61) rode and fought with the 1st Vermont

Cavalry, Buford's brigade, when the horsemen covered the final Union withdrawal from the battlefield and across Bull Run.[42]

The decisive Confederate victory at Second Bull Run prompted General Lee to attempt to cut off Pope's demoralized and retreating army. A flanking movement on the 31st of August carried Jackson's divisions eastward toward Chantilly (Ox Hill), where they met with rear elements of Pope's army on the rainy afternoon of September 1. In the engagement that followed Federal Maj. Gen. Philip Kearny was killed, as was Brig. Gen. Isaac I. Stevens. The bloody and confused fighting was a tactical draw, and the Federals withdrew as darkness descended upon the field. For the defeated Army of Virginia and the attached troops from the Army of the Potomac, it was a dismal and difficult retreat from Manassas, though not quite the rout that had ensued after the defeat at First Bull Run in 1861.

As the miserable march toward the defenses of Washington, D. C., continued, electrifying news swept up and down the column: "Little Mac was again in command!" Riding to the front with only one aide—Lt. Col. Albert V. Colburn (Class of '53) and three orderlies—George B. McClellan rejoined his beloved army. McClellan's return came to pass when the disaster on the plains of Manassas became known in the nation's capital. Realizing the desperate situation that confronted the country, and appreciating that there was no one else available who could restore order and morale to the army as quickly as McClellan, President Lincoln had reluctantly restored the general to command. It was none too soon: Lee's Army of Northern Virginia crossed over the Potomac River into Maryland on September 4, in what would prove to be the first of two large raids into Northern territory.[43]

McClellan once again impressively capitalized on his exceptional organizational skills and restored troop morale and discipline in a remarkably short time. As Lee and the Army of Northern Virginia advanced into Maryland, the Army of the Potomac was handed a golden opportunity that should have made Lee's first campaign in the North his last. With Harpers Ferry manned and in his rear, Lee divided his army. He sent Jackson with several divisions against Harpers Ferry, while the remainder of the army remained spread out west of the South Mountain range near Boonsboro. A Confederate staff officer inadvertently misplaced a set of Special Orders No. 191, which contained the disposition of the various segments of Lee's widespread army. Its discovery by Union troops offered McClellan the opportunity to defeat his nemesis in detail. McClellan is said to have exclaimed, "Here is a paper with which, if I cannot whip Bobbie Lee, I will be willing to go home!" His exclamation was prophetic, albeit not in the way he expected.[44]

At least 79 Norwich men participated in the Maryland Campaign, which includes the preliminary engagement at South Mountain on September 14. Despite the importance of his find, McClellan wasted precious hours before finally moving his army west toward the handful of gaps and passes that provided access to the far side of the mountain range and Lee's divided army. On the morning of September 14, advance elements of the Federal Ninth Corps marched into sight of the Confederate defenders at Fox's Gap. To the north about one mile at Turner's Gap, the Federal First Corps launched its assault. The Confederates, for most of the day only a thinly-spread division under D. H. Hill, waged one of the finest defensive actions of the war. The battle witnessed many acts of heroism, and it was on that day that John Gibbon's "Black Hats," who had fought so well at Groveton, earned their famous nickname "Iron Brigade." At least two Norwich men marched with the brigade at South Mountain: Capt. David A. Noyes (Class of '45), with the 6th Wisconsin, and First Lt. Charles K. Dean (Class of '45) with the 2nd Wisconsin. The brigade was involved in the difficult assault through Turner's Gap, where it lost about one-quarter of its strength. In fact, Gibbon's brigade suffered the heaviest losses of any Federal brigade in the battle. But his casualties had not gone unnoticed. Several high ranking officers, including Generals McClellan and Burnside, had witnessed the gallant advance. Later that night Joe Hooker, the brigade's corps commander, in a conversation with McClellan referred to Gibbon's men as his "iron brigade." The name stuck.[45]

As both sides fed reinforcements into the spreading battle at South Mountain, another Norwich graduate with whom we are familar, Brig. Gen. Truman B. Seymour (Class of '44), led his veteran brigade of Pennsylvania Reserves into the fight on the Frosttown Road late that afternoon. Seymour's attack up the slopes of the hillside jumped off about 4:00 p.m. and ran directly into Brig. Gen. Robert Rodes' Alabama brigade. When the assault against the defending Alabamians bogged down, the aggressive Seymour threw in his reserve regiment. He pointed toward a gorge and shouted to the regiment's commander, "Colonel, put your regiment into that corn-field and hurt somebody!" The resulting attack inflicted heavy Rebel losses and drove Rodes' men back as darkness descended on the field.[46]

The Vermont Brigade also distinguished itself in the fighting of September 14. Lieutenant Colonel Charles B. Stoughton (Class of '61), commanding the 4th Vermont Infantry, was personally singled out for his gallant handling of the regiment's assault at Crampton's Gap, the southernmost of the three mountain passes. The defile was but a few miles from Harpers Ferry and led directly into the rear of one of the Confederate columns besieging the place. William B. Franklin, the commander of the Federal Sixth Corps, was ordered to capture the pass and drive westward in order to relieve the Harpers Ferry garrison. The plan almost succeeded. After several hours of fighting, the Vermonters, in conjunction with other Sixth Corps troops, drove away the stubborn defenders and captured numerous prisoners. Stoughton's booty also included the colors of the 16th Virginia Infantry. The 4th Vermont and its commander at Crampton's Pass charged "forward. . . at the double quick. . .[its] lieutenant colonel leading the way a yard or two in front of the colors, which were flying out to the breeze," boasted an official report sent to the Adjutant General of Vermont. "Stoughton and the 4th Vermont moved "over the wall, through the woods, up the mountain sides, sweeping with irresistible force everything before us." Unfortunately for the Federals, the defending enemy remnants—bolstered by reinforcements—rallied to the west in Pleasant Valley. Overestimating the strength of the new Confederate position, Franklin declined to attack and darkness brought about an end to the action and the last hope of saving the doomed garrison.[47]

On the morning of September 15, as the besieged garrison was preparing to surrender, Clara Barton arrived at South Mountain. "My poor words can never describe to you," she later wrote of the bitterly contested field where so many Norwich men had fought, "the consternation and horror with which we descended from our wagon and trod there in that mountain pass, that field of death." Stunned by her first view of a recent battlefield, she reflected that, "There we now walked with peaceful feet, twelve hours before the ground that shook with carnage. . . .God's Angels of wrath and death had swept, and foe facing foe, freedom and treason grappled and the souls of men went out, and there side by side. . . in death mingled the northern blue and southern gray."[48]

Only hours after powder smoke had risen above the wooded crests and passes of the South Mountain range, Stonewall Jackson captured Harpers Ferry on September 15. While about 1,300 cavalrymen managed to escape, the entire infantry force of 12,000 men was surrendered, together with tons of valuable provisions and equipment. Two of the regiments that fell captive that day contained Norwich men. One of these, the 32nd Ohio, was commanded by Maj. Sylvester M. Hewitt (Class of '40), while several alumni populated the ranks of the 9th Vermont, including Maj. Edwin S. Stowell (Class of '52), Capt. Albion J. Mower (Class of '51), First Lt. William A. Dodge (Class of '64), Second Lt. Asa H. Snow (Class of '41), and Cpl. Daniel E. Wright (Class of '47).[49]

September 15 was a busy day for many Norwich alumni. Captain Elisha S. Kelley (Class of '54) had earned a reputation on the Virginia peninsula for fearlessness while leading Company E, 8th Illinois Cavalry, and thereafter as a squadron commander. In a cavalry skirmish early on September 15, Kelley rode down a lieutenant of the 9th Virginia Cavalry. With his revolver drawn, Kelley told the Virginian, who was firing at the Federals swarming around him, to surrender. The Rebel refused to do so and aimed his pistol at Kelley, planning to drop him. Unfortunately for the Southerner, he was not quick enough. Kelley aimed his pistol and shot him through the body, and the Confederate officer was unhorsed with a mortal wound. Visiting Lt. Cassius Williams of Company A, 9th Virginia Cavalry in the hospital later that day, Kelley apologized for shooting him. Politely but casually, Williams answered "I refused to surrender, and I would have shot you if I could have fired first." Captain Kelley's promising career was cut short when he was himself seriously wounded later that day while leading a charge at Boonsboro. Although he would eventually return to his unit, his wounds refused to heal, and would hemorrhage whenever he rode his horse. He was discharged for disability. Of the action of the 15th, Kelley's superior, Brig. Gen. Alfred Pleasanton, reported that "brave Captain Kelley, of the Eighth Illinois Cavalry. . .was shot while gallantly charging at the head of his squadron."[50]

After losing the mountain passes to McClellan's advancing Federals, Lee learned that Jackson had sucessfully captured the Harpers Ferry garrison. With that news he decided to stand and offer battle north of the Potomac River near the village of Sharpsburg. The Army of the Potomac's forced march toward the gathering enemy proved hot and difficult, and numerous stragglers lengthened the winding columns. This problem was not prevalent in the 9th New York ("Hawkins Zouaves"), however, for its commander, Lt. Col. Edgar A. Kimball (Class of '44) had formed a strong rear guard to catch any wayward soldiers. No one was permitted to fall out unless cleared by a surgeon, and those men were ordered into ambulances.[51]

The opposing armies gathered slowly around Sharpsburg, facing each other across Antietam Creek. Lee's army, with a large division still at Harpers Ferry and a single Potomac ford in its rear, numbered only about 35,000. McClellan, however, fielded some 75,000 men. By September 16 the stage was set for a major and potentially decisive battle. That evening, as the soldiers prepared for the morning battle most were sure was coming, Maj. Jacob Parker Gould (Class of '49) was nearly killed when a cannon shot whizzed by him in the Poffenberger Orchard. His 13th Massachusetts soldiers saw the ball smash into a corn mound directly in front of the major's mount, knocking the animal down. Gould desperately urged his startled horse to "Get up, get up. That was meant for us. Get up. Get up." It undoubtedly did the men good to see that they were not the only ones who could be frightened. When Gould was selected as the 13th's major in the summer of 1861, his appointment had initially been resented by many of the Bay Staters. His abilities and leadership skills quickly earned their respect, however, and they nicknamed him the "fighting major." It was said of Gould that ". . .he commands no man to go where he is not willing to go himself." Gould's regiment, part of George Hartsuff's brigade, Hooker's First Corps, was poised to join a planned assault early the following morning against the strongly-held plateau around the conspicuous Dunker Church.[52]

As dawn broke over the Maryland countryside on September 17, 1862, everyone knew a great battle was in the offing. Clara Barton remembered how at Antietam ". . .the bugle notes. . .The Kerner's breath, whose fearful blast would waken death.' But if like us, you had heard them this morning. . .waking us from one sleep to hasten to another. It would have lingered in your ears as they do in mine tonight." Those bugles sounded the last reveille for many Americans. As is well known, Antietam (Sharpsburg) carries with it the infamous distinction of being the most bloody day in American military history, and one in which numerous Norwich alumni distinguished themselves.[53]

Despite the seemingly decisive advantage he had gained by finding Lee's lost battle order, McClellan's cautious movements had allowed Lee the time he needed to coalesce his fragmented army. When "Little Mac" finally attacked at daybreak on the 17th, his offensive was delivered piecemeal, largely corps by corps, and so deliberately that his opponent was able to reinforce each threatened sector with units yanked from less active parts of his line. The battle began at first light when Joe Hooker's First Corps, the army's right flank element, attacked south along the Hagerstown Turnpike against Stonewall Jackson's thickly massed infantry. The rolling attack, which left thousands of dead and wounded in its wake, eventually stalled around the Dunker Church. Other Federal corps joined in the battle, driving to and beyond the church and spreading the carnage south until about noon the fighting crashed against Lee's stoutly defended center at a sunken farm lane. Although the naturally powerful position eventually gave way early in the afternoon, McClellan did not feed any reinforcements into the gap, which yawned wide and deep in the middle of Lee's vulnerable and decisively fissured army. The Federal Ninth Corps under Ambrose E. Burnside renewed the action on the army's left, and by mid-afternoon was driving into the outskirts of Sharpsburg, set to cut off and destroy Lee's battered army. It was not to be, however, for at that moment A. P. Hill's Confederate "Light" Division," which had been overseeing the Harpers Ferry surrender, arrived at precisely the right location after a 17-mile forced march and drove the Federals back toward Antietam Creek. The exhausted guns of both armies fell silent as darkness creeped across the field. Norwich men had had a hand in almost every major attack of the day.

It seems fitting that a Norwich brigadier would initiate the infantry's role in the battle. After a light engagement on the evening of the 16th in the East Woods, Brig. Gen. Truman B. Seymour (Class of '44) pushed his brigade of Pennsylvania Reserves through the timber at daybreak on the 17th. The regiments reached the Smoketown Road, on the southern edge of the woodlot, and after taking cover behind a fence, opened fire on the Confederates visible on the Mumma farm. Seymour fought his men from this position for some time, absorbing several counterattacks and a heavy artillery shelling. Later that morning when General Hooker was wounded, Seymour's division commander, Brig. Gen. George G. Meade, took over corps command. Seymour in turn, as senior brigadier, took temporary control of Meade's division. His performance was superb, and Meade lavished high praise on his subordinate. ". . . From the confidence I placed in the judgment and military skill of that officer," wrote Meade of Seymour, "I left entirely to him the management and direction of his brigade." He went on to observe that Seymour's unit was ". . . the first in action and the only one engaged with the infantry the afternoon of the 16th, and the first to commence and the last to leave on the 17th."[54]

Supporting Seymour's advance was another Norwich graduate, this one a member of the army's "long-arm." Captain Dunbar R. Ransom's (Class of '51) Battery C, 5th United States Artillery, deployed and went into action north of the East Woods, where it "played with great effect on the enemy's infantry and batteries," lauded Meade. In fact, Meade noted that he could not complete his report ". . .without calling your attention to the skill and good judgment, combined with cool- ness, with which Captain Ransom, his officers. . .and men, served his battery." When the Confederates launched one of their many counter- attacks through the disputed Miller cornfield, Meade had personally directed Ransom's fire into their masses. This fire, wrote Meade, with the assistance of infantry supports "drove the enemy back. . . .I consid- er this one of the most critical periods of the morning, and that Captain Ransom's battery is due the credit of repulsing the enemy."[55]

As Seymour's men were solidifying Federal control over the East Woods, Joe Hooker was overseeing the deployment of his men for a massive attack south along the Hagerstown Turnpike. This deploy- ment included John Gibbon's "Iron Brigade," which proceeded south from the Joseph Poffenberger Farm. The Westerners had barely stepped off at common time when disaster struck. "No sooner was the column in motion," wrote one of the soldiers after the battle, "than the enemy opened fire on us with artillery." One of the Rebel shells exploded in the midst of the 6th Wisconsin, killing and wounding many, including several in Company A. One of the fallen was Capt. David K. Noyes (Class of '45), whose foot was severed by a piece of the flying hot iron. As one eyewitness described it, ". . .the second shell exploded in the ranks, disabling 13 men, including Captain Noyes, Company A. Notwithstanding this shock, the column moved steadily forward. . . ." In all probability Captain Noyes was the first Norwich casualty of the day, although he was not the last alumnus who would fall.[56]

The Iron Brigade continued its advance, divided almost equally by the Hagerstown Turnpike. Its two left regiments, composed of part of the 6th Wisconsin and the entire 2nd Wisconsin, marched into the Miller cornfield, where it was met by severe artillery and small arms fire. Almost immediately another Norwich graduate in another Iron Brigade regiment fell when 1st Lt. Charles K. Dean (Class of '45) of the 2nd Wisconsin was knocked out of the ranks. Just a few minutes after the left wing of the Iron Brigade marched into the Miller cornfield, the 13th Massachusetts (Hartsuff's Brigade) with members boasting Norwich credentials entered the fiercely disputed ground farther east. The 13th Massachusetts' acting commander was Maj. Jacob Parker Gould (Class of '49), and Pvt. William H. Hooper (Class of '67), Company K, was following Gould's orders that morning. By 7:00 a.m., all three units (2nd and 6th Wisconsin, and 13th Massacusetts) had suffered heavy casualties, and three of the four alumni in these regiments had fallen.[57]

Major Gould's method of advancing his regiment was innovative enough to elicit comment. In an attempt to reduce casualties, Gould directed his men to advance in double columns spaced at half the normal distance while zigzagging by using directional changes (probably obliques). This movement ". . .made under a heavy fire was performed with as much precision and coolness as though the regiment was on battalion drill. It is worth mentioning to show what good use may be made of the skill and confidence acquired in constant drilling." The creative major was later cited for gallantry in action for his handling of the regiment in the Cornfield and around the Dunker Church.[58]

As the morning unfolded, Brig. Gen. Napoleon Dana's brigade found itself in a hot position. Two of Dana's regiments, Col. William R. Lee's (Class of '25) 20th Massachusetts and the 19th Massachusetts under Col. Edward Hinks, were caught in a devastating three-sided crossfire when their Second Corps brigade advanced into the West Woods. ". . .Hardly had my left regiment entered the woods," Dana later reported, "when a tremendous musketry fire opened on my left and front." The fire soon enveloped the right front of the brigade as well, and Dana's regiments quickly absorbed heavy casualties. One the these was General Dana himself, who fell wounded when a minie ball pierced his body. Dana ordered Col. Norman Hall of the 7th Michigan to assume temporary command until the brigade's senior officer, Colonel Lee, could be located. When Hall located the Massachusetts officer and offered him the brigade command, Lee ". . . positively declined to relieve me," wrote Hall, "and repeatedly desired me to give such orders as I saw fit, and he would obey them." The slaughter in the West Woods continued for some time until the Federals were eventually driven from the position by heavy Southern reinforcements. The rebuffed Federals fell back across the pasture land and fields of crops to the safety of the East Woods. Colonel Lee, largely for his role in extricating his regiment from the deadly trap, was cited for gallantry and eventually breveted brigadier general in March 1865. Fighting next to Lee's 20th that morning was the 19th Massachusetts, which was one of the last regiments to leave the West Woods. Two out of the unit's three Norwich men, however, were lost in the fighting. Major Edmund Rice (Class of '60) fell with a severe wound in his right thigh, while Capt Henry Hale (Class of '61), Company B, had a minie ball carry away all his front teeth and a part of his tongue—an unusually painful and disabling wound. Sgt. John B. Thompson (Class of '61), Company G, was the only Norwich alumnus to emerge unscathed from the bloodbath.[59]

Another battery which supported the powerful Federal attacks that morning in the seesaw combat raging in the West Woods and around the Dunker Church was headed by a Norwich alumnus. First Lieutenant Evan W. Thomas (Class of '51) and his combined Battery A/C, 4th United States Artillery unlimbered near the East Woods, where his effective fire shattered Confederate infantry and artillery. Left to his own devices, the resourceful lieutenant handled his guns well that day. "I would state that I had no infantry support during the whole engagement," were the words he used to close his report of the battle.[60]

While the Federals were being driven from the West Woods, Brig. Gen. William H. French's division (Sumner's Second Corps) drifted southward and came up against the center of Lee's line. The Confederates opposing French consisted of two brigades under D. H. Hill, deployed in a sunken farm lane that offered a naturally powerful defensive position. Regiment after regiment melted away in the face of Southern volleys as French pressed the attack with all three of his brigades. As French's attack stalled another Second Corps division, Israel B. Richardson's, moved up to assist him. One of Richardson's units was the soon-to-be-legendary Irish Brigade, led by Brig. Gen. Thomas F. Meagher. The Irishmen attacked the Bloody Lane and shot it out with the enemy at close range. Eight color bearers fell and the brigade's green flag lay in the dust. At this point Meagher cried out "Boys, raise the colors, and follow me!" The men surged forward yet again, only to be stopped dead in their tracks. As casualties on both sides mounted, neither side could advance or retreat. Richardson called upon John C. Caldwell's brigade to help break the deadlock. Caldwell aligned his regiments and attacked Hill's heavily outnumbered defenders. The tide of Federals broke through the line, forcing the Confederates rearward.

D. H. Hill was well aware of the desperate nature of the break in the line. Lee's entire center was exposed; catastrophic defeat loomed. With the Confederate line broken, elements from both sides moved to occupy a critical knoll that controlled a portion of the advancing Federal left flank. Hill gathered a small group of Southerners and personally led them into the breach. Colonel Edward E. Cross, the 5th New Hampshire's commander, suffered a head wound driving his regiment for the high ground. With blood streaming down his face and a red bandana tied on his forehead, Cross screamed for his men to "put on the war paint," and smeared gunpowder on his cheeks. His men followed suit. Whooping like Indians, they scattered the advancing Confederates. Four Norwich alumni marched into battle that afternoon with the 5th New Hampshire. One of these, Capt. Horace T. H.

Pierce (Class of '46), was the fourth man to command the regiment after three superior officers (including Cross) were shot down during the attack. Fellow alumnus Capt. Charles H. Long (Class of '55) saw his career with the Granite State regiment come to an end when he fell severely wounded. Both alumni were commended for their gallant action by Colonel Cross in his report of the fighting. Captain Long, like Pierce, survived the battle and later rose to the rank of colonel of the 1st New Hampshire Heavy Artillery, finishing the war as a brigade commander. The Second Corps 5th New Hampshire eventually earned the dubious distinction of suffering more Civil War battle-related deaths than any regiment in the Union Army.[61]

Although McClellan's attacks had driven in Lee's center, the Federal commander failed to realize just how close he was to victory. Instead of committing his reserves to exploit the breakthrough, he did nothing to justify the blood spilled to gain the sunken road position. Instead, "Little Mac" focused his attention on the left wing of his line, where Maj. Gen. Ambrose Burnside's Ninth Corps was attempting to cross the lower stone bridge over the fordable Antietam Creek. Despite repeated orders from McClellan, Burnside had delayed traversing the span for some hours. When he made a few feeble attempts, they were turned back by a regiment of Georgia troops. Urged on by McClellan, Burnside directed Brig. Gen. Samuel Sturgis to renew the attempt. Sturgis, in turn, ordered Col. Edward Ferrero's Second Brigade to advance with a two regiment front and secure the high ground beyond the creek. Ferrero selected the 51st New York and 51st Pennsylvania for the difficult assignment. General Burnside, Ferrero informed them, had requested that they take the bridge. Could they do it, he asked? Ferrero, who had suspended the Pennsylvanians' daily whiskey ration for some perceived abuse of the privilege, heard a corporal in the 51st Pennsylvania shout out, "Will you give us our whiskey, Colonel, if we make it?" Ferrero responded, "Yes, by God!" The troops cheered.

In the ranks of the 51st Pennsylvania were a pair of twin brothers, Maj. Edwin Schall (Class of '56) and Capt. Edward Schall (Class of '56), Company D, both alumni of Norwich. It was decided that instead of advancing in column along the road that hugged the river (a tactic that had been spectacularly unsuccessful thus far), the bridge would be assaulted head-on. About 12:30 p.m. the two 51sts, about

670 men, deployed and launched the attack. Unable to take the stone bridge with the first effort, the attackers massed along the banks on either side of the bridge and poured lead into the enemy on the other side. As Confederate fire slackened, the New Yorkers forded the stream while the Pennsylvanians made a mad rush across the structure. Major Schall wrote a letter on November 18, 1862 to the Montgomery County, Pennsylvania *National Defender*, of which he had been editor, poetically describing the capture of what later was derisively called Burnside's Bridge. "The task," Schall explained in the present tense to add drama to the story, "is a desperate one. . . .The Bridge must be carried. It is essential for the safety of the army and what are lives of men in comparison to the safety of the Republic." Schall's regiment, its three flags at the head of the column, "are just now moving under the musketry fire of the enemy. Several have already fallen. But we stop not. Up the steep hill we go, and wheel into close column of companies we descend." As they advanced into the ravine formed by Antietam Creek there "in full view, is the bridge. The hill on the opposite side boldly confronts us, covered with the armed legions of the rebels." Unknown to Schall or his men, the Confederates had virtually expended all their ammunition and were beginning to withdraw from their position. "We move onward at the double quick, in the face of a murderous fire. . . .The color bearers with their standards. . .push across the bridge. . .striking terror into the rebel ranks, who, panic-stricken, seek safety in flight." The far bank was secured, earning Ferrero his general's star and the Pennsylvanians their whiskey.[62]

The forced crossing complete, Burnside poured his corps over the creek. At about the same time the bridge fell, one of Burnside's divisions under Brig. Gen. Isaac P. Rodman waded his command over Snavely's Ford, about two miles below Burnside's crossing. Before long Burnside had assembled almost three divisions on a north-south axis for a drive west into Sharpsburg. Rodman's division included Col. Harrison S. Fairchild's 940-man New York brigade, which contained the flamboyantly-clad men of the 9th New York ("Hawkins's Zouaves"), under the command of Lt. Colonel Edgar A. Kimball (Class of '44). Their uniforms were based upon the gaudy trappings worn by the Algerian zouaves in the French colonial service. Although well dressed, they had but little combat experience, a trait shared with

Fairchild's other two regiments. After about two hours of preparation, the Ninth Corps finally rolled forward toward the town of Sharpsburg and Lee's lightly defended right flank. Edward Ferrero's two remaining regiments, the 21st and 35th Massachusetts, had initially provided covering fire for the earlier storming of the bridge. Although they were almost out of ammunition, they had advanced and joined the balance of the brigade on the west side of the creek. The 21st included Capt. Charles W. Davis (Class of '49), Company A, who led his men in conjunction with the rest of Ferrero's brigade and others toward the prize of Sharpsburg. Unfortunately for the Federals, they would never enter the town in any force.

As they drove forward toward the outskirts of Sharpsburg, Southern artillery bombarded the long lines of attackers. Zouave commander Nathan Kimball had his horse shot from under him in the large cornfield at the Otto Farm as his New Yorkers moved steadily against a line of Rebel artillery pieces unlimbered and firing from the top of a low but commanding ridge. Harrison Fairchild halted his brigade in a small depression and the lines were reorganized for the final thrust. The men of the 9th New York began chanting "Zou-Zou-Zou," as Edgar Kimball moved up and down their ranks encouraging them: "Bully, Ninth! Bully, Ninth! Boys, I'm proud of you! Every one of you! Don't mind me boys," he shouted, "If you want a safe place stick close to me." Kimball remained standing to motivate and inspire his men. When the advance was renewed, the Rebels withdrew two advance batteries as a pair of Southern brigades moved up into position behind a low stone wall and waited for Fairchild's regiments to approach. Within fifty yards the Confederates opened fire. Kimball's colors tumbled to the ground, as did scores of his men.[63]

One member of Company G, 9th New York, vividly described the assault against the ridge, the climax of the battle for the young zouaves:

> We were getting ready now for the charge proper, but were still lying on our faces. Lieutenant-Colonel Kimball was ramping up and down the line. . . .I only remember that as we rose and started all the fire that had been held back so long was loosed. In a second the air was full of the hiss of bullets and the hurtle of grape-shot. The mental strain was so great that i saw at that moment the singular effect mentioned, I think, in the life of Goethe on a similar occasion - the whole landscape for an instant turned slightly red.[64]

Another member of the 9th New York expressed his amazement at Kimball's almost insanely courageous actions in the fight. "Our color guards were cut down almost to a man," recalled another member of the 9th New York, "and Kimball, our hot-headed Lieut. Colonel, finally seized the flag himself and and wrapped it around him. Strange to say, he was uninjured."[65]

The attack managed to reach the stone wall, where brief pockets of hand-to-hand combat broke out before the Southerners retreated. The captured position was less than 300 yards from the outskirts of town. Other Federal regiments from other organizations were also driving the enemy from positions beyond Kimball's right front. The Norwich alumnus' regiment paid a staggering price for the small victory, a cost which may have been partly the result of the 9th's bright uniforms, which offered easy targets. Kimball carried 373 men into action that afternoon; 63% of them were killed, wounded, or missing.

As knots of Federals began entering the outskirts of Sharpsburg, and while General Lee himself looked on with no small level of concern, troops were seen advancing toward town from the direction of Harpers Ferry. A. P. Hill's exhausted Confederate division had arrived after a forced march of seventeen miles. The aggressive Southerner threw his brigades onto the field against Burnside's left flank and threw back the attack, stablizing the Confederate right flank. Within a short time only the 9th New York held the highwater mark of the Federal advance near the town's boundaries, for the other advanced regiments had fallen back. The fighting was spreading rapidly across the front and Kimball's ammunition was running low. Someone must have realized the New Yorker's desperate plight, for the 9th was ordered to withdraw. "We have the bayonets," yelled an angry Kimball to the courier who delivered the message. "What are they for?" When he was personally ordered from the field by a general officer, Kimball admonished him to "Look at my regiment! They go off the field under orders. They are not driven off. Do they look like a beaten regiment?" Kimball and his men were cited for their bravery on the field that day. Darkness and Burnside's less than strong desire to renew the attack ended the day-long battle.[66]

Although his army had come within one more division-sized attack of destruction, General Lee boldly maintained his position on the field throughout the following day, September 18. Over 4,000 dead men littered the rolling hills of western Maryland, while 18,300 lay wounded and several thousand were missing. Despite a corps of reserve troops, McClellan did nothing, pleased that he had been able to fight Lee to a standstill north of the Potomac River. On the evening of the 18th, the Army of Northern Virginia quietly slipped away south of the river. One last drama of the Maryland Campaign was played out at Boteler's Ford on the Potomac River near Sheperdstown, where Lee had left a rear guard to buy his army additional time to organize and continue south. After an artillery duel across the stream, Col. Jonathan Childs (Class of '54) and his 4th Michigan Infantry, part of Brig. Gen. Charles Griffin's brigade, George Morell's division, Porter's Fifth Corps, slipped over about sunset and routed the thin line of infantry and exhausted gunners. Childs' 300 men captured two guns and several caissons at the cost of one killed and seven wounded. The regiment was called back to the north bank after dark.[67] In the aftermath of America's costliest battle in history, Brig. Gen. Oliver O. Howard eloquently summed up its cost to the soldiers of the Republic: "They have poured out their blood like water, and we must look to God and our country for a just reward."

The Army of the Potomac spent the next several weeks in the Sharpsburg area resting and recuperating. Burnside's Ninth Corps hospitals were set up on the east bank of the Antietam. Many of Lt. Col. Kimball's 9th New York's wounded were in the field hospital located at Locust Spring. Kimball, now referred to as "Old Gunpowder" by his troops, had not only demonstrated his bravery and leadership skills on the field, but also displayed his concern for the post-battle welfare of his soldiers. In early October, Kimball marched the regimental band to a field hospital to play for the sick and wounded members of the regiment. "Their presence had a good effect on the wounded boys, who kept them busy answering questions about the regiment. The regiment appeared to be uppermost in the thoughts of each of them." The men wanted to know all the details of what was happening with their unit, "how it looked on parade; what number of men were present for duty; what kind of a camp they had; what Burnside and the other generals had said in their reports in relation to the charge of the regiment in the battle and a hundred similar questions. It was always the regiment. . . ."[68]

Although Lee had not been tactically defeated, Antietam was a significant strategic (and moral) victory for the Union. The Army of the Potomac held the field when Lee's vaunted Army of Northern Virginia retreated below the Potomac. After the disheartening string of defeats President Lincoln finally had the victory he needed—albeit a narrow one—to issue the Emancipation Proclamation. This important declaration declared that, as of January 1, 1863, all slaves in rebellious sections of the country were free. This brilliant move brought thousands of blacks into the Union army and effectively prevented European nations from officially recognizing the Southern Confederacy.

While Lincoln claimed his victory, it became obvious to many in and out of the administration that McClellan had failed to capitalize on a golden opportunity to crush Lee and effectively end the rebellion in the East. In the weeks that followed the battle, the Army of the Potomac remained stagnant in Maryland. Only a personal visit from Lincoln and a running war of words over the telegraph prompted McClellan to finally move his legions. He was too late. As the army crossed the Potomac River, Lincoln sacked McClellan. For a time angry talk circulated among some officers in the army of a possible mutiny. Two letters from Capt. Charles Bowers (Class of '52) to his wife provide insight into the impact of McClellan's removal and the attitudes of the officers and men of the 32nd Massachusetts:

> . . . This morning at 6 o'clock an order came for us to fall into line to hear the farewell address of Gen. McClellan . . . . It was short, tender, manly. He preferred no charges, made no accusations, uttered no complaints . . . . An hour later and our brigade was on the march to take our position in the line of the Grand Army of the Potomac to see for the last time our old Commander. The whole army was formed in brigades and the General rode through them all. He was accompanied by a great retinue of officers. He led them with head uncovered, bowing gracefully to each brigade as he passed, the drums ruffled and the Colors waved, the officers saluted, the men cheered. The morning was perfect. The sun shone brightly, the air was soft and delicious, the forest and the field were arrayed in their . . . green and radiant colors, and all combined to make the scene grand and imposing beyond anything I ever witnessed . . . . I think no general was ever more popular with his army than McClellan. Not even Napoleon or Washington. The men

adore him. The officers idolize him. Why he has been so suddenly removed is unknown to us . . . . One thing for certain, it has taken the
army by surprise and is spoken of by all in terms of severe, unmeasured
condemnation . . . . [69]

Bowers followed up his initial thoughts on McClellan's sacking in
another missive dated November 11, in which he addressed the issue
of army loyalty:

> . . . . Suddenly and without explanation, the favorite leader, in whom they
> trusted is removed and now all has changed to consternation and dismay. I
> suppose our own regiment is a fair specimen of all the others. As far as I can
> learn only two out of all those who hold commissions sustain the measure,
> Dr. Adams and myself. All the others either consider the act extremely inju-
> dicious at this critical juncture, or speak of it as an act of injustice and wan-
> ton ingratitude unparalleled in the world's history . . . . It is openly . . . and
> vehemently urged by leading officers that the army should disband at once
> and go home and let the government take care of itself as best it can . . . .
> Still, I think the men will soon see the folly of such a course, and a sober
> second thought after their . . . disappointment has subsided . . . .

Bowers also detailed army complaints against President Lincoln and
"the pestilent abolitionists," indicating that McClellan "lacked some
important qualities that go into making up the perfect general. I was
willing to follow McL. and I am willing to follow Burnside [who was
appointed to replace him]."[70]

Major General Winfield Scott Hancock summed up the feelings reflecting the attitude of the great majority of the army when he proclaimed, "We are serving our country, and not any man." The sacking
of McClellan, an extremely popular figure with the troops if not with
Washington and the press, proved that the Army of the Potomac was
truly "Mr. Lincoln's Army."[71]

On October 30, 1862, while the Army of the Potomac was resting
in Maryland, Col. William Lee of the 20th Massachusetts Infantry returned to Governor Andrew both stands of colors which the regiment
had received in August 1861. These were the same colors the regiment
had carried in all its battles except Ball's Bluff. "Storms and bullets had
torn them to remnants," he wrote in a letter to the governor, "[but] believe me, they are bright and untarnished."[72]

On November 7, a reluctant Maj. Gen. Ambrose Burnside assumed command of the Army of Potomac. To his credit, no one knew better than Burnside how really unfit he was to hold such a high command; nevertheless, under protest and believing it his duty to do so, he took the job. As new campaign plans were drafted, the army continued to refit and speculate as to what its next move would be. A number of new regiments had joined the army, many of them nine-month units called up by President Lincoln under the emergency decree of summer 1862, which called for 300,000 additional soldiers to put down the stubborn—and thus far successful—rebellion. Nine months was a short time within which to train troops for field operations and employ them effectively in the field. By and large, however, these regiments were populated with high quality material. Restrospect demonstrated they were the last wave of genuine volunteer units. A singular example of the best of these volunteers is the 24th Michigan Infantry, which enlisted as one of the last three-year regiments. This western outfit, which included Capt. Charles A. Hoyt (Class of '63), commanding Company C, joined the Iron Brigade that October. The regiment's reception was lukewarm at best, viewed as it was as a "green" organization. The men of the 24th Michigan would not achieve full acceptance by the brigade's other members until they too had "seen the elephant" and proven themselves worthy through courage and reliability under fire.[73]

When Burnside assumed command of the Army of the Potomac, it was encamped near Warrenton, Virginia. The plan he developed to defeat Lee's Army of Northern Virginia is considered by historians to have been quite good. Burnside intended to shift the entire army overland to the Tidewater; once there, his lines of supply would be short and he could advance on Richmond. The first major step in the plan was a rapid movement across the Rappahanock at Fredericksburg before Lee knew what he was up to; it almost worked. Both Burnside and the Army of the Potomac, unfortunately, were destined to be plagued by bad luck. While his army reached the Rappahanock well ahead of any major Rebel force, the pontoon bridges which he had ordered in advance and which were essential for the river crossing had not arrived.[74]

The 50th New York Engineers, who controlled the pontoons and in which Norwich's Lt. Col. William Pettes (Class of '27) served, had not been notified of orders to move to the Rappahanock until six days after Burnside's movement orders had originally been issued. By the time the traffic jams caused by the simultaneous movement of large pontoons and troops on the roads were sorted out and the bridges arrived, Lee was waiting on the high ground behind Fredericksburg, daring Burnside to cross and attack. After an extended period of hesitation, Burnside concluded his best hope for success was a "surprise" crossing right at Fredericksburg followed by a direct assault. The stage was set for one of the two most courageous yet futile frontal assaults ever undertaken by the Army of the Potomac.[75]

At least 76 Norwich men lay on the banks of the Rappahanock, awaiting the command to cross over and attack the waiting Confederates. For some of them, that wait marked their last days with the Army of the Potomac. The story of the gallant assault crossing of the Rappahanock and the great charges on Marye's Heights are well known to students of the war, and Norwich men participated in all aspects of the battle. The combat engineers of the 50th New York, under constant fire from Mississippi sharpshooters, suffered heavy losses attempting to construct the pontoon bridge from the shore of the Rappahanock River below the Lacy House across to Fredericksburg. Finally, the 7th Michigan, 19th Massachusetts and Col. William R. Lee's 20th Massachusetts crossed the river under fire in boats. Observing the action of the 50th New York Engineers from the Lacy House (Chatham), Clara Barton ". . . stood and watched the engineers as they moved forward to construct a pontoon bridge from the lower edge of the garden terrace to the sharp bluff on the opposite shore." After some initial success, the engineers realized that "A rain of musket balls has swept their ranks and the brave fellows lie level with the bridge or float down the stream." The men soon learned that ". . . the cellars are filled with sharp shooters and our shell will never reach them."[76]

In the Second Corps, Colonel Lee's 20th Massachusetts and Sgt. John B. Thompson's 19th Massachusetts stood out for their river crossing operation under fire, and the house-to-house fighting in Fredericksburg which followed. The street fighting in Fredericksburg, a rare occurrence in the Civil War, was particular nasty. Despite this, some units kept their aplomb. The attitude of Colonel Lee's 20th Massachusetts in the battle was recalled by its brigade commander as ". . . .he remarked that the 20th, like the regulars, did its fighting without bothering to strike heroic attitudes. Groping for the expression he wanted, he hit upon an odd one: 'The 20th has no poetry in a fight.'"[77]

Further down the river, crossing over pontoon bridges constructed by Lieutenant Colonel Pettes and his men, the 24th Michigan faced its baptism of fire. On Saturday morning December 13, 1862, as part of Maj. Gen. Abner Doubleday's division southeast of Fredericksburg, the Iron Brigade was called upon to support George Meade's division of Pennsylvania Reserves and to repel advancing Confederates. The 24th charged with a singular dash and courage earning the respect of its peers and acceptance as a full-fledged member of the "Iron Brigade." In the regiment's advance during that engagement Norwich's Captain Hoyt (Class of '63), was struck on the knee by a spent piece of shell that caused a painful contusion. When ordered to the rear by his regimental commander Hoyt refused, replying "No, Sir, I have been trying to regard this as a wound, but it won't do. I must try again," and he hobbled back into the fight with his company. Also in action on the left of the Union line with the Iron Brigade was Col. William Robinson (Class of '41) (7th Wisconsin). Robinson's handling of his regiment was singled out for special praise and he was recommended for promotion to brigadier general; it never came.[78]

Infantry actions in that section of the Union left flank were supported by a number of Norwich "red legs:" Capt. Dunbar R. Ransom's (Class of '51), Battery C, 5th United States Artillery, Capt. Frank Amsden's (Class of '59), Battery G, 1st Pennsylvania Light Artillery, 1st Lt. Evan W. Thomas' (Class of '54), Battery C, 4th United States Artillery, Capt. James A. Hall's (Class of '62), 2nd Maine Battery, and 1st Lt. Edward B. Williston's (Class of '56), Battery D, 2nd United States Artillery. Ransom, Amsden, and Hall's batteries lined up side by side; all three men, as well as Lt. Evan Thomas, were cited for their gallant conduct. Amsden had his horse killed by shrapnel and lay helplessly pinned under him for a time. General Hancock was particularly impressed with the actions of Lieutenant Thomas ". . . when this zealous young officer, receiving an order for another battery to proceed to the front . . . moved forward with his battery, and took a very advanced position upon the plain, opening with effect upon the enemy, using shrapnel." After a severe exchange of artillery fire "His position was thought to be too far in advance, on account of the enemy's musketry, and he was ordered to retire with his battery."[79]

In the Sixth Corps Vermont Brigade, which was also engaged south of the city near Deep Run Creek, Charles B. Stoughton (Class of '61), now the 4th Vermont's 20-year-old colonel, was cited for his bravery in the battle. Reporting to the Adjutant General of Vermont on the conduct of his 4th Vermont, Colonel Stoughton wrote, "The 1st Vermont Brigade has again participated in action and again distinguished itself for gallantry and courage. . . . " Summarizing the actions of his regiment, Stoughton went on to say, "My colors are completely riddled with canister and musket balls, scarcely hanging together. The top of the staff, upon which is a brass eagle, was shot away by canister, but saved and brought away."[80]

During that action, Capt. James (Jonas) H. Platt Jr. (Class of '54), Company B, 4th Vermont, was involved in a particularly selfless deed of heroism. After Platt's company had fought for an extended period and used up nearly all its ammunition, "a charge of cannister struck down half the company, killing four and wounding fourteen." Platt ordered his men back to reform, which they did, retiring in good order. Platt, after asking for volunteers, remained on the battlefield under fire where he ". . . bound up the most dangerous wounds, thus prolonging at least several lives, and, with the assistance he had summoned, bore away to the hospital, a mile distant, all who were unable to help themselves." Those who observed his actions were amazed he was unharmed and told him so. The gallant captain merely replied that "God would not let us suffer while in discharge of such a duty."[81]

Lastly, among the Green Mountain men, the 3rd Vermont commanded by Lt. Col. Thomas O. Seaver (Class of '59), performed exceptionally well in the fighting near Deep Run Creek. Seaver led his men through the ravine of Deep Run, emerging on the flank of Evander Law's Confederate Brigade. Heavy fire from Seaver's Vermonters shattered Law's advance causing over 200 casualties. Unlike the slaughter of Union troops at nearby Marye's Heights, the 3rd Vermont had light casualties and met with some success. It was in this engagement that the Vermonters first gained their reputation as peerless skirmishers, a reputation they upheld throughout the war.[82]

The Army of the Potomac's greatest glory and the height of its folly that day at Fredericksburg were the repetitive piecemeal assaults on Marye's Heights and the stone wall in the sunken road. Over the course of several hours, as many as thirteen separate attacks were made and repelled. Before it was all over 12,653 Union men were killed, wounded, captured, or missing. Nothing was accomplished except the slaughter of some of the army's bravest officers and men. Examples of courage and sacrifice abounded. Among the many units spilling their blood that day, was the newly fielded 7th Rhode Island Infantry. In its ranks were Maj. Jacob Babbitt (Class of '26), Capt. Alfred M. Channel (Class of '54), Company D, and 1st Lt. Thomas S. Brownell (Class of '54), Company I.[83]

Major Babbitt, thought by many to be too old for combat duty, was mortally wounded on the front line with his regiment during his first and last fight. Babbitt and his men were near the infamous wall and sunken road late on the afternoon of December 13 when he ascertained that the rear of the 7th Rhode Island was being fired into by friendly troops. He informed his regimental commander and was ordered to find the colonel of the regiment firing on the Rhode Islanders and put a stop to the shooting. Starting on this mission, under heavy fire from front and rear, he had not gone far when he was struck in the back by a bullet. The minie ball passed out under the left arm and then through it, making four holes and cutting a wound in the limb over a foot long. His lung was also grazed. Babbitt was removed from the field that evening but died in an army hospital in Alexandria on December 23.[84]

The after-action report of the Ninth Corps commander, Brig. Gen. Orlando B. Willcox, was particularly impressed by the actions of one of his assault brigades in which the 7th Rhode Island served. According to Willcox, "All these troops behaved well, and marched under a heavy fire across the broken plain, pressed up to the field at the foot of the enemy's sloping crest, and maintained every inch of ground with great obstinacy until after nightfall . . . . " He remembered seeing the elderly major: "Major Babbitt, of the same regiment, was mortally wounded in the gallant effort . . . . (He) fell at the head of their troops . . . ."[85]

Captain Erasmus G. Rehrer (Class of '49), Company E, 129th Pennsylvania, was wounded and cited for gallantry while serving on his brigade's staff. Captain Charles W. Davis (Class of '49) served in the 21st Massachusetts, which is credited by some as advancing closest to the Sunken Road's stone wall. Its national color bearer, Sgt. Thomas Plunkett, who was not a Norwich alumnus, set an example for high courage and sacrifice matched by few men in either army. When Plunkett's arms were blown off by a cannon shot, he refused to drop the colors, holding them with his bleeding stumps and shouting for the men not to let them fall. He clung to them until the colors were taken by another member of the twenty-first. Plunkett's blood can still be seen today on the colors of the 21st Massachusetts Infantry in the Massachusetts State House in Boston.[86]

In General Hancock's division of the Second Corps, the 5th New Hampshire went into the assault at Marye's Heights with 303 officers and men. The regiment suffered 51 officers and men killed or mortally wounded, 123 wounded, and 19 missing (presumed killed), a staggering casualty rate of 63.6%. Only three of the regiment's 19 officers, including Capt. Horace T. H. Pierce (Class of '46), who was the fourth officer to command the regiment in the battle, survived unwounded. The regiment's chief doctor, Surgeon Luther M. Knight (Class of '37), was commended for his handling of the wounded. When the Granite State men were mustered after being withdrawn from the field, only 63 men remained present for duty. It was reported that bodies found closest to the stone wall at Fredericksburg were from three regiments of the Second Corps, one of which was the 5th New Hampshire. The 5th's casualty rate at Fredericksburg was exceeded only by the Colonel Lee's 20th Massachusetts. Of the 238 officers and men fielded by Lee's regiment, 20 officers and men were killed or mortally wounded, 138 were wounded, and none were missing, a casualty rate of 68.4%. It was one of the highest casualty rates of the war. In the 19th Massachusetts, which had also fought bravely in the assault crossing of the Rappahanock and street fighting in Fredericksburg, Sgt. John B. Thompson (Class of '61), Company F, fell wounded in the assault on Marye's Heights; his regiment lost 104 men including eight color bearers, 23 of these being killed or mortally wounded.[87]

In the Fifth Corps Second Brigade, First Division that afternoon, Capt. Charles Bowers (Class of '52) and Pvt. Daniel Parmenter (Class of '63) of the 32nd Massachusetts took part in the last futile assault on Marye's Heights. Bowers wrote to his wife that "The city of Fredericksburg is a perfect picture of desolation. The buildings are either burned or perfectly riddled with shot. Men who were in all the different battles before Richmond unite in saying that the battle of Saturday surpassed in fierceness and desperation any of them. The rebels being in their entrenchments and rifle pits have suffered but little." After further collecting his thoughts, he wrote again the same day, recounting that "The streets are full of soldiers, their arms stacked and the men lying on the side walks by the side of them with their equipment and blankets on. Occasional shots from heavy guns are heard and one shell from one of them has just fallen in the city quite near us. No one was hurt by it . . . ." Troubled by the carnage he had witnessed, he wrote: "It is said the loss on our side by this conflict . . . has been very great. Some say as much as the battle at Antietam . . . the casualties have been frightful." He was proud of his men's demeanor, saying they "are behaving finely and under the circumstances deserve the greatest praise. All of you at home can never sufficiently honor the brave men who are sacrificing and suffering so much." Speaking for himself and his cause he closed by writing, "That God will give us ultimate success I firmly believe. How many of us will fall before His infinite justice will be avenged I know not."[88]

Apparently too rattled to detail his own actions, he composed himself enough by December 19 to write Lydia again that his regiment had gone into the battle ". . .at its fiercest point, about 4 P.M. Saturday, when the last great charge was made to carry the enemy's works. It was a most terrific scene, and I was proud to say the men did their duty fearlessly & nobly, deserving a better results." Charles and his men remained on the field from ". . . 3 P.M. Saturday until 10 P.M. Sunday night. All day Sunday we lay just under the brow of the hill within 40 to 60 rods of their rifle pits and batteries exchanging shots." It was a particularly stressful and difficult time. "The balls whizzed over our heads so closely we dared not lift them up and it was with great difficulty the men could load their muskets . . . . " He was personally saddened and and disappointed by the battle's outcome. "I did hope I might once be engaged in a conflict where we should come out victors. But so far it has been denied me. . . . Still. . . I tremble when I think how disastrous our defeat might have been. . . . " What Charles Bowers had not told his wife and daughter was how really lucky he had been. In the attack he was ". . . struck square in the chest by a spent bullet which did him no serious harm."[89]

A few days later, after the usual truce to recover the wounded and bury the dead, the Union army successfully withdrew across the Rappahanock River. Once again, the shaken soldiers of the Army of the Potomac were left to contemplate whether the skill of their commanders would ever match the courage displayed on the battlefield. In local buildings, such as the National Hotel in Fredericksburg and the Lacy House at Chatham, where it is said 1,200 wounded men lay in and around the house, Clara Barton and the surgeons went about their gruesome work.[90]

In Washington, the Honorable Gideon Welles (Class of '26), Lincoln's Secretary of the Navy, captured the dismal mood of the times and the difficulties high administration officials had in gathering accurate information:

December 14, Sunday.

There has been fighting for two or three days at Fredericksburg, and our troops were said to have crossed the river. The rumor at the War Department and I get only rumor is that our troops have done well, that Burnside and our generals are in good spirits; but there is something unsatisfactory, or not entirely satisfactory, in this intelligence, or in the method of communicating it. When I get nothing clear and explicit at the War Department I have my apprehensions. They fear to admit disastrous truths. Adverse tidings are suppressed, with a deal of fuss and mystery, a shuffling over of papers and maps, and a far-reaching vacant gaze at something undefined and indescribable.[91]

Immediately after Fredericksburg, Col. William R. Lee, worn out and ill through a combination of combat fatigue, his age, and his extended active service, reluctantly resigned as colonel of the 20th Massachusetts. Lieutenant Henry Abbott's letter to his brother George on December 21, 1862 summed up the incident and the regiment's feelings: "Poor old Col. Lee is . . . gone from . . . us. It fairly made my heart ache to see the brave little fellow trying to do his duty here." The men sensed Lee's life was truly imperiled. "A single week of it would have killed him outright. He is certainly the model of a plucky English officer." While many of his command would have wished to have a ceremonial departure for their beloved commander, "When he went away he wouldn't have us officers told of it. He couldn't bear to bid us good bye. He fairly broke down & shed tears when he got into the ambulance which took him away." Abbot continued his letter by writing that future United States Supreme Court Justice Oliver Wendell Holmes ". . . wrote a very good address to him to express our feelings. I trust it will do something to comfort the gallant little colonel in showing him how much his officers love . . . him."[92]

While the Army of the Potomac and fellow Vermonters were suffering at Fredericksburg, the men of the 2nd Vermont Brigade, a nine-month formation, impatiently waited their turn to fight for the Good Cause. At the time, they suffered more from disease and the stress of picket duty in "Mosby's Confederacy" than from combat. In an attempt to break the boredom and recall happier days, officers of the 12th Vermont Volunteers gathered for a belated Thanksgiving in Maj. Levi G. Kingsley's (Class of '56), log shack, christened "Shanty de Kingsley" for the occasion. Feasting on boxes of delicacies shipped from Vermont, they were able for the moment to forget their plight.[93]

Thus, while 1862 ended upon a sad and troubling note for the Union and great joy for the rebellious South, with the new year dawned new hope for the nation, and the Year of Jubilee for Black-Americans: on January 1, 1863, the Emancipation Proclamation formally went into effect.

Norwich Alumni at Gettysburg

July 1-3, 1863

= Confederate Infantry

= Federal Infantry

Ewell's Second Corps

Oak Hill

Howard's XI Corps

Reynolds' I Corps

A. P. Hill's Third Corps

McPherson's Ridge

GETTYSBURG

Cemetery Hill

Culp's Hill

MEADE

Cemetery Ridge

Battery C, 4th US

Little Round Top

Devil's Den

(July 3)

(July 2)

Pickett's Charge

(July 3)

LEE

Pegram's Battalion

Seminary Ridge

unfinished railroad

Chambersburg Pike

Pegram's Battalion (21 guns)

Herr Ridge

(July 1)

At the climax of Pickett's Charge, 20-year-old Edmund Rice (Class of '60), 19th Massachusetts Infantry, led a dramatic charge near the famous Copse of Trees which helped seal the breakthrough and defeat Pickett's men. Wounded in the attempt, Rice earned the Congressional Medal of Honor for his efforts.

Norwich alumnus Col. William Robinson (Class of '41), commander of the 7th Wisconsin Infantry of the Iron Brigade, was one of the heroes of the first day's fighting west of Gettysburg. He led his men first against Archer's Tennessee Brigade in McPherson's Woods, and then conducted a fighting withdrawal and rear guard action to Seminary Ridge and back through Gettysburg.

At dusk on July 2, 1st Lt. Evan Thomas (Class of '51) and Battery C, 4th United States Artillery, 1st Regular Brigade (Capt. Dunbar Ransom, Class of '54), played a key role in support of the suicidal assault of the 1st Minnesota. The six Napoleons kept up a withering fire into the ranks of Cadmus Wilcox's advancing Alabama regiments, helping the Minnesotans seal the breach.

IV. Chancellorsville & Gettysburg

"Clubs are Trump"
Edmund Rice '60

The New Year of 1863 brought with it the promise of emancipation, at least for slaves in states still in rebellion against the Union. The proclamation's reception in the North, as well as within the ranks of the Army of the Potomac, was mixed. A large percentage of the army opposed it, claiming they did not enlist to free slaves but to preserve the country; only a minority of the soldiers displayed any interest in fighting for black freedom. As the war dragged on, however, attitudes began to change. Simply from a pragmatic point of view, depriving the Confederacy of a key source of labor had both an economic as well as military rationale behind it. As for the idea of black soldiers, the mounting casualty lists gradually led many Northerners to feel a black man could stop a Southern bullet as well as a white one. Not surprisingly, most of the support for emancipation came from the New England states. A Vermont soldier gave vent to his feelings on the subject when he proclaimed, "Slavery must die and if the South insists on being buried in the same grave I shall see nothing but the retributive hand of God."[1]

The Vermont Brigade's "Anti-Rebel" Wilbur Fisk was of like mind. In April 1863, he wrote "There is no other way—there can be no other, for peace or for prosperity—but to fight out this rebellion to the bitter end, subjugate and destroy it." By this time, members of the Democratic Party who opposed the war, the so-called "Peace Democrats" or "Copperheads," looked to Ohio Congressman Clement L. Vallandigham for leadership. In lieu of total war against the South, the movement threatened Northern unity by preaching a message of peace, compromise and—in the eyes of the troops—defeatism. "After all the toil we have undergone, all the sufferings we have endured and dangers we have outlived," proclaimed Fisk, "it is certainly an occasion of grief and indignation to hear of those at home who are talking of peace, to be purchased by concession now." He finished by underlining he and his comrades' determination to see the war through: "There are soldiers here that would rather their bones should rot in Virginia than to have anything happen to our Government so humiliating."[2]

Despite the feeling of Fisk and many other New Englanders, other soldiers felt betrayed by Lincoln's action. These men knew they had joined the army to restore the Union, not to free the blacks. In fact, during the fall of 1862, just weeks before the formal implementation of the Emancipation Proclamation, Maj. Gen. George McClellan, despite his personal attitudes on dealing with the South, felt compelled to issue General Order No. 163. The directive reminded the troops that regardless of personal feelings, obedience was owed to governmental orders and that complaining by officers and men about emancipation must immediately cease. Feelings continued to run high. There were some who believed that a pro-slavery cabal existed within the command structure of the Army of the Potomac. Major General K. Warren actually testified to this effect before Senator Benjamin Wade's Committee on the Conduct of the War in March of 1864. Over time, however, the troops begrudgingly accepted the situation. While it played to a mixed crowd in the states, the proclamation had a decisive role in keeping both England and France from entering the war in support of the Confederacy.[3]

The New Year found the Army of the Potomac huddling in its camps around Fredericksburg. Its recent defeat the prior December left it badly demoralized. Desertions threatened to reach epidemic proportions, and the near total collapse of the commissary system contributed to rampant sickness in the camps. Four generals from the Sixth Corps, including William B. Franklin, directly approached President Lincoln to ask for the removal of Ambrose Burnside as head of the army. When Lincoln made Burnside aware of the situation and his generals' lack of confidence in his ability to command, the stunned officer tendered his resignation. Lincoln refused, and for the time being Burnside remained in command. Burnside believed that a new offensive might alter the army's mood and result in a change of fortune for the hard-luck organization. His plan was to envelope Lee's army via Banks' Ford on the Rappahannock River.

While the mid-January move showed early signs of promise, it was almost immediately crippled by atrocious weather and still more bad luck. "Here we remain fast stuck in the mud," wrote the 32nd Massachusetts' Capt. Charles Bowers (Class of '52) to Lydia. "I have not been out to the road but those who have say it looks as if the bottom had dropped out." The captain described the army's plummeting morale and how many of the troops had lost faith in the commanders. "Both officers and men do not hesitate to call the President a damned old imbecile fool and openly advocate an overthrow of the government in Washington. Gov. Andrew, Senators Sumner & Wilson are called damn fools, damned rascals & damned liars, fanatics, abolitionists."

As the men returned from fatigue duty building corduroy roads to get the artillery and supply wagons back to their original camps, Bowers recalled them singing (to the tune of old John Brown):

> Burnside's army's got stuck in the mud
> Burnside's army's got stuck in the mud
> Burnside's army's got stuck in the mud
> He can't (lord?) it over us again

As the troops, horses and mules literally foundered in a sea of mud and heavy rains, the offensive was canceled and Burnside's infamous "Mud March" came to an end, as did Burnside's tenure as commander of the army.[4]

In his place Lincoln elevated Maj. Gen. Joseph "Fighting Joe" Hooker, a solid veteran of most of the army's major battles. Hooker, who hated his press-awarded nickname, possessed genuinely impressive organizational and disciplinary skills, which he immediately set about implementing to get the army back on its feet. When he assumed command, morale was at an all-time low and unlawful absences at an all-time high. Hooker instituted a number of key reforms which served him and his successors well. Among these were a systematic program of leaves for officers and men, a reorganization of the commissary system, consolidation of the Union cavalry into a single, more potent force, and the elimination of Burnside's unwieldy "Grand Divisions." These measures and others, including a general tightening of discipline and the institution of a system of distinctive corps patches (insignia) which became very popular with the troops, did much to lift the army's spirits. Unfortunately, Hooker possessed an inflated opinion of his military abilities, was disliked by many of his fellow officers, and had the nasty habit of speaking in negative terms of just about everybody except Joe Hooker. He also tinkered with the Army of the Potomac's artillery structure, decentralizing control and parceling out batteries to the infantry units—much to the chagrin of the nominal and immensely capable Chief of Artillery, Brig. Gen. Henry J. Hunt. No one, however, doubted Hooker's personal courage or battlefield demeanor. The new commander also believed he had a better way to deal with General Lee than by launching an obvious frontal assault.[5]

As Hooker's reforms began to take effect and morale soared, two regiments of the Vermont Brigade, Thomas O. Seaver's (Class of '59) 3rd and Charles B. Stoughton's (Class of '61) 4th, took part in an epic snowball fight at Fairview, Virginia. Accepting a challenge from their large attached nine-month regiment, the 26th New Jersey, the Norwich men and their soldiers sallied forth to do battle. One enlisted man from the 26th described the event for posterity:

> The hills were covered with spectators and the eagerness to witness the novel contest knew no bounds. . . .The line being formed and everything in readiness for the contest, a red flag was raised as a signal and in a brief breath of time a strong body of the enemy drove in our skirmishers and fiercely attacked our centre. . . .the enemy were madly surging upon us in superior force and it was hardly in the power of human endurance to stand [it]. . .any longer. Gradually the center fell inch by inch, the line then wavered to and fro and finally the men broke in confusion and rolled down the hill followed by the victorious Vermonters. . . .
> The boys never rallied. Lieutenant Woods made an attempt to rally them and form them in hollow square on the fortified hill to the right. . .the Colonel was not totally deserted by his men. The Vermonters seized his horse by the bridle and made a desperate attempt to take him prisoner. The fight at this point was terrific beyond description. The men fought hand to hand. Colonel Seaver, the Achilles of the day, dashed through the combatants, seized Colonel Morrison by the shoulder and called upon him to surrender. . . .Amid the wild excitement consequent upon the shouting, the rearing and plunging of horses, the Colonel was drawn from his horse and

taken by the enemy. Most of his "staff" followed him as prisoners. . . .This fall disheartened the Twenty-sixth and only detached parties of a dozen, scattered over the field, persisted in an obstinate resistance.

Colonel Stoughton was honored with a black eye and the gallant Seaver fared little better. . . .The Vermonters fought with the determined energy characterizing them when engaging Jeff's myrmidons.[6]

One of Seaver's men, Pvt. Henry Houghton of the 3rd Vermont's Company K, recalled how he and his comrades captured the 26th New Jersey's colonel. "I remember my Company was on the skirmish line and their Colonel riding on to our skirmish line, I caught his horse by the bit and told him to surrender, but he, feeling a little ugly, tried to draw his sabre, but one of my Co. took him by the coat collar and he concluded to dismount and I took his horse to our Colonel Seaver."[7]

As his men engaged in their mock battles, Joe Hooker planned Lee's demise. While the army's morale and organization had sufficiently improved to engage it again in combat, the imminent loss of more than 16,000 veteran troops in three dozen of his nine-month and two-year regiments also prompted Hooker to act while he still had their services. Facing a more formidable fortified line across the Rappahannock River than the one Burnside had unsuccessfully attacked the previous December, Hooker refused to resort to a direct assault. Instead, he planned to use the power of maneuver to lever Lee from his fortifications in the hope of forcing a fight in the open. A key element of Hooker's plan hinged on the performance of Brig. Gen. George Stoneman's new Federal cavalry corps. Stoneman and his 10,000 horse soldiers were to move north and cross the Rappahannock River far behind Lee's flank, drive deep into his rear, and tear up the Virginia Central Railroad. While his cavalry wreaked havoc, the bulk of Hooker's infantry would move upriver and cross beyond Lee's left flank, marching down behind him while some 25,000 men from Sedgwick's Sixth Corps threatened the Confederates opposite Fredericksburg. With his supply base at Hanover Junction threatened by the resurgent Union cavalry and heavy concentrations of Federal troops behind his left, Hooker believed Lee would have to retreat, and the Federals would cross the river virtually unopposed for the pursuit.[8]

Hooker's plan was a good one, and it nearly worked. It probably would have succeeded against most opponents, but Hooker was up against the South's best field commander. "Robert E. Lee was at the peak of his powers as 1863 began," wrote one historian, "[and] Stonewall Jackson was at the peak of his fame." Lee's army, despite its battlefield successes over the last six months of 1862, had passed a difficult winter. As always, food and military supplies were scarce for both man and beast, and thus James Longstreet and most of his First Corps was detached to conduct foraging operations in southeastern Virginia near Suffolk. The Army of Northern Virginia fielded only about 61,000 men "present for duty" on March 31. Hooker's army, in contrast, numbered some 130,000 men. Still, Lee's men had battled heavy odds before, and the men were fully confident they could defeat Hooker when he moved against them.[9]

On the eastern side of the Rappahannock, the Federals were also ready and confident for a new campaign. "I may be too sanguine, I know I have been again and again disappointed," wrote Captain Bowers to his wife Lydia, "but I certainly have never felt so confident. . . as I do now. . . .I have seen defeats enough. I want to witness one good substantial victory." Even at this stage of the war, some Union men sensed that the only way the war would be won was by attrition. "I am confident the only way to end the rebellion is to defeat the armies in the field," continued the prescient Bowers, "for although there may be no end to their resources of arms and food, there is to raising men. Once defeat or capture their great army in any field and it cannot be replenished."[10]

The Chancellorsville Campaign, which involved at least 61 Norwich alumni, began splendidly for Hooker and his several corps. The campaign kicked off with the planned cavalry movement, and by the end of April, as the main advance began, Federal morale was riding high. The army's regiments averaged 433 men, most of whom were combat veterans—a level of combat strength and experience that would not be matched again for months. For once Lee was surprised by his opponent's movements, and the Federals successfully crossed the Rappahannock River at several points and were beyond and behind his left-rear before Lee could effectively react. Soon, however, the Army of the Potomac's bad luck caught up with it. A combination of poor communications, mistakes, and a lack of initiative on the part of some corps commanders—and Hooker himself—combined to foil what was otherwise a well-conceived plan.[11]

Norwich men were involved in virtually every aspect of the campaign. As part of the Hooker's preliminary movements and feints, Lt. Col. William Pettes (Class of '27) and his 50th New York Engineers played a key role in the crossing of the Rappahannock, building three pontoon bridges near Pollock's Creek, some five miles south of Fredericksburg, between April 29 and May 3. The artillery batteries of Capts. Dunbar Ransom (Class of 51) and Frank Amsden (Class of '59) effectively covered the crossing points built by Pettes. The Iron Brigade, with three Norwich men in its ranks, conducted an assault crossing of the Rappahannock River south of Fredericksburg on April 29, scattering enemy pickets and drawing praise from its superiors. Brig. Gen. Solomon Meredith, the Iron Brigade's commander, claimed Norwich alumnus Col. William W. Robinson and his men were "entitled to the admiration of their superior officers."[12]

All of these events were but preliminary efforts, and by May 1 Lee had begun to react decisively to Hooker's threat. Effective reconnaissance provided him with information that at least three Federal corps were over the Rappahannock and that Hooker had split his army into at least two parts. Lee correctly discerned that the Union force opposite Fredericksburg was a secondary effort. Splitting his own already badly outnumbered force, Lee began to shift several divisions of Jackson's Second Corps to the left toward the key crossroads of Chancellorsville. As the two armies moved towards each other, the first serious fighting of the campaign erupted about noon during a meeting engagement on the Orange Turnpike southwest of Fredericksburg and east of Chancellorsville. The Fifth Corps Regular Division, commanded by Maj. Gen. George Sykes, advanced down the Orange Turnpike with the 17th United States Infantry, Col. Sidney Burbank's brigade, deployed in the lead as skirmishers. Here the 310 men of the 17th's "Maine Regulars," with five Norwich men in the ranks, ran into advance elements of Maj. Gen. Lafayette McLaws' Division (the sole division from Longstreet's Corps with Lee's army during the campaign). In a stiff fight, the 17th drove the Confederates back and captured commanding terrain near the McGee and Lewis farms. In that action, Sgt. James W. Buel (Class of '64) was severely wounded.

After gaining an initial advantage and forcing McLaws' men back, the Northerners were about to emerge into open country when

"Fighting Joe" suddenly decided not to live up to his nickname. Much to their disgust, the Regulars were ordered to abandon the key terrain they had captured, the only open and commanding ground in the area for miles, and to pull back towards Chancellorsville. Too badly wounded to be moved, Sergeant Buel was left to the clemency of the enemy and was captured and sent to Libby Prison in Richmond. He was released later that year and discharged from the army for disability. As Buel faced an uncertain fate while lying on the field, Joe Hooker spent the remainder of May 1 defensively deploying his army in an arc facing Lee's advance. Abandoning his original plan, Hooker now hoped he could lure Lee into attacking his defenses. Hooker placed Maj. Gen. Oliver O. Howard's recently assigned Eleventh Corps, a unit in which he had little confidence, in an apparently safe area on the extreme right of the Army of Potomac's flank.[13]

The Eleventh Corps was never popular with the Army of Potomac. Although it was known as a "German Corps" because of the large number of German immigrants, particularly from New York and Wisconsin regiments, only 15 of its 26 regiments were either completely or largely foreign. The Germans, many of whom were recent immigrants, were also strong abolitionists, which gave Federal troops outside the corps another reason to dislike them. The corps' popular commander of earlier days, Maj. Gen. Franz Sigel, had recently been replaced by the gallant one-armed Oliver O. Howard, an unwelcome choice to Sigel's myriad of supporters. Howard could not speak German and had little time to get acquainted with his staff and commanders. Many of his men considered him to be patronizing and snobby. Still, ensconced on the army's far right, it appeared as though its role in the forthcoming battle would be minimal.[14]

Early on May 2, Hooker toured his army's lines and was generally pleased with what he found. He felt uneasy, however, about the Eleventh Corps right flank, which trailed off into the trackless Wilderness, a thick and wild area of tangled underbrush and second growth trees fed by meandering small streams and swampy ground. Hooker urged Howard to strengthen his line and to be particularly sensitive about his right flank, which in military parlance was "in the air"— that is, unsupported and not anchored on any natural defensive position. As he rode off, Hooker was still confident his men were well positioned to defeat Lee.

His confidence might have suffered some had he been able to eavesdrop on a fireside conference Lee and Stonewall Jackson had held the previous evening. Bolstered by sterling information from Jeb Stuart's cavalry and some local guides, the Southern commander had decided upon nothing less than a bold strike against the Hooker's unsuspecting right flank. After discussing their options and examining on a map the byways which could be used to move troops unseen around Hooker's right flank, Lee asked Jackson what he presumed to do with the information. Jackson responded that he proposed to move "his whole command" on a flank march and to strike the Federals where they least expected it. Leaving a mere two divisions of infantry with Lee, Jackson's troops were soon on the road.[15]

Among the regiments in Howard's Eleventh Corps that day was Col. William H. Noble's (Class of '26) 17th Connecticut (Brig. Gen. Nathaniel McClean's Second Brigade, Brig. Gen. Charles Devens' First Division). Part of Noble's regiment was deployed on picket duty in advance of the corps line on the endangered right flank. The wooded terrain made it difficult to discern what, if anything, was in their front. For these men much of May 2 was generally quiet. But as the hours passed, they detected signs of movement to their front. Noble later claimed his unit detected Jackson's corps on the move and tried to give warning. Unfortunately, the Federal high command did not believe the "Germans," and were instead convinced any movement of Southern troops was a retreat. The Norwich alumnus later wrote that the "disaster resulted from Howard's and Devens' utter disregard and inattention under warnings that came in from the front and flank all through the day." From his position near the Taylor House, Noble recalled that "Horseman after horseman rode into my post and was sent to headquarters with the information that. . .the rebels were massing for attack." Rather than eliciting concern and new orders, "Howard . . . insulted the informants, charging them with telling a story that was the offspring of their imaginations or their fears."[16]

Unfortunately for Howard and the Army of the Potomac, Stonewall Jackson was indeed massing in the woods. Jackson's three divisions under Robert Rodes, Raleigh Colston, and A. P. Hill, spent most of the day winding their way through the Wilderness in search of the Army of the Potomac's elusive right flank. At one crossroads, as Jackson and some of his staff officers observed the troops passing, the Army of Northern Virginia's citizen-soldier connection came to the fore. Among the passersby Jackson recognized many alumni from the Virginia Military Institute. "The Institute will be heard from today," observed Stonewall.

After some difficulty and delay, Jackson aligned his corps into three lines of battle. At about 5:45 p.m., a tidal wave of Confederates tramped through the dense woods and smashed up against the exposed Eleventh Corps flank. Several organizations put up a credible defense, Noble's 17th Connecticut among them, but any effort to stem the heavy tide was hopeless. Before long much of the corps was routing from the field. Noble tried desperately and unsuccessfully to rally his men and slow the advancing Confederates around the Taylor House. His efforts garnered nothing but a dead horse and a pair of serious wounds in the arm and leg. His regiment was one of the few units in the corps singled out for its bravery. The men of the 17th "could not fire upon the enemy while our pickets were retreating," reported the regiment's historian, "but as soon as the rebel line was unmasked by the pickets we poured in volleys into their ranks." The men fought "until being overpowered by the rapid advance of the enemy in overwhelming numbers, we were compelled to retreat, in obedience to command and in good order." In the resulting confusion "after the colonel had retreated with the right wing, which was posted in the garden, he was wounded."[17]

For a time, the fate of the Federal Army hung in the balance as the Confederate divisions caved in Hooker's right wing and drove eastward. The sheer exhausting difficulty of advancing through the thick tangled Wilderness, however, together with mounting Federal defensive efforts, a commingling of commands, and merciful darkness, ground Jackson's devastating surprise attack to an eventual halt. In the hope of launching a night attack, Jackson rashly rode out into the dark no-man's-land in order to conduct a personal reconnaissance. At the height of his military career, the moment of his greatest glory, Stonewall was mortally wounded by his own men a short time later. Despite initial hopes for his recovery, he gradually weakened and eventually died at Guinea Station on May 10.

As this tragedy was unfolding, Joe Hooker was desperately trying to save a campaign that had begun with such promise. Despite the shock of recent events, Hooker professed that he could wage a successful defensive battle. Major General John Sedgwick's Sixth Corps, however, was desperately needed to relieve the mounting pressure against Hooker, who ordered Sedgwick to drive west from Fredericksburg and link up with the main army. With Sedgwick's additional 25,000 men, perhaps the offensive might yet be renewed. In the meantime, Hooker would hold fast at Chancellorsville. For Lee's part, the loss of his key subordinate had not noticeably lessened his aggressiveness. With Jackson's old corps under the temporary command of cavalryman Jeb Stuart (it had passed to A. P. Hill for a few minutes until he also fell wounded), Lee planned to renew his attacks at first light on May 3.[18]

Despite his pre-battle bravado about defeating Lee, "Fighting Joe" could not divine a method of engaging his overwhelming superiority in numbers in such a way to bring about victory. Over the next two days, May 3-4, the Second, Third, Sixth and Twelfth Corps were involved in moderate to heavy fighting, while the First and Fifth Corps saw comparatively light action. As the battle raged, Capt. Charles Bowers (Class of '52) continued to write his letters home. "We have been posted in the woods in a nice cozy place since morning," he wrote his wife Lydia. "Our brigade is the extreme left of the line and our specific duty is to protect the [Ely's] Ford." Charles was confident the Bay Staters could hold their own. "We feel strong and entirely able to repulse any attack they can make. We have 6 batteries, 36 guns in position, among the best in the army. . .We have been busy all day making abatis. . . .Severe fighting is going on at our right."

As the hours slowly passed, Bowers began to be concerned. "Gen. Hooker was here and said this was the key to our position and must be held at all hazards. The rebels soon opened on us and all the forenoon until eleven o'clock the battle [in other sectors] raged with the greatest fury." While he still hoped for success, defeat and possibly death loomed large in his thoughts. "I hope I shall be able to chronicle in my next letter a most glorious victory." In the worst case, "if we fall, do not mourn us but rather rejoice that it was our privilege to lay down our lives in defense of our Country and freedom. We are in God's hands. . . Soon we shall all meet where separation shall never come." His faith in Gen. Hooker's abilities remained unshaken. "He is looking finely and was with us walking around yesterday P.M. The men are encouraged by his (manner). Confident that he is the man to direct. He is one of the noblest looking men I ever saw. Cannonading has just commenced again," he concluded, "I never felt better in my life. There is just excitement enough to retain me in the best condition." Bowers survived the battle without a scratch, but he did not witness his long hoped for triumph over the Confederate Army.[19]

The attacks launched by Lee early on May 3 were delivered with tremendous fury. Jackson's infantry in Stuart's capable hands gradually pushed back Daniel Sickles' Third Corps and Henry Slocum's Twelfth Corps, seizing key artillery positions at Fairview and Hazel Grove. The Union soldiers fought desperately, some under the personal supervision of their army commander. As Hooker watched Union artillerymen setting up a new gun line around the Chancellorsville House, a Southern artillery round split the porch pillar next to him. The shot knocked Hooker senseless with a severe concussion and the Army of the Potomac was suddenly leaderless. Nearby, Pvt. Henry S. Campbell (Class of '62), a member of Knap's Independent Battery E, Pennsylvania Light Artillery, helped repel a series of heavy Confederate attacks. Perhaps stirred by their proximity to the army commander, Campbell and his fellow gunners repeatedly fired canister from a position 60 yards in front of the Army of the Potomac's headquarters. Nearby, the commander of Battery A, Fourth United States Artillery, was killed and the battery nearly lost its guns to the surging enemy infantry. First Lieutenant Evan W. Thomas (Class of '51) of Battery C managed at the last moment to get the artillerists and their weapons away.[20]

For Norwich alumni, some of the most dramatic and intense fighting in the campaign took place in and around Fredericksburg and Salem Heights on May 2-3, and at Bank's Ford on May 4. Major General "Uncle John" Sedgwick had received Hooker's orders late on May 2 to drive his corps forward and link up with the main Federal army at Chancellorsville. If Sedgwick succeeded in breaking through the enemy defensive line at Fredericksburg, his corps would be in Lee's rear and a Union victory might still be possible. The problem, however, was that in order to join Hooker, Sedgwick had to assault and capture with a single corps what the entire Army of the Potomac had failed to do the previous December—Marye's Heights. Luckily for Sedgwick, the dominating terrain was but thinly-held by Jubal A. Early's Confederates, who were spread across a wide front. Sedgwick's preliminary movements against the town itself included the 19th Massachusetts, with Maj. Edmund Rice (Class of '60), Cpt. Henry Hale (Class of '61) and Hale's newly-commissioned classmate, Lt. John B. Thompson (Class of '61) in its ranks. These men helped capture Fredericksburg, which rapidly filled with Union regiments preparing to move against the formidable heights beyond.[21]

Below Marye's Heights and Lee's Hill (Telegraph Hill), nineteen Federal regiments stood ready to advance to the attack on May 3. Facing them were the Mississippians of William Barksdale's Brigade, and Harry T. Hay's Louisianians, bolstered by several batteries of artillery. The Federal attacks got under way about noon, and for a time it appeared as though history was about to repeat itself. Southern gunfire ravaged the initial assaults and drove them back. Eventually, the Federals realized the shallow nature of the Southern defensive line and managed to overwhelm the outnumbered defenders.[22]

Colonels Thomas O. Seaver (class of '59) and Charles B. Stoughton (Class of '61) led their regiments over the crest as the Vermont Brigade distinguished itself in a daring bayonet assault. Seaver in particular was singled out for his performance as commander of a "storming column" consisting of the 3rd and 4th Vermont and part of the 21st New Jersey Infantry. The colonel advanced on foot up Lee's Hill—the hill was too steep for horses—at the head of his men, just south of Hazel Run Creek, the site of Robert E. Lee's Headquarters for the December 1862 battle. The Vermonters swarmed over the crest and secured the position after a brief hand-to-hand fight. Confederate resistance, which lasted somewhat less then an hour, was desperate. A Confederate battery commander reported "firing canister. . .until the enemy was almost upon [us]." Five Confederate artillery pieces from Fraser's Pulaski and Carlton's Georgia Batteries of Cabell's Artillery Battalion were captured by Seaver's column, with the former organization suffering heavy casualties in the process. In addition to losing his guns, Fraser suffered four men killed, seven wounded, and 26 captured, with an additional 29 horses killed or captured. In his after action report, Second Division commander Albion P. Howe declared, "I desire especially to mention. . . Colonels [Lewis A.] Grant and Seaver, for the gallant and intrepid manner in which they led the storming columns to the assault (on the heights)." According to Howe, "nothing has been more handsomely or successfully done." Although Seaver was later recommended for a Medal of Honor, he did not receive the award for this action.[23]

Following its stunning success against the Fredericksburg Heights, the Sixth Corps cautiously probed forward on the Orange Plank Road toward Chancellorsville and Hooker's main body. When Lee learned of the looming disaster in his rear, he took immediate steps to deal with it by dispatching Lafayette McLaws' Division. Jubal Early, meanwhile, after the loss of the seemingly impregnable heights, regrouped in the vicinity of Salem Church in the hope of arresting Sedgwick's progress. Late in the afternoon of May 3, the converging columns clashed there, and once again Norwich men were in the thick of the fighting. Advancing astride the Orange Plank Road, troops from the New Jersey Brigade ran directly into Cadmus Wilcox's Alabamians and suffered heavy casualties. During the struggle, 1st Lt. Archibald S. Taylor (Class of '58), Company I, 3rd New Jersey, whose father, General Taylor, had been killed at Second Bull Run, was seriously wounded and initially reported as killed in action. Fortunately for Taylor, reports of his death were exaggerated and he lived for several decades after the war.

Positioned at a toll gate below Salem Church, 1st Lt. Edward B. Williston (Class of '56), commanding Battery D, 2nd United States Artillery, assisting in shattering several Confederate counterattacks while personally directing his battery's fire. Colonel Charles H. Tompkins, the Sixth Army Corps artillery commander, extolled Williston's valor and saw that he received his first brevet promotion. In his report, Tompkins described how "near the toll-gate. . .one section of Williston's was placed in the road, the other two sections on the left," in order to cover withdrawing Federal infantry. Rebels surged forward, driving the defeated Union troops before them. "The batteries opened fire over the heads of retiring troops, firing slowly at first," explained Tompkins. As the enemy attack gathered momentum, the guns fired more "rapidly. . .using canister. The enemy were checked and driven back by this fire. . . .I respectfully recommend. . .the above named officer [Williston] for brevet."[24]

Lieutenant Williston also recalled the action in his official report: "I fired 16 rounds of case [shot] as rapidly as possible. The effect of this fire proved so disastrous to the rebels that they retreated in great confusion and crossed the road to the left hand side." The soldiers on the receiving end of this hot fire "carried a large red battle flag, crossed with white, which was knocked down twice by shots from my section," added the lieutenant with some pride. Any thought the Southern infantry may have had of capturing Williston's battery ended when Williston poured canister into their approaching ranks "with great rapidity for several minutes, the effect of which was of such a character as to cause them to fall back under cover." Despite Williston's personal success, the Confederates under McLaws and Early had stopped the Sixth Corps advance cold. Hooker and John Sedgwick would not be meeting on May 3. In fact, the tables were turning, and Sedgwick found himself facing a reinforced and confident enemy.[25]

Sedgwick had reason to be alarmed. That night General Lee was formulating plans for his destruction. Alarming rumors filtered into the Sixth Corps camps. Lee, it was whispered, had arrived to face him in person, Hooker had been defeated, and James Longstreet's First Corps was arriving on the field; although gossip, it did nothing to alleviate Sedgwick's growing concern. The situation worsened somewhat the following morning, May 4, when Sedgwick received a dispatch from Hooker that he was "on his own." After his setback at Salem's Church, Sedgwick had pulled his troops into a defensive position on the hills northwest of Fredericksburg. This redeployment allowed him to cover Banks' Ford, his sole escape route across the Rappahannock River. Lee hoped that the reinforced Confederates facing Sedgwick could surround and destroy the Sixth Corps, or at least cut it off from the Rappahannock. Unfortunately for the Southerners, the attempt was slow and clumsily performed. Although Sedgwick and his men faced a series of attacks, which the troops faced with great gallantry and tenacity, they were uncoordinated and not well-delivered.

One of the serious threats against Sedgwick on May 4 fell against the Vermont Brigade and its numerous Norwich alumni, who stepped forward to solidify the line and prevent any disaster that might have befallen them on the wrong side of the river. The Green Mountain Boys were stationed with their right flank near the Orange Plank Road facing east toward Fredericksburg, essentially a second—and last—line of defense. Colonel Lewis Grant had his men lying behind the crest of a ridge, and he ordered them to stand and deliver their musketry when Harry Hays' Brigade of charging Louisianians approached within killing distance. Hays' surprised and exhausted attackers were repelled with heavy losses and swept backward with a counterattack by Capt. Alonzo Hutchinson and the 6th Vermont, which carried the day on that front. Hutchinson (Class of '62), Company B, was wounded during the counterattack and later reported killed, but he survived his severe wounds and was discharged for disability. "A little way beyond us through the smoke, the rebels could be seen," remembered Pvt. Wilbur Fisk, 2nd Vermont, who described the climax of the action on May 4. "Their officers were trying to rally them. It was a critical moment. . . .The crisis was imminent, immense consequences hung poised on a few seconds of time." As the enemy advanced once again, the Vermonters poured fire into them and "Some of the rebels were panic-stricken and running, some were rallying to renew the fight."[26]

In the desperate fight at Banks Ford, alumnus Col. Tom Seaver's (Class of '59) 3rd Vermont captured a large part of the Hays' 7th Louisiana regiment. In a gallant gesture, Seaver refused to accept the sword of the 7th Louisiana's commander, saying he declined to take it from an officer who had shown so much courage on such a bloody field. Both Colonels Seaver and Stoughton (4th Vermont) were again cited for their bravery, and Stoughton was slightly wounded in the fighting. For Seaver and his fellow alumni serving with the Vermont Brigade, a dangerous task remained to be performed before the disappointing campaign drew to a close. As the Sixth Corps began its nighttime withdrawal over the Rappahanock on the night of May 4-5, the Green Mountain Boys under Tom Seaver's personal command formed the rear guard. "Instead of marching across the river," Wilbur Fisk reported with a mixture of pride and annoyance, "we were ordered back to act as rear guard to protect the army." At first, "some of the boys thought it a poor return for brave fighting that they should be obliged to do extra duty. But it was reported. . .that Gen. Howe dare not trust any other troops but Vermonters to protect his rear at this critical time."

The 3rd Vermont's Private Houghton added a another perspective from the ranks when he penned, "it was quite a light night and we were ordered to take our cups from the outside of our haversacks and place them inside and trail our arms barrels down, that they would not glisten in the light." During this critical time, Houghton's Company K "had none killed and but three wounded, but if it had not been for the watchfulness and bravery of our Colonel T. O. Seaver, we should have fared much worse." In his report to the Adjutant General of Vermont, Colonel (later Brig. Gen.) Grant summed up his men's performance in the Chancellorsville Campaign with the simple comment, "They could not have done better."[27]

The Federals also withdrew from Fredericksburg over the Rappahannock that night. As at Banks' Ford, the demanding duty of commanding the rear guard fell once again to a Norwich graduate. This time, the task was performed by Maj. Edmund Rice (Class of '60) and elements of the 19th Massachusetts. According to Rice's brigade commander, Col. Norman J. Hall, "This last movement was accomplished almost without loss and with the utmost deliberation and regularity." During the night Major Rice "had been ordered to send a party of 30 men to a point opposite and about Falmouth, to destroy all bridges across the canal," explained the pleased colonel. "This was handsomely accomplished." Even as one bridge was cut away, "another [bridge was] uncovered and injured, the fire of the enemy preventing its perfect destruction. The bridge across the mill-race was also entirely destroyed." As the last elements of Hooker's army withdrew over the river, the Chancellorsville Campaign drew to a disappointing close. In his wake Hooker left 17,000 killed, wounded and captured, while Lee lost 13,000 men, including the much-lamented Stonewall Jackson.[28]

The defeated soldiers gathered back in their camps near Falmouth, where the dispirited Army of the Potomac settled in and took stock of its most recent setback. The frustrations of the bloody campaign emerged in the letters of several Norwich alumni. The 4th Vermont's 1st Lt. George B. French (Class of '55) wrote of the sharp fighting he had witnessed in the battles of May 3-4 near Fredericksburg. "I have no inclination to tell you what I have seen during the past ten days," wrote French in a letter home on May 11, "and what else could I write about with everything to remind me of the terrible realities of this war."

Despite the achievements of his regiment, French's letter conveyed an undertone of frustration with the outcome of the campaign. "Our Division carried the heights beyond Fredericksburg and advanced four miles beyond the town," he explained. "Monday at about 5:00 p.m. we were attacked by Jackson's Corps, which was successfully resisted, but we re-crossed at 3:00 a.m. Thursday morning after having suffered a loss in our Regiment of one killed, eight missing. . . .Other regiments suffered much more than ours." He then added, "I suppose you have received before now the published correspondence (of the battle). . .it was another 'military necessity' which compels the whole Army to come back." Massachusetts man Charles Bowers (Class of '52) was sickened by the defeat. "We are back again in our old camp reaching here at 3 P.M. yesterday," he lamented in a letter home. "I dare not write what I feel. I am mortified beyond measure." Bowers could not grasp why the powerful Union Army had not won a victory, as "it was an immense host, seemingly large enough to gobble up the whole South." The return to his camp was accompanied by heavy rain, which turned the road he was marching on into a ribbon of mud. "We then marched on to our old Camps. . .The roads were perfectly execrable. Nearly as bad as the Burnside effort. I went into them often over my boot tops."[29]

Despite Hooker's debacle in the Wilderness, the Norwich men and their Federal compatriots stoically soldiered on. In a letter to his mother, 1st Lt. Edward Stanley Abbott (Class of '64), who had experienced his first combat with Company A, 1st Battalion, 17th United States Infantry, made a prediction. Writing on May 15, just two weeks after the battle, Stanley proclaimed:

> At any rate we will whip them at last! Forty years the Hebrews wandered in search of the promised land and they reached it. We too shall surely see the fulfillment of the heavenly promise. The God of justice in heaven will yet smile on those who fight for justice on earth.
>
> I see a future for my country more noble than was ever yet permitted in any land thus far—a people just, tolerant, peaceful, giving freedom and education to a continent and true to the principles for which they have suffered. . . . Let us not count the price of that which is priceless. . . .But supposing all this and more should happen, what more beautiful death could I die?[30]

The soldiers in the Army of the Potomac were made of stern material and were amazingly resilient. After a little rest and reflection their spirit rebounded, their enthusiasm climbed, and life in the camps returned to normal. Within a mere four days of their retreat across the Rappahannock, Iron Brigade member Col. William W. Robinson (Class of '41) of the 7th Wisconsin was complaining about gambling among members of his regiment. "There is a large crowd of soldiers in the grove below," Robinson wrote, "engaged in the interesting game called chuck-a-luck. My chaplain is running his church on the other side of me, but chuck-a-luck has the largest crowd. I think this unfair," he continued, "as the church runs only once a week but the game goes on daily. I suggest that one or the other of the parties be dispersed."[31]

In the few weeks between the end of the Chancellorsville Campaign and the even more dramatic events which followed, a minor although interesting incident brought notice to a Norwich alumnus, Maj. Josiah Hall (Class of '61), a squadron commander in the crack 1st Vermont Cavalry. Shortly after the Chancellorsville fiasco, the infamous Rebel partisan, John. S. Mosby was raiding Federal positions in Fauquier County. The partisans surprised and overran an outpost of the 1st Virginia (Union) Cavalry. Some forty Union prisoners seemed destined to land in Confederate prisons at Warrenton when "a detachment of 70 men of the Fifth New York Cavalry. . .under the command of Maj. Hammond, came up, charged upon the rebels and a running fight ensued which was continued for 5 miles." During the melee "all the prisoners taken by Mosby were recaptured, with the exception of 2," while "Seventeen rebels were wounded and taken prisoner, among them 2 captains, 1 lieutenant and Dick Moran, rebel spy. Six were taken uninjured, making 23 prisoners." Near the end of the engagement, Hall's Vermont Cavalry joined in the chase, but the elusive Mosby managed to slip the tightening noose and escape his pursuers.[32]

Southern morale soared to new heights in the days following Lee's stunning victory at Chancellorsville, while morale in the Northern states slumped at the news of yet another crushing defeat. When President Lincoln heard on May 6 of the extent of the disaster, he exclaimed "My God, my God. What will the country say?" Copperheads saw the defeat as further proof that the South could not be brought back into the Union by force, and even Lincoln's closest supporters despaired of winning the war at the point of the bayonet. Lee rightly perceived that the strategic initiative in the East was his for the taking, and a debate raged within Southern command circles as to the army's next course of action. James Longstreet, Lee's trusted advisor and senior corps commander, felt that he and his divisions should be sent to reinforce Gen. Braxton Bragg's operations in Tennessee. Jefferson Davis and the Confederate War Department, meanwhile, were concerned about Maj. Gen. Ulysses S. Grant's operations against Vicksburg in Mississippi. Davis, himself a Mississippian, worried that the key stronghold would fall and communications with the Trans-Mississippi would be severed. In a conference held at Richmond on May 15, Lee convinced Davis and his cabinet that the timing was right for another raid north of the Potomac River into Maryland and Pennsylvania. By moving north, the general argued, his army could live off Yankee land rather than Virginia's, and the Peace Democrats would be provided with further ammunition with which to berate the Lincoln administration. The move might also force the Federals to withdraw from Vicksburg. Perhaps, if all went as planned, foreign recognition and independence would also follow. Lee's arguments were persuasive enough to convince Davis, and the campaign wheels began to churn.[33]

Longstreet's return to the army after his successful foraging operation around Suffolk, together with other reinforcements from the Carolinas provided Lee with nearly 75,000 men, which he reorganized into three infantry corps and six cavalry brigades. With Jackson gone, Longstreet retained his old First Corps, Richard Ewell was promoted and received Jackson's Second Corps, and a new Third Corps was formed and given to newly-promoted A. P. Hill. All three of Lee's corps commanders were West Point graduates and veterans of the Old Army.

Advance Confederate elements slipped away from the entrenchments near Fredericksburg and moved toward the Shenandoah Valley on June 3. The initial fighting of the campaign opened rather inauspiciously for the Confederates six days later when a major Union cavalry raid caught Jeb Stuart's horsemen by surprise at Brandy Station. The bloody and desperately fought engagement was the largest cavalry battle ever waged in America, and though the Northern troopers were narrowly defeated, they had never fought so well for so long against Stuart's veterans. Lee's legions continued marching north through the Valley, striking a swift and decisive blow at Winchester and Martinsburg, where some 3,500 Federals were captured. By late June the Southerners had penetrated Northern territory. Although no one realized it at the time, June 1863 marked the peak of Southern power in the Eastern Theater of the war. Within a few days, Confederate fortunes would be struck a blow from which they would never recover.[34]

As Lee's army crossed the Potomac River and tramped north, Joe Hooker and the Army of the Potomac belatedly set off in pursuit. The farsighted Lincoln realized Lee's move for what it was: a golden opportunity to destroy the bold Virginian far from his base and north of a major river. The President told his Secretary of the Navy, Gideon Welles (Class of '26), that "we cannot help beating them if we have the man." But Lincoln did not have "the man." With what can only be described as incredibly bad timing and poor judgment, a dispute over troop control broke out between Hooker and the War Department, and on June 28 Hooker asked to be relieved of command. His offer was accepted (probably to his great surprise) and the commander of the army's Fifth Corps, Maj. Gen. George Meade, assumed command of the army. Meade's army consisted of some 90,000 troops concentrated largely around the Frederick, Maryland area. Whether Meade was the general the country needed to score a victory remained to be seen. With the fate of the Republic hanging in the balance, Meade acquainted himself with his new responsibilities in the middle of what was quickly shaping up as one of the decisive campaigns of the war.[35]

Marching to confront the Army of Northern Virginia were 73 Norwich men in the ranks of at least 36 of the Army of Potomac's 278 regiments. Others served on the army's staff, the staff of Howard's Eleventh Corps, in artillery units, or on the staff of their respective division or brigade. A seventy-fourth alumnus, Capt. Thomas H. Davis (Class of '55), stood out from all the others. He, too, was marching in Pennsylvania that June as the commander of Company B, 1st Virginia Infantry, James Kemper's Brigade, George Pickett's Division, Longstreet's Corps, Army of Northern Virginia.[36]

As Lee's army had moved north, Jeb Stuart attempted to ride his Southern cavalry around the Army of the Potomac, a feat he had performed on a pair of past occasions. His troopers were screened from the marching Union infantry by the increasingly aggressive and effective

Federal cavalry. Unfortunately for Stuart and the Confederates, the shifting Federal army forced the cavalier on a circuitous route far to the east—away from Lee and his men. For a critical period Lee was without mounted reconnaissance and essentially stumbling about blind to the location, strength, and effective activities of the advancing Army of the Potomac. With his three infantry corps widely separated and living off the land, Lee feared a potential defeat in detail and ordered a concentration at the key crossroads town of Gettysburg. The furious marching pace in exceptionally hot weather was hard on the troops of both armies, but for the first time the Army of the Potomac had the additional motivation of defending a Northern state (Maryland was a border state).

A. P. Hill's Confederate corps was just west of Gettysburg on the last day of June. With Hill's blessing, Maj. Gen. Harry Heth received permission to march his division to the town, disperse any militia or cavalry found there, and seize any supplies he could find. Heth's four brigades proceeded east along the Cashtown Road (Chambersburg Pike) towards Gettysburg unaware of what was waiting for them. As the brigades of James Archer and Joe Davis approached, John Buford's Federal cavalry deployed in the fields and woods just west of town on McPherson's Ridge. Realizing the importance of the terrain below Gettysburg, Buford waged a classic holding engagement as advance elements of Maj. Gen. John Reynolds' First Corps, Brig. Gen. Lysander Cutler's Second Brigade, First Division, rushed onto the field. In the midst of this chaos, Reynolds personally positioned the six three-inch rifles of Cpt. James A. Hall's (Class of '62), 2nd Battery, 1st Maine Light Artillery. Reynolds ordered Hall to "ride forward and get between the enemy and the town; throw a few shells into them to keep them from plundering the town."[37]

The developing meeting engagement spun in favor of the defenders, albeit temporarily, when General Reynolds ordered the famed Iron Brigade—in which Col. William W. Robinson (Class of '41), 7th Wisconsin, Maj. and Acting Surgeon Henry A. Robbins (Class of '60), and Capt. Charles A. Hoyt (Class of '63), 24th Michigan, all served—into action south of the pike. The brigade had marched into Gettysburg with colors unfurled, keeping step to the tune of "The Campbells are Coming." Before long, the shrill of the fifes and the beat of the drums gave way to the cacophony of battle, as the Iron Brigade met and shredded Archer's regiments. Cutler's men performed similar work north of the roadway against Davis' brave but poorly-led men. By mid-morning, Heth's two advance brigades had been routed and troops from both armies were pouring onto the field.[38]

One of the unsung heroes of the first day's fighting at Gettysburg was the 7th Wisconsin's Norwich alumnus, Colonel Robinson. He led his regiment through intense combat in McPherson's Woods against Archer, and then conducted a fighting withdrawal and rear guard action to Seminary Ridge and through the town of Gettysburg later that afternoon. Robinson's Wisconsiners played an integral part of the First Corps effort to buy time and form a viable Union defensive line on the hills south and southeast of town. The Midwesterners of Merideth's Iron Brigade bled themselves white in the titanic struggle, though they exacted a terrible toll of enemy troops in the process. Early in the ferocious Confederate afternoon assault on McPherson's Ridge, the Iron Brigade's commander, Brig. Gen. Solomon Meredith, fell wounded. Robinson, notified of Merideth's fate upon his arrival at Cemetery Ridge, assumed command of the brigade for the remainder of the battle and the final months of 1863. On and around Seminary Ridge, Robinson had commanded the brigade's rear guard in what one author describes as the unit's "most glorious performance."[39]

The Norwich alumnus' fortunes on July 1 began well enough. As the Iron Brigade deployed and attacked with its regiments in echelon, Robinson and his men participated in a charge which largely destroyed James Archer's Confederate brigade in the ravine at Willoughby's Run. Much to their chagrin, the butternut-clad Confederates found themselves facing not some terrified local militia, but the dreaded "Black Hats" of the Army of the Potomac. Robinson's early success, however, dissipated during the afternoon hours when Heth's later rolling attack forced the defenders off McPherson's Ridge eastward to near the Seminary, where a new line was formed. There, about 4: 00 p.m., elements of three Southern divisions—Harry Heth's, Dorsey Pender's, and Robert Rodes'—struck on both sides of the Cashtown Road against the flanks and front of the Iron Brigade's barricaded position just west of the Lutheran Seminary. Despite the fact that the enemy's "ranks [initially went] down like grass before the scythe," from Robinson's fire, he knew his position could not be held. When the order came to withdraw, he explained, "I retired by the right of companies to the rear some 150 or 200 yards, halted and wheeled into line again to support the other regiments in retiring."

Like the cool veterans they were, Robinson and his Badgers poured lead into their valiant and ever advancing foes. "[We] again retired about the same distance and again wheeled into line and so on until I reached the foot of Seminary Ridge," reported Robinson after the battle. The ground between the Seminary and the town was littered with his dead and wounded. The colonel remembered how, as the 7th conducted its rear guard action, "we were exposed not only to the fire of the advancing enemy in front, but also to that from the brigade which had turned our left flank." The surging Confederate tide in "overwhelming numbers," he wrote, "had again turned our flanks. . .forming three sides of a square around us."

After a withdrawal through the town of Gettysburg to Cemetery Hill, during which he saw "men falling at every step, [and] many. . .taken prisoner," Robinson rallied the survivors. "Immediately upon my arrival at the cemetery," he remembered, "I was ordered by General Wadsworth to take command of the brigade." The 7th Wisconsin lost more men in the retreat to Cemetery Ridge than in the rest of the three day's fighting, and its overall losses were 37 men killed and mortally wounded, and 141 wounded and missing. Robinson was cited for gallantry and commended for his actions on July 1 by Maj. Gen. Abner Doubleday, who had assumed command of the First Corps after General Reynolds fell dead early in the fighting on McPherson's Ridge.[40]

Pitching in to help Robinson's tough Westerners was John Burns, an equally rugged 70-year-old local veteran of the War of 1812. The fierce aging warrior fought for a time with the Wisconsin men and was wounded several times. After the battle, when asked who he had fought with, he said "Oh, I pitched in with them Wisconsin fellers." When asked what sort of men they were, he answered, "They fit terribly. The Rebs couldn't make anything of them fellers."[41]

Concurrently with the actions of the 2nd and 7th Wisconsin regiments in McPherson's Woods and beyond, Cpt. Charles A. Hoyt (Class of '63) and his Wolverines of Company C, 24th Michigan, were also heavily engaged. Their battle experience, which included a prolonged stand up fight with an alumnus from the Virginia Military Institute (VMI) Henry K. Burgwyn, and his 26th North Carolina Infantry, resulted in the heaviest battle loss of any Union regiment. Out of the 24th Michigan's 496 men, 363 were killed, wounded, or missing. Following the fight, Col. Henry H. Morrow, the 24th's commander, reported on the actions of his regiment: "During the battle of the 1st instant, the regiment lost in killed four color-bearers. . . the flag was carried by no less than nine persons, four of the number having been killed and three wounded. All of the color-guards were killed or wounded." In the course of the fight around the Michigan colors and as the Wolverines slowly withdrew, alumnus Hoyt fell with a wound which eventually cost him a leg. "Captains Hoyt and Gordon. . .acquitted themselves honorably," reported Colonel Morrow. "Their conduct was such as to win the confidence and respect of their men and deserves the commendation of their commanding officer."[42]

After the battle Solomon Meredith, while recovering from his wounds, wrote to the Governor of Wisconsin that "The 'Old Iron Brigade' was among the first to receive the attack of a largely superior force, and the 2nd, 6th and 7th Wis., with the other regiments of the Brigade, beat back the foe and fought as only intelligent and free men can fight when defending our priceless institutions." Singling out Norwich alumnus Colonel Robinson, Meredith remarked that "Col. W. W. Robinson, of the 7th and his entire command, were the admiration of all who marked their daring conduct."[43]

A large part of the reason why the Norwich men in the Iron Brigade were driven from Seminary Ridge had to do with what transpired beyond their right flank, where other Norwich graduates were simultaneously engaged in a lopsided battle that also ended badly. By the afternoon of July 1, Brig. Gen. John C. Robinson's Second Division, Reynolds' First Corps, had taken position north of the Cashtown Pike on an extension of Seminary Ridge below Oak Hill. The dangling flank of the army was fully exposed on the north, which is exactly the direction from which Robert Rodes' Confederate division of Richard Ewell's Second Corps arrived on the field. Rodes deployed his brigades on and around Oak Hill, which dominated the Union position.

Robinson's precariously-positioned division contained the brigades of Brig. Gens. Henry Baxter and Gabriel Paul, which included, respectively, the 12th and 13th Massachusetts regiments. Both of these organizations boasted Norwich alumni, with future cadet Pvt. William H. Hooper (Class of '67) serving with the 12th, and Maj. Jacob P. Gould (Class of '49) and Capt. and Assistant Surgeon Edgar Parker (Class of '59) serving with the 13th. The actions of Hooper and his regiment on the northern end of Oak Ridge deserve special mention. The Norwich alumnus and his comrades had advanced through "the suburbs of the town and crossed the field, took possession of the right of the line," wrote one participant, which extended along the Mummasburg Road just below Oak Hill. As Hooper and his company moved into position, they found that "no enemy was visible in our immediate front, except a few skirmishers, whose position behind a stone-wall gave them an opportunity to annoy us considerable." Hooper and his comrades fixed bayonets and "moved forward at double quick and drove them at the point of the bayonet," remembered an officer. Ordered to change position, the regiment took up a spot behind a stone wall facing west with much of the rest of Baxter's brigade and waited, hidden from view while Brig. Gen. Alfred Iverson's North Carolinians advanced toward them without the benefit of skirmishers. When the order arrived, the Bay Staters stood and delivered a devastating volley that dropped the enemy by the score. The Federal fire essentially destroyed Iverson's Brigade, though Hooper fell wounded in the action. Unable to recover sufficiently to continue his service, he was discharged for disability.[44]

Within a short time Baxter's men were running out of ammunition and facing other elements of Rodes' Division, which was pressing Robinson's line. Gabriel Paul's brigade came up and assisted Baxter, deploying where Seminary Ridge meets the Mummasburg Road. Other Norwich men now found themselves in the same uncomfortable situation, on the extreme right flank of the division as one end of a V-shaped brigade line. The 13th Massachusetts, with Major Gould coolly exhorting his men to stand firm, played a large part in the initial repulse of Dodson Ramseur's advancing Confederates. When the enemy was falling back, a bayonet charge by the 13th Massachusetts netted scores of prisoners, but exposed the regiment to a devastating counterattack that essentially wrecked it as a fighting force. Paul's brigade was finally forced to retreat with the rest of the division toward town and beyond. The Massachusetts men were nearly overrun during their withdrawal, and Gould helped reassemble the survivors on Cemetery Hill. The

"Fighting Major" Gould survived Gettysburg to rise to the rank of colonel of the 59th Massachusetts. He would die at the head of a brigade from wounds received at the Battle of the Crater in July 1864 outside Petersburg. Assistant Surgeon Parker fared only marginally better. The doctor had the misfortune to receive a severe head wound while in charge of his regiment's field hospital in Gettysburg on July 1. He was discharged for disability in September 1863, but remained permanently unable to practice medicine due to the severity of his injury.[45]

Following the First Corps onto the battlefield about noon, Maj. Gen. Oliver O. Howard's Eleventh Corps marched through town and into fields north of Gettysburg. Howard planned to link his left flank with the right flank of Reynolds' First Corps (Robinson's division) and deploy his troops in an arc stretching on an axis running essentially west to east. Before his deployment could be completed, however, he was attacked on both his right and left. Rodes' Confederates caved in the developing junction of the First and Eleventh Corps, while Jubal Early's Division arrived and attacked from the north. Early's path toward Gettysburg was initially blocked by an Eleventh Corps division under Francis Barlow, who had foolishly placed his brigades on the indefensible Blocher's (later Barlow's) Knoll.

One of Barlow's brigades under Brig. Gen. Adelbert Ames took up a position behind the knoll near the county Alms House, where it acted as the division's reserve unit. Unfortunately, Jubal Early's attack collapsed Barlow's front and exposed Ames' line to an enfilading fire. One of the regiments called up by Ames to assist was Col. William H. Noble's (Class of '26) 17th Connecticut Infantry. Noble, however, had been severely wounded at Chancellorsville and was recuperating. Knowing that an important battle was about to be fought, Noble hastened into Pennsylvania from a hospital in Washington to rejoin his men on a horse he purchased just for that purpose (his former mount had been killed at Chancellorsville). Despite the pain and damage he was inflicting upon himself, the colonel rode nearly non-stop and reached the battlefield late on July 3, two days after the debacle at Blocher's Knoll. Much to his surprise, Noble was now the senior officer in his brigade, since Ames led the division after Barlow was critically wounded defending the knoll that now bears his name. Noble led the brigade into Gettysburg early on July 4, liberating the town with its thousands of wounded soldiers.[46]

The arrival of darkness and the exhaustion of troops on both sides brought the fighting to a sputtering close on July 1. Two Federal corps (First and Eleventh) had been shattered and losses were heavy. Although Lee had won a striking victory, his success had driven the Union army into a tight crescent position on high and powerful ground below the city. The Army of the Potomac's line has been often and best described as a giant fishhook, with the shank running south from Cemetery Hill toward the Round Tops, and the hook itself curved back and anchored on Culp's Hill. Federal reinforcements arrived throughout the evening and night hours, solidifying the front. General Meade, who arrived late that night, liked what he found: defensible ground and interior lines. As a result, he deployed his divisions with an eye toward defending his new position. A courier had already been sent galloping to Manchester, Maryland, about 32 miles from Gettysburg, to order forward "Uncle John" Sedgwick's Sixth Corps.

While Meade's strategy for July 2 was essentially dictated for him by terrain and happenstance, Lee's was not. Should he remain on the of-fensive or assume a defensive posture and invite attack, thereby surren-dering the initiative to his opponent? His second in command, James Longstreet, arrived in time on July 1 to study the strengthening Federal defenses and didn't like what he saw. "Old Pete" flatly stated as much, concluding the Union position was too strong to attack. Lee should move his army around the Federal left flank and get between the Army of the Potomac and Washington, counseled Longstreet wisely. The Army of Northern Virginia could select ground of its own choosing and enjoy the luxury of fighting on the defensive. Lee, with great confidence in his superb veterans, dismissed Longstreet's advice as impractical and decided instead to assault the Union left flank with Longstreet's Corps. As Longstreet attacked the Federal left, Richard Ewell would make a demonstration against Culp's Hill and other points along the Union right flank with the Third Corps, which would be turned into an actual attack should circumstances permit. It was a difficult plan dependent upon coordination and stealth.[47]

As Longstreet made preparations that morning to attack opposite the Round Tops, Maj. Gen. Dan Sickles' Federal Third Corps had taken up a position on lower Cemetery Ridge on the Union army's far left flank. Sickles, a politician with a modicum of military acumen, was unhappy with the ground he was assigned to hold. The rocky and wooded terrain was difficult to deploy on and slightly lower than the Emmittsburg Road a mile or so to the west. Believing that the enemy was about to assault his line and without orders, Sickles directed his entire corps to advance west and redeploy. One of Sickles' men marching to assume a place in the new line was 1st Lt. Charles H. Potter (Class of '47), Company B, 73rd New York. The regiment, also known as the Fourth Excelsior and 2nd Fire Zouaves, was part of the New York "Excelsior Brigade." One eyewitness vividly recorded the visual impact of the Third Corps westward march:

> The sun shone brightly on their waving colors and flashed in scintillating rays from their burnished arms, as with well-aligned ranks and even steps they moved proudly across the field. Away to the right, along Cemetery Ridge, the soldiers of the Second Corps, leaving their coffee and their cards, crowded to the front, where they gazed with soldierly pride and quickened pulse on the stirring scene. Conspicuous among the moving columns was the old Excelsior brigade, each one of its five regiments carrying the blue flag of New York. . . .They marched with no other music than the rattle of rifles on the picket line; they were inspired only with the determination to acquit themselves worthy of the State motto, which the brigade had adopted as its name.

Sickles' corps, however, was not strong enough to hold his new line, which stretched from Devil's Den northwest through the Peach Orchard and north along the Emmitsburg Road. Sickles' unauthorized movement exposed the important Round Tops behind his own left flank and opened a dangerous gap between his right flank and Winfield Hancock's Second Corps, which was still sitting atop Cemetery Ridge. General Meade exploded with anger when he discovered that Sickles—whom he disliked intensely—had unwittingly compromised the integrity of his defensive line. He was about to order Sickles to fall back when Longstreet's artillery opened fire about 4:30 p.m. By then it was too late to take any action, and the Federals would have to fight it out where they were. Longstreet's two divisions attacked en echelon, with John Hood's men striking the Round Tops and Devil's Den sector, and

Lafayette McLaws' soldiers moving against the Peach Orchard salient and the troops deployed along the Emmitsburg Road.[48]

Lieutenant Potter and the Zouaves of the 73rd New York took up position near the intersection of the Emmitsburg and Wheatfield Roads, just north of the vulnerable Peach Orchard salient. There they listened for about half an hour as Hood's attack crumbled Federal resistance beyond their left flank. Their own turn arrived soon enough when William Barksdale's Mississippians assaulted and crushed the protruding Peach Orchard position. Although Potter and his comrades managed to hold for a time, overwhelming pressure and the sheer weight of numbers forced them rearward. The New Yorkers managed a fighting retreat from the fields along the Emmitsburg Road to Cemetery Ridge, but the cost was horrendous. The 73rd regiment lost 162 of its 324 officers and men, 51 of which were killed outright. Only five other Federal regiments lost more killed at Gettysburg. The Excelsior Brigade as a whole left 778 of its 1,837 men on the field of battle.[49]

Although the Federals were putting up a stubborn defense, Longstreet's assault was sweeping almost everything before it. Evander Law's Brigade was driving over Round Top and up the slopes of Little Round Top, Jerome Robertson's famed "Texas Brigade" had penetrated the Rose Woods and was fighting for possession of Devil's Den, and other brigades were lapping up against the Stony Hill position. With McLaws' Division driving east through the Peach Orchard, the pressure exerted on the Unionists attempting to hold the Wheatfield and Wheatfield Road was overwhelming. A number of Union observers recalled seeing a member of Col. George C. Burling's brigade staff exhibiting gallantry sufficient to stand "out among the many brave acts performed that day." According to one of these officers, "while the fight was raging the hottest I noticed a mounted officer galloping back and forth along the rear of the line of our infantry in my front, exposed to both the enemy's and our own fire and I expected every moment to see him fall." The brave rider was "Captain Tommy Ayres (sic). . .of General [Burling's] staff, who fearlessly ran the gauntlet of the fire of friend and foe bearing orders to different portions of the line." Somehow Capt. Thomas W. Eayre (Class of '61), who had been detailed to Burling's staff from his own 5th New Jersey Infantry, survived

Gettysburg only to fall at Spotsylvania's "Bloody Angle," on May 12, 1864.[50]

Other units supporting the embattled Third and Fifth Corps fighting in and around the Wheatfield and Wheatfield Road that afternoon included the guns of Lt. Col. Freeman McGilvery's First Volunteer Artillery Brigade, in which Norwich's Capt. Nathaniel Irish (Class of '61), Independent Battery F, Pennsylvania Light Artillery, served. Assigned to McGilvery's staff, Irish played a signal role in helping position the Union guns covering the Peach Orchard and Wheatfield. This artillery played havoc with the advancing Confederate infantry. Irish accomplished this even though he suffered a painful wound in the process of placing his pieces. In his report on the day's actions, McGilvery recalled how "Captain Irish of Battery F, Pennsylvania Artillery. . .was hit on the thigh in the early part of the engagement by solid shot, but would not leave the field to have his wound dressed until ordered by me to do so." Despite the order, Irish was not absent long. "Notwithstanding a serious contusion which he was suffering under, [Irish] reported to me on the morning of July 3," explained McGilvery, "and remained with me during the day, ready to discharge any duty." McGilvery's guns also played an important role on July 3 by helping repulse Pickett's Charge with an effective enfilading fire on the advancing Confederate infantry.[51]

Not far from Tommy Eayre and Nathan Irish, another Norwich man was fighting for survival. At the intersection of the Wheatfield and Emmitsburg Roads, Sgt. George T. Carter (Class of '54), and his Company B of the 2nd New Hampshire distinguished themselves in combat around the Peach Orchard and Wentz House. The unit was part of Col. George C. Burling's Third Brigade, Brig. Gen. Andrew A. Humphrey's division, Sickles' Third Corps. Burling's brigade was broken up by Gen. Birney and his regiments sent to a variety of threatened areas. The 2nd New Hampshire, about 350 men, was dispatched to support Battery G, 1st New York, and deployed with its right flank facing west, and its left refused at the intersection of the Millerstown Road, facing south. Armed with a Sharp's rifle, Carter manned a sharpshooting post at the Wentz house, where he fell severely wounded. He and his New Hampshire comrades held their position for some time and even launched a small counterattack into William Barksdale's charging

Mississippians and elements of Kershaw's South Carolinians before withdrawing slowly from the field. Their stand and fighting retreat cost them 193 officers and men, 47 of whom were killed in action or died of wounds.

First Lieutenant Archibald S. Taylor (Class of '58) also saw action in the Wheatfield and Peach Orchard area. Among the hundreds falling dead or wounded in the savage fighting in the Wheatfield was 1st Lt. Charles E. Bowers, 32nd Massachusetts, who was temporarily commanding his father's (Charles Bowers, Class of '52) Company G of the same regiment. Another alumnus and member of the 32nd, Pvt. Daniel W. Parmenter (Class of '63), Company H, was lucky enough to emerge unscathed from the Wheatfield fighting.[52]

James Longstreet's sledgehammer attacks crushed David Birney's divisional front, threatened Little Round Top, captured the Peach Orchard, and swept onward, creeping up the southern end of Cemetery Ridge and the left flank of Winfield Hancock's Second Corps. One of the most dramatic episodes of the battle took place there as daylight was fading into dusk on July 2. As Cadmus Wilcox's Alabama brigade advanced deep into the thinly-held Union lines, Hancock himself ordered the 1st Minnesota to make a suicidal charge to stem Wilcox's advance. The small but critical assault ranks as one of the most dramatic events of the entire battle. Less well-known is the Norwich connection with this episode. First Lieutenant Evan Thomas (Class of '51) and Battery C, 4th United States Artillery, 1st Regular Brigade (Capt. Dunbar Ransom, Class of '54) played a role in repelling Wilcox's men. Thomas' six 12-pound Napoleon howitzers belched shell and canister in support of the 1st Minnesota, and also played a key role in beating back assaults by the 10th, 11th and 14th Alabama regiments. Holding firm, Thomas' guns kept up a withering canister fire on the advancing Confederates until their attacks disintegrated. An extract from Hancock's after-action report singled out Lieutenant Thomas: "I would mention Battery C, Fourth U.S. Artillery, commanded by Lieut. Evan Thomas," penned Hancock. "This officer is particularly mentioned for bravery and good conduct."[53]

Brigadier Gen. William Harrow, who led the brigade to which the 1st Minnesota belonged, also singled out Thomas for praise. The young Norwich man "destroy[ed] large numbers of the enemy by the very effective fire of his guns," reported Harrow. "His exertions contributed largely to checking and finally repulsing the enemy at this point."[54]

While the battle was ebbing and flowing along the Emmitsburg Road and on the southern end of Cemetery Hill, Col. Sidney Burbank's Second (Regular) Brigade, Second Division, Sykes' Fifth Corps, moved forward from its position northwest of Little Round Top in order to support Federal troops suffering in the Wheatfield. It was by all accounts an impressive spectacle. With the afternoon sun sinking slowly in the west, the well disciplined ranks of the Federal Regulars crested the right flank saddle of Little Round Top and descended into Plum Run Valley—soon to be known as "The Valley of Death." Four Norwich men, three of whom were classmates, marched with the 17th United States Infantry on the left flank of Burbank's line: 1st Lts. Edward Stanley Abbott and George W. Smith (Class of '64), 2nd Lt. Francis E. Stimpson (Class of '58), and Sgt. Eldridge H. Babbitt (Class of '64). The 17th's advance across Plum Run Valley was described after the bloody encounter by Capt. Dudley H. Chase, Company A, 2nd Battalion. "As we advanced down the slope of Little Round Top, our officers and men began to fall rapidly and as we crossed a marsh, called Plum Run, the enemy opened a most destructive fire on my regiment . . .the extreme left of our line," remembered the captain. The deadly fire emanated from the Devil's Den area. "We were thoroughly wrought up with excitement and some one yelled 'double quick.' At this we all cheered and broke into a run towards the enemy." The Confederates, continued Chase, were "firing at us from the cover of a stone wall a short distance in our front and from Devil's Den on our left flank. Our cheers were in the nature of shrieks. . . .Any of you who have had a nightmare and attempted to scream and could not, can imagine the reason we could not give forth lusty hurrahs instead of shrieks." The Regulars reached the wall of stone on Houck's Ridge, where they were "ordered to lie down," remembered the captain, "but we did not get down quickly enough to avoid a terrible flank fire from the Devil's Den. Within fifteen minutes, 150 officers and men, of our 260 in the regiment, were killed or wounded."[55]

As Burbank's Regulars struggled to hold their position, Confederates who had broken through below the Peach Orchard swarmed around their exposed right flank. The desperate fighting, which included the use of the bayonet and clubbed muskets, went against them and the brigade was ordered to retreat. "The left flank was much exposed to the enemy's sharpshooters and the left company of the Seventeenth U.S. Infantry was thrown back to confront this fire and to a more secure position under a slight rise of ground," Colonel Burbank later reported. "[I] ordered my line forward to a fence and stone wall on the edge of the woods. . .but at this moment a heavy fire was opened on our right flank. . .[and] I received orders to retire my brigade." The retreat almost became a nightmare for the Regulars, who could see the enemy "at this time moving through a wheat field to our rear and the brigade was withdrawn as rapidly and in as good order as the nature of the ground would permit." As Confederates swarmed around their flanks, "the troops were exposed to a heavy fire on both flanks and the loss of officers and men was very severe." Casualties were indeed heavy in the 17th U.S. Infantry, which suffered losses of 57.6%—the 39th highest total on the list of Union regimental losses in a single battle. Two Norwich men were mentioned in Burbank's brief and matter-of-fact report. "[The] regiment mourns as killed. . .Second [sic] Lieut. E. S. Abbot, mortally wounded. . .recently promoted from the ranks. . . .Second Lieut. F. E. Stimpson, acting battalion quartermaster, [was] distinguished for coolness and gallantry."[56]

About the same time that the Regulars fought their deadly battle along Plum Run and in the eastern skirt of the Rose Woods, Brig. Gen. George J. Stannard's (Second) Vermont Brigade, a new organization composed of five nine-month regiments containing seventeen Norwich alumni, was undergoing its baptism of fire on Cemetery Ridge near the center of the Union line. When the brigade's regiments were formed in Vermont during the fall of 1862, their basic drill and training were administered entirely by a detachment of fifteen Norwich cadets especially detailed for that purpose. Prior to the Gettysburg Campaign, their service had involved little or no combat and the men in the ranks were frustrated by the lack of direct involvement in the war effort. "Captain," one soldier informed William D. Munson (Class of '54), an officer of the 13th Vermont, "this ain't much like being home sitting on Frank Allard's steps drinking beer." Now, on the eve of their discharge back into civilian life and return to the Green Mountains, both Allard and Munson were to drink their fill of combat in Pennsylvania.[57]

When the inexperienced soldiers' opportunity to prove their mettle on July 2 and again the following day, they performed as Vermont troops always have. The brigade was called from behind Cemetery Hill to assist in repelling Brig. Gen. Ambrose Wright's Georgia brigade, which was driving deep into the Union line. "After the opening of the battle of July 2," reported Stannard in his report of the battle, "the left wing of the Thirteenth Regiment, under command of Lieutenant-Colonel Munson [Class of '54] was ordered forward as support to a battery." Although Wright's Brigade had essentially spent itself by the time the Vermonters arrived, "the right wing of the Thirteenth, under Colonel Randall. . .was granted by Major-General Hancock. . .the privilege of making the effort to retake the guns of Company C, regular battery, which had just been captured by the enemy." The Vermonters charged, and "four guns of the battery were retaken and two rebel field pieces, with about 80 prisoners, were captured." Justifiably proud, Stannard praised his troops: "Officers and men behaved like veterans," he exclaimed, "although it was for most of them their first battle and I am content to leave it to witnesses of the fight whether or not they have sustained the credit of the service and the honor of our Green Mountain State."[58]

The regular battery assisted by the Vermonters was Battery C, 5th United States Artillery, normally commanded by Capt. Dunbar R. Ransom (Class of '51). At the time, Ransom was in command of the Second Regular Brigade, Artillery Reserve of the Army of the Potomac, and his battery was under the acting command of 1st Lt. Gulian V. Wier. Ransom's men performed well on the afternoon of July 2, and Ransom himself was severely wounded in the thigh by either a sharpshooter or shrapnel, while personally positioning his guns near the Emmitsburg Road. After deploying his pieces, he was hit while courageously riding out in front of the Union positions to ensure there were no Union troops in his line of fire.[59]

As Stannard's excited Vermonters moved into line, Col. Arthur Devereux's 19th Massachusetts had taken up a position further south. The regiment, part of Hall's brigade, contained alumni Maj. Edmund Rice (Class of '60) and newly-minted Lt. John B. Thompson (Class of '61). The Bay Staters' position was intended to cover the withdrawal of the 1st Minnesota as well as elements of Gen. Humphreys' shattered

Third Corps division. Out in front of the main Union line, the Massachusetts men fired several volleys into Wright's advancing Georgians. When ordered to do so, the 19th fell back to the east up Cemetery Ridge while Maj. Rice and a line of skirmishers served as rear guard and protected the withdrawal. According to Colonel Devereux's unpublished battle report, his men "met the First Minnesota, beaten back and badly harried by the enemy, but making a desperate effort to maintain their ground." Devereux advanced the 19th Massachusetts and "easily passed through (the 1st Minnesota) with my command, marching by the flank. . . .Just as we rose the further side of the swale everything was in the direst confusion, our troops [Third Corps] were flying in great disorder and apparently no organization left." Amidst this confusion the 19th quickly "formed line of battle. . . .The enemy's line of battle followed closely upon our flying men and their artillery, running up to close quarters, used canister and grape."

Unable to fire without hitting his own men, Devereux calmly "waited until my front was clear of all the bigger fragments of our troops, then directed Colonel Mallon [42nd New York] to make his men stand up, fire a volley by the rear and front rank in succession, then to face about and regain the old line on the double quick, meaning thereby the old line of the Third Corps directly in our rear, then to halt, face about again and wait for me." At first the "successive volleys checked to a considerable extent the enemy's advance in our immediate front and gave me opportunity to face my men to the rear and move them toward the old line at ordinary quick time, but the enemy was so near that I was able to bring in with me several prisoners." Upon regaining the Cemetery Ridge line, with Rice and his rear guard still stubbornly contesting the enemy's advance, the 19th Massachusetts "passed through (the Union line), halted and faced again to the front, by the side of Mallon's Forty Second New York." With the Bay and Empire State men back on line, and Stannard's Vermonters more than holding their own, General Hancock began to sense that Longstreet's attack was about played out.[60]

Although the Federal Sixth Corps under Maj. Gen. John Sedgwick arrived too late to contribute substantially to the hard-won victory of July 2, a large number of Norwich alumni populated its ranks. On the evening of July 1, Sedgwick's men were at Manchester, Maryland, approximately thirty-two miles from Gettysburg. Peremptorily ordered by Meade to conduct a forced march in order to join the main army without delay, Sedgwick immediately thought of his hard fighting and hard marching Green Mountain Boys. "Put the Vermonters ahead and keep the column well closed up!" he directed his staff. The "Old" (First) Vermont Brigade, in which sixteen Norwich alumni served and two commanded regiments during the Gettysburg Campaign, set the marching pace and helped to ensure Sedgwick's troops were in position on the field at Gettysburg. The corps turned in a march of legendary proportions. Historian Edwin B. Coddington wrote in his classic study of the battle that when "word came that they were needed and needed in a hurry. . .they marched from ten at night until five the next afternoon with only a few breaks for coffee or now and then a short rest." Time passed agonizingly slow for the hot and thirsty soldiers. "On and on they trudged, endlessly it seemed, at first through darkness and then in the glare of the July sun, thirty-four [sic] long miles to Gettysburg." Commanders attempted every means of motivation possible to keep the troops moving. "One veteran remembered hearing the strains of band music. Catching the beat of 'Old John Brown's Body,' he noted "the men immediately strode along more briskly, as first a score, then a hundred, then a thousand and then ten thousand voices sang out the battle cry of 'Glory, Glory, Hallelujah, His Soul is marching on.'" The musicians played their hearts out as "all night long they marched at a remarkable pace to the sound of bands which alternated with the shrill of fifes and the roll of drums. Never before had their bands played on the march except when they entered a town and their performance was a 'happy inspiration.'" On July 2, however, the growing heat of the day soon "wilted the men into complete silence except for the rhythmic slap of feet on the stony pike. Some reeled and staggered as if drunk." There was a price to pay for the rapid pace set by the Vermonters. "Every now and then someone would collapse in his tracks. His comrades would quickly drag him to the grass along the roadside, place his musket beside him and then resume their places in the ranks."

"You know that the 6th Corps, except in the evening of the 2d day took no active part in the battle as a corps," wrote the Vermont Brigade's commander Col. Lewis A. Grant. "It arrived on the field a little before dark of the 2d day having marched, as General Meade says in his official report, 32 miles that day and was immediately put into line at the point of engagement." Despite the exhausted condition of the men when they reached the field, "It was a glorious sight to see our corps moving into the breach in perfect order in 5 lines of battle with colors flying and bayonets reflecting in the rays of the setting sun," remembered Grant. The timeliness of the Sixth Corps arrival did not go unnoticed, as "it was there and then that the enemy was checked, when a few minutes before the tide of battle at that point was going strongly against us." Grant, who would later be promoted to brigadier general, exaggerated the importance of the Sixth Corps arrival—but not by much. Sedgwick's men poured onto the field by way of the Baltimore Pike about 5:00 p.m. Their appearance freed up the Fifth Corps to move south toward the Round Tops, where it assisted in throwing back the Confederate assault. Sedgwick's men were eventually dispatched in the footsteps of the Fifth Corps, but only one brigade managed to take up a position and engage the enemy before the fighting ended.

After their arrival on the army's right flank behind Culp's Hill, Grant's Vermonters were dispatched to the extreme left flank of the army and faced southwest between Big Round Top and the Taneytown Road. From this position Grant could guard the baggage wagons and protect against a flanking movement into the army's rear area. Another Norwich man, Brig. Gen. Horatio G. Wright (Class of '37), commanded the First Division of the Sixth Corps. Wright's division held the center of the column of march on July 2, but arrived too late to participate in the action. Like Grant, his men also headed for the army's far left flank.[61]

The second of July had not been a repeat of Lee's spectacular victory of the previous day. After Longstreet's assault was beaten back, belated attempts by elements of Richard Ewell's Second Corps against Culp's Hill, as well as a rare night attack on Cemetary Hill, were also unsuccessful, although the Southerners managed to occupy an abandoned line of works on Culp's Hill. Despite the heavy losses he had inflicted on the defending Federals, General Lee's own army had suffered severely and his objectives for the day—essentially rolling up Meade's left and sweeping his army from Cemetery Ridge—had not been met. Lee believed his lack of success was due largely to disjointed attacks and a failure of coordination. He was still confident a victory could be obtained on July 3.

As Lee pondered his dwindling options, General Meade and his corps commanders held a council of war in the small front room of the Leister House, immediately behind the center of the Union position on Cemetery Ridge. The generals were polled as to whether to remain on the field or withdraw, and the decision was to "stay and fight it out." As the officers were leaving to rejoin their respective commands, Meade turned to Brig. Gen. John Gibbon, whose Second Corps division manned the center of the line. "If Lee attacks to-morrow," said Meade, "it will be in your front." Gibbon responded that he hoped Lee would, and that if he did, "we would defeat him."

As it turned out, both Meade's and Gibbon's predictions were accurate. Having failed on either flank, Lee decided to use the last of his fresh troops, Maj. Gen. George Pickett's Virginia division, to spearhead a three-division assault against what he believed was a relatively weak Federal center on Cemetery Ridge. The plan was as daring as it was risky, for his infantry would have to cross an open area almost a mile deep to reach the Union lines. When his infantry advanced against the enemy, cavalryman Jeb Stuart, who had finally rejoined the Army of Northern Virginia, would circle his horsemen into the Union rear, and Richard Ewell would renew his attacks against Meade's right flank. The attack was placed under Longstreet's command, even though the assaulting column contained more troops from Hill's Third Corps than his own First Corps. All of Longstreet's efforts to persuade Lee to attempt a flanking operation or call off the attack were rebuffed.[62]

Unfortunately for the Confederates, they were unable to orchestrate the evolution of the battle the next day. The Unionists on Culp's Hill spent the night preparing to dislodge Ewell's men. As dawn was breaking, Federal artillery opened on the Confederates, and Henry W. Slocum's Twelfth Corps attacked. The combat lasted seven hours and was some of the toughest of the battle. By noon it was over, and the Confederates had been knocked off the hill. One of the most dramatic moments of the fighting came when Col. Silas Colgrove's brigade was ordered to test the enemy confronting him. Colgrove, who replaced Gen. Ruger at the head of the brigade, deployed in McAllister's Woods near Rock Creek in a tight U-shaped line. The 2nd Massachusetts held the far left flank of the brigade's line and was led by Lt. Col. Charles Mudge. Within the ranks of that regiment was Company I and Norwich alumnus Lt. William E. Perkins (Class of '43). Somehow Colgrove misunderstood his orders to conduct a reconnaissance-in-force and decided to send two regiments directly against what was believed to be the Confederate left flank. The order to cross the open Spangler Meadow stunned Mudge, who asked the courier if he was sure the message was correct. After he was told it was, Mudge responded, "Well, it is murder, but it's the order."

Together with the 27th Indiana, Mudge led his men forward in a gallant but futile assault. Both units were defeated, one after the other. The 2nd Massachusetts suffered 43% casualties including Mudge, who was killed in the attempt. Observers claimed the Massachusetts men "covered [themselves] with glory," and that "few if any Regts. in the service. . .could have stood the almost simultaneous loss of half its forces & maintained as the 2d Mass. did almost perfectly the order & regularity of a battalion drill." After the battle, the remnants of the 2nd Massachusetts marched past Slocum's headquarters, where the corps commander and a large group of his staff officers bared their heads in respect to the Bay Staters and their colors.[63]

In addition to securing Culp's Hill, the Federal success removed one important aspect of the coordination Lee was seeking for his attack on July 3: Ewell would not be attacking as planned. Still, the assault went forward as ordered. In addition to Pickett Division, Johnston Pettigrew (who had replaced the wounded Harry Heth), and Isaac Trimble (in Dorsey Pender's stead) arranged their divisions opposite Cemetery Hill. A preparatory Confederate artillery bombardment, the largest ever heard on the American continent, got underway shortly after 1:00 p.m. Some 150 massed guns meant to smother the Federal position ended the solitude that had engulfed the field following the Culp's Hill victory. A similar number of Federal guns responded, and for more than one hour the pieces roared, causing a mighty sound heard as far way as Pittsburgh. Despite the intensity of the bombardment, which was designed to demoralize and soften up the Second Corps defenders, few casualties were inflicted. Hunkered down behind low stone walls and makeshift breastworks and with most of the shells falling in the rear, Hancock's soldiers eventually came to realize that the bark was worse than the bite. Finally, about 3:00 p.m. Longstreet reluctantly gave permission for Pickett to move forward. As gray and butternut-clad infantry poured from positions in the woods opposite the soon to be famous "Copse of Trees" and formed their battle lines, one of the most dramatic events of the war began to unfold.[64]

The advance of the 11,500 to 12,000 Confederate infantrymen, stretched across the landscape in an unforgettable mile-wide array, mesmerizing the Federals, who watched their disciplined and measured tread with admiration. It was surely a momentous moment, and one which remained vivid in the minds of the participants to their dying day. Federal artillery fire, which had intentionally tapered off a short while earlier, opened anew. Spherical case and round shot arched across the open fields and tore gaping holes in the advancing Southern lines. The holes were sealed up by the marching men, who continued tramping forward until they reached the Emmittsburg Road a few hundred yards from the crest of the ridge. Before too much longer the Federal infantry opened on the Confederates with rifles and muskets; artillery lining the Ridge switched from shells to canister, increasing the carnage several fold. At least one of these batteries was commanded by a Norwich man. First Lt. Evan Thomas' (Class of '54) Battery C, 4th United States Artillery, fired dozens of rounds into the massed ranks. Captain Nathan Irish (Class of '61) witnessed the event as a member of Lt. Col. Freeman McGilvery's brigade staff. Ignoring his painful wound from the previous day, Irish assisted his fellow artillerymen as they enfiladed the advancing lines of the enemy.[65]

The fire, smoke, and noise rose to epic proportions, obscuring large parts of the field. Although some of Pettigrew's men on the left had broken earlier and fallen back, a mass of North Carolinians was heading for the low stone wall in their front. What was left of Pickett's three brigades had rolled into one teeming collection of humanity. Led by the gallant Brig. Gen. Lewis Armistead, his hat fixed upon his raised sword, a few hundred Virginians spilled into the angle formed by two zig-zagging stone fences. The crisis of the battle, and what many would later call the "Highwater Mark of the Confederacy," was at hand. It was at this moment, when perhaps the fate of a nation hung in the balance, that a Norwich man's actions and courage rose to the fore.

During Pickett's Charge the 19th Massachusetts was deployed in the right-rear of Hall's brigade, southeast of the umbrella-shaped copse of trees. From this point 20-year-old Maj. Edmund Rice, who the day before had so capably led the rear guard action near the Emmitsburg Road for the 19th Massachusetts, took it upon himself to lead a dramatic counterattack to help stem the cresting Southern tide. According to the regiment's historian:

> Like a bolt of flame the little [Federal] line is launched upon the enemy on the south side of the "Clump of Trees." The first line is struck and broken through. The heroic regiment [19th Massachusetts] pauses an instant to gather breath and then, with a furious bound, goes on to the second line. As the men break through the first line, Maj. Rice is in front. With a cry "Follow me, boys!" he dashes forward and is the first man to come into contact with the second line. He is severely wounded through the thigh and falls inside the enemy's line.[66]

"I had an excellent view of the advancing lines," wrote Rice in 1887. "The men of our brigade, with their muskets at the ready, lay in waiting." As the Confederates came within range, the Unionists "opened a deadly concentrated discharge upon the moving mass in their front. Nothing human could stand it. . . .Pickett's division. . .appeared to melt and drift away." As some Federal units began to pull back from the crest, Rice remembered "some one behind me gave the quick, impatient order: 'Forward men! Forward! Now is your chance!'" The young major turned and saw that the booming voice belonged to the equally impressive Maj. Gen. Winfield Hancock. The Second Corps commander had ridden his horse up near the front line and was pointing toward the clump of trees inside the angle to the right and front of the 19th Massachusetts, about 120 yards away. Reacting to their Norwich-trained leader's order, the soldiers on "the left of the 19th responded to Rice's command and were up running towards the small clump of trees before the 42nd New York. . .had a chance to rise." According to Rice, "every foot of ground was occupied by men engaged in mortal combat, who were in every possible position which can be taken while under arms, or lying wounded or dead." As they charged forward, Rice and his men shouted "Hurrah for the white trefoil!" and "Clubs are trumps!" Realizing he could not be heard above the deafening noise, the young major:

turned toward them, raised my sword to attract their attention and mo-tioned to advance. They surged forward and just then, as I was stepping backward with my face to the men urging them on, I felt a sharp blow as a shot struck me, then another; I whirled round, my sword torn from my hand by a bullet or shell splinter. My visor saved my face, but the shock stunned me. As I went down our men rushed forward past me, capturing battle flags and making prisoners.

Fighting with Rice in that daring charge was Lt. Edward B. Thompson (Class of '61) of Company G. Thompson was one of only 39 survivors from the 19th Massachusetts who would be able to muster for its evening roll call. Another veteran of the 19th who survived the day was Thompson's classmate, Capt. Henry A. Hale (Class of '61), who had been detached from the regiment to serve on Brig. Gen. Alexander Webb's staff. Webb commanded the famous Philadelphia Brigade, which was positioned at the heart of the Southern break-through in the "Angle," where it took part in savage close quarter's fight-ing to hold the crest of Cemetery Hill.[67]

Colonel Devereux, the 19th Massachusetts' commander, recalled that "During the obstinate fight at this place, the two lines being actual-ly hand to hand, my regiment captured four regimental colors from the enemy. . . .Three of the four taken by my regiment were taken from the hands of rebel color-bearers, the fourth picked up behind the stone wall." The captured colors bore the markings of particularly distin-guished Confederate regiments. "Three of these (the Fourteenth, Nineteenth and Fifty-seventh Virginia and marked with the numbers of their regiments respectively) have been turned over to the brigade com-mander. The fourth I am unable positively to account for, but have been informed was probably carried off the field by Maj. Rice."[68]

Twenty-five years after the Civil War, when the issuance of Medals of Honor was being reviewed, Colonel Devereux submitted testimony rec-ommending Rice be awarded the medal. Referring to the Norwich alumnus' actions in the counterattack near the Copse of Trees, Devereux proclaimed:

To the daring leadership and magnificent courage of Lt. Col. Rice in that crisis much credit is due for the great success of the movement. With the cry of "Follow me, boys!" he dashed forward into the advance of the enemy, fighting with indomitable courage and fell desperately wounded inside the lines of the enemy, without doubt the leading "man in blue" who penetrated and fell within Pickett's advance. I desire to place on record in the files of the office of the Secretary of War, the following facts in regard to the repulse of Pickett's charge at Gettysburg, July 3d, 1863. . . .

The left of my regiment was the first to strike the enemy. In the advance of the men, showing, an example to all in a serious conflict was (then) Major Edmund Rice of my regiment. The lines came actually breast to breast. So near were they that a color-bearer of my regiment knocked down the color-bearer of the 14th Virginia Infantry with his color staff. In advance of all and directly in front of the men of the enemy's line, Maj. Rice was wounded and was taken from the field.

Devereux further added that Rice "received his wound while his foot was placed on a man in the enemy's front rank who had partially fallen or purposely kneeled."[69]

Attached to one of the medal recommendations sent to War Department in 1891 was a petition signed by 43 surviving members of the 19th Massachusetts. Their account of the action and their heartfelt recommendations were advanced with obvious pride, if some poetic overstatement:

> On the occasion of Pickett's Charge against our lines, formed on Cemetery Ridge, our Regiment was in position in rear of Cushing and Rorty's Batteries and when Armistead's Brigade of Pickett's Division broke through our lines at the stone wall, rolling back the remainder of our Brigade and leaving a most dangerous gap in our front, our Regiment rushed forward, through 'the clump of trees' engaging the enemy hand to hand, stemmed the tide of disaster with reckless courage, capturing four stand of colors and hundreds of enemy.
>
> This magnificent counter-charge was without doubt the salvation of the Union Army and a most vital step in the march to a restored Union.

The attached declaration continued to extoll Rice's heroic efforts:

> To the daring leadership and magnificent courage of Lt. Col. Rice in that crisis much credit is due for the great success of the movement. With the cry of "follow me boys" he dashed forward into the advance of the enemy, fighting with indomitable courage and fell desperately wounded inside the lines of the enemy. Without doubt, the leading 'man in blue' who penetrated and fell within Pickett's advance.
>
> The grand record of Lt. Col. Rice is a choice memory with the comrades who fought with him on so many glorious fields; and they now ask that for this single act of valor, that he be awarded the 'Medal of Honor' which if given, would be treasured by him above any other earthly possession.

The lead signature on the powerful declaration to the War Department was that of Cpl. Joseph H. DeCastro, the bearer of the Massachusetts state flag on July 3. DeCastro stood at Major Rice's side on that afternoon so many years before, and won his own Medal of Honor for capturing the colors of the 14th Virginia in hand-to-hand combat.[70]

Rice was finally presented his richly-deserved Medal of Honor in 1892 by Maj. Gen. Nelson A. Miles, who spoke the following words at the presentation ceremony:

> The conspicuous gallantry of Maj. Edmund Rice, of the 19th Massachusetts Volunteer Infantry, at the third day's battle of Gettysburg, where he was severely wounded, did more than the single exertion of any other officer on our side to retrieve the day, after the battle had been virtually won by Confederates who had broken our lines and were cheering and swinging their hats on our captured guns.
>
> After the line was broken, the 19th dashed in and placed themselves in the rear of the break and for twelve minutes received the enemy's fire, at a distance of less than fifteen paces. In that time one man in every two of the whole regiment and seven over, fell, including Rice, who was shot in front of his men, with his foot on the body of a fallen Confederate, he being at that time the officer fighting nearest to the enemy in the whole line. He fought till he fell. His example held them firm at a great crisis in the country's history. He held Pickett's heavy column in check with a single thin line of his regiment, till reinforcements came from right and left and thus saved the day.[71]

Norwich alumni enjoyed diametrically opposed viewpoints during Pickett's Charge. Not far from where Major Rice was leading the 19th Massachusetts forward through the Copse of Trees to stop the Southern advance was Capt. Thomas H. Davis, Company B, 1st Virginia Infantry, James Kemper's Brigade. Davis, a member of the class of 1855, managed to lead his men across the shell-swept field to the stone wall. By that time, however, the 1st Virginia had been shattered, its colors captured during fighting near the Copse of Trees. Davis was wounded and captured in the gallant but futile effort. The Norwich alumnus was sent to the Federal prison camp Johnson's Island, where he arrived on July 20, 1863.

Davis had no intention of sitting out the war on an island in the Great Lakes, however, and immediately formulated a plan of escape. Posing as Michigan woodcutters, Davis and two fellow Confederate prisoners slipped out of the camp and made their way to Canada during the 1864 New Year's day blizzard. Assisted by Southern sympathizers, the escapees took a blockade runner from Halifax, Nova Scotia to Wilmington, North Carolina. Captain Davis rejoined his regiment in time for the opening of the 1864 spring campaign. He was captured a second and final time at Sayler's Creek on April 6, 1865, and was returned to his former prison home on Johnson's Island, from which he was paroled two months later.[72]

While the tremendous struggle was being waged immediately to their north at the Copse of Trees, the 13th, 14th, and 16th Vermont regiments of Brig. Gen. George Stannard's Second Vermont Brigade, with nine Norwich men in the ranks, played a singularly important role in repulsing Pickett's Charge. At the height of the Confederate attack, Stannard noticed that General Kemper's oblique left shift across Stannard's brigade front exposed the Confederates to a flanking fire. In conjunction with orders from General Hancock, the Green Mountain men marched down from Cemetery Ridge and executed a flanking maneuver against the Virginians.

"At the commencement of the attack," reported Stannard after the fight, "I called the Sixteenth from the skirmish line and. . . as soon as the change in the point of attack became evident, I ordered a flank attack upon the enemy's column." The Vermont general swung two of his regiments (the 13th and 16th) perpendicular to the Union line and proceeded to rake the attacking enemy's exposed right flank. "The Thirteenth changed front forward on first company," Stannard remembered, "and the Sixteenth, after deploying, formed the same and formed on the left of the Thirteenth, at right angles to the main line of our army, bringing them in line of battle upon the flank of the charging division of the enemy." Their result was "a destructive fire at short range." Noticing more enemy units advancing to his rear, Stannard shifted two of his three regiments (the 14th and 16th) and performed essentially the same maneuver in the opposite direction against a small brigade of Floridians. "The Sixteenth took in charge the regimental colors of the Second Florida and Eighth Virginia Regiments and the battle-flag of another regiment," boasted Stannard. Maj. Gen. Abner Doubleday is reputed to have shouted, "Glory to God, glory to God, see the Vermonters go at it!" Indeed, it was a stunning performance.[73]

While the battle was being waged on Cemetery Ridge, a large and largely irrelevant cavalry engagement was taking place several miles to the east, behind the Union army. Here too, several Norwich men participated, riding in the Federal ranks against Jeb Stuart's horsemen. General Lee had hoped that the Confederate cavalry would create havoc in the rear of an army falling back under the hammer blow delivered by Pickett's Charge. Instead, Stuart and his troopers were met by an equally aggressive Union contingent and the two sides fought to a draw while Lee's assaulting infantry column was ripped apart.

Perhaps the most dramatic cavalry incident of the battle took place on the afternoon of July 3 south of Big Round Top. There, Brig. Gen. Judson Kilpatrick, commander of the Third Cavalry Division, foolishly ordered Brig. Gen. Elon Farnsworth to take his brigade and make a mounted charge across broken ground against veteran infantry. Disgusted by the foolish order, Farnsworth made the charge and was killed, as were a large number of his men. Elements of the 1st Vermont Cavalry took part in the action, but Maj. Josiah Hall (Class of '61), who had set off on the Gettysburg Campaign with his regiment, was sidelined by illness and missed participating in the disaster.[74]

The Battle of Gettysburg is a good representation of the vital role Norwich men played within virtually every level of the Army of the Potomac. Alumni from the rank of private to brigadier general, from rifleman to division commander and Adjutant General of the Army of the Potomac (Brig. Gen. Seth Williams, Class of '40), had assisted in beating back Lee and the Army of Northern Virginia. Out of these approximately 73 alumni, 1st Lt. Edward Stanley Abbott (Class of '64) was killed, nine others (12.3%) suffered wounds of varying severity, and twelve (16.4%) were cited for gallantry—one of whom won the Congressional Medal of Honor.[75]

The Norwich fatality, Lieutenant Abbott, led a company in the 17th U.S. Infantry, Col. Sidney Burbank's brigade. As discussed earlier, the command had advanced on July 2 from east of Plum Run toward Rose Woods, and lost almost half of its numbers in the process. Abbott was carried from the field to a Fifth Corps field hospital on the farm of Michael Fiscel, about a mile west of the Baltimore Pike behind Little Round Top. Abbott managed to telegraph his brother Edwin with the news that his wound, while serious, was probably not mortal. Edwin hastened to Gettysburg by July 10, only to learn that his brother had been dead for two days. He found Stanley's grave on a peaceful hillside near the hospital. After several frantic days trying to locate a coffin, he disinterred his brother's remains. The grave, remembered Edwin, was:

> marked carefully with wooden headboard, made from a box cover and bearing his name, rank and day of death. It was so suitable a place for a soldier to sleep, that I was reluctant to remove the body for any purpose. But the spot was part of a private farm; and as removal must come, I thought it best to take the body home. . . . Two soldiers of the Eleventh infantry, the companion regiment of the Seventeenth, had followed me to the spot—one a boy hardly as old as Stanley, the other a man of forty. As the body was lifted from the grave, this boy of his own accord sprang forward and gently taking the head, assisted in laying the body on the ground without disturbing it, a thing not pleasant to do, for the earth had received and held it for a week. I told them to uncover the face. They did so and I recognized the features. . . . I then bade them replace the folds of the gray blanket, his most appropriate shroud and lay the body in the coffin. They did so; but again the boy stepped forward and of his own motion carefully adjusted the folds as they were before. When we turned to go, I spoke to the boy and his companion. They said they knew Stanley and knowing I had come for his body, they had left camp to help me, because they had liked Stanley. 'Yes,' added the boy, 'he was a strict officer, but the men all liked him. He was always kind to them.' That was his funeral sermon. And by a pleasant coincidence, as one of the men remarked to me on our way back, the sun shone out during the ten minutes we were at the grave, the only time it had appeared in forty-eight hours.[76]

Abbott's body was returned to Beverly, Massachusetts, where it was interred in the family plot, "a pleasant place among the trees on a sloping hill, where one can see the sea in the distance and at times hear the waves upon the beach—a spot he had often admired in former times."[77]

One of Abbott's friends who was with him at Gettysburg when he fell wrote the deceased's mother that her son "was full of enthusiasm. . .and was just off a terrible march from which I expected to find him footsore, but to my surprise he told me he had such excellent shoes that he was not at all tired. He laid down his life cheerfully for what he believed to be his country's need and I believe that God accepts the sacrifice." The lieutenant's obituary, published two weeks after his death in his home town newspaper, described how "he fell mortally wounded in the breast in the fight of Thursday afternoon, July 2d, at Gettysburg, being then in command of his company and leading it in a desperate but successful charge." After he was carried from the field by fellow soldiers of the 17th U.S. Infantry, Stanley "died at the Fifth Corps Hospital, at noon on Wednesday, July 8th, peacefully and without pain, speaking often of the happiness of dying after victory and for his country." Abbott "often spoke of and wrote of the war as 'the noblest cause man ever fought for,' and his whole soul was devoted to doing his duty to his country," continued the obituary. "He died bravely as he had lived, full of trust that the Fatherly care which had so kindly watched over his short life, would bless the country and the cause for which he was so proud and happy to lay it down."[78]

The small town of Beverly was not alone in saluting Stanley Abbott. The details of his death at Gettysburg were remembered in a Harvard publication shortly after the war's end: "Early in the fight, while leading his men in a charge down a hill across a marsh and wall and up a little slope, Stanley was struck in the right breast by a mine-ball," explained the detailed article. "The shoulder strap on the light blouse he wore had worked forward and the ball, just stripping off some of its gold lace, passed through the right lung and lodged near the spine." Immediately upon being struck, Stanley "fell senseless to the ground and for some hours was unconscious. He was borne to the rear."[79]

Stanley Abbott's tombstone still stands on the hill overlooking the ocean in Beverly. The marker is inscribed as follows:

> In Memory of Edward Stanley Abbot, First Lieutenant in the 17 Infantry, U.S. Army Born at Boston, Oct. 22, 1841. Died at Gettysburg July 8, 1863. He fell, shot through the breast while leading his men in a charge near Little Round Top on the afternoon of the second day of July and died of this wound in the Field Hospital of the Fifth Army Corps. Faithful and True.[80]

Although the Confederates prepared to receive a counterattack following the disastrous repulse of Pickett's Charge, General Meade decided against the attempt. His army had also suffered heavily, and what fresh troops he had were not in a position to immediately go over on the offensive. With the battle obviously won, Meade was not about to risk losing it now. The day ended with desultory skirmishing and a heavy rainstorm. Lee's army began withdrawing from the field on the evening of July 4, and the Army of the Potomac took up pursuit. President Lincoln telegraphed Meade and thanked him for his efforts—

but pleaded with him to complete the task at hand, which was the destruction of Lee's army.

Although it was not to be, Lee's escape was a near thing. Recent heavy rains had swollen the Potomac River and made it virtually impossible, for days on end, for the Confederates to slip south across the waterway. Trapped with the Potomac at his back around Williamsport, Lee constructed a powerful series of earthworks and prepared to receive a determined assault that never came. Although Lincoln continued to urge an attack, Meade allowed a majority of his corps commanders to talk him out of the idea. Lee's army was powerfully situated and a successful Federal assault was by no means a foregone conclusion. By the time Federal skirmishers cautiously advanced toward the enemy lines on July 14, the Confederates had crossed the river to safety, ending the Gettysburg Campaign. The victory in Pennsylvania, coupled with General Grant's capture of Vicksburg and its defending army on July 4, dramatically shifted the course of the war and put to rest any thoughts of European intervention on behalf of the Confederacy.[81]

Northern elation at the victory over the seemingly invincible Lee, both inside and outside the ranks of the army, was widespread. From his hospital bed in Washington, Capt. Charles Bowers (Class of '52), captured that feeling as well as his own mixed emotions in a letter to a son. "I am so nervous I cannot write," he began. "There is the wildest excitement in Washington. The glorious fighting of our noble army for the last week is receiving the heartiest plaudits of the great multitude." The citizens and soldiers of the capital "hope before night to hear of the complete discomfiture if not surrender of Lee's Legions," he continued hopefully. "The news so far received is most encouraging." Despite his joy, Bowers couldn't help but worry about the fate of his son and comrades who had fought in the Wheatfield, and his own future. "I rejoice with trembling. Prescott and Stephenson are both reported wounded, also Gen. Barlow & fear it to be the greatest misfortune of my life not to have been in this conflict." Ending his letter home, Bowers gushed, "I have so longed to be in one victory. I could then have cheerfully exclaimed with letters 'though thy servant suffers in peace, the spirit is willing but the flesh is weak.' No one here doubts our certain victory. God grant that it may be soon."[82]

One of those who enjoyed "one victory" and who was now engaged in pursuing Lee was Col. William H. Noble (Class of '26), 17th Connecticut Infantry. In a letter to his wife on July 4, Noble described how he led his men "into Gettysburgh & to extend a line of skirmishers beyond the town. We were however in a few hours relieved and returned to the position which the Brigade had held during the fight." The army "remained here over Saturday in a drizzling rain," he continued, "Saturday night & much of Sunday was a heavy rain which God has sent to stop the flight of the foe." Finally setting off after Lee, the 17th Connecticut and its fellow units seemed "constantly on the move [with but] 3 or 4 hours of sleep each night."

While accounts of Confederate soldiers marching barefoot are commonplace, getting and keeping adequate footwear for the Federal soldiers was also a problem. "Yesterday we marched through the mud and made about 12 miles with 100 bare feet in the Regt.," explained Noble to his wife. "The poor fellows suffer terribly." Despite this inconvenience, "this army did not stop its pursuit of the enemy. We distributed in the Brigade today 200 pairs of shoes for barefoot men & this a command of not over 500 men." Admiring the endurance and pluck of the common enlisted man, Noble described one particular incident that stood out. "We yesterday went only about 10 miles, yet 6 miles of the way was ascending a single country road across a mountain. . .Yet there was no flinching though they went out of their path constantly among sharp stones & dry limbs and brambles. How they ever get up & how they followed with their bloody feet is more than I can tell."[83]

As Meade pursued the retreating Southerners from Gettysburg, an interesting engagement between the Col. Lewis Grant's Vermont Brigade and Georgia troops from John B. Hood's Division took place on July 10 at Beaver Creek (Funkstown), Maryland. The skirmish opened when John Buford's Federal cavalry overtook and engaged a portion of the Confederate rear guard. In an effort to prevent the loss of valuable wagons, some of Hood's men were ordered to drive away the pesky mounted men. Grant's Vermonters were hurried to the scene to assist Buford. Under the direction of Cols. Thomas O. Seaver (Class of '59) and Charles B. Stoughton (Class of '61), the Vermont infantry deployed in an extended skirmish line estimated (exaggerated) by some witnesses to have stretched two and a half to three miles long. Somehow they managed to hold their tenuously-thin position against repeated attempts by the enemy to break through it. Colonel Grant was amazed at the outcome of the engagement and reported that this feat—a skirmish line repeatedly driving back strong lines of infantry—was unprecedented in the history of war. Another participant described how the "Vermont brigade, under Colonel L. A. Grant, was ordered to the front as skirmishers and deployed in a piece of woods covering a front of about a half a mile." It was an unusual circumstance, noted the reporter, who explained that "in general, a skirmish-line, upon being confronted by the advance of a line of battle, is expected to retire. The Vermonters, however, did not so understand it. . . .each one holding his position, they delivered such a steady and telling fire that the enemy's line was twice repulsed." Impressed, the observer opined how "the history of war furnishes few instances such as this, yet the Vermonters did not seem to think that they had accomplished anything out of the usual line of duty."[84]

Offering a view from the ranks, the 2nd Vermont's Private Wilbur Fisk wrote of how his brigade had with "characteristic success and pluck. . . .drove the rebels and were with difficulty restrained from rushing on after the retreating foe." Fisk indicated with pride that "Mr. Johnny Rebs' thought he was going to crush our thin picket line, but the whistling minnies from our accurate rifles came most too thick and close for their courage to stand." As the action continued, "Their officers tried to urge them on," he remembered. "They shamed and threatened them; they told them that there were but few of us and we could easily be captured. Some turned on their heels and run, some rallied again to the charge. They came on a few rods further, when their ranks broke and the whole battalion, officers and all, skedaddled for their very lives. They had discovered," continued Fisk proudly if not quite accurately, "that they were blundering into a nest of Vermonters. With a few more Vermonters we could have annihilated the whole crew."[85]

The mini-victory was not without cost. Colonel Stoughton, the 21-year-old Norwich alumnus, was severely wounded in the head and lost an eye for his efforts. His promising army career (including a potential promotion to general officer), was over. Five days after the event on July 15, 1st Lt. George B. French (Class of '55), Stoughton's adjutant, wrote a letter home to his parents describing the Funkstown affair and the general frustration which followed it. "We have been continually on the march. . . .The Rebels having crossed the river and are, I understand, to cross at Berlin, just below Harper's Ferry. You will remember. . .I told you that Lee would probably be smart enough to get his army back again into Virginia," he continued. "I am one of those who believe that his Army might have been annihilated with proper management." French knew the escape of the Southern army meant hard fighting in the future for the Army of the Potomac. "I suppose [we will have] to keep marching along over the desolate fields of northern Virginia. . . . Many a weary mile we continue, encouraged by the hope of giving to the Rebellion a death blow on our own soil. The men have been ever willing and eager to fight even before this. But [the Rebels] have escaped. Perhaps its all for the best," he lamented. "But we fail to see it so. You have heard of our last engagement, I suppose, near Funkstown in which we lost one killed and twenty-three wounded (14 mortally so)," he concluded. "Colonel Stoughton was severely wounded and is now, I suppose, at home or on his way."[86]

After Lee's escape into Virginia, a general lull engulfed the Eastern Theater that would last, with the exception of the inconclusive Bristoe and Mine Run Campaigns late in the year, well into the spring of 1864. Although strategic maneuvering and heavy fighting filled the fall and winter months in the Western Theater, events in the East of a different variety occupied the nation. Resentment of the Federal Conscription law amongst the urban poor, who were not able to afford $300 for a draft substitute, led to an outbreak of lawlessness and general rioting. The situation in New York City was especially bad. Searching for scapegoats, the mobs turned on blacks and the police; dozens died in the spreading violence and bloodshed. In mid-August, several units were ordered to New York from the Army of the Potomac to enforce the Draft Law and subdue the local population.[87]

Among the organizations sent north from the front were the Vermont Brigade and Regular regiments, including the 17th U.S. Infantry, which included at least 15 Norwich men. Tom Seaver's 3rd Vermont, for example, served in both New York and Newark, New Jersey. While the duty represented a welcome break from active campaigning in the field and was mostly peaceful, Seaver and his men found themselves in a difficult situation when they were suddenly rushed to Newark. There, the Vermonters were ordered to guard a riotous new regiment of Zouaves, the 33rd New Jersey, a number of whom had tried to desert. On September 7, attempts by a mob of New Jersey men to rush past the Vermonters resulted in the killing of three "bounty jumpers" and the wounding of four others. Fortunately, that was the first and last such effort. By mid-September, most of the Army of the Potomac's units on draft duty in the cities had been relieved and returned to the front.[88]

By the fall of 1863, a number of new recruits and the first significant influx of conscripts reached the Army of the Potomac in northern Virginia. One of the results of this inundation of green troops was the implementation of additional drilling instruction, which was especially detested by veterans. The importance of well-drilled troops, however, cannot be overestimated, and the process was laborious and time-consuming. A good example of the myriad of matters green recruits needed to learn is provided by an order contained in the letters of Capt. Charles Bowers (Class of '52), Company G, 32nd Massachusetts:

Headquarters, 2d Brigade
1st Division, 5 Corps

October 8, 1863
    Brigade Drill will be substituted for Battalion Drill, tomorrow at the usual hour.

Exercises
To march in line of battle forward
To halt the line and to align it
To march forward and change direction
To march in retreat and change direction
To play each battalion into column by division,
either single or double and at any desired
distance
To march forward in line of battle, a line of
battalions in column
To Cause it to change direction
To Cause the line to march in retreat
To Cause it to change direction
To deploy the columns
Passage of a defile in front
To reform the line after having passed the defile
Passage of a defile in retreat

To reform the line

By Order of
Col. J. B. Sweitzer [89]

While the constant drilling and training may have sapped the strength out of the men, it did little to subdue the rising anger within the army over the activities of the Copperheads. Similar disgust over the issue of the necessity of a draft permeated evening campfires—especially amongst the early volunteers of the war. It was particularly difficult for these men, who had enlisted for patriotic motives during the war's early months, to comprehend why others would have to be coerced or paid large enlistment bounties to serve their nation in its hour of need. Charles Ames, a soldier of the 32nd Massachusetts, wrote on the subject to Charles Bowers' son Charlie, who was then recovering at home in Concord from the severe leg wound obtained in the Wheatfield at Gettysburg. "Men who have never been out here are afraid to come," he complained. "They know not how much they are doing against our cause, by thus holding back, & would that I could force every man able to carry a musket, to have a hand in putting down this cursed rebellion." Harkening back to the spirit of earlier days, Ames asked his friend, "What are we coming to? Is the spirit of '76 dying out? No. Thank God that we are not all cowards, that there are men who will fight for their Government until the last drop of blood is spilt. All honor to such men." Condemning the "cowards," Ames wrote that those "who dare not and will not fight, let a mark be set on them which will disgrace them forever." Appealing to those on the home front, he concluded by recommending that the "draft dodgers become the laughing stock of the community. Let no peace be had by them from day to day until the life is defeated and is writ above their remains 'here lies the body of a coward. A disgrace to his Country and his posterity.'"[90]

The relatively quiescent opponents slowly began to stir during the fall of 1863, a time when most men were probably hoping the campaigning season had ended for the year. In an attempt to utilize interior lines and bolster Braxton's Bragg's Army of Tennessee near Chattanooga, Lee dispatched General Longstreet and most of his corps in early September. The move resulted into that army's only clear-cut large victory of the war at Chickamauga on September 19-20. A concerned Federal War Department reacted to the move by transferring west the Eleventh and Twelfth Corps, under the overall command of Joseph Hooker, to reinforce the Army of the Cumberland.

These strategic chess moves did not prevent either Lee or Meade from attempting to gain an advantage over the other. In early October, Lee made an effort to outmaneuver Meade in a disappointing series of marches and actions known as the Bristoe Campaign. Its conclusion brought about Meade's effort in late November to cross the Rapidan in a surprise march to turn Lee's flank in the hopes of bringing him to battle on advantageous terms. At least 46 Norwich alumni were involved in these tedious but futile efforts to force a decisive engagement. Several alumni turned in solid performances or enjoyed experiences worthy of note.

Major Josiah Hall (Class of '61) commanded a squadron of the 1st Vermont Cavalry and had the misfortune of being wounded and captured on October 12 during the early days of the Bristoe Campaign. "During the engagement at Brandy Station on the 11th inst.," wrote his regimental commander, "Major Hall, not yet fully recovered from a recent illness, was compelled to turn over his command to Major Bennett." He "crossed the Rappahannock. . .in advance of the column and, ascertaining that the Regiment had gone to Hartwood Church, had started with a small detachment to rejoin it." Arriving in the Morrisville, Virginia area and uncertain as to the location of the regiment's camp, Hall asked for directions but was "erroneously informed by an infantry soldier—perhaps a spy or guerrilla in disguise," continued the commander's report. "[Hall] left Lieut. Grant to bring up the column and rode forward, with a single orderly to report to me." He never arrived. "It [was] feared he was captured by the guerillas who had lately lurked about that neighborhood," was the conclusion reached by Hall's superiors. The major had indeed been captured, and it would be February 1865 before he would be released, paroled, and able to rejoin his regiment. Hall was promoted to full colonel and given command of the 1st Vermont Cavalry in the last few months of the war.[91]

The only significant clash of the October campaign occurred at Bristoe Station, where Lee hoped to catch a portion of the Federal army in motion. Lieutenant Gen. A. P. Hill, commander of the Third Corps, launched a hasty and ill-planned assault on October 14 against what turned out to be the well-placed Federal Second Corps. Hill's men advanced into a trap and were slaughtered by the hundreds with no chance to respond in kind. One of the reports of this action filed by Col. Francis E. Heath (First Brigade, Second Division, Second Corps), is of interest because of its praise for Capt. Henry A. Hale (Class of '61) and its comments on the performance of the brigade's draftees. "Of the behavior of my command I cannot speak in too high terms," reported Heath proudly. "Although a large portion of it was composed of drafted men, none faltered." Singling out officers who had performed particularly well, Heath went on to "especially mention Captain Duryee. . . Captain Hale. . .and Lieutenant White. . .members of my staff, for their coolness and bravery." Major Edmund Rice (Class of '60), who led the 19th Massachusetts Infantry at Bristoe Station, echoed Colonel Heath's comments. "The men behaved admirably," he reported, "and I would state that the gallantry of the conscripts far exceeded my expectations."[92]

Another Norwich participant in the lopsided Bristoe Station action was 1st Lt. John B. Thompson (Class of 61), who served under Major Rice in the 19th Massachusetts and led the regiment's skirmishers. Thompson turned in a particularly outstanding performance when his men advanced and captured an enemy battery, securing four guns in the process. After the brigade's fire drove the enemy back, the report citing Thompson's achievement noted, "a line of skirmishers was immediately thrown forward and pushed after them. Upon the crest was a battery of five guns. The skirmishers from this brigade, under Lieutenant Thompson of the Nineteenth Massachusetts, drew four of these guns into the line." Unfortunately, Thompson's men could not recover the fifth piece which, "being dismounted. . .was not considered desirable to attempt to bring it off, as the enemy was delivering a sharp fire upon those who brought away the others." He was able to bring in "a large number of prisoners," which compounded his success. The sharp repulse effectively ended the campaign, and Lee's army withdrew below the Rappahannock River. General Meade was elated with the victory and issues a congratulatory order to his troops.[93]

A significant action followed Bristoe Station a few weeks later. On November 7, a surprise Federal attack seized a Confederate bridgehead at Rappahannock Station and captured several hundred enemy soldiers and some artillery. A number of Norwich men participated in the assault, and the whole affair was under the overall command of Brig.

Gen. Horatio G. Wright (Class of '37), temporarily commanding the Sixth Corps. Bolstered by this victory, Meade made plans to turn Lee's right flank and to unhinge his entire line with a rapid crossing of the Rapidan River on November 26. One of the prongs of Meade's offensive was led by the slothful advance of Maj. Gen William H. French's Third Corps, which allowed Confederates time to block his move with a brisk rear guard action at Payne's Farm on November 27. The fighting allowed Lee to withdraw his army to the west bank of Mine Run Creek, where it dug in and prepared for a defensive struggle. Although Meade planned to attack, General Warren, commanding the Fifth Corps, deemed it inadvisable. Meade reluctantly agreed, and the Army of the Potomac withdrew north of the Rapidan and went into winter quarters.[94]

"At day light Friday [November 27]," wrote Charles Bowers (Class of '52) in a letter home describing the campaign, "we took up our line of march and at 4 P.M. came up with the rebels in line of battle. We immediately formed line of battle and sent out skirmishers." From his position it appeared as though the enemy was avoiding an open fight, as there was "nothing but artillery and skirmishing during the afternoon. At night we fortified, expecting to be early engaged." Caught in a driving cold rainstorm, at about 8:00 p.m. Bowers and his men "received orders to march and moved for five miles in a driving rain where we remained after dark. An attack was expected here but the rain probably prevented (it)." More of the same followed the next day, when the Massachusetts soldiers "resumed our march going some five miles when we came in sight of rebel entrenchments. Here we halted and remained until Sunday P.M." Despite the powerful Southern earthworks, "at about 2 o'clock Col. Prescott called the officers together and told us it was decided to attack their works at 4. The attack was to be simultaneous at all points of the line," Bowers learned to his dismay. "The men could see how well their opponents were dug in, and in severe cold, without fires, the men prepared for what was seemingly a suicide assault. The defenses were described by one Federal general as a "summit crowned with intrenchments for infantry and artillery, strengthened by abatis." To assault the works, the men had to cross "a ravine. . .and the ground west of it. . .cleared for more than a thousand yards, rising gradually over a hundred feet, with a space well up the ascent flanked by heavy belts of timber on both sides."[95]

"At 1 Monday morning we were aroused and informed that the attack would be made," Bowers' letter continued. "At 2 we marched about 1-1/2 miles and formed our attacking lines. It was extremely cold, but the men stood it without a word of complaint." For several hours the men waited in the biting cold for the order to advance. "At 8 cannonading began and continued for a half hour. We were expecting any instant the order to advance. But 9, 10, 11, 12 o'clock came and no order." Still standing in line of battle, the men were confused and freezing. "It was so cold," recalled Bowers, "it was with great difficulty the men could keep from freezing. Some of the pickets were brought in so completely chilled that they died. By 2 o'clock there was great [uneasiness] among the men." In order to keep warm the men "formed squads and [ran] around in a circle. The afternoon passed away and just before dark it was announced the attack had been abandoned," he wrote with great relief. Another potentially climactic battle had been aborted, and "At 4 P.M. Tuesday we took up our retreat and crossed to the north side of the Rapidan at 4 A. M. Wednesday. . . .I fear I shall never see a victory."[96]

The withdrawal from before Lee's Mine Run entrenchments on the evening of December 1 was difficult and exhausting. Norwich alumnus Thomas O. Seaver (Class of '59) and his 3rd Vermont, together with the 77th New York Infantry and an artillery battery, were detailed to guard the key Rapidan crossing at Germanna Ford. Many officers in the Vermont Brigade, ten of whom were Norwich men, were "signally disappointed," as one put it, in the fall campaign's lack of substantive results. When the army went into camp around Brandy Station, the men closed out the year with a debate over enlistment. The subject centered on whether the original three-year men should reenlist for the remainder of the war, or return home when their terms of service expired in 1864. According to an officer in the 4th Vermont, "A proposition from the head of the army is before the men who have served over 2 years & have less than one to serve." Any of these soldiers or officers who reenlisted for three years "or the war, would receive $402," as well as a month's leave. This sensible government offer was an attempt to prevent a wholesale wave of expired enlistments such as occurred in 1863, when thousands of combat veterans from the two-year regiments left the army. If sufficient numbers of men did not accept the proposal, many feared that "in less than 12 months, the service [would] be barren of troops."[97]

While 1863 had indeed been a pivotal year for the Union, the spring of 1864 promised nothing but more hard fighting. The fall would also see a presidential election in November, and with the growing strength of the anti-war Democratic Party movement (the "Copperheads") in the North, the Confederacy's best hope for victory appeared to rest with the defeat of Abraham Lincoln. One of the most prominent Peace Democrats—and the man responsible for the nomination of Maj. Gen. George McClellan as that party's candidate in the 1864 election—was New York Governor Horatio Seymour (Class of '28). Seymour was an early supporter of a compromise solution to the issue of secession, but backed the war effort through contributions of his own money and by leading enlistment drives in his state. "Under no circumstances can the division of the Union be conceded," Seymour proclaimed in his inaugural address on January 1, 1863. "We will put forth every exertion of power; we will use every policy of conciliation; we will guarantee them every right, every consideration demanded by the Constitution. . .but we can never voluntarily consent to the breaking up of the union of these states or the destruction of the Constitution."[98]

When the draft riots had broken out in New York City in July 1863, Seymour was viewed by some as the instigator of the lawless. However, he immediately declared the city in a state of insurrection and called for a return to law and order, a key step prior to Federal troops being dispatched to the scene. Seymour did oppose and speak out against what he perceived to be the government's illegal excesses in the war: the draft, arbitrary military arrests, the suspension of the writ of habeus corpus, and the issuance of the Emancipation Proclamation, for example. He remained popular with many voters and was later nominated as the Democratic candidate in the presidential election of 1868. His political career ended with his narrow defeat by war hero Ulysses S. Grant.[99]

It was this same General Grant who, at the end of 1863, seemed to be the man Abraham Lincoln needed to guide the war to a successful conclusion. If anyone could decisively defeat Lee and the Army of Northern Virginia in battle, Grant, believed Lincoln, was that man.

View of Parade Ground, North and South Barracks, Norwich University, 1862 in Norwich, Vermont. *Courtesy of Special Collections, Norwich University.*

View of "Old South Barracks," with elements of the Corps of Cadets in formation, 1862. Also shown are the two six pound howitzers provided by the State of Vermont. *Courtesy of Special Collections, Norwich University.*

The nation's oldest private military college, Norwich University, Northfield, Vermont, 1996. *Courtesy of Norwich University.*

Daguerreotype of Cadet J. Samuel Gage Barker '59 in the cadet parade uniform.
Courtesy of Special Collections, Norwich University.

Colonel Jesse Gove, '49, 22nd Massachusetts Infantry. Killed in action at Gaines Mills, June 27, 1862.
Courtesy of the Massachusetts Commandery of the Loyal Legion and the US Army Military History Institute.

Private Willie Johnston, '70, 3rd Vermont Infantry, Medal of Honor winner for the Seven Days' Battles, June 25-July 1, 1862. *Courtesy of the US Army Military History Institute.*

First Lieutenant Edward Stanley Abbott, '62, 17th United States Infantry, mortally wounded July 2, 1863 at Gettysburg. *Courtesy of the Massachusetts Commandery of the Loyal Legion and the US Army Military History Institute.*

The grave of Lieutenant Abbot, Central Cemetery, Beverly, Massachusetts. *Photo courtesy of Mr. Kerry H. Shea, Norwich University Class of 1966.*

Lieutenant Colonel Edmund Rice, '60, 19th Massachusetts Infantry as he appeared in 1864. *Courtesy of the Massachusetts Commandery of the Loyal Legion and the US Army Military History Institute.*

View of Plum Run Valley ("the Valley of Death") looking west from Little Round Top. The 2nd Regular Brigade and the 17th United States Infantry fought in the left center of the photo; this is where Lieutenant Abbott fell, July 2, 1862. *Photo by author*

Cemetery Ridge looking south over the terrain on which the Second Vermont Brigade deployed to help repel Pickett's Division, July 3, 1863. *Photo by author*

Looking north to the "Copse of Trees." This photo portrays the direction and terrain of "Rice's Charge," July 3, 1863. *Photo by author*

Photo of Burnside's Bridge, September 1885. *Courtesy of the Massachusetts Commandery of the Loyal Legion and the US Army Military History Institute.*

Another view looking toward Burnside's Bridge, September 1995. *Photo by author.*

V. Norwich During the Civil War

"How Far to Derby Line?"
Anonymous cadets '65

As war consumed the country, the daily routine of university life carried on at Norwich, though at a higher pitch and with greater excitement than during peacetime. Norwich's president, the Reverend Edward Bournes, and Brig. Gen. Alonzo Jackman continued to educate and train their cadets, a select number of whom were detailed to serve as drillmasters for newly-mustered Vermont units and their recruits, as well as for student-recruits at area colleges. Between April and May 1861, Norwich cadets drilled three companies of students at Dartmouth, a 102-man company at Bowdoin College in Brunswick, Maine, and 63 students in a company at what is now Colby College in Waterville, Maine. Additional Dartmouth student companies were drilled over the course of the war upon request.[1]

At Bowdoin, student volunteers were formed into two units: the "Bowdoin Guards" (drilled by Norwich cadets) and the rival "Bowdoin Zouaves." During the daily exercises held along Maine Street, a local patriot noted for his interest in military affairs was often seen observing the drills with great interest. He was Bowdoin's professor of rhetoric, Joshua Lawrence Chamberlain. Chamberlain no doubt listened intently to the various commands issued by the Norwich cadets, and carefully watched the various formations and movements his students practiced. It would be fascinating to know what interaction, if any, took place between Chamberlain and those nameless

Norwich cadets, and what influence (if any) their sojourn at Bowdoin had on the future war hero and model citizen-soldier. How many future leaders were among the Bowdoin, Colby, and Dartmouth students drilled by Norwich cadets? At least one of note: Charles Mattocks, the student commander of the Bowdoin Guards, rose to the rank of colonel in the 17th Maine Infantry, and was awarded a Congressional Medal of Honor for distinguished gallantry at Sayler's Creek on April 6, 1865. Mattocks later served as a brigadier in the Spanish-American War.[2]

Early in the war, Norwich cadet training details were dispatched directly to the camps of newly-mustered Vermont regiments. One notable example of this process was the four-man cadet team sent to drill the 3rd Vermont Infantry at Camp Baxter, St. Johnsbury, beginning in June 1861. Cadet Charles B. Stoughton (Class of '61) was the leading member of the team, which included Cadets Thomas Eayre (Class of '61), Lorenzo Allen (Class of '63), and Edward T. Jones (Class of '62). Stoughton was nearly elected captain in the 3rd Vermont and later went on to distinguish himself as colonel of the 4th Vermont Infantry. After the initial wave of new Vermont units had formed, Norwich cadets designated as state drillmasters spent much of their time at Camp Rendezvous in Brattleboro, Vermont's principal mustering center and training depot. Between 1861 and 1865, many of Vermont's infantry regiments and more than 13,850 recruits passed through Camp Rendezvous. At least 4,660 recruits were mustered in there. Today a monument to the training site stands at the entrance to the Brattleboro Union High School, which formed a part of the original Camp Rendezvous. The Vermont 4th, 8th, 9th, 10th, 11th, 12th, 13th, 14th, 15th and 16th Infantry Regiments and 1st Light Artillery Battery were formed there and received their initial training from Norwich cadets.[3]

The firing on Fort Sumter in April 1861 led to a sharp reduction in the size of the Corps of Cadets as many students, principally upperclassmen, immediately went off to war. Those departures were eventually balanced by the entry of larger classes and by the launching of a new and innovative program based on Alden Partridge's earlier militia work. Starting in summer 1861 and continuing into 1863, specialized courses in tactics for volunteer officers, as well as for men seeking regular army commissions, were instituted. As a result, over 100 future army officers received their training in drill and advanced tactics on the Norwich campus. Unfortunately, very few of these trainees can be identified due to lost or missing records. Among those who have been identified are Col. Sumner H. Lincoln (6th Vermont Infantry), Maj. Richard Crandall (6th Vermont Infantry), Lt. Col. Thomas Henderson (7th New Hampshire Infantry), and 1st Lt. Edward Stanley Abbott. These "special military students" trained side by side with the 111 cadets on campus in September 1861. William Arba Ellis, author of the 1911 history of Norwich, reported that 100 new cadets matriculated with the Class of 1864 in the summer and fall of 1861, the largest class to enter the university up to that time. As the war dragged on, however, members of the Class of 1864 dropped out to enter the army. When the Class of '64 finally graduated, only 16 original members were awarded degrees and but seven of these were on campus to receive them, the rest having already left for the front. In 1863, an additional two year "partial course" of military study was added to the curriculum, probably as a replacement or adjunct to the "special military courses."[4]

The Norwich trustees were quick to capitalize on the university's new prestige and its unique position in the North in an attempt to strengthen enrollment, as evidenced by the following lines from the university catalogue for 1861-1862:

> The military feature of this institution is one which should particularly commend it to notice, and patronage of the public at this time. The want of men skilled in Military Science and Tactics, to take command of volunteer forces, and discipline them into effective soldiers, has been severely felt in organizing the present army of the United States. The reverses with which it has met are, without doubt, owing largely to this cause. To guard against this defect in the future, it is now generally felt, that young men should be educated thoroughly in every department of Military Sciences. In times of peace this knowledge would not incapacitate men for, nor interfere with any other business; - while in times of war, it would become invaluable to the country in training an army for efficient service.[5]

Future catalogues continued the sales pitch:

> Norwich University is the only regularly chartered Institution in the Northern States, which combines full Classical, Scientific, and Military Curricula. Its graduates have been eagerly sought after, during the pre-

sent war, as field and regimental Officers, and many of the Vermont Regiments, whose discipline and valor have shone so conspicuously in camp and field, have been officered and drilled by undergraduate as well as by graduated Cadets of this institution.[6]

According to Ellis, the wartime strength of the Norwich University Corps of Cadets did not fall below 150 and the Classes of 1862-1866 averaged 39 cadets. A review of surviving contemporary Norwich University Catalogues for the war years indicates the following:

Academic Year	Number of Cadets
1859-1860	60
1861-1862	111
1862-1863	141
1863-1864	142
1864-1865	94
1865-1866	67

The above figures do not appear to include the numerous students attending special courses in military tactics, nor can it be determined how many (if any) new cadets entered the university during the course of the academic year. A comparison of the cadets' names presented in the university history to those in extant Civil War period catalogs reveals that the total membership in wartime-era classes was larger than stated in either Ellis or contemporary catalogs:

Cadet Class	Number of Members
1861	23
1862	8
1863	32
1864	71
1865	56
1866	36
1867	62
1868	31

Clearly, all members of a given class did not matriculate simultaneously, nor were they "on campus" at the same time. If they had been, the strength of the Corps of Cadets in fall 1862, when the Classes of

1863-66 were theoretically present, would have been 195 rather than the 141 reflected in the catalog for that year. In addition, Ellis indicates the Class of 1864 had 100 members, yet only 72 names could be confirmed in surviving University records; perhaps the remaining 28 were "special military students." While it is known, however, that a number of Norwich cadets were routinely absent and assigned as drillmasters for troops being mustered in Vermont training camps, a satisfactory explanation for these disparate numbers cannot be given. In any case, while the university managed to substantially increase the size of the Corps of Cadets during the war years, fluctuations in the size and composition of the student body, combined with other special wartime requirements, were undoubtedly a source of some instability.[7]

A brief comparison between Norwich and West Point is both useful and telling. The United States Corps of Cadets at West Point numbered just over 200 cadets at any one time during the Civil War. While West Point graduated 159 officers and Norwich only 66 during the rebellion, a minimum of 55 Norwich cadets departed campus prior to their graduation to serve in the Army or Navy. These statistics do not include the more than 100 students who took special military courses at Norwich in order to qualify for regular and volunteer commissions. It is likely, therefore, that Norwich probably sent more of its alumni into Union service during the wartime years of 1861-1865 (at least 220), than did the United States Military Academy. In addition, any attempt to assess the relative contributions of each academy must take into account the fact that numerous Norwich cadets were detailed as drillmasters for troop training during their school year. No extant source indicates that members of the United States Corps of Cadets at West Point were detailed to similar duty. Lastly, comparisons between the two schools indicate that at least 36 Norwich alumni (including a number who actually graduated from Norwich) went on to attend West Point after their tenures at Captain Partridge's academy, and a minimum of 43 others served in the United States Navy and Marine Corps.[8]

Despite the ongoing distractions and disruptions of the war, Norwich students stuck to their pre-war daily routines and, moreover, numerous academy cadets remained active in fraternities and athletics. The daily cadet schedule for the war years was as follows:

. . .Reveille 5.40 A.M. Roll-call at 6. Drill, in good weather, before breakfast, which is at 7. Prayers in the Chapel at 7.45; at this time the reports of the officers for the day are read . . . . 8 to 12, study hours. 12 to 1, given for dinner, we board where we please. Roll-call at 1 P.M. Study hours till 4. 4 to 5 drill. 5 to 7, (in mid-summer 8,) supper and recreation. 7, Roll-call and study hours till Reveille next morning . . . retire at 10.[9]

Daily drill of the Corps of Cadets was normally performed in Battalion Order. For this purpose, the corps was divided into four companies (each company having its own officers) under the control of General Jackman. As part of their military training, all cadets were instructed in infantry, rifle, and artillery drill and tactics, bayonet exercises, construction of field fortifications, reconnaissance (including skirmish drill), and guard and outpost duty. The cadets routinely trained with muskets and two six-pound smoothbore howitzers issued in 1853 by the state of Vermont. By April 1864, the university armory had been fully re-equipped with a hundred new rifled Springfield muskets, sabers, assorted accompanying equipment and a good quantity of new ammunition. This new ordnance replaced the older and outdated smoothbore muskets previously used for drill, and the Springfields, combined with the Norwich artillery battery, provided the Corps of Cadets with an ample supply of serviceable weaponry in case of emergency.[10]

Several landmark events took place during the war years which served to break the daily class and drill routine at Norwich. The most remarkable of these was the organization of a volunteer cavalry company by the students of Norwich and Dartmouth in spring 1862. This unit, officially known as Company B, 7th Squadron, Rhode Island Cavalry, eventually became known as the "College Cavaliers." The College Cavaliers, a 90-day volunteer unit, have the distinction of being the only known unit of its kind during the Civil War—a company formed solely of college students who returned to their respective campuses when their tour of active duty ended.[11]

The College Cavaliers consisted of 85 students, 23 of which were Norwich cadets, and were mustered into Federal service on June 24, 1862. Norwich men held the positions of first lieutenant, second lieutenant and first sergeant in Company B, and adjutant and sergeant major in the squadron. The young horse troopers were assigned to service in the vicinity of Harpers Ferry, Maryland, just in time to face Lee's raid into Maryland in September 1862. In the siege of Harpers Ferry that followed, the College Cavaliers was part of the only Union unit to break out of the Confederate encirclement. Rather than face capture and captivity, the cadets joined a column of some 1,300 Federal horseman led by Col. Benjamin Franklin "Grimes" Davis of the 8th New York cavalry. This band of intrepid horsemen eluded General Longstreet's forces, broke out of the encirclement the night of September 15, and reached Pennsylvania without the loss of a single man. While passing through enemy lines in the darkness, they managed to capture Longstreet's 40-wagon reserve ordnance train and turn it over to Federal authorities. Due to the Antietam emergency, the cadets volunteered to remain in active service for a short time beyond their term of enlistment. There was but one loss among the cadet contingent during their tour of duty: Cadet Arthur W. Coombs (Class of '64) contacted dysentery and died. Two other cadets were captured by the Confederates and held at Libby Prison in Richmond, but were quickly released. The Norwich members of the College Cavaliers were back on campus in early October 1862, and undoubtedly regaled their classmates with tales of adventure and glory for weeks to come.[12]

Perhaps influenced by the adventures of their fellow cadets who had served with the College Cavaliers, thirteen Norwich Cadets enlisted in the 100-day 60th Massachusetts Infantry Regiment in July 1864. The young cadets deployed with their regiment to Baltimore, Maryland, but the Bay State unit was soon transferred to Indianapolis, Indiana. Far removed from the fields of glory, the soldiers performed the tedious work of garrison duty and guarded Confederate prisoners at Camp Morton. During their tenure in the Midwest, Cadet Henry H. Head (Class of '66) died of fever. Their 100-day tour extended to four months before the unfortunate cadets were finally discharged and allowed to return to campus.[13]

While the "lucky 13" were on active duty, a dramatic event took place virtually in the cadets' own backyard. On October 19, 1864, a band of some 20 to 30 Confederate raiders led by the daring Lt. Bennett H. Young successfully infiltrated the prosperous environs of St. Albans, Vermont, from their base in Montreal, Canada. Styling themselves the "5th Company, Confederate States Retributors," the raiders suddenly struck the town, looted $201,522 from local banks, and terrorized unsuspecting citizens. Before fleeing north, the band of Confederates unsuccessfully attempted to burn the town using home-made hand grenades filled with "Greek Fire." One citizen and one raider were killed and four raiders were wounded. The entire State of Vermont was stunned and, for a time, panic gripped the entire Northeast. The *Newport* (Vermont) *News* of October 27 reflected the excitement of the time: "On Thursday morning last, the good people of this village and vicinity were startled by a summons emanating from the adjutant general of the state, calling upon the arms-bearing citizens to report immediately for duty." Readers were shocked to find "that the state had been invaded by land pirates from the neighboring provinces; that the village of St. Albans had been sacked, citizens murdered in cold blood and all the crimes of the highwayman, the robber and the incendiary committed within the borders of our gallant state."[14]

Vermont Militia units had, for all practical purposes, disappeared, as their members had been mobilized, trained, and shipped to the front. With the exception of a few convalescent soldiers and provost marshal guards, the state was essentially defenseless. Searching about for sources of immediate assistance, Governor Smith telegraphed General Jackman at Norwich to enlist the aid of the state's only significant or-ganized, trained and armed military force: the Norwich University Corps of Cadets. In the fall darkness, drums beat an urgent call for an unusual evening assembly, and the cadets quickly formed into ranks before their military instructor, Union army veteran Capt. Charles N. Kent (Class of '64). Kent described what happened next: "When the ranks were aligned, [I] read the telegram, requesting all those of the cadets who would volunteer to go to Newport, if called by the gover-nor, to step one pace to the front. There was a complete forward move-ment in response. Every cadet thus expressed his wish to volunteer."[15]

Governor Smith was duly notified and the cadets were ordered to proceed to the town of Newport, located on Lake Memphremagog in northern Vermont, where intelligence indicated another Rebel raid was imminent:

Montpelier, Vt., Oct. 20, 1864

General Alonzo Jackman, Norwich, Vt.

Proceed with your infantry force, without artillery, by first train, to Derby Line, Vt. and report to Col. Grout, who has been placed in command in Orleans County. If Col. Grout is not there, assume command at that point until he arrives. Take such precautionary measures to obtain information and resist attack as you deem advisable and if necessary, organize any additional force from citizens. . . .Keep me advised of all your movements, by telegraph.

By order of the Governor,
P.T. Washburn
Adj. and Ins. General

Forming in front of their barracks, fully uniformed and equipped with their newly issued Springfield muskets, the cadets awaited the command to move out. Soon, under the command of General Jackman and Captain Kent, a full "combat ready" company of 47 cadets was on a train chugging north for Newport; the "Lake Memphremagog Campaign" had begun and the cadets were going to war![16]

The Norwich cadets seemingly arrived at Newport in the nick of time. Reports indicated a steamer filled with Rebel raiders was about to arrive from Canada. The cadets, reinforced by a motley group of nervous, haphazardly armed townspeople, formed on the Newport wharf and awaited the enemy. Also present was Lt. Frank S. Page (Class of '58) of the Veteran Reserve Corps, a one-armed veteran of the 4th Vermont. In the evening dusk, the incoming steamer suspected of carrying raiders was spotted, and the cadets were immediately deployed into battle order to receive them. A cadet who took part in the expedition recalled how "our line of battle was formed, the Cadets being on the left and the militia on the right. The efficiency of the latter was somewhat impaired by their standing in files five or six deep. The rear rank had a strange charm for many of them." As the steamer drew near, several commands were shouted, and the cadets and townsfolk fixed bayonets ("in which operation one brilliant genius was heard begging for a lantern," noted a Norwich cadet) and "stood at the 'Ready,' waiting in breathless suspense the coming of the foe."[17]

As the boat came in, an excited townsman shouted "Fire." Cadet Howard F. Hill (Class of '67) described what happened next: "Not a shot was heard; for we knew better than to fire from 'the ready.' It was owing to good drill that no one let go in the excitement." Fortunately for the boat's passengers, no one did fire: "two or three harmless looking individuals" debarked from the steamer and stared in astonishment at the massed armed force before them. Hill mused, "If that little company had fired, somebody, or more would have been 'hurted.' The writer had his eye on a spot fit for perforation. After a conference at the wharf, deep breaths were drawn and a supper at the hotel followed."[18]

After posting guards, the cadets, still expecting Confederate raiders, retired for an anxious night during which few slept. To add to the anxiety of the darkness, numerous "signal fires," undoubtedly set by Rebel raiders, were seen in the surrounding hills. The next morning the Norwich Cadets set out for the Canadian border, known locally as the "Derby Line." As the march dragged on, weary cadets shouted "How far to Derby Line?" to onlookers along their path. The contradictory answers they received led some to believe the distance was infinite rather than a mere eight miles. Finally arriving at the border, they were astonished to be informed the emergency was over and their services were no longer required. The Corps of Cadets actually did enter Canada (without arms), where Canadian authorities indicated a willingness to help their Yankee neighbors, but preferred they return to Vermont.

So ended the glorious "Campaign of Lake Memphremagog." The return to Newport was followed by the trip back to the university campus; the good citizenry had been "saved," and the honor of Vermont and the descendants of Ethan Allen fully upheld. The events surrounding the raid upon St. Albans were the closest the Norwich University Corps of Cadets came to combat duty as a unit in the Civil War.[19]

The Norwich participation in events surrounding the St. Alban's raid deserves to be remembered not for what did not occur—actual combat—but for the devotion to duty and willingness to sacrifice displayed by the young cadets. On that autumn day in 1864, the Norwich cadets demonstrated they were ready to match the deeds of their brother alumni who were then serving on other, more sanguine, fields. Unfortunately, the cadets' short period of active service has faded into the backwater of American and Vermont history.

VI. The Overland Campaign To Petersburg

"We were Simply Slaughtered"
Lemuel A. Abbott '64

On the surface, the military situation at the beginning of 1864 looked promising for the Union and bleak for the Confederacy, whose armies had passed a hard winter with inadequate rations. Despite this and the significant defeats it had suffered in 1863, morale remained generally high in the South. Looming was the Union presidential election, which promised to be a referendum on the Northern war effort. If the South could successfully avoid additional major defeats and inflict serious setbacks upon the Federals, it might yet gain its independence through the ballot box. No one was more aware of this situation than Abraham Lincoln. While he was unhappy with the progress of the war in the East, the war had gone very well in the West. And it was in the West that Lincoln believed he had finally found the man to lead the Armies of the Republic to victory. On March 9, 1864, Henry W. Halleck assumed the reins of chief of staff; more importantly, Ulysses S. Grant accepted a commission as lieutenant general and general-in-chief of the Union armies.[1]

After meeting with Lincoln and his key advisors in Washington, Grant felt it best to remain in the East and appointed his friend Maj. Gen. William T. Sherman to exercise overall command in the West. General Meade, meanwhile, retained de jure command of the Army of the Potomac, an awkward arrangement that would cause problems in the months to come. Grant's strategy for 1864 involved coordinated advances in the Shenandoah Valley and the

Virginia Tidewater area while the Army of the Potomac moved against Richmond and Lee's army from the north. In the West, Nathaniel Banks was to capture Mobile while Sherman drove against the logistically important city of Atlanta and Joe Johnston's Army of Tennessee. Grant's theory of how to achieve a victory was to press the Confederacy from several points simultaneously, thereby holding the various Southern armies in place and denying them the ability to reinforce each other as they had in the past. Though Grant's ascension to command in the East provoked varying opinions as to his ability as a commander, General Longstreet, who knew Grant from the Old Army, prophetically warned his comrades, "That man will fight us every day and every hour till the end of the war."[2]

As the Army of the Potomac lay in winter quarters, the question of the imminent discharge of its three-year veterans took center stage. Ignoring the Confederacy's example, where soldiers had to serve "for the duration," the Federal government viewed the enlistment contract as a bargain not to be broken. Unlike in 1863, when so many nine-month and two-year men were lost to the service at the end of their enlistments, the War Department now relied on appeals to patriotism and military and financial inducements to persuade the men to reenlist. These offers included a special "veteran's chevron," a 30-day furlough, and a $400 Federal bonus that was often augmented by local and state bounties. Any regiment in which 75% of its men reenlisted would retain its identity and could take furlough as a unit. Though some 100,000 proven soldiers chose to go home at the end of their terms, 136,000 reenlisted. Typical of the regiments that "veteranized" was the 19th Massachusetts. Lieutenant Colonel Edmund Rice (Class of '60) recounted how "On the 4th day of February the Regiment left Stevensburg Va upon veteran furlough of 35 days arriving in Boston Feby 8. The same day the Regt was received in Faneuil Hall by their old & beloved Commander General Hinks on the part of Governor Andrew." In contrast to the horror they were to experience in the coming months, "The day was one of happy memories to the brave survivors of the noble Regiment that nearly three years before quitted the State under the heroic Hinks to tread the Battle

Fields of the Union." The happy days at home passed all too quickly. As the Bay Staters headed back to the front, Rice proudly stated that "To the honor of the Regiment. . .during the time the Regiment was on furlough in Massachusetts no one of its members was under restraint by the Civil Authority and the Regt. reported in the field with every veteran originally furloughed."[3]

Shortly before the 19th Massachusetts returned to the front, the Army of the Potomac underwent a major reorganization. On March 24, 1864, the First and Third Corps, which had suffered so heavily in the campaigns of 1863, were disbanded, much to the disgust of their veterans. The units formerly associated with those corps were absorbed into the Second, Fifth, and Sixth Corps. In the aftermath of the reorganization, Edmund Rice's command had the honor of drilling for their new commander, General Ulysses S. Grant, at Second Division (Second Corps) headquarters. Upon completion of the drill, "The many General Officers present including the illustrious names of Grant, Meade, Hancock, Warren, Sedgwick, Gibbon & Sheridan expressed unbounded satisfaction with the admirable discipline and perfect instruction of both Regiments."[4]

On May 4, 1864, the Army of the Potomac headed south, crossed the Rapidan with 65 Norwich alumni in its ranks, and plunged into a jungle-like area known as the Wilderness. Grant and Meade planned a swift march to turn Lee's right flank and bring the Southerners to battle somewhere south of the Wilderness. To do so, the Army of the Potomac had to pass rapidly through the tangled and defensively favorable terrain before Lee could concentrate his army to oppose the advance. However, as always seemed to happen with the best laid plans of the Army of the Potomac, the scheme went awry. Remembering Hooker's effort of the previous year, Lee chose not to defend at the river but to strike at the Army of the Potomac's marching flank. If successful, the huge Federal advantage in manpower would be greatly discounted. The Union troops had not quite made it through the Wilderness when, on May 5, the two armies collided.[5]

The Wilderness consisted of almost impenetrable secondary forest growth through which cut two main roads: the Orange Plank

Road, running to and from Fredericksburg (east-west), and the Germanna Plank Road, the main north-south route. Another key route was the Brock Road, which ran generally southeast to the crossroads hamlet of Spotsylvania Courthouse. A veteran Sixth Corps staff officer described the terrain as "scrubby woods and tangled thickets [that] stretch away on every side, interminably to all appearance. The narrow roads offer the only means of going anywhere or seeing anything." If a man strayed off the roads he faced "low ridges and hollows [that] succeed[ed] each other, without a single feature to serve as a landmark and no one but an experienced woodsman with a compass could keep his bearings and position or preserve his course."[6]

In general, the Battle of the Wilderness was characterized by fierce local actions, excessive heat, confusion, and exceptionally poor visibility caused by dense smoke and the nature of the terrain. Surviving participants remembered the fight as one in which "Few of the officers and men engaged retain very definite conceptions of either time or space. They moved when the lines surged forward or back. They made the best fight they could against the seen and unseen foes in front and on right and left." As the battle developed, it was "characterized by unseen movements of troops; terrific volleys of musketry, bursting at close range from the thickets; charges through woods so dense that field officers could hardly see the line of a company." The fight was equally confusing for both sides and firsthand accounts are strikingly similar. Survivors describe the "sudden appearances and disappearances of bodies of troops, through jungles veiled in smoke; opposing brigades and regiments hugging the ground, not daring to rise for advance or retreat, yet keeping up incessant fusillades; lines rapidly thinning and ever closing up, while many dead dropped unseen in the underbrush and many wounded men crept off alone into hollows," many of them never to emerge.[7]

Grant's offensive began well enough. Warren's Fifth Corps marched on the Germanna Plank Road and bivouacked on the night of May 4-5 in the large clearing around the Wilderness Tavern, located at the road's intersection with the Orange Turnpike. On the morning of May 5, Meade's battle plan called for

General Hancock's Second Corps, which had crossed the Rapidan at Ely's Ford and camped on the old Chancellorsville battlefield, to advance from that point to Todd's Tavern via the Catharpin Road. General Warren's Fifth Corps was to advance southwest down the Orange Turnpike. If all went well, both corps would soon be clear of the Wilderness. Screening the corps' advance to the west were elements of Brig. Gen. Charles Griffin's First Division, while the 5th New York Cavalry, which was designated to be the connecting link between the main cavalry force screening the Army of the Potomac and the Fifth Corps, headed toward Parker's Store. Upon reaching that point, the Union cavalry advanced westwards down the Orange Plank Road from Parker's Store looking for Confederates. They found them—in fact, they ran into the lead elements of Lt. Gen. Ambrose P. Hill's entire corps. Lee's army was approaching the area of the Wilderness from the west, and his plan for May 5 was to send one corps of infantry down the Orange Turnpike and the other down the Orange Plank Road in the hopes of hitting the Federals in the flank and bringing them to battle (Longstreet's Corps was on the march and was not expected to arrive that day). When the butternut-clad infantry clashed with the Federal cavalry, they could not break through. Although isolated for nearly four hours, the Union cavalrymen gallantly delayed the Confederate advance and warned Warren of their approach. Confederate prisoners later stated they believed they were facing an entire Federal infantry brigade.[8]

A few miles to the north, Confederate infantry from Lt. Gen. Richard S. Ewell's Second Corps were busily digging in on a heavily wooded rise overlooking Saunder's Field, a clearing that spanned both sides of the Orange Turnpike. Ewell's presence there was a shock to Warren, who believed Lee's army to be miles away near Mine Run. As soon as Warren reported his contact on the Orange Turnpike, Meade canceled the Fifth Corps marching orders and directed Warren to "attack the enemy with his whole force." After skirmishing for much of the morning, Warren ordered Griffin to probe the enemy and determine his strength and intentions. Intense combat erupted when the Union infantry attacked Confederate entrenchments to the west of Saunder's Field.

Norwich men fighting at Saunder's Field that day included Corp. Robert C. Lord (Class of '64), 11th United States Infantry; Capt. George W. Smith (Class of '64), Company A, 2nd Battalion, and 1st Lt. Francis E. Stimpson (Class of '58), Company B, 2nd Battalion, 17th United States Infantry; and Capt. Charles Bowers (Class of '52), 32nd Massachusetts Infantry. These men advanced through heavy fire and soon found themselves locked in a whirlwind of individual combat as command and small unit integrity degenerated in the thick, dark woods beyond the Confederate trench line.[9]

This was the day that the Regular Brigade fought its last significant engagement of the war. Norwich alumni Captain Smith and 1st Lieutenant Stimpson marched with the 17th United States Infantry on the brigade's right flank and moved westward into the clearing. A Regular described the scene: "The order to advance was given and [Romeyn B.] Ayre's brigade—the strongest in numbers in the Fifth Corps and one of the best disciplined in the army—moves quietly, steadily forward, at common time and down the slope." Union observers saw how "The line is not quite exact as they first start, but by the time they reach the level ground and quicken the step, so much of the line as is in sight (for the right of the brigade was in the woods and out of sight) was as accurate and the movements as exact, as on parade." As the Regulars marched on and "reached the center of the open field, a line of fire began in their front, but nearly a brigade's length to their left." The enemy's musketry then "swept along the edge of the wood, from where the wood touched the Turnpike, to and past the brigade front, slowly, beautifully in its machine-like regularity, file-firing, past the brigade front and lost itself, out of sight and by sound, way off, in the woods to its right." Despite the heavy fire, the Regulars crashed into the enemy's line of entrenchments where, after savage combat in the smoke-filled woods, the Union charge fell apart and the survivors pulled back, recrossed Saunder's Field again under heavy fire and returned to the Union line. The already-depleted Regular Brigade, a pitiful remnant of what had once been Sykes' proud Regular Division, lost 936 men in less than 30 minutes. Smith and

Stimpson managed to survive, not knowing that each man's days with the 17th's "Maine Regulars" were rapidly coming to an end.[10]

Also engaged in the vicinity that afternoon was the 95th Pennsylvania Infantry of Horatio G. Wright's (Class of '37) First Division, Sixth Corps, in which Sgt. Maj. (later captain) John S. Carpenter (Class of '48) served. Carpenter and the Pennsylvanians moved forward and managed to link up with right flank of the Fifth Corps near Saunders' Field. They seized a small hill some 200 yards in advance of the Sixth Corps line and held on despite the burning woods. Carpenter himself was slightly wounded in the action. Later that afternoon, men from Charles Bowers' 32nd Massachusetts boldly planted their colors in the Orange Turnpike and faced west, announcing their intention to stay and fight it out.[11]

On the left of the turnpike in the woods immediately south of Saunder's Field deployed Brig. Gen. Lysander Cutler's famed Iron Brigade, which included Col. William W. Robinson (Class of '41) and his 7th Wisconsin. The brigade was now a mere shadow of the stellar fighting unit that had excelled at Antietam and Gettysburg. The Iron Brigade, which now contained many non-Western troops, found itself in a difficult situation early on the afternoon of May 5. Attempts to advance and maintain formation and troop control in the dense woods were futile. Disjointed and confused, the Iron Brigade was suddenly hit on its northern flank by George Dole's dug-in Georgia Brigade. For the first time in its history the Iron Brigade broke and ran. It rallied after a short time, however, and counterattacked with the bayonet, driving the Confederates to their second defensive line and beyond. In the process, Colonel Robinson's 7th Wisconsin captured the battle flag of the 48th Virginia. On the morning of May 6, the Iron Brigade would be back in action again, engaged in a vicious fight with the enemy's Texas Brigade. Casualties among Union field officers were heavy, and Norwich's Colonel Robinson once again found himself as acting commander of the Iron Brigade for the second time in less than a year.[12]

As the Fifth Corps became heavily engaged, both Hancock's Second and Sedgwick's Sixth Corps were on the move. About

10:30 a.m., the Federals recognized the growing significance of the Brock Road-Orange Plank intersection, and Hancock was directed toward it. Hancock's troops, however, were furthest from army headquarters and had to be reached by courier. As a result, three brigades of George Getty's Second Division, Sixth Corps, including the Vermont Brigade, were chosen to secure the critical intersection. Sedgwick's Sixth Corps began the campaign with an impressive force of 24,000 men in 49 infantry regiments. The Vermont Brigade and its Sixth Corps comrades, however, were temporarily attached to Hancock's Second Corps.

With 14 Norwich men in its ranks, the brigade arrived at the key point in time to drive away Confederate forward elements which had managed to drive within 30 yards of the intersection. About 3:00 to 3:30 p.m that afternoon, the Vermonters were ordered forward to attack General Harry Heth's Confederate division in the woods southwest of the Brock Road. The Green Mountain Boys and their Norwich men struggled through the thick underbrush, which a staff officer described as "the very centre and type of the Wilderness.

Once away from the roads, conditions only worsened as "then low ridges and hollows succeed each other, without a single feature to serve as a landmark and no one but an experienced woodsman with a compass could keep his bearings and position or preserve his course." The Federals proceeded west but did not discover the exact location of the enemy line until they were stunned by a tremendous volley delivered at point blank range.[13]

The Vermonters initially advanced with two regiments in the front line, two more in a second line, and one in reserve. As the battle developed, the entire brigade was placed into a single line of battle in order to prevent the surging Southerners from enveloping their exposed flanks. Casualties, particularly in the ranks of company and field grade officers, were unusually heavy and threatened to cripple the effectiveness of the Vermont Brigade. Despite losing 1,232 men—the heaviest casualties of any Federal unit in the Wilderness battle—the next morning the Vermonters put up a stalwart defense and played a significant role in preventing a Southern breakthrough when they repelled waves of attacking butternut-clad troops. In the desperate fighting on May 6, the brigade stood like a rock for several hours despite repeated assaults from Longstreet's veteran troops. Colonel Grant's after-action report proudly declared that "Perhaps the valor of Vermont Troops and the steadiness and unbroken front of those noble regiments were never more signally displayed. . . .They stood out in the very midst of the enemy, unyielding, dealing slaughter in front and flank."[14]

For the Green Mountain Boys, who had taken over 2,800 men into the fight, the carnage was awful. Their losses were 1,269 men killed, wounded and missing in just two days of fighting. The Battle of the Wilderness accounted for approximately 20% of all Vermonters killed in the entire war. Of the Norwich men fighting with the Vermont Brigade in the Wilderness, four (28.6%) were killed or wounded: Private John Sabine (Class of '64), Company G, 3rd Vermont, was killed in action on May 5; 1st Lt. and Adjutant George B. French (Class of '55), 4th Vermont Infantry, was severely wounded and disabled; 1st Lt. and Adjutant Sumner H. Lincoln (Class of '61), 6th Vermont and Pvt. George H. Parker (Class of '57), Company A, 4th Vermont were also wounded. The Vermonters suffered 10% of the Army of the Potomac's total casualties in the Wilderness.[15]

Colonel Thomas O. Seaver (Class of '59), 3rd Vermont, was the only regimental commander in the Vermont Brigade to emerge from the Wilderness unscathed. Both the Norwich alumnus and his regiment fought with courage and tenacity. Concerning the action in the Wilderness on May 5 and 6, Seaver wrote:

> At about 2 p. m. I was ordered to advance in line with the Fourth. Accordingly my regiment was moved forward. The skirmishers advancing, I passed them. The ground over which the regiment passed was thickly covered with trees, intercepted with a dense growth of underbrush, rendering it very difficult to move troops over, and so that nothing could be seen at a distance of more than 30 or 40 yards. After passing the skirmish line for about 200 yards, we met the enemy, who gave the first indications of his presence by delivering a full volley in our front, in consequence of which I lost many valuable lives. I had no means of guarding against this disaster. . . .After receiving the enemy's fire I ordered a charge, but the nature of the ground and the heavy fire

of the enemy rendered it impossible for me to move my men forward in such shape as to give any hope of dislodging him. . .as the line at my left had either wholly given way, or had not advanced so far, so that I received a partial cross-fire from that direction. Under the circumstances I determined to try and hold the I had, which was done until just before dark, when the regiment relieved by the Fifth Vermont, and I was directed to place my men the fortifications a few yards east of the road on which the line of battle had first been formed, where I remained until the morning of May 6, when an attack was ordered along the line. My regiment was placed in the third line. After advancing about a mile through the woods, I found that my regiment was in front, with the Second Vermont on my left, and a regiment on my right, the designation of which I do not know. . . .The regiments referred to occupied a position somewhat in advance of the main line of battle, to meet which the right and left of the advance was thrown back. My regiment occupied the position above described until about 2 p. m., when the enemy made a furious attack upon the line of the Second Corps at my left, breaking through their lines and getting in our rear. I sent an order to Lieutenant-Colonel Pingree, commanding Second Vermont, to change front to meet the new attack of the enemy in [sic], but before the order could be executed the whole left of the line had broken in confusion, and in order to save my command from capture, I was obliged to retire to the road running at right angles with the plank road [Brock Road], where I formed again to resist the farther advance of the enemy.[16]

One of Seaver's enlisted men remembered the intensity of the two-day fight in a letter home. "We marched in on the left of the Orange plank road with Scrub Oak so thick that we could not keep any formation and the first we knew of the enemy we received a volley from a line of battle within a stone's throw." In an instant, "One man at my left fell dead and a bullet went so near the face of the man in my rear that it took an eye out, two bullets went through my haversack and one through my canteen another passed so near my neck that it burned the skin then entered my blanket near my neck and when I unrolled it, I found nineteen holes in it." Private Wilbur Fisk summarized the situation faced by all Vermonters and Norwich men in the holocaust that was the Wilderness in a letter written May 9:

> The rebels gave us a warm reception. They poured their bullets into us so fast we had to lie down to load and fire. . . .We were under their fire over three hours, before we were relieved. Our regiment [2nd Vermont] lost 264 men in killed and wounded.

Observing the conditions around him, Fisk observed that "Just a little to the rear of where our line was formed, where the bullets swept close to the ground, every bush and twig was cut and splintered by the leaden balls. . . .Had the rebels fired a little lower, they would have annihilated the whole line; they nearly did as it was."[17]

In the days following the slaughter of his Vermonters in the Wilderness, Col. Lewis A. Grant drafted his report for the adjutant general of Vermont. Speaking of his brigade, in which so many Norwich men served, Grant wrote: "There has been fighting every day since and the brigade has been more or less engaged every day, but the casualties of the first two days were much the heaviest. The whole number of casualties at the present time is 1,363." He went on how "It is with sad heart I inform you of so great a loss of Vermont's noble sons, but it is with certain pride that I assure you there are no dishonorable graves." The Vermont Brigade had yet again "met the enemy in his strongholds, attacked him under murderous fire and in every face of death has repulsed with great slaughter repeated and vigorous attacks upon our lines and on no occasion has it disgracefully turned its back to the foe." He assured his commander in chief that "The flag of each regiment, though pierced and tattered, still flaunts in the face of the foe and noble bands of veterans with thinned ranks and but few officers to command, still stand by them; and they seem determined to stand so long as there is a man to bear the flag aloft or an enemy in the field."[18]

The gallant conduct of the Vermont Brigade had not gone unnoticed in the Army of the Potomac. On May 7, 1864, as the Vermonters marched past other Sixth Corps units to assume a new position on the extreme left of the line, one by one the other units of the corps cheered them for their performance. The cheers were taken up by regiment after regiment as the Vermonters filed by—a soldier's salute recognizing superior fighting men.[19]

The Vermont Brigade veterans were not the only Green Mountain men engaged in the Wilderness. First Lieutenant Lemuel A. Abbott (Class of '64), 10th Vermont Infantry, kept a diary of events, and his entry for the Wilderness fighting on May 5 notes that, "Before Captain H. R. Steele had hardly finished dressing his company, after forming line a shell from this gun exploded in the ranks of Company K, killing a private and wounding others." The incident described by Abbott is horrifying: "The shell had burst actually inside the man completely disemboweling and throwing him high in the air in a rapidly whirling motion above our heads with arms and legs extended until his body fell heavily to the ground with a sickening thud." The young lieutenant recalled how he "was in the line of file closers hardly two paces away and just behind the man killed. We were covered with blood, fine pieces of flesh, entrails, etc., which makes me cringe and shudder whenever I think of it." Injured himself, Abbott remembered that "The concussion badly stunned me. I was whirled about in the air like a feather, thrown to the ground on my hands and knees—or at least was in that position with my head from the enemy when I became fully conscious face cut with flying gravel or something else, eyes, mouth and ears filled with dirt and was feeling nauseated from the shakeup." Had he been an older and wiser man, Abbott may have reacted differently. "Most of the others affected went to the hospital," he noted, "and I wanted to but didn't give up. I feared being accused of trying to get out of a fight." Abbott returned to his men and continued the battle.[20]

On the night of May 5-6, the commanders of both armies assessed the confused situation and made plans to renew the battle. Generals Grant and Meade felt the Federals had done well enough, and planned to bring more forces to bear in the form of Ambrose Burnside's Ninth Corps. Burnside's organization, which had been transferred to the Department of the Ohio on March 19, 1863, functioned as an independent corps in the Army of the Potomac until May 24, when Grant placed Burnside directly under Meade. The primary Union effort would be centered around Hancock's drive west against A. P. Hill's front on the Orange Plank Road, supported by a general assault along the line to pin the rest of Lee's men in place. Hancock's direct opponent (Hill) was battered and disorganized, and the attack held some promise of decisive success. Robert E. Lee was concerned with simply keeping his main line intact and cohesive. Thankfully for him, his best corps commander, James Longstreet, was just a few hours away with his veteran First Corps, and was expected to reach the front before daylight.

The struggle was renewed at dawn and raged, as Grant later stated, "with unabated fury until darkness set in." As previously described, the Vermonters and Norwich men were once again in the thick of the fighting on the Orange Plank and Brock Roads. Hancock's rolling assault drove back Hill's exhausted corps and was in the process of demolishing the right wing of Lee's army when Longstreet's men arrived on the run to stem the tide and blunt the attack. Burnside's Ninth Corps took longer to get in position than anticipated, but finally filed into place left of Warren's Fifth Corps at Jones' Field. Despite the Ninth Corps arrival on the field, its presence did little to assist Hancock. Longstreet's counter-attack had stopped Hancock cold, and the Federal attack along the Orange Plank Road came to naught. As the fighting raged, it was discovered that the Federal left flank south of the Orange Plank Road and west of the Brock Road was up in the air and approachable via a concealed route through an unfinished railroad cut. By 11:00 a.m. Lee and Longstreet had gathered four brigades from several different divisions in the hope of landing a decisive blow against Hancock's Second Corps and rolling it up to the north. The surprise attack, reminiscent of Jackson's bold maneuver a year earlier and only a handful of miles away, began with great promise. Although Hancock later stated that Longstreet rolled up the left flank of his corps "like a wet blanket," Federal reinforcements, confusion, exhaustion, and Longstreet's near-fatal wounding prevented a more complete victory for the Confederates.[21]

While the Confederates were planning their flanking maneuver, a Norwich alumnus suffered a mortal wound just north of the Orange Plank Road. Charles E. Griswold (Class of '54), formerly the colonel of the 22nd Massachusetts, had left the army in 1862 following an extended illness. He felt it was his patriotic duty to return to the front after he recovered, and was commissioned colonel of the new 56th Massachusetts (1st Veterans). During the afternoon of May 6 on the Orange Plank Road, a variety of Federal units, including the 56th Massachusetts (Col. Sumner Carruth's First Brigade, Brig. Gen. Thomas Stevenson's First Division), assisted Hancock's beleaguered men as they were fending off Longstreet's counterattacks. The 56th had never been in battle, and was quickly confronted with Longstreet's veteran infantry. At a critical point in the fighting when his men began to falter before the onslaught, Griswold rushed forward and seized the national banner from the color sergeant. Waving it above his head, he shouted, "Men, stand by the flag today!" The young Norwich alumnus had scarcely uttered his challenge when a minie ball struck him in the neck. The ghastly wound resulted in a severed jugular vein which spewed his blood over the flag. Griswold fell into the arms of a corporal of the color guard and died a few moments later.[22]

Prior to the spring campaign, Griswold had a number of premonitions that this offensive was to be his last. On April 26, he gave his close friend and second in command, Lt. Col. Stephen M. Weld, a note:

> Should anything occur to me during this campaign, I want you to send all my effects that you can to my mother. . . .We are and have been good friends; I am glad you have been with me and if we don't return together, send to the same address a small black bag you will find hung around my neck—unopened. Truly Yours   CEG.

Again on May 3, Griswold enunciated his feelings for the flag he would die holding three days later. "There is something in that piece of bunting that stirs a man up to his work. You speak of the privations and unselfishness of our men, but you could not know our feelings when the colors are uncased in the field, nor of my deepened sense of duty, as my eyes rest upon them. I gladly offer my life in the good cause and I shall try to do my whole duty well." He was buried near the regimental field hospital a few hours after he fell. Weld noted in his diary that they managed to recover Griswold's corpse: "We regained the ground we had lost in the morning and found Griswold's body stripped of everything but the underclothing." Unfortunately, Weld "could not find any black bag."[23]

Another Southern flanking attack, this time against the Union far right, was undertaken early that evening when Confederate reconnaissance again discovered a vulnerable Union flank. Brigadier General John B. Gordon had discovered the weakness earlier in the day and had urged a major effort to turn and crush the enemy.

Major General Jubal Early, however, was unwilling to allow his subordinate the opportunity. Late in the day Gordon finally gained approval for the move and led three brigades against the Sixth Corps right flank. The Rebels hit Brig. Gen. Alexander Shaler's brigade like a sledgehammer, and the Federals broke and ran. Positioned to Shaler's left, Brig. Gen. Truman B. Seymour (Class of '44) refused to leave the field when his brigade line began to crumble. Instead, he rode to the scene of the action and attempted to rally his men and establish a new defensive line. The unlucky officer guided his mount through the smoke and confusion directly into the path of the advancing Confederates. Seymour wheeled and attempted to gallop to safety, but his horse was shot out from under him and he was soon captured.[24]

"General Jubal A. Early's Division of three brigades," wrote one disgusted Federal officer, "had stolen around the rear of General Shaler's veteran brigade of the First Division and the Second Brigade (formerly General Seymour's) of green men of the Third Division, Sixth Corps, which were on the right of our army in the order mentioned." The new men were "attacked vigorously both in rear and front, threw Shaler's veterans into disorder as well later as the Second Brigade, captured Shaler and created temporary confusion among the trains and hospital corps nearby. Seemingly it was the result of bad generalship by someone on our side."

On another portion of the field, the 19th Massachusetts, with Lt. Col. Edmund Rice (Class of '60) and 1st Lt. Edward B. Thompson (Class of '61), had a close call near the Wilderness Tavern. "On the morning of the 6th the Regt. advanced to relieve the front line, when it sustained a narrow escape from capture, by being flanked, lost 3 killed, 9 wounded & 17 missing." Later, "the Regt again advanced in the woods but was withdrawn and rested all night behind the works." As the deadly struggle was brought to an end by darkness and mutual exhaustion, ironically, the battle lines were just about where they had been when the battle began. The Federals had suffered nearly 18,000 casualties and the Confederates about 11,000. Little had been accomplished, and most men on both sides assumed this was the end of another failed "On to Richmond effort."[25]

It is interesting to note that Norwich men served in each of the seven Union regiments suffering the highest casualties in the Wilderness; five Norwich alumni were killed or wounded there. For those wounded alumni and other Union casualties, the horror of the fight was over, but the inhumanity of the field hospital experience was just beginning. If they were fortunate to be picked up from the field, they faced the agony of a trip by wagon or foot to Fredericksburg and Belle Plains for treatment. "The terrible slaughter of the Wilderness. . . .turned all pitying hearts and helping hands once more to Fredericksburg," wrote Clara Barton. The medical pioneer recalled that the "soil [at Belle Plain] was red clay. The ten thousand wheels and hoofs had ground it to a powder and a sudden rain upon the surrounding hills had converted the entire Basin into one vast mortar bed, smooth and glassy, as a lake and much the color of light Brick dust." Since the rail lines were not functioning, "The poor, mutilated, starving sufferers of the wilderness were pouring into Fredericksburg by thousands—and all to be taken away in army wagons across this 10 miles of alternate hills—and hollows—roots—and mud."[26]

First Lieutenant George B. French (Class of '55), adjutant of the 4th Vermont Infantry, lost his brother Quincy in the Wilderness and was himself severely wounded. Unpublished letters refer to his own situation and his brother's death. A surgeon wrote home for French on May 16 and indicated that George had "a pretty severe wound of the arm near the elbow and the bone is somewhat implicated, but not enough, I think, to give much trouble. His wound is doing very finely and his strength is steadily improving. I see no reason he should not recover rapidly with a good arm." Alluding to the rough ride and situation at Belle Plain, the surgeon described how George "was in critical condition for a day or two after being shaken up. Shaken in an ambulance for a long while, but he is now rested." French had a nurse write his parents two days later from Seminary Hospital in Georgetown. He had "left Fredericksburg on the morning of the 16th instant, remained at Belle Plain that night and arrived here last evening." His wound, he informed them, was "doing very well indeed." On the subject of his younger brother's demise, the mortified French wrote that, "It was impossible for me to learn anything very definite in relation to Quincy's death. I sent over to get the things he had. . . .I would write something to comfort you in this, our great affliction, if I could. All I can say is 'he died like a soldier. God's will be done.' There are many others who have suffered greater sacrifices in this terrible conflict."[27]

In the aftermath of what appeared to be a Federal defeat, most men on both sides expected the Federals would withdraw, regroup and prepare for another offensive, just as they had in the past. Grant, however, was a new sort of Federal commander. He had secretly dispatched a young reporter to President Lincoln with a message. When Lincoln met privately with the man and asked what the message contained, the courier answered: "He told me I was to tell you, Mr. President, that there would be no turning back." As the Army of the Potomac marched through the Wilderness during the night of May 7, to the surprise and elation of the troops, Grant made his way to the head of the column and, at a key crossroads, headed his horse south rather than north. The tired men cheered so loud that they had to be ordered to stop so as not to warn the Confederates that a movement was under way. A new era had dawned for the Army of the Potomac and for the South—the days of retreat for the Army of the Potomac were over and an unrelenting campaign of attrition had begun.[28]

As Grant headed south, a few keen observers sensed a change in the nature of fighting. In the following weeks, a relatively new aspect of warfare, which would come to characterize combat in the Eastern Theater (and had first come into large scale use in the Wilderness), took root: the widespread use of field fortifications. "The great feature of this campaign is the extraordinary use of earthworks," concluded staff officer Col. Theodore Lyman on May 18, who also believed they were a major reason for the surge in casualty rates. The astute and articulate Lyman noted:

> we arrive on the ground it takes of course a considerable amount of time to put troops in a position for attack. . . .Meantime, what does the enemy? Hastily forming a line of battle, they can collect rails from fences, stones, logs, and other materials, and pile them along the line; bayonets with a few picks and shovels, in the hands of men who work for their lives, soon suffice to cover this frame with earth and sods; and

within one hour, there is shelter high enough to cover a man kneeling, and extending often for a mile or two. When our line advances, there is a line of the enemy nothing showing but the bayonets, and the battle-flags stuck on top of the works. It is a rule that when the Rebels halt, the first day gives them a good rifle-pit; the second a regular infantry parapet with artillery in position; and the third a parapet with an abatis in front and entrenched batteries behind. Sometimes they put this three days' work into the first twenty-four hours. Our men can, and do, the same; but remember, our objective is offense—to advance. You would be amazed to see how this country is intersected with field-works, extending for miles and miles in different directions and marking the different strategic lines taken up by the two armies, as they warily move about each other.[29]

The campaign that resulted in this new breed of warfare, as noted by Lyman, was at least initially coordinated with other movements by other Federal armies. As Grant's men were moving across the Rapidan River into the Wilderness, Sherman's army group moved out against Joe Johnston in North Georgia. Major General Benjamin F. Butler's 35,000-man Army of the James was also moving, steaming up the James River on transports with orders from Grant to operate against the Southern capital. The army's spirits were high, and all seemed optimistic as to the outcome of their campaign. Butler successfully landed his men at Bermuda Hundred. Instead of moving northward, however, Butler spent several crucial days skirmishing with a small force of Confederates. Although he could have easily taken the vital railroad junction at Petersburg, he did not do so—Grant's instructions made no mention of the city. Butler's offensive, which had initially caught the Confederates by surprise, turned into a timid and faltering advance which included a sharp repulse at Drewry's Bluff on May 16. By late May, Butler had allowed himself to be bottled up on the Bermuda Hundred peninsula, and Grant began transferring troops, principally the Eighteenth Corps and units totaling nearly 17,000 men, from his Army of the James to the reduced Army of the Potomac. Butler remained stagnant in the Bermuda Hundred lines for most of the rest of the war.[30]

Serving in the Army of the James as Butler advanced toward Richmond were at least 20 Norwich alumni. Brig. Gen. Alfred H.

Terry (class unknown) commanded the First Division, Tenth Corps. In Terry's division during the campaign were Lt. Col. Thomas A. Henderson (Class of '62), 7th New Hampshire; Surgeon George C. Jarvis (Class of '52), 7th Connecticut; Assistant Surgeon John W. Parsons (Class of '63), 24th Massachusetts; Sgt. William Coffee (Class of '49), Company A, 3rd New Hampshire; Pvts. Lewis Kimball (Class of '62) Company F, 3rd New Hampshire, and Justus Washburn (Class of '62), Company D, 24th Massachusetts. Alumni serving in other units of the Army of the James included Lieutenant Elias H. Smith (Class of '61), Company D, 89th New York; Major George P. Greeley (Class of '53) and Assistant Surgeon David L. M. Comings (Class of '48), 4th New Hampshire; Capt. Frederick H. Rand (Class of '64), and 1st Lt. Henry M. Phillips (Class of '64), 4th Massachusetts Cavalry; Capts. George T. Carter (Class of '54), Company B, 2nd New Hampshire, Charles O. Bradley (Class of '63), Company C, 13th New Hampshire, Henry B. Nichols, 19th Wisconsin (Class of '52); Pvts. Albert I. Wadhams (Class of '44), Company I, 11th Connecticut and Dwight H. Kelton (Class of '64), Company B, 98th New York. Officers serving with the United States Colored Troops in Butler's expeditions included Capt. Arthur P. Morey (Class of '64), 22nd United States Colored Infantry and 1st Lt. Joseph H. Goulding (Class of '65), 6th United States Colored Infantry. Many of these men not only shed their blood for the Republic, but served with distinction throughout the campaign.[31]

At least 65 Norwich men took part with the Army of the Potomac in the battles of the May 7-21 Spotsylvania Campaign, which followed on the heels of the Wilderness action. The campaign marked the first of a series of attempts by Grant to move by his left flank and get between Lee and Richmond. If he had succeeded, the Army of Northern Virginia would have been forced to wage a decisive battle in the open. Lee, on the other hand, efficiently capitalized on his advantage of interior lines, information and support from local inhabitants, and superior knowledge of local roads and terrain to continually out pace (although sometimes just barely) the Army of the Potomac to key points. The Southerners dug in across Grant's front, hoping to force direct

Federal assaults against their powerful earthworks. Like the Wilderness before it, Spotsylvania is noted for the intensity and costliness of the fighting. It also witnessed the introduction into the army of heavy artillery regiments, which had for two years comfortably and peacefully garrisoned the forts of Washington, as combat infantry.[32]

Grant's move following the Wilderness bloodletting surprised Lee, for instead of retreating, Grant continued pressing forward. Both armies raced toward the crossroads village of Spotsylvania Court House on May 7-8. Confederate cavalry operating on the Brock Road seriously hampered the Federal advance and fought a delaying engagement with Sheridan's horsemen at Todd's Tavern. Longstreet's First Corps, now commanded by Richard H. Anderson following Longstreet's wounding on May 6, marched all night using farm roads and a newly-cut trail. The tired soldiers arrived at a key piece of terrain known as Laurel Hill just as Warren's Fifth Corps infantrymen were advancing to seize the position. A number of Norwich men saw service at Laurel Hill, and conspicuous among them was Col. William W. Robinson (Class of '41), the commander of the Iron Brigade. Laurel Hill was the scene of severe fighting through much of the campaign, although it was overshadowed by events on another part of the Spotsylvania lines.[33]

The Confederates managed to hold Laurel Hill, and soon defensive trenches spread out toward the east as more Federal and Southern troops arrived. The Confederate lines contained a salient in the shape of a large "Mule Shoe," which encompassed some high terrain and jutted out toward the Union lines. As the Federals deployed and prepared to engage the enemy, a noteworthy tragedy struck the Sixth Corps. On the morning of May 9, while he examined an artillery position near the Brock Road, beloved Maj. Gen. John Sedgwick was instantly killed by a Confederate sharpshooter. Sedgwick was succeeded by Brig. Gen. Horatio G. Wright (Class of '37), his personal choice as successor. Wright was quickly promoted to major general and led the corps with distinction for the rest of the war.[34]

The most dramatic battles of the Spotsylvania Campaign took place in and around Mule Shoe between May 10-12. The first serious engagement after the initial Laurel Hill fighting came about as a result of West Point graduate Col. Emory Upton, a Sixth Corps brigade commander who created an innovative plan to pierce the enemy lines. The attack nearly succeeded in breaking through the main Confederate line on the afternoon and evening of May 10, and resulted in a brief moment of glory for a Norwich alumnus.[35]

Upton envisaged a radical change in traditional assault tactics. Following his survey of the Mule Shoe in conjunction with army engineers, Upton detected a vulnerable section of defenses 300 yards west of the apex of the salient and a mere 200 yards beyond a tree line near the Sixth Corps forward line. He boldly proposed to break through this segment of enemy fortifications with 12 hand-picked regiments conducting a rapid ground assault with minimal artillery preparation. In lieu of the traditional attack formation (with all units on line), there would be four assault waves, each consisting of three regiments on line, with the follow-up waves in column close behind the first ranks, i.e., Upton would assault on a narrow front but in substantial depth. The plan as organized called for the first wave to penetrate the Rebel defenses and break off to the right and left, leaving the second line to continue the assault into the enemy's rear area. The second wave's advance would be supported by the third line, while the fourth line remained some 200 yards behind as Upton's reserve. Upton's effort late on the afternoon of May 10 is now recognized as one of the classic infantry attacks of military history.[36]

Among the regiments selected for the attack were three regiments of the Vermont Brigade under the leadership of a proven combat commander, thirty-year-old Col. Thomas O. Seaver (Class of '59). The Green Mountain Boys, who were specifically referred to by Upton as "elite" troops, constituted the fourth assault wave. Upton himself detailed the situation his troops faced that afternoon: "On the afternoon of the 10th an assault was determined upon and a column of twelve picked regiments was organized. . . The point of attack. . .was at an angle of the enemy's works near the Scott house, about a half mile to the left of the Spotsylvania road." Describing the formidable defenses, Upton wrote: "His entrenchments were of a formidable character with abatis in front and surmounted by heavy logs, underneath which were loopholes for musketry." Even if the Union troops broke through this line, "About 100 yards to the rear was another line of works, partly completed and occupied by a second line of battle. The position was in an open field about 200 yards from a pine wood, A wood road led from our position directly to the point of attack."[37]

According to the 5th Maine's historian:

> At six o'clock all things were ready and the artillery, from an eminence in the rear, opened a terrible fire, sending the shells howling and shrieking over the heads of the charging column and plunging into the works of the enemy. This was the signal for attack and Colonel Upton's clear voice rang out, 'Attention, battalions! Forward, double-quick! Charge!' And in an instant every man was on his feet and, with tremendous cheers, which were answered by the wild yells of the rebels, the column rushed from under the cover of the woods. . .[and with] a wild cheer and faces averted, rushed for the works. Through terrible front and flank fire the column advanced, quickly gaining the parapet. Here occurred a deadly hand-to-hand conflict.

Overcoming savage resistance, the men "Pressing forward and expanding to right and left, the second line of entrenchments, its line of battle and battery fell into our hands." For a brief time, it seemed as if a great victory was at hand when, "The column of assault had been brilliantly successful. The enemy's lines were completely broken and an opening had been made for the division which was to have supported our left, but it did not arrive."[38]

The initial results of Upton's accomplishment were impressive. His men had overrun the Confederate fortifications, captured over a thousand prisoners, several guns, and a handful of battle flags. And the fight was far from over. Thomas O. Seaver sensed the assault had reached a crisis point and without awaiting orders, rushed his men forward through heavy fire to reinforce Upton and cover his vulnerable left flank. Gershom Mott's Second Corps division, which was designated to support the attack, failed to advance and the Confederates seized the opportunity to strike back. After heavy close-in fighting it became obvious that Upton's attack would not be successful, and orders were given his men to withdraw. Though the other regiments obeyed, Seaver and his Vermonters refused to retreat, claiming they could hold the works for six months if supplied with rations and ammunition. Postwar accounts by Confederate officers specifically refer to the tenacity of the Vermonters' resistance and the difficulty they had re-capturing their lost defensive lines. General Ulysses S. Grant belatedly instructed the position be held and the Vermonters reinforced, but meanwhile a peremptory order from General Wright for Seaver to abandon his position and return to friendly lines was issued. The Vermonters, who in the interval had been joined by four companies of alumnus Seaver's 3rd Vermont, reluctantly complied. Seaver's leadership and conspicuous bravery in this action earned him a Congressional Medal of Honor twenty-eight years later.[39]

Colonel Lewis A. Grant's report of the fight, which later served as the basis for the Seaver's Medal of Honor award, stated how the "Vermont regiments, under Colonel Seaver, advanced under a most galling fire, occupied the rebel works, while the other regiments of the attacking column fell back." After holding the enemy defenses for a time, "Orders were given for all to fall back, but it failed to reach a portion who remained in the works obstinately holding them against all attacks of the enemy until late in the evening, refusing to fall back until they received positive orders to do so." Upon returning to their own lines, "The four companies of [the] Third Vermont on the skirmish line, advanced with the attacking column and a portion of them remained in the rebel works until the last. After the charge the skirmish line was re-established." Emory Upton also spoke of the Vermonter's courage when he later detailed the situation within the Mule Shoe. "The impulsion of the charge being lost," he wrote, "nothing remained but to hold the ground. I accordingly directed the officers to form their men outside the works and open fire." Upton rode back over the battlefield to bring forward Seaver and his men, "but they had already mingled in the contest and were fighting with a heroism which has ever characterized that elite brigade. . . .Our position was three-quarters of a mile in advance of the army and, without prospect of support was untenable." Upton saluted Seaver and his men by indicating that "They went forward with unflinching courage and retired only upon receipt of a written order, after having expended the ammunition of their dead and wounded comrades."[40]

Private Fisk, with his "bird's eye" view of the action as a participant in the ranks of the 2nd Vermont, saw the famous attack and
the actions of Colonel Seaver's command in his own way. "We
formed in a ravine, screened from the rebels' view, where we prepared to charge across this open space and drive the rebels out of
their rifle-pits if possible. . . .We formed in four lines of battle,
three ahead of us." The attack was begun, and "at the signal, the
first three lines sprang to their feet and rushed across the field, determined to drive the enemy or die. We followed immediately after." As Fisk, Seaver and the rest of the Vermonters charged, "The
rebels mowed the men down with awful effect, but the advancing
line was not checked. We drove the enemy out of his first line of
works and captured over 2,000 prisoners." With a Union victory
within reach, Fisk sought the reason why they had failed. He
blamed "Another brigade that was to follow on our left broke and
run before they reached the works. Of course, this made our position untenable and spoiled our victory which we had so nearly
won." The efforts of the Vermonters and their comrades had come
to naught, though "We held our position until we were nearly
flanked, hoping that re-inforcements could come, but none came
and we were reluctantly obliged to fall back. We lost heavily in
killed and wounded and so did the enemy, besides many prisoners."[41]

Henry Houghton, a member of Seaver's 3rd Vermont who supported Upton's action, remembered how "the four right companys
A, B, C, & D participated in Upton's famous charge, the rest of the
regiment was on the skirmish line at the right of the charging column." As the fight developed "the enemy undertook to break
through and turn their flank but did not succeed, they charged our
skirmish line with two lines of battle." As the enemy rushed
Houghton and his comrades, "Immediately in front of my company their colors fell three times before they got half way to our lines,
when they fell back, the last man to pick up the colors never raised
them again until he reached the inside of their works."[42]

Though Upton's attack ultimately failed, General Ulysses Grant was so impressed with his tactics that he ordered the operation repeated two days later by Major General Hancock's entire Second Corps at the apex of the "Mule Shoe." That decision led to what many regard as the most intense and savage close infantry combat of the war, and many Norwich men were destined to spill their blood that day. The attack was scheduled for dawn on May 12, and the troops spent the night moving into positions during a horrendous downpour. According to Hancock, "Birney's and Barlow's divisions moved out after dark. . .over a narrow and difficult road during a heavy rain. . . .The troops were formed just in the rear of our picket-line, about 1,200 yards from the enemy's entrenchments." Between the Union attackers and Confederate defenders, "The ground ascended sharply between our lines and the enemy's and was thickly wooded, with the exception of a clearing about 400 yards in width extending up to the enemy's works in front of the Landrum house." The heavy rain and fog forced Hancock to delay the attack until sufficient light was present to guide it. A little after 4:30 a.m., the assaulting mass of men stepped off, and "[Barlow's] heavy column march[ed] over the enemy's pickets without firing a shot, regardless of a sharp fire from the enemy's picket reserve, which was posted on the high ground on which the Landrum house stands." The assaulting regiments "continued up the slope about half way to the enemy's line, when the men broke into a tremendous cheer and spontaneously" broke into a double-quick pace. The Federals "rolled like an irresistible wave into the enemy's works, tearing away the abatis there was in front of the entrenchments with their hands and carrying the line at all points in a few moments, although it was desperately defended."[43]

The Mule Shoe was manned by Richard Ewell's Second Corps, and his men did not stand a chance of successfully defending against the attack, which was made in darkness and under the cover of fog and rain. Hancock's warriors spilled up and over the earthworks, shooting and bayonetting the stunned defenders and spreading out to the right and left. Within minutes several thousand prisoners, 20 pieces of artillery, and some 30 stands of colors were captured. The assault was so successful it bogged itself down,

for too many Union troops poured into the Confederate fortifications too quickly. Unit cohesion fell apart, and the confusion that
followed allowed General Lee and his subordinates to rally retreating survivors and send forward reinforcements from a second defensive line. The masterful Confederate response threw back the attackers, stabilized the initial breach, and regained a portion of the
outer defenses of the Mule Shoe. Hancock's determined soldiers
held fast on the far side of the earthworks, however, and both sides
found themselves engaged in furious hand-to-hand combat. At
many points on the line, the men were separated only by the narrow width of the rampart. The combatants slaughtered one another
in this manner for almost eighteen hours. The focal point of the
bloodshed has been known ever since as the West or "Bloody
Angle." A number of Norwich men found themselves in the center
of that hellish cesspool of blood, mud, and death.[44]

"At 12:30 P.M. we moved to the left marching through thick
mud and at daylight took our place in line of battle opposite the
enemy's position which was charged and taken," remembered the
19th Massachusetts' Lt. Col. Edmund Rice (Class of '60). "The
Regiment behaved with great gallantry," he boasted, "and notwithstanding the tremendous artillery fire which bore upon that part of
the line occupied by them, never faltered an instant though losing
heavily." Rice recalled how "The Regiment was the directing
Battalion, & during the charge Gen [Alexander] Webb called to
'follow the colors of the 19th.' We lost several color bearers shot
down successively before reaching the enemy's works." In the resulting close combat within the Bloody Angle, wrote one officer,
"Half of the men were killed or wounded & Lt Col Rice and several of the men being far in the advance were taken by the enemy."
Despite these losses, the 19th Massachusetts was credited with the
capture of "a large no. of prisoners, 1 color & participated in the
capture of the cannon afterward assisting in turning them on the
enemy. The Regiment was under fire until night when it was ordered to rear and rested for the night."[45]

Edmund Rice, the young hero of Gettysburg and commander of
the 19th Massachusetts (and now Confederate prisoner), had led
his men forward into the apex of the salient. Soldiers loaded and

fired in the pouring rain until they fell into the muddy trench, many struck down by simple exhaustion rather than a bullet. Fighting furiously, the men of the 19th captured the colors of the 33rd North Carolina. Rice, who again distinguished himself on the battlefield at Spotsylvania, was captured when he ventured too deeply into the enemy lines on the mistaken assumption that his colors had fallen into enemy hands during the confusion surrounding the breakthrough. He had turned to two of his officers, one of whom was 1st Lt. John B. Thompson (Class of '61), and shouted, "Where are the Colors?" Neither officer knew. They saw several hundred Confederates running back toward their own lines, and Rice mistakenly believed he had his answer. "I see a Massachusetts color and will go after it," he exclaimed. That was the last his men saw of him that day. In the days that followed, many in the regiment believed he was dead and mourned his passing.

At one point during the ensuing melee, amidst the tumult of battle and the furor of nature, one of Rice's company commanders, Capt. John G. B. Adams, began to sing the popular and stirring "Battle Cry of Freedom." The rest of the 19th Massachusetts soon took up the song and were joined by other Union regiments until thousands of men in blue were echoing the melody over the roar of cannon and musketry:

> We will welcome to our numbers the loyal, true and brave,
> shouting the battle cry of freedom
> And although they may be poor not a man shall be a slave
> shouting the battle cry of freedom.
> The Union forever, Hurrah boys Hurrah!
> Down with the traitor, Up with the star;
> While we rally round the flag, boys rally once again,
> Shouting the battle cry of freedom.

It was an inspirational and unforgettable moment for the Union troops on a day filled with terror, and the impact it may have had on their Southern counterparts can only be imagined.[46]

Before the Confederate counterattack was launched, 1st Lt. Charles H. Potter's (Class of '47) Company K of the 73rd New York, Second Corps Excelsior Brigade, succeeded in penetrating Lee's second line of defense before being forced back to the defensive works near the Bloody Angle. The New Yorkers' "moved rapidly forward over the first line of the enemy's works [which had already been taken] up to and over the second line, under a heavy fire, capturing 150 prisoners, two stand of colors and 2 pieces of artillery, one of which was turned and used against the enemy with great effect." At first, "The command succeeded in getting the prisoners, colors and guns to the rear, but being entirely unsupported and the enemy concentrating his whole fire upon it, the works so gallantly won had to be abandoned and the regiment fell back to the first line of rebel works captured." Potter's regiment "suffered more severely than at any other period in the campaign." The 73rd, however, "captured the colors of a Louisiana regiment, those of the 42nd Virginia, and those of another Virginia regiment that day."[47]

Reinforcing elements from the Sixth Corps, including the Vermont brigade, were brought up to help Hancock hold his position in the Mule Shoe. Once again, the Vermonters found themselves in the middle of another difficult engagement. The brigade, with ten Norwich men in its ranks, was originally slated to proceed with the rest of the division to the West Angle. Hancock, however, had it dispatched to assist Francis Barlow's division, which was struggling on the eastern face of the Mule Shoe. The Vermonters were unable to contribute much in that sector, and an hour or so later were recalled to a position between the East and West Angles at the tip of the Mule Shoe, where heavy Southern counterattacks were threatening to break apart Hancock's line. There the Green Mountain boys occupied some 300 yards of the defensive works and assisted in repelling the Confederate assaults.

An after-action report filed on the brigade's behalf by Colonel Grant recorded what the Norwich alumni faced during this, the war's worst day of fighting. The enemy's "most desperate efforts were being made at a point near the center of the Sixth Corps, usually known as the Angle, to which point from the left we held the rebel works and from which to the right the enemy held them." Colonel Seaver arrived soon thereafter "with the balance of the brigade and it was all put into the engagement except the Sixth Regiment, which was held in reserve in the rear of a swell of ground." It was obvious that this "was the key-point to both armies and the fighting was of the most desperate and determined character. This point held and the whole line of works must necessarily fall into the hands of the victorious party. It was emphatically a hand-to-hand fight."

The most vicious hand-to-hand combat followed, and "Scores were shot down within a few feet of the death-dealing muskets. A breast-work of logs and earth separated the combatants. Our men would reach over the breast-works and discharge their muskets in the very face of the enemy." Soldiers fighting with rifles was only part of the story. "Some men clubbed their muskets and in some instances used [wood] clubs and rails." Others reached the point where they had had enough, and "several times during the engagement those who occupied the other side of the works, finding escape impossible, would raise the white flag and when our fire slackened would jump over the works and give themselves up." The battle raged all day in the foul weather and continued into the night. "In this way the brigade was engaged for over eight hours," wrote Colonel Grant, "when it was relieved and marched to the rear. In this engagement our loss was very heavy, but the point was held and the whole line of rebel works fell into our hands. The slaughter of the enemy was terrible. The sight the next day was repulsive and sickening indeed."[48]

The view from among the Vermont Brigade's enlisted men was similarly bleak. One soldier called it "the most singular and obstinate fighting that I have ever seen during the war, or ever heard or dreamed of in my life." He recalled how, after the first Union successes, "the enemy rallied and regained all but the first line of works and in one place they got a portion of that. The rebels were on one side of the breastwork and we on the other." It is hard to imagine a more personal combat scenario. "We could touch their guns with ours. They would load, jump up and fire into us and we did the same to them. Almost every shot that was made took effect." Extreme gallantry, or temporary insanity, took hold of individual soldiers. "Some of our boys would jump clear up on to the breastwork and fire, then down, reload and fire again, until they were themselves picked off. . . .This firing was kept up all day and until five o'clock the next morning."

The following morning, when the Army of the Potomac had finally secured the Bloody Angle, Pvt. Wilbur Fisk "visited the place

. . .and though I have seen horrid scenes since this war commenced, I never saw anything half so bad as that." Some Vermonters "lay piled one on top of another, nearly all shot through the head. There were many among them that I knew well, five from my own company. On the rebel side it was worse than on ours." Looking down from the rampart into the enemy trench, Fisk recalled "the men were piled four or five deep, some of whom were still alive. I turned away from that place, glad to escape such a terrible, sickening sight." The literate young Vermonter concluded his description of the hellish field by writing, "I have sometimes hoped, that if I must die while I am a soldier, I should prefer to die on the battle-field, but after looking at such a scene, one cannot help turning away and saying, any death but that."[49]

Dozens of other Norwich men took part in the fight near the Bloody Angle. While carrying dispatches and helping control the troops in the confusion of the battle, just as he had at Gettysburg in the maelstrom of the Wheatfield, Capt. Thomas W. Eayre's (Class of '61) luck ran out, and he was shot through the heart and killed. Horatio Wright (Class of '37), commanding the Sixth Corps for only the fourth day since Sedgwick's death, demonstrated commendable personal courage after he was "struck by a piece of shell which threw him backward several feet; though greatly shaken, he insisted on remaining at the front to the close." Before the fight ended, all eight brigades of Wright's first and second divisions had been fed into the fight in and around the Bloody Angle.[50]

One of Wright's supporting units was the 95th Pennsylvania, in which Sgt. Maj. John S. Carpenter (Class of '48) served. According to one of its members, "It was not long before we reached an angle of works constructed with great skill. . . .in our front an abatis had been arranged consisting of limbs and branches interwoven into one another, forming footlocks of the most dangerous character." The initial momentum of the 95th's attack carried it up and over "the [enemy] works. . .many never to return. At this moment Lee's strong line of battle, hastily selected for the work of retrieving ill fortune, appeared through the rain, mist and smoke. We received their bolts, losing nearly one hundred of our gallant 95th." "Regardless of the heavy volleys of the enemy that were thinning our ranks," continued the witness, "we stuck to the position and returned fire." The terrible fighting conditions deteriorated further, as "the smoke, which was dense at first, was intensified by each discharge of artillery. . .but we kept up the fire in the supposed direction of the enemy. . .raising their usual yell, they charged gallantly up to the very muzzles of our pieces and reoccupied the Angle."[51]

While the drama at the Bloody Angle was unfolding, dozens of Norwich men fought on other parts of the field. For example, unsuccessful Federal supporting attacks were taking place at Laurel Hill. There, 1st Lt. Francis E. Stimpson (Class of '58), 17th United States Infantry, who had been in every battle of his regiment since the summer of 1862, fought his last fight when he fell mortally wounded. The intensity of the fighting at Laurel Hill on May 12 was confirmed by an Iron Brigade veteran, who later declared the Spotsylvania fight was "the most terrible twenty-four hours of our service in the war." To the right of the Union line at Laurel Hill fought the 32nd Massachusetts, in which Capt. Charles Bowers (Class of '52) served. The Bay Staters turned in a solid effort but were slaughtered in the attempt. The 32nd lost 103 killed and wounded out of the 190 men who assaulted the Confederate position—the greatest loss in proportion to numbers engaged it suffered in the war. "As the line of battle started," recalled the regiment's historian, "it overran the picket line [and] dashed down the little depression in their front, over the next rise of ground." The regiment's easy initial success was deceiving, for "at the foot of Laurel Hill the men, whose momentum had carried them thus far, faltered under the terrible fire and laid down within a short distance of the enemy's line of works." The soldiers were trapped. "Here the ground did not cover the left of the Regiment and while Colonel Stephenson was trying to draw his left under shelter, he saw the regiment on his right had broken and was falling back in great disorder and at once ordered the men to save themselves." The worse was yet to come, for while "the advance had been disastrous. . .as usual the retreat was far more so. In the 32nd five bearers fell before the colors reached the old position behind our works . . . .and. . . .less than thirty minutes had elapsed." Nothing had been accomplished to compensate for the loss. Later in the day, the last of the Sixth Corps units not yet engaged were called up and thrown against the eastern face of the salient. Colonel John Schall (Class of '55) of the 87th Pennsylvania led Brig. Gen. William Morris' brigade into the action (he had taken command on May 9 after Morris was wounded). His men struck the Mule Shoe and gained the outside of the entrenchments, but suffered heavily in the attempt.[52]

In the end, Hancock's grand and initially promising attack failed to break apart Lee's army, but the Northerners managed to hold their hard-won positions. During the early morning hours of May 13, Lee withdrew his exhausted veterans from the Mule Shoe to a new reserve line drawn across the base of the salient. The dawn that day brought with it Union soldiers-turned-tourists, who walked across the field to view the horrible aftermath of the previous day's fighting. "The sight the next day was repulsive and sickening, indeed," wrote Lewis Grant. "Behind their traverses and in the pits and holes they had dug for protection, the rebel dead were found piled upon each other." Enemy soldiers were still alive in the hellish pits. "Some of the wounded were almost entirely buried by the dead bodies of their companions that had fallen upon them. . . [and] many of the dead men were horribly mangled and the logs, trees and brush exhibited unmistakable signs of a fearful conflict. The rebel account of a tree over a foot in diameter being cut off by minie-balls is attested to by several Union officers."[53]

The visual impact of what visitors to the Bloody Angle saw on May 13 remained with them forever. Norwich alumnus 1st Lt. Lemuel J. Abbott (Class of '64), now commanding Company K, 10th Vermont, penned one of the best accounts of what the field looked like after the battle. "No wonder from its present appearance this place has been christened the 'Bloody Angle' and the 'Slaughter Pen,'" he exclaimed. As he walked the lines he noted that "for several hundred yards—fully a half mile or more—in the edge of the heavy oak forest of immense trees skirting an open field, enemy's works are faultlessly strong of large oak logs and dirt shoulder high with traverses fifty feet back every sixty feet or so." Looking over the rampart Abbott saw an earthwork "filled with dead and wounded where they fell, several deep nearly to the top in front, extending for forty feet more or less back gradually sloping from front to rear, to one deep before the ground can be seen. The dead as a whole as they lie in their works are like an immense wedge with its head towards the works." The picture Abbott's mind absorbed was mindboggling to observe. "Think of such a mass of dead! Hundreds and hundreds piled top of each other! . . . .two more complete dead lines of battle about one hundred feet apart the dead bodies lying where the men fell in line of battle shot dead in their tracks. The lines are perfectly defined by dead men so close they touch each other." Abbott's senses were assaulted by the human gruel spread before him:

> Many of the bodies have turned black, the stench is terrible and the sight shocking beyond description. I saw several wounded men in the breastworks buried under their dead, just move a hand a little as it stuck up through the interstices above the dead bodies that buried the live ones otherwise completely from sight. Imagine such a sight if one can! It is indescribable! It was sickening, distressing and shocking to look upon! But, above all, think if one can of the feelings of the brave men who regiment after regiment, were marched up in line of battle time and again for several days to fight with such a sight confronting them! Could anything in Hades be worse?[54]

The casualty lists sustained Abbott's conclusion that even Hell could not have been worse than Spotsylvania. The Army of the Potomac had lost another 18,000 men from all causes, elevating the total since crossing the Rapidan to more than 35,000. The Army of Northern Virginia had also lost heavily, and Spotsylvania bled away another 11,000 more men it could ill-afford to lose. Total Confederate losses over the same period numbered 23,000.

While fighting continued sporadically along the Spotsylvania lines, badly need Federal reinforcements began to arrive. While Lee could expect little help, quality soldiers were still available to augment the Army of the Potomac. The spit and polish "heavies" were joining the front line troops. The conversion of heavy artillery regiments to infantry, which averaged some 1,800 men per regiment and were as large as many of the old brigades, was very popular with the army's combat veterans. For example, as the 1st Massachusetts Heavy Artillery Regiment passed through Fredericksburg on its way to the front, it was watched by recent casualties from the Army of the Potomac's fight in the Wilderness. A wounded man shouted out, "What Regiment is that?" The answer was yelled back, "1st Mass. H. A." "For God sake," came the reply, "how many 1st Mass. regiments are there? One has just gone along; here's another and another one has been down here with us 3 years."[55]

Numerous Norwich alumni crossed the Rapidan River with their "infantry" units to reinforce the Army of the Potomac. Among them were: Majs. (later Col.) James Hubbard (Class of '57), 2nd Connecticut Heavy Artillery, and Charles Hunsdon (Class of '51), Battery M, 1st Vermont Heavy Artillery; Capts. William T. Parker (Class of '59), 1st Maine Heavy Artillery, Hunt W. Burrows (Class of '56) and James Rice (Class of '49), Battery F, 1st Vermont Heavy Artillery, and William A. Treadwell (Class of '57), Battery G, 14th New York Heavy Artillery; 1st Lts. Ellis P. Walcott (Class of '64), Battery K, 8th New York Heavy Artillery, Charles Graham (Class of '30), 15th New York Heavy Artillery, Henry C. Baxter (Class of '66), Battery D, 1st Vermont Heavy Artillery; Lts. George A. Bailey (Class of '63) and Edward Parker (Class of '62), Battery B, 1st Vermont Heavy Artillery; and First Sgt. Sardis Birchard (Class of '64), Battery L, 1st Vermont Heavy Artillery. Although they had thus far avoided active field service, their late entry into the shooting war, the heavy losses they would suffer in the months ahead more than made up for it.[56]

The impact the 1st Vermont Heavy Artillery (also known as the 11th Vermont) had on the unit it joined was typical. The former artillerists were assigned to the battered Vermont Brigade on May 15, and their arrival doubled the Green Mountain Boys fighting strength. The "heavies" brought eight Norwich men with them, and the number of alumni in the Old Brigade's ranks increased to 18, despite the casualties suffered previously in the Wilderness and around Spotsylvania. Lewis Grant's after-action report for the Spotsylvania Campaign makes clear that the 1st Vermont Heavy Artillery and the alumni in its ranks earned a place among the veteran regiments. "Special mention ought to be made of the officers and men of the Eleventh Vermont for their gallant bearing in the charge [at Spotsylvania] of May 18," he wrote. "This was the first time they had been under fire, but they exhibited the coolness and noble bearing of Vermonters and fairly stood by the side of the veteran regiments of the old brigade."[57]

Five of the large new regiments were used to form an entire new division in Hancock's Second Corps. These units were the 1st Maine Heavy Artillery, and the 2nd, 7th and 8th New York Heavy Artillery. The Maine unit would finish the war with the most battle deaths of any Union artillery regiment, even though it served in combat for less than one year. In its maiden action at Harris' Farm on May 19, another Norwich alumnus, Capt. William T. Parker (Class of '59), commanding Battery L, was killed.[58]

Another artilleryman who served with the army during the Overland Campaign and who is deserving of mention is Col. Henry S. Burton (Class of '37), 5th United States Artillery. Burton was placed in charge of the Army of the Potomac's artillery reserve and also acted as General Meade's inspector of artillery. When the decision was made to disband the army's artillery reserve during the Spotsylvania Campaign, Burton was reassigned to the army staff, and would later distinguish himself in command of the Army of the Potomac's siege artillery during the Petersburg operations.[59]

As fighting sputtered to a close at Spotsylvania, Grant doggedly stuck to his master plan despite steadily mounting losses among his best troops. Lee, conversely, had lost the initiative and was forced to respond to Grant's advances. Through careful planning and good reconnaissance, Lee was able to keep Grant on the outside of a giant circle that was slowly turning toward the James River—and Richmond. The next major clash of arms took place about twenty-five miles north of Richmond along the North Anna River from May 21-26. There, Lee placed his army in a strong position behind the river in the form of a giant "V" with the point near the center of the line behind Ox Ford. Any attempt Grant could make to cross the river could be met with a concentration of force via interior lines.[60]

As the two armies sparred along the banks, the first in a series of engagements erupted on May 23 on the left (east) of the Federal lines along the Telegraph Road when Hancock's Second Corps moved on the army's left flank to seize the Chesterfield Bridge. After a sharp fight, the Federals managed to capture an advance set of works on the north bank of the river. First Lt. Joseph S. Little (Class of '56) commanded Company A, the 93rd New York's color company in David Birney's brigade. The Norwich alumnus led the regiment's charge across the bridge under a severe enemy fire. Somehow Lieutenant Little and his comrades almost made it to far bank, driving back the Confederates before they could burn it. At the moment of victory Little fell with a mangled right leg and the Federals were driven back. He was taken to the rear, where the broken limb was amputated, and discharged for wounds on September 23, 1864. "No finer man nor braver officer ever drew a sword," wrote another member of the regimental color guard. As luck would have it, Little was the only officer in the regiment wounded in the fight for the Chesterfield Bridge. Another Union effort by Warren's Fifth Corps on the Federal right flank at Jericho Mills managed to cross the river and move south one-half mile before being met by a series of counterattacks by A. P. Hill's Confederates. Grant's army was slowly pressing up against Lee's inverted V-shaped lines.[61]

The next day at Ox Ford, the center of the line, Ambrose Burnside's Ninth Corps, was ordered to probe for weaknesses. Just south of the river, Brig. Gen. James H. Ledlie's brigade of Maj. Gen Thomas L. Crittenden's First Division paid the price for Ledlie's disastrous habit of acquiring battle courage from a liquor bottle. Ledlie's brigade contained several fine regiments, including the 35th, 56th, 57th and 59th Massachusetts, and the 4th and 10th United States Infantry. It also held four Norwich men: Col. Jacob P. Gould (Class of '49) and Capt. George W. Field (Class of '60) both of the 59th Massachusetts; Capt. Robert J. Cowdin (Class of '56), 56th Massachusetts; and Capt. Albert W. Cooke (Class of '69), 57th Massachusetts. Contrary to instructions from his division commander, Ledlie ordered his soldiers to launch a suicidal frontal assault into heavily fortified and geographically dominating enemy defensive positions. The brigade advanced gallantly in line at the common step as watching Confederate defenders yelled, "Come on Yank! Come on to Richmond!" A climactic thunderstorm broke above the attackers as they fell, butchered by the score before guns wielded by Floridians and Mississippians. The 57th

Massachusetts alone left 74 men on the field, while the 56th Massachusetts saw another 46 men fall. The Regulars fared about as badly, with the 4th United States Infantry losing 41 of 150 men engaged. Ledlie somehow avoided being disciplined and was permitted to continue in command.[62]

Fortunately for all Federals concerned, fiascoes such as the one orchestrated by Ledlie at Ox Ford did not occur with regularity. In fact, even though the recent campaigns had seen more steady combat than at any time in the war, more days involved marching than fighting. First Lieutenant John B. Thompson (Class of '61), 19th Massachusetts—who had disappeared for some time during the fighting at Spotsylvania, causing his associates to believe he had been killed—wrote about the tough marches in the Virginia heat and dust, and noted how the weather and fatigue, in addition to bullets, knocked men from the ranks. On May 24, the Bay Staters "crossed the River during the forenoon. . . .without opposition and after lying in line of battle during the middle of the day the Regt was ordered out as skirmishers." According to Thompson, the regiment moved "by the left flank for some distance [and] advanced immediately through the grounds of the Dawson Mansion crossing an open field where we engaged the enemy's skirmishers driving them over their works. The Regiment occupied these for two hours when they were flanked by the [enemy] but repulsed them with great effect. During the day 9 men were prostrated by Coup-de-Soliel [sun stroke]." Another routine day had come to a close.[63]

All of these relatively minor engagements enriched the casualty rosters and led to the dusty crossroads hamlet of Cold Harbor. Unable to crack through Lee's defenses at North Anna and realizing the brilliance of the Confederate position there, Grant pulled out on the night of May 26 in a fresh attempt to flank his opponent. Lee anticipated a Federal move west to cut the Confederates off from the Shenandoah Valley, but Grant surprised him with a march southeastward toward the Pamunkey River. The armies were now marching on familiar terrain, for much of the ground over which they tramped had been fought over during the Peninsula Campaign of 1862 and the Seven Days' Battles. As the Army of the Potomac inched its way south and east, its main base of supply was shifted from Aquia Harbor to City Point on the James River, an important logistical site captured by Ben Butler at the start of his ill-fated Bermuda Hundred Campaign. Henceforth adequate supplies were less of a problem for the Federals.

Despite the horrendous casualties he had suffered, Grant was pleased with the progress of the campaign and reported as much on May 26 to President Lincoln. "Lee is really whipped," he wrote. "I may be mistaken, but I feel that our success over Lee's army is already assured." Between May 27 and May 31, the Federal Army successfully forced a number of streams, fought a number of small engagements, and drew ever closer to the Confederate capital. By June 1, both sides were engaged in a race to seize the crossroads site at Cold Harbor. At least 69 Norwich men served with the army during this phase of the campaign, which culminated in one of the most deadly assaults in military history. Writing of that affair after the war, Ulysses S. Grant later acknowledged, "I have always regretted that the last assault at Cold Harbor was ever made." Assuredly, the troops felt the same way, for they paid a heavy price trying to break through the most formidable defenses yet seen by Union troops.[64]

On May 31, Union Cavalry under George A. Custer and Wesley Merritt tried to wrest control of the road junction at Cold Harbor from Fitzhugh Lee's Confederate horsemen, while both armies raced their infantry toward the scene. Recent reinforcements for Lee's army in the form of Robert Hoke's Southern infantrymen reached Cold Harbor first, but twice assaults were thrown back by the tenacious Federal cavalrymen. Norwich alumnus and Sixth Corps leader Horatio G. Wright conducted a grueling night march around the rear of the Union Army to relieve the fought-out troopers. Sedgwick's old "foot cavalry" trudged through the sweltering heat and dust, their lead elements tramping into sight about 9:00 a.m. on June 1. Additional Confederate attacks to oust the Federals from their defenses were equally unsuccessful, and the Cold Harbor crossroads remained firmly in Union hands.[65]

As the Sixth Corps and elements of William F. Smith's Eighteenth Corps (recently arrived from Butler's Army of the James) reached the Cold Harbor area, Grant intended to carry the

Confederate defenses as soon as possible and prevent the enemy from establishing a firm defensive line as they had at Spotsylvania. Confusion within the Eighteenth Corps as to its route of march, combined with extreme heat and poor roads, delayed Smith until the afternoon of June 1. By the time Federal attack plans were prepared, Lee had his army dug in and ready to receive an assault. Late that afternoon, elements of the Sixth and Eighteenth Corps attacked and successfully carried a few outer segments of the Southern line. On other parts of the front, however, attacks were repulsed with heavy losses—especially where Union troops ran into complex and formidable earthworks and obstructions. Grant was again faced with the unenviable task of admitting a narrow failure and extricating his army from Lee's front. His choices were as they had always been: move around either flank or, by sheer weight of numbers, attempt to break through Lee's lines and defeat him piecemeal thereafter. Believing his enemy to be nearing the point of utter exhaustion, Grant embraced the latter option.[66]

Norwich men had the misfortune of being heavily represented in all aspects of the Cold Harbor battles. Of the Sixth Corps June 1 afternoon attack, the 10th Vermont's First Lt. Lemuel Abbott (Class of '64), Company B, recorded: "our brigade soon got in motion and advanced rapidly in unbroken lines. . . .The fact is we had no support either in rear or to our right and were in a precarious situation until drawn back in continuous line of battle with the rest of the assaulting line." The day witnessed Abbott's first attempt at leading his company in battle. "It was a determined charge. . . through the woods and swamp," he remembered, and "my first experience as Company Commander in an assault and it did seem queer to step in front of my men to lead them, one of if not the youngest among them." He recalled proudly, "I was on my mettle and had I known a solid shot would have cut me in part the next second, pride would have kept me up to the rack, for the Company Commanders of the Tenth Vermont did not follow but led their men in battle."[67]

The 2nd Connecticut Heavy Artillery, of Emory Upton's Second Brigade (David A. Russell's First Division, Sixth Corps), underwent its baptism of fire in the same assault. Major James Hubbard (Class of '57) commanded a battalion in the regiment of "heavies" as it advanced toward the smoking line of entrenchments in the distance. Upton, who had earned a general's star for his spectacular tactical display on May 10, described the unit's performance in his after-action report: "At 5 p.m. . . .The Second Connecticut Artillery, under Colonel Kellogg [who was killed in the attack], was drawn up in column by battalion, forming the front three lines. . . .The Second Connecticut, anxious to prove its courage, moved to the assault in beautiful order." As the advance continued, the men crossed "an open field [and] entered a pine wood, passed down a gentle declivity and up a slight ascent. Here the charge was checked." Seventy feet in front of the works "the trees had been felled, interlocking with each other and barring all farther advance. Two paths, several yards apart and wide enough for 4 men to march abreast led through the obstructions." Despite these obstacles, "Up these to the foot of the works the brave men rushed, but were swept away by a converging fire." The battle raged in this contested space "without support on either flank, the Second Connecticut fought until 3 a.m., when the enemy fell back to a second line of works. . . .The loss of the Second Connecticut was 53 killed, 187 wounded, 146 missing; total 386."

This heavy price of June 1 was merely a down payment on what was to come over the next twelve days at Cold Harbor. Upton failed to mention in his report that the 1,400-man regiment of "heavies" had advanced to the attack with bayonets fixed and uncapped muskets. When the final loss was tallied, the regiment lost 85 killed, 221 wounded and 19 missing, most of whom could have been tabulated in either of the former categories. During the retreat, the dispirited men were rallied by the courageous Upton. Grabbing a musket, he yelled "Men of Connecticut, stand by me!" Norwich's Maj. James Hubbard, as new to combat as the men he commanded, reported to Upton that his soldiers were almost out of ammunition and unable to move the Confederates. Upton screamed at him, "If they come there, catch them on your bayonets and pitch them over your heads!" It was a lesson Hubbard would remember. For a few yards of dirt, the Sixth and Eighteenth Corps lost another 2,300 men; Lee's losses are unknown.[68]

Grant planned to launch another even larger general assault on the morning of June 2, but once again coordination was lacking.

Hancock's Second Corps temporarily lost its way during a night march, and the attack had to be postponed until the following morning, June 3. Meanwhile the enemy labored to improve their defenses. One participant remembered how "This entrenched line of the enemy was on a low hill that was quite long, ending on the right, or south, on the Chickahominy swamps, making it quite impossible to turn the position without crossing the river." Geography did indeed favor the defenders, as "On the north the hill or ridge was broken by ravines. On the east, towards Cold Harbor, it was quite a gradual slope." In addition, "along the crest of the hill was a sunken road which ran along the front of their breastworks and this made a natural defense which was utilized by the enemy." On the left wing and towards the center the terrain was "more level and though broken up by streams and swamps, were not as capable of defense. Up the slope of Watt's Hill, over the ravines and sides on the north and east, were to move the assaulting forces." Looking out toward the Confederate entrenchments through the early morning haze on June 3, the men (if not their general officers or overall commander) realized they faced an impossible task.[69]

Prior to the attack, the 57th Massachusetts' Company B commander, Cpt. Albert W. Cooke (Class of '69), noticed some strange things transpiring amongst his men. "Massachusetts men [who] had no way of knowing their fate. . .[said] their prayers and. . . wrote what many believed were their last letters home," he remembered. Fearing their loved ones would never know their fate, "Most pinned pieces of papers to their coats that had their names and regiments written on them, so that their bodies could be identified when they were killed, as they were sure they would be." Nevertheless, when the order to advance came, as they had done before and would do again, they moved out to attack the enemy. To a British analyst, the actions of the Union troops before and during the assault were indicative of something special. "A close study of the Civil War fails to reveal a moment in the history of the Union volunteer at which his courage more nearly approaches the sublime."[70]

With a great shout the general assault began about 4:30 a.m. In many areas the attack was shot to pieces and over within a handful of minutes, the men mowed down by the thousands. Most of the Confederate defenders did not believe that the main attack had been launched, so effective was their fire. In a single half hour the Army of the Potomac suffered 7,000 casualties, primarily in the Second and Sixth Corps. The historian for the latter corps recalled with no little bitterness that the attack's "management would have shamed a cadet in his first year at West Point." As it had done since the early days of the war, Norwich paid its share of the blood bounty.[71]

All along the front, the story was the same. In Hancock's Second Corps, which suffered heavily that day, Capt. David C. Beattie's (Class of '47) 164th New York Zouaves of the "Irish Legion" somehow managed to capture a segment of the Confederate breastworks before their colonel was killed and the regiment was forced back across the killing zone. A survivor of the charge recounted how "one officer alone, the colonel of the 164th New York [Col. James P. McMahon], seizing the colors of his regiment from the dying color-bearer as he fell, succeeded in reaching the parapet of the enemy's main works, where he planted his colors and fell dead near the ditch, bleeding from many wounds." Alumnus Beattie, one of the few to reach the Rebel position with his gallant commander, fell wounded and was captured there. He was later released and was awarded a brevet majority for his gallantry in the action.[72]

For many, the sudden and bloody shock of the Cold Harbor repulse numbed the senses. In the Fifth Corps, the report filed by Charles Bowers (Class of '52), 32nd Massachusetts, laconically reported the charge as follows: "June 3—Formed line of battle and charged across an open field under a heavy fire of musketry and canister. Took and held the position designed for the regiment, with a loss of 10 killed and 33 wounded."[73]

On the Sixth Corps front, the Vermont Brigade's Col. Thomas O. Seaver (Class of '59) once again deployed his regiment as skirmishers and led the brigade's advance. As Henry Houghton remembered it, they "advanced under terrific fire from artillery and musketry until within five hundred yards of their works and finding it impossible to advance farther we halted and began to dig pits with our bayonets, cups and plates and held our position until night and during the night entrenched our position." The fate of the Union troops and its Norwich men at Cold Harbor is best summed up by the contemporary diary entry of 1st Lt. Lemuel A. Abbott (Class of '64), commanding Company B, 10th Vermont: "The. . . Sixth Corps. . .were ordered to charge at 4 o'clock a.m. and not to fire a shot until we got on to the enemy's works, but the charge was not a success. We never even reached the enemy's works." As Abbott and his men leaped from their trenches, "The attack commenced on the right and ran along the line until it reached the left. We advanced under a murderous fire in our front from the enemy's artillery, sharpshooters and when in range of its main line of battle were simply slaughtered."[74]

Abbott's account also mentions the actions of the 87th Pennsylvania's commander, Col. John W. Schall (Class of '55), who had been relieved from brigade command on May 13 when another colonel superior in rank returned to the unit. "Colonel Schall, who was wounded in the arm in the assault of June first and carried it in a sling in the fight to-day, was again wounded in the same arm." Despite Schall's wound, "He is not a man to take advantage of a wound not totally disabling him to get out of a fight, evidently." Schall's actions in refusing to leave the field while wounded earned him a citation for bravery. When the 87th Pennsylvania mustered out upon completing its three-year enlistment that October, Brig. Gen. James B. Ricketts, Schall's division commander, wrote:

Colonel:

Your time having expired with that of your gallant regiment, I cannot part with you without some expression of my high appreciation of your faithful services. Always zealous and reliable, you have shown the best quality of a soldier, which would bring certain promotion, had you determined to remain in the corps, which you have ornamented by your distinguished conduct throughout the arduous summer campaign, since crossing the Rapidan in May last.

I particularly recall your gallant conduct at Cold Harbor while commanding a brigade and wounded, you nobly refused to leave the field and in the Valley where you shared in our glorious victories at Opequon and Fisher's Hill.

I part with regret from so good a soldier and wish you every success in your future life. Very sincerely your friend,

> James B. Ricketts
> Brigadier General Volunteers and Major, 1st
> United States Artillery,
> commanding 3rd Division 6th Army Corps.[75]

The Ninth Corps, Col. Edwin Schall (Class of '56), John Schall's cousin, was also present on June 3. Schall had survived the desperate charge across Burnside Bridge at Antietam and many other battles since. At Cold Harbor he commanded the 51st Pennsylvania for the last time. When the order to charge reached him, remembered one of the participants, "It was immediately done by the whole charging party. The 51st, advancing with bayonets fixed at double-quick, was met by the enemy, who were well prepared to receive a charge." The 51st continued moving forward as the Confederates "poured volley after volley into the regiment. . .until an unpropitious bullet entered the neck of Col. Edwin Schall, killing him instantly; and at the same time one struck Lieut. Isaac Fizone, of Co. D, killing him instantly also. It is generally believed the one ball killed them both."[76]

Another Norwich alumnus who was counted as a casualty that day was Capt. George T. Carter (Class of '54), commander of Company I, 2nd New Hampshire (Second Brigade, Second Division, Eighteenth Corps). Carter suffered his third wound of the war that morning shortly after the attack began. A bullet struck close to his head and threw up a cloud of dirt. "Carter's got it!" exclaimed a comrade. "No, I guess not!" replied Carter, who raised his head and immediately suffered a serious wound when a bullet struck it. Captain Robert J. Cowdin (Class of '56), Company E, 56th Massachusetts, ended his three years of hard service when he was killed in action while in command of the First Division's (Ninth Corps) pickets. Cowdin's body lay for days in the no-man's land between the lines and was never recovered. Norwich alumnus Lt. John B. Thompson (Class of '61), Company K, 19th

Massachusetts, a veteran of every Second Corps battle since the Peninsula Campaign, fell at the head of his company. His unit's actions in the one-sided slaughter were described by one of its officers: "As daylight came on, turned out formed for the charge and started on the double quick, over two lines of works, across the fields which were swept by a terrible fire of grape and canister from the enemy batteries while the musketry rolled terribly." As in other Union units, "The terrible fire of the Rebs broke our ranks and we were obliged to halt under the brow of the hill where we passed up rails from a fence near by and piled them up, with dippers and plates threw up dirt making a good line of works." As the hours wore on, "Rebel Sharpshooters were firing at any stray soldiers moving across the field. . . [and] Lieut. Thompson of Co. K [was] killed."[77]

Losses for both sides are difficult to know with any precision. Federal casualties were probably about 7,000 (killed, wounded, and captured), while Lee's were probably around 1,500. Of all the battles of the war, Norwich alumni probably suffered their greatest battle loss and bore their heaviest burden for the preservation of the Republic at Cold Harbor. At least nine Norwich men were killed in action, wounded, or captured there (13.0% of all Norwich alumni engaged). The killed included: Col. Edwin Schall (Class of '56) 51st Pennsylvania; Maj. Richard B. Crandall (Class of '62) 6th Vermont; Capt. Robert J. Cowdin (Class of '56) 56th Massachusetts; and 1st Lt. John B. Thompson (Class of '61), 19th Massachusetts. Wounded included: Col. John W. Schall (Class of '55) 87th Pennsylvania; Capt. David C. Beattie (Class of '47) 164th New York (also captured); Capt. George T. Carter (Class of '54) 2nd New Hampshire; Capt. Henry H. Hale (Class of '61), 19th Massachusetts (detailed to staff of Second Brigade, Second Division, Second Corps); and Pvt. Albert L. Wadhams (Class of '44), 11th Connecticut. The fields of Cold Harbor are indeed moistened with the blood of Norwich alumni, and somewhere on that battlefield today, in an unknown grave, sleeps Robert J. Cowdin.[78]

The agony and terror of the early morning June 3 attack at Cold Harbor continued long after its conclusion. The combatants kept up a heavy fire across no-man's land while both armies continued to improve their defenses—all the while listening to the pleadings of the thousands of wounded. Grant, unfortunately, refused to call a truce to recover the unfortunates, for to do so was to admit defeat. By the time he acquiesced and did so four days later, most of the poor men had died or were beyond salvation. "The morning of the 4th found us close to the enemy's works," reported an officer with the 19th Massachusetts, which had lost Norwich alumnus 1st Lt. John B. Thompson the previous day. "The men during the night [threw] up some works which served barely to protect them. The enemy's Sharp Shooters did great execution." Each day's routine was broken by some memorable incident. "On the 7th a truce was held and the evening & night of that day was spent quietly. On the 5th and 6th lost two men by the enemy's Sharp Shooters." The short armistice ended too quickly. "The truce which was commenced on the 7th was kept up until the morning of the 9th, when firing was resumed with spirit, the Regt. losing 6 men wounded."[79]

As the Army of the Potomac spent its last days at Cold Harbor, a large cavalry action at Trevilian Station got underway. Philip Sheridan, the Army of the Potomac's cavalry chief, had been given a free hand with his troopers on May 8, and since that time life had become miserable for Lee's horsemen. Three days later on May 11, Jeb Stuart fell mortally wounded when one of George Custer's Michigan troopers shot him in the fight at Yellow Tavern; he died the following day in Richmond. Stuart was succeeded by the able Wade Hampton, who could do little to stem the Federal cavalry's increasing dominance. While Grant and Lee confronted each other at Cold Harbor, Sheridan's 6,000 cavalry set off on another raid, this time northwestward to join Maj. Gen. David Hunter in the Shenandoah Valley and to destroy the Virginia Central Railroad. Wade Hampton and his 5,000 men rode after Sheridan in pursuit. The result was one of the largest cavalry battles of the war at Trevilian Station on June 11-12, 1864. The fight was a jumbled confusion of slashing and shooting horsemen, flanking attacks, and a climactic but unsuccessful Confederate mounted assault that almost split open Sheridan's exhausted battle line. Tactically the fight ended in a draw, but Hampton had managed to prevent Sheridan from seriously damaging the railroad or joining Hunter; Hampton, on the other hand, had been unavailable to Lee for a critical phase of the campaign.[80]

A Norwich alumnus played an important role at Trevilian Station with ramifications even the most farsighted individual could not have foreseen. First Lt. Edward B. Williston (Class of '56), commanded Battery D, 2nd United States Artillery, and his gallant actions garnered him a Congressional Medal of Honor. In fact, Williston's impressive exploits were brought to the personal attention of President Harry B. Truman nearly a century later. Truman had an intense interest in the Medal of Honor, and once stated he would rather have won the medal than be President of the United States. Major General Harry H. Vaughan, the President's personal military aide, was searching through Medal of Honor files for a Civil War artilleryman Truman could relate to, when he came upon Williston's citation. "Eureka! Here it is!" exclaimed Vaughan. Truman, like Williston, had also commanded a Battery D in combat. Extracts from the recommendation for the Norwich alumnus' award, prepared by Brig. Gen. Wesley Merritt, are worth citing:

> I have the honor to recommend that Major E. B. Williston, 3rd United States Artillery, be awarded. . .a Medal of Honor for having specially distinguished himself at the action of Trevilian Station, Virginia, June 12, 1864. . . . In the crisis of the action at Trevilian, when my lines were being pressed by an overwhelming force of the enemy, Lieutenant Williston planted three guns of his battery in an exposed but favorable position for effective work; and then personally moved the fourth gun onto the skirmish line. Using double charges of canister he, by his individual efforts, greatly aided in resisting successfully the charges of an enemy on our front. The loss of the brigade, reduced at that time in strength, was twelve (12) officers killed and wounded and two hundred twenty-two (222) men. . . .Right gallantly did the battery come up in the midst of a heavy musketry fire, we being at that time so close to the enemy their shells all flew far over us. Planting three guns of the battery in his position, where it dealt the enemy heavy blows, Lieutenant Williston moved one of his brass 12-pounders onto the skirmish line. In fact, the line was moved to the front to allow him to get an eligible position, where he remained with his gun, in the face of the strengthened enemy (who advanced to its very muzzle), dealing death and destruction in their ranks with double loads of canister.[81]

First Lt. Edward B. Williston's actions on that field exemplified Norwich's motto: "I will try."

The aftermath of the Cold Harbor assaults was grim for both sides, but especially for the Army of the Potomac. Its commanders at all levels were finally realizing that the army was exhausted to the point of burn out. In any war the boldest and bravest men always bear the greatest risks of injury, and it was no different in the spring of 1864. Since crossing the Rapidan in early May, the army had suffered casualties at the rate of 2,000 men per day. The result was that its veteran infrastructure had been ravaged. In Winfield Hancock's Second Corps, once viewed as the cream of the army, 5,092 men fell in the Wilderness, 5,457 at Spotsylvania, another 1,651 along the North Anna and Totopotomoy Creek, and 3,510 at Cold Harbor. In all, 15,710 of its best officers and men had been knocked out of action. Total losses for the Army of the Potomac since the beginning of the spring campaign essentially equaled the size of Lee's Army of Northern Virginia on May 5.

General Grant also seems to have drunk his fill of Lee's brand of warfare. Whatever Grant felt about his progress over the previous month, many of his contemporaries viewed his campaign as a failure. Lee's army had not been destroyed, nor had he been driven within the Richmond defenses. Ben Butler had not reached Richmond (or Petersburg) and had failed to seize the rail lines leading into the city. The country was in shock as cries of "Grant the butcher!" resounded in the press and from anti-war politicos. Despite these horrendous tribulations, neither Grant nor his men were willing to give up and withdraw. Morale, surprisingly, remained relatively good. Surviving veterans of McClellan's Peninsula Campaign of 1862 felt that, unlike then, they had not been defeated and were heading down the right avenue to bring the war to a conclusion. Neither Grant, his soldiers, nor President Lincoln had lost faith in ultimate victory. Indeed, Grant's unceasing hammering of Lee's Army of Northern Virginia was beginning to have an adverse effect on the Confederates. According to a Southern artillery officer, "by the time we reached Cold Harbor we had begun to understand what our new adversary meant and there, for the first time, I think the men in the ranks of the Army of Northern Virginia realized that the era of experimental campaigns against us was over; that Grant was not going to retreat. . . .and that the policy of pounding had begun and would continue until our strength should be utterly worn away."[82]

In the darkness on June 12, the Army of the Potomac slipped away from Cold Harbor, one corps at a time, in what would be Grant's finest strategic redeployment. Refusing to abandon the basic tenets of his original plan, the tenacious Federal commander put into execution a new flanking movement that completely fooled his opponent and decisively altered the strategic situation in the Eastern Theater. On June 14 Federal elements began crossing the James River on a specially-constructed pontoon bridge and heading for their new objective: the logistically important city of Petersburg, without which neither Richmond nor Lee's army could long survive. The city's defenses at this time were but lightly manned by some 2,500 regulars and militia. Although Grant ordered his two forward corps (Smith's Eighteenth and Hancock's Second) to assault the city's defenses, the effort was poorly executed and one of the conflict's finest opportunities for decisive victory slipped through the army's fingers. By the time Lee finally realized he had been outwitted, it was almost too late to save Petersburg. Confederate reinforcements were hurried south, however, and by the time Grant was able to launch his attacks in mid-June, they were handily repulsed. At least 90 Norwich men took part in these battles and the extended period of trench warfare which followed, the longest sustained operation of the war.[83]

As the Army of the Potomac's combat engineers struggled to build a 2,100 foot pontoon bridge, Maj. Gen. William F. "Baldy" Smith's Eighteenth Corps moved back through Bermuda Hundred on its way to fulfill Grant's mandate to seize Petersburg. By June 15, Smith was in position to seize the city. His advance towards Petersburg was led by the 89th New York, in which Lt. Edward H. Smith (Class of '45) served. The Eighteenth Corps had suffered heavily at Cold Harbor twelve days earlier, and Smith did not want a repeat performance outside Petersburg, which bristled with heavy defensive fortifications. As a result, he delayed the assault until he could personally complete a detailed reconnaissance. Precious hours were wasted before his men finally moved forward late in the day, and to everyone's surprise, they carried virtually every point they attacked. Rather than attacking in traditional battle lines and presenting a lucrative target for the defenders, the cautious though at times innovative Smith utilized a heavy line of skirmishers. The advance managed to overrun nearly three and a half miles of Petersburg's eastern defenses. Smith was to have had assistance from Winfield Hancock and his Second Corps, but Hancock misinterpreted his instructions and didn't offer any support.[84]

The Eighteenth Corps attack on June 15 included Capt. Charles O. Bradley (Class of '63) and his Company C, 13th New Hampshire Infantry (Second Brigade, First Division). The 13th had suffered heavily in the attack at Cold Harbor, where it lost 14 killed and 70 wounded. After Smith ordered his men forward, Bradley's regiment advanced and captured Petersburg's seemingly impregnable Battery 5. "The dirt walls rose above them 'some thirty or forty feet to the top of the parapet,' but the officers believed a determined charge would take the battery," recalled one New Hampshire soldier. Despite this obstacle, "the men scaled the sides 'on bayonets stuck in the sand, grasping grass and weeds to assist in climbing, striking their boots into the gravel.' No more than a dozen New Hampshire soldiers scrambled into the large Confederate fort." Once again, a bold bluff paid unexpected dividends when "They demanded the surrender of Capt. Nathaniel Sturdivant, commanding the artillery. . . .When he realized he lost his four guns and his men to so few Federals, Sturdivant exclaimed: 'Here are my guns double-shotted for infantry and all of us captured by a—Yankee skirmish line!" Not far from the Granite State men was Sgt. Maj. Franklin H. Walcott (Class of '64) and his 117th New York, which took part in the capture of Battery 6. The overrunning of these key points made it seem for a time that Petersburg would indeed fall to the Federals.[85]

The next several days were wasted by the Federals as poor staff work, confusing orders, languid execution, and incompetent leadership prevented a coordinated attack on the city. Meanwhile, large numbers of troops from both armies poured into the area. One of the disjointed and piecemeal Federal attacks made on June 17 included General Ledlie's Ninth Corps division. Ledlie, who had guided his men to slaughter at the North Anna while intoxicated, once again failed to personally command his troops as a result of imbibing alcohol. Colonel Jacob Parker Gould (Class of '49) filled in for the drunkard and gallantly commanded the First Division in its assault. Gould's attack offered a genuine opportunity for a Union breakthrough, and is described in a postwar paper presented to the Military Historical Society of Massachusetts: "After an hour or more spent lying in a ravine, awaiting the order and exposed to artillery fire all the time, the order to charge was given about six o'-clock." Gould and his men advanced in good order, and "with dashing courage crossed with a rush and without firing a shot, the two hundred yards separating them from the enemy's lines, the men in which had time only for one volley." Once again it seemed as though a potentially important victory was in offing, for Ledlie's men had driven away the defenders near the Shand House and had captured a substantial line of works. "The charge was perfectly successful," remembered one participant, but there were "no supports" to exploit the victory. "Hence, instead of fresh troops being marched in through this gap and taking the enemy's works in reverse to the right and left, the gallant, but disordered, division. . .was quietly allowed to remain, exposed to an enfilading fire from their right and to the ceaseless attempts of their enemy in their front to dislodge them." Gould and his men managed to hold on for several hours until "their ammunition gave out. Repeated efforts to obtain a fresh supply were made, but in vain." Finally, "about nine o'clock [p.m.] or later, the enemy, having received reinforcements in the shape of [Archibald] Gracie's Brigade from Bermuda Hundred, made a last and decisive attack and the gallant First Division of the Ninth Corps was driven out, suffering greatly in killed, wounded and prisoners."[86]

The small 17th Vermont, in which 1st Lt. William B. Burbank (Class of '55) served in Company E, also took part in the abortive Ninth Corps assault on June 17. After overrunning an important section of fortifications near the north of the Baxter Road, the 17th "moved noiselessly to and over the works in front and bayoneted all who attempted resistance." This successful bayonet attack was one of the rare documented instances in which the bayonet was actually used in hand-to-hand combat. The 17th numbered only 145 men at the time of the attack, and the unit's actions were cited by the Vermont Adjutant General: "the 17th Regiment," he noted, "after marching up a steep hill, charging impetuously forward, [drove] in the enemy's skirmishers and carried a strong line of earthworks, fully manned and capturing two guns, a caisson, six horses, seventy prisoners and the Colors and Adjutant of the 17th Tennessee. The officers and men of the regiment distinguished themselves for their gallantry in this charge and won high commendation."[87]

By June 18, both Grant and Lee were confronted with a strategic situation neither of them wanted: a siege. For Lee, being trapped within entrenchments meant a long and slow death by attrition, and his army had already been whittled down to about 50,000 men. Grant, on the other hand, was faced with the prospects of a protracted war and long casualty lists during an important election year.[88]

Some historians blame the Army of the Potomac's failure to capture Petersburg in mid-June on the "Cold Harbor Syndrome." The term was coined to describe the growing reluctance on the part of Federal commanders and their troops, in light of casualties suffered in Grant's spring campaign (particularly at Cold Harbor), to conduct determined assaults on prepared Confederate positions. Combat losses of key leaders since the crossing of the Rapidan River had reached unprecedented levels. An example from Hancock's Second Corps will suffice to demonstrate the extent of these losses: in only six weeks, the three brigades (comprised of twenty-one regiments) in John Gibbon's division had a total of 17 different brigade commanders and 40 different regimental commanders were wounded or killed. In the same period, the Second Corps lost 20 brigade commanders (killed, wounded, or missing). The cumulative result of these losses, coupled with the sheer physical exhaustion in the ranks, resulted in the ten-month siege of Petersburg.[89]

The reality of a large-scale siege, however, meant more fighting and more bloodshed. After the early failures to take Petersburg, on June 22 Grant made an attempt to stretch his lines west and break the the Weldon and Petersburg Railroad. The move was made by both the Second Corps (now under David Birney, since Hancock's old Gettysburg wound was giving him considerable trouble), and

General Horatio Wright's Sixth Corps. The two corps became separated in wooded terrain, however, and A. P. Hill's Third Corps sallied out and drove into the gap northeast of Globe Tavern and below the Jerusalem Plank Road, exploiting the advantage and inflicting about 3,000 casualties in the process. The 10th Vermont Infantry (Sixth Corps), with three alumni in its ranks, took part in the movement. First Lieutenant Lemuel A. Abbott (Class of '64) once again saw fit to comment on Col. John W. Schall's (Class of '55) actions as commander of the 87th Pennsylvania. Abbott recounted how his regiment and the Pennsylvanians "charged through the brush about two miles and captured another line of works without resistance." The attack stalled, however, and Abbott wrote about the "considerable confusion today (June 22). While on the skirmish line the Eighty-seventh Pennsylvania of our brigade came near being captured from the fact that for some unaccountable reason the picket line next on one of its flanks was withdrawn unknown to Colonel Schall." At this critical moment, "when the enemy crept through the opening and captured about a dozen men. . .seeing what was the matter, Colonel Schall, a splendid officer, took such action as was necessary and saved his regiment."[90]

Disaster struck Union forces and part of the Vermont Brigade the following day. As the Federals attempted to press forward to the Weldon rail line, William Mahone's Virginians launched a hard-hitting attack and inflicted heavy losses. Two Norwich men from the 1st Vermont Heavy Artillery were captured at the Battle of the Weldon Railroad: Lt. Edward B. Parker (Class of '62), Battery B, and First Sgt. Sardis Birchard (Class of '64), Battery L. There fate was not a glorious one. Birchard died of disease at Andersonville just eight weeks later on August 20 and is buried in grave number 6334. Lieutenant Parker managed to briefly escape his captors on October 5, 1864, only to be tracked down and badly mauled the following day by pursuing dogs. He died a week later at Columbia, South Carolina, on October 13.

A description of the horrible incident was provided by one of Parker's fellow escapees. "After leaving Branchville, Ga., the guards relaxed their vigilance somewhat and the opportunity presented itself for our escape, which we embraced and jumped from the cars."

The alarm was sounded and soon "the dogs of the neighborhood placed upon our track. . . .we resolved to reach the river, if possible, choosing death by drowning rather than by the dogs." To increase their chances of escape, the men decided to split up. As luck would have it, the dogs followed "Parker's track instead of mine, [and] thirteen bloodhounds attacked him. The horrible manner in which they tore the flesh from his limbs, his body and his arms, I cannot adequately describe." He was unable to fend off the dogs, and "With the flesh of his arms torn in shreds and the muscles of his body and limbs mangled and bleeding, he shouted: "Help me, I am being eaten up alive!" Turning back to help his friend "with the walking stick I had I could only drive off three or four of the dogs and by this time the others would be at him again." By this time, the Confederate pursuers caught up with the Union escapees. "Soon five men came up. . . .with their guns and clubs [they] had driven the dogs from Lieutenant Parker and having wrapped him in a blanket we carried him to the station near by and laid him down. From there we were taken to Columbia."

Once again in prison, the grievously wounded Parker "lingered for several days. . . .He wanted to say something but could not till just before he died, when it seemed as if all the pain had ceased and he looked up to me and said in a low whisper: 'Tell my mother I tried to do my duty. Tell—(one whom he hoped in a few months to call his wife) that in death I loved her." His friend recalled that "Lieutenant Parker's remains were buried by the rebels, just where I know not; but the soil which covers him is no longer rebel ground, but is under the authority of the flag for which he fought and for which he paid the full measure of devotion."[91]

Earlier in July 1864, while these Norwich men were wallowing in Southern prisons, the Sixth Corps, with 13 Norwich men in its ranks, was temporarily detached from the Army of the Potomac. Lee had dispatched Jubal Early and most of his corps to operate in the Shenandoah Valley in the hope he could inflict a defeat on the enemy there, draw troops away from Grant's army, and terrorize Washington, D.C. It was a desperate effort. By this time, the corps led by Norwich alumnus Horatio Wright was considered by many to be the army's best fighting and most reliable organization, and the Vermonters its best brigade. Washington officials were reeling in panic that the Rebels would reach the city before the Army of the Potomac's reinforcements could arrive. President Lincoln himself stood on the dock as a concerned onlooker when the first boat arrived on July 11. As the steamer pulled up, the president anxiously queried the initial man to step ashore: "What troops does the steamer bring?' 'It brings Major General Getty and his staff, but no troops,' was his reply. The careworn president turned away with evident disappointment, saying 'I do not care to see any major generals: I came here to see the Vermont Brigade.'" No finer compliment could have been paid to any combat unit than that statement from the nation's chief executive. Thankfully, Wright's men reached Washington as Early's exhausted Confederates approached its outer defenses. The Vermonters distinguished themselves the next day at Fort Stevens (where Lincoln was present), and the threat to the Federal capital came to an end.[92]

As the Army of the Potomac laid siege to Petersburg, and as Col. William S. Burton (Class of '37) moved his heavy siege pieces into position, Capt. Charles O. Bradley (Class of '63), Company C, 13th New Hampshire Infantry, prepared to go home. Bradley had endured a miserable war, and the 13th had recently suffered heavily in attacks at Cold Harbor and Petersburg (where he was wounded). In addition to the extended combat service he had seen with his regiment, Bradley had been seriously ill for much of the time. By late-June his doctors finally ordered him discharged. Further field service, the surgeons informed Bradley, would kill him. When he reluctantly departed his regiment, Bradley's farewell was marked by a moving tribute from his fellow officers. They described the alumnus as an "expert in drill, courageous in danger. . . firm and reliable in all places of trial and remarkable not only for his presence of mind in all places of trial, but also for his ability to provide almost instant measures of reliable action." He returned home carrying two Confederate combat banners captured by his regiment at Battery 5 in one of the first assaults on Petersburg, and presented them to the governor of New Hampshire on behalf of the 13th Regiment. After a surprisingly short recovery period, Bradley managed to rejoin the army as commander of Battery I,1st New Hampshire Heavy Artillery Regiment, on September 6, 1864. He finished the war on active service with his regiment in the defenses of Washington, and remained in the Regular Army after the end of the war.[93]

In addition to Charles Bradley, a large number of surviving veteran officers and men had begun to go home when the enlistments of their three-year regiments expired. These men felt they had done their part and were unwilling to monopolize the expression of patriotism which reenlistment implied; many stated they were ready to step aside to let others do their fair share. Among those lost to the Army of the Potomac at this time were the gallant Cols. Thomas O. Seaver (Class of '59) of the 3rd Vermont, and William W. Robinson (Class of '41) of the 7th Wisconsin, Iron Brigade.[94]

The trench warfare outside Petersburg and Richmond presaged what was to come in World War One. Miles upon miles of heavy fortifications linked with redoubts, covered ways, and obstructions scarred the once-verdant Virginia countryside. In between rested a barren no-man's land, a killing zone where the deadly sharpshooters plied their trade. The "siege" of Petersburg, however, was not a true siege, for the Confederate's were not completely encircled. While Lee's army was indeed largely pinned in place, most of the battles in the remaining months of the war occurred outside the main line of works when Grant swung elements of his army westward and Lee was forced to respond. Among these were the Weldon Railroad, Ream's Station, New Market Road, Deep Bottom, Chaffin's Farm, Poplar Springs Church, Boydton Plank Road, and the most famous of them all—which was ironically waged within the trench system—the "Battle of the Crater." Inexorably, the Union siege lines crept south and west, cutting vital roads and rail lines, while Lee desperately stretched his forces thinner to defend his logistical life lines.

Norwich men continued to excel—and die—in these now largely forgotten battles. Commanding Union artillery in front of Petersburg, Col. Henry S. Burton (Class of '37), was cited for his efforts and later earned a brevet as brigadier general. At the Second Battle of Deep Bottom on August 20, Lt. Col. Thomas A. Henderson (Class of '62), commanding the 7th New Hampshire Infantry, was mortally wounded when the artery in his hip was severed by a rifle ball during a Union assault; he bled to death within four hours. During an engagement at Chaffin's Farm not long thereafter, 1st Lt. William B. Burbank (Class of '64), 17th Vermont Infantry, distinguished himself when his regiment ran out of ammunition. He and another officer brought up an ammunition wagon and passed out the precious rounds under a severe fire, thus enabling the regiment to hold its position.[95]

While the army labored in front of Petersburg and Richmond that July, a mother took time out to remember her lost Norwich alumnus son. First Lieutenant Edward Stanley Abbott's (Class of '64) mother wrote his older brother, Maj. Henry L. Abbott, on July 8, 1864, the anniversary of Stanley's death at Gettysburg. "I have a feeling that in whatever turmoil of this horrid war you may chance to be, your heart will remind you of this first anniversary of our dear Stanley's death." As she sat in her Beverly home, Mrs. Abbott wrote how, "It comes to me here amid the calm and quiet of these everlasting hills, whence commeth my help. And when my heart would turn sorrowfully to the tent on the hillside at Gettysburg a year ago, I would remember the 'Lord gave and the Lord hath taken away—blessed be the name of the Lord.'" Fanny Larcom Abbott closed her letter with the sad observation, "It seems to me if I live for years, I can never forget him."[96]

While Mrs. Abbott mourned for Stanley, other mothers' sons were still dying, and thousands more were about to shed their blood in a spectacular failure of arms. The opposing lines between Union-held Fort Morton and the Confederate sector known as "Elliott's Salient" were separated by less than two hundred yards. Ironically, the Federal regiment that occupied a section of the line, the 48th Pennsylvania, contained a large number of experienced coal miners. The miners came up with the idea of driving a shaft beneath the enemy lines some 500 feet away, constructing a chamber at the opposite end, filling it with two tons of gunpowder, and detonating it. General Burnside thought the plan had merit and forwarded it to Meade, who opposed it, as did U. S. Grant and the army's engineers. After pleading his case, the 48th's Lieutenant Colonel Pleasants was finally allowed to proceed with his idea. If successful, the mine would be blown and a specially trained division of black troops would spearhead the attack through the breach, seal the flanks, break through the secondary defenses, and drive on to Petersburg. Other divisions would follow behind them, and a general assault upon Lee's lines would follow.

The Pennsylvanians labored for several weeks, despite Confederate suspicions and attempts to detected the mine, and by July 27 it was ready. Just before the attack, however, both Grant and Meade decided to change the plan. The black troops would not lead the assault after all, for it was feared that in the event of a disaster, the army high command would be accused of sacrificing blacks to save white soldiers. Instructed to supply a substitute division, Burnside had his three white subordinate commanders draw straws: Brig. Gen. James L. Ledlie drew the short one.[97]

Ledlie's division was the weakest and poorest of the lot and led by an alcoholic commander who disliked accompanying his troops in action. To make matters worse, there was not enough time for any specialized training prior to the detonation of the mine. Capt. Thomas W. Clarke, Assistant Adjutant General of the Second Brigade (First Division, Ninth Corps), was present at the planning meeting on the eve of the assault. "The plan as given by General Ledlie to Bartlett and Marshall and as given by Marshall to his battalion commanders, was to this effect," recalled Clarke. "The Second Brigade was formed in column of battalion front. (It made three lines of four hundred men each.)" When the mine exploded, "it was to move forward and occupy the enemy's works on the right of the crater, skirting its edge but not going into it. The First Brigade was to follow with about the same front and occupy the works on the left of the crater, but not going into it." The men were ill-prepared for this type of tactic, as they were "accustomed to line attacks and not to regimental column manouevres, were not adapted to the plan of formation designed for the colored division, with its proposed tactical conversions to right and left." It was emphasized that "after the works were reached. . . .The flanks were to be cleared before the attack on the hill. Marshall was explicit that his brigade was to confine its attention to seizing and holding as great a length of line as possible and that the work beyond [Cemetery Hill], to the enemy's rear, was to be done by other troops." Clarke recalled his brigade commander emphasizing, "When we have secured the lodgement, Ferrero will take the

Negroes through the crater, which we shall have left clear for them and see what they can do beyond."[98]

The results of another poorly planned and executed frontal assault against Confederate fortifications were predictable. The mine was exploded at 4:45 a.m. and blew a gigantic mushroom cloud of debris and humanity into the air, devastating a large stretch of the Southern trench line and leaving behind a large smoking crater 170' long, 60-80' wide, and 30' deep. After a short but critical delay, the attack finally moved forward. Instead of deviating to the right and left and fanning out down the trench lines, however, Ledlie's troops stormed into the Crater, where they milled about in confusion. Then the slaughter began.

The stunned Confederates were initially slow to respond, although artillery soon was showering the area with iron. Within a couple hours, they had sufficiently regrouped to organize a powerful counterattack. A southern division under William Mahone charged the devastated section of trenches about 8:00 a.m. and closed off the critical breach. Other Confederates methodically worked their way down the trench system until they converged on the writhing pit of Federal humanity. Rimming the smoking hole, the Confederates began shooting the almost helpless soldiers in the Crater. Brigadier General Edward Ferrero's Ninth Corps Division of United States Colored Troops was belatedly committed in a futile attempt to break through the lines, but it only made matters worse. Like those before them, the black troops also spilled into the Crater, which by this time was a boggy mass of humanity without any unit cohesion or organization. Incensed by the large scale use and presence of black troops, the Confederates fought all the harder, killing black troops even after they had surrendered. By 1:00 p.m. it was over, and the Federals found themselves exactly where they had begun the morning. Federal casualties had been extraordinarily heavy, with 3,800 killed, wounded, and captured. Southern losses were about 1,500. It was "the saddest affair I have witnessed in the war," wrote General Grant.[99]

A number of Norwich men were engaged in the July 30 bloodbath. Colonel J. Parker Gould (Class of '49) particularly distinguished himself while in command of a wing of the First Brigade,

First Division, Ninth Corps. Because of a faulty fuse, he noted, "The mine was not exploded until 4:45 a.m., which was full daylight and something of the surprise was lost, but when it did explode there was a dull roar, a tremble, a huge cloud of dust and smoke, followed by the discharge of all cannons and mortars from the Appomattox to the Plank Road." The magnitude of the explosion stunned the men, Gould reported, and a few minutes elapsed before "the [initial] troops of Ledlie's division advanced with a cheer and rushed up the sides and into the hole made by the explosion. This cheer was loud and full. I remember distinctly hearing this inspiring sound although two miles from the assault." As had happened on several occasions that spring and summer, "The first line had been captured. But alas! with this rush we stopped short; our brave men, ever ready to rush into battle when properly led, were allowed to wait in the crater until too late and when called upon to advance, it was quite useless to make the attempt." Part of the problem was a lack of leadership, and General Ledlie was again to blame. The incompetent officer had once again fortified himself with alcohol far behind the front in a bombproof, where he remained for the duration of the battle. Ledlie was finally forced from the service a few months later.[100]

Gould's brigade went in on the heels of the first line of attackers. The thickly-bearded officer tried to restore order to the chaos and push the Union troops into the Confederate rear area, but the task was beyond anyone's control. A minie ball shattered his knee, and he slumped to the ground with but little hope of escape.[101]

An eyewitness account of the wounding and evacuation of the Norwich alumnus was published in 1929 in Stoneham, Massachusetts, by 86-year-old Sgt. Robert B. Foster, late of the 59th Massachusetts. Although certainly the account is embellished after the passage of so many years, Foster's recounting corresponds to the known facts and is worth repeating. "We all knew the mine was to be exploded. Our regiment was marched up into position for the attack the night before, without any supper. We laid on our arms all night," he recalled. "The next morning we saw the debris of the fort as it was thrown high in the air, with parts of human bodies plainly discernible. Our regiment got into the crater. Col.

Gould was in command of the brigade." In the excitement of the first success, Foster "stood as near to him as I am to you at this minute, talking and laughing with him, when the fatal bullet came and struck him in the knee." The wound knocked Gould over, and Foster and from another soldier "lugged him into the shelter of the partly demolished rebel fort, only a little way from where he fell. In some manner that I can't recall we produced a stretcher and made him more comfortable upon it." The fight continued and Foster returned to his post. When it was determined that the breakthrough attempt had failed, Union soldiers began flooding to the rear. Foster found Colonel Gould, and said, "Colonel, we must get out of here." According to Foster, Gould replied, "They are shooting too briskly; we will both be killed." Not to be put off, Foster shot back, "I can't die but once. Let me try it." Gould, undoubtedly not wanting to hamper or endanger his men, said "No, I guess I better stay right here." Despite his colonel's protest, Foster refused to give in, and "after much coaxing, in which others joined, he consented to allow four of us to lift him on the stretcher and start back with him to our barracks, only a short distance back."

The trip back across no-mans' land was a harrowing and deadly trip for hundreds of Federals, and Foster left a vivid account of his journey:

> Three men took hold with me, one on each handle. We had hardly got back into the open when the man on the end with me was shot through the head and fell over dead. A bullet knocked me down, grazing my cheek and drawing blood. A second later one of the fellows ahead of me was wounded in the head and fell. I never saw him again and believe he was killed. The stretcher was on the ground and my comrade and I looked first at each other and then at the Colonel. "Come on," I said, "We can't stand here; we've got to go somewhere, or do something." Between us, he on one end and I on the other, a stretcher handle in each hand, we managed to get the Colonel back inside our own breastworks and turned him over to the hospital men. The Rebs sent lots of solid shot after us and the sand was flying in all directions as we gained the cover. The ambulance corps rushed the Colonel to the hospital, where his leg was amputated between the knee and the thigh.

The following morning, the brave Sergeant Foster visited Gould and found him cheerful and hopeful. "The surgeons did not want him to be moved, but he insisted on going home. Somewhere on the passage on the boat or on the trip from Washington to Boston. . . but while on the steamer, the stitches in his wound gave way and he bled to death before the stump could be rebound." So ended the career of the gallant Norwich alumnus.[102]

Other Norwich men who saw action in the disaster at the Crater included: Capt. Albert W. Cooke (Class of '69), Company C, 57th Massachusetts; Capt. William A. Treadwell (Class of '57), Battery G, 14th New York Heavy Artillery; Capt. George W. Webb (Class of '49), Battery F, 2nd Pennsylvania Heavy Artillery; 1st Lt. William B. Burbank (Class of '55, Company E, 17th Vermont; and First Sgt. Henry B. Mosely (Class of '59), Company B, 36th Massachusetts. Though each of these men lived through a unique experience, their accounts have been lost to history.[103]

In the days following the fiasco, confidence in Grant and the progress of the campaign reached a new low in Lincoln's circle of advisors. Gideon Welles (Class of '26) wrote on August 3 that he was "quite unhappy over this Petersburg matter—less, however, from the result, bad as it is, than from an awakening apprehension that Grant is not equal to the position assigned him. God grant that I may be mistaken," Welles continued, "for the slaughtered thousands of my countrymen who have poured out their rich blood for three months on the soil of Virginia from the Wilderness to Petersburg under his generalship can never be atoned in this world or the next if he without Sherman prove a failure." The naval secretary's diary entry continued: "A blight and sadness comes over me like a dark shadow when I dwell on the subject, a melancholy feeling of the past, a foreboding of the future. A nation's destiny almost has been committed to this man and if it is an improper committal, where are we?" Fortunately for the Republic, Welles and others proved to be wrong in their assessment of Grant but, with the election looming, it was a particularly troubling and tense time.[104]

After the Battle of the Crater, Grant settled on pressing his lines westward rather than driving through his opponent's front. The daily grind in the trenches was a horrible existence for men on both sides. Instead of dying by the hundreds or thousands in pitched battles, men fell quietly in twos and threes, victims of sharpshooters, mortars, and disease. First Lieutenant Lemuel A. Abbott (Class of '64), a twice-wounded company grade officer in the 10th Vermont, summed up the frustration of the Army of the Potomac as well as its determination. Sitting in the trenches at Petersburg that summer, Abbott confided to his diary: "I have been thinking quite seriously that I will go home this winter and fit myself for a profession—not that I am getting tired of military life but. . .[I] am undecided what I will do. I don't believe I shall be a quitter, though, for I am not weak that way. No patriot resigns in the face of the enemy when his country needs his services." While Lemuel Abbott's words and feelings are commendable, they become even more so when we examine the nature of the wounds he later suffered at Third Winchester on September 19, 1864. The unlucky Abbott had one lip shot away, both jaws crushed, and eleven teeth shot out. Despite these grievous wounds, he served through the end of the war and then for many years thereafter in the Regular Army.[105]

There was little good news for anyone in those dog days of August, but at least the 19th Massachusetts got their colonel back. Edmund Rice (Class of '60), it will be recalled, was wounded and captured at the Bloody Angle on May 12 while attempting to locate his regiment's colors. He had been put on a prison train bound for Andersonville, but as the train rolled through North Carolina at full speed, the daredevil Norwich man and several companions cut a large hole in the rail car while other prisoners sang to distract the guards. The men jumped from the speeding train and spent the next 23 days hiding by day and walking at night. After a 430-mile journey, the gaunt and exhausted party made it to friendly lines on the Ohio River. Much to their surprise, the Federals were assisted by slaves, free blacks, and Union sympathizers. Following a thirty-day sick leave in Massachusetts, Rice rejoined his regiment. He brought with him a new national color to replace the one the 19th Massachusetts had lost at the Weldon Railroad below Petersburg. By the time the old colors were lost there, fewer than 200 men were still with the regiment. From then on, only the national flag was carried by the 19th Massachusetts' soldiers.[106]

As the Bay Staters celebrated the return of their young Norwich-trained colonel, the detached Sixth Corps and 27 Norwich alumni operated in the Shenandoah Valley. The valor and steadfastness of the Green Mountain men deeply impressed the Army of the Shenandoah's new commander, Maj. Gen. Philip Sheridan, and earned his lasting respect and affection. Sheridan rolled up an impressive string of victories to which many Norwich alumni contributed. Unfortunately, the school lost several killed and wounded in the Shenandoah, with Third Winchester (September 19, 1864) taking an especially heavy toll. Captain William H. Chaffin (Class of '64), Company I, 14th New Hamsphire Infantry and a former drill instructor at Norwich, was killed by a bullet to the temple. Captains Samuel W. Shattuck (Class of '60), Sumner H. Lincoln (Class of '61), and Lemuel Abbott (Class of '64) were wounded there, as was 1st Lt. Henry C. Baxter (Class of '60), Battery D, 1st Vermont Heavy Artillery. In the culminating Union victory at Cedar Creek on October 19, Maj. Gen. Horatio G. Wright (Class of '37), particularly distinguished himself. Wright's action in reorganizing the retreating troops and the firm stand conducted by his troops in the midst of an apparent disaster allowed Sheridan the time he needed to complete his famous ride from Winchester to resume control of the army and lead it to final victory. Wright's heroic efforts in preventing a complete rout of the Union army have been all but overlooked in the shadow of Sheridan's glory. When final victory was achieved in the Shenandoah, the Sixth Corps returned to the stagnant trenches of Petersburg.[107]

Concurrently that fall, operations in front of Petersburg largely consisted of routine siege operations, heavy and constant skirmishing, and occasional larger-scale movements to extend the Union lines south and west in order to threaten Confederate supply routes. Casualties continued to rise. As the Union siege lines were extended, the line of Rebel troops defending each mile of their defenses thinned out. Large scale offensive operations by the Army of the Potomac, for all practical purposes, ceased at the end of October and were not resumed until the following spring. Edmund

Rice's report for the 19th Massachusetts's season of campaigning provides insights into the dangerous drudgery of Petersburg's siege operations. "On the 16th [October] we were again ordered down to Fort Brooks and garrisoned that work until the 24th when at short notice & under cover of night we went up to the front & relieved the 10th A. Corps in the trenches." For the next week until "the 24th of October the Regiment garrisoned successively two important works Battery 11 & Fort Rice (north of the Jerusalem Plank Road). The duty was laborious and trying in the highest degree one third of the men being constantly under arms and the remainder were usually absorbed by heavy Picket or fatigue details." The boredom was broken up by the "Artillery firing took place daily but owing to the protection afforded by Traverses & Bomb Proofs [erected by the men under direction of Colonel Rice commanding the garrison] we lost but 1 killed and 1 wounded while on the line." While Rice and his men endured these dangers, Capt. Charles W. Davis (Class of '49), Company K, 21st Massachusetts Infantry, was transferred to the command of Camp Parole for Confederate prisoners at College Green Barracks, Annapolis, Maryland, on October 21, 1864.[108]

Following the complete victory over Jubal Early's small army in the Shenandoah Campaign, the Sixth Corps was ordered back to Petersburg. During the march of Wright's troops back to the city in December 1864, an interesting anecdote, one reflecting the hardening attitudes of Confederate civilians and Union soldiers alike, is found in the correspondence of Col. Theodore Lyman of General Meade's staff. Brigadier General Truman B. Seymour (Class of '44), who had been released and paroled following his capture in the Wilderness, was marching his division through the town of Charlottesville. When the citizens of the town "told him they had had most extraordinary victories over Grant," Seymour was apparently unmoved. The Norwich alumnus "made them a speech, in which he said it didn't make any difference how many victories they had, it wouldn't do them any sort of good; that in every battle we killed off a good many of them and that we intended to keep piling up men indefinitely, until they knocked under, or were all shot!" His sentiments, not surprisingly, "enraged them much."[109]

In the months following the Battle of the Crater, Gideon Welles and many others changed their opinion of Grant and his approach to ultimate victory. He had bled Lee's army down to a mere shadow of its former self and penned it within fortifications it could never vacate. Although Grant's methodology had resulted in tens of thousands of casualties, it was clear to most observers that the tide of battle had turned. As Grant held Lee in place, William T. Sherman pushed back Joe Johnston to the gates of Atlanta, and then defeated Johnston's replacement, John Bell Hood. Atlanta's fall in early September, coupled with Sheridan's successes in the Shenandoah guaranteed the reelection of President Lincoln over opponent Gen. George B. McClellan. The Republican victory was particularly gratifying to all who wanted the war brought to a victorious conclusion. The soldiers in the Army of the Potomac, who had once viewed their army as "McClellan's Army," overwhelmingly voted for Lincoln against their former general. The veterans viewed Lincoln's triumph as "a grand moral victory gained over the combined forces of slavery, disunion, treason, [and] tyranny." As the Vermont Brigade's Wilbur Fisk so aptly put it, "Soldiers don't generally believe in fighting to put down treason and voting to let it live."[110]

The war would be fought to the finish under Lincoln's plans for the unconditional restoration of the Union and emancipation. The last hope of the South had died.

VII. 1865

"The last time on the sacred soil of Virginia."
Josiah Hall '61

The severe winter of 1864-1865 was particularly hard on the men in the Confederate trenches. Southern troops lacked proper winter clothing and, despite Robert E. Lee's best efforts, were slowly starving to death. The men of the Army of the Potomac, now supported by an immense and well developed logistical infrastructure based at City Point, had everything they needed—and more. Still, the heady days of 1861 seemed an eternity away. Some of the new Yankee regiments in the line were numbered in the 200-series. A few of these units, however, consisted almost entirely of reenlisted veterans and were among the best the Army of the Potomac had ever fielded. In those relatively quiet days of winter, one abortive attempt to end the fighting occurred. On January 31, Confederate peace commissioners came into Union lines under a flag of truce; the high-level conference which followed came to nothing. As the soldiers feared, the war had to be ended on the battlefield.[1]

By March 1865, the situation on the battle fronts was reaching crisis proportions for the battered Confederacy. Sherman's army was cutting a swath through the Carolinas as it marched north toward a rendezvous with Grant. Both Jefferson Davis and Abraham Lincoln knew that if the Army of Northern Virginia surrendered or was forced from the field, the Southern government must soon collapse. General Lee believed, however, that if he could break out of the encirclement at

Petersburg and unite with the Joe Johnston's army in North Carolina, he might yet isolate and defeat the steadily advancing Sherman and force a stalemate. The initial part of Lee's plan called for the capture of the key Union earthwork of Fort Stedman on the Petersburg siege line. On March 25, 1865, the Rebel yell pierced the darkness, signaling that the Army of Northern Virginia was on the attack for the last time. The still aggressive and plucky Confederates penetrated the Union line rapidly enough, but found they could not significantly widen the initial breach when Federal resistance rapidly stiffened. At a critical moment in the clash, the Ninth Corps Brig. Gen. John F. Hartranft, leader of the charge at Antietam's Burnside Bridge, brought up half a dozen of those higher-numbered Pennsylvania regiments and sent them on a counter charge. The Pennsylvanians stopped the Confederates cold. From a position near Fort Stedman, the Old Vermont Brigade also counterattacked. When the battered Southern survivors returned to their lines, Lee discovered that more than 4,000 of his irreplaceable veterans had become casualties.[2]

During a temporary truce to allow recovery of the fight's dead and wounded, Capt. Albert W. Cooke (Class of '69), who had commanded the 57th Massachusetts during the battle at Fort Stedman met a Confederate general officer between the lines. While they spoke, as a gesture of kindness and respect, Captain Cooke handed over a gold wedding ring that he had removed from a Southern officer who had been killed in the fight. The ring eventually found its way back to the dead officer's family.[3]

On a nearby section of the Petersburg front a segment of the enemy's entrenched picket line was seized by the 1st Vermont Heavy Artillery. In that March 25 attack, when it seemed the regiment might falter during its advance, the regiment's national colors were seized and carried forward into the enemy's works by Lt. George A. Bailey (Class of '63) of Battery M. Bailey was complimented for his bravery by General Getty and promoted to a position on Getty's staff.[4]

On the eve of that final spring campaign, the massive supply base at City Point, Virginia, had burgeoned into one of the world's largest ports. City Point boasted a half mile-long wharf and symbolized the evergrowing power of the Federal military. Here at City Point lay the huge supply dumps for ammunition and rations; here were the vast hospitals capable of treating up to 10,000 casualties; here sat the courts-martial that enforced the tightening of discipline and carried out the numerous executions; and here Lt. Gen. Ulysses S. Grant, the Commander in Chief of Union Armies, made his headquarters. The City Point hospital alone had 1,200 tents which were supplemented in winter by ninety log barracks. By the end of the war this hospital was not only the largest and best facility of its kind in America, but also its most sophisticated. It was also at City Point that the much-feared large, primitive, high-fenced outdoor internment facility for Federal military prisoners known as the "Bull Pen" had been erected. The prison was reputed to have a more severe regimen than the enemy's dreaded Andersonville facility. In a separate pen, captured Confederate soldiers were held for special transports which carried them to prison camps farther North. During the brief period of its existence, some 14,000 Confederates passed through the City Point facility on their way north. From City Point, an extremely efficient rail system, constructed and operated by the United States Military Railroad, led to sub-depots and rail stations placed at intervals behind the siege lines of Petersburg. The railroad literally delivered supplies directly into the hands of the front line troops. Twenty-five locomotives and 275 rail cars operated daily on the Petersburg Line. On an average day during the siege, the Union Army had thirty days of food and twenty days of forage on hand at City Point—a staggering 9,000,000 meals and 12,000 tons of hay and oats at a time when the enemy was literally starving in place. All in all, City Point constituted a very complex and impressive logistics operation that would not be matched again by American forces until the days of the World Wars. During its brief existence, a number of Norwich alumni either held permanent positions at the base, or passed through here on their way to the front.[5]

One of the Northern regiments assigned to garrison City Point and guard the "Bull Pen" was the 61st Massachusetts. Formed late in the war, it spent most of its active time in various duties at the supply base. In the final days of the war, the 61st Massachusetts would finally see combat in the culminating battles around Petersburg. Serving in the regiment were three Norwich men: Capts. Sebastian R. Streeter (Class of '37) and Charles E. Ashcroft (Class of '63), and First Sgt. C. Henry Moseley (Class of '59).[6]

As spring slowly spread over the Virginia countryside, it was becoming increasingly obvious to observers that the war was nearly over. Sherman was destroying the Carolinas, and the final details of the last great Union offensive in the East were being worked out by Lincoln, Grant and his staff. The last plan called for the Army of the Potomac's Cavalry Corps, with the Second and Fifth Infantry Corps, to be prepared to pursue the Army of Northern Virginia, which was to be levered from its defensive lines by a final frontal assault conducted by the Sixth and Ninth Corps. The point of attack and the details of the assault were worked out by Maj. Gen. Horatio G. Wright (Class of '37). Despite the wet, early spring weather and bad roads, the designated assault troops were ready to go by April 2. When the big offensive came the Confederate defense lines and "Fortress Petersburg" collapsed like a house of cards.[7]

In that final offensive, the powerful Sixth Corps made the main attack and its performance was particularly superb. Earlier that winter, Wright, the Sixth Corps commander, believed he had found a weak point in the defenses opposite his Second Division's lines. Referring to his reliable Vermont Brigade and its Norwich alumni, Wright predicted: "The corps will go in solid and I am sure will make the fur fly." The attack was made with the corps brigades arrayed in a wedge formation instead of the traditional lines and columns. The Vermont Brigade, the Sixth Corps most battle-tested and proven shock troops, formed the spearhead of the wedge. In addition to nine alumni still serving with the Vermont Brigade, other Norwich men played important roles in the final storming of the Petersburg defenses. These alumni included Brig. Gen. Truman B. Seymour (Class of '44), commanding the Sixth Corps Third Division; Capt. John S. Carpenter (Class of '48), Company B, 95th Pennsylvania; Capt. Lemuel A. Abbott (Class of '64), Company G, 10th Vermont; First Lt. William R. Hoyt (Class of '64) Company A and Corp. Roswell W. Hunt (Class of '42), Company D, 10th Vermont; and Lieutenant Charles W. Smith (Class of '67), Battery E, 1st Connecticut Heavy Artillery.[8]

The ground over which the Vermonters charged was relatively open, partially obstructed by stumps and branches of trees which had been cut to construct the Confederate defenses, and gently ascended toward the enemy lines. The formidable defensive works consisted of a heavy earthen rampart with a deep, wide ditch in front. The side of the defense line facing the Federal attackers bristled with heavy, sharpened stakes and four rows of abatis. The inside of the parapet was revetted with timbers and had heavy head logs positioned on top of the parapet with notches cut on their under sides through which the defenders could fire. Some twenty artillery pieces positioned in redans covered the attack zone. Although the lines were not manned as thickly as Lee or the defenders would have liked, the breakthrough sector was held by experienced and reliable North Carolina troops. At about 2:00 a.m. on Sunday morning, April 2, 1865, the assault regiments began moving into their attack positions some 700 yards away from the Confederate works. After lying in the darkness for a couple of nerve-wracking hours, the attack commenced at 4:40 a.m. In the blink of an eye, the Confederate pickets were overrun and half the distance to the defenses was covered before the Southerners could react.[9]

The Federal troops answered the enemy fire with thunderous cheers and surged forward. After a brief but fierce fight, the defenses were overwhelmed and the gate to Petersburg was kicked open. When the first phase of the offensive ended, the Sixth Corps had suffered nearly 1,100 casualties. Distinguishing themselves in the victory and cited for gallantry by Maj. Gen. George Getty, the commander of the Second Division, Sixth Corps, were alumni 1st Lt. George A. Bailey (Class of '63), 1st Vermont Heavy Artillery (for capturing two Rebel artillery pieces); Lieutenant Henry C. Baxter (Class of '66), 1st Vermont Heavy Artillery (also recommended for a brevet promotion); and Lt. Col. Charles Hunsdon (Class of '51), commander of the 1st Vermont Heavy Artillery. Hunsdon was cited for gallantry in the assault and was recommended for brevet promotion to colonel. Lastly, Pvt. John Pettis (Class of '42), Battery B, 1st Vermont Heavy Artillery was wounded in the final assault.[10]

First Lieutenant George A. Bailey demonstrated particular initiative in earning his citation. "Major Sperry of the 6th Vt. and Lieut. Bailey of the 11th Vt., assisted by a few men, captured two pieces and turned them upon the flying rebels." Unable to find the necessary primers to fire the cannon, "the pieces were discharged by firing a musket into the vent of the piece. In this manner twelve rounds were fired, when a section of artillery coming up the guns were turned over to its commander." Bailey's actions facilitated the successful advance of his fellow Green Mountain Boys.[11]

First Lieutenant Henry C. Baxter (Class of '66), a member of the division staff during the assault, gained his commendation when he and other staff officers, being without horses, "were obliged to be on foot, but notwithstanding all difficulties . . . were everywhere present throughout the entire day, cheering on the men, re-forming the lines." Baxter's actions were key to "preserving the connection of the regiments and helping on by precept and example the operations of the day."[12]

Second Lieutenant Charles W. Smith (Class of '67) was commander of Battery E, 1st Connecticut Heavy Artillery, part of the Army of the Potomac's siege artillery. Smith was cited for gallantry and breveted first lieutenant for his actions in the battle. This alumnus was placed in charge of one of three special 33-man storming parties that advanced with the lead infantry troops. As enemy batteries were overrun, Smith put his former artillery training to use and turned captured guns upon the enemy. Some 400 rounds of "liberated" ammunition were fired at the retreating Confederates, and several desperate Confederate counterattacks to regain the lost guns were repelled by Lieutenant Smith and his fellow artillerists. Meanwhile, in the old Second Corps, Lt. Daniel W. Washburn's (Class of '55), Battery I, 4th New York Heavy Artillery faced some formidable Confederate defenses near Sutherland Station. Despite savage resistance, the New York artillerists-turned-infantry broke through.[13]

When Petersburg fell on April 2, the Confederate government ordered Richmond evacuated. It was occupied by Union soldiers the following day. As the blue-uniformed soldiers tramped into the city, a large contingent of black troops proudly sang "John Brown's Body." Marching into the Confederate capital with the first elements were three Norwich alumni serving in the 9th Vermont Infantry: First Lt. William A. Dodge (Class of '64), Company B; First Lt. John Gray (Class of '52), Company K; and Corp. Daniel E. Wright (Class of '47), Company A. For the rest of the Federal army, the first few days following the fall of Petersburg and Richmond involved grueling forced marches and hard fighting. Sharp battles with the fleeing Army of Northern Virginia took place at Sayler's Creek and other places, and large portions of Lee's army either surrendered or were captured in these engagements.

At Sayler's Creek, Capt. Thomas H. Davis' (Class of '55) service as a Confederate officer ended when he was captured along with others from what was left of George Pickett's division. Realizing the end was at hand, other Confederate soldiers simply drifted away and headed home. By April 9, the old antagonists of the war's two premier armies faced each other for one last time around Appomattox Court House. Colonel Josiah Hall (Class of '61), commanding the 1st Vermont Cavalry of Custer's division, was about to make the Army of the Potomac's last attack. Hall described the event in a handwritten report to Vermont's adjutant general:

> On the ninth the fighting commenced by sunrise . . . we were soon in motion. Our brigade was in advance and my regiment in front. We moved out on the trot forcing the enemy's skirmish line back rapidly, leaving the ground to be taken up by the Fifth Corps, which came up at the double quick. After passing the enemy's entire front, and running the gauntlet from the united fire of two batteries, we came round on their flank and rear, and in full sight of their supply trains. At this point General Custer ordered me to charge the train with my regiment. I immediately made the proper disposition of the command. The front battalion had already broken into the gallop, and the others were following at a fast trot, when a staff officer of Gen'l Custer came charging down and called me to halt the regiment, saying that Gen. Lee had sent in a flag of truce, offering to surrender the army. The two rear battalions were immediately halted, but the front one had got so far that they captured the last post between us and the train before they could be halted. The regiment was at once formed in line of battle, while the preliminaries of the surrender were being gone through with. At about 5 P.M. Gen. Custer rode along the lines and announced that the terms of surrender had been agreed upon, and signed, and directed us to go into camp where we were. This was the last time the regiment was called upon to face the enemy and it was the source of much gratification to the regiment, as well as to myself, to know that we were present to see the grand rebel army of Northern Virginia find the 'last ditch.'[14]

While Hall's 1st Vermont Cavalry advanced to the attack, Lt. Col. James A. Cunningham, commanding Capt. Charles Bower's (Class of '52) 32nd Massachusetts, led the Fifth Corps infantry advance that April morning. The entire Federal corps had deployed into battle line to support the cavalry. When unit ranks had been properly aligned preparatory to receipt of the expected attack order, the command "Forward" was given. As the 32nd Massachusetts marched into range of enemy muskets, the firing suddenly ceased and an unexpected halt was ordered. The regimental historian recorded how "Colonel Cunningham, through his field-glass, seeing what seemed to be a flag of truce in our front, took the adjutant with him and, putting spurs to their horses, they dashed forward." They "met a mounted officer attended by an orderly, bearing a small white flag upon a staff. This officer announced himself as one of General Lee's staff and said that he was the bearer of a message to General Grant with a view to surrender." The chase was over.[15]

As is well known, Grant's meeting with Lee resulted in both fair and generous surrender terms for the vanquished Army of Northern Virginia. Eyewitnesses to the surrender's signing in the McClean House included Brig. Gen. Seth Williams (Class of '40), formerly Adjutant General of the Army of the Potomac and now its Inspector General. In the days leading up to the surrender, General Williams had personally carried a number of important messages between Grant and Lee. Though Grant had been generous in his surrender terms, he had nevertheless insisted that the defeated Southerners take part in a formal surrender ceremony. On April 12, under the vigilant supervision of that valiant epitome of the citizen-soldier, Maj. Gen. Joshua Lawrence Chamberlain, the remnants of the Army of Northern Virginia marched to Appomattox Court House to lay down their arms. Union units stood in formation on both sides of their path, the soldiers quietly and respectfully watching their former enemy conduct their last march.[16]

For the many sons of the Union there to witness the proceedings, it was a sublime moment. At least 30 Norwich men served in the Appomattox Campaign, and many of them were at the actual surrender ceremony. Among those who took part were Lt. Col. Edmund Rice (Class of '60), the only one of the original 37 officers of the 19th Massachusetts to endure four years of war. Other Norwich men joining Chamberlain and Rice at Appomattox included Col. Jonathan G. Tarbell (Class of '39) 91st New York Infantry; Capt. Charles Bowers (Class of '52) 32nd Massachusetts, whose regiment was placed by Chamberlain in the position of honor on the Union right; Capts.

David C. Beattie (Class of '47) 164th New York, Lemuel A. Abbott (Class of '64); and Abbott's classmate First Lt. William R. Hoyt (Class of '64) of the 10th Vermont.[17]

General Chamberlain designated the 32nd Massachusetts as the Federal unit to receive the arms and colors of the surrendering Confederate infantry. As each Southern unit stacked its arms, equipment and colors before the blue ranks, a detail of soldiers from the 32nd Massachusetts picked up the stacks from where they stood and moved them to the Union line. As more and more of their former enemies' arms were surrendered, these too were taken by the same detail and piled around the first stacks. When the ceremony was ended, there remained but a single line of stacked rifles and equipment with the Southerners' torn and tattered battle colors hanging or lying on them.[18]

For the Army of the Potomac and the Norwich men who had served in its ranks, it had been a bloody and memorable four years. At times it seemed that, no matter how brave that army's soldiers were or how hard they fought, fortune had been against them. This army was always opposed on the battlefield by the best Southern commanders and gallant troops who, during most of the battles, were fighting on their own soil in defense of their homes. At the conclusion of hostilities, General Grant wrote:

> The Army of the Potomac has every reason to be proud of its four years' record in the suppression of the rebellion. The army it had to fight was the protection to the capital of a people which was attempting to found a nation upon the territory of the United States. Its loss would be the loss of the cause. Every energy, therefore, was put forth by the Confederacy to protect and maintain their capital. Everything else would go if it went. Lee's army had to be strengthened to enable it to maintain its position, no matter what territory was wrested from the South in another quarter.[19]

Despite the surrender of Lee at Appomattox, the war dragged on for a few weeks longer in other theaters and on the oceans, and many more men from both sides lost their lives. The War to Preserve the Union, however, had been essentially brought to a conclusion on an obscure field in southwestern Virginia. Unfortunately, for the armies and the nation, there was still one great shock to come—President

Abraham Lincoln, slain by an assassin's bullet, joined the ranks of his legions of slain soldiers on April 15, 1865.

Having accomplished their mission, the troops were eager to return home. Before they did, however, a grateful nation demanded an opportunity to do them homage. The occasion came on May 23-24, 1865, in the form of the largest military review ever held in our national capital. For two days the veterans of the Army of the Potomac and of Sherman's Western armies tramped up Pennsylvania Avenue to the cheers of an ecstatic populace and the salute of their new President and Commander-in-Chief, Andrew Johnson. Joshua Lawrence Chamberlain's moving account of the Army of the Potomac's passing the presidential reviewing stand is a glowing tribute to the army, its regiments, and, by inference, the Norwich alumni in their ranks. Chamberlain noted the passing of many men and units with Norwich ties. He saw "Seth Williams, adjutant-general, steadfast as the rocky crests of Maine from which he came, whose level head had balanced the disturbances and straightened the confusions of campaigns and changes of commanders through our whole history." Then came regiments like "the trusted, sorely tried 32nd Massachusetts with unfaltering ranks. . . .the immortal 5th New Hampshire. . . .Now come those heavy artillery regiments. . . .the 1st Massachusetts. . . .the 1st Maine."[20]

Meanwhile, the Sixth Corps and Vermont Brigade, with 15 other Norwich alumni in their ranks, including Col. James Hubbard (Class of '57), who now commanded a brigade, missed the great review of the "Grand Armies of the Republic." At the time, the corps was returning to Washington from garrison duty at Danville in southwestern Virginia. The Vermonters last great field march ended on June 2 when they entered their final army camp between Munson's Hill and Ball's Crossroads, near their old 1861 base at Camp Griffin. On June 8, the entire Sixth Corps marched in its own victory parade before President Johnson in Washington. That day just happened to be one of the hottest in the city's history. Hundreds of soldiers and spectators fainted from the effects of the sun. The citizens "gave the Sixth Corps a particular welcome as being the men who, last year, saved the Capital from capture and their property from destruction." The proud Vermonters marched past the reviewing stands with their tattered battle flags wreathed in green and with evergreen sprigs (cedar or arbor of vitae), the insignia of Ethan Allen's Green Mountain Boys, in their caps. George G. Benedict, Vermont's 19th century historian, said of the brigade's flags that "Not one of the colors of the brigade, though so often flying in the very front of battle, was ever permitted to be for a moment in hostile hands." The men also drew rave reviews for their demeanor. The Vermonters were described as "the only brigade that saluted the President correctly." It was reported that in the review the men of the brigade, regardless of rank, "looked grandly; tall, sturdy, bronzed, muscular, they strode by with swinging step, fresh and bright, as if just setting out on a campaign, instead of returning homeward after four years of as terrible service as any brigade in any army of the whole republic has passed through." To the cheering onlookers the Vermonters' "torn battle flags and wasted ranks told the story of their heroism." It was said that where "there was fierce fighting, long marching, exposure, fatigue, risk to be endured, there was always the gallant Sixth Corps. They were Sedgwick's pets. The foremost among (this) host of heroes has always moved the Vermont brigade."[21]

The now legendary Vermont Brigade, in which nearly four dozen Norwich men had served and played a major role, had acquired a tremendous reputation among friend and foe alike. An anonymous postwar writer, who was neither a veteran of the brigade nor a Vermonter, penned a tribute to these model citizen-soldiers. "They were honest farmers turned vagabonds. They were simple countrymen turned heroes. They were quiet townsmen who had become rovers. They stole ancient horses and bony cows on the march. They pillaged moderately in other things." When not in combat, "They chased rabbits when they went into camp, after long marches they yelled like wild Indians when neighboring camps were silent through fatigue." Unlike some of the crack Regular and volunteer regiments, "They were ill disciplined and familiar with their officers. They swaggered in a cool, impudent way and looked down with patronizing coolness upon all regiments that were better drilled and upon the part of the army generally that did not belong to the Vermont brigade." It was a matter of note that, again unlike other units, the Green Mountain Boys "were strangely proud, not of themselves individually, but of the brigade collectively; for they knew perfectly well they were the best fighters in the

known world. They were long of limb and could outmarch the army.
They were individually self-reliant and skillful in the use of arms; and
they honestly believed that the Vermont brigade could not be beaten
by all the combined armies of the rebellion." Then, our unidentified
author reeled off some impressive facts:

> . . . .In every engagement in which this brigade took part, it was com-
> plimented for gallant conduct.
> . . . .When the Vermonters led the column on a march, their quick
> movements had to be regulated from corps or division headquarters, to
> avoid gaps in the column as it followed them. If a rapid or a forced
> march were required, it was common for Sedgwick to say, with a quiet
> smile, "Put the Vermonters at the head of the column to-day and keep
> everything well closed up."
> . . . .There were many regiments equal to the Vermont regiments in ac-
> tual battle and some that, like the Fifth New York volunteers, not only
> equalled them in fighting qualities, but greatly surpassed them in drill,
> discipline and appearance on parade. As a brigade, however, they were
> undoubtedly the best brigade in the army of the Potomac, for they not
> only fought as well as it was possible to fight, but they could outmarch,
> with the utmost ease, any other organization in the army.[22]

As demobilization went into full swing, Josiah Hall (Class of '61),
who had ended his four year military career as colonel commanding
the 1st Vermont Cavalry, submitted his last official report to the adjutant general of Vermont on July 1, 1865. His thoughts on war's end
and of his days as a citizen-soldier speak to his fellow soldiers and
brother alumni. "On the morning of June 9th. . .we broke camp for
the last time on the 'sacred soil' of Virginia, rendered truly so, by being
the last resting place of many a true and noble heart that had given its
last drop blood in defense of our common country and the glorious
old stars and stripes." The regiment "started for Burlington Vt., the
original place of rendezvous of the regiment before leaving the state."
As Hall closed this particular chapter of his and his regiment's life, he
wrote: "Permit me, here, to express my high esteem and regard for the
officers and men of the regiment, for their willing and prompt execution of every duty assigned them and with gratification and pride to
testify to the indomitable courage and bravery and heroic daring displayed by them in every engagement, which will ever be an honor to
them and the State."[23]

Not long after his discharge, citizen Hall wrote his former brigade commander, Brig. Gen. William Wells, a letter in which some of his postwar activities, attitudes, and concerns were voiced. Hall wrote how "The remainder of the Reg. is not mustered out yet. So far as I know they have not recd. any order yet to be mustered out but I have been expecting every day to hear of their arrival at Burlington." Updating Wells on some of local news, Hall went on to say: "Everything is quiet here as need be. About the only thing exciting that I hear of is of some Copperheads getting a good thrashing from some of the soldiers for not attending to their own business. As a general thing however the boys are quiet if they are let alone." Hall then queried Wells as to "How long have you been stationed at Fairfax &. . . Have the monuments on the old Bull Run field been repaired & has anything been done to prevent any further injury to them. There are plenty of rascals left in that vicinity that ought to swing." Lastly Hall wondered, "Do you think it would be safe for me to go into the Shenandoah valley to stop this fall. Am at a great loss where to go to settle. Please write soon and direct as before." As there is no record of Wells' reply, one wonders if Hall ever did revisit the Shenandoah.[24]

For many Americans who had lost friends or relatives in the war, their sense of loss and pain did not end with Appomattox. One of these was Anna Griswold, mother of Col. Charles Griswold (Class of '54). Charles' mother not only mourned him, but hoped his body might finally be recovered from its temporary resting place in the Wilderness. Thousands of soldiers from both sides who had perished in Virginia were never recovered and still lie today where they fell or were hastily buried. Anna Griswold's son, however, finally had his homecoming.

Griswold had been genuinely loved by the officers and men of the 56th Massachusetts Infantry. Even in the midst of the Battle of the Wilderness, members of the regiment carefully marked their commander's grave and hoped to return someday and recover his body. In July 1865, Mrs. Griswold was notified by Col. Stephen M. Weld, the last commander of the 56th Massachusetts and Charles' friend and comrade, that her son had been recovered and was being sent home. In February 1866 another one of Charles's friends, who coincidentally had been part of Weld's party to locate the grave and recover the body, wrote Mrs. Griswold: "You have asked me to give you some account of my visit to the Wilderness last summer, in quest of the body of your noble son, my own companion and friend." Starting out on "the morning of June 29th, 1865, I left Washington for Belle Plain, by steamboat. I was accompanied by. . .men. . .[who] were present at the burial. . .I could not, if I would, describe in words what I felt as I reviewed again the ground and recalled the scenes of carnage of that battle." After a short search, Weld and his party "came to the spot. . . where I saw for the last time our noble Colonel, your son. . . .I recalled how he looked as he stood in the open road, calm, collected, brave, encouraging all by the distinguished example of his heroism." The somber veterans apparently found it hard to tear themselves away from that now lonely and silent section of the bleak Wilderness. But, "After an hour or more passed in contemplation. . .I returned to the Brock road to search for the grave. I was unable to find it until the arrival of my companions, Hospital-Steward Martin at once directing me to the spot." The medic knew exactly where to go and "on the west side of the Brock road, opposite the end of a by-road, some two or three hundred paces north of the turnpike to Orange Court House. We found the grave undisturbed, the head-board still standing and we proceeded without delay to our melancholy task of disinterring all that remained in earthly shape of your dearly beloved son." The grim disinterment proceeded, and Weld found that "The body had been inclosed in a rude box, made of fragments, from which we transferred it with care to the sealed casket we had brought." It gave Stephen Weld satisfaction, and perhaps some psychological closure, to be be able to do this last favor for his friend:

> Thus it was, that by the valuable aid of the good and true men who volunteered to go with me, I was enabled to pay a last tribute of affection to my dear friend. . . .It was likewise a last tribute of respect paid by the officers and men of the Fifty-sixth Regiment, to one of their number, to their Commanding Officer, who had so nobly died upon the field of battle, giving up his life for the cause of human freedom and of his country.[25]

As it had for countless others, the War to Preserve the Union had finally ended for the Griswold family.

Colonel Charles Griswold, '56, 56th Massachusetts Infantry, killed in action in the Wilderness, May 5, 1864. *Courtesy of the Massachusetts Commandery of the Loyal Legion and the US Army Military History Institute.*

Officers of the Horse Artillery, 1864. First Lieutenant Edward B. Williston, '56, is shown seated second row on the right. *Courtesy of the Massachusetts Commandery of the Loyal Legion and the US Army Military History Institute.*

Colonel Thomas O. Seaver, '59, 3rd Vermont Infantry, winner of the Medal of Honor near Spotsylvania, May 10, 1864 in "Upton's Charge." *Photo courtesy of the Vermont Historical Society.*

Brigadier General Horatio G. Wright, '37, assumed command of the Sixth Corps when General Sedgwick was killed on May 9, 1864. *Generals in Blue.*

A view of the
"Bloody Angle,"
May 12, 1864,
probably taken in
the 1880s.
*Courtesy of the
Massachusetts
Commandery of the
Loyal Legion and the
US Army Military
History Institute.*

Lieutenant Colonel Edwin Schall, '56, 51st Pennsylvania Infantry, killed in action at Cold Harbor, June 3, 1864. *Courtesy of the Massachusetts Commandery of the Loyal Legion and the US Army Military History Institute.*

Brigadier General Thomas E. G. Ransom, '51, died of the effects of his wounds during the "March to the Sea," October 29, 1864. *Courtesy of Special Collections, Norwich University.*

Modern view of Cold Harbor, looking towards the Sixth Corps assault positions from Confederate defense line. *Photo by author.*

The grave of First Sergeant Sardis Birchard, '64, Battery L, 1st Vermont Heavy Artillery, at Andersonville National Cemetery. The new gravestone replaces the original damaged marker and incorrectly lists Birchard as a private. *Photo by author.*

Petersburg — modern reconstructions of Confederate defenses. *Photos by author.*

Major General Joseph A. "Fightin' Joe" Mower, '43, seated front row center, and the officers of the Twentieth Corps, summer 1865. *Courtesy of the Massachusetts Commandery of the Loyal Legion and the US Army Military History Institute.*

Colonel Jacob Parker Gould, '59, mortally wounded at the "Battle of the Crater," July 30, 1864. *Courtesy of the Massachusetts Commandery of the Loyal Legion and the US Army Military History Institute.*

Cadet Grenville M. Dodge, '51, shown in the cadet service uniform of the day. *Courtesy of Special Collections, Norwich University.*

First Lieutenant Edward B. Williston, '56, Battery "D," 2nd United States Artillery and his horse "Pony." They served together in 13 battles and engagements. Williston won the Medal of Honor at Trevilian Station, June 11, 1864. *Photo courtesy of Special Collections, Norwich University.*

VIII. Norwich Men in Other Theaters of War

"Who will follow me?"
Thomas E. G. Ransom '51

O f the 705 Norwich alumni known to have served in the War to Preserve the Union, at least 235 served in the ranks of the Army of the Potomac. In addition, 43 alumni served in the United States Navy or Marine Corps, 56 joined the Confederacy, and most of the identifiable remaining 326 fought for the Union in other theaters. In conducting the research for this study of Norwich alumni in the Army of the Potomac, considerable material was found on those Norwich men who served elsewhere. As the stated purpose of this narrative was to document Norwich alumni in that key Eastern force, a detailed and chronological account of alumni in other armies and theaters is not given here. Rather, a few of the more important alumni and their respective roles are highlighted. The brief overview provided in this chapter serves both the basic goals of this book and lays the groundwork for possible future investigations.[1]

Norwich men not only served the Union on all its war fronts, but were also found in more obscure but equally important roles in the Northern state military structures. This was particularly true of alumni who had attended and graduated from Norwich in the halcyon days of the 1820s; by the 1860s most of these men were too old for active service in the field. Among the more prominent officers filling key positions at that level was Col. William R. Lee (Class of '25). After resigning from the Army of the Potomac due to disability contracted as a regimental and brigade commander, Lee served out the remainder of the war on Governor John Andrew's staff as a brigadier general of Massachusetts state troops. Lee not only played a pivotal role in raising units and training new soldiers in the Bay State, but also personally redesigned Boston's harbor defenses. Elsewhere in New England, Brig. Gen. E. W. N. Starr (Class of '28) served as the chief drillmaster for Connecticut state troops. Starr worked in conjunction with Maj. Gen. William H. Russell (Class of '28), commander of all of Connecticut's state military forces. Russell was instrumental in raising and training troops for his state, in reorganizing the state's militia, and personally drilling the 1st and 2nd Connecticut Infantry Regiments. The quartermaster general of Pennsylvania, Brig. Gen. Reuben C. Hale (Class of '28), though seriously ill, literally worked himself to death outfitting that state's soldiers. When he was notified of Hale's death on July 2, 1863, Gideon Welles (Class of '26) commented in his diary that "A telegram this morning advises me of the death of General R.C. Hale . . . .He was the efficient Quartermaster-General of Pennsylvania, a good officer and capable and upright man. The public never had a more faithful and honest officer."[2]

Turning to those Norwich men who served in the Union's Western armies, a case can be made that their record of service was equal to, and possibly even more distinguished than, that of alumni in the Army of the Potomac. While two alumni, Maj. Gen. Horatio G. Wright (Class of '37) and Maj. Gen. Alfred H. Terry (Class unknown), rose to corps command in the East, at least three alumni did so in the West. In some cases, former Norwich cadets were singled out for particular praise by Generals Grant and Sherman. The role of citizen-soldier general officers in the Western armies was comparable in many ways to that of West Pointers in the Army of the Potomac. Norwich men served the Republic in every major battle fought in that theater of operations. For example, a minimum of 26 Norwich alumni served at Shiloh (Pittsburg Landing), 19 at Stone's River (Murfreesboro), 27 at Vicksburg, 20 at Chickamauga, 21 at Missionary Ridge, 23 at Chattanooga, 30 at Atlanta, 23 in Sherman's "March to the Sea," 10 at Franklin, and 11 at Nashville.[3]

Major General Grenville M. Dodge (Class of '51) is probably the best known Norwich alumnus to serve in the Western Theater. Prior to his historic work in the successful completion of the transcontinental railroad in 1869, Dodge was a Norwich citizen-soldier par excellence. Grenville Dodge began the war as an Iowa drillmaster before being sent to Washington on a special mission to obtain arms for his state. He met with President Lincoln and later was appointed colonel of the 4th Iowa Volunteer Infantry. He served with great distinction and gallantry as a regimental, brigade, division, and corps commander. In the early days of the war, he shared a tent with then Capt. Philip H. Sheridan. Sheridan credited Dodge with providing him critical support during a difficult period when he served as a brigade quartermaster. Had Sheridan failed in this assignment, his career would certainly have been adversely affected, if not ended. "Little Phil" recalled that "Several times I was on the verge of personal conflict with irate regimental commanders, but Colonel Dodge so sustained me before Brig. Gen. [Samuel R.] Curtis and supported me by such efficient details from his regiment—the 4th Iowa—that I shall hold him and it in great affection and lasting gratitude."[4]

As the war in the West continued, General Grant quickly became aware of Dodge's many talents and found work for this Norwich man in several capacities: as a field commander, railroad man, and in the specialized position of military intelligence officer. At Grant's direction, Dodge built up a 100-man secret service organization that was far more efficient and successful than McClellan's Pinkerton men. One historian commented that Dodge's intelligence organization "was probably the most effective secret service in the Federal army and General Grant came to rely on the information received from it. During the investment of Vicksburg many of General Dodge's secret service men operated in the rear of that objective and furnished Grant with authentic information."[5]

Dodge was often called upon to employ the civil and military engineering skills he had learned at Norwich. Grant thought highly of Dodge's activities during the Chattanooga Campaign:

> General Dodge, besides being a most capable soldier, was an experienced railroad builder. He had no tools to work with except those of his pioneers - axes, picks and spades. With these he was able to intrench [sic] his men and protect them against surprises by small parties of the enemy. As he had no base of supplies until the road could be completed back to Nashville, the first matter to consider after protecting his men was the getting in of food and forage from the surrounding country. He

had his men and teams bring in all the grain they could find, or all they needed, and all the cattle for beef, and such other food as could be found. . . .Blacksmiths were detailed and set to work making the tools necessary in railroad and bridge building. Axemen were put to work getting out timber for the bridges and cutting fuel for the locomotives and cars. . . .General Dodge had the work assigned him finished within forty days after receiving his orders. The number of bridges to rebuild was one hundred and eighty-two, many of them over deep and wide chasms; the length of road repaired was one hundred two miles.

In addition to his important and pragmatic engineering achievements, Dodge's success as a field commander resulted in his eventual rise to command of the Sixteenth Corps in the Atlanta Campaign. Grant specifically referred to Dodge as "an exceedingly efficient officer" and personally appealed to President Lincoln to ensure Dodge's promotion to major general in May 1864.[6]

During the climax of the Atlanta Campaign, Grenville Dodge was both cited for gallantry and severely wounded. General William T. Sherman, commanding the effort against the key Georgia metropolis, seems to have placed particular value not only on the services of Dodge, but also other Norwich men. In one incident, after Dodge successfully repulsed an attack by Gen. John B. Hood's men, Sherman called to him on the field and said: "'Dodge, you whipped them today didn't you?' 'Yes, Sir' Dodge replied. 'Can you do it again tomorrow?' said Sherman 'Yes, Sir,' Dodge answered and returned to his troops."[7]

In his report to Sherman of the enemy's main attack, the weight of which had fallen upon his command, General Dodge said that "The disparity of forces can be seen from the fact that in the charge made by my two brigades under Fuller and Mersey they took 351 prisoners, representing forty-nine different regiments, eight brigades and three divisions; and brought back eight battle flags from the enemy." Dodge unabashedly attributed the basis of his success as a soldier to the training he had obtained in his cadet days at Norwich. "What little success I have had in life I credit to my college training. For three years I had drummed into me a daily respect for authority, obedience to orders, the disciplining of my mind and actions, loyalty to an employer, patriotism toward my government and honor to the flag."[8]

Major General Joseph A. "Fightin' Joe" Mower (Class of '43), was another personal favorite of Grant and Sherman. Mower began the war as a captain in the 1st United States Infantry, later commanded the 11th Missouri Infantry, served for a time as commander of the Sixteenth Corps famed "Eagle Brigade," saw extensive service as a division commander, and eventually commanded the Twentieth Corps at the end of the war. Mower, wounded in action and cited for gallantry several times, drew particular praise for breaking Confederate lines at the Battle of Bentonville, North Carolina—a bold strike referred to as "Mower's Charge." The attack was so daring that General Sherman, in a rare display of temerity, recalled Mower's men and called off the attack. Before it was halted, Mower had actually overrun Joseph E. Johnson's Confederate headquarters, perhaps the only time such an event occurred in the Civil War. Mower earned brevets in the Regular Army in every grade through major general, and a recommendation for promotion to brigadier general of volunteers was submitted by Grant himself. In speaking of assigning the aggressive Mower to command of the Twentieth Corps in April 1865, Sherman proclaimed: "I had specially asked for General Mower to command the Twentieth Corps, because I regarded him as one of the boldest and best fighting generals in the whole army." Joe Mower was only 36 at the time. Prior to this, Sherman intervened with Lincoln in order to have Mower promoted to major general of volunteers. Sherman had such confidence in Mower's abilities that at one point he proclaimed: "Say to General Mower that I want him advanced and if he will whip [Nathan Bedford] Forrest I will pledge him my influence for a major-general and will ask the President as a personal favor to hold a vacancy for him." Sherman then telegraphed President Lincoln and asked that a major general's position be held for Mower, whom he described as "one of the gamest men in the service." When informed later that Mower had indeed defeated the redoubtable Forrest, Sherman exclaimed: "Tell General Mower I am pledged to him for his promotion and if Old Abe don't make good my promise then General Mower may have my place."[9]

Brigadier General (Brevet Major General) Thomas E. G. Ransom (Class of '51), was the most promising of the three sons of Colonel Truman B. Ransom (Class of '25), the president of Norwich killed in action at Chapultepec during the Mexican War. First gaining notice as a result of his gallant performance at the Battle of Fort Donelson,

Thomas Ransom rose through the ranks to command the 11th Illinois Infantry, then a brigade, a division and finally, the Seventeenth Corps. One of the earliest flashes of his courage and daring took place at the Battle of Charleston, Missouri, in 1861. Ransom was urging his men on to the charge when "a man rode up and called out 'What do you mean? You are killing our own men.' Ransom replied, 'I know what I am doing. Who are you?' The reply was 'I am for Jeff Davis.' Ransom replied, 'You are the man I am after' and instantly two pistols were drawn. The rebel fired first, taking effect in Col. Ransom's arm, near the shoulder. The Colonel fired, killing his antagonist instantly."[10]

General Ransom was repeatedly cited for conspicuous gallantry and was wounded on several occasions, sometimes severely. The effect of these injuries eventually resulting in his death by disease while on active service on October 29, 1864. A number of high ranking Federal commanders believe Ransom would have risen to even higher command had he lived. Relegated to relative obscurity today, he was nearly legendary during the war.[11]

The young Norwich-trained Ransom was viewed by contemporaries as a man born to command who was blessed with an erect carriage, possessed of a rigid moral sense based on deep rooted convictions, motivated by a strong sense of responsibility, integrity and awesome determination. General Oliver O. Howard, a great admirer of Ransom, referred to him as the "handsomest man he had ever met." In an early assessment of his abilities as a combat commander and troop leader, Maj. Gen. Ulysses S. Grant believed "Ransom would have been equal to command of a corps at least," that he was "a most gallant and intelligent volunteer officer," "as fine an officer. . .as can be found in the service," and the "best man I ever had to send on expeditions." Grant further stated that Ransom "is my best fighting man, young as he is." Citing but one example of his ingenuity, which occurred while the army was bridging the Big Black River during the Vicksburg Campaign, Grant recalled how "Ransom felled trees on opposite banks of the river, cutting only on one side of the tree, so that they would fall with their tops interlacing in the river, without the trees being entirely severed from their stumps." When this task was complete, "A bridge was then made with these trees to support the roadway. Lumber was taken from buildings, cotton gins and wherever found for this purpose. By eight o'clock in the morning. . .the troops were crossing."[12]

General Sherman referred to the 29-year-old Ransom as a "young, most gallant and promising officer." One of the more outstanding examples of his valor in combat came during the murderous general assault on the seemingly impregnable Vicksburg defenses on May 22, 1863. Ransom personally led the charge of his brigade on foot, and several of his regimental commanders fell dead or wounded (survivors of the assault would refer to Ransom's courage as "supernatural"). The attacking troops came upon what seemed to be an impassable ditch:

> The column wavered, General Ransom rushed to the head, seized the colors of the 95th (Illinois) and waving them high over his head shouted "Forward men, we must and will go into that fort! Who will follow me?" The tide was turned. The column advanced. . .and fought for a full thirty minutes across the breastworks, when General Ransom, satisfied that the position could not be carried. . . .addressed them: "Men of the 2d Brigade we cannot maintain this position; you must retire to the cover of the ravine one regiment at a time and in order. . . .The first man to run shall be shot on the spot. I will stand here and see how you do it." The movement was executed as cooly by every regiment as if on battalion drill and the command was reformed. . .without confusion and without a single straggler.

Ransom's troops, despite the attack's eventual failure, had actually managed to plant several of their colors on the enemy rampart before being repulsed.[13]

Prior to that assault, Ransom had joked with fellow alumnus Lt. Col. Joseph C. Wright (Class of '42), who was commanding the 72nd Illinois, about the fine field glass which he had been using. "Colonel, if you are killed I want you to leave that glass to me." Wright demurred, informing the young general that he had promised the glass to his son if he were killed. Later that day Wright was severely wounded while leading his regiment in the futile attack. His arm was amputated on the field and he died July 6, 1863, surviving barely long enough to know Vicksburg had fallen. The field glass was returned to his son.[14]

The May 22 attack by Ransom's brigade was big news in Illinois, and the young Norwich alumnus and his men were showered with praise. Both Ransom's corps commander, Maj. Gen. James B. McPherson, and his division commander, Brig. Gen. John McArthur, spoke of him in glowing terms. The citizens of Chicago not only presented Ransom with a gold medal commemorating his valor at Vicksburg, but also awarded him a sword, a sash, a pair of revolvers, a set of field glasses and other gifts valued at $600.[15]

The effects of three years of field service combined with his many wounds finally felled Ransom in Georgia on October 29, 1864, a month short of his thirtieth birthday. As he lay on his death bed, he stoically accepted his fate, finding solace in the fact that he was dying in the line of duty. Ransom's last coherent words were: "As a soldier I have tried to do my duty. I do not claim that all I have done was owing to patriotism alone, though I believe I have as much of that as most men." His passing was mourned by Sherman, his fellow commanders, and his troops. Ransom's body was returned to Chicago where it lay in state. On the day of his burial, his funeral cortege had to make its way through throngs of citizens on its way to the city cemetery. The *Chicago Times* reported the day "was unusually dark and gloomy. Heavy black clouds hung over the city as if the elements sympathized with the mourning of a people over the departed hero. Only on the far distant horizon the heavens were breaking into light and splendor suggestive of the glorious dawn."[16]

Many years after Ransom's death, Sherman remembered the Norwich alumnus during a speech in St. Louis, Missouri, on June 20, 1884. "War is the supreme test of manhood and an hour—a minute sometimes—reveals the spirit which is in the man; the grasp of the hand, the flash of the eye, the unspoken word which trembles on the lips. . .tell more than a volume can record." Sherman recalled, "It was during the siege of Vicksburg that I first noticed this young man. . . .I saw Ransom during the assault the 22nd of May, 1863—saw his brigade dash against the battlements to be hurled back. . . .I then marked him as of the kind of whom heroes were made." Shortly after her son's death, Ransom's mother received his major general's commission from President Lincoln, a small token of the esteem in which he was held by the Chief Executive. The spirit of the gallant Ransoms, father and son, lives on today within Ransom Hall, one of the principal cadet barracks at their Alma Mater.[17]

Far less well known and less fortunate than his illustrious brother was the youngest of Truman B. Ransom's sons, Frederick Eugene

(Class of '68). Enlisting at the start of the war in his brother Thomas' 11th Illinois infantry company, Eugene (as he was known) rose through the ranks to earn a field commission as second lieutenant. Unfortunately, he was severely wounded and captured at Fort Donelson, Tennessee, and spent a number of months in Confederate prison camps, including the notorious Libby Prison. The months spent living off the enemy's hospitality appear to have had a severe effect upon Ransom's regimen. After his release and a long recuperation period, he rejoined his regiment in time for the siege of Vicksburg, where he was again wounded. Over time, as a result of his failing health and the severe pain resulting from his wounds and imprisonment, Eugene's strength waned and he began to drink to excess. Out of respect for his brother, the regiment kept him on their rolls as long as possible.

As his conduct worsened, he was finally given the choice of being cashiered or resigning "for the good of the service." With evident regret, his regimental commander wrote to his superiors in June 1864: "I send you herewith Lieut. F. E. Ransom, E. Co., 11th Ill. Infantry. Charged with being drunk on picket yesterday 1st inst. I would say here that I have no apology to make for the man or the offense, as it is not the first time that he has committed the same crime." Despite this serious misdeed, "I must, however, for the Sake of his Family, ask an indulgence. His Father fell in Battle in Mexico, his Eldest Brother Captain [Dunbar] Ransom, now lies dangerously wounded and his other brother, Brig. Gen. Ransom is so favorably known to all Western Soldiers, as to make it unnecessary for me to speak more than his name." Concluding, Ransom's commander wrote, "I had charges prepared against the Lieut. for a previous misdemeanor and to save [the] Family from disgrace I had offered him an opportunity of resigning." Eugene finally did resign on July 6, 1864, citing "ill health," a statement which bore a large measure of truth. He went on to attend Norwich, apparently at General Dodge's suggestion and with his financial support, and then moved on to an undistinguished railroad career working for Grenville Dodge, his father's closest friend and former Norwich roommate. Ransom's final days were spent alone in the National Military Home at Fort Leavenworth, Kansas. While it seems that even in the Ransom family there was a limit to virtue, it must have been a most difficult burden for the youngest Ransom, living in the shadow of his distinguished father and brothers.[18]

In the Civil War, Norwich alumni served in the Western armies in all ranks from private to major general (corps commander). Among the other more distinguished alumni to serve in that theater was the bold cavalryman Brig. Gen. (Brevet Major General) Edward Hatch (Class of '50). Hatch served consecutively as a cavalry regimental, brigade and division commander. He led the 2nd Iowa Cavalry in the famous "Grierson's Raid," and was portrayed in the movie "The Horse Soldiers," starring John Wayne. Starting from La Grange, Tennessee, on April 17, 1863, Hatch and his 2nd Iowa were detached from Grierson's main force on April 21 and sent to destroy the important railroad bridge between Columbus and Macon. At Palo Alto, Hatch and his troopers had a sharp fight with Confederate troops and defeated them without the loss of a single man, his cavalrymen using their new Colt revolving rifles with good effect. Following the engagement, Hatch withdrew along the railroad line, destroying it as he went. A principal objective of Hatch's portion of the raid had been to decoy Confederate troops to the east, giving Grierson and the main body ample time to accomplish their mission without interference, a task which was successfully accomplished. His portion of the assignment satisfactorily concluded, Hatch and his troops successfully returned to the La Grange cavalry base on April 26.[19]

Hatch was an exceptionally successful cavalry commander, and led numerous independent operations, including a major raid into Mississippi in July 1864. In that expedition, his troops took Oxford, where Hatch made his headquarters in the home of former United States Secretary of the Interior Jacob Thompson. Thompson, at the time the Confederate Commissioner in Canada, was viewed as a particularly vile traitor. While Hatch's cavalrymen normally did very little plundering, they made an exception in the case of Thompson's house. When Mrs. Thompson appealed to Hatch for protection, he told her "that his men could take anything they wished except the chair on which he was then seated." Following the war, Edward Hatch went on to an distinguished Regular Army career in command of the 9th United States Cavalry, one of the army's two famous regiments of

"Buffalo Soldiers." While in the West, Hatch was severely wounded in action and cited for gallantry at least three times.[20]

Brigadier General William "Bull" Nelson (Class of '39) stood out in the army as a giant of a man. Standing 6' 4" tall, weighing 300 pounds and possessing a fierce temper, Nelson was not a man to be trifled with. Having served a number of years in the United States Navy, the combative Nelson switched to the army in 1861 in order to see more action. A personal friend of President Lincoln, Nelson played an important role in keeping Kentucky in the Union. At the battle of Shiloh, where he commanded a division in Maj. Gen. Don Carlos Buell's army, he helped save Grant's army and engineer a Union victory. Crossing the river by steamer during a critical moment in the fight on April 6, 1862, Nelson and his troops forced their way ashore through a horde of panic-stricken and fleeing Union soldiers. According to an eyewitness, "As the prow touched the shore, the first company jumped off and cleared a small space at the point of the bayonet. They were greeted with cries from the mob. 'We're whipped!' 'The fight is lost!' 'We're cut to pieces!'" Outraged by this rampant cowardice, to the front pushed the hulking Nelson, "his six foot, three-hundred-pound frame stretched to the fullest in an old fatigue coat and feathered hat, [and] mounted [on] Ned, his huge black horse, said to stand seventeen hands high. . . .Nelson ordered two aides positioned on each side of him and the other mounted officers in line immediately behind. Turning to his escort, Nelson shouted, 'Gentlemen, draw your sabers and trample these bastards into the mud!—Charge!' As the mounted party sprang forward, the 'skeedadlers in front tumbled over each other in abject terror. . . .with Nelson leading the way, the 36th Indiana dashed up the steep hillside shouting 'Buell!' to encourage Grant's disheartened troops."[21]

In the aftermath of the Shiloh victory, Nelson earned a promotion to major general only to be murdered a few months later by the politically well-connected Brig. Gen. Jefferson C. Davis. A particularly outrageous and publicized incident at the time, the Norwich man's demise was described by Maj. Gen. Don Carlos Buell, commander of the Army of the Ohio: "General Nelson, an officer of remarkable merit, was. . .assaulted and killed by General Davis, accompanied by Governor Morton, the very day before the army was to march against the invaders." Describing Nelson as "often rough in command, [he] was always solicitous about the well being of his troops and was held in high esteem for his conspicuous services, gallantry in battle and great energy; and his death caused much indignation among the troops that knew him best." General Buell commented how lucky he was that "The restraining influence of discipline was all that prevented an outbreak between the friends of Nelson and Davis." Following the murder, "Davis was immediately placed under arrest and the case reported to General Halleck, with the request that a court might be ordered from Washington for its trial, as the operations then in progress made it impracticable for me to spare the officers for the purpose at the moment." Buell was chagrined to learn that "Davis was released, ostensibly that the case might be turned over to the civil authority. In the end "the military authority of the Government was abased over the grave of a high officer, whose slaughter by another officer under such circumstances and as a purely military offense, it had not the character to bring to trial."[22]

Dozens of Norwich alumni who served in theaters other than the East were cited for gallantry, earned promotions or brevet promotions, were wounded, mortally wounded or killed in action. A number of these men deserve mention. Capt. Charles E. Denison (Class of '45), 18th United States Infantry, died a few days after being severely wounded in the Battle of Murfreesboro. First Lieutenant John B. T. Mead (Class of '51), served as the adjutant of the 28th Illinois at Shiloh and was mortally wounded there while rendering gallant service. Mead's home town of Bunker Hill, Illinois, erected a monument to his memory. Lieutenant Colonel Arba N. Waterman (Class of '55) was severely wounded and cited for gallantry at Chickamauga; he was soon after discharged due to the crippling nature of his wounds. Lieutenant Colonel Frederick W. Partridge (Class of '45), 13th Illinois, was a son of the founder of Norwich University and an outstanding example of the citizen-soldier idolized by his father. Partridge received several citations for valor, was wounded in action, commanded the 13th regiment in several major battles, and was breveted a brigadier general before the war's end.[23]

Chickamauga was one of the most bitterly fought battles in the Western Theater, at least 20 Norwich men participated in that two-day engagement. One of these alumni, Col. George P. Buell (Class of '56), commanded a brigade in the very midst of the chaotic and bloody combat in Viniard Field. In his official report Buell noted: "While my troops were being formed, the enemy's balls were whistling about our ears and the battle raging most fiercely, seemed approaching nearer." Rapidly preparing his men to meet the onslaught, the "formation of my command was not yet complete when everything in my immediate front and left gave way and hundreds of our own men ran through our ranks crying 'Fall back.'" Realizing the danger he and his soldiers faced, and "Knowing my front regiments could not long withstand such a shock I ordered a charge of bayonet with our rear regiment. The attempt was manfully made." Trying to force their way forward, Buell's men met "hundreds of our own men on the fence in front of them." Continuing on, "they met artillery and caissons besides the enemy's fire, so that it was impossible to form any kind of line, but notwithstanding such obstructions they gained some distance to the front. At this period my brave men, both front and rear lines, strove desperately to hold their ground. . . .Just here the slaughter was completed." Soon, however, the small brigade was "Overpowered on both front and flank my men faltered and finally fell back about two hundred yards across the field in our rear. Here my men were rallied and again they charged forward, retook the ground and also three pieces of artillery that they had lost in the first part of the action." Despite this initial success, "Again the enemy came forward like an avalanche and forced my men back a short distance. Again my men rallied and retook the same position they had formerly held. The enemy came forward a third time and were effectually repulsed and the sun went down with my command holding the field, a short distance in advance of its original position." A pause ensued and Buell's "men lay on their arms in this position until 3 o'clock in the morning of the 20th, when they moved to the left about one and a half-miles." Then, at "About half past 11 a.m. I received orders to move my Brigade by the left flank for the purpose of supporting some portion of the line to our left. We had scarcely moved one Brigade when the shock came like an avalanche on my right flank." Another crisis was upon Buell, as "At one point we advanced again from one hill to the next in front and fought the left flank of a long line of battle. . .until we were almost surrounded and flanked on our right. . . .About 4 o'clock the ammunition entirely failed, we had already taken all from the dead and wounded around us. The men fixed bayonets as a last resort to hold the hill." Buell fought on to the end, earning a brevet brigadier generalship for his wartime services to the Republic.[24]

First Lieutenant Henry Clay Wood (Class of '56), 11th United States Infantry, was one of those rare individuals whose valor in combat soared above and beyond that of his comrades. Leading a company of mounted rifle recruits at the Battle of Wilson's Creek, Missouri, on August 10, 1861, Clay was severely injured and earned a Congressional Medal of Honor for distinguished gallantry. Too badly wounded to return to the front, Wood held important staff positions in the War Department during the remainder of the Civil War, and then went on to an outstanding postwar army career, rising to the rank of brigadier general in the Regular Army.

On the West coast, Col. (Brevet Brigadier General) Thomas F. Wright (Class of '49) distinguished himself serving with several cavalry and infantry commands in California. Young Thomas served under the direction of another alumnus in California, his father. So valuable were the elder Wright's services in California and the Northwest that on September 28, 1861, he was given command of the vast Department of the Pacific. Brigadier General George Wright (Class of '22), commanded that strategically important department during the war "with sleepless vigilance, unflagging energy, and uncompromising patriotism." On July 30, 1865, Wright was on his way to assume command of the Department of Columbia when he was drowned at sea in the shipwreck of the steamer *Brother Jonathan*. Lastly in the West, 1st Lt. Julius O. Buel (Class of '61), an officer in Company L, 1st Colorado Cavalry, died of disease while on active service in the spring of 1862.[25]

Numerous Norwich men also served in operations along the eastern and gulf seaboards and in Virginia's Shenandoah Valley. Major General Alfred H. Terry (Class unknown) was one of the war's most outstanding examples of a citizen-soldier. He began his service as a 33-year-old colonel in command of the 2nd Connecticut at Bull Run. Following his discharge, Terry raised and led the 7th Connecticut Infantry. He served in turn as a brigade and division commander and eventually was promoted to lead the Army of the James' Tenth Corps. His most famous wartime accomplishment was the dramatic assault and capture of the seemingly impregnable Fort Fisher at the mouth of the Cape Fear River, North Carolina. This action sealed off the Confederacy's last port at Wilmington and earned Terry the official thanks of Congress, a promotion to major general of volunteers for distinguished gallantry, and finally a brigadier generalship in the postwar Regular Army. He went on to an equally distinguished career in the United States Army, eventually becoming the first Civil War volunteer officer to rise to the grade of major general, United States Army. In assessing Terry's abilities as a commander, Ulysses S. Grant declared: "His way was won without political influence up to an important separate command—the expedition against Fort Fisher, in January 1865. His success there was most brilliant and won for him the rank of brigadier-general in the regular army and of major-general of volunteers." Speaking of Terry's character, Grant added that he was "a man who makes friends of those under him by his consideration of their wants and their dues. As a commander, he won their confidence by his coolness in action and by his clearness of perception in taking in the situation under which he was placed at any given time."[26]

In the Shenandoah Valley, the aggressive, controversial and volatile Maj. Gen. Robert H. Milroy (Class of '43) became a scourge to Confederate civilians and soldiers alike. Milroy, a Mexican War veteran, rose rapidly from colonel of the 9th Indiana Infantry to major general of volunteers. When in command of the Mountain Department in 1862, this Norwich alumnus decisively suppressed guerrilla warfare in the western sections of Virginia, but did so through the employment of draconian means. Milroy issued an order to the effect that whenever the property of a citizen loyal to the Union was taken, or a loyal citizen killed by guerrillas, an appraisal would be taken of the losses by Federal officers, and the Confederate neighbors of that victim would be made to pay compensation. Those failing to do so would be shot. Virginians howled and the Secessionist government was outraged. The Confederacy offered a $100,000 reward for Milroy dead or alive, (it was never collected). Milroy was the field commander when Union troops were surprised and decisively defeated at the Second Battle of Winchester in June 1863. Despite his display of personal courage in that fight, Milroy was relieved of command and blamed for the loss. Stunned by the War Department's action, Milroy appealed for and was granted a Court of Inquiry. During the investigation, Milroy claimed he had been placed in an untenable situation, but that the delay he imposed on advancing Confederates during the battle bought valuable time for Union forces redeploying from Virginia to confront Lee's second invasion of the North. He was not alone in that belief. Major General Abner Doubleday stated, perhaps too strongly, that Milroy's actions "gave time to the General Government and the Governors of the loyal states to raise troops and organize resistance and it awakened the entire North to immediate action."[27]

After an extended investigation, which finally involved the direct intervention of President Lincoln, Milroy was exonerated of all charges. Despite having been cleared of any guilt in the Winchester fiasco, Milroy was permanently deprived of active field command. He believed to his dying day that the basis of his problems with the Union Army high command stemmed from his being a volunteer officer rather than a West Pointer. There may have been some merit to Milroy's complaint—he was not alone in the suspicion that certain elements in the War Department opposed the advance and success of volunteer officers. Secretary of the Navy Gideon Welles (Class of '26), for one, commented in his diary at the time of the Battle of Winchester how "The President said quietly to me he was feeling very bad; that he found Milroy and his command were captured, or would be." Welles went on how "I inquired why Milroy did not fall back—if he had not been apprised by Hooker, or from here, what Lee was doing. . . . Halleck did not move from his chair where he sat with his cigar." Upon reflection Welles realized, "From some expressions which were dropped from H.[alleck] I suspect poor Milroy is to be made the scapegoat and blamed for the stupid blunders, neglects and mistakes of those who should have warned and advised him."[28]

In a postscript to the story, Welles wrote on June 17, 1863, that "I was sorry to hear Stanton communicate an exaggerated account of Milroy's disaster, who, he said, had not seen a fight or even an enemy. [General Montgomery] Meigs indignantly denied the statement and said Milroy himself had communicated the fact that he had fought a battle and escaped. While he [Meigs] did not consider Milroy a great general, or a man of great ability, he believed him to be truthful and brave." Welles wondered, "Why should the Secretary of War wish to misrepresent and belittle Milroy?"[29]

Milroy's younger brother, Maj. John B. Milroy (Class of '45), also served the Union with courage and merit. As captain of Company A, 9th Indiana ("The Bloody Ninth") at the Battle of Shiloh, John Milroy distinguished himself by his bravery, winning a citation and a battle-field promotion to major. At Shiloh, the 9th Indiana suffered the highest casualties of any Union unit engaged and won the rare honor of being cited for its bravery (by Brig. Gen. William Nelson during the battle.) The 9th, though outnumbered two to one, held its ground against attacking forces which several times advanced to the very muzzles of their rifles, thereby saving the flank of their division from total collapse.[30]

When the United States Colored Troops were initially formed in 1863, a number of Norwich men volunteered to serve with them. Several alumni successfully passed individual reviews by strict examination boards to earn commissions or promotions into the new "sable arm." More than 20 Norwich men eventually saw service with these black units. Among them were Col. (Brevet Brigadier General) Bernard G. Farrar (Class of '45), who commanded the 6th United States Colored Heavy Artillery. This unit was widely known for its fine appearance and superior discipline. Farrar's classmate, Col. (Brevet Brigadier General) Simon M. Preston (Class of '45), 58th United States Colored Infantry, also gained prominence in assisting those eager soldiers to earn their freedom through the force of arms. Captain Daniel W. Parmenter (Class of '64), Company G, 10th United States Colored Infantry, left the ranks of the 32nd Massachusetts following Gettysburg only to be killed in action leading his men at the Battle of Plymouth, North Carolina. Those alumni who served with colored troops ran special risks—the Southerners initially viewed them as the treasonous leaders of armed slaves in revolt against the Confederacy, and had initially ordered them to be executed upon capture.[31]

Among the more distinguished alumni associated with the activities of the fledgling black troops was Maj. Gen. George C. Strong (Class of '53). Strong, who is portrayed in the climactic scene of the movie "Glory," commanded the assault brigade for the July 18, 1863, attack on Battery Wagner, South Carolina. The spearhead unit of that assault was the now-legendary 54th Massachusetts Infantry (Colored). The decision to employ the 54th Massachusetts in such a prominent role at Battery Wagner was made by Brigadier General Strong and fellow alumnus Brig. Gen. Truman B. Seymour (Class of '44), his division commander. Prior to the charge, Strong personally addressed the eager men, telling them that he too was a Massachusetts man and knew that they would uphold the Bay State's honor. Strong called the regimental color bearer forward and asked the men of the regiment who would pick up the Old Flag if the color bearer fell? Virtually the entire regiment shouted out its willingness to do so. When the 54th's commander, Colonel Robert Gould Shaw, removed the cigar from his mouth and declared "I will," the regiment responded with cheers and the attack began.[32]

Federal casualties during the storming of Battery Wagner were severe. Colonel Shaw was killed at the head of his regiment, which suffered 40% casualties. Despite the high price, the 54th Massachusetts had permanently validated the combat value of black troops. Major General Quincy A. Gilmore, who commanded operations in the Carolinas at the time, wrote that "The time of evening twilight was selected [for the attack]. . . .Brigadier General Truman Seymour organized and commanded the assaulting column, composed of Brigadier General G. C. Strong's brigade." When the attack hour arrived, "the troops went gallantly forward and gained the south-east bastion of the work and held it for more than two hours." Despite the men's bravery, "the advantages which local knowledge and the deepening darkness gave the enemy forced a withdrawal. The repulse was complete and our loss severe, especially in officers of rank." Speaking with admiration for his young brigadier's battlefield demeanor, Gilmore recalled that the "gallant Strong, who had been the first man to land on Morris Island a few days before, actually leading his entire command in that descent and in the daring assault that followed, was fatally wounded." Gilmore saw Strong "as he was being conveyed to the rear. I stopped the ambulance for a moment to ask if he was badly hurt. He recognized my voice and replied, 'No, General, I think not; only a severe flesh wound in the hip.'" Strong was taken that night to the Union hospital at Beaufort, South Carolina. But while hospitalized, Strong "was seized with a yearning desire to go home and, without my knowledge, took the first steamer for the North. Being the senior officer on board, the excitement of the trip. . .brought on lock-jaw, of which he died shortly after reaching New York." In addition to Strong, Gilmore wrote that "Colonel John L. Chatfield was mortally wounded; Colonel Haldimand S. Putnam and Colonel Robert G. Shaw were killed; and Brigadier General Truman Seymour and several regimental commanders were wounded."[33]

Strong received his commission as a full major general of volunteers shortly before he died. Fellow alumnus Seymour, the assaulting division commander, had also been wounded on the field by an artillery shell and borne to the rear. Sharing the danger of that charge with the troops at Battery Wagner were at least three other Norwich men: Maj. Thomas A. Henderson (Class of '62) 7th New Hampshire; Sgt. William Coffee (Class of '49) Company A, 3rd New Hampshire; and Pvt. Lewis Kimball (Class of '62) Company F, 3rd New Hampshire. In the assault on Battery Wagner, the 7th New Hampshire had the misfortune to suffer the heaviest officer loss by a Union regiment in a single engagement in the war when 18 officers were killed or wounded.[34]

Forty-three additional Norwich alumni served in the United States Navy and Marine Corps. The most famous of these was Secretary of the Navy Gideon Welles (Class of '26). Welles was one of President Abraham Lincoln's most trusted advisors, and was counted among Lincoln's personal friends and confidants. He was a moderating influence in the cabinet and served as the architect of the rebuilding and modernization of the wartime Union navy. As Navy Secretary, he was instrumental in the development and successful implementation of the Federal blockade of Southern ports. Among his more famous wartime decisions were those authorizing the building of the *U.S.S. Monitor* and the beginning of the transition of the United States Navy to iron ships. When the war ended, the United States had the most modern and powerful navy in the world. In addition, Welles had the honor and foresight to commission the original design for the first Congressional Medals of Honor.[35]

In the uniformed fleet, Rear Adm. Hiram Paulding (Class of '23) was one of the first naval officers appointed to that esteemed rank by President Lincoln. Put in charge of the rebuilding of the United States

Navy, Paulding worked closely with Welles and personally oversaw the outfitting of the *Monitor*, the first Union ironclad. That this ship was built at all was largely due to his foresight and guidance. In addition, Paulding played a little known though important role in providing naval support to the suppression of the infamous draft riots in New York City during July-August 1863.[36]

Captain James H. Ward (Class of '23), commander of the Potomac Flotilla in the spring of 1861, had the dubious distinction of being the first Federal naval officer killed in action in the war. Ward had commanded the Potomac Flotilla in the war's first naval engagement at Aquia Creek, Virginia, on May 31, 1861, and was felled by a minie ball in another engagement at Aquia Creek on June 27. Prior to the rebellion, Ward had been a prominent instructor at the Naval Academy at Annapolis during its infancy, and his textbook on naval science and tactics was the standard work at the academy for years. Today, the United States Naval Academy's most prominent academic building, Ward Hall, bears his name. The gallant Ward was joined in the ranks of the fallen in July 1861 by Lt. Robert E. Hitchcock (Class of '59), who was the first marine and the first Vermont officer slain in the Civil War.[37]

Other Norwich men stood out in the ranks of the Union navy. Commodore Thomas T. Craven (Class of '23) was regarded as one of the most distinguished seamen of the war. In command of the *U.S.S. Brooklyn* while the fleet ran the Confederate forts protecting New Orleans, Craven's actions were exceptionally valorous. Following the battle, Admiral Farragut exclaimed to Craven: "You and your noble ship have been the salvation of my squadron." Commodore Craven's brother, Cdr. Tunis A. M. Craven (Class of '29), set an exceptional and unique example for personal courage when he was killed in action during the Battle of Mobile Bay on August 5, 1864. Craven, who commanded the monitor *U.S.S. Tecumseh*, ordered the entire crew to evacuate his severely damaged ship after it struck a mine. As the *Tecumseh* began to sink and the crew abandoned ship, Tunis Craven and his pilot instinctively made for the narrow opening leading to exit. Craven drew back and said, in the finest traditions of the naval service, "After you, pilot." There was no afterward for Tunis—the pilot survived but Craven drowned.

Captain Charles S. Boggs (Class of '26) also earned fame and a reputation for courage in the 1862 capture of New Orleans. In command of the gunboat *U.S.S. Varuna* as the Union fleet ran by the forts protecting the city, his ship was set afire and surrounded by Rebel gunboats. Boggs gave his crew an order to "work both sides and load with grape." Although his own vessel was shot to pieces and rammed three times, Boggs sank three enemy ships before the *Varuna* finally went down with its guns still firing and flag flying. Captain Boggs was cited for gallantry and was voted a presentation sword by his native state and town. Though not the most famous naval officer of this war, Cdr. (later full Admiral) George S. Dewey (Class of '55), gained extensive combat command experience and a reputation for courage and daring which served him well in the Spanish-American War's Battle of Manila Bay in 1898. Dewey Hall at Norwich University recognizes the national legacy for gallantry and achievement of this son of Alden Partridge.[38]

Last, but certainly not least, are the Norwich alumni who chose to serve the Stars and Bars rather than the Union. They believed in and fought hard for the Confederacy as their Norwich brethren did for the Union. While the records for these men are woefully incomplete, at least 56 Norwich men fought for the South during these tragic years. Of particular note in the Confederate hierarchy was the Confederate Attorney General Thomas Bragg (Class of '28), brother of the famous Braxton Bragg. Major Stephen S. Tucker (Class of '32), died of wounds received in the defense of Mobile, Alabama. Colonel Andrew J. Dorn (Class of '41) had the unique and challenging role of commanding the Sachem Indians who fought for the Confederacy. Lieutenant Colonel Frederick H. Farrar (Class of '56) commanded the 1st Louisiana Infantry and was regarded as a most promising young officer before he fell mortally wounded at the Battle of Stone's River, Tennessee, in December 1862. Captain (Chaplain) Richard P. Johnson (Class of '29) gained a greater reputation as a drillmaster, expert swordsman and fighter than he did as a preacher. Johnson was known to his fellow cavalrymen as the "Fighting Chaplain." While serving with the renowned "Hampton's Legion," Johnston was cited for gallantry several times, and even had his horse shot out from under him during a cavalry charge. Colonel Eugene S. McClean (Class of '37) rose to prominence as assistant quartermaster general of the Confederacy.[39]

Wearing the uniform of the Confederate Navy, Commodore Josiah Tattnall (Class of '23) had turned down an admiral's rank in the United States Navy to serve Virginia and the Confederacy. Among his more important actions were defending the James River approaches to Richmond and scuttling the *C.S.S. Virginia* to prevent its falling into Union hands. Commander Ebenezer Farrand (Class of '27), commanded the naval batteries at Drewry's Bluff, Virginia, in an engagement with the Federal fleet in April 1862. He then led the Southern flotilla that attacked Union ships at City Point, Virginia, on the James River on May 15, 1862. For his actions Farrand received the thanks of the Confederate Congress for what was regarded as a "great and signal victory achieved by his fleet over the naval forces of the United States."[40]

Lastly, Capt. Thomas H. Davis (Class of '55), commanding Company B, 1st Virginia, Kemper's Brigade, Pickett's Division, Longstreet's Corps, survived all his regiment's battles, including Pickett's Charge, only to be wounded and captured within the Union line that afternoon. As previously mentioned, Davis managed to escape the Union prisoner of war camp at Johnson's Island, Ohio, and, after an extended and perilous journey through Canada and at sea on a blockade runner, returned to his unit. He was captured again at Sayler's Creek, Virginia, three days before the end of the war.[41]

IX. Postscript

"By the blood of our Alumni."
Unknown Cadet '65

*T*he Civil War stands, hopefully for perpetuity, as the bloodiest of American conflicts. The Norwich *Roll of Honor* of those who fell in defense of the Union is extensive and likely incomplete. It totals a minimum of 61 alumni (plus at least two additional Confederate officers) killed in action, died of wounds received in battle, or perished from disease or other causes. Dozens of others suffered permanently disabling wounds or were struck down by illnesses of varying severity. These men were destined to live out the rest of their often shortened lives either crippled or in a weakened state.

Evaluating the impact of Norwich University and its alumni—or those of any college—in the Civil War is difficult and somewhat subjective. Regardless, given the events, personalities and exploits detailed in this narrative, it is surprising that Norwich remains virtually unknown to students of the war. Why is this so? Perhaps one simple reason is that, unlike other more famous academies (e.g., West Point and V.M.I.), it does not contain the word "military" in its official title. Also, Norwich University itself is partially to blame. Until recently, New England's only military college has made little effort to tout its impressive history and accomplishments to the general public. Regardless of the reasons for this unfortunate anonymity, it is now possible to identify and quantify certain aspects of the Military College of Vermont's service in our Civil War. As a result, Alden Partridge's academy's contributions to the Republic at the time can be more effectively compared and contrasted to those of West Point and other military schools.

For example, the total number of men sent by Norwich to serve the Union compares favorably to that of the legendary United States Military Academy. A total of 936 West Pointers served the Republic vice some 700 men from the younger and much smaller New England academy. Conversely, 296 West Pointers served the Confederacy as compared to 56 Norwich men. In addition, unlike West Point and its Southern counterparts, Norwich sent dozens of its alumni into the naval service.[1]

An early attempt to summarize Norwich University's contribution to the Union is contained in a October 30, 1872, letter from Capt. Charles A. Curtis (Class of '61), then the military college's Commandant of Cadets, to Col. Wheelock G. Veazey, Adjutant General of the State of Vermont. Curtis, who himself was wounded and breveted for gallantry in the conflict, was working in the midst of the difficult conditions following the destruction of Norwich records in the disastrous fire of March 1866. According to Curtis,

> When the Rebellion broke out, Norwich University furnished the drillmasters for many of the companies and regiments required for the field. Previous to the battle of Bull Run, three full companies of Dartmouth students. . .were drilled by cadets of this institution; also, one company of 102 men were drilled at Bowdoin and one of 63 men at Waterville colleges. . . The Roll of Honor of N.U. contains the following number of officers as having been furnished during the late war: Maj. Gen'ls 5, Brig. Gen'ls 7, Colonels 27, Lt. Colonels 24, Majors 15, Captains 73, Adjutants 9, Lieutenants 51, Surgeons 5, Chaplains 1. In the Naval (service) there are many officers including one paymaster.

From 1872 to the publication of this work, only sporadic efforts have been made by members of the university community to update and refine Curtis' figures.[2]

As previously stated, the research for this book focused on Norwich alumni who served in the Army of the Potomac. That effort uncovered a plethora of relevant new material not contained in Norwich University records. In addition, a considerable amount of serendipitous data on alumni serving on other fronts was uncovered. Based on this author's findings, a follow-up on study of Norwich men serving in other armies and theaters would certainly yield new information on Norwich's role in the war—perhaps a considerable amount. In sum, the author found the extent and nature of Norwich alumni involvement in the War to Preserve the Union to be far more extensive than he and others previously believed. The numbers supplied in this statistical summary must be viewed as conservative, possibly considerably so, and represent the current best estimate of Norwich alumni service:

SUMMARY OF SERVICE, NORWICH ALUMNI 1861-1865

CATEGORY	ARMY OF THE POTOMAC	TOTAL UNION ALUMNI
Total Served	235	605 (705)*
Led Corp	1	5
Led Divisions	7	16
Led Brigades	22	36
Led Regiments	38	71
Regiments Served In	133	354
Held General/Flag Rank	7	33
Brevet Generals	17	37
Officers	200	516 (616)
Drillmasters	42	122
Killed	13	19
Mortally Wounded	8	18
Died of Disease	7	24
Wounded	64	94
Discharged Disabled/Ill	34	57
Cited for Gallantry	66	104
Medals of Honor	4	5
Breveted	41	77
Total Casualties (all causes)	112	192

*The totals in parentheses include the minimum number of "special military students" whose names and details of service cannot currently be identified.[3]

Analysis of data developed for this book, when compared to detailed information found in William F. Fox's *Regimental Losses in the*

Civil War, provides further insight into the question of the contribution and impact of Norwich men. Fox studied all Union army units and reports of battles and casualties. Central to his work was the identification and detailing of what have come to be known as the "300 Fighting Regiments." Comparing the identity of those units to those regiments in which Norwich alumni served shows the presence of at least one alumni in 84 (28.0%) of the "Fighting 300" regiments at some time—62 of which (73.8%) were in the Army of Potomac. Further, at least one Norwich man served in 18 (40%) of the 45 regiments identified by Fox as suffering the highest number of combat deaths (killed or mortally wounded in action). In addition, Norwich alumni served in four of the five top-ranked regiments (80%), and four alumni marched with the "most dangerous" of all Union combat regiments, the 5th New Hampshire Infantry. The 5th New Hampshire had the questionable honor of suffering the highest number of battle deaths of any infantry regiment in the Union Army. Of the four alumni who saw service in that Granite State unit, one was severely wounded and discharged for disability, a second was wounded, one went on to earn a brevet brigadier generalship, and the fourth was the unit's surgeon. At least two of the Norwich men earned one or more citations for gallantry prior to leaving the regiment.[4]

Comparison of the casualty rate percentages for the Union Army as a whole to those of Norwich men serving in the Army of the Potomac reveals the following:

	KILLED/MORTALLY WOUNDED	WOUNDED
Union Army	4.70%	11.20%
Norwich Alumni (all)	6.12%	15.39%
In Army of the Potomac	8.93%	27.23%

Analysis of the wound rate for all Union army soldiers serving in combat as compared to Norwich alumni indicates:

	UNION ARMY	NORWICH
Wounded per 1,000	11.20%	15.39%

There is no doubt that Norwich alumni, particularly those serving in the Army of the Potomac, suffered higher casualty rates for men killed in action, mortally wounded, and wounded than the Union army's statistical average. As demonstrated in this study, the service patterns of our alumni clearly reflect that most were to be found in combat units and on the front lines. Their chances of being killed or mortally wounded were greater than the average Union soldier, and they had nearly a 64% greater chance of being wounded. For the entire Union army, 112 of every 1,000 Federals were wounded in battle (11.2%); for Norwich alumni known to have served in artillery, cavalry or artillery units, the extrapolated casualty rate would be 293 per thousand (29.30%). Finally, the casualty rate for alumni serving in the Army of the Potomac was significantly higher than the norm with nearly one in three (27.23%) wounded in action.[5]

To put these casualty rates into a more familiar contemporary context, the service of Norwich alumni in the Civil War was compared to the sacrifice of her sons in the Vietnam War. Taking into account the Norwich Classes of 1960-1969, those most likely to have served during that war, some 1,500 Norwich alumni earned commissions and more than 1,000 of these served in Southeast Asia. With few exceptions, their service was entirely in the United States Army. Twenty-two Norwich men lost their lives in Southeast Asia as compared to 61 alumni who served the Union. Statistically, one in each 10 alumni serving in the Civil War made the supreme sacrifice as compared to one in each 45.45 serving in Vietnam. Thus, Norwich men serving in the Civil War were about four and a half times more likely to die than Norwich men serving in the Vietnam war.[6]

Also, in contrast to the potential officer training bases located in the Confederacy, Norwich stood unique as the lone non-Federal military college available to the Union from the inception of the war. Norwich not only continued to educate and train its cadets to be leaders and effective citizen-soldiers, but it also conducted special accelerated courses for militia, volunteer and regular officers, and for young men hoping to obtain commissions. Over and above these programs, Norwich sent hand-picked detachments of cadets to Vermont training camps to serve as drillmasters. Unfortunately, the records of the on-campus curriculum regarding the special officer training courses and related activities are sadly incomplete. Undoubtedly, some of these officers were casualties, some may have commanded regiments or higher formations, and some may have distinguished themselves in active service. Sadly, their wartime contributions can only be speculated upon at this time.[7]

It is also worthy of mention that President Abraham Lincoln, a former citizen-soldier officer himself and an associate of Gideon Welles (Class of '26), was personally aware of Norwich University and its officer training programs. When Elzey G. Burkham (Class of '66), petitioned the President for an appointment to the United States Military Academy in 1862, he was informed the entering class had been filled. President Lincoln then instructed Burkham to enter Norwich University and spend two years there, after which he would be commissioned. Lincoln also offered a commission in the United States Colored Troops to Joseph H. Goulding (Class of '65) after he had completed two years as a Norwich cadet. Goulding accepted and was commissioned into the 6th United States Colored Infantry. Lastly, in regard to the Lincoln connection, mention must be made of a prominent alumnus and important figure in the Granite State's military hierarchy, Col. Henry O. Kent (Class of '54). Kent was present during Lincoln's Gettysburg Address, serving as President Lincoln's personal military aide for the duration of his stay in that Pennsylvania town.[8]

Over the course of the war, Norwich men faithfully served the Republic in every rank from private (seaman) to major general (rear admiral). Seven are known to have risen to the rank full of major general in the Union army and 19 to brigadier general, while another six held flag rank in the Union navy. The Honorable Gideon Welles, served the entire war as Lincoln's Secretary of the Navy. In addition, at least 37 alumni were breveted to brigadier or major general for gallantry and/or outstanding service, while a number held general officer rank within the various state military organizations. A minimum of four other Norwich men served as general officers in the Confederate army, two served as commodores in the Confederate navy, and one served briefly as attorney general of the Confederacy. Norwich alumni were present at each major action of the war from Fort Sumter on April 12, 1861, to the surrender ceremony when the Army of

Northern Virginia laid down its arms four years later at Appomattox on April 12, 1865, and beyond. During that period our alumni fought in at least 254 major battles and engagements in all theaters, and suffered 192 casualties from all causes. It was both accurately and prophetically summarized by an anonymous junior cadet writing for the university's newspaper, the *University Reveille,* in March 1863, that "every field of battle during the present war has been moistened by the blood of our Alumni."[9]

There is no doubt that the service of hundreds of Norwich-trained officers and men training troops (drillmasters) and combat commanders had a decidedly positive impact on Union arms. At a time when knowledge of military affairs was desperately needed to instruct the Republic's burgeoning mass armies, Norwich men were there to serve. When the new units marched off to battle, Norwich alumni were to be found where it mattered most—in the companies (batteries), battalions, regiments and brigades of the line. To briefly recap, listed below are a few of the more outstanding Norwich-trained leaders at the tactical, operational-tactical and strategic levels, many of whom earned particular reputations for their battlefield aggressiveness:

Regimental Commanders:
Jesse A. Gove, Edgar A. Kimball, Edmund Rice,
John W. Schall, Thomas O. Seaver, and Charles B. Stoughton.

Brigade Commanders:
George P. Buell, J. Parker Gould, James Hubbard,
William W. Robinson, Seneca G. Simmons and George C. Strong.

Division Commanders:
Edward Hatch, Joseph A. Mower, William Nelson,
Thomas E.G. Ransom and Truman B. Seymour.

Corps Commanders:
Grenville M. Dodge, Joseph A. Mower, Alfred H. Terry,
and Horatio G. Wright.

Naval Warfare:
Gideon Welles, Hiram G. Paulding, Thomas T. Craven and
George Dewey.[10]

In addition to action on the battlefield, debate raged before, during and after the conflict as to the relative merits of the regular army
versus the volunteers (militia), and of the general effectiveness of West
Point graduates versus volunteer officers. These arguments continue
today. Recently a researcher argued that since antebellum West Point
was above all an engineering school, its graduates invariably employed
in battle a particular tactical engineering orientation based on firepow-
er and fortifications. Officers trained at the National Academy, it is
hypothesized, were *indoctrinated* (emphasis added) that only long-term
"regular" troops could capture strong entrenchments by direct assault.
The preponderance of high-level West Point-trained commanders on
both sides led to extensive "mirror-imaging" of combat tactics. In addition, it is argued, few West Pointers believed in the combat staying
power of "volunteer" (militia) soldiers. If true, this ill-placed lack of
confidence in citizen-soldiers likely resulted in an inclination, even in
the midst of an attack, to deliberately or passively allow the troops to
halt and shoot it out. The use of "combined arms" or "shock tactics"
was neither understood nor advocated by the majority of these "engineer" trained West Pointers. Regardless of the validity of this theory,
West Point officers certainly performed very well, in some cases exceptionally, during the conflict. It is this author's belief that many volunteer officers, particularly those with Norwich military training, did
equally well in combat and definitely provided an added value to the
Federal army. There can be no doubt that vast majority of men forming both the Union and Confederate armies were true citizen-soldiers.
In the end, it was those oft maligned citizen-soldiers, not the profes-
sionals, which won the ultimate Union victory.[11]

Gideon Welles addressed the issue of volunteer versus West Point
trained officers in 1862. Welles said that "General Scott was for a defensive policy. . . .[This] was necessary in order to adapt and reconcile
the theory and instruction of West Point to the war that was being
prosecuted." Welles also added that, "Instead of holding back, we
should be aggressive and enter their territory. Our generals act on the

defensive. It is not and has not been the policy of our country to be aggressive towards others, therefore defensive tactics are taught and the effect upon our educated commanders in the civil war is perceptible." It struck Welles, who valued his Norwich education and sent his own son to Captain Partridge's school, that "The best material for commanders in civil strife may have never seen West Point." Welles believed that "Courage and learning are essential, but something more is wanted in a good general—talent, intuition, magnetic power, which West Point cannot give." The course of the Civil War had convinced Welles that many "Men who would have made the best generals and who possess innately the best and highest qualities to command may not have been so fortunate as to be selected by a member of Congress to be a cadet."[12]

While Welles' commentary does not necessarily refer to Norwich, or to any other school for that matter, his experiences at Alden Partridge's military college must have influenced his thinking. Partridge's personal military specialty was, like other military thinkers of his day, the Napoleonic Wars and Napoleon's strategy and tactics. Unlike that of the United States Military Academy, however, the Norwich curriculum as structured under the "American System of Education" was not slanted to a single discipline or instructional approach. It was far more diversified, placed a unique emphasis on extensive field work, and was designed to stimulate creativity and innovation. In today's terms, Alden Partridge would be seen as following an "interdisciplinary approach" in educating his young cadets, and would be described as a "risk taker." Partridge's challenge to the "establishment" Regular Army over his attempts to revamp West Point, his attempts to found a national system of military colleges, his efforts to radically alter the national militia system, and his development of a novel educational system certainly demonstrate his willingness to take risks in order to fulfill his goals. Given these facts, it is likely that Partridge's military academy at Norwich produced a hefty number of like-thinking souls. Norwich-trained officers, furthermore, would certainly not have lacked confidence in the innate ability of the American citizen-soldier. In fact, Norwich cadets were taught that the American volunteer soldier was, when properly trained, *superior* to the "professional." Tens of thousands of these same citizen-soldiers were trained and commanded by Norwich drillmasters and line officers over the course of the war.[13]

Partridge's core beliefs on the merits of the citizen-soldier versus the professional military man were certainly more commonly held and widespread in the 19th century than, perhaps to the ultimate detriment of the Republic, they are in today's society. Clara Barton, an astute wartime commentator and participant who had numerous opportunities to observe, interact with and administer to both types of men, put forth her thoughts to the nation in a postwar speech. In arguing for a continued reliance on a volunteer-based force versus a professional army, Barton believed that, "The ranks of the Regular Army will be largely recruited with needy foreigners, strangers to the genius of our institutions: that the safety of the country rests essentially with those who rise from its bosom in the hour of need and peacefully retire when it is over." She warned that "The days of a nation are numbered when its common citizens refuse to fight its battles. In the days [when] a man was more precious than silver and gold had a fabulous value, the offer of a private soldier was of more worth than the gift of a Captain. Young men enough would take commissions, but who of his own free will would shoulder a musket and trudge for 2 or 3 years, through all the toils and hardship?"[14]

How, then, is the performance of Norwich men in that great and divisive Civil War to be ultimately assessed? The Union's great captains did express some contemporary opinions on the worth of Norwich alumni and on Partridge's academy. As previously noted, both Ulysses S. Grant and William T. Sherman enthusiastically praised the merits of alumni such as Dodge, Mower and Ransom. General Sherman is regarded by some scholars as this nation's first "modern" combat commander. Unlike the Army of the Potomac, where West Pointers always exercised a preponderance of control, Sherman's Western armies had numerous volunteer officers in key command and staff positions. Sherman, who witnessed the actions of many Norwich men, volunteered these insights and put forward his opinion of the impact of the sons of Alden Partridge on the Union's war effort. In the dedicatory address of the Thomas E. G. Ransom Post of the Grand Army of the Republic in St. Louis, Missouri, on June 20, 1884, Sherman declared:

Captain Alden Partridge's military school, then, as since, [is] an academy of great renown. This military school at one time almost rivaled the National Military Academy at West Point and there many a man who afterwards became famous in the Mexican and Civil Wars first drank in the inspirations of patriotism and learned the lessons of the art of war, which enabled him, out of unorganized masses of men, to make compact companies, regiments and brigades of soldiers, to act as a single body in the great game of war.[15]

Sherman then went on to proclaim that:

The reputation of the New England regiments must be attributed to the discipline and instruction received at this institution as much as to any other single factor and the "Green Mountain Boys" owe their national reputation and success largely to their training within her halls.[16]

The performance of the Vermont Brigade, to which General Sherman alludes, perhaps best exemplifies the Norwich wartime contribution. At least 44 alumni served in that brigade's ranks and 108 in all Vermont units during the war. Five of the six regiments of the Old Vermont Brigade were commanded at one time or another by a Norwich alumnus, and the brigade itself was twice led, though for short periods, by Norwich men. The Green Mountain Boys fought in some three dozen major battles and engagements and its marches in Virginia and Maryland exceeded two thousand miles. It was the only "pure" state brigade to serve throughout the war and it suffered more battle related casualties than any other similar-sized unit. While it was often in the forefront of battle and was credited with the capture of numerous Confederate colors, no brigade flag was ever in hostile hands, not even for a moment.[17]

Other generals also praised the actions of the brigade, in which so many Norwich trained officers and men served. In speaking of the Vermont Brigade's performance, Sixth Corps commander Maj. Gen. Horatio G. Wright (Class of '37) said: "As marchers they were unsurpassed and as fighters they were as good as the best, if not a little better;" their beloved former commander "Uncle John" Sedgwick would certainly have agreed. Major General Philip H. Sheridan, who shared a tent for a time during the war with Maj. Gen. Grenville M. Dodge (Class of '51), stated during an 1867 visit to the Vermont State House in Montpelier:

> When I saw these old flags I thought I ought to say as much as this: - I have never commanded troops in which I had more confidence than I had in Vermont troops and I do not know that I can say that I never commanded troops in whom I had as much confidence as those of this gallant state.[18]

Norwich University successfully maintained, albeit with difficulty, the campus' academic and military life during those days of extreme danger to the Union. She emerged from the greatest crisis in our Republic's history a better institution and with a well deserved reputation of distinguished service. The performance of her sons on and off the battlefield of our Civil War is justifiably viewed with great pride and as a ringing confirmation of Alden Partridge's beliefs as laid out in his "American System of Education." Further, the examples in courage, loyalty, perseverance and sacrifice established by Norwich alumni during the War to Preserve the Union are worthy of emulation and remembrance. Those hard earned lessons are as relevant to the nation and to the Norwich University Corps of Cadets today as they were to the men of women of the times. Norwich's nearly 200 years of service to the nation in peace and war qualifies her to stand proudly and as an equal with the great military-educational institutions of our nation. In its moment of supreme danger the Republic was fortunate. It was fortunate to have available a pool of Norwich trained citizen-soldiers—men who were the conceptual sons of Alden Partridge. These young men attended not only Alden Partridge's main school in Norwich, Vermont, but other Partridge inspired military colleges like The Collegiate and Commercial Institute in New Haven, Connecticut. If the full impact of the Norwich educational system and training on Federal and Confederate Civil War officers is to be determined, the issue requires further in-depth study and analysis. Nevertheless, the overall performance of Norwich men in the Civil War can now be viewed as documentable, important and meritorious. If not yet completely understood, the impact of our alumni's influence on the Union war effort must be viewed as undeniably positive and significant.[19]

It is regrettable that Norwich University's services to the Republic in that tragic conflict, though well known at the time, have received virtually no modern recognition and study, and are neither known nor understood by most contemporary scholars. Perhaps this oversight will be partially corrected by this book.

According to historian Edwin C. Bearss,

> Norwich's contributions to the Union may have been as significant as that of the the Virginia Military Institute to the Confederacy. . . .Because of the high profile given by Southern historians, especially Virginians, Confederate soldiers' VMI associations are common knowledge. A failure by Northern historians to trumpet corresponding Norwich association for Union military personnel, where warranted, has served to eclipse the school's and its alumni importance.[20]

Norwich University indeed "moistened fields by the blood of her alumni." Her sons firmly stood by the Union, and amply fulfilled the challenge inherent in their motto: "I Will Try."

Appendix A

ALPHABETICAL LISTING OF ALUMNI

Norwich University's Kreitzberg Library and Special Collections maintains a web site entitled "Norwich in Service to the Country." This site provides data on Norwich University and its alumni who have served in our nation's wars. Norwich's Civil War site identifier is: http://192.149.109.153/nom/nis/.

The history and records of Norwich University indicates a minimum of 705 of its alumni (graduates and former cadets) served in the Civil War. At least 56 of these fought for the South, and over 600 sided with the Union. This alphabetical list identifies these alumni, their class, unit (when known), rank, and any distinguishing aspect of their service. More than 100 other men attended Norwich as "special military students"; unfortunately most of their names are not known and, with few exceptions, they are not included in this listing. I have used the word "probable" in relation to an alumnus when information verifying absolutely a connection to Norwich and/or a unit was not available. The person so caveated, however, is very likely an alumnus and served in the unit(s) indicated. If a person is listed as "possible," it indicates there is evidence he attended Norwich and served in the unit(s) specified, but that further research and facts are needed for confirmation or denial. The use of an * indicates that the alumnus served in the Army of the Potomac.

Abbot(t), Edward S. '64*. First Lieutenant, commanding Company "A," 1st Battalion, 17th United States Infantry, mortally wounded and cited for gallantry at Gettysburg; brevet captain. He was a "special military student" March-July 1862.

Abbott, Lemuel A. '64*. Captain, Company "A," 10th Vermont Infantry, wounded at the Wilderness, severely wounded at Monocacy, severely wounded twice at Opequon Creek; drillmaster. At the Opequon he had a lip shot off, both jaws crushed, and 11 teeth shot out. Served for a time on General Sherman's staff at the end of the war and had a postwar career in the 97th United States Colored Infantry Regiment, United States Volunteers (USV) and in the Regular Army (USA).

Abbott, Walter '61. Lieutenant, United States Navy (USN).

Adams, Clinton, '48. Captain, New York artillery; his service possibly, though not likely, took place in the Mexican War.

Adams, Henry H. '65. Corporal, Company "C," 98th Ohio Infantry. He later transferred to the Regular Army and retired as a colonel.

Aiken, Walter, '54. Private, Company "D," 1st New Hampshire Infantry. While he did not enlist during the war, Aiken, when on a visit to the 1st New Hampshire, picked up a rifle and did active duty as a private without pay during the unit's service. This act was recognized by the New Hampshire legislature in 1887 and he was permanently entered on the regimental rolls.

Ainsworth, James E. '53. Captain, Company "F," 12th Iowa Infantry; resigned for ill health after the Battle of Shiloh.

Aldrich, Edward K. '66. First Lieutenant, 11th New York Infantry.

Alexander, Henry D.W. '26. Captain, Confederate States Army (CSA), Georgia Volunteers.

Allen, Charles (Cornelius) L. '66. First Lieutenant and Adjutant, Company "K," 38th Ohio Infantry.

Allen, Lorenzo D. '63*. Captain, Company "G," 3rd Vermont Infantry; discharged for disability. Reported in at least one source as dismissed from the service.

Alvord, Henry E. '63*. Captain, Company "I," 2nd Massachusetts Cavalry; First Sergeant, Company "B," 7th Squadron Rhode Island Cavalry ("College Cavaliers"); major (not mustered). Served as Assistant Adjutant General on General Hancock's staff and as the Chief Engineer on General Sheridan's staff.

Amory, Charles '24. Colonel and Assistant Quartermaster General, Massachusetts Militia; also served on the staff of the governor of Massachusetts.

Amsden, Frank P. '59*. Captain, Batteries "B," "G," and "H," 1st Pennsylvania Light Artillery; wounded in action and discharged for disability.

Arms, Austin D. '37*. Captain and Assistant Quartermaster, Vermont Volunteers.

Ashcroft, Charles E. '63*. Captain, 61st Massachusetts; also a state drillmaster mustering and training Massachusetts volunteers in 1861.

Ashe, Thomas P. '46. Colonel, CSA.

Atwood, Julius P. '48*. Lieutenant Colonel, 6th Wisconsin Infantry; resigned due to poor health; drillmaster. Took an active part in establishing the Wisconsin State Militia and in recruiting troops for the war.

Babbitt, Eldrige H. '64*. First Lieutenant 1st North Carolina Infantry (Union); severely wounded at Gettysburg as a Sergeant, 17th United States Infantry. He was also wounded in action at Fredericksburg, December 1862.

Babbitt, Jacob '26*. Major, 7th Rhode Island Infantry; mortally wounded at Marye's Heights, Fredericksburg; cited for gallantry; also served in the 10th Rhode Island Infantry.

Bachelder, John B. '49. Former lieutenant colonel in the Pennsylvania State Militia who accompanied the Army of the Potomac in some of its campaigns. Spending weeks at Gettysburg in the immediate aftermath of the battle, he made the study of that battle his life's work. His effort, summarized in The Bachelder Papers, is the outstanding 19th century study of the battle and its participants, hundreds of whom were interviewed by Bachelder. Bachelder is also responsible for the positioning of most regimental monuments on the field including the famous "High Water Mark" monument.

Bacon, Francis H. '49*. First Lieutenant, Company "K," 23rd Ohio Infantry.

Bailey, George A. '63*. First Lieutenant, Batteries "B," and "K," 1st Vermont Heavy Artillery; Corporal, Company "B," 7th Squadron Rhode Island Cavalry ("College Cavaliers"); breveted captain for conspicuous gallantry in all engagements from May 16, 1864, especially at Cedar Creek; also cited for gallantry in the assault on Petersburg. Served as a Vermont State Drillmaster in 1861.

Baker, Charles N. '59. Captain, Company "K," 2nd Michigan Cavalry; appointed a major but not mustered.

Balloch, George W. '47*. Lieutenant Colonel on the staff of Generals Winfield S. Hancock and O.O. Howard; Brevet Brigadier General, USV; also served as Captain, Company "D," 5th New Hampshire Infantry.

Bancroft, George D. '65. Second Lieutenant, 62nd Massachusetts Infantry; did not serve in field as war ended and the 62nd was not mustered.

Barker, J. (Samuel) Gage '59*. Captain, Company "A," 36th Ohio Infantry.

Barrett, Curtis S. '63. Captain and Quartermaster, Vermont Volunteers; drillmaster. Served with distinction until mustered out in October 1866.

Bartlett, John M. '47*. Private, Company "H," 12th Vermont Infantry.

Barton, Frederick A. '25*. Chaplain, 10th Massachusetts Infantry; resigned due to age and ill health. He played a key role in raising and organizing this regiment in 1861.

Bascom, Gustavus M. '60*. Lieutenant Colonel and Adjutant General, US Volunteers; Ohio state drillmaster; cited twice for gallantry at Antietam and Resaca, Georgia; breveted colonel. Credited with being "One of the ablest officers in the Army." Served on the staffs of Generals Burnside and Stoneman.

Batchelder, James E. '67*. Private, Company "E," 5th Vermont Infantry; wounded in the Spotsylvania Campaign.

Batchelder, Samuel '51. Officer, CSA.

Baxter, Henry C. '66*. Captain, Batteries "A," and "B," 1st Vermont Heavy Artillery; wounded at Cedar Creek, Virginia and cited for conspicuous gallantry; also cited for gallantry in the battles of Spotsylvania and Winchester, and in the assault on Petersburg; breveted major. He also served as aide to Brig. Gen. Lewis A. Grant, commander of the First Vermont Brigade.

Baxter, Jedediah H. '56*. Surgeon with the rank of Major, Army of the Potomac; brevet colonel; Surgeon, 12th Massachusetts Infantry. Later a brigadier general and Surgeon General of the United States. Served during the war in the Judiciary Square and Campbell Hospitals in Washington and as Chief Medical Officer, Provost Marshal General's Bureau. In charge of Campbell Hospital, one of the largest in the country, for 18 months. Served for a time in the Peninsula Campaign as a brigade surgeon.

Baxter, Luther L. '51. Colonel, 1st Minnesota Heavy Artillery; also served in the 4th Minnesota Infantry as a major.

Baxter, Portus '24. Physician; served as a military nurse at Fredericksburg, in the Wilderness, and in the Medical Corps with the 3rd Camp Detachment, Derby Line, Vermont. Served as a Vermont State agent in Washington from which place he often went to the field. Because of his interest in the men's welfare he earned the title of "the soldier's friend."

Baxter, William R. '51. Captain, Company "H," 9th Minnesota Infantry; killed in the Battle of Guntown, Mississippi, June 10, 1864.

Bayard, Albert F. '65. First Lieutenant, United States Colored Infantry; "College Cavaliers;" Private, Company "G," 5th United States Cavalry.

Bean, Eli B. '42*. Captain and Assistant Quartermaster, US Volunteers; also served in the 6th United States Cavalry; brevet major.

Bean, Sylvanus B. '34*. First Lieutenant, Company "A," 11th Maine Infantry; promoted Captain and Assistant Quartermaster; breveted major.

Beattie, David C. J. '47*. Captain, Company "I," 164th New York Infantry; severely wounded in action (upper left thigh and right groin) at Cold Harbor; captured and held at Libby Prison in Richmond, paroled on September 1; brevet major. Also suffered from typhoid fever.

Beckwith, Benjamin M. '55. First Lieutenant and Adjutant, 32nd Wisconsin Infantry; discharged for disability; Captain and Assistant Adjutant General Second Brigade, Fourth Division, Seventeenth Army Corps; on General Sherman's Staff for a time. Served as a Wisconsin State Drillmaster.

Bell, John '24. Captain and Assistant Surgeon, USA; breveted major.

Bickford, Frederick T. '55*. Musician, 5th Vermont Infantry.

Billings, C.B. '38. Served in the Union Navy.

Birchard, Sardis '64*. First Sergeant, Battery "L," 1st Vermont Heavy Artillery; captured at the Battle of Weldon Railroad June 23, 1864 and died in Andersonville Prison, August 21, 1864 of "debilitas." This condition refers to a general weakening and collapse of the vital organs from malnutrition and/or disease. Birchard is buried in grave #6334 (Section E) at Andersonville National Cemetery.

Bird, Charles S. '67. Private, Company "G," 60th Massachusetts Infantry.

Bishop, Linus D. '46. Lieutenant Colonel, 9th Illinois Cavalry; previously in Company "H;" Lieutenant Colonel, 6th United States Veteran Volunteer Infantry.

Bissell, George Henry '38. Captain, USA.

Blackburn, William H. '52. Captain, Company "G," 13th Kansas Infantry.

Blackington, William S. '66. Private, Company "G," 60th Massachusetts Infantry.

Blair, Henry W. '62?. Lieutenant Colonel, 15th New Hampshire Infantry; severely wounded in the arm at Port Hudson, Louisiana and cited for bravery. Probably one of the students in the special military courses, 1861-62.

Blodgette, George B. '67. Second Lieutenant, Massachusetts State Troops; Corporal, Company "D," 48th Massachusetts Infantry; wounded in action at Port Hudson, Louisiana.

Blois, John T. '28. First Lieutenant and Drillmaster, Michigan Volunteers.

Boardman, Napoleon '47. Captain, Battery "M," 2nd Missouri Light Artillery; also served in Company "A," 2nd Wisconsin Cavalry; brevet colonel.

Boggs, Charles S. '26. Captain, Union Navy; cited for gallantry.

Boggs, James '29. Lieutenant Commander and Surgeon, USN.

Boggs, William B. '28. Paymaster, Union Navy; became Pay Director of the Navy following the war; wounded in action.

Bomford, James V. '28*. Colonel, 8th United States Infantry; Brevet Brigadier General, USA; twice wounded in action at Perryville; cited for gallantry at the Battle of Perryville; Major, 6th United States Infantry when captured in Texas, 1861. Also served as a Lieutenant Colonel, 16th United States Infantry.

Booth, J.H., '49. Colonel, United States Volunteers; the details of his service could not be identified.

Boutelle, George V. '59*. Major, 21st New York Cavalry; Captain, Company "A," 2nd New York Infantry; Captain, Company "F," 70th New York Infantry (did not serve); breveted colonel; cited for gallantry.

Bovay, Alvin E. '41. Major, 19th Wisconsin Infantry from which he resigned due to ill health; drillmaster. Considered one of the founders of the Republican Party.

Bowen, Marcellus '68*. Private, Company "F," 1st Vermont Cavalry.

Bowers, Charles '52*. Captain, Company "G," 32nd Massachusetts Infantry; 3rd Lieutenant, Company "G," 5th Massachusetts Infantry. He may have attended one of Captain Partridge's special militia training courses rather than having been a cadet. A possible, though less likely candidate, is the Charles Bowers who served as a Corporal in the 7th Massachusetts Light Battery.

Bradley, Charles O. '63*. Captain, Company "C," 13th New Hampshire Infantry; cited by his regiment for gallantry when discharged; later served with Battery "I," 1st New Hampshire Heavy Artillery; First Sergeant, Company "I," 1st New Hampshire Infantry.

Bragg, Thomas '28. Attorney General, Confederate States of America; was the brother of Confederate General Braxton Bragg.

Breaux, Gustavus A. '47. Colonel, CSA, 30th Louisiana Infantry; alleged to have been one of the first to offer his sword to the Confederacy. Distinguished himself in combat prior to resigning for disability in 1863.

Brigham, Henry O. '48. Major and Paymaster, United States Army.

Bringhurst, Thomas F. '59*. Captain, Company "F," 2nd Pennsylvania Reserves and Company "B," 59th Pennsylvania Militia (War Service). Served for a time at Fort Mifflin in the Delaware River. Possibly served in an unidentified 90-day regiment from Philadelphia at the outbreak of the war.

Brisbane, William H. '26. Chaplain, 2nd Wisconsin Cavalry; resigned due to ill health.

Brown, Darwin T. '50. Major and Surgeon, USA.

Brown, Edward M. '44*. Lieutenant Colonel, 8th Vermont Infantry; Adjutant, 5th Vermont Infantry; resigned due to ill health; drillmaster.

Brown, Emery '67. Captain, 91st Illinois Infantry.

Brown, Leonard B. '65. Captain, 11th Illinois Infantry.

Brownell, Thomas S. '54*. First Lieutenant and Adjutant, Company "I," 7th Rhode Island Infantry; resigned for disability; also served in Company "F," First Rhode Island Infantry (90 day Militia).

Bryant, George E. '55. Colonel, 12th Wisconsin Infantry; brevet brigadier general; cited for gallantry; brigade commander; drillmaster; also served with the 8th Wisconsin. Reputed to be the first officer in the nation to volunteer himself and his unit to the government on January 9, 1861.

Buel, James W. '64*. Sergeant, 2nd Battalion, 17th United States Infantry; wounded at Chancellorsville; discharged for disability and later served as an officer in the United States Navy.

Buel, John F.L. '57*. First Lieutenant and Quartermaster, Company "G," 4th United States Infantry.

Buel, Julius O. '61. First Lieutenant, Company "L," 1st Colorado Cavalry; died of disease at Camp Weld, Colorado Territory.

Buell, George P. '56. Colonel, 58th Indiana Infantry; brigade and division commander; wounded in action at Chickamauga; drillmaster; appointed a brevet brigadier general for able management of pontoon trains; cited for gallantry at Missionary Ridge. Commander of the Special Pioneer Brigade of the Army of the Cumberland. Also breveted in the ranks of colonel and brigadier general in the Regular Army, in which he later died as Colonel, 15th United States Infantry.

Burbank, William B. '55*. First Lieutenant, Company "E," 17th Vermont Infantry.

Burkham, Elzey G. '66. Private, Company "G," 60th Massachusetts Infantry. He sought a presidential appointment to West Point from President Lincoln. As the quota was filled, Lincoln told Burkham to attend Norwich for two years and he would be commissioned in the army.

Burnham, Cyrus B. '39. Colonel, Missouri Volunteer Militia; drillmaster. Served on the governor's staff and as Quartermaster General, Commissary General, and Paymaster of Missouri.

Burnham, Hosea B. '48*. Lieutenant Colonel, 67th Pennsylvania Infantry.

Burns, Emery '55. Served as an officer in the Union Army.

Burroughs, George W. '62?. First Lieutenant, Battery "F," 3rd Massachusetts Heavy Artillery; probably one of those taking special military courses at Norwich, 1861-63.

Burrows, Hunt W. '56*. Captain, Battery "M," 1st Vermont Heavy Artillery; drillmaster; adjutant; discharged for disability.

Burton, Henry S. '37*. Colonel, 5th United States Artillery; cited for gallantry at the siege of Petersburg; artillery brigade commander; Brevet Brigadier General, USA; commanded the artillery reserve of the Army of the Potomac and the artillery of the Eighteenth Corps, summer 1864. Commander, Fort Delaware (Delaware) Military Prison. Also served as a Major, 3rd United States Artillery and Lieutenant Colonel, 4th United States Artillery.

Burton, William S. '55. Major, 3rd Michigan Cavalry; drillmaster. Provided valuable service in drilling and instructing Michigan volunteers.

Bush, Charles E. '63. Sergeant Major, 7th Squadron, Rhode Island Cavalry, "College Cavaliers;" Vermont drillmaster

Buswell, Albert '47. Private, Company "D," 8th Vermont Infantry; later Captain and Surgeon, 12th Maine Infantry.

Buttrick, George B. '56. Captain, Companies "B & E," 75th United States Colored Infantry; also served as a corporal in Company "G," 5th Massachusetts Infantry and as a sergeant in Company "G," 47th Massachusetts Infantry; discharged for disability.

Cady, Albermale '25*. Colonel, 8th United States Infantry; Lieutenant Colonel, 7th United States Infantry; Brevet Brigadier General, USA; Major, 6th United States Infantry. Spent most of the war fighting Indians in the West. He was placed in charge of the 1864 draft rendezvous in New Haven, Connecticut.

Cady, Samuel A. '64*. Corporal, Company "K," 4th Vermont Infantry; discharged disabled.

Campbell, Henry S. '62?*. Second Lieutenant, 25th United States Colored Infantry; Private, Independent Battery "E," Pennsylvania Light Artillery; wounded in action, Wauhatchie, Tennessee. Probably a special military student in 1861.

Campbell, Hugh S. '59*. Lieutenant Colonel, 83rd Pennsylvania Infantry; wounded at Malvern Hill and 2nd Bull Run; commanded his regiment during several battles in the Peninsula Campaign and later.

Carew, John E. '29. Colonel, 3rd South Carolina State Troops and 18th South Carolina Militia, Confederate States Army. In 1848, Carew headed a committee which awarded a presentation sword to General John C. Fremont.

Cargill, Charles G. '64*. Corporal, Company "H," 16th Vermont Infantry. Served as a lieutenant in the Vermont Militia after the St. Albans Raid of October, 1864.

Carpenter, Charles C. '50. Lieutenant Commander, Union Navy.

Carpenter, Edward W. '23. Commodore, Union Navy; cited for gallantry.

Carpenter, Irving S. '49. Officer, Commisary Department, US Volunteers.

Carpenter, John S. '48*. Captain, Company "H" and First Lieutenant, Company "B," 95th Pennsylvania Infantry. Enlisted as Sergeant, Company "B," 54th Pennsylvania Infantry, a unit which later became Company "B," of the 95th. Served as sergeant major of the regiment for a time.

Carter, George T. '54*. Captain, Company "B," 2nd New Hampshire Infantry; wounded in action four times: 2nd Bull Run (severely), captured and paroled; Gettysburg (severely), Cold Harbor, and Petersburg. Promoted to major but was not mustered in that rank due to the end of the war.

Chaffin, William H. '64. Captain, "Company I," 14th New Hampshire Infantry; killed at the Battle of Opequon Creek by a gunshot to the temple; drillmaster in Vermont and New Hampshire.

Chandler, Edward A. '61*. First Lieutenant, Co "F," 3rd Vermont Infantry; severely wounded at the Battle of Lee's Mills; drillmaster. Later served as a major in the Quartermaster Department. At Lee's Mill he was shot through the hand, losing three bones, and that bullet then entered his thigh.

Chandler, Julius C. '45. Sergeant, Company "G," 2nd Wisconsin Infantry; severely wounded at the Battle of 1st Bull Run; later served in Company "I," 40th Wisconsin Infantry.

Channel, Alfred M. '54*. Captain, Company "D," 7th Rhode Island Infantry; dismissed from the service August 29, 1864 by order of a general court martial, a sentence which was later revoked; also served as Second Lieutenant, Company "G," 17th Massachusetts Infantry. Contacted an intestinal disease in the service which eventually disabled and finally killed him.

Chapin, Charles J. '65. First Lieutenant; drillmaster for 11th and 15th Vermont Infantry.

Chase, Arthur '65. Captain, New Hampshire State Troops.

Chase, George E. '57*. Probably a Private, Company "G," 6th Vermont Infantry; died of disease.

Child, Oscar B. '65. First Lieutenant and Adjutant, Vermont State Troops

Childs, George W. '67. Corporal, Company "B," 6th Massachusetts Infantry.

Childs, Jonathan W. '58*. Colonel, 4th Michigan Infantry; cited for gallantry; wounded in action in the Maryland Campaign, September 1862.

Clark, Arthur E. '43. First Lieutenant, 1st Connecticut Light Battery.

Clark, John M. '50. Captain, Company "E," 144th New York Infantry and/or Major, 39th and 82nd Missouri Militia. There is clearly confusion in Ellis' historical records on this officer.

Clark, Thomas '44*. Lieutenant Colonel, 29th Ohio Infantry; wounded at the Battle of Chancellorsville while commanding his regiment; drillmaster; First Lieutenant, 19th Ohio; captured at Port Republic and later paroled; discharged disabled.

Clark, Warren '57. Captain and Drillmaster, New Hampshire Volunteers and State Troops.

Clark, William J. '61. See W.J. DePoincy, CSA.

Cleveland, James B. '55. Officer, CSA.

Coffee, William '49. Sergeant, Company "A," 3rd New Hampshire Infantry.

Coffin, Herbert G. '67*. Captain, Company "H," 56th Massachusetts Infantry; discharged for disability.

Colburn, Albert V. '53*. Lieutenant Colonel on the Army of the Potomac staff where he served as an aide and personal favorite of General McClellan; died on active duty while on Maj. Gen. John M. Schofield's staff. Also served in the 1st United States Cavalry.

Colburn, William R. '47. Major and Paymaster in the Union Army.

Collins, William F. '28. Major, Confederate North Carolina State Troops.

Colvocoresses, George M. '31. Captain, Union Navy. Retired in 1867 after 34 years service and was murdered by a robber in Bridgeport, Connecticut June 3, 1872.

Colvocoresses, George P. '66. Midshipman, United States Navy.

Commings, David L.M. '48*. Assistant Surgeon, 4th New Hampshire Infantry; served for a time at Hilton Head, South Carolina; died of disease.

Congdon, Martin V.B. '57. Served in the Union Army.

Conn, Grenville P. '54*. Surgeon, 12th Vermont Infantry; also assisted in organizing the United States Hospital at Brattleboro, Vermont. Served with distinction at the Battle of Gettysburg.

Connor, Robert E. '38. Served in the CSA.

Converse, George A. '63. Served as a midshipman in the Union Navy,

Cook, Hubbard '61. Served in the Union Army.

Cooke, Albert W. '69*. Captain, Companies "E" and "I," 57th Massachusetts Infantry; also served as First Sergeant, Company "B," 25th Massachusetts Infantry; commanded the 57th Massachusetts from March 26-April 3, 1865; also served on the staff of the Third Brigade, First Division, Ninth Corps.

Coolidge, Charles A. '63*. First Lieutenant, 7th United States Infantry; also a Private, Company "H," 3rd Battalion, 16th United States Infantry; brevet major; served for a time on the Army of the Potomac staff. Retired as a brigadier general in the Regular Army.

Coombs, Arthur W. '64. Private, Company "B," 7th Squadron Rhode Island Cavalry; "College Cavaliers;" died of disease while in the service.

Coon, Squire P. '42. Colonel, 2nd Wisconsin Volunteers; also on General Sherman's staff at the Battle of 1st Bull Run where he earned a citation. Resigned from the army in the summer 1861 after a dispute which caused some turmoil in his regiment.

Cowdin, Robert J. '59*. Captain, Company "E," 56th Massachusetts Infantry; killed at the Battle of Cold Harbor while commanding his division's pickets; his body was not recovered; also commanded Company "E," 31st New York Infantry; cited for gallantry at the Battle of Antietam.

Crandall, Richard B. '62*. Major, 6th Vermont Infantry. A special military student at Norwich in the summer of 1861. Cited as "taking special instructions under General Jackman." Killed in action at Cold Harbor by a sniper, June 7, 1864.

Craven, Thomas T. '29. Commodore, Union Navy; cited for gallantry in the attack on the forts protecting New Orleans.

Craven, Tunis A.M. '29. Commander, Union Navy; killed at Mobile Bay, Alabama where he went down with his ship "Tecumseh" while leading Admiral Farragut's attack column. Prior to the war he was the editor of the U.S. Nautical Magazine.

Crooker, Jabez C. '43. Captain, Company "I," 55th Illinois Infantry; drillmaster.

Crowninshield, Francis B. '26. Colonel, Massachusetts State Troops serving on the the staff of Governor John Andrew; sent to England to purchase weapons in spring 1861 in order to outfit New England troops.

Currier, Samuel H. '52. Captain and Assistant Surgeon, 8th Vermont Infantry.

Curtis, Charles A. '61*. First Lieutenant, 5th and 7th United States Infantry; Captain, 6th Maine Infantry; served for a time as a Maine State Drillmaster; Brevet Captain, United States Army; wounded in action. Saw extensive service against Texas forces on the Rio Grande River.

Cushman, John H. '37*. Possibly a First Lieutenant and Regimental Quartermaster, 4th Vermont Infantry.

Cushman, William H. '27. Colonel, 53rd Illinois Infantry.

Cutts, Edward H. '50. Captain, Company "C," 55th United States Colored Infantry; also served as a Private, Company "B," 8th Minnesota Infantry. The 8th Minnesota saw long and arduous service in the Sioux Indian Wars.

Dana, Stillman E. '49. Colonel, 21st Wisconsin Militia; drillmaster. An important figure in the organization and drilling of Wisconsin troops during the war.

Danforth, William C. '44*. Captain, Company "K," 16th Vermont; Captain, 18th Vermont Infantry which was not mustered due to the end of the war.

Darling, Daniel '34. Contract Surgeon, United States Army; served at the Lincoln Hospital, Washington, D.C.

Davis, Charles W. '49*. Possibly a Captain, Companies "A," and "K," 21st and Company "K," 36th Massachusetts Infantry; brevet colonel; cited three times for gallantry. Assigned as commander, Camp Parole for Confederate prisoners, College Green Barracks, Annapolis, Maryland as of October 21, 1864. If not a member of the Class of 1849, he likely attended as a special military student; he is cited as an alumnus in Norwich wartime records and by Ellis.

Davis, George A. '67*. Private, Company "G," 60th Massachusetts Infantry; Private, Company "F," 17th Vermont Infantry.

Davis, George E. '51*. First Lieutenant and Adjutant, 26th Massachusetts Infantry. Also served in the 6th Massachusetts Infantry in 1861.

Davis, Thomas H. '55. Captain, CSA, Company "B," 1st Virginia Infantry. Wounded and captured at Gettysburg during the climax of Pickett's Charge; escaped from Johnson's Island to Canada; sailed from Canada on a blockade runner to rejoin his regiment but was captured again at Sayler's Creek.

Davis, William W.H. '42*. Colonel, 104th Pennsylvania Infantry; breveted brigadier general for services at the siege of Charleston; wounded at Fair Oaks and John's Island, South Carolina; brigade and division commander; also served in Company "I," 25th Pennsylvania Infantry. It is alleged that because he was a Democrat in politics, he was not promoted to brigadier general despite commanding a brigade and a division. Wrote a history of his regiment's role in the war.

Day, Henry C. '61. Captain, Company "A," 18th Connecticut Infantry; listed as Davis in state muster rolls; discharged for disability; captured at Winchester, Virginia and later paroled.

Dean, Charles K. '45*. First Lieutenant, Company "C," 2nd Wisconsin Infantry; later served as regimental adjutant; severely wounded at Antietam; discharged for disability. Captured at Beverly Ford, Virginia, August 21, 1862 and confined in Richmond but was soon released. Recruited a company at the beginning of the war.

Dearing, Charles H. '50. Captain, 11th Georgia Infantry, CSA.

Delaney, Alfred '59. Surgeon, Pennsylvania Volunteers; brevet captain. Later served as an assistant surgeon in the Regular Army.

Denison, Charles E. '45. Captain, 18th United States Infantry; severely wounded at Murfreesboro (lost a leg) and cited for gallantry; died January 15, 1863 of wounds; also served in Company "E," 8th Illinois Infantry; brevet major.

DePoincy, William J. '61. First Lieutenant, 7th Georgia Cavalry, CSA; also known as William J. Clark. Captured at the Battle of Trevilian Station, June 11, 1864.

Derby, George H. '48. Captain, topographical engineers; died on active duty May 15, 1861.

Dewey, George '55. Lieutenant Commander, Union Navy. He served in many key posts and also with Admiral Farragut. Later promoted Admiral of the Navy and earned the title of the "Hero of Manila Bay."

Dewey, John W. '55*. Captain, Company "C," 2nd United States Sharpshooters; resigned due to disability.

Dewey, T.G. '49. Served in the Union Army.

Dewey, William S. '63. Private, Company "B," 7th Squadron Rhode Island Cavalry; "College Cavaliers."

Dicks, John W. '23. Master, Union Navy; wounded in action and taken prisoner. He was later discharged for disability.

Dixon, Luther S. '48. Drillmaster, Wisconsin Volunteers.

Dodge, Grenville M. '51. Major General and Sixteenth Corps Commander; wounded at Atlanta and Pea Ridge; cited for gallantry; a brigade and division commander; Colonel, 4th Iowa. Commander of the Department and Army of Missouri from the fall of 1864 on. Chief Engineer, Union Pacific Railroad and a key figure in the building of the transcontinental rail line following the war. Dodge City, Kansas is named in his honor.

Dodge, William A. '64. First Lieutenant, Company "B," 9th Vermont Infantry; twice wounded in action, September- October 1864; Vermont State Drillmaster; discharged due to wounds. Drilled several Vermont companies for the war in 1863.

Dorn, Andrew J. '41. Colonel, CSA; commanded the Sachem Indians.

Drew, Frederick P. '48. Major and Surgeon, USA; died of disease on active duty, at Fort Riley, Kansas where he served as Post Surgeon.

Dyer, Jay '38. Captain, Company "I," 32nd Ohio Infantry; resigned due to disability.

Dyer, William N. '39*. Probably Private, Company "D," 5th Vermont Infantry; wounded in action March 27, 1865.

Earle, Thomas A. '52. Second Lieutenant, Company "A," 25th Massachusetts Infantry.

Eayre, Thomas W. '61*. Captain, Company "I," 5th New Jersey Infantry; killed at the "Bloody Angle," Spotsylvania, by a sharpshooter while on a division staff; Vermont and New Jersey State Drillmaster; cited for gallantry at Gettysburg.

Elliot, George H. '52. Captain of engineers; considered an engineer of high scientific achievement; breveted major. He retired from the Regular Army as a colonel.

Emerson, George W. '42. Private, Company "B," 186th Pennsylvania Volunteers; died of disease.

Emery, Harvey W. '52*. Lieutenant Colonel, 5th Wisconsin Infantry; died of wounds; cited for gallantry; drillmaster.

Ensign, William H. '54. Major and Surgeon, United States Army.

Ewart, James K. '62. Captain, Company "E," 26th Ohio Infantry.

Farrand, Ebenezer '23. Commodore, Confederate States Navy (CSN).

Farrar, Bernard G. '45. Colonel, 30th Missouri Volunteers and 6th United States Colored Heavy Artillery; drillmaster; brigade commander; Brevet Brigadier General, USV. Also served as Provost-Marshal-General, Department of Missouri and on the staffs of Generals Halleck and Lyon. His 6th Heavy Colored Artillery was formerly designated the 1st Mississippi Heavy Colored Artillery and then the 5th United States Colored Heavy Artillery.

Farrar, Frederick H. '56. Lieutenant Colonel, CSA, commanding the 1st Louisiana Infantry at Shiloh and Stone's River (Murfreesboro); shot through the chest and died from this wound which he received while leading his regiment in an assault on the Union line at Stone's River. Confederate Lieutenant General Leonidas Polk said of him "This young officer was one of the most promising of the army, intelligent, chivalrous, and brave."

Farrar, William E. '56. First Lieutenant, 7th Massachusetts Battery and Quartermaster, 6th Massachusetts Infantry. Also served at Fort Monroe, Virginia for 18 months as lieutenant of an unattached Massachusetts infantry company.

Fenton, Frank B. '57. First Lieutenant, Battery "A," 2nd Illinois Artillery; served the entire war with this unit.

Field, George W. '60*. Captain, Company "D," 59th Massachusetts Infantry; also served in Company "C," 105th Illinois Infantry. May be the same man who served for a short time (June 12-August 21, 1861) in the 10th Massachusetts Infantry and was discharged for disability. There is clearly confusion on the service of this alumnus.

Field, Joseph F. '62?*. First Lieutenant, Battery "L," 2nd Massachusetts Heavy Artillery. Also served as Sergeant Major, 46th Massachusetts Infantry. Probably one of the special military students 1861-62.

Fifield, Samuel N. '50. Captain, Nebraska Volunteers.

Fiske, William '67. Private, Company "K," 43rd Massachusetts Infantry; wounded in action.

Fletcher, Frederick F. '57. Colonel, Missouri Militia; drillmaster.

Fletcher, Friend P. '39*. Private, Company "B," 12th Vermont Infantry.

Flint, Martin M. '34. Private, 40th Wisconsin Infantry. He assisted in recruiting troops for that regiment.

Folsom, George A. '65. Captain, 57th United States Colored Infantry.

Ford, Charles J. '52. Assistant Surgeon, 6th Indiana Cavalry; had charge of the hospitals at Fort Rice and Fort Randall.

Foster, Edwy W. '59*. Leader (Master Sergeant), 27th Massachusetts Infantry Band.

Fowler, John G. '58*. Corporal, Company "C," 3rd Vermont Infantry; wounded in action and captured at Savage Station in the Peninsula Campaign; discharged for disability after release from prison.

Fox, Charles '44. First Lieutenant, Company "C," 38th Illinois Infantry.

Frazer, John F. '26. Served in "Barlow's Grays," Pennsylvania Infantry.

Freeman, Norton F. '56. Colonel, New Hampshire Militia and State Drillmaster; spent time at the front studying tactics and strategy, later published a book on the subject.

French, George B. '55*. Captain and Adjutant, Companies "C" and "G," 4th Vermont Infantry; wounded in the Wilderness; later served in 26th New York Cavalry; cited for gallantry at Lee's Mills, the Seven Days, and Fredericksburg. Served in Company "E," 1st Vermont Infantry as its first sergeant.

Frizell, Joseph W. '42. Colonel, 94th Ohio Infantry; Lieutenant Colonel, 11th Ohio Infantry; Brevet Brigadier General, USV; wounded in action at Stone's River.

Fuller, Lloyd B. '64. Captain, Quartermaster Department, United States Army.

Galbraith, Frederick W. '64*. Second Lieutenant, 3rd Maine Infantry; Captain on Maj. Gen. O.O. Howard's staff; drillmaster; cited for gallantry; breveted lieutenant colonel.

Gardiner, William F. '57*. First Lieutenant, Company "E," 12th New York Infantry.

Gardner, Symmes '39. Captain, 18th United States Infantry.

Gerrish, William '64*. Private, Company "H," 1st Massachusetts Infantry; discharged for disability; First Lieutenant, 20th United States Colored Infantry; resigned.

Gillum, Henry H. '50. Captain and Quartermaster, Kansas Volunteers.

Gilman, Benjamin M. '57*. Private, Company "B," 1st Wisconsin Infantry; Private, Company "I," 12th Illinois Cavalry; discharged for disability. Possibly the Gilman that was a lieutenant in the 13th Illinois Infantry.

Gilman, George E. '67*. First Lieutenant, Company "G," 1st New Hampshire Cavalry.

Gilson, George W. '37*. Captain, 59th Massachusetts Infantry.

Gilson, James M. '40. Captain, 83rd Illinois Infantry; severely wounded and cited for gallantry at Fort Donelson; discharged for disability; drillmaster.

Gleason, Newell '49. Colonel, 87th Indiana Infantry; Brevet Brigadier General, USV; cited for gallantry at Chickamauga; drillmaster; brigade commander.

Glover, Wilson '40. Captain, Confederate States Army.

Glynn, James '23. Commodore, Union Navy.

Goddard, Henry S. '65. Second Lieutenant, Vermont State Troops.

Goodrich, Levi W. '57. Captain, Company "G," 30th Texas Cavalry, CSA.

Goodwin, William S. '64*. Private, Company "B," 7th Squadron Rhode Island Cavalry ("College Cavaliers"); First Lieutenant, 27th Massachusetts Infantry.

Gould, Edwin '57. Private, New Hampshire Infantry.

Gould, Jacob P. '49*. Major, 13th Massachusetts Infantry; Colonel, 59th Massachusetts Infantry; died of wounds received at the "Battle of the Crater," Petersburg where he suffered a compound fracture of the left knee joint from a minie ball; he was a brigade and acting division commander and was cited twice for gallantry; drillmaster; also Captain, Company "G," 13th Massachusetts Infantry; commanded the 13th Massachusetts at Antietam where he was cited for bravery and at Gettysburg. Earned the sobriquet "the fighting major" while serving in the 13th Massachusetts. Based on Clara Barton's writings, Gould was a personal and family friend.

Goulding, Joseph H. '65. Appointed a First Lieutenant, 6th United States Colored Infantry by President Abraham Lincoln. Detailed as an ambulance officer and assistant quartermaster in the Tenth, Eighteenth, and Twenty-Fifth Corps.

Gove, Jesse A. '49*. Colonel, 22nd Massachusetts Infantry; killed at Gaine's Mills, June 27, 1862 and his body was not recovered; cited for gallantry; Captain, 10th United States Infantry.

Gragg, Charles M. '65. Private, Company "B," 7th Squadron Rhode Island Cavalry ("College Cavaliers"); Private, Company "C," 42nd Massachusetts Infantry.

Graham, Charles '30*. Possibly a First Lieutenant, 15th New York Heavy Artillery.

Graham, John H. '27. Captain, Union Navy.

Granger, Brownell '57*. First Lieutenant and Adjutant, 11th Massachusetts Infantry; drillmaster; Captain of the Commisary Service; breveted major.

Granger, Charles H. '68*. Private, Company "H," 12th Vermont Infantry.

Granger, Edward M. '64*. First Sergeant, 2nd New York Cavalry; killed at Cedar Creek. He had been captured and exchanged earlier in the war.

Granger, Lyman C. '49. Assistant Surgeon, United States Navy; died of wounds on the U.S.S. "Cambridge."

Graves, George E. '46. Captain and Quartermaster, United States Volunteers.

Gray, John '52. First Lieutenant, Company "K," 9th Vermont Infantry.

Gray, John Jr. '67. Private, Company "D," 6th Massachusetts Infantry (Militia).

Gray, John S. '64. Captain, 19th Iowa Infantry.

Greeley, George P. '53*. Major and Surgeon, 4th New Hampshire Infantry; detailed as assistant operator in the Eighteenth Corps field hospital; later appointed Chief Medical Officer, Tenth Corps. His last service was as Surgeon, 9th United States Veterans Reserve Regiment.

Green, Samuel H. '65*. Private, Company "E," 2nd United States Sharpshooters, wounded in action and captured at Hatcher's Run, Virginia, October 27, 1864. Transferred to Company "G," 4th Vermont Infantry, February 25, 1865; discharged for disability.

Greenwood, William H. '52. Captain, Company "H," 51st Illinois Infantry; Lieutenant Colonel, Inspector General, Fourth Corps; cited for gallantry at Franklin and Nashville; drillmaster; brevet colonel. Also served for a time as a topographical engineer on the staff of the Cavalry Chief, Army of the Cumberland.

Griswold, Charles E. '54*. Colonel, 22nd Massachusetts Infantry; Colonel, 56th Massachusetts Infantry; killed in the Wilderness; cited for gallantry; drillmaster.

Guild, Edwin '56. Private, New Hampshire Infantry and state recruiting officer.

Hagner, Peter V. '32. Lieutenant Colonel, ordnance officer; brevet brigadier general. Served as the commander of the Watervliet, New York Arsenal. Served as a member of the Union Army's Ordnance Board and as an inspector of ordnance stores.

Hale, Henry A. '61*. Captain, Companies "C" and "H," 19th Massachusetts Infantry; severely wounded at Antietam and Cold Harbor; drillmaster; First Lieutenant, Company "E," 8th Massachusetts; cited for gallantry at Kinston, North Carolina; Captain on the staff of Second Brigade, Second Division, Second Corps staff (The "Philadelphia Brigade"); breveted lieutenant colonel.

Hale, Reuben C. '28. Brigadier General and Quartermaster, State of Pennsylvania. Very active in organizing and drilling troops, 1861-63; cited for his service by Secretary of the Navy Gideon Welles '26.

Hall, Alfred G. '55. First Lieutenant and Adjutant, 9th Connecticut Infantry; Lieutenant Colonel, 2nd Louisiana Infantry (Union) which became the 74th United States Colored Infantry. It was the second colored unit mustered into the Union Army on October 12, 1862. Hall also commanded Fort Pike near New Orleans.

Hall, Edmund '46. Lieutenant Colonel, Connecticut Volunteers; probably served with the state troops.

Hall, James A. '62?*. Lieutenant Colonel, 1st Battalion, Maine Light Artillery; Brevet Brigadier General, USV; Captain, 2nd Battery 1st Maine Light Artillery; cited for gallantry at Fredericksburg and Gettysburg; played a key role in Union actions on July 1, 1863; Colonel, 6th United States Veteran Volunteer Infantry. He may have been mistaken for James A. Hall '39 who died in 1843. Hall, born in 1835, likely attended Norwich as a special military student in 1861. The fact that he is specifically listed in the 1865 wartime Roll of Honor published in the University Reveille (see Appendix H for details) makes it likely he attended Norwich.

Hall, Josiah '61*. Colonel, 1st Vermont Cavalry; wounded in action at Bristoe Station; cited for gallantry; captured and paroled; also Captain of Company "F."

Hall, William H.H. '46*. Captain, Company "G," 6th Vermont Infantry; resigned due to ill health. Served with distinction at the Battle of Warwick Creek.

Hammond, Elisha '44*. Captain, Company "K," 20th Michigan Infantry.

Hammond, John W. '50. Second Lieutenant, Company "B," 5th California Infantry.

Hancock, Henry '43. Major, 4th California Infantry; he was active in recruiting troops at the outbreak of the war.

Handler, T.M. '46. Adjutant, US Volunteers; his service may have been in the Mexican War. It is possible he served in both wars.

Harding, Henry '54*. First Sergeant, Company "B," 12th Vermont Infantry.

Harding, William G. '28. Major General, Confederate Tennessee State Troops. Raised The Harding Light Artillery Battery and ran a munitions factory which made percussion caps for the Confederacy.

Harney, William S. '29. Brigadier General, US Volunteers; served in Missouri; Brevet Major General, USA; one of only four general officers in the United States Army when the Civil War broke out. Commanded the Department of the West.

Harris, Joseph '42. Major, Wisconsin Volunteers; paymaster.

Hartshorn, Samuel N. '56. Private, Lafayette Artillery Company, New Hampshire Militia (in federal service).

Hartstene, Henry J. '28. Captain, Confederate States Navy.

Harvey, Edward E. '51. Captain, 6th Kansas Cavalry.

Hascall, Henry B. '57. Assistant paymaster, Union Navy.

Haskell, Henry L.S. '46. Private, Company "K," 11th Illinois Infantry; discharged due to ill heath.

Hastings, Addison T. '63. Private, Company "B," 7th Squadron Rhode Island Cavalry ("College Cavaliers").

Hatch, Edward '50. Colonel, 2nd Iowa Cavalry; Brigadier General US Volunteers; drillmaster; Brevet Major General, USA and United States Volunteers; cited for gallantry at Franklin and Nashville; brigade and division commander; wounded in action. Later commanded the 9th United States Cavalry ("Buffalo Soldiers") for 23 years until his death in 1889.

Hatch, Frederick A. '56. First Lieutenant and Drillmaster, Maine State Troops. Also served on a divisional staff in the Maine State Troops.

Hatch, John E. '46. Private, Company "F," 7th Vermont Infantry; died of disease.

Haven, William B. '63. First Lieutenant, Company "K," 16th New Hampshire Infantry; First Lieutenant, Company "D," 18th New Hamsphire Infantry.

Haycock, Judson '54*. Captain, 1st United States Cavalry.

Hays, William B. '63. First Lieutenant, 7th Pennsylvania Cavalry.

Hazelton, Walter S. '64. Private, Company "B," 7th Squadron Rhode Island Cavalry ("College Cavaliers").

Hazen, Albert E. '40*. Private, Company "G," 16th Vermont Infantry.

Head, Henry H. '66. Private, Company "G," 60th Massachusetts Infantry; died of disease.

Hebard, Salmon B. '62?. Second Lieutenant, 1st Vermont Light Battery; cited for gallantry; possibly a special military student 1861.

Hebard, William '64. First Lieutenant, 138th Indiana Infantry.

Henderson, Robert '39. Served in the Confederate States Army.

Henderson, Robert '56*. Lieutenant, United States Navy.

Henderson, Thomas A. '62. Lieutenant Colonel, 7th New Hampshire Infantry; he commanded the regiment in the Bermuda Hundred Campaign until he was mortally wounded at Deep Bottom, Virginia. Henderson died when he was wounded in the hip and an artery was severed; he bled to death in four hours. He was cited for gallantry at Drewry's Bluff. He served as an aide to Colonel Putnam who commanded a brigade in the assault on Battery Wagner. Served for a time on the staff of General Truman B. Seymour '44 as Provost Marshal of Florida. He is confirmed as a "special military student" at Norwich in the summer and fall of 1861.

Henry, Horace C. '64*. First Sergeant, Company "A," 14th Vermont Infantry.

Hewitt, Sylvester M. '40. Captain, Company "I," 26th Ohio and Major, 32nd Ohio Infantry; also served in 136th Ohio Infantry. His intelligent use of the limited number of ambulances and medical supplies at Fort Donelson in February 1862, helped prevent a potential disaster for the wounded from that battle.

Hitchcock, Elisha P. '64. Captain and Vermont State Drillmaster. Drilled and instructed the 7th, 11th and 16th Vermont Infantry. Served later as a captain in the 9th Vermont Militia Regiment following the St. Albans Raid of October 1864.

Hitchcock, Robert E. '59. Second Lieutenant, United States Marines Corps, killed at 1st Bull Run when the top of his head was severed by a cannonball; first marine and first Vermont officer killed in the Civil War. Hitchcock's body was never recovered.

Hobbs, George W. '58. Second Lieutenant, 6th Massachusetts Infantry; drillmaster. Also served as an enrolling officer in Massachusetts with the rank of Captain.

Holley, George W. '28. Drillmaster, New York Volunteers.

Holley, Henry W. '50. Captain, Minnesota Volunteers; fighting Indians, 1862-1863.

Hollister, James '55*. First Lieutenant, Company "E," 1st Minnesota Volunteers; wounded in action at 1st Bull Run.

Holman, Samuel A. '49*. Chaplain, 48th and 129th Pennsylvania Infantry.

Hooper, William H. Jr. '67*. Private, Company "K," 12th Massachusetts Infantry; wounded at Fredericksburg and Gettysburg on July 1; discharged for wounds.

Hopkins, George W. '64. Captain, 22nd Indiana Infantry.

Hopkins, Henry '66. Major, 2nd Kansas Cavalry; Captain, 2nd Kansas Infantry and 3rd Kansas Independent Light Battery.

Houghton, Edmund C. '65. Officer, United States Volunteers.

Howard, Henry A. '65. Private, Company "G," 60th Massachusetts Infantry.

Howard, Henry H. '52. Colonel, Provost Marshal in Illinois.

Howard, Noel B. '60. Colonel, 2nd Iowa Infantry; brigade commander; seriously wounded at Atlanta; cited for gallantry; also served as Captain, Company "L," 2nd Iowa.

Hoyt, Charles A. '63*. Captain, Company "C," 24th Michigan Infantry; wounded in action at Fredericksburg; severely wounded at Gettysburg (losing a leg) and was discharged due to wounds; drillmaster.

Hoyt, William R. '64*. First Lieutenant, Company "A," 10th Vermont Infantry.

Hubbard, David H. '57. Captain, 4th Kansas Militia Infantry; quartermaster clerk, Thirteenth Corps. Took part in the pursuit of Quantrill's Raiders.

Hubbard, Gordon S. '56. Captain, Company "G," 88th Illinois Infantry; on the staff of General Rosecrans in the Army of the Cumberland; resigned due to illness; brevet major for gallantry in action. Also served as Assistant Inspector General of the Army of the Cumberland.

Hubbard, James* '57. Colonel and Brevet Brigadier General, USV, 2nd Connecticut Heavy Artillery; brigade commander cited for gallantry at Sayler's Creek. Also served as a captain in the 19th Connecticut Infantry prior to its conversion to heavy artillery.

Hunsdon, Charles '51*. Colonel, 1st Vermont Heavy Artillery (former 11th Vermont Infantry); Vermont Brigade commander, December 26, 1864 to January 16, 1865; cited for gallantry in the assault on Petersburg.

Hunt, John H. '56*. First Lieutenant, Company "C," 19th Maine Infantry. May possibly have been the John H. Hunt who served as an engineer, USN.

Hunt, Roswell W. '42*. Corporal, Company "D," 10th Vermont Infantry; wounded in action at Petersburg.

Hutchinson, Alonzo B. '62*. Captain, Company "B," 6th Vermont Infantry; severely wounded at Banks Ford, Virginia; discharged due to wounds.

Hutchinson, Edson '38*. Corporal, Company "K," 16th Vermont Infantry.

Hutchinson, Lewis B. '50. First Lieutenant, 15th Missouri Cavalry.

Hutchinson, Lemuel M. '46. Captain, Company "E," 8th Vermont Infantry.

Hutchinson, Samuel '?*. Served in Company "K," 16th Vermont Infantry.

Irish, Nathaniel '61*. Captain, Independent Battery "F," Pennsylvania Light Artillery; wounded in action at Gettysburg. Commanded the same battery after it was converted to heavy artillery and based at Maryland Heights (Harper's Ferry) in 1864-65.

Irving, Washington E. '30. Quartermaster, United States Volunteers.

Jackman, Alonzo '36. Brigadier General, Vermont State troops; commanded the state musters of 1860-61 and selected the units and officers for the 1st Vermont Infantry; commandant of cadets and military science instructor at Norwich; drill-master and instructor in the special military courses at the university. He also commanded the Corps of Cadets in the "Lake Memphremagog Campaign" following the Confederate raid on St. Albans in October 1864. Jackman also led hand picked detachments of cadets to Vermont training camps where he and they served as drillmasters for newly mustering units and recruits.

Jackson, John C. '51. Private, Confederate States Army in Company "F," 8th Texas Cavalry ("Texas Rangers").

Jarvis, George C. '52*. Major, surgeon, 7th Connecticut Infantry; cited for gallantry; assistant surgeon, 1st Connecticut Cavalry; Private, Company "A," 2nd Connecticut Infantry. Served for some time as Chief Surgeon, First Division, Tenth Army Corps.

Jenkins, Robert B. '40. Officer, Confederate States Army; listed in some sources as a major general.

Johnson, Richard '29. Chaplain (Captain) and drillmaster "Hampton's Legion," CSA.

Johnson, William H. '65*. Captain, Company "I," 15th Vermont Infantry.

Johnston, Daniel P. '26. Captain, Confederate States Army.

Johnston, Willie '70*. Private and Drummer, Company "D," 3rd Vermont Infantry; he was the youngest man (age 12) to win the Congressional Medal of Honor in the history of the award (for the Peninsula Campaign). The medal was presented by Secretary of War Edwin Stanton, September 16, 1863 and was only the seventh occasion when the medal was awarded. Willie transferred to the 20th Regiment, U.S. Veterans Reserve Corps in March 1864 as its drum major. Johnston is also the first Norwich alumnus and Vermonter to win the Medal of Honor.

Jones, Edward T. '62. First Lieutenant, Vermont drillmaster; died of disease; served at the front for a time with the 6th Vermont Infantry.

Kelley, Benjamin F. '26? Brigadier General, United States Volunteers. Commanded the 1st Virginia Infantry (Union) and was severely wounded at the Battle of Philippi, June 3, 1861. Spent most of the war guarding the vital Baltimore and Ohio Railroad and fending off Confederate raiders. Breveted major general on August 5, 1864. Captured by raiders on February 21, 1865 and later paroled.

Kelley, Elisha S. '54*. Major, 8th Illinois Cavalry; severely wounded at Boonsboro, Maryland; cited for gallantry; discharged for disability. Personally recruited some 100 men for the 8th Illinois Cavalry in 1861.

Kellogg, Theodore H. '62. First Lieutenant, Company "B," 7th Squadron Rhode Island Cavalry ("College Cavaliers").

Kellogg, William P. '48. Colonel, 7th Illinois Cavalry; commanded a brigade; breveted brigadier general; discharged for disability

Kelton, Dwight H. '64. Private, Company "B," 98th New York Infantry; Captain, 115th United States Colored Infantry; later served in the 10th United States Infantry. He tried to enlist in the 3rd Vermont Infantry in 1861 but was rejected as too young. Kelton later served in the Regular Army.

Kendall, Paul R. '47. First Lieutenant and Quartermaster, 12th Missouri Cavalry; drillmaster. Served as quartermaster in General Hatch's cavalry division of the Army of Tennessee.

Kent, Charles N. '64. First Lieutenant, Company "C," 17th New Hampshire Infantry; helped lead the Corps of Cadets during the St. Albans Raid in October, 1864.

Kent, Henry O. '54. Colonel, 17th New Hampshire Infantry; drillmaster; served on the governor's staff. His value as an instructor and organizer of New Hampshire troops was recognized by a special act of Congress, July 21, 1892. Kent served as a personal aide to President Lincoln during his November 1863 visit to the Gettysburg Battlefield.

Kilbourne, Byron H. '60. Second Lieutenant, Company "D," 3rd Wisconsin Cavalry. Recruited troops at the outbreak of the war.

Kimball, Edgar A. '44*. Lieutenant Colonel, 9th New York Infantry; killed by Col. Michael Corcoran of the "Corcoran Legion" after an argument near Suffolk, Virginia; cited for gallantry; commanded the 9th New York with distinction at Antietam and Fredericksburg. Called "Old Gunpowder" by his troops, he apparently had a well earned reputation for hard drinking and hard fighting. He is the principal subject of a Keith Rocco 1996 historical painting of the 9th New York Infantry at the Battle of Antietam called "Always Ready."

Kimball, Gilman '24. Brigade Surgeon and medical director for General Butler's command in Louisiana.

Kimball, Lewis '62. Private, Company "F," 3rd New Hampshire Infantry; Second Lieutenant, Company "C," 4th United States Colored Infantry; discharged for disability.

King, George L. '49. First Lieutenant and Adjutant of a Vermont Regiment; possibly in the state troops.

King, Wallace A. '59*. First Lieutenant, Company "G," 4th Michigan Infantry; Private, Company "B," 7th Squadron Rhode Island Cavalry ("College Cavaliers"); drillmaster. Recruited Michigan troops at the outbreak of the war.

Kingsley, Levi G. '56*. Second Lieutenant, Company "K," 1st Vermont Infantry; Major, 12th Vermont Infantry. Became a colonel and regimental commander in the reorganized Vermont Militia after the St. Albans Raid of October 1864.

Kinne, Aaron '56. First Sergeant, Company "H," 25th Connecticut Infantry; discharged for disability.

Knight, Luther M. '37*. Probably Major and Surgeon, 5th New Hampshire Infantry. He was commended for his actions at the Battle of Fredericksburg, December 13, 1862.

Knowles, Samuel W. '58. Second Lieutenant, Company "B," 22nd Maine Infantry; Captain, Company "G," 2nd Maine Cavalry.

Lander, Frederick W. '41*. Brigadier General, United States Volunteers; died of wounds received at Ball's Bluff; drillmaster; brigade and division commander; cited for gallantry by the Secretary of War. General McClellan, who held Lander in especially high regard, served as a pall bearer at his funeral. Lander carried out a number of secret government missions in the Southern states prior to the beginning of the war. On one mission he was sent to Texas to ensure Governor Sam Houston of Federal support. By the time he arrived, however, the Texas secessionists had already gained control of the state.

Lane, Abel G. '64. Private, Company "G," 60th Massachusetts Infantry.

Lasier, Thomas J. '64. Officer, United States Volunteers.

Lathrop, Solon H. '52*. Captain, 17th United States Infantry; Lieutenant Colonel, Inspector General, United States Volunteers; brevet colonel.

Lawrence, Arthur '58. A minister who served on General Oliver O. Howard's and William T. Sherman's staffs; although not a formally commissioned officer, he believed it was his duty to provide comfort and inspiration to the troops.

Lawrence, John B. '61. Officer, possibly in the Illinois Volunteers; apparently served as a minister and volunteer staff officer in various commands during the war.

Learnard, Oscar E. '55. Lieutenant Colonel, 1st Kansas Infantry; wounded in action.

Lee, Douglas '64. Corporal, Company "B," 7th Squadron Rhode Island Cavalry ("College Cavaliers"); died of disease.

Lee, Roswell W. '29. Colonel, Confederate States Army in the Texas Artillery.

Lee, Stephen B. '43. Lieutenant Colonel; died of disease while in the Union Army; drillmaster.

Lee, William R. '25*. Colonel, 20th Massachusetts Infantry; Brevet Brigadier General, USV; wounded in action; cited for gallantry at Antietam; brigade commander at Antietam and Fredericksburg. Chief Engineer of Massachusetts with rank of Brigadier General of State Troops; redesigned the fortifications of Boston Harbor.

Leland, Oscar H. '54. Captain, Confederate States Army in the 30th Texas Cavalry.

Lewis, Charles H. '55. Captain, 16th United States Infantry; listed as a brevet colonel in university records although there is no mention of the brevet in Heitman's Register of the United States Army.

Lewis, William E. '33. Brigadier General of Vermont Troops and drillmaster, Vermont State Troops in 1861. Helped recruit troops for Vermont regiments.

Lincoln, Francis M. '50*. Captain, Assistant surgeon, 9th Massachusetts Infantry; Major, Surgeon 35th Massachusetts Infantry; also served as surgeon, 4th United States Infantry for a short time.

Lincoln, Sumner H. '62. Colonel, 6th Vermont Infantry; cited for gallantry; wounded at the battles of the Wilderness (left knee) and Opequon Creek (left side of head), September 19, 1864. Cited for gallantry at the Battle of the Opequon. There is no identifiable record of his having been a cadet. Nevertheless, he is listed as an alumnus in Who was Who in America,1897-1942. It is likely his records were destroyed and that he was a special military student in 1861. Lincoln also served as a private in Company "B," 1st Vermont Infantry. Served in the Regular Army after the war.

Little, George '30. Colonel, Confederate States Army serving on the staff of the governor of North Carolina.

Little, James T. '39. Served in the Confederate States Army.

Little, Joseph S. '56*. First Lieutenant, Company "A," 93rd New York Infantry; Army of the Potomac Headquarters Guard; severely wounded leading a charge at the North Anna River (lost a leg); discharged for disability.

Long, Charles H. '55*. Captain, Company "G," 5th New Hampshire Infantry; Lieutenant Colonel, 17th New Hampshire Infantry; Colonel, 1st New Hampshire Heavy Artillery; severely wounded at Antietam; cited for gallantry; drillmaster; brigade commander and division commander, Twenty-Second Corps.

Longnecker, Henry C. '42*. Colonel, 9th Pennsylvania Infantry; Colonel, 5th Pennsylvania Militia on war service at Antietam; resigned due to disability; brigade commander. Active in recruiting Pennsylvania troops for the war.

Loomis, Pomeroy '56*. Sergeant, Company "C," 12th Vermont Infantry.

Lord, Charles V. '55*. Captain and Quartermaster, 2nd Maine Infantry.

Lord, Robert C. '64*. Private, Company "C," 11th United States Infantry; Second Lieutenant, 14th United States Infantry.

Lowe, Abner B. '64. Private, Company "G," 60th Massachusetts Infantry.

Lyon, Caleb '41. Officer (lieutenant colonel?) on the staff of Gen. Winfield Scott at start of war.

Mackaye (aze), James M. '25. Colonel; his Norwich records indicate he raised and commanded an unknown New York regiment at the start of the war; this service could not be verified. The Ellis history of Norwich indicates he was commissioned a colonel by President Lincoln. He can be confirmed, however, as serving on a special Presidential Commission in 1864.

Major, Augustine L.C. '41. Private, Company "E," 43rd Virginia Cavalry Battalion ("Mosby's Rangers").

Marcy, Andrew C. '61*. Private, Company "B," 12th Vermont Infantry.

Marsh, Luther R. '29. Probably a Lieutenant Colonel, New York State Troops.

Marsh, Otis M. '42. Captain, Confederate States Army in the Texas Cavalry.

Marsh, Samuel '39*. Lieutenant Colonel, 16th New York Infantry; died of wounds received at Gaine's Mills, June 27, 1862; cited for gallantry.

Marvin, Asa C. '39. Colonel, 60th Missouri Infantry (Militia) on war service; also served as First Lieutenant and Adjutant, 7th Missouri Cavalry. Played a key roll in organizing and drilling Missouri troops for the Union.

May, Charles A. '32. Lieutenant Colonel, 2nd United States Cavalry; breveted colonel.

McCollister, John Q.A. '53. Major, surgeon of 53rd Massachusetts Infantry; served as medical director of the Yorktown hospitals and in the field for two years.

McCulloch, Frederick H. '64. First Sergeant, Company "G," 60th Massachusetts Infantry.

McIntosh, George H. '25. Served as an officer in Confederate States Army in the Texas Volunteers.

McLean, Eugene E. '37. Colonel, CSA; served on the staff of Jefferson Davis and as the Assistant Quartermaster General of the Confederacy.

McNabb, John '32. Officer, Confederate States Army; said to have served as a colonel.

Mead, John B.T. '51. First Lieutenant and Adjutant, 28th Illinois Infantry; died of wounds received at Shiloh; drillmaster.

Mead, William R. '64. First Lieutenant and state drillmaster for Company "B," 14th New Hampshire Infantry.

Merrifield, William F.C. '59. Said to have served in the Union Army in an unknown capacity.

Merriman, DeForest H. '57. Lieutenant, Union Navy.

Merriman, Edgar C. '57. Commander, Union Navy.

Messenger, George '58*. First Sergeant, Company "B," 6th Vermont Infantry; also served as Commisary Sergeant, Second Division, Sixth Corps.

Metcalf, William R. '64. First Lieutenant and State Drillmaster in New Hampshire and Vermont.

Miller, John A. '44*. First Lieutenant and quartermaster, 33rd New Jersey Infantry.

Milroy, John B. '45. Major, 9th Indiana Infantry; drillmaster; cited for gallantry; elected colonel of his regiment but not mustered; discharged for ill health; also served as Captain, Company "A;" commanded his regiment for a time.

Milroy, Robert H. '43. Major General, US Volunteers; Colonel, 9th Indiana Infantry; brigade and division commander; drillmaster. A fervent abolitionist, he was the scourge of secessionists in western Virginia, he had a $100,000 price put on his head by the Confederate government; it was never collected. His defeat at the Battle of Winchester in June 1863 was a scandal at the time. He was, however, cleared of any malfeasance by a court of inquiry and returned to duty, albeit in a secondary theater. Modern scholarship has put his performance at the time in a better light.

Moore, John H. '38. Captain, Quartermaster; died on active duty.

Moores, Frederick W. '64. Assistant Engineer, Union Navy.

Morey, Arthur P. '64. Captain, 22nd United States Colored Infantry; Private, Company "B," 7th Squadron Rhode Island Cavalry ("College Cavaliers"); drillmaster; breveted major.

Morris, Henry V. '36. First Lieutenant and Adjutant, 20th Wisconsin Infantry and 8th United States Veteran Volunteer Infantry; brevet major; wounded in action; drillmaster.

Morris, Thomas E. '54*. Major, 15th Michigan Infantry; Captain, 16th Michigan Infantry; resigned May 31, 1863.

Morton, Gilbert '56. Master in the Union Navy; wounded in action at Fort Donelson, Tennessee.

Moseley, Charles Henry '59*. First Sergeant, Company "B," 36th Massachusetts Infantry; wounded in action near Petersburg.

Moses, Rufus L. '63*. First Sergeant, Company "A," 3rd Vermont Infantry.

Mower, Albion J. '51. Captain, Company "I," 9th Vermont Infantry; discharged due to disability; drillmaster. Recruited companies for the 3rd, 6th, and 9th Vermont Volunteers.

Mower, Joseph A. '46. Major General, Twentieth Corps Commander; Colonel, 2nd Missouri Infantry; cited for gallantry five times; brigade and division commander; wounded in action; Brevet Major General, USA; drillmaster. Placed in command of the District of New Orleans at war's end where he later died. He is said to have been "under fire more than any other officer in the service." Mower was wounded and captured at the Battle of Corinth; he escaped and then was recaptured and later exchanged. He was considered by Sherman to be the "boldest young officer in the army."

Mower, Oscar G. '47*. Probably Private, Company "H," 1st Vermont Infantry.

Munson, William D. '54*. Lieutenant Colonel, 13th Vermont Infantry; wounded at Gettysburg; drillmaster. Munson commanded the regiment for part of the battle on July 3rd. He served as a state recruiting officer in 1861 and recruited an artillery battery which was disbanded by Governor Fairbanks because he believed the war would not last more than a few months. Appointed colonel and given command of a regiment of Vermont Militia after the St. Albans Raid of October 1864.

Murray, Chilton '39. Served in the Confederate States Army.

Murray, John C. '38. Captain, Confederate States Army.

Myrick, Cyrus G. '40. Served in "Lesuer Tigers," Minnesota Volunteers in Indian War, 1862-1863 and in the Battle of New Ulm.

Nalle, Benjamin F. '41. Colonel, Virginia Militia; Captain, Company "A," 13th Virginia Infantry, CSA.

Needham, William C.H. '66. Private, Company "G," 60th Massachusetts Infantry.

Neil, John L. '49. Captain, 9th Kentucky Cavalry.

Nelson, William '39. Major General, US Volunteers; severely wounded at Richmond, Kentucky; shot and killed in an argument with Brig. Gen. Jefferson C. Davis; division commander; cited for gallantry. Previously served in the United States Navy but transferred to the army to see more action.

Nelson, William '62?. First Lieutenant, Company "B," 13th United States Infantry; twice cited for gallantry at Arkansas Post and Vicksburg; brevet major. Probably was a student in the special military courses, 1861.

Newman, Asahel C. '47. Clerk, United States Quartermaster Department.

Nichols, George '67. Probably a Second Lieutenant, New Jersey State Troops.

Nichols, Henry B. '62. Captain, 19th Wisconsin Infantry.

Noble, William H. '26*. Colonel, 17th Connecticut Infantry; Brevet Brigadier General, USV; severely wounded at Chancellorsville and cited for gallantry; served with distinction in South Carolina and Florida; brigade commander; captured at St. John's, Florida and later paroled. Noble was the highest ranking Union officer ever to be held at the notorious Andersonville Prison.

Nourse, Ira '45. Private, 3rd Wisconsin Cavalry.

Noyes, David K. '45*. Captain, Company "A," 6th Wisconsin Infantry; Lieutenant Colonel, 49th Wisconsin Infantry; severely wounded at Antietam where he lost a foot; also served as a recruiting officer in Wisconsin.

Noyes, Edward H. '64. Private, Company "B," 7th Squadron Rhode Island Cavalry ("College Cavaliers").

Ober, George H. '63. First Lieutenant and Drillmaster, Vermont Volunteers.

Osgood, Charles H. '64. Second Lieutenant, Brockett's Minnesota Cavalry Battalion, 5th Iowa Cavalry.

Osgood, Elbridge B. '60. Served in the Union Army.

Osgood, John H. '64. Captain, Company "G," 116th United States Colored Infantry; discharged for disability.

Otis, George E. '67. Private, Company "G," 60th Massachusetts Infantry.

Page, Frank A. '58*. Private, Company "H," 4th Vermont Infantry; severely wounded June 27, 1862 at Gaine's Mills losing his right arm; First Lieutenant, Veterans Reserve Corps; cited for gallantry at Lee's Mills; breveted captain.

Papanti, Augustus L. '65*. Private, Company "B," 7th Squadron Rhode Island Cavalry ("College Cavaliers"); Captain, 2nd Massachusetts Cavalry; severely wounded, March 31,1865.

Parker, Benjamin W. '49*. Private, Company "I," 13th Massachusetts Infantry; wounded at Antietam.

Parker, Charles E. '59. Captain, Company "E," 7th Vermont Infantry.

Parker, Edgar '59*. First Lieutenant and Assistant Surgeon, 13th Massachusetts Infantry; severely wounded in the head at Gettysburg and discharged for disability. Served with distinction at Second Fredericksburg, Chancellorsville, and Gettysburg.

Parker, Edward B. '62?*. Second Lieutenant, Battery "B," 1st Vermont Heavy Artillery; captured at the Weldon Railroad June 23, 1864; died at Columbia, South Carolina, October 13, 1864; mortally wounded by dogs during an escape attempt. He was probably a student in the special military courses, 1861-62. Also served as a Private, Company "A," 1st Vermont Infantry.

Parker, George E. '59*. Captain, Company "A," 6th Vermont Infantry.

Parker, George H. '57*. Private, Company "A," 4th Vermont Infantry; wounded in the Wilderness, May 5, 1864; assigned to the Veterans Reserve Corps.

Parker, George W. '48. Lieutenant Colonel, 79th Indiana Infantry; possibly the Parker listed as a First Lieutenant in the 6th Minnesota Infantry.

Parker, James V. '63. Private, Company "B," 7th Squadron Rhode Island Cavalry ("College Cavaliers").

Parker, James W. '48. Probably a Captain, 22nd Indiana Infantry.

Parker, William T. '59*. Captain, Battery "L," 1st Maine Heavy Artillery; killed in the Spotsylvania Campaign in the first engagement of his regiment May 19, 1864 at Harris Farm, Virginia.

Parmenter, Daniel W. '63*. Private, Company "H," 32nd Massachusetts Infantry; Second Lieutenant, Company "G," 10th United States Colored Infantry; missing, presumed dead, probably as a prisoner of war after being captured at the Battle of Plymouth, North Carolina.

Parsons, John W. '63*. Assistant Surgeon, 24th Massachusetts Infantry.

Partridge, Frederick W. '45. Lieutenant Colonel, 13th Illinois Infantry; Brevet Brigadier General, USV; cited for gallantry at Chattanooga, Lookout Mountain, and Ringold Gap; wounded in action at Chattanooga; drillmaster. He was a son of Alden Partridge, the founder of Norwich University.

Partridge, Henry L. or S. '45. Served in the Massachusetts Volunteers.

Partridge, Henry V. '92. Son of Alden Partridge, founder of Norwich University. Served as a Captain in the 10th Pennsylvania Reserves. The Ellis history indicates he attended school at Norwich, served in the war, and was awarded an A.M. degree from Norwich in 1892. While it is uncertain when he was a cadet, he is counted as an alumnus and his class dated to the year of his degree award.

Partridge, William* '49. First Lieutenant, Company "A," 43rd Wisconsin Infantry; Captain, United States Topographic Engineers.

Patch, John W. '57. Served as a Lieutenant, USA.

Patterson, Rody Jr. '63*. First Lieutenant and drillmaster, Vermont Volunteers; also served as Private, Company "B," 4th Pennsylvania Cavalry, wounded in action August 16, 1864 at Strawberry Plains, Virginia.

Paul, William P. '43. Captain and Division Quartermaster, Tennessee Volunteers, CSA. Served on the staff of General W.H. Jackson.

Paulding, Hiram '23. Rear Admiral, USN; was one of the first officers appointed to that rank. Played a key role in the outfitting of the "Monitor." Later in command of the naval base in New York City where he helped put down the Draft Riots. He led the evacuation of the Gosport Navy Yard at Norfolk, Virginia in 1861 and ensured the salvage of several vessels before the yard and its remaining vessels were destroyed and the facilities were captured.

Pearce, Henry H. '41. Captain, 11th Kansas Cavalry; First Lieutenant, 11th Kansas Infantry.

Peck, Lewis M. '59*. Captain, Company "K," 67th New York Infantry; Colonel, 173rd New York Infantry; brevet major general; cited for gallantry at Cedar Creek; wounded in action.

Peirce, Frank C. '62*. Captain, Company "A," 6th Maine Infantry; killed when he was was kicked by his horse while on duty in Sacramento, California.

Peirce, Horace T.H. '46*. Captain, Company "F," 5th New Hampshire Infantry; First Lieutenant, 1st New Hampshire Infantry; discharged for disability; cited for gallantry. Served as recruiting officer at the beginning of the war. He took command of the regiment at both Antietam and Fredericksburg when his regimental commander and more senior officers were wounded.

Penniman, Luther L. '56. Assistant paymaster, Union Navy.

Pennock, Joseph N. '46. First Lieutenant and Adjutant, 7th Missouri Cavalry; died of disease. He was the son of the first cadet to matriculate at Norwich.

Perkins, Marshall '46. Captain and assistant surgeon, 14th New Hampshire Infantry. He was in charge of the smallpox hospital at Savannah, Georgia for a time.

Perkins, Norman E.. '43*. Captain, Company "A," 12th Vermont Infantry.

Perkins, William E. '43*. Captain, Company "I," 2nd Massachusetts Infantry; wounded at Chancellorsville.

Perry, Carlton H. '23. Major, 3rd Iowa Cavalry; drillmaster; resigned due to ill health.

Pettes, William H. '27*. Colonel, 50th New York Engineers; served on the Army of the Potomac staff and in many important staff assignments in Washington. He was selected as the lieutenant colonel of the 50th New York Infantry, later the 50th Engineers, specifically because of his Norwich training. His name is sometimes seen as Pettis.

Pettis, John '42*. Private, Battery "B," 1st Vermont Heavy Artillery; wounded in action in the assault on Petersburg, April 2, 1865.

Phelps, Charles '52*. First Lieutenant, Company "I," 37th Massachusetts Infantry; discharged for disability.

Phelps, Dudley F. '64. First Lieutenant and Adjutant, 20th United States Colored Infantry. Served in the Department of the Gulf and in the Mobile Campaign. He was the Provost Marshal General of New Orleans for a time.

Phelps, Edward E. '23. Major and brigade surgeon; Chief of Brattleboro, Vermont Army Hospital; brevet lieutenant colonel. He was commended for his services at the Battle of Lee's Mills during the Peninsula Campaign. His Vermont hospital was regarded as one of the best in the nation with an unusually high patient recovery rate.

Phelps, Egbert '55. Captain, 19th United States Infantry.

Phillips, Henry M. '64. Private, Company "B," 7th Squadron Rhode Island Cavalry; First Lieutenant, Company "A," 4th Massachusetts Cavalry; cited for gallantry; brevet captain; drillmaster.

Phillips, James W. '45*. Probably Lieutenant Colonel, 18th Pennsylvania Cavalry.

Phillipes, Walter A. '62*. First Lieutenant, Company "F," 2nd Vermont Infantry; Company "H," 13th Vermont Infantry; First Lieutenant, 3rd Battery, Vermont Light Artillery; cited for gallantry; a Vermont State Drillmaster.

Pierce, John S. '46. Captain, Confederate States Army.

Pike, John B. '53. Major; Deputy Provost Marshal for New Hampshire.

Platt, Jonas (James) H. '54*. Captain Company B," 4th Vermont Infantry; captured May 30, 1864, exchanged October 16 and then discharged; cited for gallantry at the Seven Days Battles.

Porter, Benjamin F. '59*. First Lieutenant, Company "D," 8th Michigan Infantry; Captain and assistant quartermaster.

Porter, John H. '57. Captain, Assistant Surgeon and Quartermaster for a time with the 116th Illinois Infantry; breveted captain.

Porter, William '42. Captain, 48th Kentucky Infantry.

Post, Henry G. '64*. First Sergeant, Company "C," 10th Vermont Infantry; transferred to the Regulars in February 1863.

Potter, Charles H. '47*. First Lieutenant, Companies "B," "K," 73rd New York Infantry; captured at Williamsburg and paroled; later captured at Boydton Plank Road and paroled; slightly wounded in action in the Wilderness; cited for gallantry. Commanded companies "E" and "K" in the summer and fall 1864.

Potter, Charles H. '66*. Possibly a Second Lieutenant, Company "K," 12th Rhode Island Infantry; cited for gallantry.

Potter, Lorenzo D. '56. First Sergeant, 40th Wisconsin Infantry; First Lieutenant, 8th Illinois Infantry.

Powell, Cuthbert H. '31. Captain and Chaplain United States Army; served in Washington.

Prentiss, George A. '24. Commodore, Union Navy; cited for gallantry; resigned due to ill health.

Preston, Simon M. '45. First Lieutenant and Quartermaster 15th Illinois Infantry; Colonel, 58th United States Colored Infantry; Brevet Brigadier General, USV; drillmaster. Also served as an Assistant Adjutant General on the staffs of Majors General Henry W. Halleck and Horatio G. Wright. Directly commissioned in 1861 by President Lincoln.

Preston, Sylvester S. '52*. Colonel or Captain and Assistant Quartermaster, in a New York regiment or in the state troops.

Putnam, George F. '64. Private, Company "G," 3rd Massachusetts Militia Infantry.

Quimby, Asahel H. '59. Corporal, Company "D," 8th New Hampshire Infantry; severely wounded; also served as Corporal, 142nd Company, Veterans Reserve Corps.

Rand, Frederick H. '64*. First Lieutenant, Company "C," 1st Independent Battalion, 1st Massachusetts Cavalry; Captain, Company "K," 4th Massachusetts Cavalry; discharged for disability; cited for gallantry.

Ransom, Dunbar R. '51*. Captain, Battery "C," 5th United States Artillery; wounded at Gettysburg; cited for gallantry at Fredericksburg, Gettysburg, and Kearneysville, Virginia; artillery brigade commander; commanded the artillery of the Second Division, First Corps at Chancellorsville; breveted colonel. Regarded as one of the better artillerymen in the army.

Ransom, Frederick E. '68. Second Lieutenant, Company "E," 11th Illinois Infantry; severely wounded at Fort Donelson and Vicksburg; resigned due to ill health and for "the good of the service."

Ransom, Thomas E.G. '51. Brigadier General, Seventeenth Corps Commander; died of disease which resulted from his many wounds; cited for gallantry; Brevet Major General, USV; drillmaster. He was a personal favorite of Generals Grant and Sherman. His commission as a full major general arrived shortly after his death. He also commanded the 11th Illinois Infantry, various brigades and divisions, part of the Thirteenth Corps, and the Sixteenth and Seventeenth Corps. Ransom was wounded at Fort Donelson, Shiloh, and Sabine Crossroads.

Rehrer, Erasmus G. '49*. First Lieutenant, 28th Pennsylvania Infantry; Captain, Company "E," 129th Pennsylvania Infantry; seriously wounded at the Battle of Fredericksburg while serving on his brigade's staff.

Rice, Edmund '60*. Lieutenant Colonel, 19th Massachusetts Infantry; wounded at Antietam in the right leg; Gettysburg twice in the right leg and hand; and in the Wilderness; won Congressional Medal of Honor; cited for gallantry at Antietam, Fredericksburg, and the Wilderness. Rice was wounded and captured at the "Bloody Angle" May 12, 1864 but returned to his regiment after a daring escape and a 400 mile journey through enemy lines. Brevet Lieutenant Colonel, USA; promoted to Colonel, 19th Massachusetts but not mustered as his regiment had too few men on its roles. His Medal of Honor was personally presented by Maj. Gen. Nelson A. Miles in 1892. Rice remained in the Regular Army and retired as a brigadier general after service in the Spanish American War and the Phillipine Insurrection. Edmund Rice was the principal character of the Dale Gallon historical painting of the Battle of Gettysburg entitled "Clubs Are Trumps!"

Rice, Edward W. '58. Captain, served in the Union Army.

Rice, George M. '53. Private, Battery "C," 1st United States Artillery; Second Lieutenant, Battery "I," 2nd Massachusetts Heavy Artillery; dismissed from the service, January 26, 1864; enlisted in the Union Navy and died of disease at sea.

Rice, James '49*. Leader, 5th Vermont Infantry band; Captain, Battery "F," 1st Vermont Heavy Artillery; cited for gallantry at the Battle of Cold Harbor.

Rice, Thomas G. '65. First Sergeant, Company "B," 2nd Maine Cavalry; Second Lieutenant, Company "D," 4th United States Colored Cavalry; died of disease at Vidalia, Louisiana.

Rich, Clayton E. '63. First Lieutenant and drillmaster, Vermont Volunteers.

Richards, J. Swift '65. Sergeant, Company "G," 60th Massachusetts Infantry.

Richardson, Roderick J. '61. Assistant paymaster, USN.

Robbins, Henry A. '61*. Acting Surgeon, 2nd Wisconsin Infantry; cited for gallantry at Gettysburg. Probably held the rank of captain or was a contract surgeon.

Roberts, Benjamin K. '64. Captain and Assistant Adjutant General; First Lieutenant, 7th Iowa Cavalry; brevet major. Retired from the Regular Army as Brigadier General and Chief of Artillery.

Roberts, Edward E. '65. Captain, served in Connecticut Volunteers or state troops.

Robinson, Calvin L. '49. First Lieutenant, drillmaster; served as a provost marshal in Florida.

Robinson, Norman '63. First Lieutenant and Drillmaster, Vermont State Troops.

Robinson, William W. '41?*. Colonel, 7th Wisconsin Infantry, Iron Brigade; severely wounded in action below the left knee at Brawner's Farm; commanded the "Iron Brigade" for extended periods in 1863 and 1864; cited for gallantry. Discharged July 9, 1864 as his regiment had too few men to warrant a full colonel in command. Particularly distinguished himself in the fighting withdrawal from McPherson's and Seminary Ridge in the first day at Gettysburg. Also served as a colonel of the Wisconsin militia and as a drillmaster in 1861.

Rodgers, Robert S. '30. Colonel, 2nd Maryland Eastern Shore Infantry; also commanded a brigade in the Army of West Virginia. His name is sometimes seen as Rogers.

Roelofson, Frederick E. '56. First Lieutenant, Company "E," 2nd Kentucky Infantry; mortally wounded in action.

Rolfe, John M. '59*. Second Lieutenant, Company "D," 13th Vermont Infantry.

Russell, Frederick W. '51. Major, Connecticut State Troops.

Russell, William H. '28. Major General commanding Connecticut State Troops from 1862 on. In charge of drilling, equipping, and preparing all Connecticut units for field service. Russell was an excellent drillmaster and also completely reorganized the state's militia system. In 1861 he trained the 1st and 2nd Connecticut Infantry Regiments using drillmasters from his New Haven Collegiate Institute.

Saben, William '51. Captain, United States Volunteers; died in Kentucky, 1865.

Sabine, Albert '63 -First Lieutenant, 1st United States Infantry; died in the service of disease contracted during the Siege of Vicksburg.

Sabine, John '64*. Private, Companies "F" and "G," 3rd Vermont Infantry; killed in action in the Wilderness.

Saltmarsh, Edward C. '61*. Captain, Company "E," 12th Massachusetts Infantry; commissioned a First Lieutenant, United States Marine Corps.

Sanborn, George W '57*. Second Lieutenant, 11th Battery, Massachusetts Light Artillery; also served as a private in Cook's Boston Light Battery and a sergeant in the 11th Massachusetts Light Battery (nine month battery).

Sargent, Harlan P. '59. Served in the US Volunteers.

Sawyer, Francis A. '64. Private, Company "G," 60th Massachusetts Infantry.

Sayles, Charles F. '58*. Captain and Quartermaster, Army of the Potomac.

Schall, Edward '56*. Captain, Company "D," 51st Pennsylvania Infantry; Colonel, 34th Pennsylvania Militia on war duty at Readville, June-July 1863; Lieutenant Colonel, 4th Pennsylvania, 1861. He was the twin brother of Edwin Schall '56. After the war he served as Colonel, 16th Regiment, Pennsylvania National Guard and helped quell the railroads riots near Pittsburgh in 1877.

Schall, Edwin '56*. Major, 4th Pennsylvania Infantry; Colonel, 51st Pennsylvania Infantry; killed at the head of his regiment in the assault at Cold Harbor at age 29; served as a brigade commander in Tennessee; cited for gallantry. He had a presentiment of his death before Cold Harbor and made all the preparations for the disposal of his body and personal effects. He was the twin brother of Edward

Schall '56. Schall played an important role in the 51st Pennsylvania's successful assault on the Burnside Bridge.

Schall, John W. '55*. First Lieutenant, Company "K," 2nd Pennsylvania Infantry; Colonel, 87th Pennsylvania Infantry; severely wounded in the right arm at Cold Harbor but refused to leave the field; brigade commander; cited for gallantry in the Wilderness and at Cold Harbor. Later served as the Brigadier General commanding the Pennsylvania National Guard.

Schall, Reuben J. '56. Captain, Company "D," 4th Pennsylvania Infantry.

Scripture, Stephen A. '50*. Private, Company "D," 1st New Hampshire Infantry; First Lieutenant, 7th Massachusetts Infantry.

Seaver, Thomas O. '59*. Colonel, 3rd Vermont Infantry; won the Congressional Medal of Honor at Spotsylvania in Upton's attack, May 10, 1864; also served for a time as commander of the 26th New Jersey Infantry to restore discipline, December 15, 1862-January 15, 1863; Vermont Brigade commander, December 1863 and January 1864; drillmaster. Seaver was made a brigadier general and brigade commander in the reorganized Vermont Militia after the St. Albans Raid of October 1864 and would later command all Vermont State troops. Awarded his Medal of Honor on April 8, 1892 by order of Assistant Secretary of War Lewis A. Grant, his former wartime brigade commander.

Sessions, Milan H. '45. Captain, Company "G," 21st Wisconsin Infantry; recruited troops at the beginning of the war.

Sewall, William R. '51. Captain, United States Volunteers.

Seymour, Epaphroditus H. '55. Engineer, Union Navy; died of disease.

Seymour, Truman B. '44*. Brigadier General, United States Volunteers, division and department commander; Captain of Battery "H," 1st United States Artillery at Fort Sumter, April 1861; severely wounded in the assault on Battery Wagner, Charleston, South Carolina, July 18, 1863; commanded a brigade; cited for gallantry at Fort Sumter, South Mountain, Antietam, and Petersburg; Brevet Major General, USA and USV.

Shattuck, Abbott Allen '64. Corporal, Company "B," 6th Massachusetts Infantry; Captain, Company "H," 25th United States Colored Infantry; drillmaster. He distinguished himself in the capture of Mobile, Alabama.

Shattuck, Samuel W. '60. Drillmaster, Massachusetts Volunteers; Sergeant Major, 6th Massachusetts Infantry; Captain, Company "H," 8th Vermont Infantry; wounded at Opequon Creek.

Shedd, Solon '51. Major, 30th Illinois Infantry.

Shedd, Warren '40. Colonel, 30th Illinois Infantry; brigade commander and brevet brigadier general; drillmaster.

Shepard, Benjamin F. '42. Colonel, US Volunteers or of state troops.

Shields, James V.A. '41. First Lieutenant and Adjutant, 2nd Regiment, Quartermaster Employees, Washington, D.C. Was the private secretary to the Quartermaster General of the Army in 1861.

Simmons, Seneca G. '29*. Colonel, 5th Pennsylvania Reserves; died of wounds received while leading a brigade at Glendale (Charles City Crossroads), June 30, 1862; Captain, 7th United States Infantry and Major, 4th United States Infantry; cited for gallantry.

Slafter, Judson '47. First Sergeant, Company "D," 23rd Michigan Infantry, died of wounds received at Campbell's Station, Tennessee, November 16, 1863.

Slayton, Henry L. '64. Drillmaster, New Hampshire Volunteers; Captain, Company "K," 2nd United States Colored Infantry. Drilled troops in New Hampshire, New York City, and at Arlington Heights, Virginia in 1862. He was a Special Military Student.

Sleeper, Van Buren '61*. Sergeant, Company "E," 2nd Vermont Infantry.

Smalley, Henry A. '51*. Colonel, 5th Vermont Infantry; brevet brigadier general; cited for gallantry; Captain, 2nd United States Artillery. He served as a First Lieutenant, 2nd United States Artillery until appointed Colonel, 5th Vermont. He was recalled to the 2nd Artillery in October 1862 and served the rest of the was in Florida with Battery "K" of that regiment.

Smalley, Jacob M. '59. Master, Union Navy.

Smith, Alonzo E. '56. Private, Company "K," 1st Vermont Infantry.

Smith, Austin G. '?*. Private, Company "A," 18th New Hampshire Infantry.

Smith, Charles W. '67*. Private, Company "B," 7th Squadron Rhode Island Cavalry ("College Cavaliers"); Captain, Battery "I," 1st Connecticut Heavy Artillery; also served in 4th Connecticut Infantry; cited for gallantry in the assault on Petersburg; a brevet major.

Smith, Edward H. '45*. Second Lieutenant, Company "D," 89th New York Infantry and Captain, Battery "L," 10th New York Heavy Artillery. There is confusion concerning this officer in Ellis' historical records; the most likely alumnus is the captain in the 10th New York Heavy Artillery although the officer in the 89th New York may be the same man.

Smith, Elias F. '61*. Captain, Company "B," 16th New Hampshire Infantry; Captain, Company "B," 18th New Hampshire Infantry; made colonel but not mustered due to the end of the war; drillmaster. Recruited companies for the 5th, 7th, 9th, and 14th New Hampshire Volunteers.

Smith, Galen C. '48*. Private, Company "K," 18th New Hampshire Infantry.

Smith, George C. '48. First Lieutenant, 74th Indiana Infantry; severely wounded at Chickamauga.

Smith, George W. '64*. Captain, Company "E," 1st Battalion, 17th United States Infantry; severely wounded at Gettysburg and Spotsylvania; cited for gallantry at Gettysburg and Spotsylvania; breveted major; also served in Company "A," 1st Battalion, 17th United States Infantry.

Smith, Henry S. '42. Private, Company "F," 5th Vermont Infantry.

Smith, Jesse B. '65. Midshipman, United States Navy.

Smith, Nathan A.C. '53. First Lieutenant, Company "H," 12th Wisconsin Infantry and First Lieutenant, 32nd Wisconsin Infantry; resigned due to disability.

Smith, Sumner T. '60. Mate, Union Navy.

Smith, Timothy D. '37. Captain and assistant quartermaster, Minnesota Volunteers.

Snow, Asa H. '41. Second Lieutenant, Company "D," 9th Vermont Infantry.

Stancliffe, James M. '53*. First Sergeant, Company "D," 20th Connecticut Infantry; died of disease contracted in the service.

Stanyan, John M. '50. Captain, Company "B," 8th New Hampshire Infantry; severely wounded in the assault on Port Hudson; commanded the regiment in the attack on that city and was cited for gallantry; discharged for disability; drillmaster.

Starr, Elihu W.N. '28. Brigadier General and Chief Drillmaster for Connecticut State and Volunteer Troops. Exerted great efforts in the organizing and drilling of the Connecticut regiments. Colonel, 24th Connecticut Infantry for a time before it deployed to the field. Directly responsible for the commissioning and drilling of over 30 Connecticut field grade officers, possibly including general-to-be Alfred H. Terry.

Starr, William '60. Sergeant, Company "A," 3rd Battalion of Rifles, Massachusetts Volunteers.

Stebbins, Harrison '43. Second Lieutenant, 7th Ohio Light Battery.

Stedman, Joseph '59. Drillmaster and Sergeant, 6th Massachusetts Infantry; Lieutenant Colonel, 42nd Massachusetts Infantry; Colonel, 42nd Massachusetts Militia Infantry (on war service).

Steele, Benjamin H. '57. Colonel, Vermont Militia; on governor's staff; drillmaster.

Steele, Charles E. '63. First Lieutenant and Drillmaster, Vermont Volunteers.

Stillman, Dana C. '50. Colonel, Wisconsin Militia; drillmaster.

Stimpson, Francis E. '58*. First Lieutenant, Company "B," 2nd Battalion, 17th United States Infantry; died of wounds received in the attack at Laurel Hill, Virginia, May 12, 1864; cited for gallantry at the Wilderness; breveted captain.

Stockbridge, Charles '24. Chaplain, United States Navy.

Stoddard, Samuel F. '65. Musician, 8th Maine Infantry; First Sergeant, Company "F," 2nd Maine Cavalry; Captain, Maine Coast Guards; severely wounded at Marian, Florida.

Stone, Elias F. '43. Captain, 89th Indiana Infantry.

Stone, Henry '48*. Captain, Company "F," 8th Massachusetts Volunteer Infantry (Militia), 100 days; Second Lieutenant, Company "E," 8th Massachusetts Volunteer Militia, three months.

Stone, John '38. Surgeon, Confederate States Army.

Stoughton, Charles B. '61*. Colonel, 4th Vermont Infantry; Brevet Brigadier General, USV; wounded at Banks' Ford in the Chancellorsville Campaign, and severely at Funkstown, Maryland during Lee's retreat from Gettysburg, losing his right eye and was discharged for disability; cited for gallantry at the Seven Days, Crampton's Gap, and Second Fredericksburg, May 3, 1863.

Stowell, Edwin S. '52*. Captain, Company "F," 5th Vermont Infantry; Lieutenant Colonel, 9th Vermont Infantry.

Streeter, Henry B. '38. Lieutenant Colonel, United States Army or volunteers.

Streeter, Sebastian R. '37*. Captain, Company "F," 61st Massachusetts Infantry.

Strobel, Louis M. '51. Captain, Confederate States Army in Company "F," 8th Texas Cavalry ("Texas Rangers").

Strong, George C. '53. Major General, US Volunteers; mortally wounded in the assault on Battery Wagner, Charleston, South Carolina, July 18, 1863; cited for gallantry; brigade and division commander. Promoted to major general by President Lincoln after his death on July 30, 1864 in New York City.

Strong, Harvey L. '59. Officer, Confederate States Army.

Strong, William C. '56. Colonel, Confederate States Army.

Strudwick, William S. '49. Major and surgeon, Confederate States Army; said to have served with distinction.

Tanner, Robert F. '64. Officer, Pennsylvania Volunteers or State Troops.

Tarbell, Charles G. '70. Private, Company "G," 8th Vermont Infantry.

Tarbell, Jonathan G. '39*. Major, 24th New York Infantry; Colonel, 91st New York Infantry; Brevet Brigadier General, USV; cited for gallantry. Served later as Chief Justice of the Mississippi Supreme Court.

Tarr, Daniel B. '54. Captain, recruited a company of Massachusetts infantry; drillmaster.

Tattnall, Josiah '23. Commodore CSN; scuttled *C.S.S. Virginia,* which was the former *U.S.S. Merrimac,* in order to avoid its capture by the Union.

Taylor, Archibald S. '58*. Captain, Adjutant, Company "I," 3rd New Jersey Infantry; commissioned a Second Lieutenant, United States Marine Corps by President Lincoln in July 1864; severely wounded in action at the Battle of Salem Heights.

Taylor, George W. '26*. Brigadier General, US Volunteers; Colonel, 3rd New Jersey Infantry; cited for gallantry at several battles; mortally wounded at 2nd Bull Run; brigade commander (New Jersey Brigade); drillmaster.

Tenney, Otis M. '45. Major, Confederate States Army, 2nd Kentucky Cavalry.

Terry, Alfred H. '?. Major General, Tenth Corps commander; Colonel 2nd and 7th Connecticut; cited for gallantry and voted the thanks of Congress; wounded in action; Brevet Major General, United States Army; brigade and division commander. Connected to Norwich but the details are uncertain. He may have attended the Partridge inspired military academy in New Haven, Connecticut. He is cited as an alumnus in Civil War Honor Rolls published in the 1890s. It is possible, though less likely, that he was a special military student or that he attended some of Captain Partridge's militia officer training courses.

Thomas, Evan W. '51*. Captain, Batteries "A," and "C," 4th United States Artillery; cited for gallantry at Fredericksburg and Gettysburg; brevet major. His father, Brig. Gen. Lorenzo Thomas, was Adjutant General of the United States Army during the war. He was killed in action with 1st Lt. Thomas F. Wright '49, at the Battle of the Lava Beds during the Modoc War of 1873.

Thomas, Hartop P. '54. Served in the Seventeenth Corps as a sutler with the rank of private. May have also served in 3rd Wisconsin Cavalry.

Thompson, Daniel '42. Probably a Captain the 42nd Indiana Infantry.

Thompson, Edward '24. Lieutenant, United States Navy.

Thompson, John B. '61*. First Lieutenant, Companies "F," "G" and "K," 19th Massachusetts Infantry; wounded at Fredericksburg and killed in action at Cold Harbor; cited for gallantry.

Thompson, Samuel J. '48*. Captain, Company "F," 22nd Massachusetts Infantry; died of wounds received at Malvern Hill, Virginia July 1, 1862.

Thorndike, Samuel E. '57. Officer, possibly a lieutenant colonel of New York State Troops; later a brigadier general of state troops. The name is sometimes seen as Thorndyke.

Tibbetts, Charles F. '66. First Sergeant, Company "E," 21st Maine Infantry.

Tilden, Joseph G. '53. Sergeant, Massachusetts Volunteers.

Tillinghast, Charles F. '64. Second Lieutenant and Adjutant, 7th Squadron Rhode Island Cavalry ("College Cavaliers"); First Sergeant, Company "G," 60th Massachusetts Infantry.

Tilton, Charles E. '48*. Second Lieutenant, Company "K," 4th New Hampshire Infantry.

Titcomb, Albert P. '57*. First Lieutenant, Company "C," 7th Maine Infantry; Sergeant, Company "D," 30th Maine Infantry; severely wounded at Pleasant Hill, Louisiana, April 9, 1864.

Treadwell, William A. '57*. Captain, 95th New York Infantry (not mustered) in the Antietam Campaign where he served as an aide to General Abner Doubleday; Captain, Company "B," 164th New York Infantry for two months in Norfolk, Virginia (not mustered); Captain, Battery "G," 14th New York Heavy Artillery; Colonel, 1st New Jersey Veteran Infantry but the regiment was not mustered due to the end of the war; drillmaster.

Truax, Sewall '53. Major, 1st Oregon Cavalry.

Tucker, George '47*. Captain, Company "D," 4th Vermont Infantry; Drillmaster General, Army of the Potomac for a time in 1863; he supervised the drilling of a number of regiments of the Army of the Potomac. Tucker probably also served as a drillmaster for the Second Vermont Brigade in September and October 1862.

Tucker, Stephen S. '32. Major General, CSA; died of wounds received at Mobile, Alabama. His commission as a major general arrived on the day of his death.

Tucker, William H. '48*. Chief Quartermaster Clerk, Army of the Cumberland; had also served as a commissary clerk in the Army of the Potomac.

Tukey, Francis H. '59. Officer, United States Volunteers or state troops.

Tullar, Charles '23. Served in Wisconsin as the United States Provost Marshal as either a colonel or lieutenant colonel.

Turner, Thomas '55. Lieutenant and Assistant Surgeon, United States Navy.

Turpin, Walter G. '45. Major, Confederate States Army, Virginia Volunteers.

Tyler, George O. '57. Captain, Company "I," 43rd Massachusetts Infantry.

Tyler, John W.L. '48. Captain and State Drillmaster, Ohio Volunteers. He gave valuable service as an instructor in drill and tactics in many Ohio camps. He had trained various cadet corps before the war and his former cadets served in the ranks of lieutenant through major general.

Van Rensellaer, Henry '28*. Colonel and Inspector General, First and Third Corps; died of disease. First man breveted to brigadier general of volunteers who was not actually promoted to the grade after selection. Served on the staffs of Generals Winfield Scott and Irvin McDowell. Also served as Inspector General of the Department of the Ohio.

Vermilye, Washington R. '55*. Corporal, 7th New York Infantry.

Vernam, William S. '64*. First Lieutenant and Adjutant, 175th New York Infantry; Captain, Company "E," 18th New York Cavalry; discharged for disability. Also served as ordnance officer in the Third Division, Nineteenth Corps and on the staffs of various commanding officers in the Department of the Gulf. He distinguished himself in the Red River Expedition.

Wadhams, Albert L. '44*. Private, Company "I," 11th Connecticut Infantry; wounded at Cold Harbor; captured at Hanover Court House, Virginia but paroled.

Waite, Frederick T. '49. First Lieutenant and Drillmaster, Illinois Volunteers.

Walcott, Ellis P. '64*. Private, Company "B," 7th Squadron Rhode Island Cavalry ("College Cavaliers"); Sergeant, 46th New York Light Artillery; First Lieutenant, Battery "K," 8th New York Heavy Artillery; also served in 117th New York Infantry. Said to have served with distinction in the Virginia Campaigns.

Walcott, Franklin H. '64. Private, Company "B," 7th Squadron Rhode Island Cavalry ("College Cavaliers"); Sergeant Major, 117th New York Infantry.

Ward, James H. '23. Captain, Union Navy; killed at Aquia Creek, June 27, 1861; first Union naval officer killed in the war. Ward Hall at the United States Naval Academy is named after him. He commanded the Potomac Flotilla from the steamer *Freeborn* in the first naval engagement of the war at Aquia Creek, Virginia, May 31, 1861.

Ward, William H. '61. Captain, Company "B," 47th Ohio Infantry.

Ware, John M. '65. Second Lieutenant, 119th Illinois Infantry.

Warner, Stanley M. '51. Colonel, CSA, Texas Volunteers. Captured by his classmate Col. Thomas E.G. Ransom at the Battle of Fort Donelson. Warner was later placed in charge of the Camp Ford prisoner of war camp in Texas after he escaped from the Union prison camp at Camp Douglas in Chicago, Illinois.

Washburn, Daniel W. '56*. First Lieutenant, Company "G," 70th New York Infantry; later Captain, Battery "I," 4th New York Heavy Artillery; brevet major.

Washburn, Justus W.F. '62. Private, Company "B," 24th Massachusetts Infantry. He was appointed a first lieutenant in the United States Colored Troops but did not serve due to the end of the war.

Waterman, Arba N. '55. Lieutenant Colonel, 100th Illinois Infantry; severely wounded at Chickamauga; cited for gallantry; drillmaster; discharged for disability.

Webb, Charles A. '61. First Lieutenant, Company "F," 1st Vermont Infantry; Captain, 13th United States Infantry; cited for gallantry and breveted major at Vicksburg.

Webb, George W. '49*. Captain, Battery "F," 2nd Pennsylvania Heavy Artillery and 2nd Provisional Pennsylvania Heavy Artillery.

Webb, Henry '28. Engineer, Confederate States Army.

Welles, Gideon '26. Secretary of the Navy. Played a major role as a trusted advisor and friend of President Lincoln. Spearheaded the development of a modern Navy using ironclads with the launching of such ships as the *Monitor.* Welles also supervised the navy's wartime expansion, working closely with Rear Admiral Hiram Paulding '23; a major player in developing and maintaining the blockade of Southern ports. He was a moderating influence in the cabinet and after the war ensured the survival of the United States Naval Academy and its return to Annapolis, Maryland.

Welles, Samuel '59. Civil engineer, Union Navy.

Wellman, Samuel T. '66. Corporal, Battery "F," 1st New Hampshire Heavy Artillery.

Wentworth, William H. '68*. Private, 184th New York Infantry.

Wessells, Henry W. '28*. Brigadier General, US Volunteers; Colonel, 8th Kansas Infantry; cited for gallantry at Fair Oaks and Plymouth, North Carolina; brigade and division commander who also served in 6th and 18th United States Infantry; wounded in action at Seven Pines; Brevet Brigadier General, USA. He was in charge of the defense of New Berne, North Carolina and was taken prisoner when it was captured in 1864; he was later paroled.

Weston, Edmund '48*. Captain, Company "F," 1st United States Sharpshooters; resigned due to disability after turning down a promotion to lieutenant colonel of the regiment; drillmaster.

Wheeler, Holland '59. Captain, Company "A," 3rd Kansas Infantry; drillmaster. Detailed as a state ordnance officer.

Wheelwright, Charles W. '67. Private, Company "G," 60th Massachusetts Infantry.

Whipple, Thomas J. '37*. Lieutenant Colonel, 1st New Hampshire Infantry; Colonel, 4th New Hampshire; resigned due to disability; elected Colonel of the 12th New Hampshire Infantry but did not serve due to bad health.

White, Abner G. '42*. Private, Company "B," 16th Vermont Infantry.

White, Arthur W. '67. Private, Company "B," 7th Squadron Rhode Island Cavalry ("College Cavaliers"); First Lieutenant in President Lincoln's Ohio Cavalry bodyguard.

White, George R. '52. First Lieutenant and Adjutant, 11th Iowa Infantry; drillmaster. He served as a recruiting officer in Iowa at the outbreak of the war. Also served as a quartermaster for some time.

White, Thomas W. '41. Captain, CSA, Georgia Volunteers. Served as an engineer and built Fort Pulaski.

Whiting, William B. '27. Captain, United States Navy.

Whitmore, Adin H. '64*. Second Lieutenant, Company "C," 16th Vermont Infantry.

Whittier, James A.L. '66. Private, Company "G," 60th Massachusetts Infantry.

Williams, Benjamin S. '25. First Lieutenant and drillmaster, New York Volunteers and for the 117th New York Infantry.

Williams, Seth '40*. Brigadier General and Adjutant General, Army of the Potomac; on Grant and McLellan's staffs; cited for gallantry at Gettysburg and Petersburg; Brevet Major General, USA and USV. Played an important role in events surrounding the surrender of General Lee at Appomattox.

Williams, William M. '45. Probably Captain, 45th Ohio Infantry.

Williston, Edward B. '56*. Captain, Battery "D," 2nd United States Artillery; won the Congressional Medal of Honor at Trevilian Station, Virginia, May 12, 1864; cited for gallantry at Salem Heights, Gettysburg, and Winchester; Brevet Colonel, USA. Awarded the Medal of Honor on April 6, 1892, two days before Colonel Thomas O. Seaver '59. Remained in the Regular Army and retired as a brigadier general.

Wilson, Alfred C. '48. Lieutenant Colonel, 48th Kentucky Infantry.

Wilson, James '43. Lieutenant Colonel, CSA, 6th Battalion, Virginia Cavalry.

Winn, John '41. Captain, Confederate States Army, Virginia Volunteers.

Wood, Henry C. '56. First Lieutenant, 11th United States Infantry; won the Congressional Medal of Honor at Wilson's Creek, Missouri, August 10, 1861; severely wounded serving the rest of the war on the staff in Washington; cited for gallantry; Brevet Brigadier General, USA. Served on the staff of Maj. Gen. John C. Fremont. Retired from the Regular Army as a brigadier general.

Wood, Luther S. '58. Captain and Commissary, 2nd Kansas Infantry.

Woodman, Edward '65. Midshipman and Acting Ensign, United States Navy.

Woods, Joseph W. '59. Served in the Iowa Volunteers.

Woodward, Solomon E. '52. First Lieutenant, Company "B," 1st Vermont Infantry; Captain, 15th United States Infantry; cited for gallantry at Murfreesboro and Atlanta; breveted major. Served for a time as a quartermaster on the staff of General Rosecrans.

Worthen, Harry N. '57*. Major, 1st Vermont Infantry; Lieutenant Colonel, 4th Vermont Infantry; drillmaster; resigned due to ill health.

Wright, Daniel E. '47. Corporal, Company "A," 9th Vermont Infantry.

Wright, George '22. Brigadier General, US Volunteers; commanded in the Districts of California and the Pacific; Colonel, 9th US Infantry; Brevet Brigadier General, USA. Drowned in the wreck of the steamer *Brother Jonathan* July 30, 1865, while on the way to assume command of the Department of the Columbia.

Wright, Henry J. '62*. Sergeant, Company "B," 6th Vermont Infantry; First Lieutenant, 3rd Vermont Light Battery; sometimes listed as John H. Wright.

Wright, Horatio G. '37*. Major General commanding the Sixth Corps, Army of the Potomac; cited for gallantry at Rappahannock Station, Spotsylvania, Cold Harbor, and Petersburg; brigade and division commander; Brevet Major General, USA; wounded in action at the "Bloody Angle," Spotsylvania. Played a key role in planning the last assault on Petersburg. Commanded the Department of Ohio from August, 1862 to March 1863. Wright was captured and held prisoner for a time after trying to destroy the dry dock at the Norfolk Navy Yard in 1861. Later, as chief engineer of the army, he completed the construction of the Washington Monument.

Wright, James W. '48. Lieutenant Colonel, served in the Ohio Volunteers or state troops.

Wright, John Henry '63*. First Lieutenant, 3rd Vermont Light Artillery Battery; also served in Company B, 6th Vermont Infantry.

Wright, Joseph C. '42. Lieutenant Colonel, 72nd Illinois Volunteers; severely wounded in the assault on Vicksburg; died of wounds; cited for gallantry; drill-master.

Wright, Joseph W. '34. Lieutenant Colonel, Ohio Volunteers or State Troops.

Wright, Leonard J. '52. Captain, Company "B," 9th Michigan Cavalry; cited for gallantry; captured at Murfreesboro, Tennessee.

Wright, Thomas F. '49. Colonel, 2nd California Cavalry; also served in 2nd and 6th California Infantry Regiments; Brevet Brigadier General, USV for gallantry and meritorious service. He was killed in action with Capt. Evan W. Thomas '51 in the Battle of the Lava Beds in the Modoc War of 1873 while serving as a 1st Lieutenant with the 12th United States Infantry.

Wright, Thomas T. K. G. '56*. Corporal, Company "B," 6th Vermont Infantry; served in 12th Michigan Infantry; Captain, 67th United States Colored Infantry; Second Lieutenant, 57th United States Colored Infantry.

Wyck, Edward H. V. III '28. Lieutenant and Assistant Surgeon US Navy.

Wyman, George H. '47. First Lieutenant and Drillmaster, Ohio Volunteers.

Wyman, Silas W. '67. Private, Company "C," 60th Massachusetts Infantry.

Young, E. A. '65. Lieutenant, United States Army or United States Volunteers; was probably a special military student.

Appendix B

ALUMNI BY REGIMENTS

As stated in Appendix A, at least 705 Norwich alumni served in the Civil War, with an estimated 56 serving in the Confederate States Army or Navy. These figures are probably low. Nevertheless, an analysis of the available data indicates no small role for the sons of "Old N.U." Of the 605 men who served the Republic, at least seven were major generals, nineteen were brigadier generals, nine were brevet major generals, and 28 were brevet brigadier generals. Seven others reached flag rank in the United States Navy. A few key statistics demonstrates Norwich's contribution to the Civil War:

*Service in 354 of the 2,047 Union regiments (17.3%); * Alumni commanded at least five Corps, 16 divisions, 36 brigades, 71 Union regiments, and several army departments; * Alumni served in 84 of Fox's "300 Fighting Regiments" (28.0%);* Alumni served in 18 of the 45 Union infantry regiments suffering the most combat deaths (40%), and five of the nine heavy artillery regiments used as infantry (55.6%); *Alumni served in four of the five Union regiments suffering the greatest combat deaths (80.0%); * At least 61 alumni were killed in action, died of wounds, or died of disease; at least 93 were wounded in action; and at least 57 were discharged due to service incurred injury or illness; total casualties from all causes: 192 (27.2%);

The following list, broken down by state, briefly catalogs the names of alumni known to have served in combat regiments, the units in which they served, their dates of service, and key facts concerning their service. A single asterisk (*) indicates regiments from Fox's "Fighting 300"; two (**) indicates these units of the Veterans Reserve Corps were organized as infantry regiments; and a plus sign (+) indicates unit/alumnus who served in the Army of the Potomac at some time during their Civil War career.

CALIFORNIA

2nd California Volunteer Cavalry. First Lieutenant Thomas F. Wright, October 2, 1861- January 31, 1863.

2nd California Volunteer Infantry. Colonel Thomas F. Wright, October 24, 1864- July 2, 1866.

4th California Volunteer Infantry. Major Henry Hancock, September 6, 1861- October 1, 1864.

5th California Volunteer Infantry. Second Lieutenant John W. Hancock, Company B. (Dates unknown).

6th California Volunteer Infantry. Major Thomas F. Wright, February 1, 1863- October 3, 1864.

COLORADO

1st Colorado Volunteer Cavalry. First Lieutenant Julius O. Bucl, August 26, 1861- February 6, 1862; died of disease.

CONNECTICUT

1st Connecticut Light Battery. Second Lieutenant Arthur E. Clark, served to June 11, 1865.

1st Connecticut Volunteer Heavy Artillery+. Captain Charles W. Smith, Battery I, January 3, 1862-September 25, 1865.

2nd Connecticut Volunteer Heavy Artillery*+. Colonel James Hubbard, September 11, 1862-August 18, 1865; brevet brigadier general; cited for gallantry at Sayler's Creek. Also served as Captain, Battery B and as a Brigade Commander.

1st Connecticut Volunteer Cavalry+. Assistant Surgeon George C. Jarvis, December 11, 1861-October 9, 1862; transferred to the 7th Connecticut Infantry as surgeon.

2nd Connecticut Volunteer Infantry. Colonel Alfred H. Terry, May 7-August 7, 1861; Private George C. Jarvis, Company A, April 20-August 7, 1861; a 90 day regiment serving May 7-August 7, 1861.

4th Connecticut Volunteer Infantry+. First Lieutenant Charles W. Smith, Company I, June 10, 1861-January 3, 1862; this unit converted to the 1st Connecticut Heavy Artillery.

7th Connecticut Volunteer Infantry.* Colonel Alfred H. Terry, September 13, 1861- April 26, 1862; promoted to brigadier general; Surgeon George C. Jarvis, October 10, 1862-July 20, 1865.

9th Connecticut Volunteer Infantry ("The Irish Regiment"). First Lieutenant and Adjutant Alfred G. Hall, November 25, 1861-October 21, 1862; promoted Lieutenant Colonel, 2nd Louisiana Guards (Union).

11th Connecticut Volunteer Infantry*+. Private Albert I. Wadhams, Company I, November 27, 1861-November 26, 1864; wounded at Cold Harbor; captured at Hanover Courthouse, Virginia, July 6, 1863 and paroled July 8, 1863.

17th Connecticut Volunteer Infantry+. Colonel William H. Noble, July 22, 1862-July 19, 1865; wounded at Chancellorsville but returned for Gettysburg; captured at St. John's County, Florida, December 24, 1864, held at Andersonville Prison for a time, and paroled April 8, 1865.

18th Connecticut Volunteer Infantry. Captain Henry C. Day, Company A, August 8, 1862-April 25, 1865; captured at Winchester, Virginia, June 15, 1863 and paroled October 12, 1864.

19th Connecticut Volunteer Infantry. Captain James Hubbard, Company B, August 15, 1862-November 23, 1863; the unit was converted to the 2nd Connecticut Heavy Artillery at that time.

20th Connecticut Volunteer Infantry+. First Sergeant James M. Stancliffe, Company D, August 4, 1862-June 13, 1865.

24th Connecticut Volunteer Infantry. Colonel Elihu W.N. Starr, commanded the regiment from muster in November, 1862 to its field deployment; considered too old for field service.

25th Connecticut Infantry. First Sergeant Aaron Kinne, Company H, August 28,1862-May 4, 1863; discharged for disability; a nine month regiment serving in Louisiana from November 11, 1862-August 26, 1863.

ILLINOIS

2nd Illinois Volunteer Light Artillery. First Lieutenant Frank B. Fenton, Battery A, May 11, 1861-May 13, 1865.

7th Illinois Volunteer Cavalry. Colonel William P. Kellogg, July 1861-summer 1862; resigned due to typhoid.

8th Illinois Volunteer Cavalry+. Major Elisha S. Kelley; commanding officer of Company E and then commanded a squadron, September 18, 1861-September 15, 1862; discharged for wounds received at Boonsboro, Maryland, May 23, 1863; cited for gallantry.

9th Illinois Volunteer Cavalry ("Brackett's Regiment"). Lieutenant Colonel Linus D. Bishop, October 1861-October 26, 1864.

12th Illinois Volunteer Cavalry. Private Benjamin M. Gilman, Company I, October 1861-June 8, 1862; discharged for disability.

8th Illinois Volunteer Infantry*. Captain Charles E. Denison, Company E; captured first Rebel flag in Kentucky; transferred to 18th United States Infantry May 1861; First Lieutenant Lorenzo D. Potter served in the unit after September 1864.

11th Illinois Volunteer Infantry*. Colonel Thomas E.G. Ransom served in unit April 24, 1861-November 29, 1862; commander from February 15, 1862; wounded three times including severely at Shiloh; Second Lieutenant Frederick E. Ransom Company E, April 24, 1861-July 6, 1864; resigned citing health, actually allowed to resign for "the good of the service;" Second Lieutenant Henry L.S. Haskell, Company K, May 26-July 30, 1861; discharged due to illness.

13th Illinois Volunteer Infantry. Lieutenant Colonel Frederick W. Partridge, May 24, 1861-June 18, 1864; commanded the regiment for a time; cited three times for gallantry; brevet brigadier general.

15th Illinois Volunteer Infantry. First Lieutenant and Quartermaster Simon M. Preston, May 24-August 15, 1861; drillmaster and later Colonel and Brevet Brigadier General United States Colored Troops.

28th Illinois Volunteer Infantry. First Lieutenant and Adjutant John B.T. Mead, August 24, 1861-April 21, 1862; died of wounds received at Shiloh.

30th Illinois Volunteer Infantry*. Colonel Warren Shedd, served with unit as Captain, Company A, through Colonel, August 29, 1861-July 17, 1865; brevet brigadier general; Major Solon Shedd.

38th Illinois Volunteer Infantry. First Lieutenant Charles Fox, Company C, August 1, 1861-March 12, 1865.

51st Illinois Volunteer Infantry ("Chicago Legion"). Captain William H. Greenwood, Company H, December 28, 1861-March 18, 1863.

53rd Illinois Volunteer Infantry. Colonel William H. Cushman, October 11, 1861-September 3, 1862; resigned.

55th Illinois Volunteer Infantry* ("National Guards"). Captain Jabez C. Crooker, Company I, from July 1861-spring 1862; resigned due to illness.

72nd Illinois Volunteer Infantry ("1st Board of Trade"). Lieutenant Colonel Joseph C. Wright '42, August 1862-May 22 1863; died of severe wounds and leg amputation following an assault on Vicksburg.

83rd Illinois Volunteer Infantry. Captain James M. Gilson, October 22, 1862-June 26, 1865; cited for gallantry; severely wounded at Fort Donelson, February 3, 1863 and discharged for disability.

88th Illinois Volunteer Infantry ("2nd Board of Trade"). Captain Gordon S. Hubbard, September 1862-January 1, 1863, then assigned to staff, Army of the Cumberland.

91st Illinois Volunteer Infantry. Captain Emery Brown, September 8, 1862-November 4, 1863.

100th Illinois Volunteer Infantry. Lieutenant Colonel Arba N. Waterman, July 14, 1862-July 1864; cited for gallantry; severely wounded at Chickamauga and mustered out due to disability.

105th Illinois Volunteer Infantry. First Lieutenant George F. Field, Company C, September 2, 1862-July 11, 1863.

116th Illinois Volunteer Infantry. First Lieutenant and Quartermaster John H. Porter, January 9, 1864-June 7, 1865; later Captain and Assistant Surgeon.

119th Illinois Volunteer Infantry. Second Lieutenant John M. Ware, May 1864-February 1, 1865.

INDIANA

9th Indiana Volunteer Infantry ("Bloody Ninth")*. Colonel Robert H. Milroy, May-October 1861, then promoted to Brigadier General; Major John B. Milroy, August 20, 1861-July 1862; cited for gallantry, discharged due to illness; elected Colonel but not mustered due to discharge; served as Captain, Company A and acting regimental commander.

22nd Indiana Volunteer Infantry*. Captain George W. Hopkins, August 15, 1861-July 24, 1865; Captain James W. Parker, August 15, 1861-February 22, 1863.

42nd Indiana Volunteer Infantry. Captain Daniel Thompson was probably in this unit from October 1861-November 8, 1862.

58th Indiana Volunteer Infantry. Colonel George P. Buell, December 17, 1861-1865; Colonel from June 24, 1862; cited for gallantry and severely wounded at Chickamauga; served as a brigade commander in 1864 and 1865. This unit was part of the "Special Pioneer Brigade" of the Army of the Cumberland for a time.

74th Indiana Volunteer Infantry. First Lieutenant George C. Smith, August 20, 1862-August 21, 1864; severely wounded at Chickamauga and discharged for disability.

79th Indiana Volunteer Infantry. Lieutenant Colonel George W. Parker, September 2, 1862-June 7, 1865.

87th Indiana Volunteer Infantry. Colonel Newell Gleason, August 28, 1862-summer 1864; Colonel from March 23, 1863; served as a brigade commander during Sherman's "March to the Sea."

89th Indiana Volunteer Infantry. Captain Elias F. Stone, August 28, 1862-September 28, 1864.

138th Indiana Volunteer Infantry. First Lieutenant William Hebard, May-October 4, 1864; a 100 day regiment serving from May 27-September 21, 1864.

IOWA

2nd Iowa Volunteer Cavalry Regiment. Colonel Edward Hatch, August 1861-April 27, 1864; commanding the regiment from June 13, 1862; led the unit in "Grierson's Raid," April 17-26, 1863; promoted to brigadier general.

3rd Iowa Volunteer Cavalry. Major Carlton H. Perry, August 26, 1861-November 18, 1862; resigned due to ill health.

5th Iowa Volunteer Cavalry. Second Lieutenant Charles H. Osgood served in "Brackett's Minnesota Cavalry Battalion" of this regiment; mustered out May 24, 1866.

6th Iowa Volunteer Cavalry. Captain and Surgeon Charles J. Ford, 1861-1865.

7th Iowa Volunteer Cavalry. Captain Benjamin K. Roberts, July 27, 1863-December 22, 1864; promoted to Captain and Assistant Adjutant General of Volunteers.

9th Iowa Volunteer Cavalry. Major and Surgeon John Bell, March 1865-March 23, 1866.

2nd Iowa Volunteer Infantry*. Colonel Noel B. Howard, May 5, 1861-July 12, 1865; Colonel from November 8, 1864; severely wounded at Atlanta, July 22, 1864 and cited for gallantry; also served as Captain of Company L.

4th Iowa Volunteer Infantry Regiment. Colonel Grenville M. Dodge, July 6, 1861-March 1862; promoted to brigadier general.

11th Iowa Volunteer Infantry. First Lieutenant and Adjutant George R. White; served in Company H, October, 1861-April 1862.

12th Iowa Volunteer Infantry. Captain James E. Ainsworth Company F, October 1861-April 1862.

19th Iowa Volunteer Infantry. Captain John S. Gray, September 10, 1862-July 10, 1865.

KANSAS

3rd Kansas Independent Light Battery. Captain Henry Hopkins, December 9, 1861-15 October 1863; promoted to Major, 2nd Kansas Cavalry.

2nd Kansas Volunteer Cavalry. Major Henry Hopkins, 15 October, 1863-January 13, 1865.

6th Kansas Volunteer Cavalry. Captain Edward E. Harvey November 1861-November 18, 1864.

11th Kansas Volunteer Cavalry. Captain Henry Pearce, April 20 1863-September 23, 1865.

1st Kansas Volunteer Infantry*. Lieutenant Colonel Oscar E. Learnard, May 28, 1861-July 25, 1863; resigned.

2nd Kansas Volunteer Infantry. Captain and Commissary Luther S. Wood; Captain Henry Hopkins; a 90 day regiment serving from June 20-October 31, 1861.

3rd Kansas Volunteer Infantry. Captain and Ordnance officer, Holland Wheeler, Company A; organization of this regiment was not completed when the 3rd and 4th Kansas merged to form the 10th Kansas Volunteer Infantry, April 2, 1862.

4th Kansas Infantry Regiment (Militia). Captain David H. Hubbard, October 9-29, 1864.

8th Kansas Volunteer Infantry. Colonel Henry H. Wessells, September 29, 1861-February 7, 1862; resigned and was then made a Brigadier General of Volunteers; Captain and Quartermaster Henry H. Gillum.

10th Kansas Volunteer Infantry. Captain and Ordnance Officer, Henry L. Wheeler, from April 3, 1862.

11th Kansas Volunteer Infantry. First Lieutenant Henry Pearce, September 14, 1862-April 20, 1863; unit became 11th Kansas Volunteer Cavalry.

13th Kansas Volunteer Infantry. Captain William H. Blackburn, Company G September 20, 1862-June 26, 1865.

KENTUCKY

9th Kentucky Volunteer Cavalry. Captain John L. Neil, August 22, 1862-September 1863.

2nd Kentucky Volunteer Infantry. First Lieutenant Frederick E. Roelofson, Company E, June 1861-August 1862; died of wounds.

47th Kentucky Volunteer Infantry. Lieutenant Colonel Alfred C. Wilson; a one year regiment serving as mounted infantry from January 1864-April 12, 1865.

48th Kentucky Volunteer Infantry. Captain William Porter; a one year regiment serving as mounted infantry from October 26, 1863-December 19, 1864.

LOUISIANA

2nd Louisiana Volunteer Infantry ("2nd Union Guards," "2nd Corps D'Afrique"). Lieutenant Colonel Alfred G. Hall, October 12, 1862-April 4, 1864; this unit, only the second colored regiment mustered into the Union Army (October 12, 1862) became the 74th United States Colored Infantry.

MAINE

2nd Battery, 1st Maine Light Artillery+. Captain James A. Hall, November 30, 1861-August 1863; cited for gallantry at Fredericksburg and Gettysburg; promoted to lieutenant colonel.

1st Battalion, Maine Light Artillery. Lieutenant Colonel James A. Hall, August 1863-May 1865.

1st Maine Heavy Artillery*+. Captain William T. Parker, Battery L, August 21, 1862-May 19, 1864; killed in action at Harris' Farm, in the Spotsylvania Campaign during the regiment's first battle.

2nd Maine Volunteer Cavalry. Captain Samuel W. Knowles, November 30, 1863-December 6, 1865; First Sergeant Samuel F. Stoddard, Company F, November 30, 1863-June 3, 1865; severely wounded at Marian, Florida; First Sergeant Thomas G. Rice, Company B, November 16, 1863-1864 when he was commissioned Second Lieutenant, United States Colored Troops.

2nd Maine Volunteer Infantry+. Captain and Quartermaster Charles V. Lord, May 2-September 19, 1861; also served as adjutant; resigned.

3rd Maine Volunteer Infantry*+. Second Lieutenant Frederick W. Galbraith, June 22, 1863-May 18, 1864; transferred to staff.

6th Maine Volunteer Infantry*+. Captain and Drillmaster Charles A. Curtis, June 1861-June 1862, transferred to the 5th United States Infantry; Captain Frank C. Peirce, Company A, July 13, 1861-September 26, 1862; then Captain, United States Army.

7th Maine Volunteer Infantry*+. First Lieutenant Albert P. Titcomb, Company C, August 13, 1861-July 16, 1862; resigned.

8th Maine Volunteer Infantry*. Musician Samuel F. Stoddard, August 10, 1861-September 1, 1862; mustered out.

11th Maine Volunteer Infantry+. First Lieutenant Sylvanus B. Bean, Company A, November 7, 1861-November 26, 1862 then promoted to Captain of the Quartermaster Corps.

12th Maine Volunteer Infantry. Assistant Surgeon Albert Buswell, June,1865.

14th Maine Volunteer Infantry. First Sergeant Albert P. Titcomb, Company I, March 13-August 28, 1865.

19th Maine Volunteer Infantry*+. First Lieutenant John H. Hunt, Company C, August 25, 1862-October 21, 1862; resigned.

21st Maine Volunteer Infantry. Private Charles F. Tibbetts, Company E, October 1862-August 1863; a nine month regiment serving from October 14, 1862-August 25, 1863.

22nd Maine Volunteer Infantry. Second Lieutenant Samuel W. Knowles, Company B, October 10 1862-August 14, 1863; a nine month regiment serving from October 10, 1862-August 14, 1863.

30th Maine Volunteer Infantry. Sergeant Albert P. Titcomb, Company D, December 26, 1863- January 26, 1865; severely wounded at Pleasant Hill, Louisiana, April 9, 1864.

MARYLAND
2nd Maryland Eastern Shore Volunteer Infantry+. Colonel Robert S. Rodgers, October 2, 1861-October 31, 1864.

MASSACHUSETTS
Cook's Battery, Boston Light Artillery. Private George W. Sanborn, April 20-August 2, 1861; a three month (90 day) battery.

7th Independent Massachusetts Light Battery. First Lieutenant William E. Farrar, April 20, 1861-September 24, 1863.

11th Battery Light Artillery. Sergeant George W. Sanborn, August 25-1862-May 29, 1863; a ninth month battery.

11th Independent Massachusetts Light Battery+. Second Lieutenant George W. Sanborn, January 2, 1864-June 16, 1865.

1st Battalion Massachusetts Heavy Artillery. First Lieutenant George H. Elliot, Batteries E and F, August 15, 1864-June 28, 1865.

2nd Massachusetts Heavy Artillery. First Lieutenant Joseph F. Field, Battery L, June 4, 1863-September 3, 1865; Second Lieutenant George M. Rice, Battery I, August 14, 1863-January 26, 1864; dismissed from the service, he then enlisted in the United States Navy and later died at sea.

3rd Massachusetts Heavy Artillery. First Lieutenant George W. Burroughs, Battery F, August 17, 1864-June 24, 1865.

1st Massachusetts Volunteer Cavalry+ (1st Independent Battalion). Captain Frederick H. Rand, Company C, July 2, 1863-January 18, 1864.

2nd Massachusetts Volunteer Cavalry+. Captain Henry F. Alvord, Company I, November 21, 1862-August 2, 1865 (promoted major but not mustered); Captain Augustus L. Papanti, Company D, December 2, 1862-May 31, 1865; severely wounded March 31, 1865 at Dinwiddie Court House, Virginia and discharged for disability.

4th Massachusetts Volunteer Cavalry. First Lieutenant Henry M. Phillips, January 3, 1864-June 13, 1865; Captain Frederick H. Rand, Company K, January 19-August 22, 1864; discharged for disability.

1st Massachusetts Volunteer Infantry*+. Private Robert J. Cowdin Company A, October 14-November 30, 1861; transferred to the 31st New York Volunteer Infantry to accept a commission; Private William Gerrish, Company H, June 1861-October 5, 1862, discharged for disability.

2nd Massachusetts Volunteer Infantry*+. Captain William E. Perkins, Company I. February 13, 1863-May 19, 1865; severely wounded at Chancellorsville.

3rd Battalion of Rifles, Massachusetts Volunteers. Sergeant William Starr, Company A, April-July 1861; a three month (90) day battalion.

3rd Massachusetts Volunteer Infantry (Militia). Private George F. Putnam, Company G, April 16-July 22, 1861; a three month (90 day) regiment.

5th Massachusetts Militia Infantry+. Third Lieutenant Charles Bowers and Corporal George B. Buttrick, Company G, April 19-July 31, 1861; a three month (90 day) regiment serving from April 19-July 31, 1861.

6th Massachusetts Volunteer Infantry (Militia)- Captain and Assistant Surgeon John Q.A. McCollister; Possibly First Lieutenant George E. Davis, Company H; Second Lieutenant George W. Hobbs, in the Baltimore Riot; Sergeant Major Samuel W. Shattuck; Sergeant Joseph Stedman, Company B, in the Baltimore Riot; Corporal Abbott A. Shattuck, Company B, in the Baltimore Riot; a three month (90 day) regiment serving from April 15-August 2, 1861.

6th Massachusetts Volunteer Infantry (Militia). Private George W. Childs, Company B, August 25, 1862-June 3, 1863; a nine month regiment.

6th Massachusetts Volunteer Infantry (Militia). First Lieutenant and Quartermaster William E. Farrar; Corporal George W. Childs, Company B; Private John Gray Jr., Company D; a 100 day regiment serving from July 12-October 27, 1864.

7th Massachusetts Volunteer Infantry+. First Lieutenant Stephen A. Scripture.

8th Massachusetts Volunteer Infantry (Militia). First Lieutenant Henry A. Hale, Company E; Second Lieutenant Henry Stone, a three month (90 day) regiment serving from April 16-August 1, 1861.

8th Massachusetts Volunteer Infantry (Militia). Captain Henry Stone, Company F, September 15, 1862-August 7, 1863; a nine month regiment.

9th Massachusetts Volunteer Infantry*+. Captain and Assistant Surgeon Francis M. Lincoln, August 12, 1861-July 27, 1862.

10th Massachusetts Volunteer Infantry*+. Chaplain Frederick A. Barton, June 21, 1861-May 1, 1862; resigned due to health.

11th Massachusetts Volunteer Infantry*+. First Lieutenant and Adjutant Brownell Granger, June 13, 1861-April 27, 1862.

12th Massachusetts Volunteer Infantry*+. Captain Edward C. Saltmarsh, Company E, June 26, 1861-June 12, 1862; transferred to the United States Marine Corps; Major and Surgeon Jedediah H. Baxter, June 26, 1861-April 17, 1862, then he became the brigade surgeon; Private William H. Hooper Jr., Company K, June 26, 1861-April 6, 1864; wounded in action at Fredericksburg and Gettysburg and later discharged for wounds.

13th Massachusetts Volunteer Infantry+. Major Jacob P. Gould, July 16, 1861-April 21, 1864; wounded at Antietam where he commanded the regiment and was cited for gallantry; Captain and Assistant Surgeon Edgar Parker, March 13-September 18, 1863; severely wounded in the head at Gettysburg and discharged for disability; Private Benjamin W. Parker, Company I, July 16, 1861-June 11, 1864.

14th Massachusetts Volunteer Infantry. Captain Edmund Rice, April 27-July 2, 1861; his company then transferred to the 19th Massachusetts Volunteer Infantry.

17th Massachusetts Volunteer Infantry. Second Lieutenant Alfred M. Channel, Company G, August 21, 1861-January 17, 1862.

19th Massachusetts Volunteer Infantry*+. Lieutenant Colonel Edmund Rice, July 2, 1861-June 1865; won the Congressional Medal of Honor at Gettysburg, July 3, 1863; wounded at Antietam, Gettysburg, and Spotsylvania; Captain Henry A. Hale, Company B, July 1861-August 11, 1864; wounded at Antietam and Cold Harbor; became an assistant adjutant general; First Lieutenant John B. Thompson, Companies F, G and K, August 1, 1861-June 3, 1864; wounded at First Fredericksburg in the assault on Marye's Heights, and was later killed in action in the assault at Cold Harbor.

20th Massachusetts Volunteer Infantry*+ ("Harvard Regiment"). Colonel William R. Lee, July 1, 1861-December 17, 1862; he handpicked officers for this regiment; captured at Ball's Bluff and later paroled; wounded in the Peninsula Campaign; resigned due to disability; cited for gallantry at Antietam; Brevet Brigadier General of United States Volunteers, Brigadier General, Massachusetts State Troopers.

21st Massachusetts Volunteer Infantry*+. Captain Charles W. Davis, Company A and K, August 23, 1861-October 21, 1864, transferred to 36th Massachusetts Infantry and assigned as commander of Camp Parole at College Green Barracks (Annapolis), Maryland as of October 21, 1864.

22nd Massachusetts Volunteer Infantry*+. Colonel Jesse A. Gove, September 12, 1861-June 27, 1862; killed in action at Gaines Mill; Colonel Charles E. Griswold, September 12, 1861-October 16, 1862; Colonel from June 27, 1862;

resigned due to ill health; Captain Samuel J. Thompson, Company F died of wounds received at Malvern Hill July 1, 1862.

24th Massachusetts Volunteer Infantry. Captain and Assistant Surgeon John W. Parsons, April 1863-January 1866; Private Justus W.F. Washburn, Company D, April 1863-January 1866.

25th Massachusetts Volunteer Infantry*. Second Lieutenant Thomas A. Earle, Company A, September 14, 1861-September 1, 1862; resigned; First Sergeant Albert W. Cooke, Company B, September 6, 1861-January 7, 1864; transferred and promoted to Second Lieutenant, 57th Massachusetts Infantry.

26th Massachusetts Volunteer Infantry. First Lieutenant and Adjutant George E. Davis, October 18, 1861-December 4, 1863.

27th Massachusetts Volunteer Infantry*. First Lieutenant William S. Goodwin, 1863 and beyond; Band Leader Edwy W. Foster, November 1861-May 1862.

32nd Massachusetts Volunteer Infantry*+. Captain Charles Bowers, Company G, June 16, 1862-June 19, 1865; Private Daniel Parmenter, Company H, August 11, 1862-November, 1863 when he resigned to accept a promotion as a Second Lieutenant, 10th United States Colored Infantry.

35th Massachusetts Volunteer Infantry*+. Major and Surgeon Francis M. Lincoln July 28, 1862-March 10, 1863.

36th Massachusetts Volunteer Infantry+. Captain Charles W. Davis, Company K, October 21, 1864-March 3, 1865; First Sergeant C. Henry Moseley, Company B, August 4, 1862-November 11, 1864; wounded near Petersburg.

37th Massachusetts Volunteer Infantry*+. First Lieutenant Charles Phelps Company I, December 30, 1862-November 17, 1863; discharged for disability.

42nd Massachusetts Volunteer Infantry (Militia). Lieutenant Colonel Joseph Stedman, August 28, 1862-August 20, 1863; colonel from January 1863. Private Charles M. Gragg, Company C; a nine month regiment serving from November 11, 1862-August 20, 1863.

42nd Massachusetts Volunteer Infantry (Militia). Colonel Joseph Stedman, July 22-November 11, 1864; a 100 day regiment.

43rd Massachusetts Volunteer Infantry Militia ("Boston Tigers"). Captain George O. Tyler, Company I, September 12, 1862-July 20, 1863; Private William Fiske, Company K, wounded in action; a nine month regiment serving from October 23, 1862-July 30, 1863.

44th Massachusetts Volunteer Infantry. Sergeant William E. Perkins, Company F, August 29, 1862-February 13, 1863; transferred to accept promotion into the 2nd Massachusetts Infantry.

46th Massachusetts Volunteer Infantry. Sergeant Major Joseph F. Field, September 11, 1862-May 29, 1863; promoted to Second Lieutenant, 2nd Massachusetts Heavy Artillery.

47th Massachusetts Volunteer Infantry. Sergeant George B. Buttrick, Company G, October 15, 1862-March 5, 1863; discharged for disability.

48th Massachusetts Volunteer Infantry. Corporal George B. Blodgette, Company D, August 18, 1862-September 3, 1863, wounded in action at Port Hudson,

Louisiana; a nine month regiment serving from October 29, 1862-September 3, 1863.

53rd Massachusetts Volunteer Infantry. Surgeon John Q.A. McCollister, September 1862-July 1863; a nine month regiment serving from October 29, 1862-September 3, 1863.

56th Massachusetts Volunteer Infantry*+ ("First Veteran"). Colonel Charles E. Griswold, July 14, 1863-May 6, 1864; killed in action in The Wilderness; Captain Robert J. Cowdin, Company E, December 10, 1863-June 3, 1864; killed in action while in command of his division's pickets at Cold Harbor; his body was not recovered; Captain Herbert G. Coffin, Company H, January 4-April 4, 1864, discharged for disability.

57th Massachusetts Volunteer Infantry*+ ("Second Veteran")- Captain Albert W. Cooke, Company C, January 7, 1864-July 30, 1865; he commanded the regiment for a time at the end of the war.

59th Massachusetts Volunteer Infantry+. Colonel Jacob P. Gould, April 2-August 21, 1864, died of wounds (leg amputation) received at "The Crater;" Captain George W. Field, Company D, January 25-June 16, 1864, discharged for disability by War Department Order; Captain James Gilson, December 10, 1863-February 15, 1864; resigned.

60th Massachusetts Volunteer Infantry. First Sergeants Charles F. Tillinghast, Frederick H. McCulloch, Company G; Sergeant J. Swift Richards, Company G; Privates Charles S. Bird, William S. Blackington, Henry H. Head, Henry A. Howard, Abel G. Lane, Abner C. Lowe, William C.H. Needham, George E. Otis, Francis A. Sawyer, Charles S. Wheelwright, James A.L. Whittier, all serving in Company G; Private Silas W. Wyman, Company C; a 100 day regiment serving from August 1-November 30, 1864.

61st Massachusetts Volunteer Infantry+. Captain Sebastian R. Streeter, Company F, October 17, 1864-January 5, 1865; Captain Charles E. Ashcroft; possibly First Sergeant C. Henry Moseley.

MICHIGAN

2nd Michigan Volunteer Cavalry. Major Charles N. Baker, also served in Company K, October 2, 1861-August 17, 1865.

3rd Michigan Volunteer Cavalry. Major William S. Burton, September 1861-December 2, 1864.

9th Michigan Volunteer Cavalry. Captain Leonard J. Wright, Company B, December 13, 1861-November 23, 1864.

4th Michigan Volunteer Infantry*+. Colonel John W. Childs, led unit June 20-November 25, 1862; wounded in action, cited for gallantry; resigned for disability; First Lieutenant Wallace A. King, Company G, June 1861; resigned for disability in fall 1861 after spending most of his time with the unit in hospital.

8th Michigan Volunteer Infantry*+. First Lieutenant Benjamin J. Porter, Company D, April 2, 1861-May 12, 1862; transferred to the staff as a captain and assistant quartermaster.

12th Michigan Volunteer Infantry. Corporal Thomas K.G. Wright, February 20, 1862-spring 1863.

15th Michigan Volunteer Infantry. Major Thomas E. Morris, October 24, 1862-May 31, 1863; resigned.

16th Michigan Volunteer Infantry*+. Captain Thomas E. Morris, August 22, 1861-October 24, 1862; promoted to Major, 15th Michigan.

20th Michigan Volunteer Infantry+. Captain Elisha Hammond, Company K, July 26, 1862-January 26, 1863, resigned.

23rd Michigan Volunteer Infantry. First Sergeant Judson Slafter, Company D, August 12-December 31, 1862; died of wounds received at Campbell's Station, Tennessee.

24th Michigan Volunteer Infantry*+. Captain Charles A. Hoyt, Company C, July 26, 1862-November 23, 1863; wounded at Fredericksburg and Gettysburg and discharged for disability.

MINNESOTA

1st Minnesota Heavy Artillery. Colonel Luther L. Baxter; November 21, 1864-September 27, 1865.

1st Minnesota Volunteer Infantry*+. First Lieutenant James Hollister, Company E, April 29-October 22, 1861; wounded in action at 1st Bull Run; resigned.

4th Minnesota Volunteer Infantry. Major Luther L. Baxter, April 10- October 10, 1862; resigned.

8th Minnesota Volunteer Infantry. First Lieutenant Edward H. Cutts, Company B, November 1862-November 27, 1864; transferred to 55th United States Colored Infantry.

9th Minnesota Volunteer Infantry. Captain William R. Baxter, Company H, August 22, 1862-June 10, 1864; killed in action at Guntown, Mississippi.

MISSISSIPPI

1st Mississippi Colored Heavy Artillery. Colonel Bernard G. Farrar, January 21-March 11, 1864; unit redesignated 5th United States Colored Heavy Artillery.

MISSOURI

2nd Missouri Light Artillery. Captain Napoleon Boardman, Batteries E, M, February 23, 1864-June 1865.

7th Missouri Volunteer Cavalry. First Lieutenant and Adjutant Asa C. Marvin, May 1-July 29, 1862; First Lieutenant and Adjutant Joseph N. Pennock, December 1862-March 31, 1865.

11th Missouri Volunteer Cavalry. Captain Leonard B. Brown, March 28, 1863-July 27, 1865.

12th Missouri Volunteer Cavalry. First Lieutenant and Quartermaster Paul R. Kendall, September 29, 1863-April 9, 1866.

15th Missouri Volunteer Cavalry. First Lieutenant Lewis B. Hutchinson, November 1, 1863-July 1, 1865.

11th Missouri Volunteer Infantry*. Colonel Joseph A. Mower, August 1861-November 20, 1862; led the unit from May 3, 1862; promoted to brigadier general.

30th Missouri Volunteer Infantry. Colonel Bernard G. Farrar, September 1862-January 21, 1864, then Colonel, 6th United States Colored Heavy Artillery.

60th Missouri Volunteer Militia (on war service). Colonel Asa C. Marvin, October 13, 1862-March 12, 1865.

NEW HAMPSHIRE

1st New Hampshire Heavy Artillery. Colonel Charles H. Long, April 17, 1863-June 15, 1865; Colonel from September 29, 1864; earlier, Captain, Battery A; Captain Charles O. Bradley, Battery I, September 6, 1864-June 15, 1865; Corporal Samuel T. Wellman, Battery F, June 1864-June 1865; Private Samuel N. Hartshorn, August 1-September 23, 1864.

1st New Hampshire Volunteer Cavalry+. First Lieutenant George E. Gilman, Company G, August 9, 1864-June 30, 1865.

2nd New Hampshire Volunteer Cavalry. Captain John M. Stanyan, December 1863-May 1865.

1st New Hampshire Volunteer Infantry. Lieutenant Colonel Thomas J. Whipple, April 21-August 9, 1861; First Lieutenant Horace T.H. Peirce, Company G, April 20-August 9, 1861; First Sergeant Stephen A. Scripture, CompanyD, June 5-August 9, 1861; First Sergeant Charles O. Bradley, Company I, April 20-August 9, 1861; Private Walter Aiken, Company D; a 90 day regiment serving from May 1-August 9, 1861.

2nd New Hampshire Volunteer Infantry*+. Captain George T. Carter, Company B, November 5, 1861-December 19, 1865, wounded in action four times, twice severely; promoted to major but not mustered; Captain and Assistant Surgeon George P. Greeley, May 3-June 3, 1861.

3rd New Hampshire Volunteer Infantry*. Sergeant William Coffee, Company A, August 12, 1861-July 20, 1865; Private Lewis Kimball, CompanyF, August 9, 1862-July 18, 1864.

4th New Hampshire Volunteer Infantry+. Colonel Thomas J. Whipple, August 20, 1861-May 18, 1862, resigned due to disability; Major George P. Greeley August

20, 1861-October 23, 1864; Captain and Assistant Surgeon David L.M. Commings, August 1862-August 1, 1863, died of disease; Second Lieutenant Charles E. Tilton, September 18, 1861-January 16, 1862; resigned.

5th New Hampshire Volunteer Infantry*+. Major and Surgeon Luther M. Knight, September 13, 1861-May 18, 1863; Captain Charles H. Long Company G, October 12,1861-November 6, 1862, severely wounded at Antietam; Captain Horace T.H. Peirce, Company F, October 12, 1861-January 29, 1863, distinguished himself at Antietam; commanded the regiment for a time at both Antietam and Fredericksburg; First Lieutenant George W. Balloch, Company D, October 23-November 11, 1861, reassigned to a brigade staff as acting commissary.

7th New Hampshire Volunteer Infantry*. Lieutenant Colonel Thomas A. Henderson, November 4, 1861-August 16, 1864; mortally wounded at Deep Bottom, Virginia; cited for gallantry.

8th New Hampshire Volunteer Infantry. Captain John M. Stanyan, Company B, September 14, 1861-October 16, 1863; severely wounded while leading his unit in the second assault at Port Hudson, Louisiana, June 14, 1863; discharged for disability; Sergeant Asahel H. Quimby, Company D, December 5, 1861-April 10, 1864; severely wounded in action.

12th New Hampshire, Volunteer Infantry*+. Colonel Thomas J. Whipple, elected Colonel, September 1862 but did not deploy with the unit due to ill health.

13th New Hampshire Volunteer Infantry+. Captain Charles O. Bradley, Company C, August 8, 1862-June 10, 1864; discharged for disability but later joined the 1st New Hampshire Heavy Artillery.

14th New Hampshire Volunteer Infantry. Captain William H. Chaffin, Company I, January 11, 1863-September 19, 1864; killed in action at Opequon Creek; Captain and Assistant Surgeon Marshall Perkins, September 23, 1862-July 8, 1865.

15th New Hampshire Volunteer Infantry. Lieutenant Colonel Henry W. Blair, October 6, 1862-August 13, 1863, severely wounded at Port Hudson, Louisiana; a nine-month regiment serving in the Department of the Gulf.

16th New Hampshire Volunteer Infantry. Captain Elias F. Smith, September 1862-August 20, 1863; Second Lieutenant William B. Haven, Company K, October 21, 1862-August 20, 1863.

17th New Hampshire Volunteer Infantry. Colonel Henry D. Kent, October 30, 1862-April 16, 1863; Lieutenant Colonel Charles H. Long, October 23, 1862-April 17, 1863; Major Henry W. Blair; First Lieutenant Charles N. Kent, Company C, December 1, 1862-April 17, 1863; formation of this regiment was not completed and its companies were reassigned to the 2nd New Hampshire Volunteer Infantry.

18th New Hampshire Volunteer Infantry+. Captain Elias F. Smith, Company B, September 20, 1864-June 10, 1865; elected colonel but not mustered due to the end of the war; First Lieutenant William B. Haven, Company D, September

1863-June 10, 1865; Private Galen C. Smith, March 27-May 6, 1865; Private Austin G. Smith, September 3, 1864-June 10, 1865.

NEW JERSEY

1st New Jersey Veteran Volunteers. Colonel William A. Treadwell, 1865; regiment not mustered due to the end of the war.

3rd New Jersey Volunteer Infantry*+. Colonel George W. Taylor, June 4, 1861-May 9, 1862; mortally wounded at 2nd Bull Run and died September 1, 1862; named Brigadier General, May 9, 1862; First Lieutenant Archibald S. Taylor, Company I, June 1861-July 2, 1864; served as adjutant; severely wounded at Chancellorsville and later transferred to the United States Marine Corps.

5th New Jersey Volunteer Infantry*+. Captain Thomas W. Eayre, Company I, August 28, 1861-May 12, 1864; killed in action at the "Bloody Angle" while serving on the division staff.

26th New Jersey Infantry⌐. Colonel Thomas O. Seaver, 3rd Vermont Infantry, placed in temporary command of this unit to restore discipline, December 15, 1862-January 15, 1863; a nine month regiment assigned to the First Vermont Brigade.

33rd New Jersey Volunteer Infantry+. First Lieutenant and Quartermaster John A. Miller, August 29, 1863-July 17, 1865.

NEW YORK

46th New York Independent Battery. Second Lieutenant Ellis P. Walcott, May 23-July 10, 1864.

4th New York Heavy Artillery+ ("Irish Brigade"). Captain Daniel W. Washburn, Battery I, September 10, 1864-September 26, 1865.

8th New York Heavy Artillery*+. First Lieutenant Ellis P. Walcott, Battery K, June 11, 1864-June 4, 1865.

10th New York Heavy Artillery+ ("Black River Artillery," "Jefferson County Regiment"). Captain Edward H. Smith, Battery L, August 8, 1862-June 23, 1865 (see Appendix A).

14th New York Heavy Artillery*+. Captain William A. Treadwell, Battery G, December 5, 1863-December 18, 1864.

15th New York Heavy Artillery+. Possibly First Lieutenant Charles Graham, August 1863- December 5, 1864.

2nd New York Volunteer Cavalry+ ("Harris' Light Cavalry"). First Sergeant Edward M. Granger, March 1863-September 19, 1864; killed in action at Winchester, Virginia.

18th New York Volunteer Cavalry. Captain William S. Vernam, Company E, May 5-August 4, 1865.

21st New York Volunteer Cavalry. Major George V. Boutelle, October 15, 1863-May 1865.

26th New York Volunteer Cavalry (Frontier). Captain George B. French, Company F, January 26-June 26, 1865.

50th New York Volunteer Engineer Regiment+. Colonel William H. Pettes, September 10, 1861-July 5, 1865; Colonel from June 3, 1863. This unit was originally formed as infantry but was converted to engineers by General George B. McClellan.

2nd New York Volunteer Infantry+. Captain George V. Boutelle, Company A, May 1861-May 26, 1863; a two year regiment.

7th New York Volunteer Infantry+. Possibly Corporal William R. Vermilye.

9th New York Volunteer Infantry+ ("Hawkins Zouaves"). Lieutenant Colonel Edgar A. Kimball, April 1, 1861- April 12, 1863; cited for gallantry; commanded the regiment at Antietam and Fredericksburg; shot and killed by Col. Michael Corcoran, 69th New York Infantry at Suffolk, Virginia.

11th New York Volunteer Infantry ("Ellsworth Fire Zouaves"). First Lieutenant Edward K. Aldrich; a two year regiment; the unit was disbanded in May 1862.

12th New York Volunteer Infantry+. First Lieutenant William F. Gardiner, Company E, October 18, 1861-May 17, 1862.

16th New York Volunteer Infantry+. Lieutenant Colonel Samuel Marsh, April 1861-June 27, 1862; in command at 1st Bull Run and before Richmond, mortally wounded at Gaine's Mills.

24th New York Volunteer Infantry+ ("Oswego County Regiment"). Major Jonathan G. Tarbell, May 17-December 26, 1861; then Colonel, 91st New York.

31st New York Volunteer Infantry+ ("Baxter's Light Guard" "Montezuma Regiment"). Captain Robert J. Cowdin, Company E, November 30, 1861-June 4, 1863; a two year regiment.

50th New York Volunteer Infantry+. Lieutenant Colonel William H. Pettes, September 18-October 22, 1861. Reformed as 50th New York Engineers by order of General George B. McClellan, October 22, 1861.

67th New York Volunteer Infantry+ ("First Long Island Regiment"). Captain Lewis M. Peck, Company K, June 24, 1861-October 11, 1862; wounded in action at Fair Oaks; transferred to 173rd New York as a Lieutenant Colonel.

70th New York Volunteer Infantry*+ ("First Excelsior"). Captain George V. Boutelle, Company F, May 11 1863 (appointed but did not serve); First Lieutenant Daniel W. Washburn, Company G, June 27-August 8, 1861.

73rd New York Volunteer Infantry*+ ("Fourth Excelsior"). First Lieutenant Charles H. Potter, Companies B and K, July 10, 1861-June 29, 1865; wounded in action in the Wilderness and cited for gallantry; captured at Williamsburg in May 1862 and Hatcher's Run, October 1864; paroled on both occasions.

89th New York Volunteer Infantry+ ("Dickinson Guard"). Second Lieutenant Edward H. Smith, Company D, September 30, 1861-June 17, 1865 (see Appendix A).

91st New York Volunteer Infantry+ ("Albany Regiment"). Colonel Jonathan G. Tarbell, December 26, 1861-March 13, 1865; led unit from February 11, 1865; promoted to brevet brigadier general, March 13, 1865.

93rd New York Volunteer Infantry*+ (Morgan's Rifles). The regiment served as the Army of the Potomac Headquarters Guard, May 1862-May 1864; First Lieutenant Joseph S. Little, Company A, September 23, 1861-September 23, 1864; severely wounded in action at North Anna, discharged for disability from wounds (leg amputation); brevet captain.

95th New York Volunteer Infantry+ ("McCombs Plattsburgh Regiment"). First Lieutenant William A. Treadwell, September 1862 (appointed but not formally mustered) served with the regiment and on General Abner Doubleday's staff during the Maryland Campaign.

98th New York Volunteer Infantry ("Malone and Lyons Regiment"). Private Dwight H. Kelton, CompanyB, January 29-October 14, 1864; transferred and commissioned Captain, 115th United States Colored Infantry.

117th New York Volunteer Infantry* ("4th Oneida Regiment"). Sergeant Major Franklin H. Walcott, November 25, 1862-June 1864; Sergeant Ellis P. Walcott, November 25, 1862-June 11, 1864; transferred and promoted to Second Lieutenant, 8th New York Heavy Artillery.

144th New York Volunteer Infantry. Captain John M. Clark, Company E, August 15, 1862-June 25, 1865.

164th New York Volunteer Infantry*+ ("Corcoran Legion"). Captain David C. J. Beattie, Company I, May 12, 1862-July 15, 1865, wounded in action at Petersburg and Cedar Creek; captured at Petersburg and paroled; brevet major; Captain William A. Treadwell, Company B, September 13-October 14, 1862 (appointed but not mustered); a zouave unit.

173rd New York Volunteer Infantry ("4th National Guard"). Colonel Luther M. Peck, October 11, 1863-May 11, 1865; brevet major general, cited for gallantry at Cedar Creek, Virginia.

175th New York Volunteer Infantry. First Lieutenant and Adjutant William S. Vernam, September 24, 1862-September 17, 1864.

184th New York Volunteer Infantry+. Private William H. Wentworth, August 1864-July 1865; a one year regiment formed in October 1864.

NORTH CAROLINA
1st North Carolina Volunteer Infantry (Union). Second Lieutenant Eldridge H. Babbitt, March 1864-July 27, 1865.

OHIO
7th Independent Battery Ohio Light Artillery. Second Lieutenant Harrison Stebbins, January 3, 1862-August 11, 1865.

11th Ohio Volunteer Infantry. Lieutenant Colonel Joseph W. Frizell, June 5-July 20, 1861; a three month regiment serving from April 18-July 20, 1861.

19th Ohio Volunteer Infantry. First Lieutenant and Drillmaster Thomas Clark, June-August 1861.

23rd Ohio Volunteer Infantry*+. First Lieutenant Francis H. Bacon, Company K, June 1, 1861-December 26, 1862.

26th Ohio Volunteer Infantry. Captain Sylvester M. Hewitt, Company I, June 5-July 26, 1861; Captain James K. Ewart, Company E, July 24, 1861-December 2, 1862.

29th Ohio Volunteer Infantry*+. Lieutenant Colonel Thomas Clark, August 13, 1861-June 19, 1863; wounded at Chancellorsville.

32nd Ohio Volunteer Infantry. Major Sylvester M. Hewitt, July 26, 1861-January 13, 1863; Captain Jay Dyer, Company I, August 31, 1861-April 10, 1862; discharged for disability. The regiment was captured at Harper's Ferry and later paroled.

36th Ohio Volunteer Infantry*+. Captain James Samuel Gage Barker, Company A, July 27, 1861-November 14, 1864.

38th Ohio Volunteer Infantry*. First Lieutenant and Adjutant Charles, L. Allen, Company K, September 1, 1861-December 9, 1863.

45th Ohio Volunteer Infantry. Captain William M. Williams, August 19, 1862-June 12, 1865.

47th Ohio Volunteer Infantry. Captain William H. Ward, Company B, June 15, 1861-August 9, 1864.

94th Ohio Volunteer Infantry. Colonel. Joseph W. Frizell, July 1862-February 22, 1863; severely wounded at Stone's River, Tennessee and forced to resign.

98th Ohio Volunteer Infantry*. Corporal Henry H. Adams, Company C, February 2, 1864-June 26, 1865; discharged for disability.

136th Ohio Volunteer Infantry. Captain and Surgeon Sylvester M. Hewitt, July 5-August 31, 1864; a 100 day regiment serving from May 18-August 31, 1864.

OREGON

1st Oregon Volunteer Cavalry. Major Sewall Truax, November 29, 1861-November 19, 1864.

PENNSYLVANIA

Independent Battery E, Pennsylvania Light Artillery+. Private Henry S. Campbell, August 1862-March 16, 1864; transferred and promoted Second Lieutenant, 25th United States Colored Infantry.

Independent Battery F, Pennsylvania Light Artillery+. Captain Nathaniel Irish, January 13, 1862-June 26, 1865; wounded in action at Gettysburg and cited for gallantry. The battery was converted to heavy artillery in fall 1863 and posted to Harper's Ferry for the duration of the war.

1st Pennsylvania Volunteer Light Artillery+. Captain Frank P. Amsden, Batteries B,G, and H, May 11, 1861-May 25, 1863; wounded in action and retired for disability.

2nd Provisional Pennsylvania Heavy Artillery+. Captain George W. Webb, Battery F, April 20-September 5, 1864; this unit was a temporary regiment formed to hold surplus men from its parent regiment the 2nd Pennsylvania Heavy Artillery.

2nd Pennsylvania Heavy Artillery. Captain George W. Webb, Battery F, December 18, 1861-May 6, 1865.

4th Pennsylvania Volunteer Cavalry+. Private Rody Patterson Jr., Company B, February 16, 1864-July 5, 1865; wounded in action August 16, 1864 at Strawberry Plains, Virginia.

7th Pennsylvania Volunteer Cavalry*. Possibly First Lieutenant William B. Hays.

18th Pennsylvania Volunteer Cavalry+. Probably Lieutenant Colonel James W. Phillips, December 1862 June 1865.

2nd Pennsylvania Volunteer Infantry. First Lieutenant John W. Schall, Company K, April 20-July 25, 1861; a 90 day regiment serving from April 20-July 26, 1861.

4th Pennsylvania Volunteer Infantry. Lieutenant Colonel Edward Schall; Major Edwin Schall; Captain Reuben J. Schall, Company D; a 90 day regiment serving from April 20-July 27, 1861.

5th Pennsylvania Militia Infantry+ (war service). Colonel Henry C. Longnecker, September 11-27, 1862, resigned due to disability after Antietam.

2nd Pennsylvania Reserves+ ("31st Volunteers"). Captain Thomas F. Bringhurst, Company F, May 28-August 27, 1861.

5th Pennsylvania Reserves*+ ("34th Volunteers"). Colonel Seneca G. Simmons, June 21, 1861-June 30, 1862; mortally wounded in the battle of White Oak Swamp, Virginia while commanding his brigade; captured and died next day.

9th Pennsylvania Volunteer Infantry. Colonel Henry C. Longnecker, April 24-July 27, 1861; a 90 day regiment serving from April 20-July 27, 1861.

10th Pennsylvania Reserves*+ ("39th Volunteers"). Captain Henry V. Partridge, July 1, 1861-July 26, 1862; resigned.

25th Pennsylvania Volunteer Infantry. Captain William W.H. Davis, Company I, June-August 1861, a 90 day regiment serving from April 18-August 1, 1861.

28th Pennsylvania Volunteer Regiment*. First Lieutenant Erasmus G. Rehrer, served three months in the unit probably from May-August 1862.

34th Pennsylvania Militia Infantry (war service). Colonel Edward Schall, July 3-August 10, 1863 in the Philadelphia and Reading, Pennsylvania areas during Lee's Invasion.

48th Pennsylvania Volunteer Infantry*+. Chaplain Samuel A. Holman, October 1, 1861-January 2, 1863.

51st Pennsylvania Volunteer Infantry*+. Colonel Edwin Schall July 27, 1861-June 3, 1864; Colonel from June 1, 1864; killed in action leading a charge at Cold Harbor; Captain Edward Schall, Company D, August 16, 1861-April 14, 1863.

54th Pennsylvania Volunteer Infantry. Sergeant John S. Carpenter, Company B, September 11-December 31, 1861; this company became Company B, 95th Pennsylvania Volunteer Infantry.

59th Pennsylvania Militia Infantry (War Service). Captain Thomas F. Bringhurst, Company B, July 1-September 9, 1863; an emergency unit posted at Philadelphia during Lee's Invasion and the draft riots.

67th Pennsylvania Volunteer Infantry+. Lieutenant Colonel Hosea B. Burnham, October 31, 1861-October 30, 1864.

83rd Pennsylvania Volunteer Infantry*+. Lieutenant Colonel Hugh S. Campbell, August 21, 1861-May 14, 1863; wounded in action at Malvern Hill and 2nd Bull Run; commanded the regiment in several engagements.

87th Pennsylvania Volunteer Infantry+. Colonel John W. Schall, September 12, 1861-October 13, 1864; Colonel from May 9, 1863; wounded in action at Cold Harbor; also served as a brigade commander.

95th Pennsylvania Volunteer Infantry*+. Captain John S. Carpenter, Company H, January 1, 1862-September 17, 1865; also served as a first lieutenant in Company B and as the sergeant major of the regiment from May 27, 1863-August 20, 1864.

104th Pennsylvania Volunteer Infantry+. Colonel William W.H. Davis, September 5-June 1865; also served as a brigade commander and department commander; brevet brigadier general.

129th Pennsylvania Volunteer Infantry+. Captain Edward G. Rehrer, CompanyE, August 1, 1862-May 18, 1863; severely wounded at Fredericksburg while serving on the brigade staff; a nine month regiment serving from August, 1862-May 18, 1863.

186th Pennsylvania Volunteer Infantry. Private George W. Emerson, Company B, December 5, 1864-August 15, 1865.

RHODE ISLAND

7th Squadron, Rhode Island Cavalry ("College Cavaliers"). Company B, Henry E. Alvord; George A. Bailey; Albert F. Bayard; Charles E. Bush; Arthur W. Coombs (died on active service); William S. Dewey; William S. Goodwin; Charles M. Gragg; Addison T. Hastings; Walter S. Hazelton; Theodore H. Kellogg; Wallace A. King; Douglas Lee; Arthur P. Morey; Edward H. Noyes; Alfred L. Papanti; James V. Parker; Henry M. Phillips; Charles W. Smith; Charles F. Tillinghast; Ellis P. Walcott; Francis H. Walcott; Arthur W. White; unit served from June 24-October 2, 1862; a three month (90 day) unit.

1st Rhode Island Volunteer Infantry (Militia). Private Thomas S. Brownell, Company F, April 17-August 1, 1861; a three month (90 day) regiment serving from April 20-August 2, 1861.

7th Rhode Island Volunteer Infantry+. Major Jacob Babbitt, September 1-December 23, 1862; mortally wounded at Fredericksburg in the assault on Marye's Heights; Captain Alfred M. Channel, Company D, September 4, 1862-August 1, 1864; dismissed from the service by order of a general court martial which was later revoked and he was restored to his rank; First Lieutenant and Adjutant Thomas S. Brownell, Company I, September 4, 1862- January 1, 1863; re-signed for disability.

10th Rhode Island Volunteer Infantry. Major Jacob Babbitt, June 9-September 1, 1862; transferred to 7th Rhode Island Infantry; a three month (90 day) regiment.

12th Rhode Island Volunteer Infantry+. Second Lieutenant Charles H. Potter, Company K, October 13, 1862-July 29, 1863; cited for gallantry.

UNITED STATES TROOPS

5th United States Colored Heavy Artillery. Colonel Bernard G. Farrar, March 11-April 26, 1864; unit redesignated 6th United States Colored Heavy Artillery.

6th United States Colored Heavy Artillery. Colonel Bernard G. Farrar, April 26, 1864-May 8, 1865, Brevet Brigadier General; this unit was 1,800 men strong and became noted for its discipline, drill, and overall efficiency.

4th United States Colored Cavalry. Second Lieutenant Thomas G. Rice, Company D, July 19, 1864-October 5, 1865; contacted fever and died at Vidalia, Louisiana.

2nd United States Colored Infantry. First Lieutenant Henry L. Slayton, Company K, September 24, 1863-January 1866; this unit was the second Federal colored unit raised.

4th United States Colored Infantry. Second Lieutenant Lewis Kimball, July 19, 1864-January 23, 1865; discharged for disability.

6th United States Colored Infantry. First Lieutenant Joseph H. Goulding, September 24, 1863-September 20, 1865.

10th United States Colored Infantry. Second Lieutenant Daniel W. Parmenter, Company G, November 11, 1863-April 20, 1864; died of wounds received at Plymouth, North Carolina, probably while a prisoner of war.

20th United States Colored Infantry. First Lieutenant William Gerrish, February 4, 1864-July 20, 1864; resigned; First Lieutenant Dudley F. Phelps, March 5, 1864-October 7, 1865.

22nd United States Colored Infantry. Captain Arthur P. Morey, January 30, 1864-October 16, 1865.

25th United States Colored Infantry. Captain Abbott A. Shattuck Company H, January 3, 1864-December 6, 1865.

45th United States Colored Infantry. Captain Edward H. Cutts, Company C, June 1864-May 13, 1865.

57th United States Colored Infantry. Captain George A. Folsom, March 11 1864-May 1865; Second Lieutenant Thomas K.G. Wright, December 1863-June 14, 1864.

58th United States Colored Infantry. Colonel Simon M. Preston, April 25, 1864-April 30, 1866.

67th United States Colored Infantry. Captain Thomas K.G. Wright, June 14, 1864-May 8, 1865.

74th United States Colored Infantry ("2nd Louisiana Guards, Corps D'Afrique"). Lieutenant Colonel Alfred G. Hall, October 12, 1862- October 27, 1865. This unit was the second colored regiment mustered into the Union Army, October 12, 1862.

75th United States Colored Infantry ("3rd Corps D'Afrique"). Captain George Buttrick, Companies B & E, September 1863-November 1865.

115th United States Colored Infantry. Major Dwight H. Kelton, October 14, 1864-May 1865.

116th United States Colored Infantry. Captain John H. Osgood, Company G, July 21, 1864-January 1, 1865; discharged for disability.

1st United States Artillery. Captain Truman B. Seymour, Battery H, December 1860-April 14, 1861; Private George M. Rice, Battery C, January 20-August 8, 1863; discharged for promotion into the 2nd Massachusetts Heavy Artillery.

2nd United States Artillery+. Captain Edward B. Williston, Battery D, April 1861-April 1865; won the Congressional Medal of Honor at Trevilian Station, Virginia, June 12, 1864; Captain Henry A. Smalley, Battery K, October 1, 1862-August 3, 1865.

3rd United States Artillery+. Major Henry S. Burton; First Lieutenant Dunbar R. Ransom, Battery E, April-September 1861.

4th United States Artillery+. Lieutenant Colonel Henry S. Burton, July 25, 1863 then Colonel 5th United States Artillery, August 11, 1863-May 15, 1865, cited for gallantry; brevet brigadier general; commanded the artillery reserve, Army of the Potomac, summer 1864; Captain Evan W. Thomas, Battery A, for a period at Antietam and Chancellorsville, and Battery C, May 14, 1861-May 1, 1865; cited for gallantry at Fredericksburg and Gettysburg.

5th United States Artillery+. Colonel Truman Seymour, commanded the unit in the defense of Washington, December 31, 1861-March 5, 1862; cited for gallantry five times and promoted to brigadier general; Colonel Henry S. Burton; also commanded the artillery reserve and siege artillery of the Army of the Potomac; Captain Dunbar R. Ransom, Battery C, 1862-August, 1864; severely wounded in action at Gettysburg; brevet colonel; also commanded an artillery brigade.

1st United States Cavalry+. Captain Judson Haycock, August 26, 1861-November 12, 1864; First Lieutenant and Adjutant Albert V. Colburn, to 1 July 1861 then promoted to staff as a Captain and Assistant Adjutant General to General

George McClellan; died on active duty; First Lieutenant Henry C. Wood June 27, 1856-May 14, 1861; transferred to the 11th United States Infantry.

2nd United States Cavalry. Lieutenant Colonel Charles May; resigned April 20, 1861.

5th United States Cavalry+. Private Albert F. Bayard, Company G, April 1865.

6th United States Cavalry+. Captain Eli B. Bean, February 29, 1864-October 30, 1865.

1st United States Infantry. First Lieutenant John Sabine, February 19, 1862-September 29, 1863; died of disease contracted at Vicksburg.

4th United States Infantry+. First Lieutenant and Quartermaster John F.L. Buell Company G, August 5, 1861-November 6, 1862; Major (Surgeon) Francis M. Lincoln.

5th United States Infantry. First Lieutenant Charles A. Curtis, April 28, 1862-September 27, 1865.

6th United States Infantry+. Major Henry W. Wessells, January 6-September 29, 1861; promoted to Brigadier General of United States Volunteers; cited three times for gallantry; captured at San Lucas Springs, Texas, May 9, 1861 with his regiment and later paroled; Major James V. Bomford, January-April, 1861; Major Albermale Cady, January 27, 1853-June 6, 1861.

7th United States Infantry+. Lieutenant Colonel Albermale Cady, June 6, 1861-October 20, 1863; designated Colonel, 8th United States Infantry; Captain Seneca G. Simmons, January 1-June 21, 1861; promoted to Colonel, 5th Pennsylvania Reserves; First Lieutenant Charles A. Coolidge, July 21, 1864-May 1865; First Lieutenant Charles A. Curtis, April 14-April 28, 1862; transferred to the 5th United States Infantry.

8th United States Infantry+. Colonel Albermale Cady, October 20, 1863-May 18, 1864; retired; Colonel James V. Bomford, April 1861-October 10, 1864; severely wounded twice at the Battle of Perryville; cited for gallantry; Colonel, 8th United States Infantry, May 18-October 10, 1864; retired as a brevet Brigadier General.

9th United States Infantry. Colonel George Wright, led the regiment 1855-October 1861; promoted to brigadier general and department commander.

10th United States Infantry. Captain Jesse A. Gove, April 1-November 9, 1861; promoted to Colonel, 22nd Massachusetts Infantry.

11th United States Infantry+. Captain Henry C. Wood, May 14, 1861-June 24-1861; severely wounded and won the Congressional Medal of Honor at Wilson's Creek, Missouri August 1861; promoted to a staff assignment in the Adjutant General's Office in Washington where he served for the remainder of the war; Corporal Robert C. Lord, Company C, 7 March 1864 April 3,1865; promoted to second lieutenant, 14th United States Infantry.

13th United States Infantry. Captain Charles A. Webb, August 10, 1862-September 20, 1866; cited for gallantry at Vicksburg, brevet major; First Lieutenant

William Nelson, Company B, September 5, 1861-end of war; cited for gallantry at Arkansas Post and Vicksburg; brevet major.

14th United States Infantry+. Second Lieutenant Robert C. Lord, March 1865 to the end of the war.

15th United States Infantry. Captain Samuel E. Woodward, August 5, 1861-September 30, 1866; cited for gallantry at Stone's River and at Atlanta.

16th United States Infantry. Lieutenant Colonel James V. Bomford; Captain Charles H. Lewis, August 5, 1861-July 28, 1864; Private Charles A. Coolidge, Company H, 3rd Battalion, October 23, 1862-July 21, 1864; transferred to the 7th United States Infantry as a Second Lieutenant.

17th United States Infantry+ ("Maine Regulars"). Captain Solon H. Lathrop, August 5, 1861-August 20, 1862 then transferred to staff; First Lieutenant Edward S. Abbot, Company A, First Battalion, July 1, 1862-July 2, 1863, died of wounds received at Gettysburg; cited for gallantry and breveted captain; Captain George W. Smith, Company A, 2nd Battalion and Companies A and E, First Battalion, May 10, 1862-October 19, 1865, wounded at Gettysburg and Spotsylvania; cited twice for gallantry; First Lieutenant Francis E. Stimpson, Company B, 2nd Battalion, July 31, 1862-May 12, 1864, mortally wounded at Laurel Hill in the Spotsylvania Campaign; Sergeant Eldridge H. Babbitt, June 7, 1862-July 2, 1863, severely wounded at Gettysburg; Sergeant James W. Buel, June 1, 1862-December 10, 1863; wounded at Chancellorsville, captured and held in Libby Prison until he was discharged for disability.

18th United States Infantry*. Lieutenant Colonel Henry W. Wessells, February-May 1865; Captain Charles B. Denison May, 1861-January 15, 1863, severely wounded at Stone's River, Tennessee; cited for gallantry and later died of wounds in hospital; Captain Symmes Gardiner, May 14, 1861-November 13, 1863.

19th United States Infantry. Captain Egbert Phelps, May 14, 1861-March 18, 1865.

1st United States Sharpshooters*+ ("Berdan's Sharpshooters"). Captain Edmund Weston, Company F, August 15, 1861-August 2, 1862; resigned due to disability after refusing promotion to Lieutenant Colonel of his regiment.

2nd United States Sharpshooters*+ ("Berdan's Sharpshooters"). Captain John W. Dewey, Company C, October 19, 1861-February 20, 1863, discharged for disability; Private Samuel H. Green, Company E, December 18, 1863- February 25, 1865; wounded in action and captured at Hatcher's Run, Virginia, October 27, 1864; paroled and later transferred to Company G, 4th Vermont Infantry.

2nd United States Veteran Reserve Corps**. Colonel James A. Hall, March-June 1865.

6th United States Veteran Reserve Corps. Lieutenant Colonel Linus D. Bishop, March-June 12, 1865.

8th United States Veteran Reserve Corps. First Lieutenant Henry J. Morris, November 1863- August 3, 1865.

9th United States Veteran Reserve Corps. Major and Surgeon George P. Greeley, January 1865.

20th United States Veteran Reserve Corps. Drum Major Willie Johnston, March 1-December 15, 1864.

VERMONT

1st Vermont Volunteer Heavy Artillery*+ (former 11th Vermont Volunteer Infantry). Colonel Charles Hunsdon, November 2, 1863-August 25, 1865; Colonel from May 23, 1865; Captain George A. Bailey, Battery M, August 1862-August 25, 1865; cited for gallantry; Captain Hunt W. Burrows, Battery M, August 22, 1862-September 1, 1864; served as adjutant and discharged for disability; Captain James Rice, Battery F., August 12, 1862-April 28, 1865, cited for gallantry; First Lieutenant Henry C. Baxter, Battery D, December 12, 1863-June 24, 1865; wounded in action at Cedar Creek, Virginia and cited for conspicuous gallantry; Second Lieutenant Edward B. Parker, Battery B, August 8, 1862-October 13, 1864, captured at the Weldon Railroad, June 23, 1864; died trying to escape from prison in South Carolina, October 13, 1864; First Sergeant Sardis Birchard, Battery L, June 27, 1863-June 23, 1864; taken prisoner at the Weldon Railroad, VA, died in Andersonville August 21, 1864, where he is buried in grave #6334; Private John Pettis, Battery B, December 7, 1863-June 29, 1865; wounded in action in the assault on Petersburg.

1st Battery Vermont Light Artillery. Second Lieutenant Salmon B. Hebard, January 15, 1862-July 11, 1862.

3rd Battery Vermont Light Artillery+. First Lieutenant Walter A. Phillipes, December 12, 1863-February 13, 1865; discharged for disability; First Lieutenant J. Henry Wright, January 1, 1864-May 29, 1865.

1st Vermont Volunteer Cavalry*+. Colonel. Josiah Hall, October 17, 1861-June 21, 1865; rose from private to colonel; wounded in action and was captured and later paroled; Private Marcellus Bowen, Company F, September 5, 1864-June 21, 1865.

1st Vermont Volunteer Infantry. Major Henry N. Worthen, April 26-August 15, 1861; First Lieutenant Charles A. Webb, Company F, April-August, 1861; First Lieutenant Solomon E. Woodward, Company B, April 26-August 15, 1861; Second Lieutenant Levi G. Kingsley, Company K, March 3-August 15, 1861; First Sergeant George B. French, Company E, May 2-August 15, 1861; Privates Edward B. Parker, Company A, April 26-August 15, 1861; Sumner H. Lincoln, Company B, Oscar G. Mower, Company H, and Alonzo E. Smith, Company K, May 9-August 15, 1861; a three month (90 day) regiment serving from May 9-August 15, 1861.

2nd Vermont Volunteer Infantry*+. First Lieutenant Walter A. Phillipes, Company F, May 20-December 31, 1861; dismissed from the service by a General Court

Martial but later served in other units; Sergeant Van Buren Sleeper, Company E, May 13, 1861-August 1, 1863 when he transferred to the Signal Corps.

3rd Vermont Volunteer Infantry*+. Colonel Thomas O. Seaver, May 1861-July 16, 1864; Colonel from January 15, 1863; won the Congressional Medal of Honor near Spotsylvania Court House, May 10, 1864; Captain Lorenzo D. Allen, Company G, May 27, 1861-November 24, 1862 when discharged for disability; First Lieutenant Edward A. Chandler, Company F, May 1861-July 27, 1864; pensioned for wounds received at Lee's Mills, Virginia; First Sergeant Rufus L. Moses, Company A, December 12, 1863-July 11, 1865; Corporal John G. Fowler, Company C, July 21, 1861-December 2, 1862; wounded and discharged for disability; Private and Drummer Willie Johnston, Company D, May 1, 1862-February 5, 1864 when he transferred to the Veterans Reserve Corps; youngest soldier ever to win the Medal of Honor (Peninsula Campaign) at age 12; Private John Sabine Companies F and G, May 30, 1862-May 5, 1864; killed in action in the Wilderness.

4th Vermont Volunteer Infantry*+. Colonel Charles B. Stoughton, August 11, 1861-February 2, 1864, Colonel from November 5, 1862; severely wounded in action and breveted brigadier general; Lieutenant Colonel Henry N. Worthen, August 26, 1861-July 16, 1862; resigned due to health; Captain George F. Tucker, Company D, September 4, 1861-February 22, 1862 when resigned due to health; Captain Jonas (James) H. Platt, Company B, August 30, 1861-November 21, 1864, captured May 30, 1864 and exchanged October 16, 1864; First Lieutenant and Adjutant George B. French, Companies C and G, September 3, 1861-September 30, 1864; severely wounded in action in the Wilderness; Corporal Samuel A. Cady, Company K, September 12, 1861-May 19, 1862; Private Samuel H. Green, Company G, February 25- July 15, 1865; transferred from the 2nd United States Sharpshooters and later discharged for disability; Private Frank A. Page, Company H, August 1861-December 12, 1862, when discharged for wounds received at Lee's Mills; Private George H. Parker, Company A, August 19, 1861-May 5, 1864; wounded in action in the Wilderness and assigned to the Veterans Reserve Corps.

5th Vermont Volunteer Infantry*+. Colonel Henry A. Smalley, July 30, 1861-September 10, 1862 when he was ordered back to his regular army regiment; Captain Edwin S. Stowell, Company F, September 4, 1861-June 21, 1862; transferred to the 9th Vermont Infantry as a Major; First Lieutenant and Adjutant Edward M. Brown, August 24, 1861-January 9, 1862 then transferred to 8th Vermont as a Lieutenant Colonel; Musicians Frederick T. Bickford, August 29, 1861-April 11, 1862 and James Rice, August 14, 1861-April 11, 1862; Private William N. Dyer, Company D, August 21, 1861-June 29, 1865; wounded in action; Private James E. Batchelder, Company E, December 18, 1863-September 22, 1864 when he was discharged for wounds received at Spotsylvania, May 12, 1864; Private Henry S. Smith Company F, August 25, 1862-June 19, 1865.

6th Vermont Volunteer Infantry*+. Colonel Sumner H. Lincoln, October 15, 1861-June 26, 1865, twice wounded in action and cited for gallantry; Major Richard B. Crandall, October 15, 1861-June 7, 1864, killed in action at Cold Harbor by a sniper; Captain William H.H. Hall, Company G, October 9, 1861-April 26, 1862, discharged due to fever; Captain Alonzo B. Hutchinson, Company B, October 5, 1861-May 4, 1863; severely wounded at Bank's Ford, Virginia and discharged for disability; Captain George E. Parker Jr., Company A, October 4, 1861-October 21, 1862; Sergeant George Messenger, Company B, September 7, 1861-October 28, 1864; Sergeant Henry J. Wright, Company B, September 7, 1861-July 25, 1864; Private Thomas K.G. Wright, Company B, September 6, 1861-February 20, 1862; Private Edwin J. Chase, Company G, September 2, 1861-January 15, 1862; died of disease.

7th Vermont Volunteer Infantry. Captain Charles E. Parker, Company E, January 1, 1862-October 22, 1863 when he resigned due to ill health; Private John E. Hatch, Company F, February 17-August 8, 1862; died of disease.

8th Vermont Volunteer Infantry. Lieutenant Colonel Edward M. Brown, January 9, 1862-December 23, 1862 when he resigned due to ill health; Captain Lemuel M. Hutchinson, Company E, July 23, 1862-June 1865; Captain Samuel W. Shattuck, Company H, January 15, 1863-June 6, 1865, greatly distinguished himself and was wounded in action at Cedar Creek, Virginia; Captain and Assistant Surgeon Samuel H. Currier, December 10, 1861-November 30, 1862; Private Albert Buswell Company D, January 4, 1864-June 18, 1865; Private Charles G. Tarbell, Company G, January 4, 1862-February 26, 1864; transferred to signal corps.

9th Vermont Volunteer Infantry. Lieutenant Colonel Edwin S. Stowell, June 21, 1862-May 11, 1863; Captain Albion J. Mower, Company I, June 30, 1862-July 8, 1863 when he resigned due to disability; First Lieutenant William A. Dodge, Company B, May 29, 1862-June 6, 1865, twice wounded in action in the Shenandoah; First Lieutenant John Gray, Company K, March 1862-August 28, 1865; Second Lieutenant Asa H. Snow, Company D, June 17, 1862-December 11, 1864; Corporal Daniel E. Wright, Company A, June 3, 1862-June 13, 1865. The regiment was captured at Harper's Ferry, Maryland in September 1862 but was later paroled.

10th Vermont Volunteer Infantry*+. Captain Lemuel A. Abbott, Company G, July 28, 1862-June 22, 1865; wounded in action on three separate occasions; possibly Captain George E. Davis, Company D, August 8, 1862-June 22, 1865 (see Appendix A); First Lieutenant William R. Hoyt, Company A, September 23, 1863-June 29, 1865; First Sergeant Henry G. Post, Company C, July 16, 1862-February 12, 1863 when he transferred to the regular army; Corporal Roswell W. Hunt, August 1, 1862-June 22, 1865; wounded in action.

11th Vermont Volunteer Infantry. See 1st Vermont Volunteer Heavy Artillery.

12th Vermont Volunteer Infantry+. Major Levi G. Kingsley, September 19, 1862-July 4, 1863; First Lieutenant and Assistant Surgeon Grenville P. Conn,

September 19, 1862-July 15, 1863; Captain Norman E. Perkins, Company A, August 23, 1862-July 14, 1863; First Sergeant Henry Harding, Company B, August 19, 1862-July 14, 1863; Sergeant Pomeroy Loomis, Company C, September 23, 1862-July 14, 1863; Private Friend P. Fletcher Company B, August 23, 1862-July 14, 1863; Privates John M. Bartlett, Charles H. Granger, Company H, and Andrew C. Marcy, Company B; a nine month regiment serving from October 4, 1862-July 14, 1863.

13th Vermont Volunteer Infantry+. Lieutenant Colonel William D. Munson, September 6, 1862-July 14, 1863; commanded the regiment for a time at Gettysburg and was wounded in action; Second Lieutenant John M. Rolfe, Company D, September 6, 1862-January 30, 1863; First Sergeant Walter A. Phillipes, Company H, August 19, 1862-July 21, 1863; a nine month regiment serving from October 10, 1862-July 14, 1863.

14th Vermont Volunteer Infantry+. First Sergeant Horace C. Henry, Company A, August 27, 1862-July 30, 1863; a nine month regiment serving from October 14, 1862-July 15, 1863.

15th Vermont Volunteer Infantry+. Captain William H. Johnson, Company I, August 1862-January 15, 1863; resigned.

16th Vermont Volunteer Infantry+. Captain Samuel Hutchinson, Company K, October 1862-January 8, 1863; resigned; Captain William C. Danforth, Company K, October 1, 1862-August 10, 1863; Second Lieutenant Adin H. Whitmore, Company C, October 16, 1862-August 10, 1863; Corporal Charles G. Cargill, Company H, September 18, 1862-August 10, 1863; Corporal Albert E. Hazen Company G, September 4, 1862-August 10, 1863; Private Edson Hutchinson Company K, October 23, 1862-August 10, 1863; Private Abner G. White, Company B, August 28, 1862-August 10, 1863; a nine month regiment serving from October 23, 1862-July 23, 1863.

17th Vermont Volunteer Infantry*+. First Lieutenant William B. Burbank, Company E, April 9, 1864-July 14, 1865.

18th Vermont Volunteer Infantry. Captain William C. Danforth; the regiment was not mustered due to the end of the war.

WISCONSIN

2nd Wisconsin Volunteer Cavalry. Chaplain William H. Brisbane, October 31, 1861-June 19, 1862 when he resigned due to ill health; First Lieutenant Napoleon Boardman Company A, October 8, 1861-February 27, 1864, promoted to Captain, Battery M, Second Missouri Light Artillery.

3rd Wisconsin Volunteer Cavalry. Second Lieutenant Byron H. Kilbourne, Company D, October 19, 1861-August 15, 1862; Privates Ira Nourse and possibly Hartop P. Thomas.

1st Wisconsin Volunteer Infantry. Captain George E. Bryant, Company E, April 27-August 21, 1861; Private Benjamin M. Gilman, Company B, April 27-August

21, 1861; a three month (90 day) regiment serving from April 27-August 21, 1861.

2nd Wisconsin Volunteer Infantry*+. Colonel Squire P. Coon, April 24-July 30, 1861; transferred to brigade staff and then resigned; First Lieutenant and Adjutant Charles K. Dean, April 22, 1861-May 28, 1863; severely wounded at Antietam; Acting Surgeon Henry A. Robbins, June-November, 1863; Sergeant Julius C. Chandler, Company G; severely wounded at 1st Bull Run and discharged for disability, November 5, 1861.

5th Wisconsin Volunteer Infantry*+. Lieutenant Colonel Harvey W. Emery, May 28, 1861-September 20, 1862; resigned due to wounds.

6th Wisconsin Volunteer Infantry*+. Lieutenant Colonel Julius P. Atwood, May 28-September 14, 1861; resigned due to poor health; Captain David K. Noyes, Company A, April 26, 1861-September 17, 1862; severely wounded (lost foot) at Antietam and discharged for disability.

7th Wisconsin Infantry*+. Colonel William W. Robinson, August 15, 1861-July 9, 1864; severely wounded in action at Brawner's Farm (2nd Bull Run); commanded the "Iron Brigade" at Gettysburg and from the Rapidan to Petersburg in Grant's Overland Campaign; led the regiment from February 3, 1862; discharged when his regiment was reduced in numbers beyond the point where it was authorized a colonel.

8th Wisconsin Volunteer Infantry ("Live Eagle Regiment"). First Lieutenant and Drillmaster George E. Bryant, April-September 1861; then transferred and promoted to Colonel, 12th Wisconsin Volunteers, September 27, 1861.

12th Wisconsin Volunteer Infantry. Colonel George E. Bryant, September 27, 1861-May 1865; First Lieutenant Nathan A.C. Smith, Company H, October 25, 1861-August 4, 1862; resigned due to disability.

19th Wisconsin Volunteer Infantry. Major Alvin E. Bovay, December 31, 1861-September 29, 1863; discharged for disability; Captain Henry B. Nichols, March 19, 1862-April 29, 1865.

20th Wisconsin Volunteer Infantry. First Lieutenant and Adjutant Henry V. Morris, May 1862-November 1863.

21st Wisconsin Volunteer Infantry. Captain Milan H. Sessions, Company G, August 26, 1862-December 1864.

32nd Wisconsin Volunteer Infantry. First Lieutenant and Adjutant Benjamin M. Beckwith, September 6, 1862-June 11, 1864, discharged for disability; possibly First Lieutenant Nathan A.C. Smith.

40th Wisconsin Volunteer Infantry. First Sergeant Lorenzo Potter; Privates Julius C. Chandler Company A, Martin M. Flint; a 100 day regiment serving from June 14-September 16, 1864.

43rd Wisconsin Volunteer Infantry. First Lieutenant William Partridge, Company A, September 14, 1864; a one year regiment serving from September 14, 1864-June 24, 1865.

49th Wisconsin Volunteer Infantry. Lieutenant Colonel David K. Noyes, January 28-November 8, 1865.

Appendix C

BATTLES AND ENGAGEMENTS

At least one or more Norwich alumni served in each of the following 254 Civil War battles and engagements:

Adairsville, Georgia, May 17, 1864.
Aldie, Virginia, June 17, 1863.
Allatoona, Georgia, October 5, 1864.
Allegheny Mountain, West Virginia, December 13, 1861.
Antietam, Maryland, September 17, 1862.
Appomattox Campaign, Virginia, March 29-April 9, 1865.
Appomattox Station, Virginia, April 8, 1865.
Arkansas Post, Arkansas, January 10-11, 1863.
Arrowfield Church (Swift Creek), Virginia, May 9, 1864.
Atlanta, Georgia, May-September 1864.

Ball's Bluff, Virginia, October 21, 1861.
Banks Ford, Virginia, May 4, 1863.
Baton Rouge, Louisiana, August 5, 1862.
Bayou de Glaize, Louisiana, May 18, 1864.
Belmont, Missouri, November 7, 1861.
Bentonville, North Carolina, March 19, 1865.
Bermuda Hundred, Virginia, June 2, 1864.
Bethesda Church, Virginia, May 30-1 June, 1864.
Big Bethel, Virginia, June 10, 1861.
Big Black River Bridge, Mississippi, May 17, 1863.
Bisland Fort, Louisiana, April 12-13, 1863.
Blackford's Ford, Maryland, September 19, 1862.
"Bloody Angle," Virginia, May 12, 1864.
Boydton Road, Virginia, October 27, 1864.
Brandy Station, Virginia, June 9, 1863.
Brandy Station, Virginia, October 11, 1863.
Brandy Station, Virginia, 10 November 1863.
Brawner's Farm, Virginia, August 28, 1862.
Brice's Cross Roads, Georgia, June 10, 1864.
Bristoe Station, Virginia, August 27, 1862.

Bristoe Station, Virginia, October 14, 1863.
Brooke's Turnpike, Virginia, March 1, 1864.
Brook's Church, Virginia, May 12, 1864.
Buffington Island, Ohio, July 19, 1863.
Burgess Mill, Virginia, October 27, 1865.
Cabin Creek, Indian Territory, July 1-2, 1862.
Camden, North Carolina, April 19, 1862.
Campbell's Station, Tennessee, November 16, 1863.
Catlett's Station, Virginia, August 22, 1862.
Cedar Creek, Virginia, October 19, 1864.
Cedar Mountain, Virginia, August 9, 1862.
Centreville, Louisiana, April 12-13, 1863.
Chaffin's Farm, Virginia, September 29, 1864.
Champion's Hill, Mississippi, May 16, 1863.
Chancellorsville, Virginia, May 2-4, 1863.
Chantilly, Virginia, September 1, 1862.
Chaplin Hills, Kentucky, October 8, 1862.
Charlot, Missouri, October 25, 1864.
Charlston, Missouri, August 19, 1861.
Charlston, South Carolina, August 21-December 31, 1863.
Charlston, West Virginia, August 21, 1864.
Chattanooga, Tennessee, September 24-November 23 1863.
Cheat Mountain, West Virginia, October 3-4, 1861.
Chickamauga, Georgia, September 19-20, 1863.
Chickasaw Bluffs (Chickasaw Bayou), Mississippi, December 29, 1862.
Clover Hill (Appomattox Court House), Virginia, April 9, 1865.
Cloyd's Mountain, Virginia, May 9, 1864.
Cold Harbor, Virginia, June 1-12, 1864.
Corinth, Mississippi, Siege of, April 29-May 30, 1862.
Corinth, Mississippi, October 3-4, 1862.
Crampton's Gap, Maryland, September 14, 1862.
"The Crater," Virginia (Siege of Petersburg), July 30, 1864.
Cross Keys, West Virginia, June 8, 1862.

Darbytown and New Market Roads, October 7, 1864.
Deep Bottom, Virginia, July 27-28, 1864.
Deep Bottom, Virginia, August 14-16, 1864.
Dinwiddie Court House, Virginia, March 30-31, 1865.
Dranesville, Virginia, December 20, 1861.
Drury's Bluff, May 12-16, 1864.

Elk Creek, Indian Territory, July 17, 1862.
Ezra Chapel, Georgia, July 28, 1864.

Fair Oaks, Virginia, May 31, 1862.
Fair Oaks and Darbytown Road, Virginia, October 27, 1864.
Falling Waters, West Virginia, July 2, 1861.
Farmington, Mississippi, May 3, 1862.
Farmville, Virginia, April 7, 1865.

Fauquier White Sulphur Springs, Virginia, August 24, 1862.
First Bull Run, Virginia, July 21, 1861.
Fisher's Hill, Virginia, September 21-22, 1864.
Fitzhugh's Crossing, Virginia, April 29-30, 1863.
Five Forks, Virginia, April 1, 1865.
Fort Donelson, Tennessee, February 13-16, 1862.
Fort Fisher, North Carolina, January 15, 1865.
Fort Gaines, Alabama, August 3-8, 1864.
Fort Harrison, Virginia, September 28-October 1, 1864.
Fort Henry, Tennessee, February 6, 1862.
Fort Hindman, Arkansas, January 10-11, 1863.
Fort Macon, North Carolina, April 25, 1862.
Fort Morgan, Alabama, August 8-23, 1864.
Fort Pulaski, Georgia, April 10-11, 1862.
Fort Stedman, Virginia, March 29, 1865.
Fort Stevens, District of Columbia, July 12, 1864.
Fort Sumter, South Carolina, April 12, 1861.
Fort Wagner, South Carolina, Assault of July 11, 1863.
Fort Wagner, South Carolina, Assault of July 18, 1863.
Franklin, Tennessee, November 30, 1864.
Franklin's Crossing, Virginia, June 6, 1863.
Fredericksburg, Virginia, December 13, 1863.
Fredericksburg, Virginia, May 3-4, 1863.

Gaine's Mill, Virginia, June 27, 1862.
Gainesville, Virginia, August 28, 1862.
Gettysburg, Pennsylvania, July 1-3, 1863.
Gilbert's Ford, Virginia, September 13, 1864.
Glendale, Virginia, June 30, 1862.
Golding's Farm, June 27-28, 1862.
Goldsboro, North Carolina, December 14-17, 1862.
Goldsboro, North Carolina, March 24, 1865.
Grierson's Raid, Mississippi, April 17-May 2, 1863.
Groveton, Virginia, August 27, 1862.
Guntown, Mississippi, June 10, 1864.

Hagerstown, Maryland, July 6, 1853.
Hanover Courthouse, Virginia, May 27, 1862.
Harper's Ferry, Virginia, September 12-15, 1862.
Harris' Farm, Virginia, May 19, 1864.
Hatcher's Run, Virginia, February 5-7, 1865.
Haw's Shop, Virginia, May 28, 1864.
Hicksford Expedition, Virginia, December 7-12, 1864.
High Bridge, Virginia, April 7, 1865.

Irish Bend, Louisiana, April 14, 1862.
Island #10, Missouri (on Mississippi River), March 15-April 8, 1862.
Iuka, Mississippi, September 19, 1862.

Jackson, Mississippi, May 14, 1863.
Jackson, Mississippi, Siege of, July 10-17, 1863.
Jericho Mill, Virginia, May 23, 1864.
Jerusalem Road, Virginia (see Weldon Railroad).
Jonesboro, Georgia, August 31-September 1, 1864.

Kelly's Ford, Virginia, March 17, 1863.
Kelly's Ford, Virginia, November 7, 1863.
Kelly's Store, Virginia, January 30, 1863.
Kenesaw Mountain, Georgia, June 27, 1864.
Kernstown, Virginia, March 23, 1862.
Kernstown, Virginia, July 24, 1864.
Knoxville, Tennessee, Siege of, November 14-December 17, 1863.

Labadiesville, Louisiana, October 27, 1862.
Laurel Hill, Virginia, May 8-12, 1864.
Lee's Mill, Virginia, April 16, 1862.
Leggett's Hill (Bald's Hill), Georgia, July 20-21, 1864.
Lewis Farm, Virginia, March 29, 1865.
Little Rock Expedition, Arkansas, August 1-September 14, 1863.
Lookout Mountain, Tennessee, November 24-25, 1863.
Lost Mountain, Georgia, June 15-17, 1864.
Lovejoy Station, Georgia, September 2-5, 1864.
Lynchburg, Virginia, June 17-18, 1864.

Malvern Cliff, Virginia, June 30, 1862.
Malvern Hill, Virginia, July 1, 1862.
Malvern Hill, Virginia, August 5, 1862.
Malvern Hill, Virginia, July 28, 1864.
Manassas Gap, Virginia, July 23, 1863.
Martinsburg, West Virginia, July 25, 1864.
Marye's Heights, Virginia, May 3, 1863.
McDowell, Virginia, May 8, 1862.
Mechanicsville, Virginia, June 26, 1862.
Middletown, Virginia, May 24, 1862.
Mine Run, Virginia, November 26-28, 1863.
Middleburg, Tennessee, December 24, 1862.
Missionary Ridge, Tennessee, November 24-25, 1863.
Mobile, Alabama, March 17-April 12, 1865.
Monocacy, Maryland, July 9, 1864.
Morton's Ford, Virginia, October 11, 1863.
Mount Jackson, Virginia, May 3, 1862.
Murfreesboro, Tennessee, (see Stone's River).
Nashville, Tennessee, December 15-16, 1864.
Natural Bridge, Florida, March 6, 1865.
New Berne, North Carolina, March 14, 1862.
New Market, Virginia, May 15, 1864.
New Orleans, Louisiana, April 20-27, 1862.

North Anna River, Virginia, May 9, 1864.
North Anna River, Virginia, May 21-26, 1864.

Oak Grove, Virginia, June 25, 1862.
Olustee, Florida, February 20, 1864.
Opequon Creek, Virginia, September 19, 1864.
Orchard Knob, Tennessee, November 23-24, 1863.
Ox Ford, Virginia, May 24, 1864.

Payne's Farm, Virginia, November 27, 1863.
Peach Orchard, Virginia, June 29, 1862.
Peach Tree Farm, Georgia, July 19-20, 1864.
Pea Ridge, Arkansas, March 7, 1862.
Peebles Farm, Virginia, September 29-October 1, 1864.
Perryville, Kentucky, October 8, 1862.
Petersburg, Virginia, June 9, 1864.
Petersburg, Virginia, Assault of June 15, 1864.
Petersburg, Virginia, Assault of June 18, 1864.
Petersburg, Virginia, Siege of, June 15, 1864-April 2, 1865.
Petersburg, Virginia, Final Assault on, April 2, 1865.
Pickett's Mills, Georgia, May 27, 1864.
Pine Knob, Georgia, June 15-16, 1864.
Pleasant Hill, Louisiana, April 9, 1864.
Plymouth, North Carolina, April 18, 1864.
Poplar Springs Church, Virginia, September 29-October 2, 1864.
Port Gibson, Mississippi, May 1, 1863.
Port Hudson, Louisiana, Assault of May 27, 1863.
Port Hudson, Louisiana, Assault of June 14, 1863.
Port Hudson, Louisiana, Siege of, May 24-July 9, 1863.
Port Republic, Virginia, June 9, 1862.
Prairie Grove, Arkansas, December 6-7, 1862.

Rappahannock Bridge, February 5-7, 1863.
Rappahannock Station, Virginia, November 7, 1863.
Raymond, Mississippi, May 12, 1863.
Reams Station, Virginia, August 25, 1864.
Red River Campaign, Louisiana, April 22-May 21, 1864.
Resaca, Georgia, May 14-15, 1864.
Richmond, Kentucky, August 30, 1862.
Richmond, Virginia, April 3, 1865.
Rich Mountain, Virginia, July 11, 1861.
Ringold, Georgia, November 27, 1863.
Roanoke Island, North Carolina, February 7, 1862.

Sabine Crossroads, Louisiana, April 18, 1864.
Sayler's Creek, Virginia, April 6, 1865.
Salem Church, Virginia, May 3, 1863.
Salem Heights, Virginia, May 4, 1863.

Savage Station, Virginia, June 20, 1862.
Savannah, Georgia, December 10-21, 1864.
Secessionville, South Carolina, June 16, 1863.
Second Bull Run, Virginia, August 29-30, 1862.
Selma, Alabama, April 2, 1865.
Seven Days' Battle, Virginia, June 26-July 2, 1862.
Shenandoah Valley, August 1-31, 1864.
Shiloh, Tennessee, April 6-7, 1862.
Smithfield Crossing, West Virginia, August 29, 1864.
South Mountain, Maryland, September 14, 1862.
Spotsylvania Courthouse, Virginia, May 7-21, 1864.
Springhill, Tennessee, November 29, 1864.
Stevensburg to Richmond Raid, February 28-March 4, 1865.
Stone's River, Tennessee, December 31, 1862-January 2, 1863.
Stony Creek, Virginia, June 28-29, 1864.
Suffolk, Virginia, Siege of, April 13-May 4, 1863.

Taylor's Hole Creek, North Carolina, March 16, 1865.
Todd's Tavern, Virginia, May 7-8, 1864.
Tom's Brook, Virginia, October 8-9, 1864.
Totopotomy River, Virginia, May 28-31, 1864.
Totopotomy, Virginia, June 2, 1864.
Trevilian Station, Virginia, June 11-12, 1864.
Tupelo, Mississippi, July 13-15, 1864.
Turner's Gap, Maryland, September 14, 1862

Upperville, Virginia, June 21, 1863.

Vicksburg, Mississippi, Assault of May 19, 1863.
Vicksburg, Mississippi, Assault of May 22, 1863.
Vicksburg, Mississippi, Siege of, May 19-July 4, 1863.

Ware Bottom Church, Virginia, May 18-20, 1864.
Wauhatchie, Tennessee, October 29, 1863.
Waynesboro, Virginia, March 2, 1865.
Weldon Railroad, Virginia, August 18-21, 1864.
West Point, Virginia, May 7, 1862.
White Oak Road, Virginia, 29 March 1865.
Wilderness, Virginia, May 5-6, 1864.
Williamsburg, Virginia, May 5, 1862.
Wilson's Creek, Missouri, August 10, 1861.
Winchester, Virginia, March 23, 1862.
Winchester, Virginia, May 25, 1862.
Winchester, Virginia, June 13, 1863.
Winchester (Kernstown), Virginia, July 24, 1864.

Yellow Tavern, Virginia, May 11, 1864.
Yorktown, Siege of, Virginia, April 5-May 4, 1862

Appendix D

UNION ROLL OF HONOR

Killed in Action
Abbot, Edward S. '64; Babbitt, Jacob '26; Baxter, William R. '51; Chaffin, William H. '64; Cowdin, Robert J. '59; Crandall, Richard B. '62; Craven, Tunis A.M. '29; Eayre, Thomas W. '61; Gove, Jesse A. '49; Granger, Edward M. '64; Griswold, Charles E. '54; Henderson, Thomas A. '62; Hitchcock, Robert E. '59; Parker, William T. '59; Parmenter, Daniel W. '63; Sabine, John '64 Schall, Edwin '56; Thompson, John B. '61; Ward, James H. '23.
TOTAL: 19

Died of Wounds
Denison, Charles E. '45; Emery, Harvey W. '52; Gould, Jacob P. '49; Granger, Lyman C. '49; Kimball, Edgar A. '44; Lander, Frederick W. '41; Marsh, Samuel '39; Mead, John B.T. '51; Nelson, William '39; Parker, Edward B. '62?; Roelofson, Frederick E. '56; Simmons, Seneca B. '29; Slafter, Judson '47; Stimpson, Francis E. '58; Strong, George C. '47; Taylor, George W. '26; Thompson, Samuel J. '48; Wright, Joseph C. '42.
TOTAL: 18

Died of Disease
Ainsworth, James E. '53; Buel, Julius O. '61; Birchard, Sardis '64; Chase, Edwin J. '57; Colburn, Albert V. '53; Commings, David L.M. '48; Coombs, Arthur W. '64; Drew, Frederick P. '48; Emerson, George W. '42; Hale, Reuben C. '28; Hatch, John E. '46; Head, Henry H. '66; Jones, Edward T. '62; Lee, Douglas '64; Lee, Stephen B. '43; Moore, John H. '38; Pennock, Joseph N. '46; Ransom, Thomas E.G. '51; Rice, George M. '53; Rice, Thomas G. '65; Saben, William S. '50; Sabine, Albert '63; Seymour, Epaphroditus H. '55; Van Rensselaer, Henry '26 .
TOTAL: 24
Grand Total: 61

Appendix E

THOMAS SEAVER'S MEDAL OF HONOR

This appendix summarizes material from the National Archives and Records Administration Medal of Honor file for Col. Thomas O. Seaver, 3rd Vermont Volunteer Infantry (B986-VS-1862). Seaver was awarded his medal 28 years after he displayed "conspicuous gallantry near Spotsylvania Court House" as part of a general review of Medals of Honor presented during the war and new nominations based on revised War Department criteria.

Analysis of the sequence and timing of the nomination and decision process, a summary of Seaver's combat actions, endorsements to the nomination, the individuals involved in the award process, the delivery of the medal, and Seaver's acceptance letter provide interesting insights into his case. The recommendation that a Medal of Honor be presented Colonel Seaver was initiated by General Theodore S. Peck, Adjutant General of the State of Vermont, located in the City of Burlington, March 16, 1892. In his nomination statement Peck requested the medal be presented for "distinguished and gallant conduct at the storming of Marye's Heights, May 3, 1863." Peck refers the War Department to Official Reports prepared at the time by Brevet Major General Lewis A. Grant, Seaver's wartime commander in the Vermont Brigade.

The recommendation was logged into the War Department on March 21, 1892. The same day, Assistant Secretary of War Lewis A. Grant, Seaver's former commander mentioned above, referred the nomination to the Major General Commanding the United States Army (J.M. Schofield) for action. The next day, Schofield returned the nomination to Grant recommending approval but stating that:

> From so long a record embracing numerous acts of distinguished gallantry, it is difficult to select that one for which a medal should be awarded, as
> being the most distinguished of all. I respectfully suggest that General L.A. Grant select himself the special act of distinguished bravery
> for which the medal should be awarded, since he from his personal knowledge of the circumstances is best able to make that selection....

On March 24, 1892, a mere nine days after the nomination was mailed from Vermont and less than four days after its arrival at the War Department, Assistant Secretary of War Grant declared, "Let the medal issue (be) for distinguished gallantry in action near Spotsylvania Court House, May 10, 1864." Given the bureaucratic processes inherent to the War Department, a 72-hour review process, which seemingly included the preparation of an impressive eight page typewritten synopsis of Seaver's battle actions and commendations, is remarkable.   On March 25, 1892, a letter announcing approval of Seaver's award was sent to the Adjutant General of Vermont, and on April 8 the medal itself was transmitted to Seaver via registered mail. Colonel Seaver's acknowledgement of receipt and thank you letter to the War Department were sent from Woodstock, Vermont, on April 15, 1892:

> Maj. F.E. Ainsworth
> My Dear Major
>
> Your kind letter preceding the one transmitting the medal was gladly rcvd. The kind words in your letter and those in the letter of other friends give an added value to the medal itself and without these I could hardly attach much value to it. I am not at all surprised that the War Dept. was greatly perplexed what to give me a medal for and on the whole it was bestowed for "general cussedness."
>
> Truly Yours
> T.O. Seaver

The total time elapsed from the initiation of Seaver's nomination to the mailing of his letter of acceptance was only thirty days. Thomas O. Seaver certainly deserved his Medal of Honor as this book, his war record, and the documentation in his award file amply demonstrate. Nevertheless, his case must have been positively influenced by his comrade and former brigade commander Lewis A. Grant's position as Assistant Secretary of War. Grant singled out his performance in the Spotsylvania Campaign as the most conspicuously gallant act of a combat career marked by deeds of bravery, ranking it superior to his performance at Marye's Heights a year earlier (the action for which he was originally nominated). The author believes strong circumstantial evidence and the timing of events in the award's approval process show Seaver's name likely surfaced in the War Department during the review of potential Civil War officer Medal of Honor candidates, probably by Assistant Secretary of War Grant himself. The expeditious handling of the Seaver case by all concerned, and a nomination supported by an impressive typewritten battle account based on wartime Official Reports rather than by handwritten supporting evidence common at the time, smacks of ongoing "background research" and document preparation prior to the formal medal request by General Peck. In addition, Seaver's acceptance letter, though clearly stating surprise at the turn of events, specifically cites his appreciation of the kind words of his "friends." The award of a Medal of Honor at any time is a rare event. The fact that Thomas O. Seaver's award was processed so rapidly, without a hint of dissent, and linked to an action other than that for which he was originally nominated, represents a clearly exceptional if not unique case.

Appendix F

HOW MANY SERVED: THE DIFFERING NUMBERS

Source	Officers	Enlisted	Unknown	Total
1865 Reveille	160 (incomplete)	"numerous"	none	160+
1872 Curtis Letter	246	?	none	246+
1890 White Paper	250	"many"	none	250+
1896 Honor Roll	281	46	17	344
1898 Ellis History*	424	46	15	485
1911 Ellis History	521	115	none	636
Kimball Book	500+	?	?	500+
1965 Gwin Study**	434	77	5	516
This study	**562**	**78**	**18**	**658**

*First systematic attempt at identifying alumni who served in the Civil War.

Actual Estimated Total: 758+ (includes more than 100 unidentified men who received commissions following attendance as "special military students)."

As stated in this study, the exact total of alumni who served and their ranks will never be known due to the destruction of records in the fire of March 13-14, 1866, and confusion in Norwich University records. All the above sources, with the exception of the author's database, are located in the Norwich University Special Collections and can be accessed there.

* * Not completed or published

Appendix G

RESEARCH GAPS

In conducting research for "*By the Blood of Our Alumni*," I quickly realized I had struck the tip of an historically fascinating iceberg. The more I dug, the more I found. The more I found, the more I realized I had more to discover. For example, it was a fortuitous discovery that the outstanding 19th century historian of the Battle of Gettysburg, Lt. Col. John B. Bachelder ("The Bachelder Papers"), was an alumnus of the Class of 1849. It seems that when Ellis wrote his History of Norwich University, he misspelled Bachelder's name (with a "t") and only listed his initials rather than his first and middle names. For others who are interested in Norwich University's role in The War to Preserve the Union, a proverbial "gold mine" awaits them. Listed below are a few of the research tasks which await the historian, as well as areas of investigation which offer potentially high returns:

* The extensive Norwich archives housed in the Kreitzberg Library need to be comprehensively indexed, studied, and analyzed. The publication of a catalog of available holdings, especially those related to the Civil War, is particularly essential to researchers. This effort was begun under the able supervision of Ms. Julie Bressor, a former Archivist and Head of Special Collections. (see also the reference to the Civil War web site in Appendix A).

* Files developed by the comprehensive study and analysis of our alumni and school archives will eventually be computerized and placed "on line," as has been accomplished for other military colleges (Virginia Military Institute, for example). The establishment and maintenance of a computer database of alumni, particularly of names found nowhere except in rare 19th century university catalogs, would be particularly helpful to researchers. Analysis of apparent gaps in the names of matriculated cadets for the "wartime classes" of 1860-1866 would be historically important and likely to lead to the identification of additional veterans of the conflict. A computer database of Norwich alumni from 1820-1870 has been developed by this author and a copy is in the possession of the Norwich Special Collections.

* The issue of the "other" military colleges founded by Alden Partridge, as well as those established by his followers, needs to be studied. Several of these schools, partic-

ularly those in the South such as the academy in Portsmouth, Virginia, flourished before the Civil War. A 1997 study on Southern military colleges and their alumni in the war entitled *The Young Lions: Confederate Cadets at War* (Stackpole) by James L. Conrad, completely ignores Alden Partridge and these military colleges.

* The compilation of a comprehensive and accurate list of Southerners who attended Norwich and its forerunner, The American Literary, Scientific, and Military Academy, could yield a number of surprises. There are indicators that the role of Alden Partridge and other Norwich alumni in the prewar establishment of the Virginia Military Institute and The Citadel, in the Civil War itself, and their overall impact on the Confederacy is more significant than currently believed.

* Research on Union alumni who fought in the West, in coastal operations, in the Navy and Marine Corps, and with United States Colored Troops has only begun. Indicators discovered during research for this book show the accomplishments of Norwich alumni in the West will match, if not surpass, those who served in the Army of the Potomac.

* Selective detailed biographies of Norwich men who fought in the war, particularly some of those who fought at the brigade and regimental level, should be produced. The careers and performance of combat leaders like Edward Hatch, Thomas O. Seaver, Charles B. Stoughton, Edmund Rice, and Thomas E.G. Ransom, offer many lessons of current relevance. For example, Hatch not only was a major cavalry leader in the Western Theater, but also played a key role in the organization and command of black troops in the postwar years.

* The detailed study of Norwich University itself in the immediate prewar years and during the conflict, especially as compared and contrasted to sister institutions such as the VMI and The Citadel, would provide valuable insights into the development of our citizen-soldiery, highlight potential differences in education and military training between the "citizen-soldier academies" and the Federal academy, thereby providing new and potentially significant data and provide new avenues of analysis.

* Why do figures on the total strength of the Corps of Cadets and the identification of members of the Corps provided by William Arba Ellis in his two histories of Norwich University conflict with data found in contemporary university catalogs? Ellis had access to information not only from these catalogs, but also possibly to documents and catalogs that may now be lost (such as lists of Special Military Students). In addition, Ellis also had access to members of the staff, faculty and Cadet Corps who were on campus before, during, and immediately after the war. It is unfortunate that these differences in his and the author's data cannot be reconciled. Are the answers eventually to be found in the Special Collections at Norwich?

*Attempts at identification of the 100-plus short-term students who attended Norwich in 1861-62 in order to qualify for commissions have been frustrated to date by a lack of sources. The few special students which the author has been able to identify performed with great merit. What other surprises await discovery when more of these men have been identified? As of the date of this publication, a review of the more important surviving Vermont Civil War newspapers has yielded but limited results.

* Lastly, there is clearly a need for further compilation and analysis of accurate data concerning Norwich University and Alden Partridge's citizen-soldier programs. As indicated in the preface, this book is primarily historical narrative rather than historical analysis. Nevertheless, a number of potential interesting and significant analytical issues were raised. For example:

- What was the impact of Norwich and its alumni on the organization, training, and combat performance of New England regiments--particularly those from Vermont and Massachusetts? Generals William T. Sherman and U.S. Grant rated those services highly.

- What was the real role of Norwich University alumni and Alden Partridge in the establishment of military schools and training in Virginia, particularly in the context of the founding of the VMI and the setting up of on-campus military training at the University of Virginia? Is VMI possibly a "Partridge inspired" institution?

- What role, if any, did the numerous Norwich alumni in South Carolina play in the founding of the Citadel?

- Was there a difference in the way West Pointers and Norwich men trained troops and led them in combat? If so, was it a result of their education and training at their respective schools? What was the impact of these differences?

- Why did Norwich alumni in the Army of the Potomac become casualties at a rate significantly higher than the norm for the Union Army?

- What was the impact of alumni who attended other Partridge academies or schools founded by his disciples? For example, Lt. Col. William W. Dudley, 19th Indiana ("Iron Brigade") attended The Collegiate and Commercial Institute in New Haven, Connecticut. He lost a leg at Gettysburg and was breveted brigadier general for gallantry. How many more like him are there, where did they serve, and what was their impact?

Appendix H

PITFALLS IN THE NORWICH RECORDS

I often had difficulty deciding whether or not to include an alumnus as a potential Civil War veteran. One of the following such examples of that dilemma is quite clear, while one is far more difficult to interpret.

Captain James A. Hall, Class of 1843 or 1862? A detailed review of Norwich publications, cadet catalogs, and wartime Rolls of Honor initially seemed straightforward enough: the famous Maine artilleryman James A. Hall, born in 1835, was a Norwich alumnus who served with high courage and great distinction in the war. In fact, Captain Hall was featured in an article by this author on Norwich men at Gettysburg (see bibliography). After including extensive, high impact and high interest materials on Hall in this book, I discovered a potential "glitch" in the story. Norwich catalogs of the late 1830's list a James A. Hall who, upon further research, may have been a second Hall. Or was he? The James A. Hall listed in these catalogs died in 1843. No other James A. Hall was found catalogs of the period, specifically those in which the Class of 1843 were listed. Several interpretations are possible: the only James A. Hall to have attended Norwich died in 1843; there were two James A. Halls, one of which served in the Civil War; or, that a "Captain Hall" attended Norwich, quite likely as a special military student in 1861, but was not listed in the university catalogs and is one of the "missing 100."

Of particular importance, I believe, is the fact that the first major Civil War Roll of Honor published by Norwich in 1865 lists James A. Hall of the 2nd Maine Battery as an alumnus. Is this because professors and cadets remembered him being on campus in 1861? It is hard to imagine instructors such as Gen. Alonzo Jackman, a permanent fixture on campus from 1836 and who knew every cadet, would confuse Capt. James A. Hall of Maine with Cadet James A. Hall who died in 1843. Furthermore, in possibly pertinent and related data, Norwich produced a number of distinguished Civil War artillerymen, including Truman Seymour, Dunbar Ransom, Edward Williston, Frank Amsden, and Evan Thomas. Norwich had obtained artillery pieces from the state in the early 1850s and ensured its cadets were trained on them. It appears more likely that the Captain Hall received his training as a special wartime military student than by "on the job training." After reaching these conclusions I felt that, despite a potential injustice to my alma mater and to Captain Hall's particularly distinguished actions at Fredericksburg and Gettysburg, that extensive details of his wartime accomplishments should be omitted from the text. Perhaps it was wiser to err on the side of historical conservatism and exclude extensive reporting on Hall, but I could easily have overachieved in this matter.

Second example: Lieutenant Colonel Walter H. Hubbard. When I discovered the career of this apparent alumnus from the Class of 1852, who was cited in several Rolls of Honor, I was impressed. A lieutenant colonel and veteran of the famed First Vermont Brigade, wounded in action, and cited for gallantry; all in all, a sterling example of our citizen-soldiery. To my chagrin, I later discovered that there were at least two Walter H. Hubbards in Vermont: the war hero (who did not attend Norwich), and a confirmed Norwich alumnus. The Norwich man apparently moved to the Midwest on the eve of the war and was involved in a retail business there during the conflict. Both myself and Norwich researchers who had gone before me had been fooled by identical names and initials into believing the war hero was an alumnus. Similar problems could have occurred with other potential alumni.

In sum, the potential errors and pitfalls encountered in a work such as this, with so many missing records and few firsthand accounts, are numerous. I trust I have eliminated as many errors and misidentifications as I could; no doubt some deserving alumni have been omitted and possibly others, who were not alumni, mistakenly included. Hopefully historians and researchers who come after me will develop new data, make corrections, and improve this baseline effort.

ENDNOTES

1. ORIGINS

1. W.F. Beyer and O.F. Keydel, editors, *Deeds of Valor: How America's Civil War Heroes Won the Congressional Medal of Honor* (Detroit, 1903), p. 235. Hereinafter cited as Beyer and Keydel, *Deeds of Valor*; Edmund Rice, "Repelling Lee's Last Blow at Gettysburg," *Battles and Leaders of the Civil War*, Vol. III (New York, 1956), pp. 387-390. Hereinafter cited as *Battles and Leaders*; Edmund Rice file, *Special Collections*, Kreitzberg Library, Norwich University (NU), Northfield, Vermont. Hereinafter cited as *NU Special Collections* with file name; References to the author's extensive personal computerized records of Norwich matriculants are cited in the text as the Poirier, *Alumni Database*. Other cross references to the authors files used in this text are cited, for example, as Poirier, *Appendix A*. This file is a synthesis of all the various sources of data on Norwich alumni found and used during the project. Details and sources for individual alumni service and achievements are available through the author. Edmund Rice's actions at Gettysburg have been captured in an impressive Dale Gallon Civil War historical painting commissioned by Norwich University. The painting was unveiled in a formal ceremony at Norwich on October 3, 1996, and is now permanently displayed in the university's Medal of Honor Room as a tribute to Maj. Edmund Rice (Class of 1860), First Lt. John B. Thompson (Class of 1861), and to all Norwich alumni who served in the War to Preserve the Union. The painting featuring Rice, with the kind permission of Mr. Gallon and Norwich University, also serves as the book jacket for this work. The "clash of the flags" portrayed in the painting was reported in a Gettysburg newspaper as early as July 1865, see "An Incident at Gettysburg," *Adams Sentinel* (Gettysburg, Pennsylvania, July 25, 1863), p. 1. It is ironic that the commander of the 14th Virginia, Col. James G. Hodges, attended the Partridge founded Portsmouth Literary, Scientific, and Military Academy in Virginia. Thus, the two pivotal units in the incident were led by citizen-soldiers educated and trained in the Norwich tradition.

2. At least four Norwich alumni, Rear Adm. Hiram Paulding Class of 1823), Commodores Josiah Tattnall Class of 1823), John H. Graham Class of 1827), and Samuel Partridge Class of 1822), saw service in the War of 1812, several years prior to the actual founding of the university, William Arba Ellis, *Norwich University, Her History, Her Graduates, Her Roll of Honor*, Vol. I of three Volumes (Montpelier, Vermont, 1911), pp. 2-3. Hereinafter referred to as Ellis, *Norwich University*. Norwich is second only to West Point in seniority among American military colleges, the national academy having been established in 1802.

3. Ellis, *Norwich University* I, pp. 2-3; *Bugle Notes* (West Point, New York, 1959), pp. 26-27; Gary Thomas Lord, "*Alden Partridge: Promoter of an 'American System' of Education*," Annual Meeting of the American Military Institute, Lexington, Virginia, 14 April 1989, pp. 3-5. Hereinafter referred to as Lord, *Alden Partridge*. Dr. Lord's paper is not widely available but copies can be obtained from the Norwich University library.

4. Lord, *Alden Partridge*, p. 11; Ellis, *Norwich University* I, p. 6; *Ibid.*, pp. 2-3.

5. Brian Smith and Gary T. Lord, *Norwich University 1819* (Louisville, Kentucky, 1995), p. 33. Hereinafter referred to as Smith and Lord, *Norwich University 1819*; Lord, *Alden Partridge*, p. 8. In the early days of the A.L.S.& M.A., more than 25 years before the establishment of the United States Naval Academy at Annapolis, a number of active duty naval officers studied naval science at Norwich. In addition, many alumni entered into the naval service before the Civil War.

6. Ellis, *Norwich University* I, p. 209.

7. William A. Ellis, *Norwich University: Her History, Her Graduates, Her Roll of Honor* (Concord, New Hampshire, 1898), p. 3. Hereinafter cited as Ellis, *Norwich University 1898*. Prior to 1825, 73 cadets from the South, including 45 from South Carolina, attended Norwich. In 1826, 102 of 296 members of the Corps of Cadets were southerners; Ellis, *Norwich University* I, pp. 7-8; Ellis, *Norwich University* I, p. 6; Association of Collegiate and Professional Students, *The University Quarterly* (New Haven, Connecticut, April 1861), p. 416. Hereinafter referred to as *The University Quarterly*. Lord and Smith, *Norwich University 1819*, p. 42; Ellis, *Norwich University 1898*, p. 3; Robert Gwin, unpublished manuscript, *The Contribution of Norwich University to the Civil War*, Norwich University Special Collections (Northfield, Vermont, 1965), pp. 126-127. Hereinafter referred to as Gwin, *Norwich in the Civil War*; Ellis, *Norwich University* I, pp. 9, 73. Lord, *Alden Partridge*, pp. 16-18.

8. Lord, *Alden Partridge*, p. 28; Alden Partridge, "Discourse on Education," in Francois Peyre-Ferry, *The Art of Epistolary Composition* (Middletown, Connecticut, 1826), pp. 269-271; the entire lecture is found on pp. 263-280.

9. Ellis, *Norwich University* I, p. 13; *Ibid*, pp. 128-131. With the exception of 1861 (see below), commencement exercises were held even if no diplomas were to be awarded. It became the setting for alumni reunions (Founders Day), patriotic speeches, cadet drills, and religious services.

10. Ellis, *Norwich University* I, pp. 15-16, p. 21; *Ibid.*, pp. 25-28.

11. Ellis, *Norwich University* I, p. 60-62; *Ibid.*, pp. 63-69; Ellis, *Norwich University 1898*, pp. 3-4; Ellis, *Norwich University* I, pp. 139-140. The various relocations of the institution and the devastating fire of March 13-14, 1866, are undoubtedly factors in modern difficulties identifying all cadet matriculants for the years before and during the Civil War. For example, Ellis, *Norwich University 1898*, p. 7 specifically refers to records of classes attending between 1828-1836 as lost; see also Gwin, *Norwich in the Civil War*, p. 5. A number of alumni have been identified during research for this book for whom no attendance record has yet been found at Norwich. There are others who are listed as alumni in contemporary and early post-Civil War university research on the conflict who are not cited by Ellis in the 1911 three-volume history of Norwich, and who cannot currently be confirmed or excluded from having attended Norwich. It is clear, however, that other alumni, perhaps a substantial number, remain to be identified. In addition, Norwich University has stated on several occasions since the Civil War that the record of military service of our alumni in that conflict, particularly that of Southern alumni, is substantially incomplete, for example, see *The Rutland Weekly Herald*, August 17, 1865 p. 4. These facts are the basis for concluding that figures presented in this book for the total number of alumni in service during the war are conservative and, in many cases, the details of their service and accomplishments incomplete. It is also possible that some men who claim to have been alumni or who have been identified as Norwich alumni are not, in reality, former cadets. Lastly, the names of more than 100 students who took special military and tactics courses to qualify as officers during the Civil War, an undoubtedly important group, have yet to be found and may never be recoverable.

12. Ellis, *Norwich University 1898*, p.7; *Ibid.*, pp. 42, 74. It goes without saying that the opening of The Virginia Military Institute in 1839 and the Citadel in 1842 further reduced, although it did not stop completely, the number of Southern cadets attending Norwich.

13. Ellis, *Norwich University 1898*, pp. 14-15.

14. Homer White, *History of Norwich University, 1890* (Northfield, Vermont, 1891), p. 10. Hereinafter referred to as White, *Norwich University, 1890*. Since spring 1997, the Norwich University Corps of Cadets has worn the traditional pre-war Partridge created uniform for dress parades and formal occasions--" *La plus sa change, la plus sa reste la meme chose.*"

15. Ellis, *Norwich University* I, p. 91; Ellis, *Norwich University 1898*, pp. 13, 42-43. For a time, Captain Partridge actually presided over a "rival" academy called the American Literary, Scientific, and Military University in Norwich; Ellis, *Norwich University* I, p. 91; statement attributed to Truman B. Ransom (Class of 1825), quoted in Smith and Lord, *Norwich University 1819*, p. 13.

16. Lord, *Alden Partridge*, p. 21; Thomas H. Ellis, "Letter to Alden Partridge," May 9, 1835, *The Partridge Papers*, Norwich University Special Collections; Keith E. Gibson, Director of Virginia Military Institute Museum Programs, letter to the author, April 3, 1996. The full impact of Partridge and his "American System of Education on the establishment of VMI and The Citadel is likely substantial and constitutes an appropriate subject for future study.

17. Lord, *Alden Partridge*, pp. 19-23; John Bigelow Jr., *Chancellorsville* (New York, 1995), p. 16. Hereinafter referred to as Bigelow, *Chancellorsville*; Ellis, *Norwich University* I, pp. 395-402; the Virginia Military Institute founded in 1839, was the other. The Charlottesville program of course, is the earliest example at a civilian campus of what would evolve into the Reserve Officer Training Corps (R.O.T.C.) of later years. "List of Student Subscribers to Captain Partridges Course of Lectures delivered at the University of Virginia 1835-1836," *The Partridge Papers*, Norwich University Special Collections; William Couper, *One Hundred years at V.M.I.*, Four Volumes (Richmond, Virginia, 1939), Vol. III, pp. 123-124.

18. Ellis, *Norwich University* II, pp. 211-212.

19. Ellis, *Norwich University* I, pp. 402-404; Poirier, *Alumni Database*. Serendipitous discoveries made during research for this book indicate the numbers of Norwich men serving in these wars, particularly the Mexican War, are probably much higher than Ellis believed.

20. Poirier, *Alumni Database*; Ellis, *Norwich University* I, pp. 403-404. Colonel Thomas H. Seymour (Class of '28) later served as commander of the 12th United States Infantry.

21. Ellis, *Norwich University* I, p. 126.

22. Ellis, *Norwich University* I, p. 126-127.

23. Ellis, *Norwich University 1898*, p. 15; *Ibid.*, pp. 14, 4-5

24. C.B. Stoughton, T.W. Eayre, and F.C. Peirce, editors, *University Reveille* , Vol. 2, No. 1 (Norwich, Vermont, April 1861), p. 4. The author unsuccessfully attempted to identify the names and number of Southern cadets on campus when the war began. Most likely, they would have returned to their native states as Southern cadets at West Point did. Unfortunately, no copy of the 1860-1861 Catalogue listing members of the corps of cadets for that period has survived in the Norwich Special Collections.

2. BULL RUN & BALL'S BLUFF

1. Ellis, *Norwich University* II, p. 372. A brevet was a commission promoting an officer to a higher rank without awarding him the pay commensurate with that rank. Brevets provided a limited authority to act in the higher rank under specified circumstances and could be awarded for gallantry, service, or a combination of the two. The use of brevets was widely employed by the United States Army, particularly in the later stages of the war; see Morris Schaff, *The Spirit of Old West Point, 1858-1862* (Boston, 1908), pp. 246-247, and Roger D. Hunt & Jack D. Brown, *Brevet Brigadier Generals in Blue*, reprint (Gaithersburg, Maryland, 1990), pp. v-xx. Hereinafter referred to as Hunt and Brown, *Brevet Brigadier Generals in Blue*.

2. George Blood French, "To Calvin & Valeria French," April 14, 1861, in unpublished letters provided to the author by Ms. Linda Margaret Farr Welch.

3. Bigelow, *Chancelorsville*, p. 16; Philip Katcher, *The Civil War Source Book* (Facts on File Inc., New York, 1992), pp. 229-231. It should be noted that the Confederacy did not establish a national military academy during its existence. The military colleges in Virginia were the Virginia Military Institute and Alden Partridge's academy at Portsmouth, The Virginia Literary, Scientific, and Military Academy (renamed The Virginia Collegiate Institute).

4. W.H. Johnson, J.V. Sweeter, and J.C. Boy, editors, Vol. 5, No. 1, *The University Reveille* (Norwich, Vermont, April 1864), p. 5.

5. *The University Quarterly*, Vol. IV- July and Oct. 1861, p. 143; *University Reveille,* Vol. 3, No. 1, April 1862, p. 4.

6. Ellis, *Norwich University 1898*, p. 78. Ellis, in his 1911 history indicates that a graduation was held on August 13-14, 1862, but no programme of its events had survived which may account for conflicting reports about the graduation situation in 1862; Ellis, *Norwich University* I, p. 131; Poirier, *Alumni Database;* University Reveille, Vol. 5, No. 1 (Norwich, Vermont, April, 1864), p. 5.

7. Poirier, *Alumni Database;* United States War Department, *The War of the Rebellion: A Compilation of the Official Records of the Union and Confederate Armies*, 70 volumes in 128 parts (Washington, D.C., 1880-1901, Series 1, Vol. 2, pp. 6-9. Hereinafter cited as *OR*, followed by appropriate volume and part, all books are series 1 unless otherwise noted; George G. Benedict, *Vermont in the Civil War*, Volume I (The Free Press Association, Burlington, Vermont, 1886), pp. 11-12. Hereinafter cited as Benedict, *Vermont in the Civil War*. At the end of 1860, Jackman commanded the only organized and functional brigade of Vermont State Militia. Ellis, *Norwich University* II, p. 269; Howard Coffin, *Full Duty: Vermonters in the Civil War* (Woodstock, Vermont, 1993), p. 52. Hereinafter cited as Coffin, *Full Duty.*

8. Peter H. Haraty, *History of the Vermont National Guard* (Burlington, Vermont, 1982), p. 96. Hereinafter cited as Haraty, *Vermont National Guard;* Poirier, *Alumni Database;* Ellis, *Norwich University* II, p. 269; Benedict, *Vermont in the Civil War* I, pp. 19-20; Peck, *Revised Roster of Vermont Volunteers*, p. 5; Jackman and Vermont's Adjutant General H.H. Baxter worked in concert to select the regiment's companies and officers. The 1st Vermont's Major was Harry N. Worthen (Class of '57), whose "Bradford Guards" were considered to be one of the best drilled militia companies in the state. Worthen later served as lieutenant colonel of the 4th Vermont. Norwich alumnus Sumner H. Lincoln (Class of 1862?) began his service as a private in the 1st Vermont and later rose to command the Vermont Brigade's 6th Regiment.

9. Ellis, *Norwich University 1898*, pp. 77-78; Washburn, *Vermont AG Reports, 1863*, pp. 55-56, for associated costs to the state of Vermont. Beginning in the spring of 1862, the recruit and unit rendezvous camp at Brattleboro, Vermont was the site of most of these cadet training assignments. In the fall of 1862, Norwich cadets drilled the entire Second (New) Vermont Brigade (12th, 13th, 14th, 15th, and 16th Vermont Volunteers) before it left the state; Washburn, *Vermont AG Reports, 1864*, p. 6; Benedict, *Vermont in the Civil War* I, p. 405. Author records and Poirier, *Alumni Database* (also see Appendix B); Leon Burr Richardson, *History of Dartmouth College*, Volume II (Hanover, New Hampshire, 1932), p. 504; Stephen G. Abbott, *The First Regiment New Hampshire Volunteers in the Great Rebellion* (Keene, New Hampshire, 1890), p. 95 (for Norwich cadets at Dartmouth); Ellis, *Norwich University* I, p. 405; Gwin, *Norwich in the Civil War*, pp. 2-3. These men, of course, are not counted as alumni. For an interesting sidelight involving Norwich, Bowdoin, and the legendary Joshua Lawrence Chamberlain, see Chapter 5. Many alumni who fought for the South also served as drillmasters; Poirier, *Alumni Database.*

10. Poirier, *Alumni Database;* Ellis, *Norwich University 1898*, pp. 76-77; *The Reveille*, Vol. IV, No. 1 (Northfield Vermont, Oct., 1884), p.5.

11. William Gilham, *Manual of Instruction for the Volunteers and Militia of the United States* (Baltimore, Maryland, 1861). Hereinafter referred to as *Gilham;* Paddy Griffith, *Battle in the Civil War*, (Camberly, Surrey, England, 1986), p. 100. Hereinafter referred to as Griffith,

Battle in the Civil War, Ellis, *Norwich University* I, pp. 405-408 and Vol. II, pp. 421-22. At least 42 alumni served as drillmasters in units assigned to the Army of the Potomac, Poirier, *Alumni Database*, Gwin, *Norwich in the Civil War*, pp. 100-105; Ellis, *Norwich University 1898*, pp. 76-77.

12. Charles C. Calhoun, *A Small College in Maine: Two Hundred Years of Bowdoin* (Brunswick, Maine, 1993), p. 184; Ellis, *Norwich University* I-III; Poirier, *Appendix A*; also see Chapter 9.

13. Philip S. Paludan, *A People's Contest: The Union and the Civil War* (New York, 1988), pp. 132-33; the author's *Alumni Database* indicates that at least 513 of the 714 alumni from the Classes of 1820-1861 who were living, who were not too old, and for whom information was available, served in the war.

14. Participation of these 241 alumni at a rate equal to alumni whose wartime activities are known would add 207 additional Norwich men to the known total of 656 participants. Given the author's research, the current lack of knowledge on alumni who fought for the South, the activities of the "missing" 241, the "unknown" special military students, and those alumni whose records of matriculation are lost, an estimate of about 950 total Norwich alumni serving in the Civil War appears reasonable. Several previously unknown alumni have been identified during research in archival records, primary and secondary sources, and unit histories. Particularly for those who were officers, or initially enlisted men who later earned commissions, it was found in those sources that their recommendation for commissions and/or positions was at least partially based on their attendance "at Capt. Partridge's Academy" or "at the Military Academy in Norwich, Vermont;" Ellis, *Norwich University* I, p. 478. A major fire on the Norwich campus March 13-14, 1866, destroyed the University's major building and some records. A significant example of an alumnus whose attendance at Norwich was unknown prior to this study, is Col. William W. Robinson, commander of the 7th Wisconsin Volunteer Infantry Regiment and of the famed Iron Brigade. His connection to Norwich was revealed in the *History of the Iron Brigade*, 4th Ed. (see below) and in material provided by the Wisconsin Historical Society (see below). Information developed since that time, including material from Wisconsin archives, indicates Robinson probably attended Norwich sometime in the period 1836-41.

15. James I. Robertson Jr., *Soldiers Blue and Gray* (University of South Carolina Press, Columbia, 1988), p. 4. Hereinafter referred to as Robertson, *Soldiers Blue and Gray*. Charles Bowers letter, April 21, 1861, *Massachusetts Historical Society* (Boston, Massachusetts), *Civil War Microfilm Collection*, Part II, Reel 15. Hereinafter referred to as Bowers Letters, *MHS* and the appropriate reel (15 or 16). Bowers' son Charles E. (Charlie) Bowers, later served with his father in Company "G," 32nd Massachusetts Infantry (June 1862-October 1864). Charlie was severely wounded in action at Gettysburg and eventually discharged for disability. In order to facilitate readability, some letters have been edited by the author.

16. Bowers Letters, *MHS*, Reel 15.

17. S.T. Learnard to Oscar A. Learnard, April 24, 1861, Norwich University Special Collections. Despite his mother's wishes that he remain a civilian, Oscar O. Learnard (Class of 1855) spent two years serving as the lieutenant colonel of the 1st Kansas Volunteer Infantry.

18. These seven alumni were Assistant Surgeon J.Q.A. McOllister (Class of '53), First Lt. and Regimental Quartermaster W.E. Farrar (Class of '56), Second Lt. G.W. Hobbs (Class of '58), Sgt. J. Stedman (Class of '59), Corp. G.W. Childs (Class of 1867), Corp. A.A. Shattuck (Class of '64), and Pvt. G.F. Otis (Class of '67). Sergeant Major S.W. Shattuck (Class of '60) caught up to his regiment in Washington after the Baltimore incident; Leo T. Baldwin, "First Blood in Baltimore," in *America's Civil War*, November 1995 (Leesburg, Virginia, 1995), pp. 34-36. The statistics on alumni class, war service, and unit associations were gathered from wartime *Rolls of Honor* in the Norwich University *Reveille*, 1863-65, and that of 15 April, 1896, from the Norwich University History of 1898, from the vastly expanded university history published in 1911, from federal and state records, and from unpublished primary source

data such as letters and diaries. For a summary of the author's complete roll of known alumni names, classes, service, and units, see Poirier, *Appendices A* and *B*.

19. Poirier, *Alumni Database* and *Appendix B.*

20. James B. Fry, "McDowell's Advance to Bull Run," *Battles and Leaders* I, p. 173. Joseph R. Carr, "Operations of 1861 About Fort Monroe," *Battles and Leaders* I, pp. 148-151; *Benedict, Vermont in the Civil War* I, pp. 42-55; Ellis, *Norwich University* II, pp.460, 523, 576; the Norwich men of the 1st Vermont at Big Bethel were First Lt. Solomon E. Woodward (Class of '58) and Pvt. Sumner H. Lincoln (Class of '62?) Company "B;" Second Lt. Levi G. Kingsley (Class of '56), Company "K," and Pvt. Elias F. Smith (Class of '61), Company "K." Bruce Catton, *The Centennial History of the Civil War. The Coming Fury,* Three Volumes (New York, 1961-63), Vol. One, pp. 436-437. Hereinafter cited by author and volume; William Tecumseh Sherman, *Memoirs of General W.T. Sherman* (New York, 1990) pp. 196-197. Hereinafter cited as Sherman, *Memoirs.*

21. Baxter would later serve on General McClellan's staff, be placed in charge of the 1,500 bed Campbell General Hospital in Washington, and serve as Chief Medical Officer for the Provost Marshal General's Bureau; *Benedict, Vermont in the Civil War* II, p. 787; Irwin Silber, compiler and editor, *Songs of the Civil War,* (New York, 1995), p. 11. Hereinafter referred to as Silber, *Songs of the Civil War;* Timothy J. Reese, *Syke's Regular Infantry Division, 1861-1864: A History of Regular United States Infantry Operations in the Eastern Theater* (Jefferson, North Carolina, 1990), p.33. Hereinafter cited as Reese, *Sykes' Regulars.*

22. Fry, *Battles and Leaders* I, p. 194; See Poirier, *Appendix B.*

23. Material listing alumni in the paragraphs immediately preceeding this reference are from the author's *Alumni Database;* William C. Davis, *Battle at Bull Run* (Mechanicsburg, Pennsylvania, 1977), pp. 183-83. Hereinafter cited as Davis, *Bull Run;* Appendix B; Alan T. Nolan, *The Iron Brigade: A Military History,* 4th Edition (Bloomington, Indiana, 1994), pp. 9-10, 324. Hereinafter cited as Nolan, *Iron Brigade; OR,* Vol. 2, pt. 1, pp. 351 and 371. Interestingly Sherman, who would later render high praise to Norwich for its services in the war, stated that Coon "was a good-hearted gentleman, who knew no more of the military art than a child; whereas his lieutenant colonel Peck, had been to West Point, and knew the drill," Nolan, *Iron Brigade,* p. 10. Sherman said this despite the fact that Coon had spent at least three years at Norwich where he must have picked up some military knowledge in that time! Although Sherman may have been ignorant of Coon's background, perhaps this event foreshadowed the West Point-Volunteer rivalry which became particularly virulent in the eastern armies. Regardless of Sherman's opinion of Coon, he later surrounded himself with volunteer officers in the west. Two Norwich alumni in particular, Maj. Gen. Joseph A. Mower (Class of '46) and Brig. Gen.Thomas E. G. Ransom (Class of '51), ranked among his personal favorites; see also Catton, *Mr. Lincoln's Army,* pp. 121-122, for additional details on the West Point-Volunteer controversy which was a major issue to contemporaries. It is also worthy of note that when the history of the 2nd Wisconsin was written, several officers and enlisted men of the unit protested the treatment of Coon and wrote the unit historian who then included their letters in the his unit history. In them, Coon was commended for his actions before 1st Bull Run and in the battle itself; George H. Otis, *The Second Wisconsin Infantry,* reprint (Dayton, Ohio, 1984), pp. 107-10, 113-15; *OR,* Vol. 2, pt. 1, p. 373.

24. Davis, *Bull Run,* pp. 220-21; Poirier, *Appendix B;* Catton, *The Coming Fury,* pp. 461-62; *OR,* Vol. 2, pt. 1, pp. 431-434.

25. Ellis, *Norwich University* II, p. 622; Benedict, *Vermont in the Civil War* I, pp. 75-76; Gwin, *Norwich in the Civil War,* p. 3. The first Norwich alumnus, and also the first Union naval officer known to have been killed in the war, was Capt. James H. Ward (Class of '23), United States Navy, and commander of the Potomac Flotilla; he was killed in action at Aquia Creek, June 27, 1861.

26. Catton, *The Coming Fury*, pp. 467-471; Bruce Catton, *The Civil War: Mr. Lincoln's Army*, reprint, Volume One (New York, 1984), p. 38. Hereinafter cited as *Catton* with appropriate volume.

27. Catton, *Mr. Lincoln's Army*, pp.42-43. The 2nd Maine went "on strike" and wished to return home with the 90-day regiments, but the 2nd's men had enlisted for two and three years; 63 of them spent the rest of the war breaking rocks in the disciplinary barracks on the Dry Tortugas off Florida. A different tack was used with the 79th New York: refusing to perform prescribed duties, they were surrounded with fully armed regular battalions of infantry and cavalry and a regular artillery battery. Suitably impressed, they returned to duty. McClellan took their colors away and kept them for a month before they were restored to the regiment with an appropriate flourish. Frederick H. *Dyer, A Compendium of the War of the Rebellion*, reprint, Vol. I (Dayton, Ohio, 1978), p.272. Hereinafter cited as Dyer, *Compendium* with appropriate volume; Francis T. Miller, *The Photographic History of the Civil War*, Ten Volumes (Hartford, Connecticut, 1910), Vol. I, p. 337. Hereinafter referred to as Miller, *Photographic History*, Benedict, *Vermont in the Civil War* II, p. 777. Colburn had been sought by the governor of Vermont to command the 3rd Vermont but his services had been in the Regular Army were deemed "too valuable to lose;" Benedict, *Vermont in the Civil War*, Vol. I, pp. 127-128.

28. Nolan, *Iron Brigade*, p. 38. An alumnus' name followed by a '? class designator indicates uncertainty as to, or the non-availability of, that alumnus' class designation; W. K. Wright, *"Band of Brothers": The Record of Company B, Seventh Wisconsin Volunteer Infantry*, Unpublished Typescript, 1971, pp. 40-41. Hereinafter referred to as Wright, *7th Wisconsin*; Silber, *Songs of the Civil War*, p. 21; Miller, *Photographic History* IX, p. 156; Glenn Tucker, *High Tide at Gettysburg: The Pennsylvania Campaign* (New York, 1958), p.109. Hereinafter referred to as Tucker, *High Tide at Gettysburg*; Silber, *Songs of the Civil War*, pp. 22-23.

29. Phillipe, Comte de Paris, "McClellan Organizing the Grand Army," *Battles and Leaders* II, pp. 112-22; Catton, *Mr. Lincoln's Army*, pp. 45-50; Ellis, *Norwich University* II, pp. 160-161; George A. Bruce, *The Twentieth Massachusetts Volunteer Infantry, 1861-1865* (Cambridge, Massachusetts, 1906), pp. 23, 30-68. Hereinafter cited as Bruce, *Twentieth Massachusetts*; Robert Garth Scott, editor, Fallen Leaves: The *Civil War Letters of Major Henry Livermore Abbott* (Kent, Ohio, 1991), pp. 50-51. Hereinafter referred to as Scott, *Fallen Leaves*.

30. Richard B. Irwin, "Ball's Bluff and the Arrest of General Stone," *Battles and Leaders* II, pp. 128-130.

31. Scott, *Fallen Leaves*, pp. 66-67.

32. Bruce, *Twentieth Massachusetts*, p. 54; Catton, *Mr. Lincoln's Army*, pp. 48-49; *OR*, Vol. 5, pt. 1, pp. 317-320; Ellis, *Norwich University* II, pp. 337-338; *Ibid.*, pp. 638-643, 649; Ernest L. Waitt, compiler, *History of the Nineteenth Regiment Massachusetts Volunteer Infantry, 1861-1865* (Salem, Massachusetts, 1906), pp. 22-31. Hereinafter cited as Waitt, *Nineteenth Massachusetts*; Ellis, *Norwich University* II, pp. 337-38. When General Lander died in March 1862, General McClellan issued a General Order of the Army of the Potomac mourning his passing and citing his services, and also served as a pall bearer at Lander's funeral; Robert Hunt Rhodes, editor, *All for the Union: The Civil War Diary and Letters of Elisha Hunt Rhodes* (Lincoln, Rhode Island, 1985), p. 48; Bruce, *Twentieth Massachusetts*, pp. 64-65, 74; Catton, *Mr. Lincoln's Army*, p. 50.

33. Miller, *Photographic History* VII, p. 47; Bruce, *Twentieth Massachusetts*, p. 69.

34. Benedict, *Vermont in the Civil War* I, p. 95; Poirier, *Alumni Database*, Ellis, *Norwich University 1898*, p. 95; Theodore S. Peck, *Revised Roster of Vermont Volunteers and Lists of Vermonters Who Served in the Army and Navy in the War of the Rebellion, 1861-66* (Montpelier, Vermont, 1892), pp. 50, 496-647. Hereinafter cited as Peck, *Revised Roster of Vermont Volunteers*.

35. Nolan, *Iron Brigade*, pp. 36-37, 307. The couple was married on May 9, 1862.

36. See Poirier, *Appendices A* and *B* for the names of these alumni and the regiments they served in. Classes and names are drawn from *Norwich University* and other records as compiled

in the author's *Alumni Database*. It is also worth noting that surgeons from Massachusetts and Vermont, a number of whom were alumni, were deemed the most qualified in the army. In fact, Vermont's testing of candidates was not only the strictest of any state, but also the candidates military rank was determined by his final standing on the exams; Benedict, *Vermont in the Civil War* I, p.125; George Worthington Adams, *Doctors in Blue, The Medical History of the Union Army in the Civil War* (New York, 1952), pp. 10-11.

37. Philippe, Comte de Paris, "McClellan Organizing the Grand Army," *Battles and Leaders* II, pp. 116-122; Catton, *Mr. Lincoln's Army*, pp. 60-63.

3. THE PENINSULA CAMPAIGN THROUGH FREDERICKSBURG

1. Stephen W. Sears, *To the Gates of Richmond: The Peninsula Campaign* New York, 1992), pp. 9-10, 13-14, 21-22. Hereinafter referred to as Sears, *The Peninsula Campaign*.; United States Congress, Joint Committee on the Conduct of the War, extracts from the *Report of the Joint Committee on the Conduct of the War 1863-1866*, two volumes (Milwood, New York, 1977) Vol. I, pp. 242, 250, 578-581. Hereinafter cited as U.S. Congress, *Wade Committee*; William J. Miller, "Logistics, Friction and McClellan's Strategy for the Peninsula Campaign," in William J. Miller, editor, *The Peninsula Campaign of 1862* (Campbell, California, 1995), pp. 132-134.

2. Poirier, *Alumni Database*. These regiments included, but are not limited to, the 8th Illinois Cavalry; 19th, 20th and 22nd Massachusetts; 4th Michigan; the 5th New Hampshire; 16th New York; 5th and 10th Pennsylvania Reserves; 83rd Pennsylvania; the First Vermont Brigade--2nd, 3rd, 4th, 5th and 6th Vermont; 4th and 17th United States Infantry; 1st and 2nd United States Sharpshooters; and the 5th Wisconsin.

3. Sears, *Peninsula Campaign*, pp. 38-39; Catton, *Mr. Lincoln's Army*, pp. 66-67, 73-75.

4. Wilbur Fisk, Emil and Ruth Rosenblatt, editors, *Hard Marching Every Day: The Civil War Letters Private Wilbur Fisk* (University Press of Kansas, 1992), pp. 20-21. Hereinafter referred to as Fisk, *Hard Marching*. Private Fisk was not a Norwich alumnus but his letters to a Vermont newspaper describing combat involving the 2nd Vermont and the Vermont Brigade, in which dozens of Norwich men served, are worth citing. He wrote under the pseudonym "Anti-Rebel." Sergeant Van Buren Sleeper, a Norwich alumnus, served in the same company (Company "E") of the 2nd Vermont but is not mentioned in Fisk's letters; Benedict, *Vermont in the Civil War* I, pp. 137-140, 249-266.

5. Benedict, *Vermont in the Civil War* I, p. 265; *OR* 11, pt. 1, p. 377; Ellis, *Norwich University* II, pp. 566-567, 656; Linda Margaret Farr Welch, "Memories of George Blood French," in *Families of Cavendish*, Vol. 3 (publication pending), Hereinafter cited as Welch, *Families of Cavendish*; John E. Balzer, editor, *Buck's Book: A View of the 3rd Vermont Infantry Regiment* (Bolingbrook, Illinois, 1993), pp. 34-35, 42-43. Hereinafter referred to as Balzer, *Buck's Book*.

6. Eric Scheirson, editor, *The Private Letters and Diaries of Captain Hall* (Glendale, California, 1974), p. 178.

7. Scott, *Fallen Leaves*, p. 119.

8. *OR* 11, pt. 1, pp. 289, 312-313, 399-400; Frank Moore, *The Civil War in Song and Story, 1860-1865*, reprint (P. F. Collier, Publisher, 1892), p. 99. Hereinafter referred to as Moore, *The Civil War in Song and Story; OR* 11, pt. 1, p. 291.

9. Ellis, *Norwich University* II, pp. 450-451; *OR* 11, pt. 1, pp. 288-289, 400.

10. Sears, *The Peninsula Campaign*, pp. 78-84; George T. Stevens, *Three Years in the Sixth Corps*, (Albany, New York, 1866), pp. 54-55. Hereinafter referred to as Stevens, *Three Years in the Sixth Corps*; Poirier, *Alumni Database*; Ellis, *Norwich University* II, pp. 505-506, 651-652, 665, 611; U.S. Congress, *Wade Committee* I, p. 324-325.

11. *OR* 11, pt. 1, pp. 372-374; Benedict, *Vermont in the Civil War* I, p. 249; William F. Fox, *Regimental Losses in the Civil War, 1861-1865* (Albany, New York, 1898), p. 116. Hereinafter cited as Fox, *Regimental Losses*; Ellis, *Norwich University* II, pp. 653-654, pp. 502-503.

12. Ellis, *Norwich University* II, pp. 196-197; U.S. Congress, *Wade Committee* I, p. 411; Pettes' name is sometimes seen in contemporary accounts and *Official Records* as Pettis; C. Dale Marshall, "Ordnance: The 50th New York Engineers," in *America's Civil War*, November 1995 (Leesburg, Virginia, 1995), p. 10; Ellis, *Norwich University* II, p. 598; *OR* 11, pt. 1, p. 177.

13. Sears, *The Peninsula Campaign*, pp. 95-96, 108-110; *OR* 11, pt. 1, pp. 304-305, 927-928; Ellis, *Norwich University* II, pp. 344-345, 506-507, 664; William W. H. Davis is also the author of the *History of the 104th Pennsylvania Regiment* (Philadelphia, Pennsylvania, 1866), p. 108. Hereinafter cited as Davis, *104th Pennsylvania.*; Poirier, *Alumni Database.*

14. Sears, *The Peninsula Campaign*, pp. 117-124; *OR* 11, pt. 1, pp. 813-815. Under Lee's tutelage, the 20th gained a reputation as "one of the very best regiments in the service. It also was destined to suffer the highest loss of any unit from Massachusetts; Fox, *Regimental Losses*, p. 164; Stewart Sifakis, *Who Was Who in the Civil War* (New York, 1988), p. 383. Hereinafter referred to as Sifakis, *Who Was Who in the Civil War.*

15. Ellis, *Norwich University* II, 449-451; William H. Powell, *The Fifth Army Corps, Army of the Potomac*, reprint (Dayton, Ohio, 1984), p. 114. Hereinafter cited as Powell, *Fifth Corps*; John L. Parker, *History of the Twenty-Second Massachusetts Infantry* (Boston, 1887), p. 49. Hereinafter cited as Parker, *Twenty-Second Massachusetts*. The 22nd Massachusetts lost 69 killed, 153 wounded and 124 missing in action at Gaine's Mills; Fox, *Regimental Losses*, p. 166.

16. Sears, *Peninsula Campaign*, p. 237; Ellis, *Norwich University* II, pp. 301-302; Reese, *Syke's Regulars*, pp. 87-88.

17. Sears, *Peninsula Campaign*, p. 243; Amos M. Judson, *History of the Eighty-Third Regiment Pennsylvania Volunteers*, reprint (Dayton, Ohio, 1986), p. 273. Hereinafter cited as Judson, *Eighty-Third Pennsylvania*. Campbell commanded the 83rd during nearly all its 1862 battles due to the absence of its colonel, Strong Vincent. The 83rd Pennsylvania acquired such a high reputation for its drill and precision that General McClellan rated it first in Porter's division. Historian Glenn Tucker's claim that the excellence of the 83rd's discipline and drill was due solely to Strong Vincent, its commander who was absent sick leave for much of the 1862 campaign period; Tucker, *High Tide at Gettysburg*, pp. 257-258. While I have no intention of denigrating Vincent's superb accomplishments, this author believes the 83rd's reputation may have been due as much to Lt. Col. Campbell and his Norwich military education, training and experiences as a drillmaster. Strong, though without question an efficient and gallant commander, had no similar background. In addition, Campbell's performance and battlefield wounds must have gained him the respect if not the admiration of the troops. This regiment eventually suffered the heaviest losses of any unit from Pennsylvania; Fox, *Regimental Losses*, p. 282.

18. Ellis, *Norwich University* II, p. 502-503; Benedict, *Vermont in the Civil War* I, p. 293; Fox, *Regimental Losses*, p. 150; Peck, *Revised Roster of Vermont Volunteers*, p. 81; Poirier, *Alumni Database*.

19. Richard A. Sauers, "The Pennsylvania Reserves: General George A. McCall's Division on the Peninsula," in *The Peninsula Campaign of 1862*, Volume I (Campbell, California, 1995), pp. 34-36, 39-40. Hereinafter referred to as Sauers, *Pennsylvania Reserves*; Ellis, *Norwich University* II, pp. 320-322; Sears, *Peninsula Campaign*, pp. 294-295, 299; Sauers, *Pennsylvania Reserves*, p. 42; L. Van Loan Naisawald, *Grape and Canister, The Story of the Field Artillery of the Army of the Potomac, 1861-1865* (New York, 1960), pp. 82-85. Hereinafter referred to as Naisawald, *Grape and Canister*,

20. Powell, *Fifth Corps*, pp. 139-140; Ellis, *Norwich University* II, pp. 627-628; Naisawald, *Grape and Canister*, p. 116; Bruce, *Twentieth Massachusetts*, pp. 126-132; Ellis, *Norwich University* II, pp. 637-643.

21. Ellis, *Norwich University* II, pp. 235-236; Sears, *Peninsula Campaign*, p. 232; *OR* 11, pt. 1, pp. 163-164; Ellis, *Norwich University* II, p. 615.

22. Catton, *Mr. Lincoln's Army*, p. 85.

23. Sears, *Peninsula Campaign*, pp. 308-312; Wm. Y.F. Ripley, *Vermont Riflemen in the War for the Union 1861 to 1865: A History of Company F, First United States Sharpshooters* (Rutland, Vermont, 1883), pp. 54-55. The 1st and 2nd United States Sharpshooters were considered peerless skirmishers and are reputed to have killed more enemy soldiers than any units in the army; Fox, *Regimental Losses*, p. 419; Ellis, *Norwich University* II, p. 615.

24. Sears, *Peninsula Campaign*, p. 325; Walker, *Fifth Corps*, p. 168.

25. Griffith, *Battle in the Civil War*, p. 37; Naisawald, *Grape and Canister*, p. 131; Parker, *Twenty-Second Massachusetts*, p. 134.

26. Reese, *Sykes' Regulars*, pp. 97-99; Poirier, *Alumni Database.*

27. Powell, *Fifth Corps*, p. 177; Ellis, *Norwich University* II, p. 529. Colburn served on McClellan's staff from July 31, 1861 to November 10, 1862.

28. Ellis, *Norwich University* II, p. 546; Poirier, *Alumni Database.*

29. Peck, *Revised Roster of Vermont Volunteers*, pp. 85, 741; Beyer and Keydel, *America's Medal of Honor Recipients*, p. 814; Benedict, *Vermont in the Civil War* I, pp. 140-141; Coffin, *Full Duty*, p. 112; *Norwich University Catalog*, 1866-67 (Northfield, Vermont), p. 8. Willie drummed for his company until February 1864 when he transferred to the 20th Regiment, Veterans Reserve Corps. He later returned to the 3rd Vermont and was discharged in July 1865. Johnston entered Norwich by summer 1866. To date, a total of seven Norwich alumni have been awarded the Congressional Medal of Honor: five in the Civil War, one in the Philippine Insurrection and one in World War II.

30. Bowers Letters, *MHS*, Reel 15.

31. Catton, *Mr. Lincoln's Army*, pp. 89-92; Sears, *The Peninsula Campaign*, pp. 350-355.

32. Bowers Letters, *MHS*, Reel 15.

33. *Ibid.*

34. Thomas O. Seaver, *Medal of Honor File*, National Archives and Records Service, Records Group 94, File B986-VS-1862, Box 21. Hereinafter referred to as Seaver, *Medal of Honor File.*

35. Catton, *Mr. Lincoln's Army*, pp. 88-95, 18-33; *OR* 12, pt. 2, p. 406-408; Henry Codman Ropes, *The Army Under Pope* (New York, 1881), p. 57. Hereinafter referred to as Ropes, *The Army Under Pope*; Miller, *Photographic History* II, p. 43.

36. Ellis, *Norwich University* II, pp. 235-236; Camille Baquet, *The First Brigade, New Jersey Volunteers* (State of New Jersey, 1910), pp. 35-36. Hereinafter cited as Baquet, *The New Jersey Brigade*; Miller, *Photographic History* IX, pp. 74-75.

37. *OR*, 12, pt. 1, pp. 364-365; John J. Hennessy, *Return to Bull Run: The Campaign and Battle of Second Manassas* (New York, 1993), pp. 209-214. Hereinafter cited as Hennessy, *Return to Bull Run*; Alan D. Gaff, *Brave Men's Tears:The Iron Brigade at Brawner Farm* (Dayton, Ohio, 1988), pp. 81-85, 156-157; *OR* 12, pt. 2, pp. 337, 377-378; Ropes, *The Army Under Pope*, pp. 77-78. See also Alan D. Gaff, *On Many A Bloody Field: Four Years in the Iron Brigade* (Bloomington, Indiana, 1996), p. 163. Hereinafter referred to as Gaff, *Bloody Field*. It is worthy of note that recent scholarship indicates, despite the development of the enhanced-range musket rifle, the average Civil War engagement took place at the remarkably short range of 127 yards. At Brawner's Farm, the future Iron Brigade and the Stonewall Division stood and fought it out for three hours. Given the deadlier, more accurate weaponry and reports by survivors of the intensity of the musketry, no one should have survived. Their casualty rate, however, averaged 4.71 per minute--severe, though hardly men falling in droves.

Factors such as battlefield smoke caused by black powder propellants, inaccurate (high) firing by the troops and terrain conditions (the slope of the land) undoubtedly helped keep the casualty rates lower than they would have been in a smoke-free, level terrain, stand up battle; Stuart L. Koehl, "Civil War was Really Napoleonic," *The Washington Times* (Washington, D.C., February 3, 1996), p. B3; Nolan, *Iron Brigade*, p. 89, 96; Poirier, *Alumni Database*. Records indicating his class have not been found and may have been among records referred to previously as lost, Ellis, *Norwich University 1898*, pp. 3-4; Gaff, *Brave Men's Tears*, pp. 73-74. First Lieutenant Charles K. Dean (Class of 1845), served as adjutant of the 2nd Wisconsin at the time; Lieutenant Dean, however, had been captured at Beverly Ford, August 21, 1862 and was in Libby Prison, Richmond during the Battle of Brawner's Farm. He was paroled in time to rejoin the 2nd Wisconsin for the Battle of Antietam where he was severely wounded in the Cornfield; unpublished Dean letter to State Historical Society of Wisconsin, Madison, September 3, 1889; Ellis, *Norwich University* II, pp. 383-384; Gaff, *Brave Men's Tears*, p. 175; W.K. Wright, Ed., *Civil War Voices*, Unpublished Typescript (State Historical Society of Wisconsin, Madison, 1971), p. 76.

38. James Longstreet, "Our March Against Pope," *Battles and Leaders* II, p. 522-523; Ropes, *The Army Under Pope*, pp. 102-104;.

39. Hennessey, *Return to Bull Run*, pp. 209-214; Poirier, *Alumni Database*;

40. *OR* 12, pt. 1, pp. 318-323; Hennessy, *Return to Bull Run*, pp. 248-251, 254-258. Not far from Sergeant Carter and the 2nd New Hampshire, classmate Col. Charles E. Griswold (Class of '54) was now commanding Jesse Gove's beloved 22nd Massachusetts in Charles Robert's brigade. The regiment does not appear to have taken an important role in the fight, although the balance of the brigade was heavily engaged; Ellis, *Norwich University* II, pp. 544-545. It is logical to conclude that at least part of the 22nd's reputation for discipline and battlefield courage stemmed from the efforts on its Norwich commanders.

41. Judson, *83rd Pennsylvania*, p. 87; Hennessy, *Return to Bull Run*, pp. 356-357; Poirier, *Alumni Database*; Naisawald, *Grape and Canister*, p. 146.

42. Hennessy, *Return to Bull Run*, pp. 408-410, 416, 480; Reese, *Sykes' Regulars*, pp. 105-106, 123-126; Poirier, *Alumni Database*.

43. George B. McClellan, "From the Peninsula to Antietam," *Battles and Leaders* II, p. 550; Hennessy, *Return to Bull Run*, pp. 451-459.

44. Catton, *Mr. Lincoln's Army*, p. 129; Stephen W. Sears, *Landscape Turned Red: The Battle of Antietam* (New York, 1983), pp. 114-121. Hereinafter cited as Sears, *Battle of Antietam*. A compelling and fresh examination of the controversy surrounding the question of who lost Special Orders 191 identifies the staff officer who lost them; See Wilbur D. Jones, "Who Lost Lee's Lost Orders?" in *Civil War Regiments: A Journal of the American Civil War*, Vol. 5, No. 3 (1997), pp. 1-26.

45. Sears, *Battle of Antietam*, pp. 141-142; Poirier, *Alumni Database*; Nolan, *The Iron Brigade*, pp. 129-130.

46. John Michael Priest, *Before Antietam, The Battle for South Mountain* (Shippensburg, Pennsylvania, 1992, pp. 233-237. Hereinafter referred to as Priest, *Battle for South Mountain*; Daniel H. Hill, "The Battle of South Mountain, or Boonsboro," *Battles and Leaders* II, p. 574; *OR* 19, p. 268.

47. *OR* 19, pt. 1, p. 408; Benedict, *Vermont in the Civil War* I, pp. 163-164, 328-339; William B. Franklin, "Notes on Crampton's Gap and Antietam," *Battles and Leaders* II, p. 594; Thomas W. Hyde, *Following the Greek Cross Or, Memories of the Sixth Corps* (Boston, 1897), pp. 96, 103-106. Hereinafter referred to as Hyde, *Sixth Corps*; Coffin, *Full Duty*, p. 131. Timothy J. Reese, "Howell Cobb's Brigade at Crampton's Gap," in *Blue & Gray Magazine*, Volume XV, Issue 3 (Columbus, Ohio, 1998), pp. 17-19, 56.

48. Library of Congress, *Clara Barton Papers*, Containers 152-153, Reel 107, pp. 55-56. Hereinafter referred to as Clara Barton Papers, *LoC*. Clara Barton, naturally, was not a Norwich alumnus. The author chose to include quotations from some of her writings in order

to assist the reader in visualizing events in which so many of our alumni took part. Her ability to describe what she personally witnessed during the war is striking. Henry Kyd Douglas, "Stonewall Jackson in Maryland," *Battles and Leaders* II, pp. 618, 625-627.

49. See Chapter 5 for details of the Norwich "College Cavaliers'" escape from Harper's Ferry; Poirier, *Alumni Database* and *Appendix B*; Coffin, *Full Duty*, pp. 127-129.

50. Priest, *Before South Mountain*, pp. 52, 56, 317-318; Ellis, *Norwich University* II, p. 545-546; *OR* 19, pt. 1, pp. 210, 212.

51. John W. Schildt, *The Ninth Corps at Antietam*, reprint (Gaithersburg, Maryland, no date), pp. 57-59. Hereinafter referred to as Schildt, *Ninth Corps at Antietam*.

52. Sears, *Battle of Antietam*, pp. 158-161, 175-179; Austin C. Stearns, *Three Years with Company K*, Arthur A. Kent, editor (Rutherford, New Jersey, 1976), p. 125; William B. Stevens, *History of Stoneham* (Stoneham, Massachusetts, 1891), p. 85. Hereinafter referred to as Stevens, *History of Stoneham*. Ellis, *Norwich University* II, p. 448; *OR* 19, pt. 1, p. 216.

53. Clara Barton Papers, *LoC*, Containers 152-153, Reel 107, pp. 65-66. Kerner is a derivation of an Irish-Scottish word for soldier.

54. Sears, *Battle of Antietam*, pp. 184-186; *OR* 19, pp. 268-271; Francis B. Heitman, *Historical Register and Dictionary of the United States Army* (Washington, D.C., 1903), p. 875. Hereinafter cited as Heitman, *Register*; *OR* 19, Part 1, pp. 268-71; Jacob D. Cox, "The Battle of Antietam," *Battles and Leaders* II, pp. 635-636.

55. *OR* 19, pt. 1, p. 271; Naisawald, *Grape and Canister*, p. 201.

56. *OR* 19, pt. 1, p. 254; Nolan, *Iron Brigade*, pp. 137-138. Noyes obtained an artificial foot and recovered sufficiently to serve later in the war as Lieutenant Colonel of the 49th Wisconsin; Ellis, *Norwich University* II, pp. 389-390; Rufus R. Dawes, *Service With the Sixth Wisconsin Volunteers* (Marietta, Ohio, 1890), pp. 87-88. Hereinafter cited as Dawes, *Sixth Wisconsin*; John M. Priest, *Antietam: The Soldier's Battle* (Shippensburg, Pennsylvania, 1989), p. 33. Hereinafter cited as Priest, *Antietam: The Soldier's Battle*.

57. Colonel William W. Robinson (Class of '41) of the 7th Wisconsin missed Antietam as he was recovering from wounds received at Brawner's Farm and would not rejoin his regiment for several weeks. The 2nd Wisconsin would suffer the highest (proportionate) percentage of combat deaths of any unit in the Union Army; Fox, *Regimental Losses*, p. 393; Nolan, *Iron Brigade*, p. 130; Ellis, *Norwich University* II, p. 384; Daniel H. Hill, "The Battle of South Mountain, or Boonsboro," *Battles and Leaders* II, pp. 575-577; Jacob D. Cox, "The Battle of Antietam," *Battles and Leaders* II, pp. 638-639; Priest, *Antietam: The Soldier's Battle*, pp. 48-49. Poirier, *Alumni Database*. The 13th Massachusetts gained a fine reputation as a fighting regiment and its troops were cited as "superior material;" Fox, *Regimental Losses*, p. 471.

58. Griffith, *Battle in the Civil War*, p. 108; *OR* 19, pt. 1, p. 261. Comparing complex movements executed on the battlefield to a unit's performance of similar maneuvers on a drill field appears to be a standard Civil War battle means of praise. It is fair to say , however, that the actions referred to were certainly difficult and considered to have been well done under trying circumstances, thus reflecting great credit on the officers and troops.

59. Sears, *Battle of Antietam*, pp. 223-229; Ellis, *Norwich University* II, pp. 160-161. Colonel Lee assumed command of his brigade on September 19, *OR* 19, pt. 1, pp. 321-322; Waitt, *Nineteenth Massachusetts*, pp. 137-138, 141, 143, 388.

60. *OR* 19, pt. 1, pp. 284, 402, 485; Cox, "The Battle of Antietam," *Battles and Leaders* II. p. 646; Naisawald, *Grape and Canister*, pp. 212-213.

61. *OR* 19, pt. 1, pp. 277-278, 285-287; Sears, *The Battle of Antietam*, pp. 242-247, 251-252; D.P. Conyngham, *The Irish Brigade and Its Campaigns* (New York, 1867), pp. 305-306; Poirier, *Alumni Database*; Ellis, *Norwich University* II, pp. 403, 561-562, 665.

62. *OR* 19, pt. 1, pp. 448-449; Sears, *The Battle of Antietam*, pp. 270-274, 265-267; Samuel P. Bates, *History of the Pennsylvania Volunteers*, Seven Volumes (Harrisburg, Pennsylvania, 1869), Vol. III, p. 7 (Edwin); p. 13 (Edward). Hereinafter cited as Bates,

Pennsylvania Volunteers, Thomas H. Parker, *History of the 51st Regiment of Pennsylvania Volunteers and Veteran Volunteers* (Philadelphia, 1869), pp. 232-236. Hereinafter cited as Parker, *51st Pennsylvania*. Cox, "The Battle of Antietam," *Battles and Leaders* II, pp. 651-653; William Parsons, "Letters of the Fifty-First," *The Bulletin of the Historical Society of Montgomery Country*, Volume XIII, Number 3 (Montgomery Country, Pennsylvania, fall 1962), pp. 230-231; Sears, *The Battle of Antietam*, pp. 266-267.

63. Sears, *The Battle of Antietam*, pp. 262-268, 276-282; Priest, *Antietam: The Soldier's Battle*, pp. 281-283; *OR* 19, pt. 1, p. 451; of Kimball's 373 Zouaves present at Antietam, 240 were casualties--a loss rate of 64.34%; Ellis, *Norwich University* II, pp. 370-371.

64. David L. Thompson, "With Burnside at Antietam," *Battles and Leaders* II, pp. 661-662.

65. Edward A. Longacre, editor, *From Antietam to Fort Fisher: The Civil War Letters of Edward King Wightman, 1862-1865* (Cranbury, New Jersey, 1985), p. 38. Hereinafter referred to as Longacre, *From Antietam to Fort Fisher*.

66. Priest, *Antietam, The Soldiers Battle*, pp. 281-283; *OR* 19, pt. 1, p. 451; Brian C. Pohanka, *Always Ready: The 9th New York Hawkins Zouaves At Antietam* (Keith Rocco, private publishing, 1996), pp. 2-3. Hereinafter referred to as Pohanka, *Always Ready*.

67. Sears, *The Battle of Antietam*, pp. 302-308; Walker, *Fifth Corps*, pp. 294-295.

68. *OR* 19, pt. 1, p. 308; Schildt, *The Ninth Corps at Antietam*, pp. 122-124. Kimball would again command the regiment at Fredericksburg and would, tragically, be murdered by Brig. Gen. Michael Corcoran at Suffolk, Virginia April 12, 1863. The incident was described by a member of the 9th New York. Apparently, Kimball's men were in charge of camp guard when General Corcoran, drunk according to some accounts, "attempted to pass a sentinel without the countersign and Kimball, who happened to be near, backed the soldier." An argument followed and "Corcoran drew his pistol and fired a shot, striking the Colonel in the throat and dropping him from his horse." Despite his wound "the lion-hearted old man was up again in a moment and with his sword drawn, contemptuously calling upon Corcoran to 'fire again." Kimball's carotid had been struck, however, and he soon collapsed to rise no more." The regiment was outraged and the next morning "when the facts came to (the) knowledge of the men, they cried and swore at a terrific rate and the least favoring sign from any of their officers would have caused the fiercest kind of an attack by the regiment on the whole Corcoran legion." Fortunately, the men were restrained by their officers; Longacre, *From Antietam to Fort Fisher*, pp. 38, 59, 125. Kimball had a reputation as a "hard-figthing and hard-drinking officer;" *Ibid.*, pp. 249, note 21, p.97. He apparently was one of those officers that the men loved and/or hated, but would follow anywhere in a charge.

Other Norwich men who served at Antietam included another Norwich graduate First Lt. John F.L. Buel (Class of '57), led Company G, 4th United States Infantry and performed fine service in command of skirmishers; Reese, *Sykes' Regulars*, pp. 150-151. The Chaplain of the 48th Pennsylvania, Chaplain Samuel A. Holman (Class of '49), helped treat the wounded and provided religious comfort to the men during and after the battle. Holman not only survived the fight at Antietam, but was also present at ceremonies held in honor of the Pennsylvania regiments on September 17, 1904, the forty-second anniversary of the battle. Holman led the invocation at the dedication of the monument to Pennsylvania units and for his own beloved 48th; Schildt, *The Ninth Corps at Antietam*, pp. 178, 183-184. Captain and Assistant Surgeon Francis M. Lincoln (Class of '50), 35th Massachusetts, spent this day and many thereafter in field hospitals. The 35th's association with Ferrero's brigade made it quite likely that Dr. Lincoln had the opportunity to meet and work with the famous Clara Barton, who was present treating the wounded at Antietam. Clara Barton had a particular affinity for Massachusetts regiments and was made an honorary member of the 21st Massachusetts; Stephen B. Oates, *A Woman of Valor: Clara Barton and the Civil War* (New York, 1994), pp. 84-90. Hereinafter cited as Oates, *Woman of Valor*.

69. U.S. Congress, *Wade Committee* I, p. 509; Bowers Letters, *MHS*, Reel XVI, frames 881-884. The two pontoon bridges used by the Army of the Potomac to cross the Potomac River were built by part of the 50th New York Engineers under the command of Lt. Col. William H. Pettes (Class of '27); New York Monuments Commission, *New York at Gettysburg,* 3 Vols. (Albany, New York, 1900), Vol II, p. 1091. Hereinafter referred to as *New York at Gettysburg*; Miller, *Photographic History* II, pp. 56-57.

70. Bowers Letters, *MHS*, Reel XVI, frames 886-889.

71. Francis A. Walker, *Great Commanders: General Hancock* (New York, 1894), p. 57. Hereinafter referred to as Walker, *General Hancock*; Catton, *Mr. Lincoln's Army*, pp. 192-195.

72. Bruce, *Twentieth Massachusetts*, p. 179.

73. Catton, *Mr. Lincoln's Army*, pp. 195-196. Burnside apparently also took the command to ensure it would not be given to General Hooker whom he intensely disliked; McPherson, *Battle Cry of Freedom*, pp. 570-571; O.B. Curtis, *History of the Twenty-Fourth Michigan of the Iron Brigade* (Detroit, 1891), pp. 65-66, 101-103. Hereinafter cited as Curtis, *Twenty-Fourth Michigan*. The phrase "seen the elephant" was applied to those soldiers who had actually been in combat; as combat veterans, they were said to "have seen the elephant."

74. Catton, *Glory Road*, p. 233.

75. *Ibid.*, pp. 234-236; *Poirier*, Alumni Database.

76. Edward J. Stackpole, *The Fredericksburg Campaign*, 2nd edition (Harrisburg Pennsylvania, 1991), pp. 65-66, 70-73, 75-77, 79-80, 133-136. Hereinafter referred to as Stackpole, *The Fredericksburg Campaign*; Stackpole, *The Fredericksburg Campaign*, pp. 83-84, 133-136; Poirier, *Alumni Database*; Clara Barton Papers, *LoC*, Containers 152-153, Reel 107, notes in ledger dated January 22-January 31, 1866 and lecture notes (undated) pp. 9-11. Colonel Lee, due to a steadily worsening health, had returned to Massachusetts, shortly before the battle, returning after its conclusion.

77. Bruce, *Twentieth Massachusetts*, pp. 194-222 (for the regiment's role in the battle); Waitt, *Nineteenth Massachusetts*, pp. 169-194 (for the regiments role in the battle); Catton, *Glory Road*, pp. 243-244; Francis A. Walker, *History of the Second Army Corps*, second edition (New York, 1891), pp. 149-150. Hereinafter cited as Walker, *Second Corps*.

78. Catton, *Glory Road*, pp. 227-228, 234-236. A number of these nine month volunteers were men who had previously wished to enlist but for various reasons felt they could not sign up for the full two or three year term; Curtis, *Twenty-fourth Michigan*, p. 103; *OR* 21, pt. 1, pp. 475-477. Colonel Robinson not only appears to have compiled a fine combat record as a regimental commander, but also acted as commander of the Iron Brigade for two extended periods in 1863 and 1864, including part of the Battle of Gettysburg, the Rapidan and Mine Run Campaigns, the Wilderness, Spotsylvania and Cold Harbor. His actions in serving as commander of the First Corps rear guard in the withdrawal from McPherson's Woods to Seminary Ridge, through Gettysburg, to Cemetery Ridge, though little known are particularly noteworthy and are covered in detail in Chapter 4.

79. *OR* 21, pt. 1, pp. 229, 231, 458-459, 522; O'Reilly, *Prospect Hill* , p. 59; Naisawald, *Grape and Canister*, p. 249; Ellis, *Norwich University* II, p. 627. For more information on Captain Hall and his probable Norwich connection, see Appendix H. Hall greatly distinguished himself at Fredericksburg and Gettysburg and there are extensive primary source materials and official reports on his actions in those engagements. These accounts have been deliberately omitted from this text.

80. *OR* 21, pt. 1, pp. 532-533; Poirier, *Alumni Database*; Washburn, *Vermont AG Reports, 1863;* Benedict, *Vermont in the Civil War* I, pp. 343-345; Poirier, *Alumni Database*.

81. Otis F.R. Waite, *Vermont in the Great Rebellion* (Claremont, New Hampshire, 1869), p. 287. Hereinafter referred to as Waite, *Vermont in the Rebellion*; *OR* 21, pt. 1, pp. 532-533; Frank A. O'Reilly, *The Fredericksburg Campaign, "Stonewall" Jackson at Fredericksburg: The Battle of Prospect Hill*, 2nd edition (Lynchburg, Virginia, 1993), pp. 168-172. Hereinafter re-

ferred to as O'Reilly, *Prospect Hill; OR* 21, pt. 1, p. 647 (Hill); *OR* 21, pt. 1, p. 662 Pender); Earl J. Hess, *The Union Soldier in Battle: Enduring the Ordeal of Combat* (Lawrence, Kansas, 1997), p. 108. Hereinafter referred to as Hess, *The Ordeal of Combat.*.

82. *OR* 21, pt. 1, pp 532-533; Benedict, *Vermont in the Civil War* I, pp. 344-346. The 3rd Vermont's troops were considered to be unusually fine physical specimens, averaging 5' 10 1/2" in height and weighing 161 pounds; Fox, *Regimental Losses*, p. 148; George W. Parsons, *Put The Vermonters Ahead: The First Vermont Brigade in the Civil War* (Shippensburg, Pennsylvania, 1996), p. 42. hereinafter referred to as Parsons, *First Vermont Brigade.*

83. Stackpole, *The Fredericksburg Campaign*, pp. 214-215; Poirier, *Alumni Database* and *Appendix B*; *OR* 21, pt. 1, p. 311;.

84. Ellis, *Norwich University* II, p. 54; William P. Hopkins, *The Seventh Regiment Rhode Island Volunteers in the Civil War 1862-1865* (Providence, Rhode Island, 1903), pp. 46-47. Hereinafter referred to as Hopkins, *Seventh Rhode Island.*

85. *OR* 21, pt. 1, pp. 311-313.

86. Ellis, *Norwich University* II, p. 456; Oates, *Woman of Valor*, p. 113; the gallant Plunkett was awarded a Medal of Honor for his courage at Fredericksburg in 1866; the color he carried is now in the Massachusetts State House. When Plunkett died, "his flag" was brought to Worcester, Massachusetts from the State House and used to cover his casket. This is the only occasion a Massachusetts color has ever left the State House once it was deposited there; Clara Barton Papers, *LoC*, Containers 152-153, Reel 107, lecture notes, pp. 49-50.

87. Stackpole, *The Fredericksburg Campaign*, pp. 205-214; Fox, *Regimental Losses*, pp. 35-36; *OR* 21, pt. 1, pp. 231-232, 234-235; Walker, *Second Corps*, pp. 172, 186-187, 194; Ellis, *1898*, p. 541; The Adjutant General, *Massachusetts Soldiers, Sailors and Marines in the Civil War: Index to Army Records* (Boston, 1937), pp. 409-410. Captain Edmund Rice (Class of '60) and First Lt. Henry Hale (Class of '61), were not on the field with the 19th Massachusetts at the fight, both men were recovering from severe wounds received in Antietam's West Woods.

88. Stackpole, *The Fredericksburg Campaign*, pp. 215-217; *OR* 21, pt. 1, p. 433; Bowers Letters, *MHS*, Reel 16, frames 1005-09, frames 1010-1013.

89. Bowers Letters, *MHS*, Reel 16, frames 1034-1036, 1001-1004.

90. Stackpole, *The Fredericksburg Campaign*, pp. 226-235; Oates, *Woman of Valor*, pp. 114-120. A significant part of the research for this book was done within the Lacy House, in a room used to treat wounded soldiers, thanks to the courtesy of members of the National Park Service based there.

91. Gideon Welles, *The Diary of Gideon Welles*, 3 Volumes (Boston, 1911), Vol. I, pp. 191-192. Hereinafter referred to as Welles, *Diary.*

92. Scott, *Fallen Leaves*, p. 154. The Holmes referred to is, of course, Captain Oliver Wendell Holmes the future great Supreme Court Justice.

93. George Grenville Benedict, *Army Life in Virginia: Letters From the Twelfth Vermont Regiment* (Burlington, Vermont, 1895), pp. 80-83. Hereinafter referred to as Benedict, *12th Vermont.*.

4. CHANCELLORSVILLE AND GETTYSBURG

1. McPherson, *Battle Cry of Freedom*, pp. 495-502, 508-510; Robertson, *Soldiers Blue and Gray*, pp. 10-11.

2. McPherson, *Battle Cry of Freedom*, pp. 493-494, 559-560, 591-592; Fisk, *Hard Marching*, p. 67.

3. McPherson, *Battle Cry of Freedom*, pp. 493-354, 494-496, 496-500, 502-506, 559; U.S. Congress, *Wade Committee* I, p. 519; vol. II, p. 311.

4. Catton, *Glory Road,* pp. 271-277; McPherson, *Battle Cry of Freedom,* p. 584; Stephen W. Sears, *Chancellorsville* (Boston, 1996), pp. 14-22, hereinafter cited as Sears, *Chancellorsville;* Bowers Letters, *MHS,* Reel 16, frames 1145-1148.

5. Catton, *Glory Road,* pp. 305-309; Sears, *Chancellorsville,* see pp. 54-83 for the full details of Hooker's actions and reforms.

6. Moore, *Civil War Song and Story,* pp. 310-311. Stoughton (Class of '61) and Seaver (Class of '59), knew each other both at Norwich and in the army. "Jeff's myrmidons" refers to Jeff Davis' troops. A feu d'enfer is French for "hellfire."

7. Henry Houghton, "The Ordeal of Civil War: A Recollection," in *Vermont History,* Volume 41, Number 1 (Montpelier, Vermont, 1973), p. 32. Hereinafter referred to as Houghton, *Recollection.*

8. Sears, *Chancellorsville,* pp. 108-135; U.S. Congress, *Wade Committee* II, pp. 219, 241-242, 315-316.

9. Sears, *Chancellorsville,* pp. 45, 112-114.

10. Bowers Letters, *MHS,* Reel 16, frames 1338-1341; Sears, *Chancellorsville* (Boston, 1996), pp. 436-438, 504-505.

11. Bigelow, *Chancelorsville,* p. 27; Poirier, *Alumni Database.*

12. *OR* 25, pt. 1, pp. 215, 258-259, 266-67, 273-274; Catton, *The Glory Road,* pp. 319-321; Bigelow, *Chancelorsville,* pp. 196, 206-207; Sears, *Chancellorsville,* pp. 147-148, 155-159, 174-175; Poirier, *Alumni Database.*

13. Reese, *Sykes' Regulars,* pp. 210-15; *OR* 25, pt. 1, pp. 540-541; Ellis, *Norwich University* II, p. 710. Captain George W. Smith, 1st Lts. Edward Stanley Abbott and Francis E. Stimpson (Class of '58), and Sgts. James W. Buel and Eldridge H. Babbitt, fought with the 17th that day. Except for Stimpson, all the Norwich men were from the Class of 1864, and it is assumed that they knew of each others' presence with the regiment. Sears, *Chancellorsville,* pp. 205-213, 420, 504-505. Sears' research puts Hooker's withdrawal into a better context and indicates his decision to withdraw was probably sound based on the available intelligence.

14. Catton, *The Glory Road,* pp. 325-327; Sears, *Chancellorsville,* pp. 235-238.

15. Sears, *Chancellorsville,* pp. 233-235.

16. Sears, *Chancellorsville,* pp. 240-243, 264-265; Edward Marcus, editor, *A New Canaan Private in the Civil War: Letters of Justus M. Silliman, 17th Connecticut Volunteers* (New Canaan, Connecticut, 1984), p. 24. Hereinafter referred to as Marcus, *17th Connecticut.* Abner Doubleday, *Chancellorsville and Gettysburg* (Charles Scribners Sons, New York, 1881-83), pp. 28-29. Hereinafter referred to as Doubleday, *Chancellorsville and Gettysburg.* While Doubleday is considered a generally unreliable writer, his data is used here with an appropriate note of caution. It is a matter of some interest that the inventor of the sewing machine, Elias Howe, although clubfooted and in his forties, served with Noble's regiment although he was never officially mustered. His son, Elias Jr., served in the 17th Connecticut from August 28, 1862 to the end of the war.

17. Sears, *Chancellorsville,* pp. 240-243, 260-272, 362-363; Ellis, *Norwich University* II, pp. 184-185; Bigelow, pp. 296-297; Marcus, *17th Connecticut,* pp. 31-34; *OR* 25, pt. 1, pp. 638-640.

18. Sears, *Chancellorsville,* pp. 293-297, 302-306, 312-314, 446-448.

19. Sears, *Chancellorsville,* pp. 357-359; Bowers Letters, *MHS,* Reel 16, frames 1354-1359, 1375-1380.

20. Sears, *Chancellorsville,* pp. 314-337; James P. Brady, compiler, *Hurrah for the Artillery: Knap's Independent Battery E, Pennsylvania Light Artillery* (Gettysburg, Pennsylvania, 1992), pp. 217, 234. Hereinafter referred to as Brady, *Knap's Battery.* Henry Campbell's Norwich training was specifically cited when his commander submitted his nomination papers for a commission. Campbell's Norwich experience, combined with commendable service with the unit from August 1862 on, played a key role in his obtaining a commission in the United States

Colored Troops. Campbell was probably one of the special military students on campus in 1861-62; *OR* 25, pt. 1, pp. 309-310.

21. Sears, *Chancellorsville*, pp. 347-353; *OR* 25, pt. 1, pp. 358-360; Poirier, *Alumni Database*.

22. Sears, *Chancellorsville*, pp. 353-357.

23. *OR* 25, pt. 1, pp. 599-600, 602-603; Ernest B. Ferguson, *Chancellorsville 1863: The Souls of the Brave* (Alfred A. Knopf, 1992), pp. 255-262. Hereinafter referred to as Ferguson, *Chancellorsville*. Stevens, *Three years in the Sixth Corps*, pp. 194-200; Parsons, *First Vermont Brigade*, pp. 49-50; Benedict, *Vermont in the Civil War* I, pp. 264, 365-366. William Barksdale lost over 600 men from his brigade, of which about half were captured; Ellis, *Norwich University* II, p. 622; *OR* 25, pt. 1, pp. 812, 839-840; Washburn, *Vermont AG Report, 1864*, pp. 78-79. In the assault upon Marye's Heights, the Sixth Corps captured five battle flags and 15 pieces of artillery, including guns from the famous Washington Artillery battery. Nine of these guns were successfully carried off to Union lines. See Huntington W. Jackson, "Sedgwick At Fredericksburg and Salem Heights," in *Battles and Leaders* III, p. 232. See Appendix E for additional details on Seaver's career and his Medal of Honor recommendation and award.

24. Sears, *Chancellorsville*, pp. 371-372, 378-386; Baquet, *The New Jersey Brigade*, p. 449; Ellis, *Norwich University* II, p. 615. The regimental history of the 3rd New Jersey lists Taylor as killed in action at Chancellorsville. His former comrades obviously lost track of his 1864 transfer to the United States Marines, as well as his extended postwar overseas career; Ellis, *Norwich University* II, pp. 578-581; Heitman, *Register*, p. 1044; *OR* 25, pt. 1, pp. 564-566, 597-599. In addition, the 95th Pennsylvania, in which alumnus Sgt. (later Capt.) John B. Carpenter (Class of '48) served, lost 23 killed, 110 wounded, and 20 missing in action at Salem Church, a total of 153 men. Fox, *Regimental Losses*, p. 285.

25. *OR* 25, pt. 1, p. 598.

26. Sears, *Chancellorsville*, pp. 386, 390-394, 398-403; *OR* 25, pt. 1, pp. 604-608; Ellis, *Norwich University* II, p. 664; Poirier, *Alumni Database*, Washburn, *Vermont AG Reports, 1863*, pp. 74-79. Fisk, *Hard Marching*, p. 79.

27. Fisk, *Hard Marching*, p. 84; Washburn, *Vermont AG Reports, 1863*, p. 76-77; Houghton, *Recollection*, p. 33; Peck, *Revised Roster of Vermont Volunteers*, p. 69; *OR* 25, pt. 1, pp. 602-607.

28. *OR* 25, pt. 1, pp. 358-359; Sears, *Chancellorsville*, pp. 405-414, 424-426, 428-429.

29. George Blood French letter "to Calvin and Valeria French," from unpublished correspondence in the possession of Linda Margaret Farr Welch and supplied to the author; Bowers Letters, *MHS*, Reel 16, frames 1381-1384.

30. Catherine Abbot, "A Soldier's Life and Death in Family Letters," *The Washington Times* (Washington, D.C., July 9, 1994), p. B-3. The author's attempts to contact Mrs. Abbot through *The Washington Times* in order to ascertain if additional letters from Stanley Abbot existed were unsuccessful.

31. Curtis, *Twenty-Fourth Michigan*, p. 138.

32. *OR* 25, pt. 1, pp. 1105-1106; Louis N. Boudrye, *Historic Records of the Fifth New York Cavalry, First Ira Harris Guard* (Albany, New York, 1865), pp. 55-56. Hereinafter referred to as Boudrye, *Fifth New York Cavalry*; Washburn, *Vermont AG Reports, 1863*, pp. 85-87.

33. Glenn Tucker, *High Tide At Gettysburg* (New York, 1958), pp. 15-27; McPherson, *Battle Cry of Freedom*, pp. 645-647.

34. McPherson, *Battle Cry of Freedom*, pp. 648-651.

35. Catton, *Glory Road*, pp. 376-377; U.S. Congress, *Wade Committee* II, pp. 475-487; Welles, *Diary*, pp. 340-348 (for events preceding Gettysburg).

36. McPherson, *Battle Cry of Freedom*, pp. 651-652. Some of the material from this Gettysburg section appeared in Robert G. Poirier, "Norwich at Gettysburg: The Citizen-Soldier Academy's Contribution to Victory," *The Gettysburg Magazine*, Number Fourteen,

January 1996, pp. 113-128. The data in that article has since been modified and updated; Poirier, *Alumni Database.* One of the little-known facts surrounding the battle and its aftermath is that nineteenth century Gettysburg historian John B. Bachelder was an alumnus of Norwich (Class of '49); Ellis, *Norwich University* III, p. 641; David L. and Audrey J. Ladd, editors, *The Bachelder Papers,* 3 vols. (Dayton, Ohio, 1994-95), vol. 1, p. 9. In an impressive effort, Bachelder spent 84 days on the ground at Gettysburg immediately after the battle, as well as two months in the field hospitals, writing the accounts of wounded men. He also visited the winter camp of the Army of the Potomac and interviewed officers and men from virtually every unit engaged in the battle; Ladd and Ladd, *Bachelder Papers* 2, pp. 736-737. Bachelder is also credited with playing a major role in the positioning of many of the monuments currently seen on the battlefield; Charles F. Morse, *History of the Second Massachusetts Regiment of Infantry* (Boston, 1882), p. 4.

37. McPherson, *Battle Cry of Freedom,* pp. 652-653; Richard S. Shue, *Morning at Willoughby Run, July 1, 1863* (Gettysburg, PA, 1995), p. 88; Tucker, *High Tide at Gettysburg,* p. 108; *OR* 27, pt. 1, pp. 245-246, 359-360.

38. Ladd and Ladd, *Bachelder Papers* 1, pp. 322-323; Tucker, *High Tide at Gettysburg,* pp. 108-110.

39. Wright, *Seventh Wisconsin,* pp. 188-189; Nolan, *Iron Brigade,* pp. 233-252; Doubleday, *Chancellorsville and Gettysburg,* p. 130; Tucker, *High Tide at Gettysburg,* pp. 164-165; Ladd and Ladd, *Bachelder Papers* 2, p. 943.

40. *OR* 27, pt. 1, pp. 254, 279-280; Ladd and Ladd, *Bachelder Papers* 1, pp. 300-301, 640-643; Tucker, *High Tide at Gettysburg,* p. 111; Wright, *Seventh Wisconsin,* p. 190; Fox, *Regimental Losses,* p. 397.

41. Frank A. Haskell, *The Battle of Gettysburg* (Sandwich, Massachusetts, 1993), p. 13.

42. Fox, *Regimental Losses,* pp. 2, 390. For more details on the casualties at Gettysburg, see John W. Busey and David G. Martin, *Regimental Strengths and Losses at Gettysburg* (Hightstown, New Jersey, 1994); *OR* 27, pt. 1, pp. 270-271; Tucker, *High Tide at Gettysburg,* pp. 145-149; Curtis, *Twenty-fourth Michigan,* pp. 155-166. It is worth noting that Lt. Col. William W. Dudley, 19th Indiana,"Iron Brigade," had a Norwich connection: he attended the Partridge-inspired and Norwich clone "Collegiate and Commercial Institute" in New Haven, Connecticut. Colonel Dudley was severely wounded and lost a leg trying to rally his men during the severe fighting on July 1. He was later breveted brigadier general for his gallantry in the battle. Long, *Brevet Brigadier Generals in Blue,* p. 176. Biographical data on the 20-year-old Dudley suggests he attended preparatory classes in his native Vermont and may have also attended Norwich for a brief period. Nolan, *Iron Brigade,* p. 114. Dudley is not, however, considered an alumnus for the purposes of this book.

43. Wright, *Seventh Wisconsin,* pp. 203-204.

44. Ladd and Ladd, *Bachelder Papers* 2, p. 1021. The actions of the 12th Massachusetts in repulsing the attack by Alfred Iverson's Brigade resulted in the capture of some 400 prisoners. Poirier, *Alumni Database.* For a relatively new study on the first day's action, see David G. Martin, *Gettysburg July 1* (Conshohocken, PA, 1995), pp. 253-54.

45. *OR* 27, pt. 1, pp. 297-298; Ellis, *Norwich University* II, pp. 447, 622; Martin, *Gettysburg, July 1,* pp. 251-252; Arthur H. Kent, ed., *Austin C. Stearns, Three Years with Company K* (Cranbury, New Jersey, 1976), p. 205. Surgeon Parker and the regimental commander of the 13th Massachusetts, Col. Samuel H. Leonard, were both treated together in Jennie McCreary's house on Chambersburg Street near the town square. The McCreary House was probably the site of Parker's field hospital; Martin, *Gettysburg, July 1,* pp. 456-457.

46. McPherson, *Battle Cry of Freedom,* p. 654; Ellis, *Norwich University* II, p. 185; *OR* 27, pt. 1, pp. 715-718; Gregory A. Coco, *A Strange and Blighted Land: Gettysburg: The Aftermath of a Battle* (Gettysburg, PA, 1995), pp. 149-248; Ladd and Ladd, *Bachelder Papers* 1,

pp. 138-139 and vol. 2, p. 747; the 17th Connecticut lost 197 of the 386 men engaged, a 51% casualty rate; Busey and Martin, *Strengths and Losses*, p. 263.

47. McPherson, *Battle Cry of Freedom*, pp. 654-657.

48. McPherson, *Battle Cry of Freedom*, pp. 656-657; *New York at Gettysburg*, vol. 1, p. 40; Harry W. Pfanz, *Gettysburg: The Second Day* (Chapel Hill, 1987), p. 145. While marching up from Emmitsburg the day before, a farmer demanded twenty-two cents from the regiment for pulling his fence down! The 73rd's outraged regimental commander, much to the delight of the troops, ordered him into the ranks and marched him six miles before releasing him; Ladd and Ladd, *Bachelder Papers 2*, pp. 845-847; vol. 3, pp. 1978-1979.

49. *New York at Gettysburg*, vol. 1, p. 56; vol. 2, p. 603; Pfanz, *Gettysburg: The Second Day*, pp. 323-326, 330-331; Ladd and Ladd, *Bachelder Papers 1*, pp. 225-226. An excellent firsthand account of the fighting by the 73rd New York and Excelsior Brigade around the Peach Orchard and Emmitsburg Pike was written by Capt. Frank E. Moran, 73rd New York, and is found in Ladd and Ladd, *Bachelder Papers 2*, pp. 772-775; Busey and Martin, *Strengths and Losses*, p. 265.

50. Pfanz, *Gettysburg: the Second Day*, pp. 170-171, 229, 514-515, and note 17; Ladd and Ladd, *Bachelder Papers 1*, pp. 175-177. The intensity of the fighting is related by Capt. John Bigelow, 9th Massachusetts Battery, where he recalls that McGilvery had "his horse during his approach riddled with bullets;"Ibid.

51. Pfanz, *Gettysburg: The Second Day*, p. 312; *OR 27*, pt. 1, p. 884. On the afternoon of July 3, McGilvery's brigade, like Evan Thomas' Battery "C," 4th United States Artillery, leveled a devastating oblique fire on the advance of James Kemper's Brigade during Pickett's Charge; Ladd and Ladd, *Bachelder Papers 3*, p. 1,900. Because its losses had been so severe in previous battles, Irish's battery, Independent Battery "F," had been merged with Independent Battery "C," to form Independent Battery "C/F," Pennsylvania Light Artillery; Ladd and Ladd, *Bachelder Papers I*, pp. 430-434, 440-441; Fairfax Downey, *The Guns of Gettysburg* (New York, 1987), p. 149.

52. Fox, *Regimental Losses*, p. 137; *OR 27*, pt. 1, pp. 573-575; Martin A. Haynes, *Second Regiment, New Hampshire Volunteer Infantry* (Lakeport, NH, 1896), pp. 170-177; Gary G. Lash, "A Pathetic Story: The 141st Pennsylvania (Graham's Brigade) At Gettysburg," in *The Gettysburg Magazine*, #14 (January, 1996), pp. 89-90. Carter's company was armed with Sharps repeating rifles. Haynes, *Second New Hampshire*, p. 182; *OR 27*, pt. 1, pp. 571-573; Francis J. Parker, *The Story of the Thirty-Second Regiment Massachusetts Infantry* (Publishers, Boston, 1880), p. 172; Jay Jorgensen, "Anderson Attacks The Wheatfield," in *The Gettysburg Magazine*, #14 (January, 1996), p. 74. Captain Charles Bowers missed his first battle since joining the regiment in spring 1862; he had the misfortune--or perhaps good fortune--to be kicked in the hip by a horse in early June and was in a Washington hospital. Bowers Letters, *MHS*, Reel 16, frames 1487-1488. The 32nd Massachusetts suffered 13 killed, 62 wounded and five captured, a casualty rate of 33.1% of the 242 men engaged. Busey and Martin, *Strengths and Losses*, p. 248; Poirier, *Alumni Database*.

53. *OR 27*, pt. 1, pp. 371-377, 410-411, 420, 424-425; Haskell, *Battle of Gettysburg*, pp. 45-46; Naisawald, *Grape and Canister*, p. 400; Pfanz, *Gettysburg: The Second Day*, pp. 375-376; Edwin B. Coddington, *The Gettysburg Campaign: A Study in Command* (New York, 1968), p. 423; Ladd and Ladd, *Bachelder Papers 3*, p. 1,900. Thomas' battery lost one man killed and 17 wounded, an 18.9% casualty rate. Busey and Martin, *Strengths and Losses*, p. 260.

54. *OR 27*, pt. 1, p. 420; Ladd and Ladd, *Bachelder Papers 1*, pp. 256-259; *OR 27*, pt. 1, p. 241. For example, Hall's Battery fired 695 rounds. The average expenditure per gun was 106 rounds. Downey, *The Guns of Gettysburg*, pp. 119-120.

55. Reese, *Sykes' Regulars*, p. 243; Poirier, *Alumni Database*; Dudley H. Chase, "Gettysburg." *Military Order of the Loyal Legion of the U.S., Commandery of Indiana, War*

Papers, Volume 1 (Indianapolis, Indiana, 1898), pp. 301-302. For more information on the roll of the Regulars at Gettysburg, see Pfanz, *Gettysburg: The Second Day*, pp. 296-302.

56. Reese, *Sykes' Regulars*, pp. 243-245, 250, 253-258. Burbank's Regular Brigade suffered the loss of 40 of its 80 officers and 408 of its 900 enlisted men. *New York at Gettysburg* 1, p. 55; Pfanz, *Gettysburg: The Second Day*, pp. 297-298, 301; Ladd and Ladd, *Bachelder Papers* 1, p. 593, vol. 3, pp. 1686-1687; *New York at Gettysburg* 1, p. 55; *OR* 27, pt. 1, pp. 644-645, 650-651; Fox, *Regimental Losses*, p. 36. Busey and Martin, *Strengths and Losses*, p. 263. Lieutenant Abbot's more famous older brother, Capt. Henry Larcom Abbot, rose to command the 1st Connecticut Heavy Artillery and the siege artillery of the Army of the Potomac at Petersburg. He was named a brevet major general of volunteers, Brevet Brigadier General, United States Army, and eventually retired as Colonel of Engineers in the Regular Army; Sifakis, *Who's Who in the Civil War*, p. 1; Regis de Trobriand, *Four Years With The Army of the Potomac* (Boston, 1889), pp. 502-503. Abbott was a new first lieutenant at the time of his death and was breveted captain for his gallantry in the "Valley of Death" at Gettysburg. Stimpson's rank is incorrectly reported.

57. "State Drill Officers," *University Reveille*, vol. 4, No. 1 (Norwich, Vermont, March 1863), p. 6. Coffin, *Full Duty*, pp. 180-185; *Vermont National Guard*, p. 106.

58. The left wing (second battalion) consisted of companies D, F, H, I and K. Ralph Orson Sturtevant, *Pictorial History: The Thirteenth Vermont Volunteers 1861-1865* (Burlington, Vermont, 1911), p. 261; *OR* 27, pt. 1, pp. 349-350; G. G. Benedict, *Vermont at Gettysburg: A Sketch of the Part Taken by The Vermont Troops* (Burlington, Vermont, 1870), pp. 6-7; Haskell, *Battle of Gettysburg*, p. 67; Pfanz, *Gettysburg: The Second Day*, pp. 415-416, 514 (note 114); Ladd and Ladd, *Bachelder Papers 1*, p. 95, vol. 3, pp. 1969-1971. Colonel Francis V. Randall, 13th Vermont, who distinguished himself at Gettysburg, later became the Vice President of Norwich University, Ellis, *Norwich University* 1, p. xiv. Randall received his early military training as a member of Brig. Gen. Alonzo Jackman's (Class of '36) Vermont Militia staff in 1860-61. As a result of this experience, he was able to obtain a commission as captain, Company "F," 2nd Vermont Infantry. Robert Gwin, "Colonel Francis Voltaire Randall and Pickett's Charge at Battle of Gettysburg," Robert Gwin File, *Special Collections*, Norwich University, Northfield, Vermont. It is also possible that Randall spent time at Norwich as a special military student.

59. *OR* 27, pt. 1, pp. 352, 874, 879-880; Naisawald, *Grape and Canister*, pp. 377-378. Pfanz, *Gettysburg: The Second Day*, pp. 358-359. Wier never recovered from the disgrace of losing his guns, apparently blaming himself for the episode and committed suicide after the war.

60. Pfanz, *The Second Day at Gettysburg*, pp. 379-380. Lieutenant Colonel Mallon, the commanding officer of the 42nd New York, was under Colonel Devereux's immediate command. National Archives and Record Service, War Department, Record and Pension Service, *Colonel Michael Devereux File*, unpublished official report on the Gettysburg Campaign, May 1, 1878. While written 15 years after the event, the report was written from Devereux's contemporary field notes and is believed accurate. McPherson, *Battle Cry of Freedom*, pp. 659-661.

61. James A. Sawicki, *Infantry Regiments of the US Army* (Dumfries, Virginia, 1981), pp. 339-340; Benedict, *Vermont in the Civil War 1*, p. 385. Today, the 172nd United States Armor Regiment (Vermont National Guard) traces its lineage to elements of the Old Vermont Brigade. The modern citizen-soldiers proudly display the slogan "Put the Vermonters Ahead" on its crest as its regimental motto. Sawicki, *Infantry Regiments*, p. 339; Stevens, *Three Years in the Sixth Corps*, pp. 226-228, 239-241. The Vermont Brigade eventually took up a position on the extreme left of the army, between Big Round Top and the Taneytown Road. The 2nd and 3rd Vermont (Col. Thomas O. Seaver, Class of '59) constituted the front line of the brigade, while the 4th Vermont (Col. Charles B. Stoughton, Class of '61) was on the picket and skirmish lines; Ladd and Ladd, *Bachelder Papers 1*, pp. 98, 122-123, 375. The Vermont Brigade,

given that it led the march from Manchester, Maryland, was in the Sixth Corps first battle line (if it led all the way, which is probable); Ellis, *Norwich University* II, pp. 260-261; *OR* 27, pt. 1, pp. 661-666; Benedict, *Vermont in the Civil War* I, p. 388; Washburn, *Vermont AG Reports, 1863*, pp. 83-84.

62. McPherson, *Battle Cry of Freedom*, pp. 660-661; John Gibbon, "The Council of War on the Second Day," in *Battles and Leaders* 3, pp. 313-314.

63. Harry W. Pfanz, *Gettysburg: Culp's Hill and Cemetery Hill* (Chapel Hill, North Carolina, 1993), pp. 286, 341-350. It has not been satisfactorily determined whether the attack order was actually given, whether it was a mistake, or whether the assault resulted from a misinterpretation of instructions. Nevertheless, it was made over the protests of the commander of the 2nd Massachusetts. *OR* 27, pt. 1, pp. 813-817; Poirier, *Alumni Database*. The regiment was considered by many to be the best officered unit in the Union Army; Fox, *Regimental Losses*, p. 156. The 2nd Massachusetts suffered 23 killed, 109 wounded, and four missing of 316 men engaged. Busey and Martin, *Strengths and Losses*, p. 256; Coddington, *A Study in Command*, p. 475; Ladd and Ladd, *Bachelder Papers* 1, pp. 146-147, 156-158. Positioned on the extreme right of the Union line on Culp's Hill, where it saw only limited action, was Independent Battery E (Knap's Battery), Pennsylvania Light Artillery, in which Pvt. Henry S. Campbell (Class of '62) served. Brady, *Knap's Battery*, pp. 247-248.

64. McPherson, *Battle Cry of Freedom*, pp. 661-662.

65. McPherson, *Battle Cry of Freedom*, p. 662; Downey, *The Guns of Gettysburg*, pp. 144-156; Poirier, *Alumni Database*; *OR* 27, pt. 1, pp. 238-243.

66. McPherson, *Battle Cry of Freedom*, p. 662; Waitt, *Nineteenth Massachusetts*, p. 240.

67. Waitt, *Nineteenth Massachusetts*, p. 245, 257; Fox, *Regimental Losses*, p. 163. The 19th suffered nine killed, 61 wounded, and three missing, a casualty rate of 46%. Busey and Martin, *Strengths and Losses*, p. 283. The 14th, 53rd and 57th Virginia, as might be expected, also suffered severe losses in their gallant charge. In fact, the 14th, 53rd and 57th Virginia are among those regiments whose losses cannot be determined as most of their cadre was killed, captured or wounded. It is safe to say, however, that their total casualties were probably above 60%; Busey and Martin, *Strengths and Losses*, pp. 277, 283; Poirier, *Alumni Database*; National Archives and Records Administration, Pensions and Records Division, John B. Thompson File, Muster Roll, Company "G," 19th Massachusetts Infantry, July 30, 1863.

68. *OR* 27, pt. 1, p. 444. The colors in question, the battle flag and staff of the 53rd Virginia Infantry, was used by Major Rice as a crutch when he left the field after the repulse of Pickett's Charge. Rice presented the 53rd Virginia's colors to the wounded General Hancock at the Second Corps Field Hospital; Waitt, *Nineteenth Massachusetts*, p. 242; Haskell, *Battle of Gettysburg*, pp. 95-96, 121. Most of the more than 500 battle flags captured by Union forces during the war were returned to their respective states in 1905. Virginia flags, as well as those which were unidentified, were sent to Richmond, where most are currently stored in The Museum of the Confederacy. The colors of the 19th Virginia, also captured by the 19th Massachusetts, are on loan from The Museum of the Confederacy to the Gettysburg National Park. The 14th Virginia's colors (2nd bunting) are apparently in a private collection in New York, although The Museum of the Confederacy believes they possess the flag the 14th carried at Gettysburg (3rd bunting) in its collection. Photos of the 14th Virginia and 19th Massachusetts were used to ensure the accuracy of their portrayal in Dale' Gallon's painting, "Clubs Are Trumps." For additional information, see Richard Rollins, ed., *The Return of the Battle Flags* (Redondo Beach, California, 1995). Many Southern battle flags remain in private hands, such as the 14th Virginia's; others reside in various state archives (such as those of Iowa, Minnesota, and Wisconsin).

69. Arthur F. Devereux, "Some Account of Pickett's Charge at Gettysburg," *Magazine of American History*, vol. 18, 1887. The color bearer referred to is Cpl. Joseph H. De Castro.

Bachelder Papers, vol. 3, pp. 1,609-1,610, 1882 (115n); Edmund Rice file, Norwich University, *Special Collections.*

70. National Archives, War Department, Record and Pension Division, *Edmund Rice Military File,* letter dated August 28, 1891, 19th Massachusetts Regimental Association. This file contains other letters of recommendation for the Medal of Honor and various data, including a recommendation by Maj. Gen. Francis C. Barlow, dated January 3, 1866, that Rice be made a brevet brigadier general for his services in the war. Although he states that his recommendation was belated and would have been made at the time "had he known so many were to be awarded," Barlow went on to write that Rice "is one of the most meritorious officers he had ever known in the service." The recommended brevet was rejected by Lt. Gen. Ulysses S. Grant.

71. Frank E. Edwards, *The '98 Campaign of the 6th Massachusetts, U.S.V.* (Boston, 1899), pp. 129-130; Ladd and Ladd, *Bachelder Papers* 3, pp. 1874-1882.

72. *New York at Gettysburg* 1, p. 536; Rollins, *Battle Flags,* p. 4; Ellis, *Norwich University* II, p. 565; Benedict, *Vermont at Gettysburg,* p. 24. Roger Long, Letter to Author concerning Thomas H. Davis, December 17, 1995.

72. Ellis, *Norwich University* II, p. 565; Thomas Davis File, Norwich University, *Special Collections;* author's personal papers.

73. *OR* 27, pt. 1, p. 350; Coffin, *Full Duty,* p. 195; Benedict, *Vermont at Gettysburg,* pp. 14-20; Benedict, *12th Vermont,* pp. 159-181. These three Vermont regiments, which served only for nine months, were significantly larger than the average Federal regiments on the field that day. Their respective strengths were: 13th Vermont: 719 officers and men; 14th Vermont: 729 officers and men: 16th Vermont, 735 officers and men. The 12th and 15th Vermont regiments, with several Norwich men in their ranks were, much to their disgust, detailed to guard supply trains; Coddington, *A Study in Command,* p. 799 (120n); Tucker, *High Tide at Gettysburg,* pp. 361-362, 367. The Second Vermont Brigade suffered 45 killed, 274 wounded, and 32 missing in the three regiments engaged (about 1,950 men). Busey and Martin, *Strengths and Losses,* p. 241.

74. *OR* 27, pt. 1, pp. 993, 996-997; Poirier, *Alumni Database;* Miller, *Photographic History 4,* p. 232; Dr. Elliot W. Hoffman, Letter to the Author, February 15, 1996. The 1st Vermont Cavalry gained a fine reputation and was noted as "one of the best mounted regiments in the service." Fox, *Regimental Losses,* p. 145.

75. Poirier, *Alumni Database.*

76. Coco, *A Strange and Blighted Land,* pp. 111-113.

77. Coco, *A Strange and Blighted Land,* p. 113.

78. Abbot, "A Soldier's Life and Death in Family Letters," p. B3; Lieutenant E. Stanley Abbot obituary, *The Beverly Citizen* (Beverly, Massachusetts, July 25, 1863), p. 1.

79. Sever & Francis, *Harvard Memorial Biographies,* 2 vols. (Cambridge, MA, 1866), vol. 1, pp. 426-427.

80. Information and photos provided by Kerry H. Shea, Norwich University Class of 1966.

81. McPherson, *Battle Cry of Freedom,* pp. 663-667. See LoC, *Wade Committee 2,* for testimony concerning General Meade actions.

82. Bowers Letters, *MHS,* Reel 16, frames 1541-1542. Bowers later learned his son had been wounded and was in contact with the Adjutant General of the Army concerning Charlie's case on July 21, 1863; Charles E. Bowers File, National Archives and Records Administration, Pension Division.

83. Noble also mentions the death of his second-in-command in his letter. An interesting sidelight to this incident lies in one of the more famous ghost stories of the Gettysburg battlefield. Lieutenant Colonel Fowler was killed when his head was blown off by a Rebel cannonball. Since that time, dozens of allegedly reliable sightings of Fowler's headless body , which

continue to this day, have been made on and around the site of the 17th Connecticut's battle-field of July 1, 1863 at Barlow's (Blocher's) Knoll. The lack of adequate footwear is more commonly mentioned in conjunction with Confederate forces. It is less well known that a lack of shoes was a problem for Union troops as well, the experience of Noble's men being duplicated in the Fifth Corps 140th New York Infantry. The assistant surgeon of that unit, Matthias Lord, wrote to his sister on July 12, 1863, that the men had literally "marched out of their shoes" prior to the battle. Bruce A. Bennett, from "An Addendum to The Supreme Event in its Existence: The 140th New York on Little Round Top," in the Gettysburg Discussion Group, on the Internet (erols.com), 1996; Colonel William H. Noble, unpublished letter of July 6th, 1863, *Lewis Leigh Collection*, Books, 43, 44, 45, U.S. Army Military History Institute, (Carlisle Barracks, Pennsylvania).

84. Martin T. McMahon, "From Gettysburg To The Coming Of Grant," *Battles and Leaders 4*, pp. 81-82; Washburn, *Vermont AG Reports*, 1863, pp. 83-84.

85. Fisk, *Hard Marching*, pp. 122-123.

86. Washburn, *Vermont AG Reports, 1863*, p. 84. Stoughton was breveted a brigadier general of volunteers for his gallantry; Ellis, *Norwich University* II, pp. 653-645; Stevens, *Three Years in the Sixth Corps*, pp. 262-264. George Blood French, to "Calvin and Valeria French," from unpublished correspondence in the possession of Linda Margaret Farr Welch.

87. McPherson, *Battle Cry of Freedom*, pp. 608-611.

88. Benedict, *Vermont in the Civil War* I, p. 144; Parsons, *First Vermont Brigade*, p. 66; Houghton Recollection, p. 33.

89. Bowers Letters, *MHS*, Reel 16, frame 1673.

90. Bowers Letters, *MHS*, Reel 16, frames 1552-1553.

91. McPherson, The *Battle Cry of Freedom*, p. 681; *OR* 29, pt. 1, pp. 232, 279. See also William D. Henderson, *The Road to Bristoe Station: Campaigning with Lee and Meade, August 1-October 20, 1863* (Lynchburg, VA, 1987), pp. 278, 283-285, 331; Washburn, *Vermont AG Report, 1864*, p. 210; Ellis, *Norwich University* II, pp. 652-653. For the regulations on paroles, see LoC, *Wade Committee 2*, p. 206.

92. *OR* 29, pt. 1, p. 279.

93. Henderson, *The Road to Bristoe Station*, pp. 185, 252; *OR* 29, pt. 1, pp. 283, 285; Henry L. Abbott, *Fallen Leaves: Civil War letters of Major Henry L. Abbott* (Kent, 1991), pp. 208-209, 224; McMahon, "From Gettysburg To The Coming Of Grant," p. 84.

94. For additional details on both the Bristoe and Mine Run Campaigns, see A. A. Humphreys, *Gettysburg to the Rapidan: The Army of the Potomac July 1863 to April 1864* (New York, 1883), pp. 23 -30, 37-46, 49-70.

95. Bowers Letters, *MHS*, Reel 16, frames 1775-1780; Humphreys, *Gettysburg to the Rapidan*, p. 63.

96. Bowers Letters, *MHS*, Reel 16, frames 1775-1780.

97. Washburn, *Vermont AG Report, 1864*, pp. 39-40. Benedict, *Vermont in the Civil War* I, pp. 144-145, 406-410; Samuel E. Pingree to Augustus Hunton, November 19, 1863, *Pingree Letters*, Vermont Historical Society, Montpelier, Vermont; Stephen M. Pingree to Augustus Hunton, October 8 and December 8, 1863, *Pingree Letters*; Houghton, *Recollection*, p. 35.

98. Although he received substantial criticism for his positions during the war, Governor Seymour never advocated a divided Union and considered himself a patriot. He lost the presidential election of 1868 to General Grant by a mere 305,000 votes; Ellis, *Norwich University* II, pp. 215-217. Seymour apparently never lost the boldness and aggressiveness he had shown as a youth: when he was a cadet he had been suspended from the university for joining a midnight raid on the town commons, Ellis, *Norwich University 1898*, p. 36.

99. Numerous references to Governor Seymour's part in suppressing the New York City Draft Riots can be found in *OR* 27, pt. 2. See also Sifakis, *Who Was Who in the Civil War*, p. 582.

5. HOW FAR TO DERBY LINE?

1. Leon Burr Richardson, *History of Dartmouth College*, Volume II (Hanover, New Hampshire, 1932), p. 504; Stephen G. Abbott, *The First Regiment New Hampshire Volunteers in the Great Rebellion* (Keene, New Hampshire, 1890), p. 95 (for Norwich cadets at Dartmouth); Gwin, *Norwich in the Civil War*, pp. 2-3.

2. *Norwich in the Civil War*, pp. 2-3; Alice Rains Trulock, *In the Hands of Providence: Joshua Chamberlain in the American Civil War* (Chapel Hill, 1992), p. 60; Philip N. Racine, editor, *Unspoiled Heart: The Journal of Charles Mattocks of the 17th Maine* (Knoxville, Tennessee, 1994), pp. xvi-xix, 288-289.

3. Peck, *Revised Roster of Vermont Volunteers*, p. 67; "The Third Regiment," *Walton's Daily Journal and Watchman*, Montpelier, Vermont, July 11, 1861, p. 2; Ellis, *Norwich University 1898*, pp. 77-78; Washburn, *Vermont AG Reports, 1863*, pp. 55-56; "Camp Baxter, St. Johnsbury," *The Vermont Journal* (Windsor, Vermont, June 15, 1861), p. 8; Mary R. Cabot, editor, *Annals of Brattleboro 1681-1895*, Volume II (Brattleboro, Vermont, 1922), pp. 767, 786-787; Coffin, *Full Duty*, pp. 68, 120; Benedict, *12th Vermont*, pp. 5-7.

4. Ellis, *Norwich University 1898*, p. 408. Unfortunately, only 72 of these 100 matriculants can be identified and the others may be unidentified "special military students." See University Trustees, *Catalogue of the Corporation, Officers and Cadets of Norwich University for the Academic Year, 1863-64* (Norwich, Vermont, November 1863), pp. 12-13, 15; see also the *Catalogue for 1864-65* (Norwich Vermont, November 1864), pp. 9-10, 12; Poirier, *Alumni Database*. This two year course at Norwich may have been alluded to by President Lincoln (see Chapter 9). It should also be noted that the current Montpelier Campus of Norwich University (formerly Vermont Junior College) was the site of Sloan Army General Hospital during the last two years of the Civil War. Some of the original hospital buildings survive and are in use today.

5. University Trustees, *Catalogue of the Corporation, Officers and Cadets of Norwich University for the Academic Year 1861-62* (Norwich, Vermont, November 1861), p. 12.

6. University Trustees, *Catalogue of the Corporation, Officers and Cadets of Norwich University for the Academic Year 1862-63* (Norwich, Vermont, October 1862), p. 11.

7. Ellis, *Norwich University* III, pp. 650-653; Ellis, *Norwich University 1898*, p. 19; Poirier, *Alumni Database*. This is the last prewar catalog; no catalog for the academic year of 1860-1861 was found in the Norwich University archives. University catalogs also refer to cadets entering at any point during the previous year, but does not identify them. For example, see *Norwich University Catalogue for the Academic Year 1863-64* (Norwich, Vermont, November 1863), p. 13 note. Further complicating attempts to compile accurate totals for the Norwich University Corps of Cadets in a given year is the fact that the corps roster was not broken down by class until 1863. While the question of the total numbers of cadets at Norwich at any one time may seem "much ado about nothing," it does point out the difficulties in identifying alumni, including those who may have served in the Union forces; Ellis, *Norwich University 1898*, p. 408. The presence on campus of more than 60 special military students in 1861, with over 100 students taking special military courses between 1861-63, however, could account for the apparent disparity in Ellis' totals for the number of cadets in the Cadet Corps at a given date; see Norwich University, Special Collections, *Norwich University Catalogues, 1859-1865*.

8. Katcher, *The Civil War Source Book*, p. 178. Figures for cadets who attended the national academy but did not graduate are not provided. Ellis, *Norwich University* III, 649-653.

Ellis, *Norwich University 1898*, p. 408; Poirier, *Alumni Database*, Gwin, *Norwich in the Civil War*, pp. 126-127.

9. *University Reveille*, Vol. 3, No. 1, (April 1862), pp. 1-6; Ellis, *Norwich University* I pp.122-23; Ellis, *Norwich University 1898*, p. 76; *University Reveille*, Vol. 3, No. 1 (Norwich, Vermont, April, 1862), p. 5. For modifications to this daily routine initiated after the war see White, *Norwich University 1890*, p. 8.

10. Association of Collegiate and Professional Students, *The University Quarterly* (New Haven, Connecticut, April, 1861), p. 146; University Trustees, *Catalogue of the Corporation, Officers and Cadets of Norwich University for the Academic Year 1861-62* (Norwich, Vermont, November 1861), p. 11; Ellis, *Norwich University*, Vol. I, p. 119; *University Reveille*, Vol. 5, No. 1 (Norwich, Vermont, April 1864), p. 6. The potential "emergency" turned out be the St. Albans raid of October 1864, when the newly issued armaments were put to good use; P. P. Pitkin, *Report of the Quarter-Master General of the State of Vermont, October 1, 1865* (Montpelier, Vermont, 1865), p. 8.

11. Ellis, *Norwich University* I, p. 410; Unknown Author, "Seventh Squadron Rhode Cavalry," Norwich University *Special Collections* (Northfield, Vermont, no date), pp. 1-3.

12. Sears, *Landscape Turned Red*, pp. 150-153; Ellis, *Norwich University* I, pp. 412-413; John G. Walker, "Jackson's Capture of Harper's Ferry," *Battles and Leaders* II, p. 611; Julius White, "The Capitulation of Harper's Ferry," *Battles and Leaders* II, pp. 613-614; Bradley Finfrock, "Harrowing Nighttime Escape From Harper's Ferry," *The Washington Times* (September 9, 1995), p. B3; Ellis, *Norwich University* I, p. 414; Dyer, *Compendium* II, p. 1628.

13. *University Reveille*, No. 1 (April 1865), p. 2; Dyer, *Compendium* II, pp. 1267-1268.

14. Peter T. Washburn, *Report of the Adjutant & Inspector General of the State of Vermont from Oct. 1, 1864, to Oct. 1, 1865* (Montpelier, Vermont, 1865), pp. 96-100; Hereinafter referred to as Washburn, *Vermont AG Report, 1865*; Sifakis, *Who Was Who in the Civil War*, pp. 736-737; *Vermont National Guard*, pp. 116-118. The event was actually made into into a 1954 Hollywood movie titled "The Raid," starring Van Heflin, Anne Bancroft, Lee Marvin, Richard Boone, Peter Graves and Claude Akins; *Newport News* (October 27, 1864), p. 1; Ellis, *Norwich University 1898*, p. 61. The excitement caused by this raid would not be matched again in Vermont until a contingent of Norwich cadets descended upon the staid capital of Montpelier in May 1963. The cadets were in town to conduct a now fabled "panty raid" at the all-female Vermont Junior College. Coming as it did before full-blown American involvement in the Viet Nam War, the event caused quite a sensation. The panty raid has since become a part of cadet and local folklore, even finding its way into the Norwich University *Cadet Handbook*. New cadets, called Cadet Recruits (Rooks) in the Norwich vernacular, are required to memorize key segments of the handbook. The legendary "Great Panty Raid" (justifiably so in the author's opinion) is now viewed as a historically significant event; Norwich University Corps of Cadets, *Cadet Handbook* (Norwich University, Northfield Vermont, 1996), p. 16. Unfortunately, or more likely luckily, the author, a cadet recruit himself at the time, missed out on the event. However, his roommate, James E. Fewer (Class of 1966), is a bona fide "veteran" of the action and narrowly escaped capture and draconian punishment at the hands of members of the irate Commandant of Cadets' staff. The young ladies appear to have been in cahoots with senior leaders of the cadet raiders and had apparently emptied the stores in Montpelier and Barre, Vermont, of all varieties of undergarments prior to the event.

15. Ellis, *Norwich University* I, pp. 416-418; Washburn, *Vermont AG Report, 1863*, pp. 52-53; *Vermont AG Reports, 1865*, pp. 96-97.

16. Washburn, *Vermont AG Report, 1865*, Appendix B, p.13; *University Reveille*, Vol. 6, Number 1 (April 1865), p. 2. The cadets were prepared to bring at least one of their brass six-pound howitzers with them. However, at the last moment, another telegraph message from the governor specified that only "infantry forces" were needed--that telegram no doubt serious-

ly disappointed the cadet gun crew; P.P. Pitkin, *Report of the Quarter-Master General of the State of Vermont, October 1, 1865* (Montpelier, Vermont, 1865), p. 8; Ellis, *Norwich University* I, pp. 416-418.

17. *University Reveille*, No. 1 (Norwich, Vermont, April, 1865), p. 2.

18. Ellis, *Norwich University* I, p. 419. Ellis, *Norwich University 1898*, p. 63; *University Reveille*, Number 1 (April, 1865), p. 2.

19. It is noteworthy that at a Vermont National Guard encampment in 1894, it was revealed that the Confederate "signal fires" observed in the hills around the town in October 1864, had actually been lit by St. Alban's boys who felt it was their bound duty to keep things stirred up! Ellis, *Norwich University 1898*, p. 63; *University Reveille*, Number 1 (April, 1865), p. 2.

6. THE OVERLAND CAMPAIGN TO PETERSBURG

1. McPherson, *Battle Cry of Freedom*, pp. 718-719; Ulysses S. Grant, *Memoirs and Selected Letters: Personal Memoirs of U.S. Grant, Selected Letters 1839-1865* (New York, 1990), p. 469. Hereinafter cited as Grant, *Memoirs*.

2. Grant, *Memoirs*, pp. 478-479; Catton, *A Stillness at Appomattox*, pp. 483-484; McPherson, *Battle Cry of Freedom*, p. 722.

3. McPherson, *Battle Cry of Freedom*, pp. 719-720; Edmund Rice, *19th Massachusetts Infantry, Draft Report for 1864,* from the Private Collection of Steven J. Nitch (Near Petersburg, Virginia, December 16, 1864), pp. 1-2. Hereinafter referred to as Rice, *1864 Report, 19th Massachusetts Infantry*.

4. Dyer, *Compendium* I, pp. 284, 294; Rice, *1864 Report, 19th Massachusetts Infantry*, pp. 2-3.

5. Poirier, *Alumni Database*; McPherson, *Battle Cry of Freedom*, pp. 723-724; *OR* 36, pt.1, p. 437.

6. These "plank" roads were so named because the dirt (mud) surface had been "corduroyed" with actual planks; R. Wayne Maney, *Marching to Cold harbor: Victory & Failure, 1864* (Shippensburg, Pennsylvania, 1995), 25. Hereinafter cited as Maney, *Marching to Cold Harbor*; Stevens, *The Sixth Corps in the Wilderness*, p. 191.

7. Benedict, *Vermont in the Civil War* I, pp. 418, 422; Carol Reardon, "The Other Grant: Lewis A. Grant and the Vermont Brigade in the Battle of the Wilderness," in *The Wilderness Campaign*, edited by Gary Gallagher (Chapel Hill, North Carolina, 1997), p. 16; "The Fighting of the First Brigade in the Wilderness," *The Caledonian*, St. Johnsbury, Vermont, June 10, 1864, p. 1.

8. Gregory A. Mertz, "No Turning Back: The Battle of the Wilderness," Part I, *Blue & Gray Magazine* (Columbus, Ohio, April 1995), p. 12. Hereinafter referred to as Mertz, *No Turning Back*; Gordon C. Rhea, *The Battle of the Wilderness* (Baton Rouge, Louisiana, 1994), pp. 94-99. Hereinafter referred to as Rhea, *Battle of the Wilderness*; Edward Steere, *The Wilderness Campaign: The Meeting of Grant and Lee*, reprint (Mechanicsburg, Pennsylvania, 1994), pp. 88, 114. Hereinafter referred to as Steere, *The Wilderness Campaign*; John Michael Priest, *Nowhere to Run: The Wilderness, May 4th & 5th, 1864* (Shippensburg, Pennsylvania, 1995), pp. 42-43. Hereinafter referred to as Priest, *Nowhere to Run*; Nowhere to Run, pp. 114-115, 263-264; Andrew A. Humphreys, *The Virginia Campaign of '64 and '65* (New York, 1881-83; Archive Society reprint, 1992), Part I, p. 24. Hereinafter cited as Humphreys, *The Virginia Campaign*.

9. Rhea, *Battle of the Wilderness*, pp. 100-102; Steere, *The Wilderness Campaign*, pp. 152-154; Mertz, *No Turning Back* I, p. 19; Priest, *Nowhere to Run*, pp. 67-68, 77; Poirier, *Alumni Database*.

10. Reese, *Syke's Regulars*, pp. 301-304; Steere, *The Wilderness Campaign*, pp. 152-155; Maney, *Marching to Cold Harbor*, p. 28.

11. Steere, *The Wilderness Campaign*, pp. 106-107, 246-247; Priest, *Nowhere to Run*, pp. 97-98; John B. Carpenter, *Military Record #10550-B-80*, National Archives Records and Pension Division, Washington D.C. Hereinafter referred to as Carpenter, *#10550-B-80*.

12. Rhea, *The Battle of the Wilderness*, pp. 157-162; Steere, *The Wilderness Campaign*, p. 161; Wright, *Seventh Wisconsin*, pp. 228, 302-303; Nolan, *Iron Brigade*, p. 274; Gregory A. Merz, "No Turning Back - The Battle of the Wilderness," Part II, in *Blue & Gray Magazine*, Volume XII, Issue 5 (Columbus, Ohio, June 1995), p. 13.

13. Mertz, *No Turning Back*, I, pp. 49-51; Hazard Stevens, "The Sixth Corps in the Wilderness," February 14, 1887, *Papers of the Military Historical Society of Massachusetts*, Volume IV (Wilmington, North Carolina, 1989), pp. 178, 191. Hereinafter referred to as *PMHSM*.

14. Mertz, *No Turning Back* I, pp. 49-51 and Part II, pp. 12-22; *OR* 36, pt. 1, pp. 696-697, 709-710; Steere, *The Wilderness Campaign*, pp. 204-07; Washburn, *Vermont AG Reports, 1864*, pp. 171-174; Rhea, *Battle of the Wilderness*, pp. 190-92, 310-312; Benedict, *Vermont in the Civil War* I, pp. 424-425, 428-431; William P. Shreve, "The Operations of the Army of the Potomac, May 13-June 2, 1864," February 14, 1881, Vol. IV, *PMHSM*, pp. 317-318; *OR* 36, pt. 1, p. 699; Rhea, *Battle of the Wilderness*, pp. 310-12; Humphreys, *The Virginia Campaign* I, p. 32.

15. Mertz, *No Turning Back* I, pp. 49-51; *Buck's Book*, p. 78; Poirier, *Alumni Database*. *OR* 36, pt. 1, p. 701; Waite, *Vermont in the Rebellion*, pp. 169-172; Benedict, *Vermont in the Civil War* I, p. 434; Fox, *Regimental Losses*, p. 116. The 6th Vermont alone suffered 34 killed, 155 wounded and seven missing for a total of 196 casualties; Fox, *Regimental Losses*, p. 151; see also Benedict, *Vermont in the Civil War* I, p. 223. George B. French was pensioned in 1867 as a result of the wound he suffered in the Wilderness. In later years, it affected his ability to write and was one of the reasons he resigned his job as Clerk of Windsor County, Vermont, in March, 1885; see *Families of Cavendish*. In addition, while French's Civil War correspondence has survived, nothing in these letters refers to action in the Wilderness. Linda Welch, who is preparing an extensive publication on the family, believes this is related to the loss of George's younger brother in that battle. Apparently, George had persuaded his parents to let the boy enlist telling them it would help him to "grow up;" he may well have blamed himself for his brother's death.

16. Rhea, *Battle of the Wilderness*, pp. 196-197; Washburn, *Vermont AG Reports, 1864*, pp. 41, 171-173; *OR* 36, pt. 1, pp. 709-710; Priest, *Nowhere to Run*, pp. 152-156.

17. Houghton, *Recollection*, p. 35; Fisk, *Hard Marching*, p. 215.

18. *OR* 36, pt. 1, pp. 695-96; Washburn, *Vermont AG Reports, 1864*, pp. 174-175.

19. Washburn, *Vermont AG Reports, 1864*, pp. 175-176; Benedict, *Vermont in the Civil War* I, p. 439; Stevens, *Three Years in the Sixth Corps*, pp. 304-310. In addition, the Second Division, Sixth Corps, in which the Vermont Brigade fought, suffered the largest loss of any division in a single battle during the war--2,994 men killed, wounded and missing; Fox, *Regimental Losses*, p. 115.

20. Lemuel Abijah Abbott, *Personal Recollections and Civil War Diary* (Free Press Printing Co., Burlington, Vermont, 1908), pp. 44-45. Hereinafter referred to as Abbott, *Civil War Diary*.

21. Mertz, *No Turning Back* II, pp. 10-20; Dyer, *Compendium* I, p. 313; Noah Andre Trudeau, *Bloody Roads South: The Wilderness to Cold Harbor, May-June 1864* (New York, 1989), pp. 240-241. Hereinafter referred to as Trudeau, *Bloody Roads South*.

22. Ellis, *Norwich University* II, p. 545; Stephen Minot Weld, *War Diary and Letters of Stephen Minot Weld*, 2nd Edition. (Boston, 1979), p. 286. Hereinafter referred to as Weld, *Letters*. Griswold felt his death was imminent that morning when, as he accepted a cup of cof-

fee from one of his officers, he stated "I suppose this is the last breakfast I shall eat." Anna Griswold, *Charles Griswold* (Boston, 1866), pp. 18-19. Hereinafter referred to as Griswold, *Charles Griswold.*

23. Weld, *Letters*, pp. 280-281, 288; Griswold, *Charles Griswold*, pp. 20-21; emphasis in original; *Unpublished diary of Doctor Horatio S. Soule, 56th Massachusetts*, Fredericksburg and Spotsylvania National Military Park, entries for May 6-7, 1864. In a sequel to the black bag story, five years after the war Weld met a young woman who asked him if he had been with Colonel Griswold when he was killed; Weld replied he had. She then asked if Weld had seen the locket Charles had worn around his neck. Weld answered no but that Griswold had asked him to retrieve it if he was killed and send it to his mother. The woman then indicated it had been her picture in the locket.

24. Mertz, *No Turning Back* II, pp. 20, 48-49; Rhea, *Battle of the Wilderness*, p. 420. Seymour, following adventures as a prisoner of war in Charleston, South Carolina, where he would be placed with other officers directly in the line of fire of the Union Fleet, was paroled in time to rejoin the Army of the Potomac in time for its final campaigns. Stevens, *Three Years in the Sixth Corps*, pp. 311-312; George R. Agassiz, editor, *Meade's Headquarters 1863-1865: Letters of Colonel Theodore Lyman from The Wilderness to Appomattox* (Boston, 1922), p. 99. Hereinafter referred to as Lyman, *Meade's Headquarters*; Steere, *The Wilderness Campaign*, pp. 441-442; Humphreys, *The Virginia Campaign* I, pp. 49-50.

25. Mertz, *No Turning Back* II, p. 49; Abbott, *Civil War Diary*, p. 48; Rice, *1864 Report, 19th Massachusetts Infantry*, pp. 3-4.

26. Poirier, *Alumni Database*; Fox, *Regimental Losses*, p. 445. Those regiments were the 2nd and 4th Vermont, 93rd New York, 5th Vermont, 57th Massachusetts and 3rd and 6th Vermont. Clara Barton Papers, *LoC*, Containers 152-153, Reel 107, lecture notes, pp. 18-19.

27. George Blood French, "To Calvin & Valeria French," May 16 and May 18, 1864, in unpublished letters provided to the author by Ms. Linda Margaret Farr Welch.

28. Mertz, *No Turning Back*, pp. 49-50; Catton, *A Stillness at Appomattox*, p. 514; Steere, *The Wilderness Campaign*, pp. 465-466.

29. Lyman, *Meade's Headquarters*, pp. 99-100.

30. William Glenn Robertson, Back Door to Richmond: *The Bermuda Hundred Campaign, April-June 1864* (Newark, Delaware, 1987), p. 55, 139-149. Hereinafter referred to as the Robertson, *Bermuda Hundred Campaign*; Humphreys, *The Virginia Campaign* I, pp. 137-159. Of particular interest is the first large-scale use of wire entanglements by the Army of the James. These proved to be a rather unpleasant surprise to attacking Confederate; Robertson, *Bermuda Hundred Campaign*, pp. 180 fn. 23, 185; John Horn, *The Petersburg Campaign, June 1864-April 1865* (Conshohocken, Pennsylvania, 1993), pp. 16-29. Hereinafter referred to as Horn, *The Petersburg Campaign.*; Robertson, *Bermuda Hundred Campaign*, p. 235. The Eighteenth Corps returned to the Bermuda Hundred for a brief period following the Battle of Cold Harbor, minus the 3,000 casualties they suffered there. Horn, *Bermuda Hundred Campaign*, p. 241. Although the Eighteenth Corps was moved to join the Army of the Potomac, the main part the troops who redeployed with it were drawn from the Tenth Corps. *Ibid.*, p. 246.

31. Robertson, *Bermuda Hundred Campaign*, p. 256. Alfred H. Terry, given his illustrious military career, represents one of the most significant enigmas concerning our alumni. For additional details on the question, see the entry on General Terry in Appendix A, Poirier, *Alumni Database.*

32. William D. Matter, *If It Takes All Summer, The Battle of Spotsylvania* (Chapel Hill, North Carolina, 1988) pp. 297-298. Hereinafter referred to as Matter, *If It Takes All Summer*, pp. 488-489; The General's Tour, "The Battles at Spotsylvania Court House, Virginia, May 8-21, 1884, in *Blue & Gray Magazine*, Vol. I, Issue 6 (Columbus, Ohio, 1984), pp. 35-36. Hereinafter referred to as Blue & Gray Magazine, *Spotsylvania.* Poirier, *Alumni Database.*

33. Poirier, *Alumni Database*, Blue & Gray Magazine, *Spotsylvania*, p. 36.

34. Ellis, *Norwich University* II, p. 260-261; Stevens, *Three Years in the Sixth Corps*, pp. 192-195. Following the Battle of Gettysburg, Capt. Oliver Wendell Holmes Jr. joined Wright's staff as an aide. He served in that position until his term of service ended July 17, 1864. Holmes, of course, went on to become a legendary Supreme Court Justice; Bruce, *Twentieth Massachusetts*, p. 358; Humphreys, *The Virginia Campaign* I, p. 71.

35. Matter, *Spotsylvania*, pp. 156, 195; Blue & Gray Magazine, *Spotsylvania*, pp. 36-39.

36. *OR* 36, pt. 1, pp. 667-669; Matter, *Marching to Cold Harbor*, pp. 44-45; Charles Lawrence Pierson, "The Operations of the Army of the Potomac May 7-11, 1864," November 10, 1879, Vol. IV, *PMHSM*, pp. 224-225; Stevens, *Three Years in the Sixth Corps*, pp. 330-332; *Grant's Campaigns*, pp. 267-270; George W. Bicknell, *History of The Fifth Maine Volunteers* (Portland, Maine, 1871), pp. 312-316. Hereinafter referred to as Bicknell, *Fifth Maine*; Griffith, *Battle in the Civil War*, p. 152.

37. *OR* 36, pt. 1, pp. 667-668; Grant, *Memoirs*, pp. 267-268.

38. Bicknell, *Fifth Maine*, p. 314; *OR* 36, pt. 1, p. 668; Humphreys, *The Virginia Campaign* I, pp. 84-86; Grant, *Memoirs*, pp. 268-269.

39. McHenry Howard, "Notes and Recollections of Opening of the Campaign of 1864," April 16, 1883, Vol. IV, *PMHSM*, pp. 107-109; Waite, *Vermont in the Rebellion* I, pp. 174-175; Ellis, *Norwich University* II, p. 622; Beyer and Keydel, *America's Medal of Honor Recipients*, p. 895.

40. *OR* 36, pt. 1, pp. 668, 702-703; Thomas O. Seaver, *Medal of Honor File* (See also Appendix D); Washburn, *Vermont AG Reports, 1864*, pp. 176-177; Ellis, *Norwich University* II, pp. 668-669; Grant, *Memoirs*, pp. 269-270.

41. Fisk, *Hard Marching*, pp. 220-221.

42. Houghton, *Recollection*, p. 35.

43. *OR* 36, pt. 1, pp. 334-335; Grant, *Memoirs*, pp. 280-283; Walker, *Second Corps*, pp. 468-470.

44. Walker, *Second Corps*, pp. 468-470; Howard, Vol. IV, *PMHSM*, pp. 114-115; Francis Channing Barlow, "Capture of the Salient," January 13, 1879, Vol. IV, *PMHSM*, p. 258; Humphreys, *The Virginia Campaign* I, pp. 92-94; Grant, *Memoirs*, pp. 283-284; Catton, *A Stillness at Appomattox*, pp. 533-535; Matter, *Spotsylvania*, pp. 245-267; Grant, *Memoirs*, pp. 285-286.

45. Waitt, *Nineteenth Massachusetts*, p. 308; Kenneth C. Turino, editor, *The Civil War Diary of Lt. J.E. Hodgkins* (Camden, Maine, 1994), pp. 85-86. Hereinafter referred to as the Turino, *Hodgkins Letters*. General Webb's appeal to "follow the colors of the 19th Massachusetts" makes sense when it is noted in Rice's 1864 report to the Adjutant General of Massachusetts that his regiment was the Second Corps "battalion of direction" for the May 12 assault and that its state color was white--most states bore blue colors; Rice, *1864 Report, 19th Massachusetts Infantry*, pp. 5-6.

46. Waitt, *Nineteenth Massachusetts*, pp. 308-312, 368; Moore, *Songs of the Civil War*, pp. 18-19; Turino, *Hodgkins Letters*, p. 85; John B.G. Adams, *Reminiscences of the Nineteenth Massachusetts Regiment* (Boston, 1899), pp. 90-91. Thompson may have been wounded here as he is mistakenly reported for a time as having died of wounds received May 12 vice killed in action at Cold Harbor, June 3; *Thompson File*, Muster Roll, Company "G," 19th Massachusetts, June 30, 1865.

47. *OR* 36, pt. 1, p. 505; Rhea, *Spotsylvania*, pp. 209-213; Rollins, *Battle Flags*, pp. 11-13. The actual totals are three colors taken, not two as stated in the 73rd New York's *Official Report*. Rollins' *Battle Flags* lists the colors of the 13th Louisiana and 56th Virginia as captured on May 12, 1864 by the 73rd. These units, however, were not listed in the Army of Northern Virginia's Order of Battle for that engagement.

48. Lewis A. Grant, "Review of Major General Barlow's Paper on the Capture of the Salient at Spotsylvania, May 12 1864," March 14, 1881, Vol. IV, *PMHSM*, pp. 268-271; Stevens, *Three Years in the Sixth Corps*, pp. 333-335; Matter, *Spotsylvania*, p. 215; *OR* 36, pt. 1, pp. 703-704; Humphreys, *The Virginia Campaign* I, pp. 98-100; Walker, *Second Corps*, pp. 472-475; Washburn, *Vermont AG Reports, 1864*, p. 177.

49. Fisk, *Hard Marching*, p. 221. The Vermont Brigade, in the one week period following their crossing of the Rappahanock with 2,800 men, suffered the loss of 1,645 men killed, wounded and missing in the Wilderness and Spotsylvania; Fox, *Regimental Losses*, p. 116.

50. Ellis, *Norwich University* II, p. 657; *OR* 36, pt. 1, p. 491; Robert McAllister, "McAllister's Brigade At The Bloody Angle," *Battles and Leaders* IV, p. 176; Ellis, *Norwich University* II, p. 619; Walker, *Second Corps*, p. 476; Matter, *Spotsylvania*, pp. 218, 250-252.

51. G. Norton Galloway, "Hand-to-Hand Fighting at Spotsylvania," Vol. IV, *Battles and Leaders*, p. 171; Matter, *Spotsylvania*, p. 217; Ed Raus, "Hell's Half Acre: The Fight for Bloody Angle," in *Blue & Gray Magazine*, (Columbus, Ohio, June-July 1984), pp. 44-45. The 95th Pennsylvania lost 135 men killed, wounded and missing at Spotsylvania, May 12; Fox, *Regimental Losses*, p. 285.

52. Poirier, *Alumni Database*. Also wounded on May 12 was Pvt. James E. Batchelder (Class of '67), Company E, 5th Vermont. He was discharged on September 22, 1864, in order to accept an appointment to West Point, one in a long line of Norwich men to do so. He graduated in June 1868 and was commissioned a second lieutenant in the 2nd United States Cavalry. Ellis, *Norwich University* III, p. 98; Parker, *Thirty-Second Massachusetts*, pp. 214-215; Henry H. Meachum, *The Empty Sleeve: The Life and Hardships of Henry H. Meachum* (Springfield, Massachusetts, 1869), pp. 15-16; Matter, *Spotsylvania*, pp. 228-229, 357, 416 fn. 23, 24; *OR* 36, pt. 1, p. 570; Catton, *A Stillness at Appomattox*, p. 535.

53. *OR* 36, pt. 1, p. 704; Stevens, *Three Years in the Sixth Corps*, pp. 201-02.

54. Abbott, *Civil War Diary*, pp. 57-59.

55. Alfred S. Roe and Charles Nutt, *History of the First Regiment of Heavy Artillery Massachusetts Volunteers* (Boston, 1917), p. 151. Companies of heavy artillery regiments are designated as "batteries" in this text in order to more clearly differentiate these units from the old line infantry regiments.

56. Poirier, *Alumni Database*. For example, the 1st Maine Heavy Artillery suffered the heaviest loss of any unit in the army and in the assault on "The Crater"; the 14th New York Heavy Artillery distinguished itself by capturing a Rebel color while losing 132 total casualties. Later, in the Rebel assault on Forth Stedman in March 1865, the 14th fought their way out of the fort after being overrun and helped save the key position of Fort Haskell; Fox, *Regimental Losses*, pp. 125, 190; Washburn, *Vermont AG Reports, 1864*, p. 178.

57. *OR* 36, pt. 1, p. 706; Poirier, *Alumni Database*. The 1st Vermont Heavy Artillery had originally been known as the 11th Vermont Infantry before being converted to an artillery unit on December 10, 1862. Officially, it was redesignated the "First Artillery, Eleventh Vermont Volunteers." Benedict, *Vermont in the Rebellion* II, p. 346. The old designation was routinely used, however, in official reports and by other Vermont units when referring to their "heavies."

58. *OR* 36, pt. 1, pp. 337-338; Fox, *Regimental Losses*, p. 125; Heitman, *Register* I, p. 6; Shreve, Vol. IV, *PMHSM*, pp. 298-299; *OR* 36, pt. 1, p. 150; Horace H. Shaw and Charles J. House, *First Maine Heavy Artillery 1862-1865* (Portland, Maine, 1903), p. 112; Grant, *Memoirs*, pp. 319-320.

59. *OR* 36, pt.1, pp. 285-287; Ellis, *Norwich University* II, pp. 282-283; Naisawald, *Grape and Canister*, pp. 464, 487.

60. Maney, *Marching to Cold Harbor*, pp. 55-57, 61-62.

61. J. Michael Miller, *The North Anna Campaign, "Even to Hell Itself," May 21-26, 1864*, 2nd Edition (Lynchburg, Virginia, 1989), p. 60. Hereinafter referred to as Miller, *North Anna Campaign*.; Dyer, *Compendium* I, pp. 937-940; Miller, *Photographic History* III, p. 71. The

93rd New York had served as the Army of the Potomac Headquarters Guard from May 21, 1862, to April 10, 1864. It was much favored on account of its superior discipline, drill and general efficiency. Nevertheless, it was a fighting regiment as its performance in the summer of 1864 would show; Fox, *Regimental Losses*, p. 218; David H. King, A. Judson Gibbs and Jay H. Northrup, *History of the Ninety-Third Regiment, New York Volunteer Infantry* (Milwaukee, Wisconsin, 1895), pp. 554-555. See also *New York at Gettysburg* II, pp. 713, 716.

62. Poirier, *Alumni Database* and *Appendix B*; Miller, *North Anna Campaign*, pp. 102-107; Warren Wilkinson, *Mother May You Never See the Sights I've Seen: The Fifty-Seventh Massachusetts Veteran Volunteers in the Last Year of the Civil War* (New York, 1990), pp. 138-139. Hereinafter referred to as Wilkinson, *Fifty-Seventh Massachusetts*; Fox, *Regimental Losses*, p. 83.

63. Rice, *1864 Report, 19th Massachusetts Infantry*, pp. 7-8.

64. Maney, *Marching to Cold Harbor*, pp. 61-70; Grant, *Memoirs*, pp. 176, 588; Poirier, *Alumni Database*.

65. Maney, *Marching to Cold Harbor*, pp. 89-99.

66. Catton, *Stillness at Appomattox*, pp. 551-553; Maney, *Marching to Cold Harbor*, pp. 90-91; Washburn, *Vermont AG Reports, 1864*, pp. 180-81; Martin T. McMahon, "Cold Harbor," *Battles and Leaders* IV, p. 215; William Farrar Smith, "The Eighteenth Corps At Cold Harbor," *Battles and Leaders* IV, pp. 222-224; Charles H. Porter, "The Battle of Cold Harbor," December 12, 1881, *PMHSM* IV p. 333; Humphreys, *The Virginia Campaign* I, pp. 180-182.

67. Abbott, *Civil War Diary*, pp. 71-72.

68. *OR* 36, pt. 1, p. 671; Fox, *Regimental Losses*, p. 178; Maney, *Marching to Cold Harbor*, pp. 105-108.

69. Maney, *Marching to Cold Harbor*, pp. 119-120, 136; *PMHSM* IV, pp. 333-334.

70. Maney, *Marching to Cold Harbor*, p.130; *Grant's Campaigns*, p. 451; Wilkinson, *Fifty-Seventh Massachusetts*, pp. 151-152.

71. Maney, *Marching to Cold Harbor*, pp. 139-158; Catton, *A Stillness at Appomattox*, pp. 553-556; Stevens, *Three Yeats in the Sixth Corps*, pp. 210-211; Lyman, *Meade's Headquarters*, pp. 143-148; Humphreys, *The Virginia Campaign* I, pp. 182-187.

72. Maney, *Marching to Cold Harbor*, pp. 139-140; *OR* 36, pt. 1, p. 464; Poirier, *Alumni Database*; Humphreys, The Virginia Campaign 1, p. 184; Matter, *Spotsylvania*, p. 298; Trudeau, *Bloody Roads South*, pp. 285-286. In twenty-two minutes, Hancock's Second Corps lost 3,510 casualties including six colonels killed and two general officers severely wounded. *General Hancock*, pp. 222, 228; McMahon, "Cold Harbor," *Battles and Leaders* IV, p. 217; Grant, *Memoirs*, p. 454; Frederick Phisterer, *New York in the War of the Rebellion*, 3rd Edition, Vol. I (Albany, 1912), p. 320.

73. *OR* 36, pt. 1, p. 571.

74. Houghton, *Recollection*, pp. 37-38; Abbott, *Civil War Diary*, p. 74; the 10th Vermont lost 28 killed, 131 wounded and three missing in action in this battle; Fox, *Regimental Losses*, p. 152. Stevens, *Three Years in the Sixth Corps*, pp. 351-352; Porter, *PMHSM* IV, pp. 335-336.

75. George R. Prowell, *History of the 87th Regiment Pennsylvania Volunteers* (York, Pennsylvania, 1901), p. 270; *OR* 36, pt. 1, p. 727.

76. Henry W. Ruoff, ed., *Biographical and Portrait Cyclopedia of Montgomery Country, Pennsylvania* (Philadelphia, Pennsylvania, 1895), p. 54; Parker, *51st Pennsylvania Volunteers*, p. 560; *OR* 36, pt. 1, pp. 952-953; Fox, *Regimental Losses*, p. 270. Edwin's parents had his body shipped home for burial where it was interred in the Montgomery, Pennsylvania, cemetery. An obelisk was erected over his grave with the following inscription: "...on the outbreak of the Southern Rebellion, he offered his services to his country and held successively the offices of Major of the 4th Regt, of Pa. Vol. for 3 months and then Major, Lieut. Colonel and Colonel in the Battles of Roanoke Island, Newbern, Camden, Second Bull Run, Chantilly, South

Mountain, Antietam, Fredericksburg, Vicksburg, Jackson, Campbell Station, Siege of Knoxville, Wilderness, Spotsylvania and Cold Harbour in which last, while gallantly leading on his men, he was shot through the neck and instantly killed. 'A dutiful son and affectionate brother, a faithful friend, a brave soldier, an efficient officer, a sincere Christian."

77. Haynes, *Second New Hampshire*, p. 238; Ellis, *Norwich University* II, p. 629; Waitt, *Nineteenth Massachusetts*, p. 356; Rice, *1864 Report, 19th Massachusetts Infantry*, p. 23; Turino, *Hodgkins Letters*, p. 91; Poirier, *Alumni Database*.

78. Poirier, *Alumni Database*.

79. Rice, *1864 Report, 19th Massachusetts Infantry*, pp. 9-10.

80. See Walbrook Davis Swank, *Battle of Trevilian Station: The Civil War's Greatest and Bloodiest All Cavalry Battle* (Shippensburg, Pennsylvania, 1994).

81. Ellis, *Norwich University* II, pp. 578-581; Sifakis, *Who's Who in the Civil War*, pp. 162, 587, 632; Poirier, *Alumni Database*; Theodore F. Rodenbough, "Sheridan's Trevilian Raid," *Battles and Leaders* IV, p. 234. *OR* 36, pt. 1, pp. 849-851.

82. Walker, *General Hancock*, p. 228; Horn, *The Petersburg Campaign*, p. 35. Humphreys, *The Virginia Campaign* I, pp. 191, 199-204; Catton, *A Stillness at Appomattox*, pp. 563-567; George Cary Eggleston, "Notes On Cold Harbor," *Battle and Leaders* IV, p. 230.

83. Horn, *The Petersburg Campaign*, pp. 35-40; Catton, *A Stillness At Appomattox*, pp. 573-577; Poirier, *Alumni Database*.

84. Horn, *The Petersburg Campaign*, pp. 55-57; Noah Andre Trudeau, *The Petersburg Campaign: Wasted Valor June 15-18, 1864* (H.E. Howard Inc., Lynchburg, Virginia, p. 22. Hereinafter referred to as Trudeau, *Wasted Valor*; Noah A. Trudeau, *The Last Citadel: Petersburg, Virginia, June 1864-April 1865* (Boston, 1991), pp. 40-41. Hereinafter referred to as Trudeau, *The Last Citadel*; Humphreys, *The Virginia Campaign* I, pp. 207-209.

85. Trudeau, *The Last Citadel*, pp. 17, 31-33; Poirier, *Alumni Database*.

86. Trudeau, *Wasted Valor*, pp. 93-99. As he had done before and would do again, Ledlie's use of alcohol before battles resulted in the actual combat command falling to one of his subordinates. In this case it was Colonel J. Parker Gould. Gould seems to have received little credit or notice for the times when he had to lead the troops in Ledlie's absence or, as at the North Anna, carry out his foolish orders. Don Lowry, *Fate of the Country: The Civil War from June to September 1864* (Hippocrene Books), New York, 1992), pp. 54-55. Hereinafter referred to as Lowry, *Fate of the Country*; John C. Ropes, "The Failure to Take Petersburg on June 16-18, 1864," February 17, 1879, *PMHSM* V, p. 171-172; Charles H. Porter, "The Petersburg Mine," January 12, 1885, *PMHSM* V, pp. 223-224; Trudeau, *Wasted Valor*, p. 94; *Wilkinson, Fifty-Seventh Massachusetts*, pp. 174-175; Humphreys, *The Virginia Campaign* I, p. 218.

87. Horn, *The Petersburg Campaign*, pp. 61-62; Trudeau, *Wasted Valor*, pp. 65-67; Poirier, *Alumni Database. Humphreys, The Virginia Campaign* I, pp. 217-218. Though it was in service for only a year, the 17th Vermont lost more men in battle than 75% of all Union regiments. Fox, *Regimental Losses*, p. 153; Washburn, *Vermont AG Reports, 1864*, p. 76.

88. Catton, *A Stillness at Appomattox*, pp. 578-580.

89. Trudeau, *Wasted Valor*, pp. 137-138, 141-142. Military history reveals that a severely weakened corps of combat leaders at the company, battalion and regimental level always results in serious reductions in aggressiveness and offensive spirit; Trudeau, *Wasted Valor*, pp. 60, 137-138.

90. Abbott; *Civil War Diary*, pp. 86-87.

91. Benedict, *Vermont in the Civil War* II, pp. 357-362, 366-371, 394; Ellis, *Norwich University* II, pp. 709, 732; Fox, *Regimental Losses*, p. 60.

92. Benedict, *Vermont in the Civil War* I, pp. 485-486, Poirier, *Alumni Database*.

93. S. Millet Thompson, *Thirteenth Regiment New Hampshire Volunteers* (Cambridge, Massachusetts, 1888), pp. 419-421; Ellis, *Norwich University* II, pp. 671-672.

94. Benedict, *Vermont in the Civil War* I, p. 149; Nolan, *Iron Brigade*, p. 276; Poirier, *Appendix B.* Robinson apparently came under strong criticism for the Iron Brigade's poor performance at the North Anna River on May 23, 1864. Regardless of whether he was at fault, the Iron Brigade of that time was not the unit of past days. The performance question rapidly became moot when Robinson's Brawner Farm wound reopened and the 7th Wisconsin shrunk to a size no longer warranting a full colonel as commander. See also Gaff, *Many a Bloody Field*, pp. 353-356.

95. Henry F.W. Little, *The Seventh Regiment New Hampshire Volunteers in the War of the Rebellion* (Ira C. Evans, Printers, Manchester, New Hampshire, 1896), p. 293; Poirier, *Alumni Database*; Dyer, *Compendium*, pp. 947-956; *OR* 36, pt. 1, pp. 278-279, 282-283, 800-801; Ellis, *Norwich University* II, pp. 282-283.

96. Catherine Abbot, "A Soldier's Life and Death in Family Letters," *The Washington Times* (Washington, D.C., July 9, 1994), p. B3. Stanley's brother survived the war and went on to a distinguished career in the Regular Army. Fanny Larcom Abbot, widowed at age 40, mourned Stanley until her death in 1883. Henry's uncle, Joseph Hale Abbot, named a son born December 13, 1863, Edward Stanley in memory of his soldier nephew; thus, his name was carried on.

97. Horn, *The Petersburg Campaign*, pp. 97-105.

98. Michael A. Cavanaugh and William Marvel, *The Battle of the Crater, "The Horrid Pit," June 25-August 6, 1864*, 2nd edition (Lynchburg, Virginia, 1989), pp. 4-13, 17-19. Hereinafter referred to as Cavanaugh and Marvel, *The Horrid Pit.*; Wilkinson, *Fifty-Seventh Massachusetts*, pp. 238-239; Humphreys, *The Virginia Campaign* II, pp. 254-260, 263.

99. Cavanaugh and Marvel, *The Horrid Pit*, pp. 52-53; Catton, *A Stillness at Appomattox*, pp. 599-608; Horn, *The Petersburg Campaign*, pp. 108-19; William H. Powell, "The Battle of the Petersburg Crater," *Battles and Leaders* IV, pp. 551-560.

100. Porter, *PMHSM* V, pp. 229-230.

101. Horn, *The Petersburg Campaign*, p. 118; *OR* 36, pt. 1, pp. 534, 539, 920-921; Humphreys I, p. 218; Stephen M. Weld, "The Petersburg Mine," March 27, 1882, *PMHSM* V, pp. 207-211; Wilkinson, *Fifty-Seventh Massachusetts*, pp. 241-242; Poirier, *Alumni Database*; Ellis, *Norwich University* II, p. 448.

102. Frank C. Damon, "Interesting Story Regarding Colonel J. Parker Gould," in the *Stoneham Independent* (Stoneham, Massachusetts, July 26, 1929), p. 2. Gould was specifically cited as having the respect of his troops and of being an officer who "was always out in front of his troops and never shirked his duties;" Wilkinson, *Fifty-Seventh Massachusetts*, p. 224. Gould was apparently a very well known Massachusetts officer. In fact, in a letter of September 14, 1864, from Clara Barton to her lifelong friend Annie Childs, she mentions Gould's death in a manner which indicates he was clearly known to Annie and to other members of both the Barton and Childs families. William Barton, *The Life of Clara Barton*, Volume 1 (New York, 1922), p. 292; Joseph K. Barnes et. al. *The Medical and Surgical History of the War of the Rebellion (1861-1865)*, six volumes (Washington, D.C., 1875-83), Vol. 2, pt. 1, p. 614, pt. 2, pp. 655, 697, 805, 824, pt. 3, pp. 127, 175, 432. The average Civil War death rate for amputations was 26% (28.5% for leg amputations such as Gould's); Horn, *The Petersburg Campaign*, pp. 117-118; Cavanaugh and Marvel, *The Horrid Pit*, pp. 108, 112-114; Weld, *PMHSM* V, p. 210; Henry Goddard Thomas, "The Colored Troops at Petersburg," *Battles and Leaders* IV, pp. 563-567. In 1866, Federal troops returned to The Crater to recover the men buried on the field. Six hundred and sixty-nine bodies were recovered, none of which could be identified and reinterred in the new Poplar Grove Cemetery. Not all bodies were recovered, however, and in 1931 another 29 Union skeletons were recovered during construction of a gold course. It is quite likely that additional unrecovered Union and Confederate remains lie today in the Crater.

103. Poirier, *Alumni Database*.

104. Welles, *Diary* II, p. 92.

105. Abbott, *Civil War Diary*, p. 83; E.M. Haynes, *A History of the Tenth Regiment Vermont Volunteers, with Biographical Sketches*, 2nd edition (Rutland, Vermont, 1894), p. 409.

106. Delos Phillips, 17th Michigan Infantry Diary, May 23-June 23, 1864, *Civil War Times Illustrated*, typescript (U.S. Army Military History Institute, Carlisle Barracks, Pennsylvania); Waitt, *Nineteenth Massachusetts*, pp. 343-344; Ellis, *Norwich University* II, pp. 639-640. The colors lost at the Weldon Railroad were retrieved and returned to the regiment after the end of the war and reside today in the Massachusetts State House in Boston; Rice, *1864 Report, 19th Massachusetts Infantry*, p. 12.

107. Committee of Publication, *A Memorial of the Great Rebellion Being a Brief History of the Fourteenth Regiment, New Hampshire Volunteers, 1862-1865* (Boston, 1882), p. 397; *Alumni Database*. Chaffin is buried in the Winchester (Virginia) National Military Cemetery; Catton, *A Stillness At Appomattox*, pp. 634-639, 642-645; Poirier, *Alumni Database* and *Appendix A*; Don Lowry, *Dark and Cruel War: The Decisive Months of the Civil War*, September-December 1864 (New York, 1993), pp. 325-327, 384; Fox, *Regimental Losses*, p. 78; Theodore C. Mahr, *Early's Valley Campaign The Battle of Cedar Creek: Showdown in the Shenandoah October 1-30, 1864* (Lynchburg, Virginia, 1992), pp. 134, 172.

108. William R. Driver, "The Siege of Petersburg after the Capture of the Weldon Railroad," *PMHSM* V, pp. 310-315; Rice, *1864 Report, 19th Massachusetts Infantry*, pp. 19-20; Adjutant General's Office, War Department, *Special Orders No. 362*, October 24th, 1864.

109. Lyman, *Meade's Headquarters*, pp. 299-300.

110. McPherson, *For Cause &Comrades*, pp. 146-147; Fisk, *Hard Marching*, p. 276.

---

7. 1865

1. Humphreys, *The Virginia Campaign* II, pp. 309-311; Dyer, *Compendium* I, p. 227. In addition, the white troops of the Army of the James were reorganized into the Twenty-fourth Corps and the African-American troops into the Twenty-fifth Corps. General Ferrero's division of African-Americans in the Ninth Corps was eventually added to the Twenty-fifth Corps; Catton, *A Stillness at Appomattox*, pp. 653-654.

2. Stevens, *Three Years in the Sixth Corps*, pp. 243-245; George L. Kilmer, "Gordon's Attack at Fort Stedman," *Battles and Leaders* IV, pp. 580-583; Trudeau, *The Last Citadel*, pp. 337-350.

3. John Anderson, *History of the 57th Massachusetts Volunteers* (Printers, Boston, 1896), p. 264; George L. Kilmer, "Gordon's Attack at Fort Stedman," *Battles and Leaders* IV, pp. 580-583. The 57th Massachusetts, although in active service for less than one year, suffered one of the highest percentages of battle deaths in the army. For example, in the Wilderness, the regiment lost 57 killed, 158 wounded and 30 missing in action, a loss of 245 of the 546 men engaged; Fox, *Regimental Losses*, p. 175.

4. Benedict, *Vermont in the Civil War* II, p. 386.

5. Catton, *A Stillness at Appomattox*, pp. 647-648; Petersburg National Battlefield, *City Point Unit*, informational brochure (no date); Trudeau, *The Last Citadel*, p. 132.

6. Poirier, *Alumni Database* and *Appendix B*.

7. Catton, *A Stillness at Appomattox*, pp. 659-660. It should be noted that Sumner H. Lincoln (Class of '62?) had risen from the rank of private, 1st Vermont Infantry in April 1861 to command of his regiment, the 6th Vermont, by October 21, 1864. At that time Lincoln was promoted to major in recognition of "his gallantry and fitness for command." Lincoln, who was likely a "special military student" in 1861, finished the war as colonel of the 6th Vermont and went on to become a brigadier in the regular army. He was in the hospital with fever when the final assault on Petersburg was made. Benedict, *Vermont in the Civil War* I, p. 229.

8. Trudeau, *The Last Citadel*, pp. 366-367; Humphreys, *The Virginia Campaign* II, pp. 366-371; Poirier, *Alumni Database*.

9. Catton, *A Stillness at Appomattox, pp. 669-671*; Mr. Jerry Wooten, Pamphlin Park Staff Historian, provided these notes and unpublished materials from a file on the Vermont Brigade which he generously opened to the author, February 24, 1996, pp. 7-13. The breakthrough sector is very well preserved and now forms part of the privately owned Pamphlin Park site at Petersburg, Virginia. Hereinafter referred to as Wooten, *Pamphlin Park Files.*

10. Wooten, *Pamphlin Park Files*; Hazard Stevens Report, Sixth Corps, April 2, 1865, *Personal Narratives of the Events in the War of the Rebellion being Papers read before the Rhode Island Soldiers and Sailors Historical Society*, Sixth Series, No. 8 (Providence, Rhode Island, 1904), pp. 14, 39; *OR* 46, pt. 1, pp. 960, 968; Washburn, *Vermont AG Report, 1865*, p. 39, and Appendix C, p. 9. In a visit to the Vermont Brigade's combat area, now located within the Pamphlin Park site near Petersburg, the author had an extended opportunity to inspect the ground and talk to the Park Historian, Mr. Jerry Wooten. The Pamphlin Park Headquarters sits in the breakthrough sector and Mr. Wooten informed the author that the Vermonters literally "would have charged through the front doors of the Visitor's Center." Conversation with author and materials provided from the personal files of Mr. Jerry Wooten, February 24, 1996.

11. Washburn, *Vermont AG Reports, 1865*, Appendix C, pp. 7-8.

12. Washburn, *Vermont AG Reports, 1865*, Appendix C, p. 9.

13. *OR* 46, pt. 1, pp. 671-673; Trudeau, *The Last Citadel*, pp. 392-394; Poirier, *Alumni Database.*

14. Humphreys, *The Virginia Campaign* II, pp. 366-372, 380-384; Poirier, *Alumni Database*; Stevens, *Three Years in the Sixth Corps*, pp. 249-255; Josiah Hall File, *Special Collections*, Kreitzberg Library, Norwich University; Grant, *Memoirs*, pp. 728-729. While Hall was a prisoner in Richmond, two junior officers from the 1st Vermont Cavalry were promoted over him, an unusual if not unique occurrence. It appears there was some "politicking" amidst in the regiment; Hall eventually obtained his due, although his belated promotion may well have cost him a general's star or at least a brevet to that rank; Dr. Elliot W. Hoffman, letter to the author, February 15, 1996.

15. Parker, *Thirty-Second Massachusetts*, pp. 252-253.

16. Ellis, *Norwich University* II, pp. 322-323; Warner, *Generals in Blue,* pp. 562-563; Horace Porter, "The Surrender at Appomattox Court House," *Battles and Leaders* IV, p. 730; Powell, *Fifth Corps*, pp. 846-847; Humphreys, *The Virginia Campaign* II, pp. 391-392.

17. Chamberlain, *The Passing of the Armies*, pp. 259-269; Joshua Lawrence Chamberlain, *Bayonet! Forward* (Gettysburg, PA, 1994), p. 227; Poirier, *Alumni Database* and *Appendix B.*

18. Parker, *Thirty Second Massachusetts*, pp. 255-256.

19. Grant, *Memoirs*, p. 712.

20. Chamberlain, *The Passing of the Armies*, pp. 332-361.

21. Benedict, *Vermont in the Civil War* I, pp. 610-614, 619-620; Washburn, *Vermont AG Report, 1865*; p. 42; Coffin, *Full Duty*, p. 352; Houghton, *Recollection*, p. 48; "The Vermont Troops," *The Vermont Journal*, (Montpelier, Vermont, June 17, 1865), p. 1; "The Green Mountain Boys," *Walton's Daily Journal*, July 1, 1865, p. 1; Stevens, *Three Years in the Sixth Corps*, pp. 268-269.

22. Moore, *Civil War in Song and Story*, pp. 335-336.

23. Josiah Hall File, *Special Collections*, Kreitzberg Library, Norwich University.

24. Hall is referring to the 1st Vermont Cavalry. The other regiments mentioned are Vermont infantry regiments; Elliot W. Hoffman, copy of unpublished letter of Josiah Hall to William Wells, 11 July, 1865 from the *Wells Papers.*

25. Griswold, *Charles Griswold*, pp. 46-50; Weld, *Letters*, p. 401.

8. NORWICH MEN IN OTHER THEATERS OF WAR

1. There is no doubt that some of these 326 alumni, particularly those whose units could not be specifically identified, served in the Army of the Potomac. In addition, it proved impossible, as indicated in the text, to trace the military career of the more than 100 officers who had attended Norwich as "special military students." See Poirier, *Alumni Database* and *Appendix A.* The seeming disparity in adding the total number of alumni serving in various fields is due to the fact that several had dual service. That is, they served in both the Army and/or the Navy or Marine Corps.

2. Ellis, *Norwich University* II, pp. 162, 227, 211; W.A. Croft and John M. Morris, *The Military and Civil History of Connecticut During the War of 1861-1865* (New York, 1868), p. 65; Welles, *Diary* I, p. 354.

3. Norwich University, *The Reveille*, Vol. XXX, No. 7 (Northfield, Vermont, April 15, 1896), p. 105; Poirier, *Alumni Database.*

4. While in the city, Dodge met and apparently made a lasting positive impression on President Abraham Lincoln. See J.R. Perkins, *The Life of General G.M. Dodge* (Indianapolis, Indiana, 1929), pp. 82-84. Hereinafter referred to as Perkins, Life of General Dodge.

5. Perkins, *Life of General Dodge*, p. 105.

6. Grant, *Memoirs*, pp. 423-424, 637, 556.

7. Ellis, *Norwich University* II, pp. 477-487; Grant, *Memoirs*, p. 737. According to Dr. Gary Lord, Norwich University's historian, General Dodge was struck in the head by a minie ball while at one of Sherman's officers meetings. When he fell, the other officers were stunned and feared Dodge had been killed. However, as General Sherman observed Dodge's wound, he commented that since Dodge had been hit in the head, he would recover--of course, he did. The bullet was placed on a watch chain and used thereinafter by Dodge. It is now in the possession of the Norwich University Museum; Sherman, *Memoirs,* p. 934; *OR* 38, pt. 3, pp. 47, 369-372; Lowry, *Fate of the Country*, p. 235.

8. Grant, *Memoirs*, pp. 505-506 note; J. R. Perkins, *Trails, Rails and War: The Life of General G.M. Dodge* (Indianapolis, Indiana, 1929), p. 10.

9. Fox, *Regimental Losses*, p. 120; Poirier, *Alumni Database*; *OR* 47, pt. 1, pp. 391-403; Mark L. Bradley, *Last Stand in the Carolinas: The Battle of Bentonville* (Campbell, California, 1995), pp. 60, 380, 410-412; Lowry, *Fate of the Country*, pp. 786; Ellis, *Norwich University* II, p. 401; Grant, *Memoirs*, p. 282; Ellis, *Norwich University* I, p. 819; Lowry, *Fate of the Country*, p.70. Forrest is General Nathan Bedford Forrest, CSA; Sherman, *Memoirs*, pp. 316-317.

10. Ellis, *Norwich University* II, pp. 491-495; Lew Wallace, "The Capture of Fort Donelson," *Battles and Leaders* I, p. 418; Moore, *Civil War in Song and Story*, p. 228.

11. Jim Huffstodt, *Hard Dying Men: The Story of General W.H.L. Wallace and General T.E.G. Ransom and their "Old Eleventh" Illinois Infantry in the American Civil War (1861-1865)*, (Bowie, Maryland, 1991). Hereinafter referred to as Huffstodt, *Hard Dying Men.* Extensive use of contemporary materials and Ransom's letters to Grenville M. Dodge (Class of '51), his close friend and classmate, in *Hard Dying Men* amply demonstrates the extent of his contemporary fame and reputation.

12. Huffstodt, *Hard Dying Men*, pp. 184-186; Grant, *Memoirs*, pp. 353, 385, 527-529; *OR* 22, pt. 2, p. 130; Warner, *Generals in Blue*, p. 390; "Death of General Ransom," *The Vermont Journal* (Windsor, Vermont, November 12, 1864), p. 1.

13. *OR* 24, pt. 1, pp. 296-299; Huffstodt, *Hard Dying Men*, pp. 142-146; Sherman, *Memoirs*, p. 636; Grant, *Memoirs*, p. 492; Ellis, *Norwich University* II, pp. 350-351.

14. Huffstodt, *Hard Dying Men*, p. 143; Ellis, *Norwich University* II, pp. 350-351.

15. Huffstodt, *Hard Dying Men*, p. 155.

16. Ellis, *Norwich University* II, pp. 491-495; Huffstodt, *Hard Dying Men*, p. 191; Sherman, *Memoirs*, p. 636.

17. *The National Tribune* (Washington, D.C., July 10, 1884), p. 1; *The Reveille*, Vol. IV, No. 1 (Norwich University, Northfield, Vermont, October 1884); Grant, *Memoirs*, pp. 493-494; Gwin, *Norwich in the Civil War*, p. 3.

18. Huffstodt, *Hard Dying Men*, p. 220; Ellis, *Norwich University* III, pp. 123-125. In his regimental commander's endorsement to Eugene Ransom's resignation, which was submitted on June 16, 1864, "almost habitual intoxication and continued venereal diseases" were also included as reasons for his recommending approval, *Ibid.*, p. 221.

19. Ellis, *Norwich University* II, pp. 470-471; Miller, *Photographic History* IV, p. 132.

20. Ellis, *Norwich University* II, pp. 470-471; Lowry, *Fate of the Country*, pp. 327-328. Hatch himself seems to have garnered more than his fair share of the loot, for his headquarters wagon was reportedly loaded with paintings, china and glassware when the troops departed Oxford; Warner, *Generals in Blue*, p. 215-216.

21. Wiley Sword, *Shiloh: Bloody April* (Dayton, Ohio, 1974), pp. 357-358. Hereinafter referred to as Sword, *Shiloh, Bloody Shiloh*; Ellis, *Norwich University* II, p. 309; *OR* 30, pt. 1, pp. 323-326; Ulysses S. Grant, "The Battle of Shiloh," *Battles and Leaders* I, pp. 474-476; Don Carlos Buell, "Shiloh Reviewed," *Battles and Leaders* I, pp. 492-495, 506-507, 524-525.

22. Sword, *Shiloh, Bloody Shiloh*, p. 358; Ellis, *Norwich University* II, p. 309. That officer was Union Brigadier General Jefferson C. Davis. Davis avoided court martial due to his important political connections. Although he rose to corps command, he was never promoted. Indiana Governor Oliver P. Morton's influence with the government and the importance of Indiana's role in the war, apparently were key factors in his protege Davis never being tried. Don Carlos Buell, "East Tennessee and the Campaign of Perryville," *Battles and Leaders* III, pp. 43-44. The murder was apparently incited by Nelson slapping Davis after Davis had thrown a crumpled paper into Nelson's face after an argument. For details see the referenced article p. 43, note and J. Montgomery Wright, "Notes Of A Staff Officer At Perryville," *Battles and Leaders* III, p. 60-61; Warner, *Generals in Blue*, pp. 115-116.

23. Poirier, *Alumni Database*; Ellis, *Norwich University* II, pp. 495, 562, 390-391.

24. *OR* 30, pt. 1, pp. 654-657; Ellis, *Norwich University* II, pp. 574-575; Charles E. Belknap, *History of the Michigan Organizations at Chickamauga, Chattanooga and Missionary Ridge 1863* (Lansing, Michigan, 1897), pp. 131-132.

25. *OR* 3, pt. 1, p. 56; Ellis, *Norwich University* II, pp. 581-582; "The Opposing Forces at Wilson's Creek," *Battles and Leaders* I, p. 306; Ellis, *Norwich University* II, pp. 458, 259-260; Heitman, Vol. I, p. 1054; Warner, *Generals in Blue*, pp. 574-575.

26. Warner, *Generals in Blue*, pp. 497-498;Thomas O. Selfridge, Jr., "The Navy at Fort Fisher," *Battles and Leaders* IV, pp. 655-657; *The Reveille*, Vol. XXX, No. 7, p. 105. There is some confusion in Norwich records concerning General Terry's status as an alumnus. As a result, discussion of Terry's wartime role in this work has reluctantly been minimized, perhaps unjustly so. General Terry appears as an alumnus in several issues of the cadet newspaper *The Reveille*, and in various Norwich Rolls of Honor. Terry is not, however, listed as such in the 1911 Ellis, *History of Norwich University*. Terry was given command of the 2nd Connecticut and later the 7th Connecticut while Maj. Gen. William H. Russell (Class of '28) and Brig. Gen. E.W.N. Starr (Class of '28) dominated the Connecticut state military structure. While it would not have been unprecedented for Terry to have been given such commands with limited or no military training or experience, the "Norwich connection" is a more likely reason. If Terry did not actually obtain his military training on the Norwich campus as a cadet or as a special military student, he may well have trained at the Partridge inspired "Commercial and Collegiate Institute" in New Haven, of which the same William H. Russell (Class of '28) was president for many years. To compound the problem, Ellis' alumni listings have also been found to contain some omissions and errors; Grant, *Memoirs*, pp. 668-670, 772.

27. Ellis, *Norwich University* II, pp. 360-361; Doubleday, *Chancelorsville and Gettysburg*, p. 95. See also Jesse Bowman Young, *The Battle of Gettysburg: A Comprehensive Narrative* (New

York, 1913), pp. 115-118. Additional modern support to the view that Milroy acted properly at Winchester and possibly assisted Union efforts to counter Lee's invasion are given in Edwin C. Fishel, *The Secret War for the Union: The Untold Story of Military Intelligence in the Civil War* (New York, 1996), pp. 444-453, 572-574.

28. *OR* 27, pt. 2, pp. 196-197 (conclusions). The complete transcript of the Court of Inquiry and President Lincoln's ruling can be found in *OR* 27, pt. 2, pp. 88-201; Margaret B. Paulus, *Papers of General Robert Huston Milroy*, Vol. 1, (Private Printing, 1965), pp. 1-4, 102, 488-491, Vol. IV, pp. 57-59. Milroy's anti-West Point feeling may have stemmed not only from his admiration of Alden Partridge and the citizen-soldier tradition, but also from his failing to gain a commission in the army upon graduation with a master's degree in military science from Norwich in 1843. At the time, West Point did not award degrees. Ulysses S. Grant's own chief of staff, Brig. Gen. John A. Rawlins, believed there was serious cause for alarm in the existence of a West Point "Old Boy Network." Rawlins, a volunteer officer, found his influence with Grant, very substantial during 1861-1863, waning from 1864 on, partly due to Grant's surrounding himself with West Pointers in the Army of the Potomac. Rawlins believed these men deliberately crowded out non-academy officers. For details see Robert F. James, "Inspired Profanity Was Tool of Grant's Aide," *The Washington Times* (Washington, January 7, 1995), p. B1. Strong pro- or anti-West Point feelings were not exclusive to the Northern armies. Brigadier General Robert A. Toombs of Georgia once remarked that the epitaph of the Confederate Army should read "Died of West Point;" John Roberts, "West Pointers A Dominant Force on Both Sides," *The Washington Times* (Washington, September 30, 1995), p. B1; Welles, *Diary* I, p. 329. See also Grant associate General John A. Logan, *The Volunteer Soldier of America* (R.S. Peale & Company Publishers, 1887), pp. 581-584 for additional views on the subject.

29. Welles, *Diary* I, pp. 332-333. Ironically, it was Montgomery Meigs (a West Pointer), who had a distinguished career as Quartermaster General of the Army, who vigorously defended Milroy from his accusers.

30. Miller, *Photographic History* I, p. 207; Ellis, *Norwich University* II, p. 388.

31. Ellis, *Norwich University* II, pp. 385-386, 379, 680; Heitman, *Register*, p. 180; Poirier, *Alumni Database*.

32. *OR* 28, pt. 1, pp. 16, 208, 344, 362; Stephen R. Wise, *Gate of Hell: Campaign for Charleston Harbor* (Columbia, South Carolina, 1994), p. 102.

33. Quincy A. Gilmore, "The Army Before Charlston in 1863," *Battles and Leaders* IV, pp. 59-60. The national color of the 54th Massachusetts was saved by Sergeant William H. Carney, an African-American freeman from New Bedford, Massachusetts, this author's home town. Sergeant Carney, though wounded four times and severely injured, managed to crawl back to Union lines with the national color where he told the men "The Old Flag never touched the ground." He became the first African-American to win the Congressional Medal of Honor. The Carney Academy (formerly the Carney Elementary School) in New Bedford, Massachusetts, is located close to the author's former home in that city; Beyer and Keydel, *Deeds of Valor*, p. 258. Wise, *Gate of Hell*, pp. 108, 114; Poirier, *Alumni Database*.

34. Ellis, *Norwich University* II, p. 534.

35. Ellis, *Norwich University* II, pp. 252-254; James Russell Soley, "The Union and Confederate Navies," *Battles and Leaders* I, pp. 623-624.

36. Ellis, *Norwich University* II, pp. 190-191; Soley, "The Union and Confederate Navies," *Battles and Leaders* I, pp. 616-618; *OR* 27, pt. 2, pp. 878-879, 882-883.

37. *OR* 51, pt. 1, p. 19; Ellis, *Norwich University* II, pp. 247-248, 622.

38. Ellis, *Norwich University*, II, pp. 65-66, 88-90; Fox, *Regimental Losses*, p. 537, note. Boggs went on to achieve further fame in the naval service and eventually retired as a rear admiral.

39. Ellis, *Norwich University* II, pp. 68, 242, 325, 577, 153-154, 275; *OR* 1, pt. 1, pp. 645-646, 655; *OR* 20, pt. 1, pp. 658, 672.

40. Ellis, *Norwich University* II, pp. 110-111, 233-235; John Taylor Wood, "The First Fight of Iron-Clads," *Battles and Leaders* I, pp. 705-707, 709-711. Farrand was later promoted to commodore.

41. Ellis, *Norwich University* II, p. 565.

9. POSTSCRIPT

1. Emory Upton, *The Military Policy of the United States* (New York, 1904), pp. 236-242; Young, *The Battle of Gettysburg*, p. 335; Poirier, *Alumni Database*.

2. Charles Curtis to Wheelock Veazey Letter, October 30, 1872, in the Norwich University *Special Collections*. See Appendix F for the various estimates of Norwich men participating in the Civil War. Waterville College is now Colby College, Waterville, Maine; Gwin, *Norwich in the Civil War*, pp. 3-4.

3. The total number of alumni breveted, cited for gallantry, serving as drillmasters, wounded in action, and killed in action will undoubtedly rise following a detailed research effort on non-Army of the Potomac and Confederate alumni--an increase that would perhaps be significant. Nearly 90% of Norwich alumni serving in the Union's armed forces were officers. Unfortunately, the scope of the impact and role of the over 100 special military student alumni in the war effort can only be speculated upon at the current time. The few special military students who are known and are mentioned in this text, however, certainly performed very well.

4. Poirier, *Alumni Database* and *Appendix B*.

5. Fox, *Regimental Losses*, p. 48; Burke Davis, *The Civil War: Strange & Fascinating Facts* (New Jersey, 1994), p. 215; Poirier, *Alumni Database*. The figures per thousand for alumni are extrapolated due to the fact that less than 1000 alumni served in the war.

6. Melanie L. Bent, Norwich University Office of Alumni Affairs, *Letter to Author*, February 12, 1996, pp. 1-2. Following the Civil War, Norwich men sacrificed their lives in the Indian Wars (with at least one officer with Lt. Col. George A. Custer at the Little Big Horn), at least two lost their lives in the Spanish-American War, 16 Norwich men gave their lives in World War I, 87 in World War II, three in Korea, 22 in Viet Nam, and one in Operation Desert Storm. Over 1,600 alumni served in World War II (1,300 as officers), and hundreds more in World War I, Korea and Desert Storm. The Corps of Cadets was called to active duty in both World Wars and there were no commencements in 1918 and from 1943-46. In a program bearing similarities to the indoctrination of "special military students" in the Civil War, nearly 2,000 pilots, navigators and bombardiers were trained on the Norwich campus after the cadets were called to active duty during World War II. See Robert O. Gwin, *The History of Norwich University*, Volume IV (Northfield, Vermont, 1965), pp. 46, 334-336.

7. See Chapter 5 for additional details. The identities of only a few of the men who attended Norwich as special military students are known. As detailed in the text, however, each of these distinguished himself while on active service.

8. Ellis, *Norwich University* II, p. 748; Poirier, *Alumni Database*; Peck, *Revised Roster of Vermont Volunteers*, p. 718; Norwich University, *Special Collections* and the Norwich University Museum.

9. Poirier, *Alumni Database*; no naval engagements are included in this total. Editorial staff, *University Reveille*, Vol. 4, No. 1 (Norwich, Vermont, March 1863), p. 4.

10. Poirier, *Alumni Database* and *Appendices A and B*.

11. Griffith, *Battle in the Civil War*, pp. 124-127; Stuart L. Koehl, "Modern Civil War Was Really Napoleonic," *The Washington Times* (Washington, D.C., February 3, 1996), p. B3. General Emory Upton, U.S.M.A. Class of 1861, was a clear exception to this trend. From the

Southern perspective, much has been written on the "value added" provided the Confederate Army, particularly to the Army of Northern Virginia, by alumni of the Virginia Military Institute. This author believes that further research on Norwich alumni and those of Alden Partridge's Norwich "spinoff" academies in the South will likely show they had a similar "value added" to the Confederacy. In addition, this author believes that such a study would show that the a large measure of the effectiveness of the Army of Northern Virginia was derived from the presence of thousands of V.M.I. graduates and alumni of the Alden Partridge's various academies in its ranks rather than solely from its West Pointers.

12. Welles, *Diary* I, p. 85.

13. For example, Generals Milroy, Ransom, Hatch, Strong and Seymour, as well as regimental commanders such as Edgar Kimball, Thomas Seaver and Edmund Rice are specifically and repeatedly cited for their unusual aggressiveness. Alden Partridge, *Lecture on Education* (Middletown, Connecticut, 1828), pp. 263-280; Gwin, *Norwich in the Civil War*, pp. 100-105. Thousands of other volunteers could have also come from Partridge-influenced and trained alumni from schools such as the Collegiate and Commercial Institute in New Haven, Connecticut.

14. Clara Barton Papers, *LoC*, Containers 152-153, Reel 107, p. 86.

15. Reprint of the speech of General William T. Sherman, *The Reveille*, Vol. IV, No. 1 (Northfield Vermont, October, 1884), p. 5. For an example of the involvement of Norwich cadets in training Vermont regiments, see Peck, *Revised Roster of Vermont Volunteers*, p. 67.

16. Ellis, *Norwich University 1898*, pp. 76-77. For example, the training of all the regiments of the "New" (Second) Vermont Brigade by Norwich cadets in fall 1862 as per "State Drill Officers," *University Reveille*, Vol. 4, No. 1 (Norwich, Vermont, March 1863), p. 6.

17. Poirier, *Alumni Database*; Benedict, *Vermont in the Civil War* I, pp. 618-619. Efforts by the Adjutant General of Vermont in 1865 (Brig. Gen. Peter T. Washburn) and in the early 1890s (Brig. Gen. Theodore S. Peck) to ascertain from the War Department the exact identity and number of Confederate colors captured by Vermont units were unsuccessful; see Washburn, *Vermont AG Report, 1865*, pp. 25-26, Appendix B, pp. 10-11 and Peck, *Revised Roster of Vermont Volunteers*, p. iv.

18. Benedict, *Vermont in the Civil War* I, p. 619.

19. Ellis, *Norwich University* I, p. 397; between three and four thousand cadets attended the New Haven school, many of whom attained distinction in the Civil War.

20. Edwin C. Bearss, "Introduction: Gettysburg Revisited," *The Gettysburg Magazine*, Issue Number Fourteen (Dayton, Ohio, January 1996), p. 6. Two of Mr. Bearss' ancestors, including Congressional Medal of Honor winner Brigadier General Hiram "Hike em" Bearss, USMC, Class of 1898, are Norwich alumni.

Bibliography

MANUSCRIPTS

Dartmouth College, Hanover New Hampshire Unpublished Civil War materials in the possession of Linda M. Welch, Native-American Department.
Fredericksburg and Spotsylvania National Military Park, Fredericksburg, Va. Diary of Dr. Harry Soule, 56th Massachusetts.
The Historical Society of Montgomery County, Norristown, Pennsylvania
File on Edward and Edwin Schall, and file on John W. Schall.
The Library of Congress, Washington, D.C.
Clara Barton Papers; particularly her diary and Civil War related materials in Reel 107 (Containers 152-153).
The Massachusetts Historical Society, Boston, Massachusetts
Letters of Charles and Charles E. Bowers (32nd Massachusetts), Civil War Microfilm Part XIII, Reels 15-16.
Special Collections, Kreitzberg Library, Norwich University, Northfield, Vermont
William Arba Ellis Papers (Background to History of Norwich University, 1911). These papers include in some cases unpublished letters, photos, and wartime information. Files on the following individuals were specifically used: Edward S. Abbott, George W. Balloch, Albert V. Colburn, Thomas W. Eayre, Jacob P. Gould, Oscar E. Learnard, Pomeroy Loomis, William D. Munson, William H. Noble, Edgar Parker, Dunbar R. Ransom, Thomas E.G. Ransom, Edmund Rice, Thomas O. Seaver, George W. Smith, Archibald S. Taylor, Evan Thomas, and Edward B. Williston.
Gwin, Robert. *The Contribution of Norwich University to the Civil War* (Norwich University Special Collections, Norwich University, Northfield, Vermont, circa 1965.
Military College of Vermont, Corps of Cadets, *Handbook, 1996-97.*
Norwich University Catalogs (1820-67) listing members of the Norwich University Corps of Cadets and their hometown for a given academic year; e.g. 1856-57. Particularly the following: University Trustees. *Catalogue of the Corporation, Officers, and Cadets of Norwich University for the Academic Year 1861-62.* Norwich, Vermont, November, 1861. University Trustees. *Catalogue of the Corporation, Officers, and Cadets of Norwich University for the Academic Year 1862-63.* Norwich, Vermont, October, 1862.
Norwich University. *Rules and Regulations of The Military College of Vermont, Corps of Cadets,* 177th Edition. August 1996.
Norwich University. *Corps of Cadets, Standards, Organization and Procedures Manual.* August 1996.
The Alden Partridge Papers.
Painter, Jacqueline S., editor. *The Trial of Captain Alden Partridge, Corps of Engineers.* Norwich University Library, Northfield, Vermont, 1987.

The Truman B. Ransom Papers.

The University Quarterly. April 1861, July 1861, October 1861.

University Reveille. Vol 2, No. 1, April 1861; Vol 3, No 1, April 1862; Vol. 4, No. 1, March 1863; Vol. 5, No. 1, April 1864; Vol. 6, No. 1, April 1865; Vol. IV, No. 1, October 1884; April 15, 1896.

Cadet matriculation (muster) roles for the period 1835-70.

Unpublished materials dealing with various subjects such as the "College Cavaliers."

White, Homer. *History of Norwich University.* C.N. Whitmarsh, Northfield, Vermont, 1891.

State Historical Society of Wisconsin, Madison, Wisconsin

Charles K. Dean Papers.

W.K. Wright Papers.

Civil War Voices.

We Band of Brothers: The Record of Company B, Seventh Wisconsin Volunteers.

State House Flag Project, State of Massachusetts, Boston, Massachusetts

Photos and data on various Massachusetts Civil War Flags (Courtesy of Stephen Hill).

Steven J. Nitch Collection

Lieutenant Colonel Edmund Rice. *Report of Operations, 1864* (Initial Draft), 19th Massachusetts Veteran Volunteer Infantry, directed to the Adjutant General of Massachusetts (In the Field, Near Petersburg, December 16, 1864), 24 pages.

United States Army Military History Institute, Carlisle, Pennsylvania

Civil War Times Illustrated Collection.

Delos Phillips, 17th Michigan. Diary.

Lewis Leigh Collection.

Colonel William H. Noble, 17th Connecticut. Letter.

Massachusetts Commandery of the Military Order of the Loyal Legion.

Photos of Edward S. Abbott, Charles E. Griswold, Jacob P. Gould, Jesse Gove, Willie Johnston, Joseph A. Mower and Staff, Edmund Rice, Edwin Schall, Edward B. Williston, "Bloody Angle," Spotsylvania, Burnside Bridge, Staff of the 19th Massachusetts Infantry.

Roger D. Hunt Collection.

James A. Hall, Photo.

The National Tribune (Washington, D.C.)

Issues of May 17, 1883, June 28, 1883, November 29, 1883, May 1, 1884 June 20, 1884, November 20, 1884, January 28, 1897, and February 4, 1897.

United States National Archives,Records Group 393

Unpublished Regimental and Special Orders and records of the Second Vermont Brigade, and the 12th, 13th, and 15th Vermont Volunteer Infantry Regiments. Military and/or pension files for David C. J. Beattie, Charles Bowers, Charles E. Bowers, John. Carpenter, Alfred M. Channel, James A. Cunningham, Charles W. Davis, Michael Devereux, Jacob Parker Gould, Charles Hunsdon, Nathaniel Irish, Charles H. Potter, Edmund Rice (Including Medal of Honor File), William W. Robinson, Thomas O. Seaver (including Medal of Honor File, John B. Thompson, and Daniel W. Washburn.

OFFICIAL COMPILATIONS

Adjutant General. *Record of Service of Connecticut Men in the Army and Navy of the United States During the War of the Rebellion.* Case, Lockwood, and Brainard Co., Hartford, Connecticut, 1889.

Adjutant General. *Report of the Adjutant General of the State of Illinois, 1861-1866.* Three Volumes. Baker, Balhache and Company Printers, Springfield, Illinois, 1867 (first two volumes), Volume Three, 1886.

Adjutant General. *Records of the Massachusetts Volunteers, 1861-1865.* Two Volumes. Wright & Potter Printers, Boston, 1868.

Adjutant General. *Record of Service of the Michigan Volunteers in the Civil War.* Volume 17. Ihling Bros. & Everard, Kalamazoo, Michigan, 1906.

Adjutant General. *Revised Register of Soldiers and Sailors of New Hampshire in the War of the Rebellion, 1861-1866.* A.D. Ayling and K.A.C. Evans, Printers, Concord, New Hampshire, 1895.

Adjutant General's Office. *Official Register of the Volunteer Force of the United States Army of the Years 1861, 1862, 1863, 1864, 1865.* Ten Volumes. Adjutant General's Office, Washington, D.C., 1865.

Adjutant General. *Annual Reports of the Adjutant General of the State of New York.* J.B. Lyons & Co., Albany, New York, 1900-01.

America's Medal of Honor Recipients: Complete Official Citations. Highland Publishers, Golden Valley, Minnesota, 1980.

Axline, H.A., Adjutant General. *Official Roster of the Soldiers of the State of Ohio in the War of the Rebellion, 1861-1866.* The Ohio Valley Press, Cincinnati, 1888.

Ayling, Augustus D. *Revised Register of the Soldiers and Sailors of New Hampshire in the War of the Rebellion 1861-1866.* Ira C. Evans, Public Printer, Concord, New Hampshire, 1895.

Davis, Major George B., Leslie J. Perry, civilian expert, Joseph W. Kirkley, civilian expert. Compiled by Captain Calvin D. Cowles, 23rd U.S. Infantry. *The Official Military Atlas of the Civil War.* Washington, Government Printing Office, 1891-1895. Reprint, Gramercy Books, New York, 1983.

Harrison, Noel G. *Gazetteer of Historic Sites Related to the Fredericksburg and Spotsylvania National Military Park.* Two volumes. Fredericksburg and Spotsylvania National Military Park, 1986.

Heitman, Francis B. *Historical Register and Dictionary of the United States Army.* General Printing Office, Washington, D.C., 1903.

Medal of Honor Recipients, 1863-1978. Washington, D.C.: Government Printing Office, 1979.

New York Monuments Commission. *New York at Gettysburg.* Three volumes. Lyon Printers, Albany, New York, 1900.

Peck, Theodore S. *Revised Roster of Vermont Volunteers and Lists of Veterans Who Served With the Army and Navy of the United States.* Watchman Publishing Company, Montpelier, Vermont, 1892.

United States War Department. *The War of the Rebellion: A Compilation of the Official Records of the Union and Confederate Armies.* One Hundred-Thirty volumes. Washington, D.C.: Government Printing Office, 1880-1901.

Washburn, Peter. *Reports of The Adjutant and Inspector General of The State of Vermont (1862, 1863, 1864, 1865).* Walton's Steam Printing, Montpelier, Vermont.

PUBLISHED PRIMARY SOURCES

NEWSPAPERS

Burlington, Vermont, *The Burlington Weekly Sentinel,* 1861-65.
Hyde Park, Vermont, *Lamoille Newsdealer,* 1861-1865.
Montpelier, Vermont, *Vermont Watchman and State Journal,* also known as *Walton's Daily Journal,* 1861-65.
Rutland Vermont, *Daily Herald,* 1862-1865.
Rutland, Vermont, *The Rutland Weekly Herald,* January-December, 1861.
St. Johnsbury, Vermont, *The Caledonian,* 1861-65.

PUBLISHED PRIMARY SOURCES

(Includes autobiographies, Diaries, Journals, Memoirs, Reminiscences and Unit Histories)

Abbott, Henry L. *Siege Artillery in the Campaign Against Richmond.* D. Van Nostrand Publisher, New York, 1868.

Abbott, Lemuel Abijah. *Personal Recollections and Civil War Diary.* Free Press Printing, Burlington, Vermont, 1908.

Abbott, Stephen G. *The First Regiment New Hampshire Volunteers in the Great Rebellion.* Sentinel Printing Co., Printers, Keene, New Hampshire, 1890.

Adams, John B.G. *Reminiscences of the Nineteenth Massachusetts Infantry.* Wright & Foster Printing Co., 1899.

Agassiz, George R., editor. *Meade's Headquarters, 1863-1865: The Letters of Colonel Theodore Lyman from the Wilderness to Appomattox.* Massachusetts Historical Society, Boston, 1922.

Anderson, John. *History of the 57th Regiment Massachusetts Volunteers.* E.B. Stillings and Co., Printers, Boston, 1896.

Anonymous. *History of the First Connecticut Heavy Artillery.* Hartford, Connecticut, 1893.

Bachelder, John B. '49, David L. and Audrey J. Ladd, editors. *The Bachelder Papers,* Three Volumes. Morningside House Inc., Dayton Ohio, 1994-95.

Balzer, John E., editor. Buck's Book, *A View of the 3rd Vermont Infantry Regiment.* Balzer & Associates, Bolingbrook, Illinois, 1993.

Baquet, Camille. *History of the First Brigade, New Jersey Volunteers from 1861-1865.* Published by the State of New Jersey, 1910.

Bartlett, A.W. *History of the Twelfth Regiment New Hampshire Volunteers in the War of the Rebellion.* Ira C. Evans, Pinter, Concord, New Hampshire, 1897.

Bates, Samuel P. *History of the Pennsylvania Volunteers.* Seven Volumes. Harrisburg, Pennsylvania, 1869.

Benedict, George Grenville. *Army Life in Virginia: Letters From the 12th Vermont Regiment.* Free Press Association, Burlington, 1895.

Bicknell, George W. *History of the Fifth Regiment Maine Volunteers.* Hall L. Davis, Portland, Maine, 1871.

Boies, Andrew J. *Record of the Thirty-Third Massachusetts Volunteer Infantry.* Fitchburg, Massachusetts, 1880.

Boudrye, Louis N. *Historic Records of the Fifth New York Cavalry, First Ira Harris Guard.* S.R. Gary, Albany, New York, 1865.

Bowen, James L. *History of the Thirty-Seventh Regiment Massachusetts Volunteers.* Clark W. Ryan & Co., New York, 1884.

Carley, Kenneth. *Minnesota in the Civil War.* Ross & Haines, Inc., Minneapolis, Minnesota, 1961.

Carpenter, George N. *History of the Eight Regiment, Vermont Volunteers, 1861-1865.* Deland & Barton, Boston, 1886.

Child, William. *A History of the Fifth Regiment New Hampshire Volunteers in the American Civil War.* R.W. Musgrove Printer, Bristol, New Hampshire, 1893.

Committee of Publication. *A Memorial of the Great Rebellion Being a Brief History of the Fourteenth Regiment, New Hampshire Volunteers, 1862-1863.* Franklin Press, Boston, 1882.

Committee of the Regimental Association. *History of the Twenty-Fifth Regiment Massachusetts Volunteers, 1862-1865.* Mills, Knight & Co., Printers, Boston, 1884.

Committee of the Regiment. *History of the Thirty-Sixth Regiment Massachusetts Volunteers 1862-1865.* Press of Rockwell and Church, Boston, 1884.

Cook, Benjamin F. *History of the Twelfth Massachusetts Volunteers.* Boston, 1882.

Curtis, O.B. *History of the Twenty-Fourth Michigan of the Iron Brigade.Known as the Detroit and Wayne Country Regiment.* Winn and Hammond, Detroit, Michigan, 1891.

Davis, C.E. *Three Years in the Army: The Story of the 13th Massachusetts Volunteers.* Estes & Lauriat, Boston, 1894.

Davis, William W.H. *History of the 104th Pennsylvania Regiment.* James A. Rogers Printers, Philadelphia, Pennsylvania, 1866.

Dawes, Rufus. *Service With the Sixth Wisconsin Volunteers.* E.R. Alderman & Sons, Marietta, Ohio, 1890.

De Troibriand, Regis, (translated by G.R. Dauchy). *Four Years With the Army of the Potomac.* Ticknor and Company, Boston, 1889.

Doubleday, Abner. *Chancellorsville and Gettysburg.* Charles Scribners Sons, New York, 1881-1883. Reprint, The Archive Society, Harrisburg, Pennsylvania, 1992.

Dyer, Elisha. *Annual Report of the Adjutant General of the State of Rhode Island & Providence Plantations For the Year 1865,* Volume I. E.L. Freeman and Sons, Providence, Rhode Island, 1893.

Dyer, Frederick H. *A Compendium of the War of the Rebellion.* Two Volumes. Reprint by Morningside Press, Dayton, Ohio, 1994.

Emilio, Luis F. *A Brave Black Regiment: The History of the 54th Massachusetts.* Reprinted Capo Press, New York, 1995.

Fox, William F. *Regimental Losses in the American Civil War, 1861-1865.* Brandon Printing Company, Albany, New York, 1898. Reprint. Morningside Press, Dayton, Ohio, 1985.

Galloway, G. Norton. *The Ninety-Fifth Pennsylvania Volunteers (Gosline's Zouaves) In the Sixth Corps.* Philadelphia, Pennsylvania, 1884.

Gibbon, John. *Personal Recollections of the Civil War.* Reprint. Morningside Press, Dayton, Ohio, 1978.

Gilham, Major William. *Manual of Instruction for the Volunteers and Militia.* Charles Desilver, Philadelphia, Pennsylvania, 1861.

Graham, M.J. *The Ninth Regiment New York Volunteers (Hawkins Zouaves).* New York, 1900.

Grant, U.S. *Memoirs and Selected Letters: Personal Memoirs of U.S. Grant: Selected Letters, 1839-1865.* Literary Classics of the United States Inc., New York, 1990.

Hanson, John W. *Historical Sketch of the Old Sixth Regiment of Massachusetts Volunteers During its Three Campaigns.* Lee and Shepard, 1866.

Haynes, E.M. *A History of the Tenth Regiment, Vermont Volunteers with Bibliographical Sketches,* 2nd edition. The Tuttle Company, Rutland, Vermont, 1894.

Haynes, Martin A. *A History of the Second Regiment, New Hampshire Volunteer Infantry in the War of the Rebellion.* Lakeport, New Hampshire, 1896.

Hopkins, William P. *The Seventh Regiment Rhode Island Volunteers in the Civil War 1862-1865.*

The Providence Press, Providence, Rhode Island, 1903.

Houghton, Henry. "The Ordeal of Civil War: A Recollection," in *Vermont History*, Volume 41, Number 1, Winter 1973.

Huffstodt, Jim. *Hard Dying Men: The Story of General W.H.L. Wallace, General T.E.G. Ransom, and their "Old Eleventh" Illinois Infantry in the American Civil War (1861-1865)*. Heritage Books Inc., Bowie, Maryland, 1991.

Humphreys, A.A. *Gettysburg to the Rapidan: The Army of the Potomac, July 1863 to April 1864*. Charles Scribners Sons, New York, 1883.

— *The Virginia Campaign of 1864 and 1865*. Two parts. Reprint. The Archive Society, Harrisburg, Pennsylvania, 1992.

Hyde, Thomas W. *Following the Greek Cross or Memories of the Sixth Army Corps*. The Riverside Press, Cambridge, Massachusetts, 1897.

Ingersoll, C.M. *Catalogue of Connecticut Volunteer Organizations*. Brown and Gross, Hartford, Connecticut, 1869.

Jackson, Lyman. *History of the Sixth New Hampshire Regiment in the War for the Union*. Republican Press Assc., Concord, New Hampshire, 1891.

Joint Committee on the Conduct of the War, extract. *The Battle of Bull Run*. Kraus Reprint Co., Milwood, New York, 1977.

— *The Battle of Balls Bluff*. Kraus Reprint Co., Milwood, New York, 1977.

Judson, Amos M. *History of the Eighty-Third Regiment, Pennsylvania Volunteers*. B. F. H. Lynn, Publisher, Erie, Pennsylvania, 1865.

King, David H., A. Judson Gibbs, and Jay H. Northrup. *History of the Ninety-Third Regiment, New York Volunteer Infantry*. Swain & Tate Co. Printers, Milwaukee, Wisconsin, 1906.

Kirk, Hyland C. *Heavy Guns and Light: A History of the 4th New York Heavy Artillery*. C.T. Dillingham, Publisher, New York, 1890.

Koystal, K.M. *Field of Battle: The Civil War Letters of Major Thomas J. Halsey*. National Geographic Society, Washington, D.C., 1996. (11th New Jersey).

Little, Henry F. W. *The Seventh Regiment New Hampshire Volunteers in the War of the Rebellion*. Ira C. Evans, Printer, Manchester, New Hampshire, 1896.

Longacre, Edward G., editor. *From Antietam to Fort Fisher: The Civil War Letters of Edward King Wightman*. Fairleigh Dickinson University Press, Cranbury, New Jersey, 1985. (9th New York)

McGregor, Charles. *History of the Fifteenth Regiment New Hampshire Volunteers in the War of the Rebellion*. 1900.

Marcus, Edward, editor. *A New Canaan Private in the Civil War: Letters of Justus M. Stillman, 17th Connecticut Volunteers*. New Canaan Historical Society, New Canaan, Connecticut, 1984.

Meachum, Henry H. *The Empty Sleeve: The Life and Hardships of Henry H. Meachum*. Springfield, Massachusetts, 1869 (Thirty-Second Massachusetts).

Meade, George. George Gordon Meade, Editor. *The Life and Letters of George Gordon Meade*, Two Volumes. Charles Scribner's Sons, New York, 1913.

Newell, Joseph K. *Annals of the 10th Regiment Massachusetts Volunteers in the Rebellion*. C.A. Nichols & Co., Springfield, Massachusetts, 1875.

No Author. *Journal of the History of the Twenty-Ninth Ohio Veteran Volunteers, 1861-1865, Its Victories and Its Reverses*. J. Hamp Secheverell, Cleveland, Ohio, 1883.

Osborne, William H. *History of the Twenty-Ninth Regiment of Massachusetts Volunteer Infantry in the Late War of the Rebellion*. Albert J. Wright, Printer, Boston, 1877.

Otis, George. *The Second Wisconsin Infantry*. Reprint. Morningside House Inc., Dayton, Ohio, 1984.

Parker, Francis J. *The Story of the Thirty-Second Massachusetts Infantry*. C.W. Calkins & Co., Publishers, Boston, 1880.

Parker, John L. *History of the Twenty-Second Massachusetts Infantry: Henry Wilson's Regiment.* Avery Rand Co., Boston, 1887.

Parker, Thomas H. *History of the Fifty-First Regiment of Pennsylvania Volunteers and Veteran Volunteers.* King and Baird printers, Philadelphia, Pennsylvania, 1869.

Parsons, George W. *Put the Vermonters Ahead: The First Vermont Brigade in the Civil War.* White Mane Publishing Company, Shippensburg, Pennsylvania, 1996.

Paulus, Margaret B. *Papers of General Robert Huston Milroy.* Three volumes. Private Printing, 1965.

Powell, *The Fifth Army Corps.* Reprint. Morningside Bookshop, Dayton, Ohio, 1984.

Priest, John Michael, editor-in-chief. *Captain James Wren's Diary.* White Mane Publishing Co., Inc. Shippensburg, Pennsylvania, 1990. (Company B, 48th Pennsylvania).

— *One Surgeon's Private War: Doctor William W. Potter of the 57th New York.* White Mane Publishing Company Inc., Shippensburg, Pennsylvania, 1996.

Prowell, George R. *History of the Eighty-Seventh Regiment, Pennsylvania Volunteers.* York, Pennsylvania, 1901.

Pullen, John J. *The Twentieth Maine: A Volunteer Regiment in the Civil War.* Revised Edition. Morningside House Inc., Dayton, Ohio, 1991.

Quint, A.H. *The Record of the Second Massachusetts Infantry, 1861-1865.* Boston, 1867.

Reese, Timothy J. *Syke's Regular Infantry Division, 1861-1864: A History of Regular United States Infantry Operations in the Civil War's Eastern Theater.* McFarland & Company Inc., Publishers, Jefferson, North Carolina, 1990.

Racine, Philip N., editor. *Unspoiled Heart: The Journal of Charles Mattocks of the 17th Maine.* The University of Tennessee Press, Knoxville, 1994.

Rhodes, Elisha Hunt, Robert H. Rhodes, editor. *All for the Union: The Civil War Diary and Letters of Elisha Hunt Rhodes.* Vintage Books, A Division of Random House, New York, 1985.

Ripley, William Y.W. *Vermont Riflemen in the War for the Union, 1861 to 1865: Company F, First United States Sharpshooters.* Tuttle & Co. Printers, Rutland, Vermont, 1883.

Roe, Alfred S. *The Twenty-Fourth Regiment Massachusetts Volunteers, 1861-1866.* Twenty-Fourth Veteran Association, Worcester, Massachusetts, 1907.

— *History of the First Regiment of Heavy Artillery Volunteers.* Commonwealth Printers, Boston, 1917.

Rogers, Edward H. *Reminiscences of Military Service in the Forty-Third Regiment Massachusetts Infantry During the Great Civil War, 1862-1863.* Franklin Printers, Boston, 1883.

Rood, Hosea W. *Story of the Service of Company E, and of the Twelfth Wisconsin Regiment Veteran Volunteer Infantry in the War of the Rebellion.* Swain & Tale Co. Printers and Publishers, Milwaukee, Wisconsin, 1893.

Rosenblath, Emil and Ruth. Editors. *Hard Marching Every Day: The Civil War Letters of Private Wilbur Fisk.* University Press of Kansas, Lawrence, Kansas, 1992.

Sawicki, James A. *Infantry Regiments of the U.S. Army.* Wyvern Publications, Dumfries, Virginia, 1981.

— *Cavalry Regiments of the U.S. Army.* Wyvern Publications, Dumfries, Virginia, 1985.

Schneirson, Eric, editor. *The Private Letters and Diaries of Captain Hall.* London Book Co., Glendale California, 1974. (6th Vermont Volunteers)

Scribner, Benjamin F. *How Soldiers Were Made; or The War As I Saw It.* New Albany, Indiana, 1887. (38th Indiana Veteran Volunteers)

Shaw Horace H. and Charles J. House. *The First Maine Heavy Artillery 1862-1865.* Portland, Maine, 1903.

Sherman, William Tecumseh. *Memoirs of General W.T. Sherman.* Literary Classics of The United States, Inc., New York, 1990.

Smith, John Day. *The History of the Nineteenth Regiment of Maine Volunteer Infantry, 1862-1865.* Great Western Printing Company, Minneapolis, Minnesota, 1909.

Speed, Thomas. *The Union Regiments of Kentucky*. Courier-Journal Job Printing Company, 1897.

Stearns, Austin C. Arthur A. Kent, editor. *Three Years With Company K.* Associated University Presses Inc., Cranbury, New Jersey, 1976.

Stevens, C.A. *Berdan's United States Sharpshooters in The Army of the Potomac*. Reprint. Morningside Press, Dayton, Ohio, 1972.

Stevens, George T. *Three Years in the Sixth Corps*. S.R. Geary, Albany, New York, 1866.

Stevens, Hazard. "Sixth Corps, April 2, 1865," *Personal Narratives of the Events in the War of the Rebellion being Papers read before the Rhode Island Soldier's and Sailor's Historical Society*, Sixth Series, No. 8. Providence, Rhode Island, 1904.

Sturtevant , Ralph Orson. *Pictorial History: The Thirteenth Vermont Volunteers 1861- 1865*. Compiled by Eli. N. Peck. Burlington, Vermont, 1911.

Swinton, William. *Campaigns of the Army of the Potomac*. New York, 1866.

Thompson, Millett. *Thirteenth Regiment New Hampshire Volunteers*. Riverside Press, Cambridge, Massachusetts, 1888.

Turino, Kenneth C. Editor. *The Civil War Diary of Lt. J.E. Hodgkins*. Picton Press, Camden, Maine, 1994.

U.S. Congress, Joint Committee on The Conduct of the War. Joint Report of The Committee on The Conduct of the War. *The Army of the Potomac*. Two volumes. Reprint. Kraus Reprint Co., Milwood, New York, 1977.

Waitt, Ernest Linden. *History of The Nineteenth Regiment Massachusetts Volunteers*. Salem Press, Salem, Massachusetts, 1906.

Walcott, Charles W. *History of The Twenty-First Regiment, Massachusetts Volunteers, 1861-1865*. Houghton, Mifflin & Company, Boston, 1882.

Walker, Aldace F. *The Vermont Brigade in the Shenandoah Valley*. The Free Press Association, Burlington, Vermont, 1869.

Walker, Francis. *History of The Second Army Corps*, second edition. Charles Scribners Sons, New York, 1891.

Webb, Alexander S. *The Peninsula: McClellan's Campaign of 1862*. Reprint. Archive Society, Harrisburg, Pennsylvania, 1992.

Weld, Stephen Minot Weld. *War Diary and Letters of Stephen Minot Weld*. Second Edition. Massachusetts Historical Society, Boston, 1979.

Welles, Gideon. *The Diary of Gideon Welles*. Three volumes. Houghton Mifflin Co., Boston, 1912.

Wilkinson, Warren. *Mother, May You Never See The Sights I Have Seen: The Fifty-Seventh Massachusetts Veteran Volunteers In The Army of the Potomac*. Harper Collins Publishing Inc., New York, 1990.

Woodbury, Augustus. *A Narrative of the Campaign of the First Rhode Island Regiment in the Spring and Summer of 1861*. Sidney S. Rider, Providence, Rhode Island, 1862.

PUBLISHED SECONDARY SOURCES

Abbot, Catherine. "A Soldier's Life and Death in Family Letters," *The Washington Times*, July 9, 1994.

Abell, Sam and Brian Pohanka. *The Civil War: An Aerial Portrait*. Thomasson-Grant, Charlottesville, Virginia, 1987.

Adams, George Worthington. *Doctors in Blue: The Medical History of the Union Army in the Civil War*. Henry Schumann, New York, 1952.

Allan, Stacy D. "Shiloh! The Campaign and First Day's Battle," in *Blue & Gray Magazine*. Blue & Gray Enterprises, Columbus Ohio, February 1997.

Andrews, C.C., editor. *Minnesota in the Civil and Indian Wars*. Pioneer Press, St. Paul, Minnesota, 1891.

Arnold, James R. *The Armies of U.S. Grant*. Arms and Armour Press, London, 1995.

Atkinson, C.F. *Grant's Campaigns of 1864 and 1865: The Wilderness and Cold Harbor*. Hugh Rees Ltd., London, 1908.

Author Unknown. *Obituary, Edward Stanley Abbot.*. Beverly Massachusetts, July 25, 1863.

Author unknown. "An Incident at Gettysburg" in the *Adams Sentinel*. Gettysburg, Pennsylvania, July 25, 1865.

Author unknown. "Roll of Honor of Norwich University," in the *Rutland Weekly Herald*, Rutland, Vermont, August 17, 1865.

Baker, Dean Paul. *The Partridge Connection: Alden Partridge and Southern Military Education*. PhD Thesis, University of North Carolina, Chapel Hill, 1986.

Baldwin, Leo. T. "First Blood in Baltimore," *America's Civil War*, November 1995, Cowles History Group, Leesburg, Virginia, 1995.

Barnard, Henry. *Military Schools and Courses of Instruction in the Science and Art of War*. E. Steiger, New York, 1872.

Barrett, John G. *The Civil War in North Carolina*. University of North Carolina Press, Chapel Hill, 1963.

Belknap, Charles E. *History of the Michigan Organizations at Chickamauga, Chattanooga, and Missionary Ridge 1863*. Robert Smith Printing Co., Lansing Michigan, 1897.

Benedict, G.G. *Vermont at Gettysburg: A Sketch of the Part Taken by the Vermont Troops*. The Free Press Association, Burlington, Vermont, 1870.

—*Vermont in the Civil War*. A History. Two Volumes. The Free Press Association, Burlington, Vermont, 1886.

Bennett, Edwin C. *Musket and Sword or the Camp, March, and Firing Line*. Coburn Publishing Company, Boston, 1900.

Bigelow, John Jr. *Chancellorsville*. Reprint. Smithmark Publishers, New York, 1995.

Bowen, James L. *Massachusetts in the War, 1861-1865*. Clark W. Bryant Co., Springfield, Massachusetts, 1889.

Bowers, John. *Chickamauga and Chattanooga: The Battles That Doomed the Confederacy*. Harper Collins, Publishers, New York, 1994.

Bradley, Mark L. Last Stand in the Carolinas: The Battle of Bentonville. Savas Publishing Company, Campbell, California, 1995.

—"Last Stand in the Carolinas: The Battle of Bentonville, March 19-21, 1865," in *Blue & Gray Magazine*, Volume XIII, Issue 2, December 1995.

Brady, James P. *Hurrah for the Artillery! Knap's Independent Battery "E," Pennsylvania Light Artillery*. Thomas Publications, Gettysburg, Pennsylvania, 1992.

Buel, Clarence C. and Robert U. Johnson. *Battles and Leaders of the Civil War*. Four Volumes. New York, 1887.

Buono, Anthony. "General George Stannard," in *America's Civil War*, Leesburg, Virginia, July, 1996.

Burnett, William G. *Andersonville*. Eastern National Park and Monument Association, 1995.

Busey, John W. and David G. Martin. *Regimental Strengths and Losses at Gettysburg*, fourth edition. Longstreet House, Hightstown, New Jersey, 1994.

Cabot, Mary R. *Annals of Brattleboro 1681-1895*, Volume II. Press of E.L. Hildreth & Co., Brattleboro, Vermont, 1922.

Calhoun, Charles C. *A Small College in Maine: Two Hundred Years of Bowdoin*. Bowdoin College, Brunswick, Maine, 1993.

Calkins, Chris M. *Thirty-Six Hours Before Appomattox*. Farmville Herald, 1980. - *The Final Bivouac: The Surrender Parade at Appomattox and the Disbanding of the Armies*, 2nd edition. H.E. Howard Inc., Lynchburg, Virginia, 1988.

— "The Battle of Five Forks: Final Push for the South Side," in *Blue & Gray Magazine*, Volume IX, Issue 4, April 1992.

—*From Petersburg to Appomattox*. Farmville Herald, 1993.

Castel, Albert. *Decision in the West: The Atlanta Campaign of 1864*. Univ. Press of Kansas, Lawrence Kansas, 1992.

Catton, Bruce. *Civil War*. Three Volumes, reprint. The Fairfax Press, New York, 1984.

Cavanaugh, Michael A. *The Battle of the Crater: "The Horrid Pit," June 25-August 6, 1864*, 2nd edition. H.E. Howard Inc., Lynchburg, Virginia, 1989.

Chadwick, Albert G. *Soldier's record of the Town of St. Johnsbury, Vermont, in The War of the Rebellion, 1861-65*. (C.M. Stone & Co., St. Johnsbury, Vermont, 1883).

Chamberlain, *The Passing of the Armies*. Reprint. Stan Clark Military Books, Gettysburg, Pennsylvania, 1994.

Chase, Dudley H. "Gettysburg," in the *Military Order of the Loyal Legion of the U.S., Commandery for the State of Indiana, War Papers*, Volume I, Indianapolis, Indiana, 1898.

Cheeks, Robert C. "Little Phil's Fighting Retreat," in *America's Civil War*, Volume 9, Number 6, Leesburg, Virginia, 1996.

Cist, Henry M. *The Army of the Cumberland*. Charles Scribner's Sons, New York, 1883. - *Bayonet! Forward*. Stan Clark Military Books, Gettysburg, Pennsylvania, 1994.

Coco, Gregory A. Editor. *From Ball's Bluff to Gettysburg and Beyond: The Civil War Letters of Private Roland E. Bowen, 15th Massachusetts Infantry, 1861-1864*. Thomas Publications, Gettysburg, Pennsylvania, 1994.

— *A Strange and Blighted Land. Gettysburg: The Aftermath of a Battle*. Thomas Publications, Gettysburg, Pennsylvania, 1995.

Coddington, Edwin B. *The Gettysburg Campaign: A Study in Command*. Charles Scribner's Sons, New York, 1968.

Coffin, Howard. *Full Duty: Vermonters in the Civil War*. The Countryman Press Inc., Woodstock, Vermont, 1993.

Conklin, Eileen F. *Women at Gettysburg 1863*. Thomas Publications, Gettysburg, Pennsylvania, 1993.

Couper, William. *One Hundred Years at V.M.I.*, Four Volumes. Garrett and Massie, Richmond, Virginia, 1939.

Croffut, W.A. and John M. Morris. *The Military and Civil History of Connecticut During the Civil War of 1861-1865*. Ledyard Bill Publisher, New York, 1868.

Crotty, Daniel G. *Four years Campaigning in the Army of the Potomac*, reprint. Belle Grove Publishing Co., Kearny, New Jersey, 1995.

Cullen, Joseph C. *The Siege of Petersburg*. Eastern Acorn Press. Harrisburg, Pennsylvania, 1992.

Damon, Frank C. "Interesting Story Regarding Colonel J. Parker Gould," in the *Stoneham Independent*, Stoneham, Massachusetts, July 26, 1929.

Davis, Burke. *The Civil War: Strange and Fascinating Facts*. Wings Books, New York, 1994.

Davis, William C. *Gettysburg: The Story Behind the Scenery*. KC Publications Inc., 1993. - *Battle at Bull Run: A History of the First Major Campaign of the Civil War*. 2nd edition. Stackpole Books, Mechanicsburg, Pennsylvania, 1995.

Davis, William W.H. "The Siege of Morris Island," in *The Annals of War*, Morningside House, Inc., reprint, Dayton, Ohio, 1988.

Denney, Robert E. *Civil War Medicine: Care & Comfort of the Wounded*. Sterling Publishing Co., Inc., 1994.

Downey, Fairfax. *The Guns at Gettysburg*. David McKay Company Inc., New York, 1987.

Editorial Staff, "Gettysburg - The First Day, July 1, 1863," in *Blue & Gray Magazine*, Volume V, Issue 2, November, 1989.

— "The Battles at Spotsylvania Court House, Virginia. May 8-21, 1864," in *Blue & Gray Magazine*, Volume I, Issue 6, 1987.

Eicher, David J. *The Civil War In Books: An Analytical Bibliography.* University of Illinois, Urbana, 1997.

Ellis, William Arba. *History of Norwich University: Her History, Her Graduates, Her Role of Honor.* The Rumford Press, Claremont, New Hampshire, 1898. - editor. *Norwich University, 1819-1911.* Three Volumes. The Capital City Press, Montpelier, Vermont, 1911.

Fairbanks, Edward T. *The Town of St. Johnsbury: A Review of One Hundred Twenty- Five Years.* The Cowles Press, St. Johnsbury, Vermont, 1914.

Farley, Paul, Printers. *Civil War Tales.* New Oxford, Pennsylvania, 1983.

Finfrock, Bradley. "Harrowing Nighttime Escape from Harpers Ferry," *The Washington Times* (Washington, D.C., September 9, 1995).

Fishel, Edwin C. *The Secret War For The Union: The Untold Story of Military Intelligence in the Civil War.* Houghton Mifflin Company, Boston, 1996.

Frassanito, William A. *Antietam: The Photographic Legacy of America's Bloodiest Day.* Charles Scribners Sons, New York, 1978.

Furgurson, Ernest B. *Chancellorsville 1863: The Souls of the Brave.* Alfred A. Knopf, Inc., New York, 1992.

Gaff, Alan D. *Brave Men's Tears.* Second edition, revised. Morningside Press, Dayton, Ohio. 1988.

—*On Many A Bloody Field: Four Years in the Iron Brigade.* Indiana University Press, Bloomington, 1996.

Gallagher, Gary W., editor. *The Second Day at Gettysburg.* The Kent State University Press, Kent, Ohio, 1993.

—*The Third Day at Gettysburg & Beyond.* The University of North Carolina Press, Chapel Hill, 1994.

—*The Fredericksburg Campaign: Decision on the Rappahanock.* The University of North Carolina Press, Chapel Hill, 1995.

—*The Battle of Chancellorsville.* Eastern Monument and Park Association, 1995. *Chancellorsville: The Battle and Its Aftermath.* The University of North Carolina Press, Chapel Hill, 1996.

Geier, Clarence R. Jr. and Susan E. Winter, editors. *Look to the Earth: Historical Archaeology and the American Civil War.* The University of Tennessee Press, Knoxville, Tennessee, 1994.

Graham, Martin F. and George F. Skock. *Mine Run: A Campaign of Lost Opportunities, October 21, 1863-May 1, 1864.* Second edition. H.E. Howard Inc., Lynchburg, Virginia, 1987.

Greene, A. Wilson. *The Second Battle of Manassas.* Eastern Monument and Park Association, 1995.

Griffith, Paddy. *Battle in the Civil War.* Field Books, Camberly, Surrey, England, 1986.

Groene, Bertram Hawthorne. *Tracing Your Civil War Ancestor.* Revised edition. John F. Blair, Publisher, Winston-Salem, North Carolina, 1973.

Gwinn, Robert O. *The History of of Norwich University, 1912-1965,* Volume IV. Northfield, Vermont, 1965.

Happel, Ralph. *Salem Church.* Eastern National Parks & Monuments Association, 1980.

Halstead, Murat. *The Life and Achievements of Admiral Dewey.* Our Possessions Publishing Company, Chicago, Illinois, 1899.

Haraty, Peter H., editor. *History of the Vermont National Guard.* Queen City Printers Inc., Burlington, Vermont, 1982.

Harmon, Ernest N. *Norwich University - Its Founder and His Ideals.* Presented at a meeting of the Newcomen Society, Norwich University, Northfield, Vermont, October 6, 1951.

Harrison, Noel G. *Fredericksburg Civil War Sites, April 1861-November 1862.* Volume 1. H.E. Howard Inc., Lynchburg, Virginia, 1995. - *Fredericksburg Civil War Sites, December 1862-April 1865,* Volume 2. H.E. Howard, Inc., Lynchburg, Virginia, 1995.

Haskell, Frank A. *The Battle of Gettysburg.* Reprint. Chapman Billies Inc., Sandwich, Massachusetts, 1993.

Hassler, Warren W. *Crisis at the Crossroads: The First Day at Gettysburg.* University of Alabama Press, 1970.

Headley, P.C. *Massachusetts in the Rebellion: A History of the Historical Position of the Commonwealth in the Civil War of 1861-1865.* Walker, Fuller, and Company, 1866.

Hemenway, Abby maria. *The Vermont Historical Gazetteer,* Volume I. A.M. Hemenway, Burlington, Vermont, 1868.

Henderson, William D. *The Road to Bristoe Station: Campaigning with Lee and Meade, August 1-October 20, 1863.* Second Edition. H.E. Howard Inc., Lynchburg, Virginia, 1987.

Hennessy, John J. *Return to Bull Run: The Campaign and Battle of Second Manassas.* Simon & Schuster, New York, 1993.

Historian, Staff of Richmond National Battlefield Park, "From the North Anna to the Crossing of the James," *Blue & Gray Magazine,* Volume XI, Issue 4, April, 1994.

Holsworth, Jerry W. "Uncommon Valor: Hood's Texas Brigade in the Maryland Campaign," *Blue & Gray Magazine,* Volume XIII, Issue 6, August 1996.

Horn, John. *The Petersburg Campaign.* Combined Books, Conshohocken, Pennsylvania, 1993.

Howe, Thomas J. *The Petersburg Campaign: Wasted Valor, June 15-18, 1864.* Second Edition. (H.E. Howard, Inc., Lynchburg, Virginia, 1988)

Hunt, Roger D. & Jack R. Brown. *Brevet Brigadier Generals in Blue.* Olde Soldier Books, Inc. Gaithersburg, Maryland, 1990.

Ide, Horace K., Dr. Elliott W. Hoffman, editor. "The First Vermont Cavalry in the Gettysburg Campaign," *The Gettysburg Magazine,* Number Fourteen, January, 1996.

James, Robert F. "Inspired Profanity Was Tool of Grant's Aide," *The Washington Times,* January 7, 1995.

Jones, V.C. *First Manassas: The Bull Run Campaign.* Historical Times Inc., Harrisburg, Pennsylvania, 1992.

Jorgensen, Jay. "Anderson Attacks The Wheatfield," *The Gettysburg Magazine,* Number Fourteen, January, 1996.

Katcher, Philip. *The Civil War Source Book.* Facts on File Inc., New York, 1992.

Kelly, Dennis. *Second Manassas: The Battle and Campaign.* Eastern Acorn Press, Harrisburg, Pennsylvania, 1982.

Koehl, Stuart L., "Modern Civil War Was Really Napoleonic," *The Washington Times,* February 3, 1996.

Krick, Robert K. *Lee's Colonels: A Biographical Register of the Field Officers of the Army of Northern Virginia,* 4th Edition, revised. Morningside House Inc., Dayton, Ohio, 1992.

Kross, Gary. "Gettysburg Vignettes," *Blue & Gray Magazine.* Volume XIII, Issue 3, Winter, 1996.

Lash, Gary G. "A Pathetic Story: The 141st Pennsylvania (Graham's Brigade) at Gettysburg," *The Gettysburg Magazine,* Issue Number Fourteen, January, 1996.

Linderman, Gerald F. *Embattled Courage: The Experience of Combat in the American Civil War.* MacMillan Inc., New York, 1987.

Livermore, Mary A. *My Story of the War: A Woman's Narrative of Four Years Personal Experience.* A.D. Worthington and Company, Hartford, Connecticut, 1891.

Logan, John A. *The Volunteer Soldier of America.* R.S. Peale & Company, Publishers, 1887.

Lord, Gary Thomas. *Alden Partridge: Promoter of an American System of Education.* Presented at the Annual Meeting of the American Military Institute. Virginia Military Institute, Lexington, Virginia, 14 April, 1989.

Lowry, Don. *No Turning back: The Beginning of the End of the Civil War.* Hippocrene Books, New York, 1992. - *Fate of the Country: The Civil War from June-September 1864.* Hippocrene Books, New York, 1992.

—*Dark and Cruel War: The Decisive Months of the Civil War, September- December 1864.* Hippocrene Books, New York, 1993.

Luvaas, Jay and Harold W. Nelson. *The U.S. Army War College Guide to the Battles of Chancellorsville and Fredericksburg.* South Mountain Press Inc., Carlisle, Pennsylvania, 1988.

Mahr, Theodore C. *Early's Valley Campaign The Battle of Cedar Creek: Showdown in the Shenandoah October 1-30, 1864.* H.E. Howard Inc., Lynchburg, Virginia, 1992.

Maney, R. Wayne. *Marching to Cold Harbor: Victory and Failure, 1864.* White mane Publishing Co., Inc., Shippensburg, Pennsylvania, 1995.

Marshall, C. Dale. "Ordnance: The 50th New York Engineers," *America's Civil War,* November, 1995, Cowles History Group, Leesburg, Virginia, 1995.

Marvel, William. *The Battle of Fredericksburg.* Eastern National Park and Monument Association, 1993.

Martine, David G. *The Chancellorsville Campaign: March-May, 1863.* Combined Books, Conshohocken, Pennsylvania, 1991.

—*Gettysburg July 1.* Combined Books, Inc., Conshohocken, Pennsylvania, 1995.

Marvel, William. *The Battle of Fredericksburg.* Eastern National Park and Monument Assc., 1993.

Matter, William D. "The Oak Tree at Spotsylvania," in *Blue & Gray Magazine,* Volume I, Issue 6, June-July 1984.

—*If It Takes All Summer: The Battle of Spotsylvania.* University of North Carolina Press, Chapel Hill, North Carolina, 1988.

Mertz, Gregory A. "No Turning Back - Part I, The Battle of the Wilderness," in *Blue & Gray Magazine,* Volume XII, Issue 4, April 1995.

—"No Turning Back - Part II, The Battle of the Wilderness," in *Blue & Gray Magazine,* Volume XII, Issue 5, May 1995.

Miller, Francis T. Editor. *The Photographic History of the Civil War.* Ten volumes. Reprint. Eastern Press, Norwalk, Connecticut, 1995.

Miller, J. Michael. *The North Anna Campaign: Even to Hell Itself," May 21-26, 1864.* 2nd Edition. H.E. Howard Inc., Lynchburg, Virginia, 1989. - Strike Them a Blow: Lee and Grant at the North Anna River," in *Blue & Gray Magazine,* Volume X, Issue 4, April 1993.

Miller, Richard F., and Robert F. Mooney. *The Civil War: The Nantucket Experience.* Wesco Publishing, Nantucket, Massachusetts, 1994.

Miller, William J., editor. *The Peninsula Campaign,* two volumes. Savas Woodbury Publishers, Campbell, California, 1995.

Moore, Frank, collector and arranger. *The Civil War in Song and Story, 1860-1865.* Reprint by P.F. Collier, Publisher, 1892.

Mosocco, Ronald A. *The Chronological Tracking of the Civil War.* James River Publications, Williamsburg, Virginia, 1994.

Naisawald, L. Van Loan. *Grape and Canister: The Story of the Field Artillery in the Army of the Potomac, 1861-1865.* Oxford University Press, New York, 1960.

Nesbitt, Mark. *Through Blood & Fire: Selected Civil War Papers of Major General Joshua Chamberlain.* Stackpole Books, Mechanicsburg, Pennsylvania, 1996.

Nofi, Albert A. *The Gettysburg Campaign: June-July 1863.* Combined Books, Ponshohocken, Pennsylvania, 1993.

Nolan, Alan T. *The Iron Brigade: A Military History.* Fourth Edition. Indiana University Press, Bloomington, Indiana, 1994.

O'Reilly, Frank A. *"Stonewall" Jackson at Fredericksburg: The Battle of Prospect Hill December 13, 1862,* 2nd edition. H.E. Howard, Inc., Lynchburg, Virginia, 1993.

Palfrey, Francis Winthrop. *The Antietam and Fredericksburg.* Reprint. The Archive Society, Harrisburg, Pennsylvania, 1992.

Papers of the Military Historical Society of Massachusetts. Volume IV. *The Wilderness Campaign, May-June 1864*. The Military Historical Society of Massachusetts, Boston, 1905. - Volume V. *Petersburg, Chancellorsville, Gettysburg*. The Military Historical Society of Massachusetts, Boston, 1906.

Parsons, William T. "Letters from the Fifty-First," in *The Bulletin of the Historical Society of Montgomery County*. Volume XIII, Number 3, Fall, 1962.

Perkins, J.R. *Trails, Rails and War: The Life of General G.M. Dodge*. The Bobbs- Merrill Company, Publishers, Indianapolis, Indiana, 1929.

Pitkin, P.P. *Report of the Quarter-Master General of the State of Vermont, October 1, 1865*. Walton's Steam Printing Establishment, Montpelier, Vermont, 1865.

Pfanz, Donald C. *The Depot Field Hospital at City Point*. National Park Service, 1988. *Abraham Lincoln At City Point, March 20-April 9, 1865*, 2nd Edition. H.E. Howard, Inc., Lynchburg, Virginia, 1989.

Pfanz, Harry W. *Gettysburg: The Second Day*. University of North Carolina Press, Chapel Hill, 1987.

—*Gettysburg: Culp's Hill and Cemetery Hill*. University of North Carolina Press, Chapel Hill, 1993.

Philadelphia Weekly Times. *The Annals of the War*. Morningside House Inc., reprint, Dayton, Ohio, 1988.

—*The Battle of Gettysburg*. Eastern Monument and Park Association, 1995.

Phisterer, Frederick. *Statistical Record of the Armies of the United States*. Charles Scribners Sons, New York, 1881-1883.

—*New York in the War of the Rebellion*. Third edition. Five volumes. Albany, New York, 1912.

Poirier, Robert G. "Norwich at Gettysburg: The Citizen Soldier Academy's Contribution to Victory," *The Gettysburg Magazine*, Issue Number Fourteen, January, 1996.

Priest, John Michael. *Antietam: The Soldier's Battle*. White Mane Publishing Co., Inc. Shippensburg, Pennsylvania, 1989.

—*Before Antietam: The Battle for South Mountain*. White Mane Publishing Co., Inc. Shippensburg, Pennsylvania, 1992.

—*Nowhere to Run: The Wilderness, May 4th & 5th, 1864*. White Mane Publishing Co., Inc. Shippensburg, Pennsylvania, 1994.

Raus, Ed. "Hell's Half Acre: The Fight for the Bloody Angle," *Blue& Gray Magazine*, Volume I, Issue 6, June-July 1984.

Ray, J.P. *The Diary of a Dead Man, 1862-1864*. Eastern Acorn Press, 1995.

Reid, Whitelaw. *Ohio in the War: Her Statesmen, Generals and Soldiers*. Volume 2. Moore, Wilstach, and Baldwin Publishers, New York, 1868.

Rhea, Gordon C. *The Battle of the Wilderness, May 5-6, 1864*. L.S.U. Press, Baton Rouge, Louisiana, 1994.

—*The Battles of Wilderness & Spotsylvania*. Eastern National Park Monument Association, 1995.

Richardson, Leon Burr. *The History of Dartmouth College*, Volume II. Dartmouth College Publications, Hanover, New Hampshire, 1932.

Roberts, John. "West Pointers a Dominant Force on Both Sides," *The Washington Times*, Washington, October 2, 1995.

Robertson, John. *Michigan in the War*, revised edition. W.S. George & Co., Lansing, Michigan, 1882.

Robertson, William Glenn. *Back Door to Richmond: The Bermuda Hundred Campaign, April-June 1864*. University of Delaware Press, Newark, Delaware, 1987.

Rollins, Richard, editor. *The Returned Battle Flags*. Rank and File Publications, Redondo Beach, California, 1995.

Ropes, John Codman. *The Army Under Pope*. Charles Scribner's Sons, New York, 1881.

Schaff, Morris. *The Spirit of Old West Point.* Houghton, Mifflin Company, Boston, 1908. - *The Battle of the Wilderness.* Reprint. The Archive Society, Harrisburg, Pennsylvania, 1994.

Scott, Robert Garth. Editor. *Fallen Leaves: The Civil War Letters of Major Henry Livermore Abbott..* The Kent State University Press, Kent, Ohio, 1991.

Schouler, William. *A History of Massachusetts in the Civil War.* Boston, 1879.

Sears, Stephen W. *Landscape Turned Red: The Battle of Antietam.* Ticknor & Fields, New York, 1983.

—*To The Gates of Richmond: The Peninsula Campaign.* Ticknor & Fields, New York, 1992.

—*Chancellorsville.* Houghton Mifflin Company, Boston, 1996.

Sever and Francis. *Harvard Memorial Biographies,* 2 Volumes. University Press, Welch, Bigelow & Co., Cambridge, Massachusetts, 1866.

Shannon, Fred Albert. *The Organization and Administration of the Union Army 1861- 1865.* The Arthur H. Clark Company, 1928.

Sheldon, N.L. *Norwich University.* Norwich University, Northfield, Vermont, 1899.

Schildt, John W. *The Ninth Corps At Antietam.* Olde Soldier Books Inc., Gaithersburg, Maryland, no date.

Sifakis, Stewart. *Who Was Who in The Civil War.* Facts on File Publications, New York, 1988.

Smith, Brian W. and Gary T. Lord, *Norwich University 1819.* Harmony House, Louisville, Kentucky, 1995.

Spencer, James. *Civil War Generals: Categorical Listings and a Biographical Directory.* Greenwood Press, New York, 1986.

Stackpole, Edward J. *The Fredericksburg Campaign.* Second edition. Stackpole Books, Harrisburg, Pennsylvania, 1991.

Steere, Edward. *The Wilderness Campaign: The Meeting of Grant and Lee.* Reprint. Stackpole Books, New York, 1994.

Stevens, William B. *History of Stoneham, Massachusetts.* F.L. & W.F. Whittier, Stoneham, Massachusetts, 1891.

Strock, G. Michael. *Andersonville National Cemetery.* Williams Printing Company, Atlanta, Georgia, 1983.

Suhr, Robert Collins. "Firing the Norfolk Navy Yard," in *America's Civil War,* Leesburg, Virginia, November 1996.

Swank, William Davis. *Battle of Trevilian Station.* Beidel Printing House Inc., Shippensburg, Pennsylvania, 1994.

Sword, Wiley. *Shiloh: Bloody April.* Morningside House Inc., Dayton Ohio, 1974.

Symonds, Craig L. *Gettysburg: A Battlefield Atlas.* The Nautical and Aviation Publishing Company of America, Baltimore, Maryland, 1992.

Thomas, Emory. *Richmond: The Peninsular Campaign.* Eastern Acorn Press, Harrisburg, Pennsylvania, 1980.

Todd, Frederick P. *American Military Equipage 1851-1872,* Volume II. The Company of Military Historians, Providence, Rhode Island, 1972.

Townsend, George Alfred. *Campaigns of a Non-Combatant and His Romaunt Abroad During the War.* Blelock & Company, New York, 1866.

Trudeau, Noah Andre. *Bloody Roads South: The Wilderness to Cold Harbor, May- June 1864.* Little, Brown, and Company, Boston, 1989.

—*The Last Citadel: Petersburg, Virginia, June 1864-April 1865.* Little, Brown & Company, Boston, 1991.

—*Out of the Storm: The End of the Civil War, April-June 1865.* Little, Brown, and Company, Boston, 1994.

—*The Siege of Petersburg.* Eastern Monument and Park Association, 1995.

—*The Campaign to Appomattox.* Eastern Monument and Park Association, 1995.

Trulock, Alice Rains. *In the Hands of Providence: Joshua Chamberlain and the American Civil War.* University of North Carolina Press, Chapel Hill, 1992.

Tucker, Glenn. *High Tide At Gettysburg.* The Bobbs-Merrill Inc., New York, 1958.

—*Chickamauga: Bloody Battle in The West.* Bobbs-Merrill Inc., New York, 1961.

Von Deck, Joseph F. "Dismal Day at Dismal Swamp," in *America's Civil War,* Leesburg, Virginia, July 1996.

Waite, Otis F. *Vermont in The Great Rebellion.* Tracy, Chase, and Company, Claremont, New Hampshire, 1869.

—*New Hampshire in The Great Rebellion.* Tracy, Chase & Company, Claremont, New Hampshire, 1870.

Walker, Francis. *General Hancock.* D. Appleton and Company, New York, 1894.

Warner, Ezra J. *Generals in Blue: Lives of The Union Commanders.* Louisiana State University Press, Baton Rouge, Louisiana, 1993.

Welles, Gideon. "The First Iron-Clad Monitor," in *The Annals of War,* Morningside House Inc., reprint, Dayton, Ohio, 1988.

Wells, Dean M., "Ewell Seizes the Day at Winchester," in *America's Civil War,* Leesburg, Virginia, March 1997.

Wert, Jeffrey D. *From Winchester to Cedar Creek: The Shenandoah Campaign of 1864.* South Mountain Press, Carlisle, Pennsylvania, 1987.

Western Historical Society. *The History of Sauk County Wisconsin.* Chicago, 1880.

Whitman, E.S. and Charles H. True. *Maine In The War For The Union: A History of The Part Borne by Maine Troops In The Suppression of The American Rebellion.* Nelson Dingley & Co. Publishers, Lewiston, Maine, 1865.

Wise, Stephen R. *Gate of Hell.* University of South Carolina Press, Columbia, South Carolina, 1994.

Young, Jesse Bowman. *The Battle of Gettysburg: A Comprehensive Account.* Harper & Brothers Publishers, New York, 1913.

Index

The names of alumni and units contained in Appendices A and B are not cited in the index as those sections consist of alphabetical and numerical listings which make individuals and units easy to find. Units listed in this index are infantry unless otherwise noted.